Ona B. Forrest.
July 1955

FREE

# APPROACHES TO ECONOMIC DEVELOPMENT

ii

# APPROACHES TO
# ECONOMIC DEVELOPMENT

NORMAN S. BUCHANAN

*and*

HOWARD S. ELLIS

NEW YORK · The Twentieth Century Fund · 1955

PRINTED IN THE UNITED STATES OF AMERICA BY

WM. F. FELL COMPANY, PHILADELPHIA, PENNSYLVANIA

# FOREWORD

WHAT ACCOUNTS for the fact that two thirds of the world's people still work and live much as their ancestors did while the other third have forged ahead to ever higher levels of productivity and well-being? In other words, why has economic and technological progress since the Industrial Revolution been limited to such a small fraction of the world's area and population?

Why, and how, does economic development take place? What are the factors—social, political and cultural, as well as economic—that promote, or inhibit, a nation's capacity to achieve a better life for its citizens? Are there any common factors that can be identified as essential to the process of economic growth, wherever it takes place? To what extent can the economic development of the underdeveloped regions be accelerated by "importing" techniques and capital from the developed countries? What are some of the implications of our present knowledge of this subject for American and world policy with regard to economic development?

These were some of the questions that the trustees of the Twentieth Century Fund had in mind in asking Norman S. Buchanan and Howard S. Ellis to undertake the present study. Both authors are professors of economics at the University of California, Berkeley, and both have participated in earlier Fund studies—Norman Buchanan as co-author of *Rebuilding the World Economy*, issued in 1947, and Howard Ellis as one of the six contributors to the symposium *Financing American Prosperity*, brought out in 1945.

Professors Buchanan and Ellis have made a perceptive and thoughtful appraisal of their subject. Readers, both lay and professional, may well feel grateful for their skill as writers, since their text attains interest and clarity to a degree not often encountered in scholarly treatises.

Their conclusions, in the main, are soberly hopeful but at no point do they attempt to minimize difficulties, or turn away from realities. They are well aware of the insistent pressures that surround us today. They see the vast stirring of underprivileged peoples. They recognize that unless the free nations of the world can offer some sympathetic help and guidance, large and critical segments of mankind may succumb to the false and facile lures of the Marxist conspiracy and thus participate in their own betrayal and add to the free world's peril.

The authors also see that economic development is by no means a matter of economics alone. Throughout this study they show a notable grasp of personal, social, cultural and political factors that always influence, and frequently determine, the course that economic events will take.

v

As for the division of labor in writing the book, Norman Buchanan assumed primary responsibility for Chapters 1 and 2, part of Chapter 3, Chapters 4 through 11 and Chapter 19, and Howard Ellis for the others. The final product, of course, necessarily was a joint effort. The Fund wishes to express its appreciation to both authors, and to all who assisted them in any way, for what we believe will prove to be a significant contribution to the understanding of a major problem of our time.

J. FREDERIC DEWHURST, *Executive Director*
*The Twentieth Century Fund*

330 WEST 42D STREET
NEW YORK 36, N. Y.
JANUARY 3, 1955

# PREFACE

THIS BOOK undertakes a general analysis of the problem of the economic development of the underdeveloped areas. As economists we have, naturally, given rather more attention to the economic aspects of the development problem than to others perhaps equally important. However, economic analysis, being itself general in character, is not ill-suited to the study of economic development. Capital accumulation and saving, monetary policy and inflation, tax systems and fiscal policy, balance-of-payments problems and foreign borrowing, specialization and trade, scarcity and economy, resource allocation and productive efficiency, population and income—these and related matters are topics on which economists have long dwelt. Presumably, this body of analysis has relevance to the development problems of the underdeveloped areas. To the best of our ability, however, we have also drawn upon other disciplines when we felt that economic analysis alone did not suffice. The problem of the sustained accumulation of productive capital in underdeveloped areas, for example, is scarcely comprehended by reference to liquidity preference schedules in relation to the quantity of money and the marginal efficiency of investment. Thus the study attempts to be general in the sense that it is not exclusively economic. Similarly, it is not focused on particular geographical areas; so far as possible, it is intended to apply to those problems that appear to be common, in greater or smaller degree, to nearly all the so-called underdeveloped areas.

From one point of view, economic development can be said to be a new term for a process long familiar. In the past two centuries the average material well-being of the inhabitants of many countries of the world has improved remarkably if one may judge from the criteria that appear to be relevant for such judgments. To be sure, what is envisaged and sought after by the underdeveloped areas in the middle of the twentieth century is not identical with what has occurred in times past. Nevertheless, the record of past instances of development perhaps has more application to the present-day problems than might be supposed. At any rate, we incline toward this belief, and we have therefore included historical sketches of development in England, France, Germany, Japan and Russia. It is not presumed that these will satisfy the professional economic historian; they are too brief and too avowedly selective for that. They are intended, however, to suggest certain points which appear pertinent to the problems facing the underdeveloped countries in our time.

At one time, interest in the United States in these problems might have been mainly academic. This is far from true today. Both in the sphere of national foreign policy and through membership in the United Nations and its affiliated agencies the United States must reckon with the aspirations of the underdeveloped areas and, presumably, help these countries realize their objectives. This implies something more than voting funds for dollar assistance through an abhorrence of poverty and sympathy for the underfed. Its heavy obligations at home and elsewhere abroad leave the United States only limited resources for assisting the underdeveloped areas in their struggle for material betterment. This means that what resources are expended toward this end should be wisely committed: the attack should be directed at the heart of the development problem, not merely its surface manifestations. Moreover, tangible assistance for development should be joined with wise policies in other directions that work toward similar or at least harmonious objectives of American foreign policy as a whole.

From the time we first began our study in the summer of 1951 we have been acutely aware that we were running grave risks in attempting to sketch on such a large canvas. No two persons, no matter how assiduous, could hope to examine, comprehend and integrate the bewildering mass of materials on the subject of the underdeveloped areas and their development problems. Moreover this mass is growing visibly day by day. We are quite certain, therefore, that we have overlooked some studies we might have examined with profit. For these sins of omission we apologize sincerely. We must also point out that our manuscript was virtually completed at the end of the summer of 1953 and that this accounts for the regrettable fact that we make no reference to several important studies since published. Although an earlier publication date would have been highly pleasing to all concerned, unfortunately that proved to be quite impossible.

We are indebted and grateful to many persons for their advice and assistance. For brief periods, or on particular topics, we had research assistance from Charles F. Haywood, James F. Mahar, Dr. Leon A. Mears of San Francisco State College and Dr. Norman Zellner of the University of California at Davis. Professor Erskine McKinley of the University of Indiana worked part time for more than a year as general research assistant. His perceptive and imaginative approach to our problems and difficulties helped us appreciably. Frances J. Toler, our secretary and typist, contributed far more than she might suppose to our endeavors by her unfailing good humor and endless patience in the face of all difficulties. Josephine Haywood, Dolores Hiskes, and Jeanne Trahan assisted Mrs. Toler in typing and reconciling the various copies of the manuscript as it evolved into its present form.

Professor M. K. Bennett of Stanford University, Professor J. B. Condliffe of the University of California at Berkeley, Richard H. Demuth of the

International Bank for Reconstruction and Development, Washington, D. C., and George Wythe of the U.S. Department of Commerce read the manuscript in substantially its present form with extreme care and contributed many helpful suggestions and criticisms for which we are exceedingly grateful. Professor Arthur Geddes of the University of Edinburgh and Professor George J. Stolnitz of Princeton University contributed helpful criticisms of an earlier draft of Chapter 5.

Gloria Waldron Grover improved the readability of the manuscript by rooting out some of our obscurities in style and expression; she also added most of the sideheads. Finally, the staff of the Twentieth Century Fund and its director—Evans Clark until August 1953 and since then J. Frederic Dewhurst—have, from the start, lightened our task considerably by the grace and considerateness of their friendly cooperation. We extend our sincere thanks to all these persons. Friends, colleagues and professional acquaintances have been unfailingly helpful at all times.

NORMAN S. BUCHANAN
HOWARD S. ELLIS

# CONTENTS

## Part I: AN ANALYTICAL VIEW OF THE PROBLEM

## Part II: ECONOMIC DEVELOPMENT AS RECORDED HISTORY

## Part III: ACHIEVING DEVELOPMENT IN THE CONTEMPORARY WORLD

# APPENDICES

# FIGURES

# TABLES

Contents                                                    xiii

*Part I*

# AN ANALYTICAL VIEW OF
# THE PROBLEM

# 1. What Is an Underdeveloped Area?

A GRADIENT AND NOT A CLIFF separates the underdeveloped areas of the world from the developed areas when countries and regions are placed in an array. At the extremes the contrasts are dramatically sharp, but in the middle ranges blurring is unavoidable. Nevertheless, to follow the now widely used terms appears to be the desirable course, even though to generalize on this basis will stretch the facts a bit at times. For nowadays the usage is nearly universal and a satisfactory classification into more categories is not easily devised.

Present usage would put much of Asia and Africa, the Near and Middle East, southeastern Europe, the Caribbean and most of Central and South America in the underdeveloped category. On the other hand, the developed areas would include Western Europe, the U.S.S.R., northern North America, Japan, Australia and New Zealand, and the Union of South Africa. The developed areas are mostly in the temperate zones. Though China and Chile are also in the temperate zones, the underdeveloped areas tend to lie either in the tropics—Indonesia, the Malay Peninsula and much of India, South America and Africa—or in the adjacent fringes of the temperate zones.

Loose generalizations about the underdeveloped areas as a whole, however, can easily be misleading because the countries or areas usually so categorized differ greatly in the degree to which they can be called underdeveloped by acceptable objective tests. Colombia and Ceylon, for instance, are usually referred to as underdeveloped countries and so are Egypt and Ecuador along with Nigeria and Nicaragua. But a generalization that would fit both Ceylon and Egypt might require appreciable qualification if applied to Nigeria. Similarly, if Western Europe is an already developed area it ought also to be kept in mind that to lump Spain and Portugal together with Denmark and Germany makes an uneven loaf too. Finally, there are often sharp contrasts between different regions within the same national boundaries: Michigan as against Mississippi, for example, or São Paulo, Brazil, as compared with Mato Grosso.

## THE MEANING AND MEASUREMENT OF UNDERDEVELOPMENT

An economically underdeveloped country is one which on the average affords its inhabitants an end product of consumption and material well-being appreciably inferior to that provided by the economies of the developed countries. The underdeveloped countries are often called "poor" countries. Poor is a relative term. The citizen of first century Rome was materially poorer than today's resident of Copenhagen or Colombo. But he was not poor compared with people living on the outskirts of the then Roman world, for example in Germany or Macedonia. Similarly, the average resident of Colombo today may be better off than he was a century ago but badly off as against the average resident of Stockholm today.

## Comparative Nature of Concept

Thus, the concept is, first of all, a comparative one and refers to the performance record of a country's economy. Outside the economic sphere, an underdeveloped country may be highly developed—in art, religion, philosophy or social organization, for example. To designate a country as underdeveloped also implies that its present economic performance—as evidenced by the average of consumption and material well-being—could be improved by means which are known and understood. If the underdeveloped countries were to use their existing productive resources more effectively and if, too, they were to augment the productive resources at their disposal, their people would get an appreciably better end product of consumption and material well-being than they are now getting. The task is not easy, and simple remedies are not ready to hand. Nevertheless, if much of what is routine practice in the developed countries could be transferred and applied in the underdeveloped countries, their residents would be distinctly better off than they are now.

Underdevelopment means poor economic performance as evidenced by the comparatively low average of consumption and material well-being of the people, plus the potentiality of improvement through the application of known means.[1]

## The Potentiality of Improvement

If a low average of material well-being were wholly explainable by immutable facts of physical environment or human nature, it would have to be accepted, like the weather, with resignation and despair. Yet such a view appears untenable. To be sure, there is no magic device which can immediately catapult an area to a much higher material plane. But more than a little is known about the nature of the changes required and the means by which they can be brought about.

1. The above concept is much broader than use of the term "underdeveloped" to mean only the presence of underdeveloped "natural" resources such as basic raw materials or hydroelectric power sites. This usage seems much too restricted. While most underdeveloped countries doubtless have some unutilized natural resources of this type which could be exploited, this will usually not be the main avenue by which economic betterment will be attained. Moreover, the existence of such natural resources is not a necessary prior condition to development.

Among the reasons for believing that the average level of material welfare in the underdeveloped areas can be greatly improved is that two centuries ago, or more recently in many cases, consumption and material well-being in the now developed countries were little better than they are in most underdeveloped areas today. Although such comparisons are treacherous, accounts of life in seventeenth- or early eighteenth-century Europe portray the people as living under conditions remarkably similar to those now found in many underdeveloped areas. These societies, however, subsequently developed and progressed sufficiently to provide a vastly improved material welfare. By present standards, though not by his, life in Hobbes's England was "poor, nasty, brutish and short," yet the circumstances which made it so have given way to others which afford the average person both a longer and a better life.

Clearly these changes had no single cause. The evolution of the Western world since the eighteenth century has been multiform and complex. Yet out of it all emerged an average of consumption and material well-being for the individual that is richer in texture and variety and available to more people over a longer life span. Furthermore, and perhaps most important of all, the changes wrought appear to be progressive and in a measure self-generating, so that further gains are still in prospect.

Unfortunately, the underdeveloped countries of today have undergone no similar transformation. Average material welfare in these areas has not improved appreciably in modern times. Modes of thought remain essentially unchanged. Their societies, in the main, neither generate change from within nor easily accommodate it when it impinges from without.

If these countries should develop—as many appear determined to do—the ensuing changes will probably not be wholly different from those which have brought about improvement of material welfare in the western world. This is not to say that the underdeveloped countries must repeat altogether the recent economic history of Western societies. The task may be easier and the time span shorter. But it is unlikely that the changes will be wholly different in character or that the dislocations, adjustments and adaptations which the developed countries have experienced can be altogether avoided. Moreover, the process of development as it has already occurred presumably has relevance in more ways than one to the problem of the material advancement of the now underdeveloped countries.

### INDEXES OF DEVELOPMENT AND UNDERDEVELOPMENT

International comparisons of human well-being are conceptually difficult and often statistically impossible. Among the reasons for these difficulties is the fact that many developed and nearly all underdeveloped countries have not compiled the relevant statistical data. The process of collecting and compiling reliable statistics demands sophistication and is expensive. Moreover, until recently, few countries saw any need for even the most elementary national statistics.

Even were the desired statistical data available, however, international comparisons of human well-being would still involve sticky, often insoluble, problems of interpretation. Societies have their own cultures, and each culture has its own scale of values. This diversity means that identical physical facts may have different significance for human well-being in different cultures. Few indexes of well-being would be placed at the top of the value scale in all cultures. Consequently international statistical comparisons may give misleading results. Furthermore, different particular indexes will almost certainly rank countries in different order. Ideally, one would like some over-all index of human well-being which would overcome the "weighting problem" implicit in partial indexes. But at present this ideal cannot be fully realized.

A further fact—often overlooked—is that human well-being is not wholly reducible to quantitative terms. Psychological, anthropological and sociological studies seem to show that nonmaterial drives and achievements are fundamental in all social groups, and that how well or how poorly a particular society provides for their expression will notably raise or lower the individual's sense of well-being. Related studies seem to indicate, moreover, that some highly developed societies with high material standards of living leave the individual rather badly off in these nonmaterial respects—both absolutely and by comparison with societies that are less highly developed in an economic sense.

Peace of mind and contentment cannot be bought as commodities, while frustration and dissatisfaction are often free goods. But since these elements of human well-being do not lend themselves to statistical recording—especially for comparative purposes as between countries or areas—they tend to be glossed over or disregarded in international comparisons. This is even more likely if, as has often been true, the statistical compilations used to compare developed and underdeveloped areas tend to reflect the value scales of the already developed areas.

International comparisons of human well-being must be gingerly handled and cautiously interpreted. They can lend themselves all too readily to false inferences and conclusions. Still worse, well-intentioned persons may find them a ready springboard for action programs verging on the grotesque.

*Two Kinds of Measures*

Keeping in mind the limitations just mentioned, statistical data bearing on development or underdevelopment in different countries may be conveniently divided into two groups. Group I would include those which indicate the quality and texture of life as "end product." That is, the statistical measure portrays some aspect of life which can be regarded as good or bad in itself, rather than as a means to, or an explanation of, something else desirable or undesirable. For example, higher life expectancy at birth or lower infant mortality or "better health" are presumably desirable as ends in themselves rather than as means to something else.

Group II, on the other hand, would include those statistical findings which tend to portray economic performance and therefore to explain, or at least to correlate with, a poor end product of life as a whole as recorded by data of the first type. For example, a low agricultural productivity per person or per acre is presumably neither good nor bad in itself. But it may partially explain why diets are deficient and why the incidence of certain deficiency diseases is strikingly high in a particular area.

Indexes in Group I variously express the fact that the underdeveloped countries are poor; those in Group II suggest some of the reasons for the low quality of life and the lines along which remedial action could proceed. The indexes in Group I are more likely to display the composite effects of a number of interacting causes. For example, a high rate of infant mortality will usually not be solely a matter of diet or maternal health; it will also reflect the availability of medical care and prevailing sanitary practices. Though multiple causation may also be present in Group II data, the factors at work and their relative importance will usually be easier to disentangle.

Some statistical indexes may belong in both groups. According to the point of view, they are either end results or they help to explain why the over-all end product is what it is. For example, an endemic disease such as malaria may be undesirable by its very nature; but it may also seriously affect the energy and endurance and thus the productivity of the labor force. Illiteracy is another example. The statistical tabulations which follow in this chapter and the next, however, usually fall into one or the other of the two broad types.

## INDEXES OF LIFE AS END PRODUCT

There are few wholly satisfactory indexes of the general texture of life as end product in one area or one historical period as against another. An acceptable index of life as end product should be free from subjective influences, and either wholly outside the value scales dominating the cultures of the countries being compared or present as common elements in all. These are severe limitations, particularly so in view of the paucity of statistical data relating to most underdeveloped areas. Nevertheless, some few are available.

*Life Expectancy*

Life expectancy is surely one such index. So far as can be learned, people in all societies in all times and places have seemed to prefer life to death. Regardless of how they rank other values, people consider longer individual and average life expectancy desirable ends. This is not to say that in all cultures people prefer longer life to the realization of all other ends. This is manifestly *not* the case. But, other things being equal, a longer life is regarded as better than a shorter life.

As Edmund Halley suggested in 1693, in offering one of the first life tables ever prepared, its "Uses are manifold, and give a more just Idea of the State and Condition of Mankind, than any thing extant that I know of."[2]

A table of life expectancies shows, for a given population, the age to which an individual may, on the average, expect to survive. For example, it has been estimated that the life expectancy at birth of white males in the United States was 48.2 years in 1900–1902 but had risen to 64.4 in 1945 and to 65.9 in 1949. Similar figures for Massachusetts in 1789 indicate an expectancy of only 34.5 years. A computation of expectation of life can of course be made for any age from birth onward.[3]

While life expectancies are by no means available for all countries, those that are available show striking contrasts. In the countries usually regarded as underdeveloped, life expectancy at birth frequently falls short of that in developed countries by 20 or even 25 years. In Scandinavia, England and most of Western Europe, life expectancy at birth in the period before World War II was above 60 years and sometimes above 65. In India, China, Indonesia and the rest of Asia, as well as most of the Arab world, the comparable figure was probably more often below 40 than above. In Latin America, expectancies may have been somewhat higher. (See Table 1-1.) In the U.S.S.R. before World War II, the figure is reported at 46.7 for males; it has probably climbed somewhat in the postwar years. Since the end of the war, life expectancies have improved appreciably in some underdeveloped areas because of falling mortality rates, as they have in almost all developed areas.

2. As quoted in A. Wolf, *A History of Science, Technology, and Philosophy in the XVIth and XVIIth Centuries*, Allen and Unwin, London, 1935, p. 610. Halley's paper, "An Estimate of the Degrees of Mortality of Mankind drawn from curious tables of the Births and Funerals at the City of Breslaw; with an Attempt to ascertain the Price of Annuities upon Lives," appeared in 1693. Until his paper appeared, life insurance, although already used in the sixteenth century, was akin to a game of chance or a wager. Earlier tabulations of the number of deaths in relation to population and the causes of death were made by John Graunt (1620–1674), Sir William Petty (1623–1687) and Gregory King (1648–1712). See *ibid.*, pp. 587–608. But it was only in the eighteenth century that any serious efforts were made to calculate the population in France, Germany, Sweden and England. See also D. V. Glass, "The Population Controversy in Eighteenth-century England, Part I: The Background," *Population Studies*, July 1952, pp. 69–91.

3. Life expectancy tables are computed for a given population cohort (say 100,000 live births) by recording the numbers actually removed by death in each age year. These may then be used to get an average age of death, which is the average life expectancy at birth. It is not a highly refined statistical measurement at all; moreover, small differences between countries, especially underdeveloped countries, may not be significant because of possible imperfections in the raw data.

TABLE 1-1. EXPECTATION OF LIFE AT SPECIFIED AGES

(*Average number of years of life remaining to persons of exact age specified,
if subject to mortality conditions of period indicated*)

| | | Age in Years | | |
|---|---|---|---|---|
| Country | Period of Data | 0[a] | 5 | 15 |

Developed Countries

| | | | | |
|---|---|---|---|---|
| United States | 1900–1902[b] | 49.3 | 55.0 | 46.8 |
| | 1909–1911[b] | 51.0 | 56.2 | 48.3 |
| | 1939–1941 | 63.8 | 62.6 | 53.2 |
| England and Wales | 1910–1912 | 53.4 | 58.5 | 50.0 |
| | 1920–1922 | 57.6 | 60.2 | 51.6 |
| | 1930–1932 | 60.8 | 61.7 | 52.7 |
| Sweden | 1901–1910 | 55.8 | 58.6 | 50.6 |
| | 1911–1920 | 58.0 | 58.3 | 50.1 |
| | 1921–1930 | 62.1 | 62.2 | 53.3 |
| | 1931–1940 | 65.0 | 63.8 | 54.6 |
| | 1941–1945 | 68.4 | 66.1 | 56.7 |
| Netherlands | 1900–1909 | 52.2 | 58.9 | 50.4 |
| | 1910–1920 | 56.1 | 59.9 | 51.3 |
| | 1921–1930 | 62.7 | 63.3 | 54.2 |
| | 1931–1940[c] | 66.4 | 65.0 | 55.8 |

Intermediately Developed Countries

| | | | | |
|---|---|---|---|---|
| Italy | 1901–1911 | 44.5 | 55.3 | 47.3 |
| | 1921–1922 | 50.0 | 57.7 | 49.5 |
| | 1930–1932 | 54.9 | 60.5 | 51.8 |

Underdeveloped Countries

| | | | | |
|---|---|---|---|---|
| Southern North America | | | | |
| Guatemala[d] | 1939–1941 | 36.5 | 48.8 | 41.7 |
| Mexico | 1929–1933 | 37.0[e] | .. | 39.4 |
| Panama[f] | 1941–1943 | 52.0 | 55.1 | .. |
| Costa Rica[e] | 1927 | 41.0 | .. | .. |
| Puerto Rico[g] | 1939–1941 | 44.5 | .. | .. |
| Jamaica[h] | 1940–1942 | 53.1 | 55.2 | 46.4 |
| South America | | | | |
| Brazil[i] | 1920 | 37.4 | 47.8 | 40.1 |
| Chile | 1930 | 36.6 | 51.1 | 43.2 |
| | 1940 | 38.9 | 51.5 | 43.2 |
| Colombia[e] | 1939–1941 | 46.0 | .. | .. |
| Africa | | | | |
| Egypt | 1927–1937 | 30.9 | .. | .. |
| | 1936–1938 | 38.6 | 54.0 | 46.8 |
| Middle East | .. | .. | .. | .. |

(*Continued on page 10*)

TABLE 1-1. EXPECTATION OF LIFE AT SPECIFIED AGES—Continued

| | | Age in Years | | |
|---|---|---|---|---|
| Country | Period of Data | $0^a$ | 5 | 15 |
| Underdeveloped Countries—continued | | | | |
| **South Asia** | | | | |
| India[j] | 1901–1911 | 23.0 | 35.2 | 30.6 |
| | 1921–1931 | 26.7 | 37.8 | 31.4 |
| Korea[h] | 1938 | 48.9 | 55.1 | 47.3 |
| **Southeast Asia** | | | | |
| Thailand[k] | 1937–1938 | 40.0 | 51.9 | 43.7 |
| **Southeastern Europe** | | | | |
| Bulgaria | 1899–1902 | 40.2 | 51.0 | 45.4 |
| | 1925–1928 | 46.3 | 56.8 | 49.3 |
| Greece | 1920 | 44.7 | 52.9 | 45.6 |
| | 1926–1930 | 49.9 | 56.7 | 49.3 |

*Source:* United Nations, *Statistical Yearbook, 1949–50*, New York, 1950, pp. 54–63, unless otherwise specified.

a. Life expectancy figures exclude stillbirths.
b. Based on data for ten death-registration states of 1900.
c. Including war losses.
d. Based on data for Department of Guatemala only.
e. *Point Four*, U. S. Department of State, Publication 3719, January 1950, pp. 115–16.
f. Excluding tribal Indians.
g. Kingsley Davis, *The Population of India and Pakistan*, Princeton University Press, Princeton, 1951, p. 62.
h. United Nations, *Statistical Yearbook, 1951*, New York, 1951.
i. Based on data for the Federal District and thirteen cities.
j. Including Burma. Figures for India computed by Kingsley Davis in his book cited above are as follows:

| | Age in Years (Males Only) | | | | |
|---|---|---|---|---|---|
| | 0 | 10 | 20 | 30 | 40 |
| 1911–1921 | 19.4 | 26.7 | 25.5 | 21.6 | 17.9 |
| 1931–1941 | 32.1 | 41.2 | 35.0 | 29.0 | 23.3 |

k. For Bangkok municipal area.

Average life expectancy is the net result of a wide variety of causes—diet, disease, infant and maternal health, exposure to hazards, availability of medical care, sanitary practices, etc. As such, it supplies an over-all measure of what a particular society affords as end product to the people who compose it. There can be little question that improved life expectancy is indicative of improved well-being, especially if the improvement is appreciable.

*Mortality*

Where detailed vital statistics are unavailable or too unreliable for the computation of life expectancies, one has to resort to correlative measures such as crude death rates or infant mortality rates.[4] Here, as in the case of life expectancies, countries usually regarded as underdeveloped compare

4. The compilation of life expectancies for underdeveloped areas is difficult not merely because deaths are incompletely recorded but also because many of the people literally do not know their own age, so that their age at death cannot be recorded accurately.

TABLE 1-2. CRUDE DEATH RATES AND INFANT MORTALITY RATES FOR
SELECTED COUNTRIES, 1938

| Country | Infant Mortality Rate | Crude Death Rate |
|---|---|---|
| | (Number of Deaths in First Year of Life per 1,000 Live Births) | (Number of Deaths, Exclusive of Stillbirths, per 1,000 Population) |
| **Africa** | | |
| Egypt | 163.4 | 26.3 |
| Mauritius | 162.5 | 29.2 |
| **Central America and West Indies** | | |
| Costa Rica | 123.1 | 17.7 |
| El Salvador | 117.2 | 19.1 |
| Guatemala | 101.1 | 26.3 |
| Honduras | .. | .. |
| Mexico | 128.0 | 22.9 |
| Panama | .. | 14.2 |
| Barbados | 221.3 | 21.4 |
| Jamaica | 129.2 | 16.8 |
| Panama Canal Zone | 36.7 | .. |
| Puerto Rico | 121.0 | 17.7 |
| **South America** | | |
| Argentina | 105.3 | 11.8 |
| Chile | 235.7 | 23.5 |
| Colombia | 156.5 | 17.3 |
| Ecuador | 141.5 | .. |
| Venezuela | 138.7 | 18.3 |
| Surinam | 58.7 | 12.6 |
| **Asia** | | |
| Ceylon | 161.4 | 21.0 |
| China (Formosa) | 145.7 | 20.0 |
| India | 167.1 | 23.7 |
| Korea | 101.0 | 17.6 |
| Thailand | 93.6 | 15.1 |
| Federation of Malaya | 149.4 | 20.4 |
| **North America** | | |
| United States | 51.0 | 10.6 |
| **Europe** | | |
| Denmark | 58.7 | 10.3 |
| Norway | 37.3 | 9.9 |
| Sweden | 42.5 | 11.5 |
| United Kingdom: England and Wales | 52.7 | 11.6 |
| **Far East** | | |
| Japan | 115.0 | 17.7 |
| **U.S.S.R.**[a]  Male | 198.9 | .. |
| Female | 163.6 | .. |

*Source:* United Nations, *Demographic Yearbook, 1952*, New York, 1952, pp. 264, 320.

a. Figures are conjectural and are for 1938–1940. See Frank Lorimer, *The Population of the Soviet Union: History and Prospects*, League of Nations, Geneva, 1946, p. 124.

unfavorably with developed countries. In prewar years, the crude death rates—number of deaths, exclusive of stillbirths, per 1,000 population—ranged between 16 and 23 in the underdeveloped areas as against 10 to 14 in the developed countries. The picture of infant mortality is even more dismal. In the developed countries, the prewar infant mortality rate—number of deaths in the first year of life per 1,000 live births—was usually between 40 and 60, whereas in underdeveloped countries the rate was usually above 100 and sometimes above 200. (See Table 1-2.[5]) Joseph J. Spengler even reports the surely incredible figure of over 500 for Iran.[6] In 1949 in Sweden, on the other hand, the infant mortality rate had been cut to 23.2!

*General Health*

The general health of a population as an index of human well-being is closely akin to life expectancy—indeed one of its determinants. The health of a population cannot be portrayed by any single measure, but it is mostly independent of cultural differences and can be objectively measured, at least in part.[7] If many eradicable diseases or debilitating ailments—such as malaria, diphtheria, dysentery, hookworm or trachoma—are endemic to some areas but almost absent in others, one may almost certainly conclude that the people in the infected areas have poorer health and, therefore, less well-being.

The general health of the people in underdeveloped areas—as measured by the incidence and mortality rates for certain common diseases—compares unfavorably with the more developed regions. Disease is more widespread and it takes a heavier toll. Although comprehensive figures apparently are not available, the United Nations reports, for example, that the death rate from diphtheria in Costa Rica, Puerto Rico or Colombia is 6 to 9 times that in the United Kingdom; from malaria, it may be 10 to 100 times greater; and for "other infectious or parasitic diseases" 10 to 15 times greater. Such preventable scourges as malaria and enteritis take a huge toll in underdeveloped areas, while only heart disease is shown as a significant killer in developed countries. (See Table 1-3.)

5. The reader will observe that, if the data in Table 1-2 are reliable, some underdeveloped countries, for example Surinam and Thailand, have death rates lower than Japan, which would not be considered underdeveloped by most people. Also one wonders if the infant mortality rate in the U.S.S.R. was, in fact, higher than in India.

6. Joseph J. Spengler, "Economic Factors in the Development of Densely Populated Areas," *Proceedings* of the American Philosophical Society, February 1951, p. 39*n*.

7. It seems necessary to confine the comparisons to diseases for which medical science has evolved effective means of control or of alleviation. Cancer and heart diseases are important causes of death in many highly developed countries and they also account for a certain number of deaths in underdeveloped countries as well, but so far medical science has not developed means for substantially reducing the incidence of these ailments. By contrast, although people in the more developed countries still die of malaria or typhoid or tuberculosis, medical science has been able to cut the incidence of these diseases substantially in the last half century and similar techniques would presumably be as efficacious in the underdeveloped areas.

TABLE 1-3. DEATH RATES BY CAUSE IN SELECTED COUNTRIES
(*Deaths per 100,000 Population*)

| Country | Year | Diph-theria | Malaria | Smallpox | Typhus Fever | Diarrhea, Enteritis | Diseases of the Heart | Other Infectious or Parasitic Diseases |
|---|---|---|---|---|---|---|---|---|
| Mauritius | 1949 | 5.2 | 204.4 | .. | .. | 196.5 | 69.4 | 39.3 |
| Canada | 1947 | 1.1 | 0.0 | .. | 0.0 | 15.8 | 255.2 | 4.7 |
| Costa Rica | 1947 | 5.8 | 100.6 | 0.3 | 0.9 | 214.4 | 69.0 | 132.9 |
| United States | 1947 | 0.6 | 0.1 | 0.0 | 0.2 | 5.6 | 321.2 | 5.3 |
| Puerto Rico | 1947 | 4.0 | 19.6 | .. | 0.4 | 172.9 | 99.8 | 24.8 |
| Colombia | 1948 | 4.5 | 27.2 | 7.1 | 14.3 | 143.5 | 62.5 | 63.0 |
| Surinam | 1948 | 2.2 | 10.9 | .. | 1.6 | 48.9 | 126.6 | 31.5 |
| Ceylon | 1947 | 1.7 | 66.3 | 0.0 | .. | 69.8 | 36.6 | 88.8 |
| Japan | 1947 | 4.3 | 0.6 | 1.0 | 0.2 | 130.0 | 62.3 | 37.1 |
| Denmark | 1947 | 1.2 | .. | .. | .. | 9.3 | 244.0 | 11.7 |
| Norway | 1947 | 2.5 | 0.1 | .. | .. | 7.5 | 135.6 | 10.3 |
| United Kingdom | 1947 | 0.6 | 0.0 | 0.0 | 0.0 | 14.9 | 338.8 | 7.3 |

*Source:* United Nations, *Demographic Yearbook, 1951,* New York, 1951, pp. 396–419.

If the death rates from eradicable diseases are so high in the under-developed areas the incidence rates must also be high, with all that this implies for human suffering and misery. While precise data on the incidence of certain diseases are unavailable, Joseph J. Spengler has recently stated:

. . . malaria affects 300 million persons per year, killing 3 million and causing a loss of 20–40 days per person afflicted per year; schistosomiasis, a debilitating rural disease like malaria, afflicts 20–30 million people in the Near East alone and millions more in Africa, Asia and Latin America; filariasis cases number about 189 million per year in underdeveloped countries; yaws, widespread in tropical countries, afflicts over one million in Haiti alone; hookworm and other intestinal parasites debilitate millions; cases of syphilis number 20–100 millions and those of gonorrhea 2–3 times as many. There is high incidence also in many under-developed countries of diseases accompanied by high mortality (e.g., smallpox, typhus, cholera, plague, kala azar, some fevers) or by disability (e.g., trachoma, leishmaniasis).[8]

All this—even if the statement is somewhat exaggerated—represents well-being with a huge minus sign. And what is more, with present knowl-edge, the incidence of these diseases could be reduced by large percentages at only moderate cost.

### Food, Clothing and Shelter

"Food, clothing and shelter" was long the familiar phrase to designate man's minimal needs, and even today the degree to which a society pro-vides these needs is some measure of its over-all achievement. Unfortunately,

8. Spengler, *loc. cit.,* pp. 38–39n.

however, they only partly lend themselves to meaningful comparisons. Social custom, religious convictions, cultural patterns and geographical and climatic factors tend to make comparison exceedingly difficult and even, at times, meaningless.

One may be reasonably sure that people everywhere dislike being hungry or without protection from the elements. But eating and housing are everywhere something more than taking in calories and being sheltered from the rain. Yet the "something more" is likely to be so indigenous to each culture as often to defy objective comparison. What measures are available on these fundamentals of life are thus likely to be only indirectly revealing. Minor differences in calorie intake are likely to be due to food preferences or cultural differences; only a very low calorie intake probably signifies a hunger diet. On the other hand, where the calories are obtained almost entirely from cereals and/or potatoes, this is more likely to be by force of circumstances than by consumer preference.

In the United States before World War II, calories per person were estimated at 3,249, of which 30–40 per cent were from cereals and potatoes; in India the calorie intake was about 2,021, of which 60–70 per cent was from cereals or potatoes. In India the calorie intake may be too low and too largely composed of cereals to give the population resistance to disease and the energy needed for the day's work. Estimates have been made of the amount and sources of calories consumed in a number of countries in prewar years. (See Appendix 1–1.) Although these estimates are doubtless subject to a wide margin of error, they nevertheless indicate the inferior position of the underdeveloped countries relative to the developed countries. Those that are underdeveloped consume considerably fewer calories, and the amount that they consume consists to a much greater degree of cereals and potatoes.

An interesting study by M. K. Bennett compares prewar consumption and material well-being in 31 countries by means of 19 nonmonetary indicators.[9] Bennett groups his 19 indicators under six headings: Food and Tobacco; Health; Housing and Clothing; Education and Recreation; Transport and Communication; and, lastly, Balancing Indicators. His method is to set at 100 for each indicator the highest absolute figure found among the 31 countries, and then to express the absolute figures for the other 30 countries in that series as percentages of this figure. Since 19 series are used, the maximum rating any country could possibly score would be 1900, and it would score that figure only if it stood highest among the 31 countries in every one of the 19 indicators of consumption and material

9. M. K. Bennett, "International Disparities in Consumption Levels," *American Economic Review*, September 1951, pp. 632–49. Bennett stresses the dangers of misinterpretation in reasoning from differences in patterns of consumption in different countries to differences in well-being.

well-being. No country scored this maximum, but the United States did get the highest score among the 31 countries included in the tabulation. Bennett reports that:

The nearest competitor, Canada, scored only about four-fifths as many points; and the lowest-ranking nation, French West Africa, only about one-sixth as many. The gradient from highest scorer downward was initially steep and thereafter more gradual. Only six countries—Canada, Australia, the United Kingdom, Germany, France, and Argentina—scored more than half as many points as the United States. There were 13 countries which scored from a fourth to a half as many points as the United States, and 11 countries which scored less than a fourth as many.[10]

The results of Bennett's calculations are shown graphically in Figure 1.

*Per Capita Income*

Finally, per capita income computations are also indicative of the quality of life as end product. These have often been used to compare underdeveloped areas with one another and with the more developed countries. And when used cautiously they can be enlightening. Nevertheless, they can easily be misleading.[11] As a Latin American writer has expressed it,

A North American is interested in knowing the national income of the various Latin American countries expressed in dollars—the only currency which for him has a definite meaning in terms of commodities and services. The basket of goods bought by North Americans is, nevertheless, different from that bought, for example, by Brazilians or Panamanians. Tastes and habits differ widely; natural conditions in the various countries are such that goods readily and cheaply available in the United States are rarities or delicacies in Latin America, and vice versa . . . clothing, buildings, transportation, almost everything is subject to regional differentiation which prevents any sort of accurate inter-country comparison of national incomes or standards of living.[12]

10. *Ibid.*, p. 640. The details of the 19 series cannot be reproduced here but are fully explained in the article. Dr. Bennett in private correspondence has made the following interesting comment on his calorie figures: "I now take issue strongly with the idea that figures on estimated calorie consumption per head indicate anything at all about relative well-being. These are estimates pertaining to a five-year period. They pertain to 'calories at retail level,' not to ingestion, and thus include household waste . . . I would not again use even calories per 100 pounds of humanity as an indicator, much less calories per head. There is no such thing as continuing chronic calorie shortage over years; what there is is sporadic shortage associated with war or crop failure."

11. Simon Kuznets has called attention to this in a recent article: "in studying temporal changes and spatial differences in statistical indices it is necessary to consider the bias introduced by the changing or different proportion of the measurable to the total. But recognition of this bias is not assurance of ability to adjust for it.

"A notable case of this difficulty, which becomes a pitfall when overlooked, is provided by national income, the most comprehensive measure of a country's economy and a gauge of its total current output. The customary exclusion from this total of services rendered within the household, and of other services not designed for the market, means that at any given time the measure covers only part of the total volume of economic goods produced; that over time, in a country in the process of industrialization, the proportion of total economic activity covered by the measure increases; and that at a given time the measure is more complete for industrialized than for underdeveloped countries. Yet it is widely employed with inadequate or no correction at all for these biases." Simon Kuznets, "Statistical Trends and Historical Changes," *Economic History Review*, 2d Series, Vol. III, No. 3, 1951, p. 275.

12. Loreto M. Dominguez, "National Income Estimates of Latin American Countries" in *Studies in Income and Wealth*, Vol. 10, National Bureau of Economic Research, New York, 1947, p. 236.

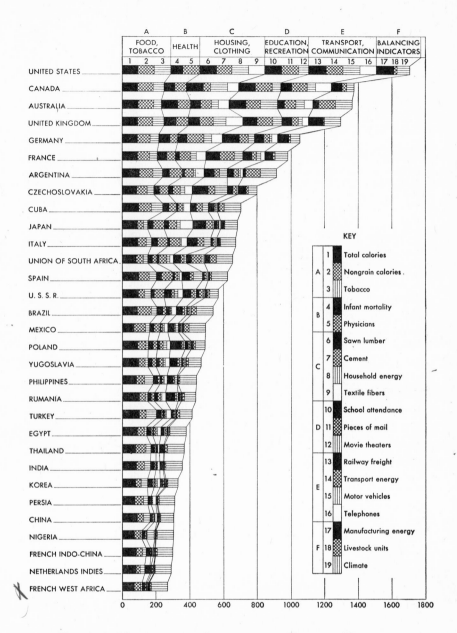

FIGURE 1. NONMONETARY INDICATORS OF RELATIVE NATIONAL
CONSUMPTION LEVELS, IN 31 COUNTRIES, AROUND 1934–1938

Source: M. K. Bennett, "International Disparities in Consumption Levels," *American Economic Review*, September 1951.

16

Any visitor in a foreign country will readily confirm the high cost abroad of stubborn adherence to his customary pattern of living and consumption. The conversion of money figures in national currencies to some common currency, say U.S. dollars, is another difficulty which raises problems too numerous and complex to be dealt with here.[13]

### Special Difficulties of Computation

These and similar difficulties are particularly acute in the case of the underdeveloped countries. Perhaps the worst stumbling block is the fact that in many underdeveloped areas so much of "production" and "consumption" occurs wholly outside the market economy and therefore cannot be interpreted according to the usual principles of valuation and exchange.[14] Economic activity is often almost indistinguishable from social behavior in general. In developed countries, the services of housewives may legitimately be excluded in reckoning national income. But if the wives sow, cultivate and harvest the entire food supply, exclusion of their services is surely absurd. Apparently, too, in some underdeveloped regions—China, for example—"income in kind" and services rendered gratis are exceedingly common. These are not easily valued and totaled.[15]

Other difficulties arise from the great variation among countries in the range, scope and conception of government activities. The services of governments of underdeveloped countries often bear little similarity to those accepted in more developed countries where national income calculations have been developed. While one cannot be positive in these matters, the likelihood is that per capita income comparisons between developed and underdeveloped countries usually tend to exaggerate rather than to understate the gap between them in real terms, large as that gap undoubtedly is.

The reasons for this belief are numerous; some of them, however, are subjective and so not easily substantiated. For the more highly developed countries, consumers' durable goods and investment goods bulk large in the computations and tend to skew the results. Many of these goods are as much a measure of the degree of urbanization as they are of material welfare. The fact that the already developed countries are nearly all in the temperate zones and the underdeveloped countries mostly in the tropical

13. See, however, Morris A. Copeland, Jerome Jacobson and Bernard Clyman, "Problems of International Comparisons of Income and Wealth" in *ibid.*, pp. 136–59; Ta-Chung Liu and Shan-Kwei Fong, "The Construction of National Income Tables and International Comparisons of National Incomes"; Phyllis Deane, "Measuring National Income in Colonial Territories," in *Studies in Income and Wealth*, Vol. 8, National Bureau of Economic Research, New York, 1946. See also Phyllis Deane, *The Measurement of Colonial National Incomes*, Cambridge University Press, Cambridge, 1948. This volume contains estimates for Northern Rhodesia, Nyasaland and Jamaica.

14. The common technique of valuing such production at prices in adjacent markets often cannot be used because the markets do not exist or because the amount passing through them is but a tiny fraction of the whole. See *The Measurement of Colonial National Incomes*, pp. 153–58.

15. See Liu and Fong, *loc. cit.*, pp. 95*ff.*

latitudes also tends to make the per capita income figures higher in the developed countries because so much effort must be spent there in protection from the elements. The commercialization of agriculture in the developed countries, in contrast to many underdeveloped countries, also tends to overstate the differences between them. Lastly, the simple fact that the statistical data are plentiful for the developed countries and often nearly non-existent for the underdeveloped countries tends to mean that many things get "counted in" in the developed countries, while comparable items are omitted from the totals for the underdeveloped countries. This last may be only an extension of the general rule that income figures as between rural and urban areas tend to exaggerate the margin (in real terms) between them. And this is particularly true if price differentials between rural and urban areas are disregarded in the income comparisons. Underdeveloped countries are of course predominantly agricultural.[16]

Notwithstanding these difficulties, comparisons of per capita income are used frequently to suggest international differences in the flow of goods and services. For example, 1939 per capita income in the United States, according to one widely used estimate, was $554, in Argentina $218, in Bulgaria $109, in Indonesia $22. In the first 15 of 53 countries ranked in descending order of per capita income (Table 1-4), all but one (Argentina) had populations with low growth potential (Type 1: birth rates and death rates largely under control). On the other hand, of those countries ranking from 26th to last place in per capita income, 25 had populations with high growth potential (Type 3: neither birth rates nor death rates in reasonably secure control, although death rates, but not birth rates, generally falling) and only three had populations in transitional growth (Type 2: death rates, but not birth rates, coming under control).

*Polarization Shown by Indexes*

It was stated at the beginning of this chapter that an underdeveloped country is one which affords its people a comparatively poor end product of consumption and material well-being and that this relatively poor economic performance could be improved by means which are known, understood and have already been applied by the developed countries. Objective measures of net economic performance have demonstrated the validity of the first part of this statement. Whether the measure was expectation of life at birth, death rates, infant mortality rates, the health of the people, con-

16. For an interesting discussion of some of the theoretical and statistical difficulties inherent in rural-urban and international comparisons of real incomes, see Nathan Koffsky, "Farm and Urban Purchasing Power," with comments by Margaret G. Reid, D. Gale Johnson and E. W. Grove; and Hans Staehle, "The International Comparison of Real National Income; A Note on Methods," with comments by Abram Bergson, Dorothy Brady and Eleanor M. Snyder, Morris A. Copeland and William Vickrey, in *Studies in Income and Wealth*, National Bureau of Economic Research, Vol. 11, New York, 1949, pp. 156–272. See also Bennett, *loc. cit., passim.*

TABLE 1-4. PER CAPITA INCOME, POPULATION AND POPULATION GROUPS OF
53 COUNTRIES, 1939

| Country | Per Capita Income | Rank | Population | Population Type |
|---|---|---|---|---|
| | (U.S. Dollars per Year) | | (Thousands) | |
| Total | .. | | 1,836,145 | |
| **Upper income group (over $200):** | | | | |
| United States | $554 | 1 | 131,416 | 1 |
| Germany | 520 | 2 | 69,317 | 1 |
| United Kingdom | 468 | 3 | 47,778 | 1 |
| Switzerland | 445 | 4 | 4,206 | 1 |
| Sweden | 436 | 5 | 6,341 | 1 |
| Australia | 403 | 6 | 6,997 | 1 |
| New Zealand | 396 | 7 | 1,642 | 1 |
| Canada | 389 | 8 | 11,368 | 1 |
| Netherlands | 338 | 9 | 8,834 | 1 |
| Denmark | 338 | 10 | 3,825 | 1 |
| France | 283 | 11 | 41,950 | 1 |
| Norway | 279 | 12 | 2,937 | 1 |
| Belgium | 261 | 13 | 8,396 | 1 |
| Eire | 248 | 14 | 2,946 | 1 |
| Argentina | 218 | 15 | 13,132 | 2 |
| **Middle income group ($101–$200):** | | | | |
| Union of South Africa | 188 | 16 | 10,251 | 2 |
| Finland | 184 | 17 | 3,684 | 1 |
| Chile | 174 | 18 | 4,940 | 2 |
| Austria | 166 | 19 | 6,650 | 1 |
| U.S.S.R. | 158 | 20 | 196,500 | 2 |
| Italy | 140 | 21 | 43,864 | 1 |
| Greece | 136 | 22 | 7,200 | 2 |
| Czechoslovakia | 134 | 23 | 15,239 | 1 |
| Hungary | 125 | 24 | 9,129 | 1 |
| Bulgaria | 109 | 25 | 6,308 | 2 |
| **Lower income group ($100 and below):** | | | | |
| Cuba | 98 | 26 | 4,253 | 3 |
| Yugoslavia | 96 | 27 | 15,703 | 2 |
| Poland | 95 | 28 | 35,090 | 2 |
| Japan | 93 | 29 | 72,520 | 2 |
| Venezuela | 92 | 30 | 3,650 | 3 |
| Egypt | 85 | 31 | 16,650 | 3 |
| Palestine | 81 | 32 | 1,502 | 3 |
| Costa Rica | 76 | 33 | 639 | 3 |
| Colombia | 76 | 34 | 8,986 | 3 |
| Peru | 72 | 35 | 7,000 | 3 |
| Panama | 71 | 36 | 620 | 3 |
| Ceylon | 63 | 37 | 5,922 | 3 |
| Mexico | 61 | 38 | 19,380 | 3 |
| Uruguay | 56 | 39 | 2,147 | 3 |
| Dominican Republic | 51 | 40 | 1,650 | 3 |
| Haiti | 50 | 41 | 2,600 | 3 |

(*Continued on page 20*)

TABLE 1-4. PER CAPITA INCOME, POPULATION AND POPULATION GROUPS OF
53 COUNTRIES, 1939—Continued

| Country | Per Capita Income | Rank | Population | Population Type |
|---|---|---|---|---|
| | (*U.S. Dollars per Year*) | | (*Thousands*) | |
| Nicaragua | 50 | 42 | 883 | 3 |
| Guatemala | 48 | 43 | 3,260 | 3 |
| Bolivia | 47 | 44 | 3,400 | 3 |
| Honduras | 45 | 45 | 1,090 | 3 |
| El Salvador | 45 | 46 | 1,745 | 3 |
| Brazil | 46 | 47 | 40,900 | 3 |
| Ecuador | 44 | 48 | 3,000 | 3 |
| Paraguay | 39 | 49 | 970 | 3 |
| India | 34 | 50 | 382,000 | 3 |
| Philippines | 32 | 51 | 16,300 | 3 |
| China | 29 | 52 | 450,000 | 3 |
| Indonesia | 22 | 53 | 69,435 | 3 |

*Source:* U.S. Department of State, *Point Four*, Publication 3719, January 1950, pp. 113–14.

Type 1. *Low growth potential.* Birth rates below 25 per thousand population. Low death rates. Small natural increase with prospect of relatively stationary populations in the future.

Type 2. *Transitional growth.* Birth rates 25–35. Both birth and death rates generally falling. Rapid population growth.

Type 3. *High growth potential.* Birth rates over 35. Death rates (but not birth rates) generally declining. Rapid growth in absence of civil disturbance, famine, and epidemic.

The birth rates refer to average annual figures for the period 1931–40. Official vital statistics were used where available, though for a number of countries these were corrected to take account of apparent under-reporting of births. Birth rates were estimated from other demographic information for countries lacking official vital statistics.

sumption as revealed by certain nonmonetary indicators or by per capita incomes, the broad results were essentially the same: one group of countries tended to cluster at the favorable end of the scale; another and much larger group fell more or less regularly and consistently at the unfavorable end. The order of rank among those countries at the lower end was of course not always the same with each measure of net economic performance. Nevertheless, the broad picture is unmistakable: one group of countries rates relatively well on the indicators, the other group quite poorly. Thus, provided the criteria are accepted, countries can be roughly differentiated into those which provide their inhabitants a relatively good end product of consumption and material well-being and those which do not.

The indexes that have been used to distinguish between countries which generally afford their residents a relatively poor life and those which do much better in this respect do not indicate in themselves to what degree or along what lines the end product can be improved. Answers to this question will necessarily depend upon a variety of factors—the reasons for the low level of economic performance at present, the ease or difficulty with which the barriers to better performance can be removed, the kinds of positive measures introduced, the possibility of outside assistance, and a host of related considerations. Even the most cursory glance at the underdeveloped countries from this point of view shows that they differ appreciably in their potentiality for bettering the lot of their people. And unfortunately, it is by no means true that those countries which stand most in need of betterment have the greatest potentiality for improvement.

## WHAT IS ECONOMIC DEVELOPMENT?

If underdeveloped areas can be distinguished from the already developed countries by means of certain indexes of life as end product—that is, monetary and nonmonetary indicators which suggest economic performance and material well-being—then presumably a country could be said to be achieving development if these indexes showed sustained improvement. If the phrase "real income per person" is used as a shorthand expression for all these partial indicators of material well-being taken together, then development implies raising real income per person. In other words, viewed broadly, what is underdeveloped in the underdeveloped areas is their real income potentialities; development means exploiting these potentialities. The real income potential of the land and the people, together with what capital equipment and technical knowledge they now have or can obtain, is for the underdeveloped areas appreciably above the level of real incomes which now prevail.

### A Broad Concept

Underdevelopment of real income potentialities is clearly a broader concept than underdevelopment of natural resources or lack of industrialization. Either exploitation of natural resources or industrialization or both might lead to higher real incomes in a particular underdeveloped area; but the concept of development is broader than either. To say that a country is underdeveloped does not necessarily imply that it has an abundance of untapped natural resources or that it should be industrialized. Development consists in making those changes—nearly all will require use of resources to some degree—which will most effectively realize the real income potentialities of a particular area.

What these changes will be probably cannot be answered by general economic analysis. The most promising approach for some areas may be via a more efficient use of the productive resources already in hand, for example, the labor force or land as a factor of production; for others, the important obstacles to higher real incomes may be a dearth of entrepreneurial abilities and productive capital equipment or socio-cultural factors. Regardless of these differences, development means developing the real income potentialities of the underdeveloped areas by using investment to effect those changes and to augment those productive resources which promise to raise real incomes per person.

The phrase "economic resources available to an area" has little meaning unless the state of the industrial arts or technology of the particular area is specified. Coal was not an economic resource to the Welsh or the English in 1066, nor is uranium an economic resource to the native tribes of the Belgian Congo today. What is a productive resource in any area depends a good deal upon the technical and industrial sophistication of the people who inhabit it. Consequently, the more literate, skilled and knowing the people become, the more numerous are the productive resources external to themselves which are available to them for augmenting their real incomes. The nonhuman resources tend to be a variable, dependent upon the character of the human productive resources.

The emphasis in the above is to identify development with those changes and investments which lift real incomes per person—as measured by various monetary and nonmonetary indicators of material well-being—closer to their potential level. Presumably, developmental changes should be of a kind and type which generate a sustained growth in real incomes. A temporary upsurge in material well-being followed by a recession to the initial levels could scarcely be called development.

While the foregoing probably corresponds to the common understanding of the term development, an awkward difficulty remains: What of the case where, despite important changes and sizable investments of a developmental character, real income per person does *not* increase over time, but instead a larger population gets an unchanged average income? Can one still say there has been development? Probably so. For it must be conceded that if the economy over time is able to support larger and larger numbers at the same level of material welfare, then welfare has improved: had developmental changes *not* been instituted, some persons now alive would not have survived, or if they had, they would have been less well off than they now are. Though this conclusion may seem paradoxical it appears to be the more reasonable of the alternatives.

The case is of more than hypothetical interest. In countries with high birth rates and falling death rates, a goodly share of the benefits of what would usually be regarded as developmental projects will take the form of increased numbers in the population rather than appreciably higher real incomes per person. The case of India comes to mind at once.[17]

17. See Chapter 5.

# 2. The Determinants of Real Income:

## Resources and Their Productivity in Underdeveloped Areas

THE FLOW OF OUTPUT, and hence average real incomes, in any society depends upon the productive resources available to it; how effectively these are used; and the cultural, social and political framework within which all economic activity in the particular society is carried on. These three factors broadly determine the level of total output and thus per capita incomes at any point in time. Similarly, efforts to raise real incomes in any area can be classified initially according to whether they attempt to augment the productive resources available, to improve the efficiency with which resources are used, or, lastly, to modify the socio-cultural environment in ways that either increase the available productive resources or enlarge the output they yield.[1]

In any actual society, of course, the three major factors or determinants have numerous cross relationships. But before examining these intricacies let us first attempt to give more content to the three determinants.[2]

### BASIC DETERMINANTS OF TOTAL OUTPUT

Real income per person may be low primarily because the productive resources available—though efficiently used—are so poor in quality or so deficient in quantity that little, if any, greater output can be had from them. If so, a better end product for the inhabitants depends upon augmenting the quantity and improving the quality of the area's productive resources. Since labor is a basic resource, people who are illiterate, diseased and undernourished, for example, are necessarily poor workers who will have a low output per person. Or if virtually all the arable land is already being cultivated efficiently, then a greater agricultural output would require more capital in production. Even areas that are already densely populated may

1. At least theoretically, income distribution in underdeveloped areas could be a problem. The existing aggregate output could conceivably give most of the people a better end product if it were not so badly skewed in its distribution: a few have far too much, many have far too little.

Although incomes are badly distributed in most underdeveloped areas, this factor appears to be of minor *direct* importance in explaining the low incomes of the bulk of the population. Incomes are *not* low primarily because output is badly divided. However, the indirect effects of a more nearly equal income distribution upon the size and composition of total output might be appreciable. Also, a badly skewed income distribution has important indirect effects upon output through the kind of social system, governmental organization, fiscal and tax arrangements and economic motivation likely to be associated with gross inequalities.

2. Consideration of the socio-cultural factor is mostly postponed to Chapter 4.

be acutely short of certain *kinds* of human skills or special abilities—entrepreneurs, innovators, administrators, for example. Thus the kinds and quantities of productive factors available are an important determinant of average real income.

### Resource Utilization

Real income per person may also be low, however, partly because the country does not use the productive resources it already has as effectively as it might. The land, the capital equipment and the labor force as they now are—poor quality and all—could be made to yield an appreciably larger output.

In the underdeveloped areas, this present inefficiency in resource use or underutilization of productive resources will necessarily be found chiefly in agriculture since the population is now mostly employed in agriculture. Better systems of crop rotation—without additional land, labor or capital —would often improve output. The seasonality of agriculture often means that much of the labor force is nearly idle for long intervals when instead it might be productively occupied. And there may be other people who are only nominally engaged in agricultural production in the sense that if they were withdrawn, total output would not decline. These are only a few examples. Of a different sort are inefficiencies in production which arise from the geographical and occupational immobility of the labor force. The low level of real incomes in underdeveloped areas is thus not simply a matter of insufficient resources, but also of the inefficiency with which present resources are being used.

Some observers would insist that perhaps the primary reason why productive resources in underdeveloped areas are often unutilized or inefficiently employed is the great dearth of persons with organizational and administrative skills in nearly all branches of private and public life. Entrepreneurs and entrepreneurial abilities are in short supply. The qualities of leadership combined with organizational and administrative skills are said to be all too rare in the underdeveloped areas. Were these skills more plentiful and more widely diffused and applied, the other resources would yield a better product and the present environment would be seen to contain far more resources than are now believed to exist. The inefficiency with which some resources—land and labor, for example—are currently used is attributable in part to the fact that a particular kind of productive factor, entrepreneurial and organizational ability, is in short supply.[3]

3. Consideration of some of the reasons for this dearth of entrepreneurial abilities in underdeveloped areas is postponed to Chapter 4 since the reasons for it appear to be primarily social and cultural. The importance of entrepreneurial and organizational abilities is well demonstrated by J. B. Condliffe in *The Commerce of Nations*, Norton, New York, 1950, pp. 677–95. For a particularly graphic account of the tragic consequence of the absence of such organizational and administrative abilities see Peter G. Franck, "Economic Planners in Afghanistan," *Economic Development and Cultural Change*, February 1953, pp. 323–40.

## The Socio-Cultural Environment

The third major factor in the flow of output and hence of real incomes in any area is the social, cultural or political environment within which the existing productive resources are used and increments thereto must be effected. Output and income per person in any society depend not alone on the kinds and quantities of productive resources available and how these are utilized in production, but also on those more intangible but no less "real" conditions which formal economic analysis is likely to pass over. If the Hindu religion attaches special significance to the cow, it seems a bit forced to say that the people of India make less than full and effective use of their cattle as an economic resource. Similarly, if the value system of a society assigns a low prestige index to entrepreneurial abilities or to comparable personality traits like leadership, initiative, imagination and organizational ability displayed in other spheres, then it is more reasonable to say that social and cultural factors inhibit economic achievement than to say that these abilities are untapped.

This category is clearly an omnibus affair. It includes a wide variety of institutions, mores and habits of thought which reflect the value systems and religious tenets dominant within the area or country. Among many other things, it would include the legal and political organization of the society, the structure of family organization and the values which dominate it, the extent to which work, creativeness and productive activity are held in esteem or treated with disdain. All in all, this factor relates to the whole environment which surrounds the use of productive resources in the society and the conditions within which economic resources must be reallocated and increased in number and kind.[4]

## A Necessary Caution

This formulation of three determinants of income, however, calls for a word of caution. As formulated, the quality of life as end product, real income per capita, etc., has been treated as the result, the dependent variable, which is determined by certain identifiable causal factors. The answer to the question, Why do underdeveloped areas have the low incomes they do? has been put in terms of three groups of causal factors which tend to fix the level of total output and, hence, income per person. While this formulation is analytically useful, it is also true that the low productivity which "explains" the low incomes in underdeveloped areas is itself partly the result of poor diet and poor health which make people lethargic, of incomes

4. For various economic approaches to this range of problems see Moses Abramovitz, "The Economics of Growth" in Bernard F. Haley (Ed.), *A Survey of Contemporary Economics*, Vol. II, Irwin, Homewood, Illinois, 1952, pp. 132–78, especially pp. 138–44; W. W. Rostow, *The Process of Economic Growth*, Norton, New York, 1952, Chapter 2 and *passim;* and Joseph J. Spengler, "Economic Factors in the Development of Densely Populated Areas," *Proceedings* of the American Philosophical Society, February 1951, pp. 20–53.

per capita so low that they leave little beyond bare consumption needs from which to accumulate capital goods, of a cultural environment which checks the incentive to greater efficiency in production.

The very quality and texture of life as end product is thus in part the explanation of why it is what it is. It is paradoxically true that people are poor in underdeveloped areas simply because they are poor. In other words, there is no simple causal relation between the end product and the factors which make the end product what it is; rather, the relation is one of complex interdependence and interaction between the variables, much after the fashion of the general equilibrium theory in economics of the relation between product prices and factor prices.

Much of this paradox arises from the fact that people are at one and the same time a factor in production and the recipients of the end product which flows from all the factors of production used in combination. Hence one can say that when people are ridden with malaria or when they have diets so poor that they are easy victims to epidemic diseases, they are badly off: the end product of the economy is poor. But one can equally well say that they have these diseases mainly because they produce so little and that one of the reasons why they produce so little is the fact that their illnesses seriously reduce their working effectiveness.

### Differences among Countries

Notwithstanding this interdependence, the relative importance of the three causal factors mentioned above is quite uneven among the underdeveloped areas. In some, the evidence suggests that the crux of the problem of low incomes lies in the socio-cultural environment rather than in any acute shortage of productive resources relative to the population. In others, the populations are so large and the available capital equipment and arable land so small in quantity or poor in quality that even the most favorable socio-cultural environment might not suffice appreciably to raise real incomes per person. In Egypt, for example, the productivity of agriculture per unit of land area is notably higher than in most underdeveloped areas. Consequently, higher real incomes must probably be sought mainly in other directions. But the same could not be said of parts of Latin America, where the income potentialities in agriculture are far from fully exploited.

In other words, while all three elements—factor supply, factor use and the socio-cultural environment—are probably of some causal importance in accounting for the low incomes in all underdeveloped areas, their relative importance as between one country and another is very uneven. Consequently, the most effective way to raise real incomes will not be everywhere the same. Economic development will necessarily mean different things in different areas simply because the factors which account for the low level of real incomes at present are not of equal importance in all countries and because, too, the means or directions by which these incomes can be improved are not everywhere equally promising.

## LABOR AND ITS PRODUCTIVITY

Unlike land and capital, human beings are at once a factor in production and the end purpose of economic activity as a whole. Viewed as "labor," human beings are an agent of production; viewed as people, they alone have wants and needs to be satisfied by the productive process. Here the emphasis is entirely upon labor as a factor in production.

Broadly speaking, the productivity of human labor when combined with land and capital resources depends upon the numbers and skills of the total population and the energy, drive, regularity and ingenuity with which these are applied in productive activity. The total population in relation to usable land area or to the available stock of capital goods does not constitute the effective labor force. The age and sex composition of the population and the mortality rates and fertility rates at various ages, along with social and cultural factors, chiefly determine the size of the labor force or the supply of labor. But even this statement is only approximately correct, since it takes no account of the varying amounts of time that members of the labor force may be willing or able to devote to productive activity. Also it does not measure differences in relative efficiency. Two equal populations might have identical proportions "in" the labor force yet in one of them more people might be involuntarily idle for several months each year and also measurably less efficient when actually working. Economically, therefore, the two labor forces of the same actual numbers are of unequal significance. Countries differ appreciably in this regard.

### Demographic Differences

Leaving aside for the moment unemployment and differences in the average skill or efficiency per person in the labor force, the contrast between the developed and underdeveloped areas is demographically most striking in three respects. First, in the underdeveloped areas characteristically a much higher proportion of the total population is in the younger age groups. Second, the mortality rates in these younger age groups are appreciably higher. Third, those who do escape death in childhood and reach a productive age have, on the average, fewer productive years remaining to them.

Available evidence shows that, on the average, in the underdeveloped countries about 40 per cent of the population is below 15 years of age as against only 25 per cent in the more developed countries. Thus the underdeveloped areas have about 15 fewer persons per 100 inhabitants who are old enough to work and be productive than the developed countries—assuming of course that children do not work before the age of 15. (See Table 2-1.)

TABLE 2-1. AGE DISTRIBUTION OF POPULATION IN
REGIONS OF THE WORLD, 1947

| | Estimated Percentage of Population | | |
| Region | Under 15 Years | 15–59 Years | 60 Years and Over |
|---|---|---|---|
| World | 36 | 57 | 7 |
| Africa | 40 | 55 | 5 |
| America | | | |
| United States and Canada | 25 | 64 | 11 |
| Latin America | 40 | 55 | 5 |
| Asia[a] | | | |
| Near East | 40 | 54 | 6 |
| South-Central Asia | 40 | 56 | 4 |
| Japan | 37 | 55 | 8 |
| Remainder of Far East | 40 | 55 | 5 |
| Europe[b] | | | |
| North-West-Central Europe | 24 | 62 | 14 |
| Southern Europe | 30 | 59 | 11 |
| Eastern Europe[b] | 34 | 59 | 7 |
| Oceania | 28 | 62 | 10 |

Source: United Nations, *Demographic Yearbook, 1949–50*, New York, 1950, p. 15.
a. Excluding Asiatic part of the U.S.S.R.
b. Including Asiatic part of the U.S.S.R.

The underdeveloped areas are even worse off in the productivity of their numbers than these figures suggest, because a larger proportion of the group "under 15" in these areas is made up of children under 5 or under 10 years of age. Young children not only have no productivity but they pre-empt the working time of many adults. For example, in Egypt in 1937, 39.2 per cent of the total population was below the age of 15, 27.2 per cent was below age 10 and 13.4 per cent below age 4. By contrast, in the United States in 1940 only 25 per cent of the population was below age 15, 16.1 per cent below age 10 and 8 per cent below age 4. These figures, moreover, probably understate the differences because of underreporting of young children in the census and the use of rounded figures for the ages of young children.[5]

5. Joseph J. Spengler points out that these differences in the age composition of the populations of developed and underdeveloped areas are principally the result of the fall in mortality in the developed countries. He also suggests that this improved age composition may have "increased per capita productive capacity perhaps 10–25 per cent and . . . made age structures such as the American about one-sixth more productive than those of Asia and Latin America." See his chapter entitled "Population Theory" in Bernard F. Haley (Ed.), *A Survey of Contemporary Economics*, Vol. II, Irwin, Homewood, Illinois, 1952, p. 106.

*Waste in Costs of Dependency*

Any society necessarily uses productive resources in the rearing and training of its children. From the economic point of view, this is a social investment which will yield benefits as the children advance into the productive years. Unfortunately, in the underdeveloped areas, these social investments yield smaller returns than in the more developed countries for two reasons. The first is that a sizable proportion of the dependency outlays yield no return at all because of the high infant and juvenile mortality rates: many of those born and reared through part of childhood never reach an age at which productivity could commence.[6] Moreover, in some underdeveloped areas, the ceremonies attendant upon birth, death and burial impose a further drain on resources that could be better used in other ways were mortality rates not so high in relation to birth rates.

The second reason why underdeveloped countries get smaller returns from the outlay costs of dependency is that a child who has reached the age of 15 may look forward to fewer years of productive work before his demise. The expectation of life at age 15 in Sweden in 1941–1945 was 56.7 years and in the United States in 1939–1941 it was 53.2 years. In contrast, life expectancy at age 15 in Guatemala was only 41.7 years (1939–1941); in Mexico, 39.4 (1929–1933); in Brazil, 40.1 (1920); in Korea, 47.3 (1938); and in India, only 31.4 years (1921–1931). The gap is thus appreciable.

QUALITATIVE DIFFERENCES

The labor supply in underdeveloped areas has so far been discussed chiefly in terms of the numbers in the population, their age distribution and the time span of their economically productive years. The assumption implicit in this treatment was that productive efficiency per person in the labor force was uniform: that one might reason from the numbers and composition of the labor force, their average life expectancy, and so on, to the supply of labor. This is patently false, since average efficiency per member of the working population differs appreciably between one underdeveloped area and another, and differs markedly as between developed areas and underdeveloped areas.

*Factors in Inefficiency*

Unfortunately, no general index of the economic efficiency of labor is available which can be used to compare countries with one another. One can only infer probable efficiency from certain collateral facts which, *a priori*, seem to be associated with efficiency. For example, a population

---

6. The relevant data on infant mortality have already been presented in Table 1-2. But juvenile mortality rates are also appreciably higher in underdeveloped areas. In the more developed countries mortality rates in the age category 1–4 years range from about 1.5 per 1,000 (Sweden, 1947) to 4.0; in the underdeveloped countries the comparable range is perhaps 25 to 70.

with a literacy rate of, say, 90 per cent is certain to be more efficient economically than one where the rate is 10 per cent. The tasks people will be able readily to perform where literacy is the rule will differ vastly from those people will be able to perform where it is the exception. Consequently, a high rate of illiteracy is prima facie evidence that a whole range of skills will be lacking because illiterates cannot acquire these skills. Similarly, a nation having few schools or teachers, or where people normally spend only a brief period in school, has, by definition, less effective means for imparting many skills to its people.

Labor efficiency is also affected by the energy people have available for the work in hand. Apart from cultural and social factors, which will be considered separately, this is probably largely a matter of diet and disease. Diets below the biological minimum requirements and endemic disease induce lethargy and apathy. People are often too ill to work at all, and even when they are at work they may lack the energy to be efficient producers. On both counts, the average annual output of the population is reduced.

*Evidences of Inefficiency*

In spite of the absence of any over-all index of labor efficiency by which directly to compare countries with one another, certain useful inferences can probably be drawn from such collateral facts as those just mentioned. And as might be supposed, the indirect evidence available suggests a marked gap between average labor efficiency in underdeveloped areas and that in the more developed countries.

In the underdeveloped areas, the proportion of illiterates ranges from 40 per cent to 90 per cent as against 4 to 8 per cent in the more developed countries.[7] Educational facilities are also far less abundant in the underdeveloped countries. Whereas in the underdeveloped countries the number of elementary school teachers per 1,000 population seems to vary from 0.63 (Haiti) to 2.4 (Mexico), the developed countries have ratios of from 4 to 5—more than twice as many. Technical schools and higher schools are much fewer in relation to the population in underdeveloped regions and are sometimes almost nonexistent.[8]

The profound effect of poor diets, endemic disease and lack of medical and hospital care upon the energy, and thus the efficiency, of labor in underdeveloped areas has been touched upon in Chapter 1. Mortality from tuberculosis ranges from 41 per 100,000 in the Netherlands to over 400 in

7. See United Nations, *Statistical Yearbook, 1949–50*, New York, 1950, Table 163, pp. 486ff. Generally speaking, the illiteracy rate is higher among females than among males and higher for the older age groups than for those in the earlier years. Ordinarily, illiteracy is expressed in terms of percentage of the population 10 years of age and over.

8. The United Nations classifies educational institutions under four headings: primary, secondary, technical and higher. For most underdeveloped countries there are few entries in the higher classifications, There are exceptions, however; for example, although the United Nations' *Statistical Yearbook, 1949–50*, gives no data on India or China, it is well known that these countries have long had universities.

# TABLE 2-2. INDICATORS OF LOW AVERAGE PRODUCTIVITY

| Country | Tuberculosis Death Rates per 100,000 Population (1939) | Percentage of Population Age 10 and Over Illiterate (about 1930) | Physicians per 1,000 Population | Elementary School Teachers per 1,000 Population |
|---|---|---|---|---|
| United States | 47 | below 5 | 1.37 | 4.29 |
| Germany | 50 | " 5 | .69 | 2.63 |
| United Kingdom | 62 | " 5 | 1.13 | 4.11 |
| Switzerland | 80 | " 5 | .84 | 3.01 |
| Sweden | 75 | " 5 | .94 | 4.03 |
| Australia | 40 | " 5 | .94 | 3.78 |
| New Zealand | 60 | " 5 | 1.00 | 4.58 |
| Canada | 53 | " 5 | .95 | 5.43 |
| Netherlands | 41 | " 5 | .83 | 4.10 |
| Denmark | 34 | " 5 | 1.03 | 4.51 |
| France | 137 | 5 | .73 | 3.77 |
| Norway | 86 | below 5 | .93 | 3.80 |
| Belgium | 68 | 6 | .80 | 5.73 |
| Eire | 113 | below 5 | .67 | 4.23 |
| Argentina | 103 | 17 | 1.05 | 5.24 |
| Union of South Africa | low | 60 | .41 | 1.28 |
| Finland | 190 | 14 | .45 | 3.68 |
| Chile | 264 | 24 | .63 | 2.54 |
| Austria | 40 | below 5 | 1.07 | 3.99 |
| U.S.S.R. | 160 | 19 | .76 | 3.65 |
| Italy | 76 | 22 | .87 | 3.41 |
| Greece | 128 | 41 | .86 | 2.17 |
| Czechoslovakia | 124 | below 5 | .76 | 2.31 |
| Hungary | 148 | 9 | .97 | 3.50 |
| Bulgaria | 138 | 31 | .65 | 4.18 |
| Cuba | 76 | 35 | .63 | 3.18 |
| Yugoslavia | 234 | 45 | .31 | 1.52 |
| Poland | 195 | 27 | .32 | 3.10 |
| Japan | 207 | below 10 | .87 | 3.47 |
| Venezuela | 233 | 63 | .41 | 0.94 |
| Egypt | 52 | 86 | .21 | 1.58 |
| Palestine | 56 | 69 | 1.38 | .. |
| Costa Rica | 172 | 35 | .25 | 4.74 |
| Colombia | low | 44 | .29 | 1.41 |
| Peru | high | 90 | .19 | 1.93 |
| Panama | 119 | 47 | .21 | 3.41 |
| Ceylon | 62 | 60 | .15 | .. |
| Mexico | 56 | 62 | .51 | 2.40 |
| Uruguay | 101 | 30 | .71 | 2.99 |
| Dominican Republic | medium | 71 | .20 | 1.45 |
| Haiti | high | 90 | .09 | 0.63 |
| Nicaragua | medium | 57 | .28 | 2.15 |
| Guatemala | medium | 72 | .11 | 1.24 |
| Bolivia | medium | 92 | .15 | 1.62 |
| Honduras | low | 68 | .11 | 1.45 |
| El Salvador | high | 73 | .16 | 1.81 |
| Brazil | 250 | 62 | .31 | 1.97 |
| Ecuador | high | 80 | .24 | 1.03 |
| Paraguay | 102 | 65 | .28 | 3.34 |
| India | 283 | 91 | .12 | 1.27 |
| Philippines | 298 | 51 | .26 | 1.76 |
| China | 400–500 | 85 | .04 | 1.73 |
| Indonesia | high | 92 | .02 | .. |

Source: U.S. Department of State, Point Four, Publication 3719, January 1950, pp. 115–16, 122–23.

China; the number of physicians per 1,000 population from 1.38 in Palestine and 1.37 in the United States to .02 in Indonesia. (See Table 2-2.) While
the data are fragmentary and imprecise, they point to one of the primary
causes of the low efficiency of labor in underdeveloped areas.

### Mobility and Productivity

One of the striking features of the labor force in most underdeveloped
areas is its relative immobility—geographical, occupational and social. The
allocation of the labor force appears to be based much more on caste, class,
custom, tradition or similar social sanction than on personal preferences
and abilities. Consequently good talent may go unutilized and obvious
ineptness may go uncorrected. Market considerations such as cost and
returns play a smaller part than in developed countries in determining how
the labor force is utilized in production.

While geographical mobility is partly held in check because of poor communications and transport, the social and cultural factors governing entry
and exit into various callings appear to be considerably more important.
The usually greater rigidity of class distinctions and class lines in underdeveloped areas, which often virtually preclude vertical mobility, must also,
it would seem, inhibit diligence, imagination and ingenuity among members of the labor force. If "advancement" to a higher social class and "de-
motion" to a lower are both nearly impossible, then neither the spur of
ambition nor the fear of failure will be of much importance as a factor in
labor output.

## LAND AND CAPITAL RESOURCES

Land, regarded as an economic resource, implies not mere area alone but
its climatic complement, topography, soil, vegetation cover, water tables,
mineral content, waterways and much else besides. Together these determine what useful products can be obtained when land is combined in production with labor and capital equipment.

Some characteristics of particular land areas are virtually immutable,
with important consequences for their potential productivity. Man cannot
change the winds of Patagonia, the heavy rains in parts of the tropics or the
monsoons in India. On the other hand, judicious investment of labor and
capital in irrigation works, transport facilities, harbor developments, fertilizers and so on can often greatly increase the output even from poor land.
Similarly, technical advances in agricultural science may convert barren
wastes into fruitful fields. For example, in recent decades improved strains
of wheat have pushed the boundaries for the economical production of this
crop much closer to the poles.

The physical and economic geography of particular underdeveloped areas must be left to specialized studies with maps of topography, rainfall, soil, mineral deposits and the like. Economic development, moreover, depends not so much on the physical characteristics of the land areas where low incomes prevail as on the possibilities of raising these incomes by combining the land with other productive agents to yield a larger output.

### Cultivable Land

Only about 7 per cent, or 2.6 billion acres, of the 35.7 billion acres of the earth's surface is believed to be suitable for agricultural production. Of these 2.6 billion acres, about 60 per cent is now used for the production of food, including grain feeds for livestock, while the remaining 40 per cent produces nonedible crops or stands idle.

TABLE 2-3. LAND IN RELATION TO POPULATION, ABOUT 1940

| Continent | Land Adapted to Agricultural Production | Land Used for Food Crops, Including Grain Fed to Livestock | *Acres per Capita* Adapted to Agricultural Production | *Acres per Capita* Used for Food Crops, Including Grain Fed to Livestock | Food Crops: Yield per Harvested Acre |
|---|---|---|---|---|---|
| | *(Millions of Acres)* | | | | *(Lbs. Dry Weight)* |
| World | 2,580 | 1,529 | 1.19 | 0.70 | 1,003 |
| Asia | 600 | 476 | 0.52 | 0.41 | 1,046 |
| Europe | 890 | 477 | 1.55 | 0.83 | 976 |
| North America | 570 | 317 | 3.10 | 1.72 | 1,058 |
| Africa | 240 | 152 | 1.53 | 0.97 | 643 |
| South America | 220 | 83 | 2.47 | 0.93 | 1,066 |
| Oceania | 60 | 24 | 5.45 | 2.18 | 740 |

*Source:* Adapted from Joseph J. Spengler, "Aspects of the Economics of Population Growth, Part II," *Southern Economic Journal,* January 1948, p. 252.

But this world figure of 60 per cent is the result of averaging out wide disparities among the continents. North America, for example, is estimated to have 570 million acres of land suited to agricultural production, of which 317 million acres, or 55 per cent, is now devoted to food production. In South America, only 37 per cent of the 220 million acres of comparable land is used for food production. But in Asia, 79 per cent of the usable 600 million acres is already being used to produce food. When these figures are reduced to a per capita basis, the land scarcity in Asia shows up even more sharply. Asia has only .52 acre per capita suited for agriculture and only .41 acre per capita devoted to food production. In North America, the corresponding per capita figures are 3.10 and 1.72 acres, or roughly six times and four times as much. (See Table 2-3.)

Even these statistics do not show the marked differences among individual countries. Insofar as a global picture can be conveyed, Figures 2 and 3

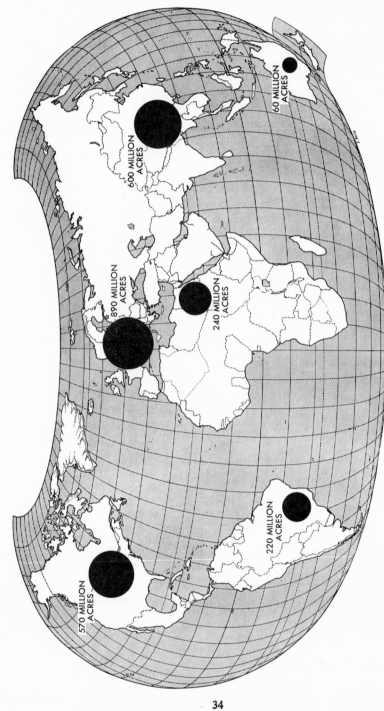

FIGURE 2. LAND SUITABLE FOR AGRICULTURE IN EACH CONTINENT

*Source:* W. S. and E. S. Woytinsky, *World Population and Production,* Twentieth Century Fund, 1953.

The area of land suitable for agriculture in each continent is represented by black circles on the same scale as the respective continent.

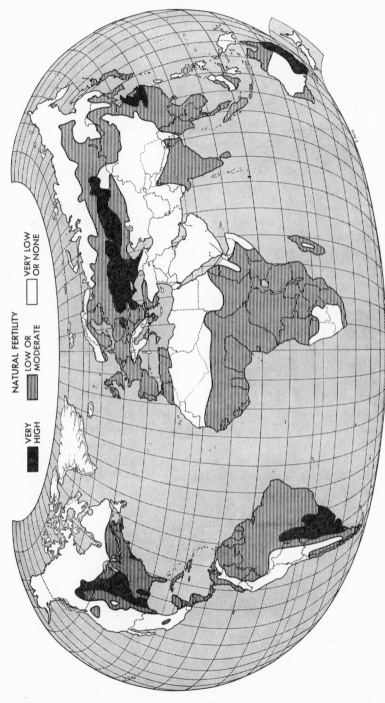

FIGURE 3. GEOGRAPHIC DISTRIBUTION OF LAND IN EACH CONTINENT BY NATURAL FERTILITY

*Source:* W. S. and E. S. Woytinsky, *World Population and Production,* Twentieth Century Fund, 1953.

NATURAL FERTILITY

VERY HIGH

LOW OR MODERATE

VERY LOW OR NONE

come about as close to portraying the "facts" as can be done in summary form.[9]

Only a few underdeveloped areas appear to have much potentially productive land which is not already in use. One index sometimes used to indicate the possibilities of further land development is the percentage that the area of unused but potentially productive land area forms of that already in use. On this basis, Nicaragua (827 per cent), Brazil (155 per cent), India (57 per cent), Burma (64 per cent), Syria (147 per cent), Tunisia (109 per cent) and Liberia (150 per cent) all appear to have at least half as much unused but potentially productive land as they have land already in use.[10] These figures are not to be taken too literally, however, and their usefulness is limited by the lack of comparable data for many other underdeveloped countries. Moreover, the phrase "potentially cultivable" implies a host of assumptions as to the "other conditions" necessary to realize this potential. The underdeveloped areas as a whole—and especially those with already large populations—probably do not have large unused but potentially cultivable land areas. Much of the unused land is little more than desert. In the Middle East, for example, "desert comprises 95 per cent of area of Egypt, 80 per cent of Jordan, 40 per cent of Israel (35 per cent of Palestine), 33 per cent of Iraq, 25 per cent of Iran and Syria and 20 per cent of the Anglo-Egyptian Sudan; figures are approximate."[11]

### Implications of Land Scarcity

Some underdeveloped areas already suffer so much from acute overcrowding on the land that, barring technological progress or large investments, the prospects for higher incomes through further intensification of land use are not encouraging. Others are in a more favorable position. In India, for example, the ratio of the arable land in hectares (one hectare = 2.47 acres) to the agricultural labor force was already 1.04 in 1947; that is, each agricultural laborer had on the average 1.04 hectares of land with which to work.[12] In Indonesia, the comparable figure was 0.797. Turkey, on the other hand, had 3.087 hectares per agricultural worker, Mexico 5.26 and Venezuela 31.94. As compared with Canada's 28.37, Egypt had only 0.57 and Japan 0.34.[13]

9. As a friendly critic has pointed out, however, there are no really accurate data as to what lands are suited to agricultural production among those that are not actually cultivated at present: the tendency is to list uncultivated lands as incapable of cultivation or at least economically uncultivable. In a good many underdeveloped areas, however, only a modicum of reliable information exists concerning the productive potential of lands not now in use. Moreover, the usability of land, as of other resources, is a function of the level of technical knowledge in the population and the degree of economic development.

10. Computed from Appendix 2-1 by dividing the figure in column 6 by that in column 4.

11. United Nations, *Review of Economic Conditions in the Middle East* (Supplement to *World Economic Report, 1949–50*), 1951, New York, 1951, Table 30, p. 64.

12. Note that these figures relate land area to the *labor force* and not to total population as in Table 2-3.

13. Figures for these and other countries are shown in Appendix 2-1, which is a summary of data on the relation between land and people in agriculture.

A low ratio of land area to labor force in agriculture is not necessarily associated with low income per person: Switzerland (1.22), Belgium (1.60) and the Netherlands (1.89) are all examples of the contrary. When the ratio drops below one hectare of arable land, however, the probabilities are that per capita income will also be at a very low figure, say less than $100.

Thus to a limited extent scarcity of land accounts for the low incomes of the underdeveloped areas. Unfortunately, however, the large potentially cultivable land areas that are known to exist are mostly either in already developed countries such as Canada, Australia and the United States or in underdeveloped countries that are remote from the overcrowded countries, for example in Latin America. Consequently, at least for the present, no appreciable increase in incomes is in prospect merely through making more land available to those who need it. Better incomes will have to come chiefly from better use of existing land resources. From the point of view of its productive contribution, moreover, land varies widely in "quality." Yet the underdeveloped countries, by and large, are less able than others to make full use of the potential productivity of their best land or to modify or overcome the deficiencies of their poorer land: their people lack the technical knowledge and real capital resources which, if combined with existing land resources, could provide higher real incomes.

### PRODUCTIVE CAPITAL RESOURCES

Productive capital resources are those used primarily to further the output of final consumption goods and services. They include factory buildings, machinery and equipment, transport facilities, water, sewerage and irrigation works, communication facilities, public buildings, laboratories, schools, land improvements, work animals, livestock, inventories of raw materials and goods-in-process, etc. Apart from these productive capital goods, all societies possess other capital goods which yield a direct flow of consumption goods and services. These consumption capital goods, which include dwellings, churches, shrines, museums, chattels and consumers' durable goods, afford comfort, satisfaction and pride to a people within their particular cultural environment.

Most countries have gradually accumulated capital goods of both types over the centuries. But the developed countries have greater stocks of each per capita, and especially of productive capital goods. Development, industrialization and productive capital accumulation have gone hand in hand in the now high income countries over the past one hundred and fifty years.

### Contrasts among Countries

Direct comparisons of the productive capital resources of developed and underdeveloped countries, by an inventory method, for example, is impossible because adequate data are not available. Nevertheless, the indirect evidence on the dearth of productive capital goods in the underdeveloped areas is sufficiently convincing.

The very fact that incomes are so low in the underdeveloped areas is itself indicative of capital scarcity. The same deduction can be drawn by reasoning along the following lines. In the underdeveloped countries the labor force is predominantly in agriculture; hence, what productive capital there is must be primarily in agriculture unless there are other industries which use much capital and relatively little labor. The meager data available, however, suggest that the workers outside agriculture—say, usually, less than a third of the total—are primarily in commerce and transport, in manufactures and handicrafts, and in administration, domestic service, etc.[14] Of these activities only manufactures and transport are likely to be conducted with any appreciable amount of capital equipment.[15] Consequently, the capital equipment in agriculture must account for the bulk of the total in the underdeveloped areas. But all the evidence is that agriculture in underdeveloped areas is not abundantly supplied with capital.

### Capital Resources in Agriculture

The real capital resources in agriculture may be classified roughly under three heads: (1) direct capital input in the form of seeds, fertilizers, work animals, farm tools and machinery, etc.; (2) fixed capital installations used directly in agriculture such as drainage systems, irrigation facilities, storage tanks, buildings, farm roads; (3) ancillary capital installations serving agriculture along with other economic activities such as electrical power, road and rail transport facilities, communication systems, which contribute indirectly to agricultural productivity. Good facilities for the transport of crops are no less important than silos or hoes.

The available statistical data under these three headings, however, are fragmentary and at times difficult to interpret.

14. A Burmese census of 1931 shows 69 per cent of the gainfully occupied population in agriculture, 13 per cent in manufacturing and handicrafts, 14 per cent in commerce and transport and 4 per cent in administration, domestic service, etc. See International Labor Office, *Economic Background of Social Policy*, New Delhi, 1947, p. 4, and Chapter 4. Egypt had 11 per cent of its gainfully employed population in manufacturing and handicrafts, Mexico and India each had 13 per cent as of about 1930, according to *Industrialization and Foreign Trade*, League of Nations, Geneva, 1945, pp. 26–27.

15. Manufactures in the underdeveloped areas seem to display certain essential similarities even though generalization is hazardous. While basic producers' goods industries—iron and steel, metallurgy, engineering and chemicals—are scarcely present in modern form, local handicraft industries do provide some of their simpler products either for domestic use or even for export—for example, simple tools, dyestuffs, salt, matches, soap and glass. Direct foreign investment has typically concentrated upon the processing of primary products for export and often, too, upon transport facilities necessary to get primary products to world markets. Examples from the Far East include petroleum (Indonesia), tin (Malaya, Indonesia, etc.), rice milling (Siam and Burma), tea (Ceylon and India), sugar (Philippines, Indonesia, etc.), coconuts (Philippines), sawmilling (Siam and Burma). A third type of industry is the manufacture of consumers' goods for the home market or for export to other underdeveloped countries. Here, textiles and tobacco, financed either by local or foreign capital, are likely to predominate. The overwhelming importance of textiles as measured by the number of persons employed is striking: this industry often accounts for over 50 per cent of those employed in manufactures in underdeveloped countries.

*Direct Capital Input in Agriculture*

As for direct capital input, the more advanced countries use more fertilizer and more pesticides than the underdeveloped countries. If tons of fertilizer per 1,000 hectares of arable land are used as a measure of fertilizer-capital input, the five largest consumers among the developed countries, around 1948–1949, were Belgium (294.8), the Netherlands (283.1), New Zealand (246.8), Switzerland (166.6) and Germany (131.5).[16] In the underdeveloped countries, the amount used rarely rises above 2 tons per 1,000 hectares and is below one ton in India (0.55), Indonesia (0.709), Syria (0.218) and Burma (0.057).

Fertilizer consumption is determined by the type of agriculture as well as by the degree of economic development. It is likely to be greater in those underdeveloped countries where plantation agriculture is practiced. Egypt uses more tons (54.3) of fertilizer per 1,000 hectares of arable land than does the United States (29.6). Argentina uses less than either India or Indonesia, while Korea is a substantially heavier consumer (20.4 tons) than most Latin American countries and even some central and southeastern European countries.

Similarly, the few figures available on pesticide consumption indicate much higher consumption in the more developed countries.[17]

The underdeveloped countries, as one would expect, use more work animals and fewer tractors than the developed countries. (See Appendix 2–2, column 8.) Their working livestock includes asses, mules, buffaloes, camels, oxen and horses according to the type of agriculture and the level of poverty. In many underdeveloped areas, of course, work animals and human muscles are close substitutes for each other.

*Fixed Capital Installations*

Fixed capital resources used either directly or indirectly in agriculture are doubtless exceedingly sparse in underdeveloped areas. All indirect evidence —such as energy consumption per capita, railway mileage in relation to area, motor vehicles or telephones in relation to population—emphasizes the enormous gulf between the developed and underdeveloped areas in the amount and variety of their fixed capital resources. For example, whereas the United States consumes 37.6 horsepower-hours of all kinds of energy per capita per day and the United Kingdom 27.1, the amount consumed in Haiti, Bolivia, India, China and Indonesia is 0.5 or less.

As for transport, China, Paraguay, Nicaragua, Peru and Venezuela all have less than 5 miles of railway per 1,000 square miles of area while

16. The fertilizers included are commercial nitrogenous fertilizers (N), commercial phosphoric acid ($P_2O_5$) and commercial potash fertilizers ($K_2O$). See United Nations, *Yearbook of Food and Agriculture*, New York, 1949, Tables 74–76.

17. *Ibid.*, Table 78.

Belgium, Germany, Switzerland and the United Kingdom have over 200. Differences are even greater if the measure used is ton-miles of freight carried per capita per year. India and Finland, for instance, both have 26 miles of railroad per 1,000 square miles of area, but the number of ton-miles of freight carried per capita per year is 60 in India and 508 in Finland. The underdeveloped areas not only have fewer miles of railways, but what mileage they have is used less intensively.[18]

The meager data on real capital resources in agriculture in underdeveloped countries suggest that they compare quite unfavorably with the more developed countries. Land scarcity or inefficiency of labor is not offset by capital abundance. But since industry is typically of minor importance this is the same as saying that aggregate capital resources available are exceedingly small compared with the more developed countries.[19]

### Differences in Kinds of Productive Capital Resources

Among the many contrasts between the underdeveloped countries and the more well-to-do countries none is perhaps more striking than the differences in productive real capital resources. The high-income countries possess certainly more real capital per person; but, perhaps even more important, their capital is more diversified in type and serves economic welfare in ways which have no real counterpart in underdeveloped areas.

Among the most important of these services of capital in high-income countries are the huge investments in "general purpose" capital goods— railways, highways, telephone and telegraph installations, river and harbor developments, electric power facilities, flood control and irrigation works, educational facilities and the like. All these contribute enormously to the effectiveness with which human skills and natural resources can yield out-

---

18. The broad picture on ancillary and "general purpose" capital goods will be found in Appendix 2–2, from which the figures above are drawn.

19. The omission of any explicit reference to plantation agriculture from the foregoing discussion of real capital resources in agriculture in underdeveloped areas deserves a word of explanation. Plantation agriculture is typically much more highly capitalistic than subsistence agriculture, so that some of the foregoing comments would not be relevant. Indeed, the plantation is probably more similar to an industrial undertaking in its methods of finance, organization and control than to indigenous agriculture. Typically, the capital has come from abroad, the manager also, and the product is largely marketed abroad. In other words, plantations might be regarded as overseas outposts of advanced economies rather than as segments of underdeveloped economies that directly permit the local populations to finance imports. The contribution of plantations to the welfare of underdeveloped countries is made indirectly through their contribution to exports after deduction of capital charges, profits and wages of the foreign personnel. On a net basis, therefore, their contribution to the financing of imports would be about equivalent to the wages and other outlays paid directly to the native workers on the plantation. Though substantially less than the f.o.b. value of the exported products of the plantation, this still amounts to a sizable sum annually but probably quite small per person in the underdeveloped area. In other words, the contribution of the capital invested in plantations to real incomes in underdeveloped areas would not usually raise appreciably the general average or much modify the general argument in the text. In any case, whatever modification is necessary is perhaps better approximated by an examination of export statistics than by estimates of capital invested in plantations.

Among the principal products of plantation agriculture are tea, coffee, rubber, cocoa, coconut, cinchona, cotton, cinchona bark, abacá, tobacco, sugar, sisal and various vegetable oils. For an interesting discussion of some economic aspects of plantation agriculture see C. R. Fay, "Plantation Economy," *Economic Journal*, December 1936, pp. 620–44.

put through the specialization of persons in productive activities and the specialization of production by geographical areas. The combination of specialization and power and transport facilities is so effective that only a comparatively small fraction of the working population in the high-income countries is needed to produce the basic necessities of life while the remainder can engage in manufactures, service industries, etc., which make life richer and more varied. But these activities are also carried on with a substantial complement of real capital resources, so that output per person in manufacturing, for example, is generally strikingly higher than in the underdeveloped countries wherever any comparison is possible. Thus the high-income countries have more productive capital per person and use most of it in types of economic activity which are almost nonexistent in the underdeveloped areas.

## Rate of Accumulation

Beyond the fact that the developed countries have more capital per person, they are adding to these stocks more rapidly than the underdeveloped countries. Whether measured against existing stocks of capital or against national incomes, capital accumulation proceeds faster in the already developed countries. Indeed, the problem of capital in the underdeveloped countries is not so much that of providing a stock of real capital goods—a once-and-for-all proposition—as it is to create those conditions and attitudes which generate capital accumulation as a continuing process. For today's capital goods will often be obsolete tomorrow, and tomorrow's requirements probably cannot be foreseen today; a country must maintain a steady flow of new investment if, year in and year out, it is to realize its real income potentialities.[20]

### FACTOR COMBINATIONS AND THEIR PRODUCTIVITY

Labor, land and capital complement one another as agents of production in the sense that usually no production is possible without some amount of

20. The amount of savings in relation to national income in underdeveloped areas is undoubtedly low, but accurate statistical information is rarely available. Perhaps most authorities would agree with the generalization made recently by the United Nations' experts: "In most countries where rapid economic progress is occurring, net capital formation at home is at least 10 per cent of the national income, and in some it is substantially higher. By contrast, in most under-developed countries net capital formation is not as high as 5 per cent of the national income, even when foreign investment is included." United Nations, *Measures for the Economic Development of Under-Developed Countries*, New York, 1951, p. 35. Home-financed investment in India is said to be about 2.5 per cent of national income. See *The Colombo Plan for Co-Operative Economic Development in South and South-East Asia*, Cmd. 8080, H.M.S.O., London, 1950, p. 54. In much of the rest of Southeast Asia the rate is doubtless no higher. See *ibid.*, *passim* and United Nations, *Economic Survey of Asia and the Far East 1950*, New York, 1951, pp. 121–25 and *passim.*

The familiar generalization that savings are a small fraction of national income in underdeveloped countries may not apply to certain Latin American countries, for example Brazil, Chile and Mexico, where rates comparable to (or greater than, as in Brazil) those in developed countries are said to prevail. See Simon G. Hanson, *Economic Development in Latin America*, Inter-American Affairs Press, Washington, 1951, pp. 188 *ff.*, where it is alleged (p. 190) that "The ineffective mobilization of available domestic capital constitutes the real challenge."

all three. Only rarely, however, do the technical conditions of production require that the agents be used in a fixed proportion to give a desired product. One agent—labor, for example—can be used in partial substitution for another, say capital equipment. It is possible to dig a ditch or build a road by using many men with shovels or a few men with machinery. Or again, farming can be conducted by the methods of the homesteader using a quarter section and his own labor or by many laborers on a small plot. The agents of production can be substituted for one another, within limits, to produce the same end product. But the limits of substitution are clearly finite, not infinite.

## A Special Problem in Underdeveloped Areas

This imperfect substitutability of the factors of production goes far to explain the low per capita level of output, and hence of real incomes, in the underdeveloped areas. If labor were completely substitutable for land and capital equipment in production, then the dearth of land and capital relative to labor in the underdeveloped areas would make no difference: output per person could be just as high as in the high-income countries. In fact, however, real output per person is necessarily lower because of the limited range over which labor can be substituted for land or capital to obtain the same total output.

The possibilities of substitution among the agents of production differ enormously according to the type of final product. In electric power production, for example, the range over which more labor and less capital can be used is narrowly restricted. In raising cotton or in the manufacture of certain types of cotton textiles, the range is much broader. But in all cases the limits of substitution are short of infinity.

Broadly speaking, the stubborn fact of less-than-infinite substitutability among the factors of production, in conjunction with the inequality of endowments as between different countries and regions, goes far to explain the marked differences between countries in the relative costs and prices of the same or similar goods. In a country with abundant labor and little capital equipment, goods which take much labor in their production will be relatively cheap; for example, craft goods such as filigree jewelry, tooled leather goods and all kinds of personal services. On the other hand, goods that require large amounts of scarce capital equipment and relatively little labor will be much more expensive in these countries than in more developed countries where capital equipment is more abundant. The converse is observed in countries like the United States where the relative scarcity of the productive factors is reversed: refrigerators and automobiles are relatively cheap but hand tailoring, watch repairs, maids and butlers come high.

The consequence is that the consumption patterns in different countries tend to conform to these differences in relative product prices, which in turn reflect the relative supplies of the factors of production and the technical possibilities of substitution among them. There may be a large demand for home haircutters in the United States but almost none at all in China.

### Limitations of Substitution

The possibilities of substituting the cheap for the dear in consumption—and what is cheap and what is dear in any area depends largely upon the relative scarcities of productive factors—are severely limited in underdeveloped areas. In other words, the fact that personal services are so cheap in underdeveloped areas does not mean that the people there can get along without food or clothing or shelter: a certain consumption of these goods is essential. Moreover, to take food as an example, the possibilities of substitution, both on the side of consumption and on the side of production, are soon exhausted: the substitution of other items for food in consumption is limited; the substitution of labor for land in food production is limited.

The underdeveloped areas therefore cannot fully adjust their consumption habits to their endowment of productive factors, nor can they completely substitute abundant labor for scarce land and capital in production to supply their consumption needs and wants. They can substitute partially in consumption and partially in production, but in neither are the possibilities of substitution unlimited. Consequently, output, consumption and material well-being are all at a lower level than they would be if the possibilities of substitution were greater or if the factor endowments were less disproportionate.

### Consequences of Limited Substitutability

If underdeveloped areas are characterized by relatively abundant labor and relatively scarce land and capital equipment, this must mean that per capita output is low and will remain low as long as this disproportion persists.[21] Moreover, the worse the disproportion becomes, the lower will be per capita incomes. Economic necessity will force the substitution of labor for land or capital equipment wherever possible in the struggle to raise total output. But if the possibilities of substitution are finite, as the evidence indicates they are, then it follows that further increments in the labor factor, with unchanged quantities of land and capital equipment, will no longer add anything to total output. The marginal physical product of the labor factor becomes zero: no further increases in total output from

21. In some underdeveloped areas—parts of Latin America, for example—the land supply is not notably deficient even though capital equipment is relatively scarce. Here part of the explanation for the low incomes lies in the fact that institutional or social factors prevent the land from being used in production as efficiently as it might be or even from being used at all.

merely applying more labor are possible. If population increases beyond this point and still more labor is applied with the existing land and capital equipment, total output will remain the same and output per person will fall. The average person will be worse off because more people have to be fed and these additional people add nothing to total output.

The degree of this disproportion between the labor factor and the complementary production factors of land and capital equipment will of course determine how low real incomes per capita will be.[22] For present purposes, two groups are worth distinguishing: first, those underdeveloped areas in which the marginal physical product of labor, primarily agricultural labor, while possibly quite low, is still greater than zero, so that if labor were withdrawn from agriculture total farm output would decline; second, those others in which the marginal physical product of labor has already fallen to zero, so that some labor—perhaps more than a modest fraction of the labor force in some underdeveloped areas—could be withdrawn without reducing total output.

The second group includes nearly all those underdeveloped countries which are usually referred to as "overpopulated," such as India, Java, and other areas in Southeastern Asia, Egypt and some other Arab countries, parts of Southeastern Europe, as well as much of the Caribbean. Most of Latin America and even some countries in Asia fall in the first group. Theoretically, the dividing line between the two groups is whether or not the marginal physical productivity of labor in agriculture has already fallen to zero. It may have fallen below zero outside agriculture as well, but since most of the labor force is in agriculture the rest can be neglected for the time being.

### Disguised Unemployment

These overpopulated or densely populated underdeveloped countries in which some labor might be withdrawn from agriculture without reducing output are usually said to have "disguised unemployment" or "overemployment" in agriculture. This phenomenon is not a mere figment of the economic theorist's imagination, even though precise estimates of its amount and extent are at present impossible. According to W. Arthur Lewis, an English economist who has closely observed underdeveloped areas in the Caribbean and the Orient, "Indian economists estimate conservatively that a quarter of the rural population is surplus, in the sense that its removal from the land would make no difference to agricultural

22. This disproportion of the factors of production also accounts to a considerable degree for the great disparity in incomes among persons in underdeveloped areas. Landowners will have high incomes from the very fact that land is scarce; moneylenders who have command over liquid resources which can be made the means of acquiring capital for production or consumption purposes will be well paid for the accommodation they supply.

output."[23] W. E. Moore, in his *Economic Demography of Eastern and South-eastern Europe*, suggests that perhaps 35 to 45 per cent of the population dependent on agriculture in that region adds little or nothing to output.[24] Similar conclusions have been drawn with respect to other underdeveloped areas.[25]

If the facts are as alleged by these and other observers, namely, that in many densely populated underdeveloped areas perhaps as much as 25 per cent of the agricultural labor force could be withdrawn without diminishing output, there is a strong presumption that this economically unproductive portion of the labor force could be turned to better account in other directions.

## Seasonal Idleness

Even in those underdeveloped areas in the first group, where population on the land is not so large that the addition of more labor would not increase production, seasonal unemployment of the labor force often runs high. Seasonal unemployment in agriculture is everywhere prevalent to some extent, but in the more economically advanced countries it is not accompanied by low levels of material well-being and it probably amounts to less loss of working days per year because of greater diversification in production and because of the greater possibilities for direct farm investment in improvements during slack periods. Insofar as seasonal idleness exists, it also offers a potential for improved welfare.[26]

Thus disguised unemployment in the densely populated underdeveloped areas and seasonal idleness in the others represent failure to utilize an economic resource. Whether effective means can be devised for the utilization of this labor potential that now runs to waste will be examined in a later chapter. Certainly with the organization of production that now prevails in most underdeveloped areas, and with the disproportion between labor and other productive factors that now severely limits further substitu-

23. W. Arthur Lewis, "Reflections on South-East Asia," *District Bank Review*, December 1952, p. 11.

24. League of Nations, Geneva, 1945, pp. 61–75 and appendices.

25. See, for example, Doreen Warriner, *Land and Poverty in the Middle East*, Royal Institute of International Affairs, London, 1948; also her earlier study, *Economics of Peasant Farming*, Oxford University Press, London, 1939, which relates to eastern and southeastern Europe.

In order to avoid possible misunderstanding, it should be stressed that the notion of excess population in agriculture used in the text relates to the numbers or the fraction of the working force or total population that might be withdrawn from agriculture without any absolute fall in output. The marginal physical product of labor is already zero.

A quite different concept of excess population in agriculture is one which makes the criterion whether or not the level of living in agriculture with these numbers can be "decent" or "acceptable," that is, does it fall below the level that the social conscience or social policy allows? The notion of "submarginal" farmers as the term has been used in the United States is of this kind. It does not imply that the marginal physical product of labor on those farms is zero, only that it is unconscionably low.

26. The seasonal variation in agriculture in underdeveloped areas is a huge topic with striking differences from area to area. For an unusually interesting account of certain seasonal features in Indonesian agriculture, see the remarks of Egbert DeVries in *Formulation and Economic Appraisal of Development Projects*, Vol. I, United Nations, Lahore, 1951, pp. 357–67 and *passim*.

tion between them, there is little reason to believe that the problem will solve itself. Indeed, if allowed to drift, it is likely to become worse rather than better. For disproportion means low incomes, and low incomes imply little possibility of capital formation out of savings. Yet it is the shortage of capital, and of land, relative to labor that is a primary cause of the low incomes.

## WAYS TO INCREASE OUTPUT AND REAL INCOMES

Insofar as the low incomes of the underdeveloped areas have their root cause in the lack of proportion among the productive factors of labor, land and capital, and in the limited possibilities of technical substitution among them, there are only three types of change by which output and incomes can be improved.

### Technical Changes

First, output from existing productive factors could be increased by means of technical changes that make it easier to substitute abundant labor for relatively scarce capital equipment and land. A spate of innovations that were capital-saving or land-saving or both would raise total output.

This is not inconceivable. The adaptations need not be completely new techniques or methods of production; the techniques of production used in some underdeveloped areas are much inferior to those already in use in other underdeveloped areas where labor is also abundant and about equally cheap compared with land and capital. These better techniques need to be transferred and applied. Point IV "technical assistance" programs are often essentially of this character. More generally, greater specialization and division of labor in the underdeveloped areas is probably feasible and would tend to raise total output. The precise forms of specialization would undoubtedly vary greatly from country to country and region to region.

Apart from adapting and applying superior techniques already in use elsewhere, genuine land-saving or capital-saving innovations might be developed to meet the special problems of the underdeveloped areas. Unfortunately, most innovations and technical advances now originate in the already developed countries where labor is the relatively expensive factor, rather than land or capital. Hence new techniques in the developed countries mainly tend to save labor. But in the underdeveloped areas it is land-saving or capital-saving innovations that are needed, simply because they are the relatively scarce and costly factors. Logically there is no reason why capital-saving innovations are not just as possible as laborsaving innovations. They are not likely, however, to originate in the already developed areas.

## Greater Demand for Labor-Using Products

Second, any change in the structure of domestic and world demand for final products in favor of those using relatively more labor in their production would tend to raise incomes in countries where labor is abundant. In other words, a shift in domestic and world demand toward goods that the underdeveloped areas are well equipped to supply would raise incomes in those areas. Doubtless this is a far less promising approach for the time being than technical adaptations and innovations. But it should not be dismissed.

The possibilities of altering the composition of the *present* demand for final products within underdeveloped areas themselves in this direction are surely almost negligible; most of the possibilities of substitution in consumption have already been exploited to the full. But the same cannot be said of increments in consumption. If some development does occur in the underdeveloped areas, then so far as possible increments in consumption might be made to take forms that economize scarce land and scarce capital resources in favor of abundant labor services.[27]

Any change in demand in the world outside the underdeveloped areas in favor of products with a high labor content would necessarily be favorable to incomes in the underdeveloped areas. For example, if the demand for Oriental rugs—a product that requires a minimum of materials and immense amounts of labor—should greatly increase, incomes in the producing areas would rise. The same would be true for certain types of pottery, filigree work, fine laces, hand-patterned fabrics, etc. Many Japanese exports to the more developed areas were products with a high labor content. The possibilities for the now underdeveloped countries along similar lines are surely worth exploring. Raw materials and primary products generally, while not final products in the sense of consumers' goods, are of course a prime example of labor-using output with a wide market outside the underdeveloped areas. All the indications are for a strong upward secular trend in the demand for foods and industrial raw materials which would tend to raise incomes in the producing countries. A wise policy would attempt to gear production to the satisfaction of this demand.

## Correcting the Basic Lack of Proportion

Third, and finally, real incomes in the underdeveloped areas can be raised by removing the existing disproportion among the factors of produc-

27. From the point of view of development, the spectacle of certain underdeveloped areas that had acquired substantial foreign exchange reserves during World War II squandering these reserves after the war on imported consumers' durable goods, trashy trifles and the like does not represent the ideal way of achieving increments in consumption. And the point here does not rest on the fact that the goods were imported, even though that raises considerations of its own; the same could be said if the increased consumption took the form of domestically produced substitutes which required plentiful supplies of capital goods in their production.

tion that is economically responsible for the low level of output. This is undoubtedly the most important means of all and it may take two forms. First, the relationships among the factors can be improved by increasing land and capital relative to labor. Since the possibilities of augmenting the land resources in many underdeveloped countries are severely limited, the major stress is likely to be upon increasing productive capital equipment. The other possibility is to shrink the supply of labor relative to the quantities of land and capital equipment. Internal migration, international migration, or a fall in birth rates relative to death rates, appear to be the only means by which changes in labor supply could better the relationships among the productive factors.

Clearly, the two approaches are not mutually exclusive: capital can be made more plentiful and labor made less abundant. The one does not preclude the other. Both may not be equally feasible in all underdeveloped areas, however, and therefore they must to some extent be viewed as two alternative means to a single objective.

### The Triangular Pattern

Thus, apart from social, political and cultural changes that improve the environment within which all economic activity is carried on in the underdeveloped areas, the economic means to greater output and improved real incomes are basically three: technical changes and innovations that improve the flow of output from existing resources; shifts in demand within and without the underdeveloped areas that increase the demand for their abundant labor supply; and, finally, improvements in the relationships among the productive factors, through increasing the quantities of the relatively scarce land and capital factors or reducing the superabundance of the labor factor or by doing both at the same time. All three measures, whether undertaken singly or in combination, would have the desired result of raising output and real incomes.

#### DYNAMIC FACTORS IN DETERMINATION OF REAL INCOME

Even a brief survey of labor, land and capital resources in the underdeveloped areas suffices to indicate that scarcity of productive resources and inefficiency in their use, given the possibilities of substitution among them, must account to a large extent for the low average real incomes of the people. All the same, however, one cannot entirely escape the uncomfortable feeling that this is not the whole story, particularly if the inference is that adding more economic resources would assuredly raise real incomes. Certainly most underdeveloped countries are "resource poor" as compared with the more developed countries; but differences in resource endowment, important as they are, do not suffice either as an explanation or as an index of the range in real incomes.

The observable differences in real incomes between the developed and underdeveloped countries seem to be explicable only by passing from static to dynamic factors. An inventory of productive resources is inescapably static. Changes in resources, changes in their use through time and changes in the level of real incomes resulting therefrom are dynamic factors. And these, in turn, must be traceable to certain traits and characteristics of flesh and blood people and the interests and bents that they display and pursue within their social environment. It must suffice here merely to illustrate these generalizations by a few examples.

The people of any area are not likely to make the most of the resources at their disposal unless they are, in a sense, dissatisfied with the end product that those resources currently supply. If the "standard of living"—the patterns of consumption to which people aspire—is not above the "level of living" of their present patterns of consumption, then the level of living of the group is not likely to rise. In other words, perhaps a prerequisite to better living is an aspiration to better living *plus* the conviction that it is worth striving for and working for. Without this conviction a man is unlikely to tackle his job with the gusto, ingenuity and perception that make for high productivity and, more important, for secularly rising productivity. While these comments sound banal, reflection suggests that one of the most striking general differences between people in developed and people in underdeveloped areas is precisely this difference in attitude toward the day's work and the morrow's promise.[28]

Persons who possess ingenuity and aspiration to a marked degree and who combine them with organizational and administrative abilities of a high order are usually among the most effective instrumentalities for material progress. These are the entrepreneurs. Whatever their motivations—a point much in dispute—they seem to possess a peculiar knack for seeing how productive resources may be used in unfamiliar ways to produce a better result. Moreover, they have the skill required to organize people, tools, equipment and segments of land into a functioning unit of production —something more than the mere sum of the parts. In economies with a secularly rising level of material well-being entrepreneurs do much to ease it cumulatively upward year after year by their restless search for better ways of doing things and their almost implacable dissatisfaction with the gap between the realized and the realizable. This is a dynamic factor of peculiar importance for material progress that seems to be largely absent in

28. The reasons for this difference are doubtless complex. But surely one of them is the plain fact that past experience in most underdeveloped areas gives no grounds for believing that aspiring to a higher standard or struggling to attain it has much changed the level of living that most of the people actually realized. Aspirations and strivings must sooner or later bear fruit or people will cease to hold or pursue them.

the underdeveloped areas. Entrepreneurial abilities, organizational skills and administrative talents seem to be scarce both in absolute amount and, even more so, in relation to size of the labor force as a whole.

Innovations, another important dynamic factor in high income countries, are also strikingly rare in underdeveloped areas.[29] Except in the most general terms, little is known about what factors are responsible for the stream of innovations that is so characteristic of the more developed countries. The spread of literacy, education and scientific knowledge doubtless affords a partial explanation; but further explanation usually trails off in vague references to the "socio-cultural environment" and the like. The absence of innovations in the underdeveloped countries is at least equally puzzling; here again the level of education does not seem sufficiently to account for the obvious facts. Innovations, however, whatever their explanation, are fully as important as productive resources in accounting for the secular rise in real incomes per person in the now developed countries and for the persistently low level of real incomes over much of the rest of the globe.

These admittedly loose generalizations are intended only to inject a note of caution—particularly when joined with the different dynamics of population in developed and underdeveloped countries to be explored in Chapter 5—against the easy inference that shortages of productive resources or inefficiencies in their use adequately explain the persistently low level of real incomes in the underdeveloped areas. Along with social and cultural factors, they do tend to explain why incomes are as low as they are in the historical present. But they do not altogether account for the *persistence* of low incomes in the past and the prospects of continuing low incomes in the foreseeable future if other factors do not intervene. Dynamic factors such as those just alluded to must also be woven into the analysis.

29. Whether innovators should be regarded as the only true entrepreneurs, as Schumpeter cogently argued, or as a group at least logically separate is of no particular relevance in the present context.

# 3. Capital Accumulation and Allocation

THE DEVELOPMENT OF THE REAL INCOME potential of the underdeveloped areas by a more effective utilization of existing productive resources and by augmenting the resources available constitutes the essence of economic development. Insofar as development is to be achieved through increasing productive resources, this means adding to the real capital stock.

The manner and timing by which real capital resources are accumulated and allocated is fraught with complexities in any economy. Many economists have argued that upon it depends full employment and steady economic progress in well-developed countries such as the United States. In a static economy, however, in which capital resources are not increasing and in which technical change and innovation are absent, most of the troublesome economic problems of capitalistic economies cease to exist, at least in theory. Consequently, the underdeveloped economies, which are virtually "static" in these respects (though not in the full sense of theoretical economic models), are largely free from such problems as "achieving full employment" or preventing uneven rates of economic growth. At the same time, however, they suffer from the perhaps still worse difficulty that real incomes per person—far from increasing at uneven rates—scarcely improve at all. Instead, they remain, as they have long been, at a level of poverty for most of the population. One of the primary reasons for this persistent poverty is the fact that there is little or no accumulation of productive real capital resources and virtually no technological progress.

To point to the absence of real capital formation for productive purposes in underdeveloped areas, however, is merely to pose the problem. How can the lack of real capital resources be overcome? The question divides itself for analysis into two parts: first, how to *initiate* productive capital formation and carry it forward; second, how to *allocate* or distribute these capital increments among various possible uses. The two problems are closely interrelated.

## PRODUCTIVE AND UNPRODUCTIVE CAPITAL ACCUMULATION

Nearly all "civilizations" have accumulated capital in the sense that, for considerable periods, their total production has exceeded their total consumption by an appreciable margin. During their period of vigorous development, civilizations perhaps usually display a high rate of capital accumu-

51

lation; at their zenith, net accumulation often approaches zero; while in their decline, they suffer more loss of capital than they replace: the capital inheritance is not even maintained. The Egyptians, the Babylonians, the Greeks, the Romans and the Carthaginians, each in their time, created pyramids, temples, public buildings, roads, aqueducts, fortifications, and the like, which show clearly that current output was not entirely consumed. The medieval castles and cathedrals, the Louvre and Versailles, Drottningholm and Schönbrunn afford examples from more recent history of periods in which consumption was less than total production. There was "capital accumulation" of a sort.

"Capital goods" such as these—and examples could be drawn from almost any underdeveloped area—are of a special kind: they usually pertain to the social, religious or ceremonial side of the particular culture. Neither in their creation nor in their utilization, in most instances, is their economic productivity of the least concern. They are more similar to community consumers' durable goods, such as parks or museums, than to capital goods used for further production like railway bridges or steel mills.

Most societies before the modern era and most underdeveloped areas today have accumulated capital goods not for productive purposes but for *noneconomic* purposes. This is to use the term capital goods, or capital formation, in the broad sense of any excess of current output over current consumption. For study of the process of economic development, however, this usage is not altogether satisfactory; some further analysis is necessary.

*The Concept of "Investment"*

The depression of the 1930s produced a large literature on employment theory and national income analysis that popularized a very loose usage of the term "investment." This usage, while not formally identifying "investment" with productive capital formation, makes it so easy to pass from one to the other that they are often used almost as synonyms. This Keynesian type of economic analysis tends to classify the output of any period as either "consumption" or "investment." Similarly, all expenditures in any period are treated as either for consumption purposes or for nonconsumption purposes. The twofold classification is exhaustive. Since traditionally— at least in private enterprise economies—most of the nonconsumption outlays were used for additions to productive plant and equipment or inventories, that is, what the ordinary citizen usually thought of as investment, it became common practice to treat all of them as investment outlays. Thus all output or all expenditure in any period was regarded as either for consumption or for investment as a matter of convenient definition.

In the context of depression and unemployment problems, however, it was soon realized that while under "normal" conditions most nonconsumption expenditures were paid out for productive capital goods, their employment-income effect did not, in fact, depend upon their being used for new factories or new machinery; building a new art gallery or a new golf course, or putting unemployed mural painters to work would do just as well. So long as the focus is upon short-run changes in aggregate incomes and employment, all outlays for nonconsumption purposes are similar in their effects: they raise total employment and thus money incomes and real incomes alike. A new stadium and a new steamship are both investment insofar as their construction creates employment.[1]

The reason such employment policies are effective in developed countries is that the money incomes paid out in stimulating investment—in the broad sense described above—will mostly be spent for consumption goods, the output of which must rise, once excessive inventories have been sold off. If the process continues, the analysis contends, the rising prosperity will force the consumption goods industries to order more raw materials, machinery and plant; more money will have to be paid to produce these; and so on, with further "rounds of spending," as the economy works toward full employment with higher total money and real incomes.

## Underdeveloped Countries and the "Investment Multiplier"

Regardless of the applicability of this analysis to already developed countries, it can be decidedly misleading if applied without modification to the problems of employment and capital formation in underdeveloped areas. For in underdeveloped countries, total output is difficult to increase in the short run: greater money outlays generated by investment, in either the broad or the narrow sense, do not raise output in the consumption goods industries, but only raise prices.

The fundamental reason why total output tends to be limited lies in the excessive lack of proportion between labor and other factors of production which was stressed at the end of the preceding chapter. If the addition of more workers in agriculture in densely populated underdeveloped areas cannot increase agricultural production, and if in the other underdeveloped areas output cannot expand because social or cultural factors withhold potentially usable land from the relatively abundant laborers, then increased money expenditure must raise prices. Disproportion among the factors available for production precludes a rise in agricultural output; but

1. This usage, as might be expected, has caused no little confusion. It will be seen at once that the term investment becomes exceedingly broad and thus includes—from the employment point of view—a whole host of things to which the calculus of costs and returns in the private acquisitive sense is quite inapplicable. In the language of the market place, investment has always meant an individual's commitment of funds—owned or borrowed—with the expectation of gaining an income and/or an appreciation in value from the acquisition of an asset. Consequently, an investment decision meant weighing alternative asset purchases according to the straightforward criteria of potential, realizable income or realizable appreciation. But this kind of calculation is obviously inapplicable to playground construction or similar unemployment relief projects, which are investment only from the point of view of employment or in national income analysis.

because agricultural output is much the most important segment of the economy, this means that total output is virtually inelastic in the short run. Thus the "investment multiplier" analysis, so highly regarded for its illumination of the problem of raising total *real* incomes in developed countries by merely increasing money incomes, is not applicable to the underdeveloped countries because of the inelasticity of their total output. Prices and money incomes can rise, but *not* real output and real incomes.

## CAPITAL FORMATION IN UNDERDEVELOPED AREAS

The importance of capital accumulation in the development process is accepted on all sides. Since total output in the underdeveloped areas cannot rise so long as the disproportion among productive factors remains as it is, and since the most feasible way to better the proportions between labor and the other productive factors is to augment the capital supply, the problem, then, is to effect such changes as will generate a positive rate of productive capital formation. Without resort to assistance from outside the economy, the means by which an economy can effect a positive rate of productive capital formation on its own are rather limited.[2]

### The Capital Accumulation Process

In nonmonetary terms, an economy whose productive resources are entirely occupied in creating consumption goods for current consumption and in maintaining its inherited stock of capital equipment is one that is *not* accumulating capital. Capital accumulation means that the flow of total output from year to year is so constituted that at each year's end the kinds and quantities of useful capital equipment in existence are superior to those of the year before.

There are essentially only two ways in which capital accumulation can occur, although there may be variants of the second. First, some resources engaged in providing goods and services for current consumption can be shunted over into the production of capital goods. In this instance, the flow of consumption goods is diminished while that of capital goods is increased; the fraction of total productive resources devoted to capital goods production is raised, that devoted to consumption goods reduced. The second method of accumulating capital equipment is to increase total output in such a fashion that the increase consists entirely of capital equipment. Here, the increased flow of capital goods is not, as in the first case, *a substitute for* a portion of the flow of consumption goods, but *an addition to* the previous flow of consumption goods.

2. Foreign borrowing as a means of capital accumulation is considered in Chapter 17.

In either of these methods of capital formation the value of the flow of total output over a given period will exceed the value of the flow of consumption goods by the amount of capital formation that has occurred. Total output will equal the value of the consumption goods produced, plus the value of the capital goods produced. But total *income* will exceed total *consumption:* the difference will be savings. In other words, the very fact that capital formation has occurred during any period means that, on the income side, savings in equivalent amount have been made. At the close of any period, savings equal to the value of the capital formation will be a necessary concomitant of the fact that capital accumulation has occurred.

## Some Inherent Problems

The purely formal reasoning according to which savings are necessarily equal to the value of the increase in real capital at the end of any period must not obscure the fact that, in a monetary economy, the process by which this equivalence is realized may raise difficulties. Whether capital goods output is increased by means of a reduced output of consumption goods or by increasing total output without changing the amount of consumption goods produced, the money spent for consumption goods is likely to raise prices of these goods unless steps are taken to prevent it.

The reason is fundamentally the same in both cases. In the first case, incomes will be paid to factors of production—laborers, for example—for making capital goods, and the income receivers, if unrestrained, will spend as much as before on a diminished flow of consumption goods. The prices of consumption goods will necessarily rise. In the second case, those who produce capital goods, and so raise the total value of output, must be paid money incomes; and these incomes spent against a flow of consumption goods that is no larger than before must here, too, cause their prices to rise.[3]

If capital formation is *not* to generate a rise in consumers' goods prices in this manner, then money outlay for these goods must be checked by taxation, by rationing or by a rise in voluntary saving. Ideally, money outlay per time period must be checked by an amount equal to that currently paid out to the factors of production engaged in producing capital goods. If, for example, only labor were used as a productive factor in road construction, then, if the government during the period of construction siphoned off from total money incomes an amount equal to the total wage bill in road construction during that time period, consumers' goods prices would not rise, unless of course some other change also intervened.

3. This is why full-employment policies, in developed countries also, will degenerate into inflation if pushed beyond the point at which most of the unemployed resources have already been drawn into employment.

*Capital Formation from Disguised Unemployment*

If disguised unemployment of labor and heavy seasonal unemployment in agriculture are widespread in underdeveloped areas, as they in fact are, then these people could, at least theoretically, be organized for certain types of capital goods production without reducing agricultural output. They add nothing to output now. Their withdrawal therefore would not cut output below its present level. Capital goods production would increase, not at the expense of consumption, but because total output had been raised.

In other words, the second method of capital accumulation—an increase in capital goods output without a decline in consumption goods output— may be applicable in the underdeveloped areas. Certain cautions and elaborations, however, are necessary to carry this prescription beyond the level of theoretical analysis.[4]

*Checking Consumption*

First, the argument rests on the assumption that the workers left in agriculture, that is, those not drawn off permanently or seasonally into the production of capital goods, will not increase their total consumption as a consequence of the fact that some laborers have been drawn off. Similarly, those who were idle and are now transferred to capital goods production must be able to consume as much as they did before. This implies effective methods of securing from the workers left in agriculture a fraction of their product equal to the proportion of the total labor force now engaged in producing capital goods. For example, if 15 per cent of the farm labor force is drawn off into capital goods production, then the workers left in agriculture must consume no more than 85 per cent of their unchanged output. This will require taxing arrangements or rationing schemes to assure a proper division of the food supply between those engaged in its production and those engaged in capital goods production. If, for example, capital goods are mostly being produced in the towns and food in the country, the peasants may not be willing to supply food to the urban dwellers, especially where the towns have no goods to offer in return. In this instance, total consumption would be so badly allocated that the production of capital goods would have to stop. Consequently, the price-market arrangements or the planning authorities would have to prevent consumption goods from being so badly distributed that capital formation came to a halt.

4. The possibility of using disguised unemployment as a means of capital accumulation in underdeveloped areas has been analyzed by several writers. It is implicit, if not explicit, throughout K. Mandelbaum, *The Industrialization of Backward Areas*, Blackwell, Oxford, 1945. Perhaps the clearest exposition of the basic theory, however, is James S. Duesenberry, "Some Aspects of the Theory of Economic Development," *Explorations in Entrepreneurial History* (mimeographed), Vol. III, No. 2.

*Financial and Other Problems*

The second problem is financial. If people are to be drawn into making capital goods they have to be paid, and the money to pay them must come from somewhere. If the government should tax away in each period an amount equal to the incomes paid for capital goods production, then it would have a sort of revolving fund from which it could continue the process of capital formation indefinitely. But it would need money at the start to establish the revolving fund.

The third problem is that the argument as usually formulated implies that the people drawn out of agriculture can be assigned to capital goods production in the immediate vicinity. Otherwise, there will be additional transport costs, new housing costs, and so on, and perhaps serious family and social dislocations as well. Furthermore, the capital goods to be so produced must not require any special equipment or technical services from abroad which would cause a drain on the foreign exchange reserves.

In spite of these qualifications, there appear to be many types of capital goods which underdeveloped areas could produce for themselves in this manner. Improved roads, irrigation ditches, swamp drainage, storage reservoirs, construction of schools and other public buildings, river improvements, docks or even airfields—all these need little more than human labor, the simplest of tools and someone to organize and direct the labor force. The absence of people able and willing to direct such undertakings is usually the basic handicap here; otherwise it is hard to understand why such capital investments are not already common practice in the underdeveloped areas. In parts of Iran and Iraq, for example, a recent observer reports that the villagers are apparently unable to organize themselves sufficiently well to keep even the existing irrigation dams and ditches in repair.

If some few technical specialists or some special types of equipment could be brought in from outside, many other projects would also be feasible. Added to the direct gain in productivity which such capital goods make possible are the benefits derived from developing community organization for self-improvement and betterment. Out of such efforts may grow a new community attitude toward local problems and the means to their solution. Ingenuity and determination may dislodge resignation and apathy.

*Capital Formation by Diverting Resources*

Most underdeveloped areas probably consume something less than their whole current output. Many of them have substantial inheritances of collective consumers' durable goods—temples, shrines, churches, palaces, etc. —which they manage to maintain and even to augment. People "save," too, insofar as they personally consume less than they produce, and they "invest" these savings in hoards of such directly usable consumers' goods as cloth, grain and oil, or in precious stones and metals.[5] In this respect, the underdeveloped areas today differ very little, so far as one can determine, from most premodern societies. But this resemblance only emphasizes the fact that the investment of savings in productive capital goods is a distinctly modern phenomenon. While many societies have not currently consumed all of their annual output, only the relatively high-income economies have translated the difference into productive capital goods which raise output and therefore consumption per person.

The underdeveloped areas also resemble many earlier societies in that they devote an appreciable fraction of their productive resources, especially human services, to supporting a few persons in luxurious idleness or in various kinds of ceremonial activities. The *ancien régime* in France, for example, kept a large part of the population occupied in supplying goods and services for the nobles, the court and the high clergy. In some, though by no means all, underdeveloped areas today, productive resources are similarly deployed. Their socio-political structure is such that economic resources that might be used for productive capital formation are used instead for supplying special types of consumption goods from which most people draw only vicarious satisfaction. Surely one of the most striking features of most underdeveloped areas is the virtual absence of productive capital formation concurrent with an enormous "waste" of labor, judged by the standards of high-income countries.

### Savings as a Source of Capital Accumulation

The other possible internal source of capital formation in underdeveloped areas is through lowering output of consumption goods in favor of increasing the production of capital goods. This is the process of capital formation so heavily stressed by the classical economists: the accumulation of capital through savings.

Theoretically, any underdeveloped area can acquire more real capital if it is willing to diminish consumption. But how far the government will be willing to go in this direction, or how far it will dare to go, will depend upon the modal level of consumption and upon the possible social and political repercussions of reducing it. In some very poor underdeveloped areas, consumption is already so low that any reduction would almost certainly raise death rates. In others, the government could lower consump-

---

5. As Adam Smith put it long ago, "In those unfortunate countries, indeed, where men are continually afraid of the violence of their superiors, they frequently bury and conceal a great part of their stock, in order to have it always at hand to carry with them to some place of safety, in case of their being threatened with any of those disasters to which they consider themselves as at all times exposed." *The Wealth of Nations* (Everyman's Library), Vol. I, Dutton, New York and Dent, London, 1910, p. 250.

tion without seriously injuring the people, but if it did so, it would almost certainly be driven out of office. Consequently, little can be said in general terms about how much capital underdeveloped areas may be able to accumulate by deliberately cutting consumption. The amount may be considerably larger than is usually assumed, however.[6]

Thus the underdeveloped areas have three means available by which, without resort to foreign borrowing, they can accumulate productive real capital resources internally: by using disguised unemployment or seasonal idleness in agriculture wherever this condition exists; by transferring labor and other productive resources from nonproductive capital formation and ceremonial activities to productive capital formation; and by cutting consumption to release factors of production to produce capital goods. None of these possibilities is likely to occur automatically. But to assume that the underdeveloped areas cannot devise effective means to exploit these potential sources of capital formation seems unnecessarily pessimistic.

### Capital Formation via Saving from Increased Output

If productive capital formation is achieved in the underdeveloped areas by means similar to those just explored, then total output in any period will necessarily be increased by the value of the capital goods so produced in that period. But this is not the whole story. The capital goods are not museum pieces. They are instruments of production. This means that they will make the total output in the economy greater than it would have been without them. The composition of this increased output and the time when it is received largely determine what disposition can be made of it.

If the capital goods created are mostly general-purpose capital goods and improvements, such as better land drainage, better storage facilities, irrigation facilities, then the increased output will be mostly in the form of farm products, and these should appear without long delay. Schools, on the other hand, will not show immediate results in higher output but only long-run results as they make people literate and train them in new skills. Better roads will perhaps have highly diffused effects on output through reduced transport costs, improved communication and a larger marketable surplus. A large reforestation scheme or the drainage of a big swamp might not for several years yield any product that could be consumed by the people or used for further investment. But in all cases the capital formation will raise total output, because total productive resources have been increased.

6. A sharp rise in voluntary saving, an alternative possibility theoretically, is probably most unlikely in view of the social, political and cultural environment that prevails in most underdeveloped areas. Even highly developed economies have had little success in greatly increasing voluntary saving in times of war or other crises. Individual income receivers have to be restrained in their consumption by rationing, priority schemes, payroll deduction plans, etc., in order to prevent inflation and to free productive resources for the production of war matériel.

An underdeveloped area that is determined to develop rapidly, however, will see to it that much the greater portion of this increased production is used for further capital goods production rather than consumed. If the increase takes the form of greater agricultural production, then this can be used to support still more people in capital goods production; fewer people are needed to supply the food requirements. It could also be exported and the proceeds used to buy machinery and other capital equipment that cannot be produced at home. Capital accumulation becomes cumulative and tákes on new forms. The point to be stressed is that the *increment* in output which the capital formation has made possible need *not* be consumed, but can be devoted to pushing capital formation still further.

Because people in underdeveloped areas are poor, the tendency will be for them to consume the increased output unless they are somehow prevented from doing so. The tendency to consume more will be very strong. What fraction should be consumed and what invested is largely a political question which will call for different answers in different countries. But there is no need to assume that the authorities have no choice but to allow it all to be consumed. If the country so desires, it can cause nearly the entire increment in output to be invested.[7]

Once capital formation is started, therefore, the way to speed development is to save and invest a large fraction of the increment in output that results from the fact that there is now more capital. From this point forward, the process can simply repeat itself. The basic difficulty is to get productive capital formation started initially.

## CAPITAL ACCUMULATION AND ALLOCATION IN DEVELOPED ECONOMIES

The accumulation and allocation of productive capital in highly developed economies is arranged in one way in countries that organize their economic life in a system of predominantly unregulated prices and markets, as does the United States, and in another in countries with a system of centralized economic planning, like the U.S.S.R. Despite striking differences between the two methods, there are remarkable similarities because of the very nature of the problem of capital accumulation and allocation.

7. This formulation does not take into account the difficulties posed when population is also increasing. Clearly, if the rate of capital accumulation is known, and the increments in output occasioned by having more capital are also known, then the rate of growth in total output of consumption goods is determinable. The degree to which this rate of growth of output of consumption goods exceeds or falls short of the rate of growth of population will determine the degree of rise or fall in real incomes per capita. If population *is* growing, then all the increment in output can be saved only if the government and the people are willing to accept a fall in the average real income. For an interesting discussion of these and related problems see H. W. Singer, "The Mechanics of Economic Development," *Indian Economic Review*, August 1952, pp. 1–18. The population problem is treated in Chapter 5, below.

### UNPLANNED ECONOMIES

The capital and investment market in unplanned economies serves both to mobilize the savings of income receivers and to channel these savings into alternative uses. This process, which has become highly institutionalized in the United States, will be so familiar to most readers that a few comments will suffice. Its essential features are, first, that no central authority decides what fraction of their total incomes people must save, that is, not spend for current consumption; second, that no authority determines what fraction of the total output in any period will consist of productive capital goods rather than consumption goods. Apart from tax levies, social security deductions and undistributed profits, each income receiver decides how much of his income he will save. Those in charge of business firms, in turn, decide what kinds and types of capital goods, if any, could be profitably added to, or substituted for, their existing capital equipment, and on this basis they order their purchase or construction.

In unplanned economies this decision-making to invest further in capital equipment tends to be specialized in "entrepreneurs" who have close familiarity with the probable yields to be had from further capital increments in particular enterprises in view of the present and prospective constellation of costs and prices. The prospective yield rate on the acquisition cost of a particular capital good in a particular use is nowadays usually referred to as the "marginal efficiency" of that type of investment. The marginal efficiency of different types of investments will usually differ at any moment; over time it will show striking variations. The very fact that much investment already has been committed to the construction of factories for making radios, for example, will tend to lower the marginal efficiency of investment in radio manufacturing: in other words, investment along any one line is likely soon to show prospects of falling returns and so engender its own decline. On the other hand, the perfection of some new invention, such as television, will create new opportunities for capital investment because the invention raises the marginal efficiency of investment in that use. Indeed, the economic history of any highly developed economy records how investment has flowed in endless succession into one industry after another as investments already made, inventions, discoveries, and so on, altered the marginal efficiency of investment in particular uses.

If business firms are to realize their investment plans, however, they must get funds, that is, they or others must relinquish their savings for the purposes proposed. If radio manufacturers want to build more factories, they can do so only if they already have the necessary funds themselves or can persuade others to supply them. In economies like that of the United States, individual savers are likely to delegate decisions whether to advance or withhold funds to specialized investing institutions—banks, insurance companies, trust companies, mortgage companies, investment trusts, etc. These institutions, as well as individual savers who make their own choices, are guided chiefly by the performance record of established firms, usually corporations, in the various industries, and by what they judge the future returns on additional capital investments are likely to be.

Thus, in a market economy the savers, with their accompanying institutions, on the one hand, and those in charge of firms, on the other, together constitute the "capital market." This market performs the function of mobilizing that fraction of aggregate income which people decide not to spend for current consumption and of allocating it among the alternative proposals for adding to the productive capital equipment for this or that particular use. It must be remembered, however, that the funds made available for investment by personal income receivers are often supplemented, at times substantially, by credit creation through the banking system or by the fiscal operations of the central government.[8] If full employment already prevails, direct government financing of productive capital goods creation unmatched by comparable tax collections or increased voluntary saving must eventuate in inflation. The same result will follow from unrestrained credit creation by the banking system. If unemployment prevails, however, monetary expansion will tend to raise output and employment, rather than to push up prices.

### CENTRALLY PLANNED ECONOMIES

In centrally planned economies, the planning authority must solve essentially the same problems: first, the rate at which the economy will plan to make net additions to the capital stock each year—5 per cent, 15 per cent or whatever; second, how this annual aggregate should be allocated among alternative uses, given the end purposes of the planning authority.

The upper limit of the rate of internal capital accumulation in planned economies is set by the minimum level to which aggregate consumption may be lowered without reacting dangerously on human efficiency. All output above this minimum consumption requirement could, theoretically, consist of capital goods production. How closely to approximate this theoretical maximum will be a matter of judgment. No general principles seem to be clearly applicable.

The planning authority will also determine the allocation of new investment. Presumably, increments in the production of certain goods are more to be desired than in others; consequently, more capital goods will be added

8. During World War II, for example, the United States government expended for war and other purposes a good deal more than it collected in tax revenues; much of this expenditure was to finance the production of real capital goods necessary to produce war matériel.

in these industries. The concept of the marginal efficiency of investment is applicable here also, although the content of "anticipated net returns" is presumably different, perhaps radically different, from that used in market economies. It would seem that the allocation problem would be handled in somewhat the same way as, in unplanned economies, the military general staff decides what kinds of war matériel and how much of each would come closest to realizing its task of assuring "preparedness" or winning the victory. Each sector of the economy, or each branch of the military, presents its claims, and the central planning authority, or the general staff, ultimately decides on a solution. In neither case is there a handbook setting forth the marginal efficiency of investment in alternative uses. Physical and engineering data may be superabundant but no market mechanism exists to reduce these to a common money denominator for purposes of comparison. Hence, whereas in unplanned economies certain types of real investments are made outside the market at all times, and others in special circumstances, in planned economies all investment allocations are presumably left to the judgment of the central planning authority. Which method is the more likely to give "desirable" results is not here at issue.[9]

A centrally planned economy, no less than an unplanned economy, is likely to generate inflationary pressures if in trying to force capital accumulation it spends more for this purpose than it has siphoned off in tax revenues. Although all prices, including consumers' goods prices, may be fixed by the planning authority rather than left to the market, total money incomes after taxes may exceed goods available to consumers at the established prices. If so, either the "official" prices will not be the actual ruling prices or rationing will be unavoidable. To avoid inflationary pressures, the planning authority must therefore finance its investment projects by drawing off tax revenue from income recipients at nearly the same time-rate as it spends to create capital goods. Central economic planning does not by itself free an economy from the risk of investment-induced inflation.

Thus the capital accumulation and allocation problem under central economic planning basically resembles that encountered in unplanned

9. It is usually said that the volume and allocation of investment is inherently superior in centrally planned economies because in price-market economies the volume of saving tends to be largely a function of the distribution of income—those with higher incomes providing most of the saving—whereas, in planned economies, the planning authorities can determine, wisely though arbitrarily, total saving and its allocation. See Oskar Lange and Fred M. Taylor (edited by Benjamin E. Lippincott), *On the Economic Theory of Socialism*, University of Minnesota Press, Minneapolis, 1938, pp. 84, 108–09.

This contention is at least doubtful if the planning authorities must perforce delegate authority to the managers of the trusts because of the impossibility of making all decisions at the highest echelon. If the trust managers control productive resources in their own sphere there is little to prevent them from making direct investments in their plants—provided they are meeting their quotas—without the knowledge of the central planning authorities. Hence total investment may be greater than the planning authorities had planned; it may also be less, as for example where the managers are not meeting their current output quotas and use for current production resources intended for investment. The actual volume and allocation of investment may therefore diverge appreciably from the planning authorities' decisions. This possibility becomes a strong probability with the present level of administrative efficiency in many underdeveloped areas.

economies. Some of the differences are really superficial. Consequently, whichever route the now underdeveloped countries may choose, many of the basic problems in capital accretion and allocation will be the same and unavoidable in either case.[10]

## CRITERIA FOR THE ALLOCATION OF INVESTMENT IN DEVELOPMENT

So far the discussion of capital accumulation in underdeveloped areas has centered on the problems and difficulties of achieving a positive rate of productive capital accumulation. The emphasis was upon ways and means by which the annual flow of output could be made to consist partly of capital goods and not almost entirely of goods for current consumption. Once capital formation has been initiated and is proceeding—or could proceed by means already discussed—then the problem of allocating new investment inevitably arises. What kinds and types of capital equipment should be accumulated? To what points within the economy should new investment be directed? If the range of choices is wide, what criteria should determine the allocation of capital investment?[11]

### Labor Abundance and Size of Venture

Since the most pervasive economic feature of underdeveloped areas is the abundance of labor in contrast to the shortage of capital, a strong presumption exists that capital should be used sparingly relative to labor wherever there is a choice of methods of production. In agriculture, for example, although more capital would be used, the methods of production would still remain labor-intensive instead of being highly mechanized. For the capital investment required to mechanize farming would have greater productivity if invested elsewhere in the economy. Capital investment would presumably add more to total output if it were diffused in many directions rather than concentrated.

A strong presumption also prevails in favor of small ventures. The small unit permits a greater diffusion of superior methods of production. Since

10. In all probability, capital accumulation for development in most underdeveloped countries will not proceed either entirely by central planning or entirely through private capital markets. In order to get development under way some central planning by the government appears to be almost unavoidable. Moreover, in greater or smaller degree, there will have to be a public sector of the economy (just as in unplanned economies) and, at least for this sector, investment will have to be planned. In a sense, therefore, a free choice between the two possible methods distinguishable in theory does not exist in fact.

11. Although economic analysis usually treats the allocation problem and the problem of the rate of capital accumulation as separate problems, they are often not separable. This is especially likely to be true in underdeveloped areas. For example, in the initial stages of development a country may be forced to accumulate capital entirely out of disguised unemployment in agriculture. If so, there will be very restricted choice as to the kinds of capital goods that can be accumulated; and the sum total of the capital goods thus accumulated will determine the rate of accumulation for the economy. On the other hand, if capital is accumulated mostly by cutting consumption, then the possibilities of alternative allocations of investment are much wider. Finally, the range of choice will be wide, rather than narrow, with regard to the allocation of new investment achieved by high rates of saving out of increments in output.

economic progress depends in good measure on imitation, it is desirable that as many persons as possible should participate in the new productive techniques and catch the spirit of the times. The dearth of experienced managers also argues for small ventures. Large undertakings, to be efficient, require management skills of an extremely high order, and only rarely are these indigenous to underdeveloped areas. Moreover, a pattern of smaller ventures affords greater opportunities for management training. A final advantage of small-scale projects is the reduction of risk: results can be more quickly assessed and corrected than in the giant investment scheme.

The criterion of diffusion does not, however, imply that it should displace the basic test of productivity; or at least it does not suggest that conspicuous deviations from productivity would be justified for the sake of diffusion alone. There are often limits to the gains of small-scale units and diffusion: past a certain point, the small unit may become technically impossible or uneconomical. The newly developing country may in these circumstances find it desirable to concentrate investment of certain types in certain regions, leaving to the passage of time and the process of imitation of one region by another the general diffusion of the new productive techniques and equipment.

Occasionally, for example in chemical processes such as the manufacture of synthetic fertilizers, the *only* technique may be highly capital-intensive; low wages will then be of no avail in inducing the use of more labor. Assuming the availability of the wherewithal to construct the plant, this technical fixity of proportions would be a matter of no concern in many of the lightly populated countries of South America and in parts of Africa and the Near East. But in the densely populated Orient, this technical fact may be embarrassing or even dangerous. A giant oil refinery may make only a small draft upon native labor. Even if it is in native ownership, whether private or public, the great mass of the population may derive only slight and indirect benefits: government revenues may increase through the yield of public investments or through taxes upon private projects, but the mass of unskilled laborers or peasants may go their way largely unaffected by the industrial revolution. Thus a "dual economy" is created. Too few people gain any acquaintance with modern technology and, because of its capital-intensive methods of production, the refinery draws too few persons into new employments in comparison with numerous small projects dispersed widely over the area.

*Productivity: Risk Factor*

The theoretically "ideal" allocation of investment according to the test of productivity—that investment in no particular industry be halted until the rate of return has been brought down to the general level of returns prevailing elsewhere—may be singularly difficult to apply in many under-developed areas. A sophisticated attitude toward capital yields is not widely diffused, and often the requisite data are completely lacking. Initially, therefore, public or private investment may have to proceed upon somewhat ill-defined convictions as to general and most probable yields, rather than upon the "sieve of interest rates" in any precise sense. Transport and communications, for example, may be chosen as a field for concentrating investment until more precise business and economic calculations are possible. This is a different problem from that of estimating the gains of investment in such activities as public health and education, which are *always* difficult or impossible to measure in exact monetary terms.

Risk is a further investment criterion which may be decisive even in developed economies in choosing among particular lines offering equal marginal returns. In underdeveloped countries, the timing of income returns may affect the risk factor. Industries with especially protracted "gestation periods"—requiring many months or years of construction—may be unwelcome or impossible, despite prospects of eventual high returns, because of the risk of incorrect forecasts of demand as well as the prolonged deprivation of consumers. Furthermore, the shrinkage of consumer income increases the risk of inflation. The poverty of these regions enforces economy and caution not only in the use of capital but also in the assumption of risks.

## Complementary Industries

The fact that the increase of production in any segment of the economy requires progress everywhere, particularly in complementary industries, may seem to justify a high investment rate and rapid industrialization. Despite its superficial plausibility, this argument actually does not appear to be well founded. The intricate interrelations of industries and services may tax the analytical powers of both public and private investors. And the very difficulty of the problem is as much a reason for caution as the mutual interdependence is a reason for "a rapid advance on all fronts." A solution cannot be evolved from general arguments but must be painfully worked out for each scene and for each change of the times.

## Balance of Payments

Finally, in any consideration of investment criteria for developing countries comes the frequently crucial matter of the balance of international payments. If investment goes too heavily into the production of goods for domestic consumption and too lightly into production of goods which either increase exports or diminish imports, deficits in the foreign balance may develop. If investment is increased, money incomes will tend to increase and a portion of these larger incomes will be spent for imports. Consequently, the exchange control authority or national bank will have to anticipate this result and will have to take into account a possible chronological lag of demand for imports behind increased investment.

### THE IMPORTANCE OF CAPITAL

The strategic factors in economic development are numerous. Present and future net reproduction rates of their populations are bound to determine the future course of per capita income in underdeveloped countries. Effective government and efficient administration are indispensable to economic progress. A case could be made for the view that the introduction of improved techniques supplies the one essential ingredient of economic development. In particular countries one or another of these forces may be the crucial factor; and the list of crucial factors could be considerably extended. Nevertheless, the one most nearly *omnipresent* limiting factor, one that frequently is also the most *severe*—apart perhaps from entrepreneurial and managerial skills, which are often equally important—is the sheer scarcity of the wherewithal for material progress: It does *not* follow, however, that a country's "need" for capital is necessarily matched by a comparable ability to absorb capital into productive uses, even were it available in abundance from external sources. Absorptive capacity depends not on need alone, but also on a variety of other factors which are mostly noneconomic.

A paradoxical characteristic of underdeveloped economies is that a large part of their slender supply of capital is embodied in ceremonial, esthetic and symbolic forms. But low incomes are bound to persist unless capital is devoted to increasing the flow of goods—both consumers' and producers' goods. Hence the problem of capital involves not only the matter of availability of capital, but also the allocation of capital to its most productive uses. So formidable is the problem of accumulating or borrowing enough capital for development purposes that the equally important problem of suitable allocation of capital to particular industries, firms and instruments may suffer relative neglect. Like nearly all genuinely economic problems, the problem of progress is an exercise in managing or husbanding scarce resources; and the husbandry pertains not merely to the painful birth of capital, but to the equally painful denial of capital to one particular use in order to achieve a higher productivity elsewhere.

### Investment Concept Broader for Development Problems

While investment and its allocation lie close to the heart of the economic development problem, it should be stressed that the investment concept as applied to development has often to be used in a broad sense.

In developed economies, capital investment usually means productive investment, that is, additions to productive plant and equipment, inventories and foreign exchange reserves. The implication is that these are the means by which higher real incomes per person in those economies will be achieved. But this is often *not* the case in underdeveloped countries. At their present stage of development, wiping out illiteracy or endemic disease may do more to raise real incomes per person than putting up factories or increasing the number of machines. But if the essential meaning of investment is the commitment of productive resources with the objective of increasing the level of output, then, applied to underdeveloped areas, the term will necessarily embrace certain undertakings not usually included for countries where development has already passed beyond the early stages. A broader concept of investment is often necessary for the underdeveloped areas. Whether the quest for higher real incomes is made via increasing the stock of capital equipment in the form of transport facilities, storage warehouses, better roads, or via increasing the efficiency of the workers by health and sanitation programs, expansion of educational facilities to reduce illiteracy or provide technical training, or via inducing modifications in age-old cultural patterns which impede labor mobility or fortify group antagonisms, all these approaches have this in common: they require the expenditure of resources in the form of manpower, materials and supplies. They are all a species of capital investment intended to raise total output and average real incomes.

## In Different Kinds of Societies

Economies that are "planned" and "unplanned" in varying degrees ranging from totalitarian to *laissez faire* reveal sharp contrasts in ownership and control. There may also be significant differences in the distribution of wealth and income, and in the system of economic incentives for supplying labor and risking capital. The contrasts are much less sharp, however, in regard to problems of production, including the problem of capital allocation. John Stuart Mill probably overstated the matter somewhat in saying that "the laws and conditions of the production of wealth partake of the character of physical truths."[12] But whatever their economic systems, the underdeveloped areas will face many common problems: how far to press industrialization relative to agricultural development; what public services to launch and how far to carry them; how to articulate domestic production with foreign economies, and the like. Differences of climate, of religion, of cultural history will probably account for larger differences in the character of their investment programs than will types of economic organization.

12. John Stuart Mill, *Principles of Political Economy* (Gonner ed.), Longmans, New York, 1909, p. 199.

An illustration of this is in the degree to which disguised unemployment in underdeveloped areas, especially in agriculture, can be made a source of capital formation. The problem is essentially one of moving the surplus labor into other, more productive agricultural pursuits or into industry without expanding the total consumption of all labor—at least so long as capital formation remains the sole objective. This is equally a basic problem for a socialized or for a liberal economy. Both need to consider also the costs of transporting or transplanting labor, including the costs of housing and of the public services attached to population centers. Both have to devise means of coping with inflationary pressures.

## Mores More Important than Systems

All this amounts to saying that economic systems per se are probably less important for the major *directions* and *forms* of investment than are the local social and economic mores, the objective facts of environment, and the cultural, aesthetic and religious values of the particular society. Economic systems of the most varied kinds can be adapted to these divergent facts and ends; the history of economic development of widely different nations in the Occident and the Orient testifies to this fact. Production economics is not highly dissimilar among various economic systems; if distribution and tastes are given, techniques and costs objectively determine the optimal methods of production, and these in turn determine the broad outlines of capital *allocation*.

The rate of capital *accumulation* is something else again. This is, to employ Mill's phrase, "a matter of human institution only," at least above a very low level of physical subsistence. Being a matter of "human institution," the desirable and achievable rate of saving enters immediately into the realm of politics and political philosophy.

Many of the most important problems in capital accumulation and capital allocation are questions that must be answered in the institutional context of the particular country. In the words of the Professor of Colonial Affairs at Oxford University:

Neither the mere "expenditure" of capital nor the application of force can solve the real problems of our time. We are faced not with problems of "spending" capital but investing in those multitudinous personal and social forms which can grow only in conjunction with the always unique social heritage of different individuals and societies.[13]

What is unquestionable, however, is the vital necessity of deliberate accumulation of capital and rigorous allocation policies wherever a country is bent on economic development.

13. S. Herbert Frankel, *Some Conceptual Aspects of International Economic Development of Underdeveloped Territories* (Essays in International Finance, No. 14), International Finance Section, Princeton University, May 1952, p. 22.

### THE CONTROVERSY OVER THE RATE OF CAPITAL ACCRETION

Among those concerned with the problems of underdeveloped areas perhaps no cleavage of views is sharper and deeper than that concerning the rate of capital accumulation necessary to put the underdeveloped areas squarely on the road to economic progress. It would perhaps be more precise to say that the divergent views of two schools of thought on the whole process of economic development are more strikingly obvious in the issue over the rate of capital accumulation than anywhere else. The issue is fundamental.

One group is convinced that only a very rapid rate of real capital accretion is capable of jolting the underdeveloped countries into sustained development. The argument has many facets and takes various patterns. First, almost all underdeveloped areas, it is pointed out, are so bound by tradition, so hampered by outworn cultural institutions, so socially and economically static, and frequently so pressingly overpopulated that only "big" investment projects, "large" capital increments and the like can hope to clear the way to economic development. Hence, it is argued, a high rate of capital accretion must be achieved forthwith—to which it is often added that if this is not done the problem will become steadily and alarmingly worse.

These contentions are usually fortified by emphasizing that the "real" obstacles to economic development are generally poor health, endemic disease, poor sanitation, bad diet, hunger, illiteracy, dearth of educational facilities, poor housing, and the like. Only large capital outlays can remove these obstacles, it is said, and such undertakings, by their very nature, must be under state auspices. On the more narrowly economic side, the state must also undertake large irrigation and electric power projects, harbor development, roads and other forms of transport, and push into industry and manufactures by actually creating the necessary facilities. It is argued that only such full-scale efforts, requiring large capital investment, are capable of jolting the underdeveloped areas out of the slough of poverty and despair in which they now stagnate economically and ferment socially.

### Attitude toward the State

Members of this first group are likely to consider the state as the ideal entrepreneur and to stress the necessity and virtues of central economic planning. They tend to distrust consumer sovereignty, resource allocation through market processes, the price system and so on, as against central direction and control of economic affairs from some apex within the state administration. They would contend that the experience of the U.S.S.R., though they deplore some of the consequences of its ruthless single-mindedness, shows clearly what can be done by this method and offers—with one important modification—the only workable blueprint for the now underdeveloped areas.

The modification is this: whereas the U.S.S.R. developed its economy almost entirely out of real capital domestically accumulated, the presently underdeveloped areas should and must get much of their capital accretion from the high-income countries. In brief, the argument usually proceeds by the following steps: only a large investment program will do the job; the underdeveloped areas are exceedingly poor and so cannot provide the capital domestically; hence much of the capital to carry out the necessary investment project must come from abroad. Moreover, since many of the most needed projects are highly capital-intensive, will not yield early returns, and the returns are so diffused in their effects as to be nonappropriable by fiscal measures, and because such projects will not directly either diminish import needs or increase exports, they must be financed from abroad either by very long term loans at nominal interest rates or, preferably, by large outright grants.

Views closely resembling these have been widely held by political leaders in many underdeveloped countries. Official publications of the United Nations seem frequently to consider particular problems against some such analysis of the economic process by which development can be achieved. And some independent scholars follow similar reasoning. Let us call all these Group I.

## The More Gradual Approach

The contention of Group I that really large capital injections are virtually the only way to replace stagnation with economic development is not everywhere accepted. A second group insists that large capital injections such as Group I proposes would be either, at best, wasted or, at worst, fatal, because of the nature of the problem. This second group believes that a more gradual, if less dramatic, approach to capital and other problems in underdeveloped areas would be more effective, both immediately and over the long run.

Members of this second group are no less sociological in their conception of economic development problems than those in Group I. They do, however, tend to emphasize somewhat different sociological factors. In particular, they stress—what they believe experience to demonstrate—that drastic changes which are carried through largely with foreign finance and foreign technicians are unlikely ever to establish a foundation within the society for sustained economic advance. They hold that once the large foreign aid and direction are withdrawn, stagnation will certainly reappear.

In other words, they question the soundness of externally imposed cultural changes as a basis for economic development unless accompanied by ruthlessness and force of a kind, degree and duration which they find morally unacceptable.

They would argue, for example, that even programs for improving health by eliminating certain endemic diseases are likely to be only temporarily beneficial if most of the staff and facilities are not locally developed and if the economy does not provide an economic base to support such an undertaking. People in the area have to be specially trained to understand not only the immediate task but also the fundamental importance of good public health and how to get it, keep it and pay for it. This means training physicians, nurses, attendants, health officials, etc., within the country, and also, equally important, inducing its leaders in public and private life to think along wholly unfamiliar lines. Malaria can probably be eradicated entirely by epidemiologists from the outside, as it was by the American armed forces in some places during World War II; but this falls far short of reorienting and training a people in such a way that they are thenceforth capable of handling their own public health problems.

Consequently, Group II argues that, while theoretically the capital additions suggested by Group I could be effected by large grants or loans from without, these would not assure economic development.

Apart from these fundamental differences of view on the essential nature of social and economic changes and how they can be brought about, members of Group II have specific criticisms as well. They point out, for example, that the only feasible assault on ignorance, bad health, disease, etc. —indeed, on most of the "basic" difficulties in underdeveloped areas—is through people thoroughly familiar with the local languages, customs and mores, grouped, if need be, about a core of foreign specialists. A foreign agency can contribute vaccines but it cannot educate a population. In relation to the underdeveloped areas as a whole, there is no more than a handful of specialists available for such work. Assistance of this kind does not take much capital from abroad in any usual sense. Above all else, it takes time.

*Emphasis on the Market and Internal Savings*

Members of Group II also tend to deny that central economic planning with its attendant administrative problems is manifestly a superior approach to the development problem for most underdeveloped areas. They would put more emphasis on market processes, prices, individual effort, personal ingenuity, and less on the omniscience of central government bureaus. They would argue, too, that perhaps the Soviet experience illustrates not so much the wisdom of central planning authorities in forcing a high rate of capital accumulation as the results sometimes obtainable by ruthless discipline imposed after a seizure of power by force and violence.[14]

Thus those in Group II do not believe that the highroad to economic progress for the underdeveloped areas must necessarily lie in a prodigious rate of capital growth, especially if this means large capital injections from abroad. They believe that nonviolent social change can be effected rapidly enough by *internal* capital accumulation; a substantially faster rate would risk either social collapse or merely superficial modifications. Hence they stress the primary importance of domestic capital accumulation rather than large loans or grants from abroad. They concede, of course, the potentialities of technical assistance and foreign loans, provided the borrowers acknowledge balance-of-payments problems and recognize the reality of international economic relationships. In all this, it would appear, they rest their case on their conviction that sustained economic development requires a social and cultural environment markedly different from that now found in most underdeveloped areas; that large capital commitments cannot create this environment in a brief period; and that, therefore, a rate of capital growth so great that it must come mostly from abroad is not the key to the problem of the underdeveloped areas.

The cleavage between Group I and Group II is fundamental. And while this cleavage is clearly apparent on the unresolved question of the rate of capital accumulation necessary for economic development, it is present if not so obvious in a host of other issues as well. The issue of capital accumulation has particular pertinence for the United States, because it is usually from this source that Group I proposes to finance the high rate of capital formation allegedly necessary.

Despite its importance, however, the issue is likely to remain unsettled for a long time. There seems little prospect of resolving it one way or another by a priori reasoning, by appeals to historical experience or by scientific analysis. This is partly because the social sciences are at present unable to supply a table of weights for the component factors in a problem as complex as this, and partly because different analysts start from different systems of ultimate values. A Marxist or Fabian socialist will have one set of answers; a Friedrich Hayek or a Paul Hoffman another; and in between will be nearly all the colors of the spectrum. Similarly, even careful historical analysis runs into difficulties: on the one hand, the same objective "facts" carry different inferences for different students while, on the other, no historical case of economic development is ever without its unique features.

14. It is worth observing that the postwar development of the "iron curtain countries" on the Russian model has not been accompanied by capital injections from the U.S.S.R.; quite the reverse probably. But disciplinary officials have been exported in abundance. In Soviet central Asia "development was probably accomplished with a rather moderate amount of net capital assistance, and possibly zero net assistance, from the rest of Russia," according to Warren Wilhelm, "Soviet Central Asia: Development of a Backward Area," *Foreign Policy Reports*, February 1, 1950, p. 224.

# 4. Social and Cultural Factors in Development

THE QUALITY AND QUANTITY OF THE FACTORS of production in their relation to one another do not alone determine a society's economic productivity, or how much and how rapidly this productivity can be increased. What real incomes these factors will yield in combination depends upon the whole social and cultural environment within which economic activity is pursued. In any society, this environment tends to be the external expression of the fundamental religious, moral and cultural beliefs and aspirations of the people who compose that society. Moreover, these ultimate values tend to manifest themselves in certain religious, social, political and cultural institutions which prescribe the way of life for the people and determine the motivations and behavior patterns to which they will respond.[1]

## VALUE SYSTEMS IN ECONOMICALLY UNDERDEVELOPED AREAS

The observation is commonplace that a society is all of a piece and that one cannot detach one part from the rest, even for analytical purposes, without running the risk of misconception or self-delusion. This may be even more true of the underdeveloped than of the developed countries. In peasant societies, the social, cultural and even religious aspects of land cultivation, for example, are interwoven with the purely economic end of food production to a degree not matched in farming in more developed countries. Where the economic and noneconomic aspects of land and other resource utilization are closely integrated in a cultural whole, the patterns of prescribed behavior may be highly inimical to efficient economic performance and strongly resistant to innovations that would improve it.

The importance of socio-cultural factors in economic efficiency can be seen also from another angle. The economic approach to development tends to stress—as Chapters 2 and 3 have done—that productivity in underdeveloped areas is low because there is a disproportion among the factors

1. As economists, the writers should perhaps state here that they fully realize they are stepping out of their depth in attempting to deal with problems of culture and cultural change. The subject is one of such vast proportions as to repel all but the most foolhardy. Nevertheless, they are struck repeatedly by the importance of the noneconomic elements in economic development problems. Even so, the writers wish to make it quite clear that in drawing attention to certain social, cultural and religious factors which seem to inhibit economic development, they do not say or intend to imply that these "must" or "should" be rooted out. This would be presumptuous in the extreme. If, however, economic development *is* considered a desirable end—as they believe, though others may not—then these noneconomic factors do seem to be at times in conflict with it.

Few references will be made to the vast literature in this field. Apart from published sources, however, the authors wish to acknowledge the enlightenment received from the as yet unpublished papers presented at two conferences sponsored by the Social Science Research Council: the first, "Economic Growth in Selected Countries," held in April 1952 and the second, "The Near East—Social Dynamics and the Cultural Setting," held in October 1952.

74

of production, shortage of capital, adherence to outmoded techniques, and so on. The implication is that if capital were made available or new techniques were introduced, productivity would increase and real incomes would rise. This does not necessarily follow. Despite more capital equipment or the demonstration of better production methods, no rise in output will occur if the socially accepted goals or the culturally accepted values assign little importance to material achievements, such as greater production. If material accomplishments are little esteemed, people will devote little effort to achieving them. In other words, although greater output will be impossible without more capital and improved techniques, the mere provision of these does not assure that output and material welfare will increase.

In the final analysis, whatever is accomplished in any society is accomplished by the people who compose it. Hence, what they will actually accomplish depends as much on the drives and motivations that compel them as on the economic resources at their disposal. As Thomas R. Malthus observed long ago:

. . . the powers of production, to whatever extent they may exist, are not alone sufficient to secure the creation of a proportionate degree of wealth. Something else seems to be necessary in order to call these powers fully into action . . . Unless the estimation in which an object is held, or the value which an individual, or the society places on it when obtained, adequately compensates the sacrifice which has been made to obtain it, such wealth will not be produced in future.[2]

Even the most superficial comparison of the value scales and correlative institutional forms in underdeveloped and developed countries shows striking contrasts. Such contrasts necessarily reflect differences in the historical experience of different societies. Only a Toynbee or a Spengler would attempt to explain why the contrasts in values and institutions are as they are and to what origins they are historically traceable.

### Different Sources of Values

Broadly viewed, the dominant values in the economically developed countries stem from Greek and Roman civilization, the Judaic-Christian religious system, the Renaissance, the Reformation and the Enlightenment.[3] Among many of the economically less developed countries, on the

2. T. R. Malthus, *Principles of Political Economy*, 2d edition, William Pickering, London, 1836, p. 361 (London School of Economics reprint, 1936). Malthus seems to have believed strongly in what, following James S. Duesenberry (*Income, Saving and the Theory of Consumer Behavior*, Harvard University Press, Cambridge, 1949), has been called "the demonstration effect," that is, that people will adopt new consumption patterns and work hard to finance them when those new patterns have been set by persons above them in the social scale.

3. The ideals, the values, the mores, the intellectual atmosphere and the points of view that have evolved from these origins are now exceedingly complex. Nevertheless, they are still fundamentally the animating spirit behind the institutional framework of Western society. And, with the exception of the U.S.S.R., all societies that are economically highly developed are Western in orientation if not in geographical location.

other hand, the dominant values and points of view have their origins in non-Christian religions—Islam, Buddhism, Confucianism, Hinduism and many others. In the words of Professor F. S. C. Northrop:

The mentality of the Middle East stems from the prophet Mohammed and embraces the thought of Arabian, Persian and Turkish Islam. The Islamic mentality holds sway from the northwest tip of Africa, opposite Gibraltar, eastward by way of Egypt through the entire Middle East, Pakistan and Indonesia to the Philippines.

The mentality of the Far East rises out of Hinduism, Buddhism, Taoism and Confucianism. (Some objection . . . can be made against lumping Confucianism with the other three.) The Far Eastern mentality embraces present-day India (except for her remaining Moslem minority), Tibet, Burma, Thailand, Ceylon, Bali, Indo-China, China, Korea and Japan.[4]

These doctrines have been largely untouched by the ideas and attitudes generated by the development of scientific thought in Western society over the past three centuries. Similarly, the whole body of Western thought since the eighteenth century known as "political and economic liberalism" has scarcely tinged the prevailing outlook in many of these economically underdeveloped areas. The contrasts between the two groups are enormous and have been described from many points of view. A recent writer, for example, speaks of the "open society" and the "closed society."

The open society is one which recognizes the freedom of man to shape his own destinies in accordance with the findings of a scientifically enlightened empiricism . . . Primitive man lives in a stable and tradition-dominated world, a closed society, where external forces seem to determine the conditions of human existence. To perceive and conform to the requirements of these extra-human forces is the primary problem.[5]

Whatever may be the most incisive or perceptive way to put the contrast, the fact remains that the "culturally recognized values" in the economically underdeveloped countries are often strikingly different from those which prevail in the economically developed countries, and that these differences bear directly upon present economic achievements in the underdeveloped countries and the means and possibilities for their improvement. Let us consider a few of the more important.

*The Individual in Relation to His Social Environment*

Few conceptions basic to the Western world view are more important in their range and implications than those associated with "the inherent dignity of man" or "individualism." These terms and others like them epitomize a whole body of economic, political and social relationships that characterize Western society: the conceptions of citizenship, of the state and

4. F. S. C. Northrop, "The Mind of Asia," *Life*, December 31, 1951, p. 39.

5. F. M. Watkins in a review of *The Open Society and Its Enemies*, by Karl B. Popper (Princeton University Press, Princeton, 1950), *Canadian Journal of Economics and Political Science*, November 1951, p. 570.

of government; the principles of private property, individual initiative and independence; the conviction that knowledge, education and learning are valuable in their own right and open to all rather than the prescribed privilege of a small minority; the belief that creativeness and self-expression are among the highest manifestations of man as man.

The dominant philosophical preconceptions in many underdeveloped areas are often directly antithetical to the Western view of individualism. Instead of the individual, the stress is rather upon the family or clan as the inviolable social unit. Social organization tends to be more rigidly hierarchical and stratified. While a caste system is not everywhere formalized, as in India, social transgressions are usually so severely stigmatized that they occur infrequently. Social and occupational mobility are severely restricted. Education tends to be formalized and often esoteric: it bears little, if at all, upon the problems of day-to-day living. All these factors in combination tend to promote attitudes of resignation and acceptance rather than ambition and ingenuity. Group loyalties and group relations tend to outweigh logic and rationality in the approach to problems of everyday living. More attention is devoted to preserving the delicate balance of social organization than to devising better means of providing for the basic material needs of the whole group.[6]

*Rationalism, Secularism and Materialism*

Western society tends to be rationalistic in approach and secular in outlook. There is enormous faith in "the scientific approach" to secular affairs. Few things are deemed to be immutable because preordained. Change is to be expected and encouraged. The individual does not accept his personal status with resignation; and for society as a whole the *status quo* only shows the possibilities of further progress. The prevailing attitude toward both the physical and the social environment is rationalistic and materialistic rather than fatalistic or metaphysical—one of scientific detachment rather than traditional or religious absolutism. The secular and the non-secular in human affairs are separate and distinguishable.

The prevailing cultures of certain economically underdeveloped countries, by contrast, seem to be characterized by a world outlook reminiscent of medieval Europe. The late Carl Becker once described this view of life in these words:

Existence was thus regarded by the medieval man as a cosmic drama, composed by the master dramatist according to a central theme and on a rational plan.

6. Consider the following, for example, by a scholar with wide experience in the Near East: "The person who is not loyal first of all to his family and village is regarded as being something of a traitor, and, therefore, the pressure is for staunch loyalty to the smaller unit.

"This feature of life in the Near East is still abundantly evident in the village and tribal feuds which continue today in such highly-developed countries as Egypt and Iraq." W. Wendell Cleland, "Social Conditions and Social Change," *Journal of International Affairs*, Winter 1952, p. 12.

Finished in idea before it was enacted in fact, before the world began written down to the last syllable of recorded time, the drama was unalterable either for good or evil. There it was, precisely defined, . . . The duty of man was to accept the drama as written, since he could not alter it; his function, to play the role assigned.[7]

The views of medieval Christianity and the outlook of Buddhism, Confucianism, Taoism, Mohammedanism, Hinduism and the other non-Western religions or philosophies are of course quite dissimilar at many important points.[8] Yet the *implications* of these beliefs for *economic* affairs, as these are understood in the Western world, appear to be somewhat similar.

Secular affairs are considered inseparable from the nonsecular: the distinction lacks meaning. This is true of the Middle East, for example. It is said that "The Koran provides for the believer not only the forms and content of his worship, but also a complete rule of life and a social and legal system (Shari'a)."[9] Material achievements pale to insignificance before the appeal of the mystical entity that is the universe. Man is expected to disdain the relative and transitory in favor of the absolute and the timeless. Acceptance, resignation, compassion, piety and reverence come close to being the proper descriptive terms.[10]

### Underdeveloped Countries in the West

In Latin America and the Caribbean, the dominant value systems do not derive from Oriental philosophies or religions. Yet here, too, economic achievements have traditionally been assigned a relatively low rank in the cultural value scale. Perhaps the most striking cultural contrasts between these regions and the more economically developed countries are, on the one hand, less complete separation between church and state and, on the other, the persistence well into the twentieth century of value systems and codes of behavior usually associated with a landholding, semifeudal aristocracy.

The forms, as a rule, rather than the full substance of political and economic liberalism were transplanted from Europe and the United States

7. Carl L. Becker, *The Heavenly City of the Eighteenth-Century Philosophers*, Yale University Press, New Haven, 1932, p. 7.

8. F. S. C. Northrop states that "The Oriental portion of the world has concentrated its attention upon the nature of all things in their emotional and aesthetic, purely empirical and positivistic immediacy . . . the East tends to concentrate its attention upon this differentiated aesthetic continuum in and for itself for its own sake." *The Meeting of East and West*, Macmillan, New York, 1946, p. 375. Just what this means, however, occupies a good part of Professor Northrop's book.

9. Royal Institute of International Affairs, *The Middle East: A Political and Economic Survey*, Oxford University Press, London, 1950, p. 50.

10. "The peasant in whose mind is firmly established the idea that Allah has decreed from the beginning of time his present existence and condition, sees little use in trying to change the will of Allah and goes along patiently accepting the *status quo*, hoping for a happier setting in his next existence." Cleland, *loc. cit.*, p. 12.

during the nineteenth century; but they appear not to have taken firm root in the new soil.[11] The organization of society appears to be more similar to pre-eighteenth-century Europe than to late eighteenth-century Europe or even late seventeenth-century England. Whether this is because these lands were all colonies until after the Napoleonic wars—when some of the fervor had gone from the revolutionary phrases, slogans and concepts—or, rather, as some would contend, because they have continued as primary producers for world markets overseas, is not here at issue.

Regardless of the cause, the countries of Latin America give the strong impression that neither political nor economic liberalism, nor any similar revolutionary movement, has yet swept away the feudal values and the feudal organization of society inherited from the colonial era.[12] Land ownership, for example, seems to be valued rather more for the cultural and social prestige it affords than for its worth as an agent of production. Education, even higher education, emphasizes formal learning along classical and traditional lines with surprisingly little attention—at least until very recently—to the pure or the applied sciences. To be a "gentleman" and to lead a "gentleman's" life is still an objective widely esteemed and widely pursued.

The pervasiveness of the Church in all phases of social life in Latin America is much broader and deeper than in the more economically developed countries, though probably less far-reaching than in many Oriental cultures. Because neither Spain nor Portugal had to accommodate the Protestant Reformation, their colonies were founded and developed in accordance with the views on the relation between church and state then prevailing in the mother countries. These views seem to have persisted with only minor changes long after the colonies gained their political independence.

The strong position of the Church in Latin America also seems to have retarded scientific speculation and intellectual boldness: the Catholic Church has never encouraged and at times not even accepted these values.[13] Traditionally, too, the Catholic Church has strongly stressed the impor-

11. Even so, one is a little taken aback by statements like the following in William S. Stokes's *Honduras: An Area Study in Government* (University of Wisconsin Press, Madison, 1950): "The slogan 'to the victors belong the spoils' means, in Honduras, that personal and partisan factors dominate all phases of administration at every level in government" (p. 191); "Parties seldom recognize the legal and moral right of their opponents to register and vote. The political faction in control of local government is almost always reluctant to permit members of rival groups to register, and in some cases, it may even be dangerous for a citizen to demand his legal rights" (p. 231); "Correspondingly, all those who have not been 'for' are adjudged to have been 'against,' and in the field of politics they must make their peace with the victors, leave the country, or reconcile themselves to persecution" (p. 295). These quotations are taken almost at random from the study.

12. The importance of the institution of slavery should also not be overlooked.

13. This is not to suggest that the Protestant faiths were usually strong for "scientific speculation" and "intellectual boldness." Often quite the contrary. Nevertheless, the Protestant revolt tended to separate church and state so that the aversion of the particular faiths or sects to scientific thought had diminished force.

tance of the family, family ties and family obligations against the alternative view of the importance of the individual and the fullest development of his talents, interests and personality. Finally, and more or less parenthetically, the value scales promulgated and fostered by the Church have appreciably influenced demographic patterns and the forms and types of real capital formation that have so far occurred.[14]

Thus even the most cursory glance at the value scales that are dominant in underdeveloped countries discloses that they differ appreciably from those characteristic of economically more developed countries. These values strongly affect the drives and motivations to which the people in these areas will respond, how they will approach the problem of getting a living from the resources available to them, and, not least, the responses they will make to the efforts of their governments and their leaders to achieve economic development.

### INSTITUTIONAL FORMS IN RELATION TO ECONOMIC DEVELOPMENT

The ultimate values of any society display themselves most concretely in the institutional forms by which the people organize their social life. By their very nature, these are almost invariably complex in their structure and intricate in their workings, according to anthropologists and sociologists. These institutional forms extend over all phases of social life—kinship and family relations, property relations, differentiation of function between persons, and the hierarchy of authority in social and political affairs, to name only a few. Fortunately, not all these aspects of social organization are immediately relevant to problems of economic development. But some few of them seem so clearly to affect current and potential economic performance in underdeveloped areas that they must be briefly noted.

### *Government and Administration*

In many economically underdeveloped countries, the concepts and attitudes underlying government and administration differ so greatly from those in the economically developed countries that they are not well adapted for the planning and execution of programs of economic development. The concept of "sovereignty" or the derivative concept of "the state," in the Anglo-European or American sense, for example, is alien or unfamiliar. Such concepts do not constitute the foundation of government authority and administration in the economically underdeveloped countries. The primary loyalties and responsibilities that people recognize tend instead to be those of the person-to-person type—the member of the family

---

14. The importance of the Church in these respects is clearly seen in miniature from even a superficial comparison between the Canadian provinces of Quebec and Ontario. Quebec has many elaborate churches and other religious structures, but it has less productive capital equipment and substantially higher birth rates than its neighbor province.

to the family group or the individual to his racial or religious group. Nepotism and ethnic or religious loyalties in public administration are, of course, not unknown in developed countries, but they are much less a part of the normal order of things.

In underdeveloped areas, moreover, people tend not to distinguish in thought or practice between the hierarchy of the social structure and the logically quite separate concept—at least in Western thought—of the relation between the individual and the state. The notion of political rights and obligations attaching to persons as persons, without regard to social status, ethnic origin or religious belief, is usually absent. Those persons highest in the hierarchy *are* the state or the government. Rights and privileges are a function of class, occupation or lineage rather than the very basis of the concept of citizenship.

## Attitudes toward Government

The implications of these preconceptions and attitudes for the actual functioning of government are that the people at the top interpret their position as one of indisputable right rather than one of public responsibility —and similarly at the successive steps downward in the hierarchy of authority and administration. Seen from the underside, it is taken for granted that the authorities or the officials are primarily occupied only with maintaining or strengthening their own interests. The concept of the "general welfare" or the notion of "the public servant" is usually neither expected nor exemplified in the practice of government and public administration.

These attitudes have naturally been reinforced by the fact that for centuries past in many economically underdeveloped countries governments have done little else but collect taxes and maintain order. In other words, the great masses of the people have encountered their government officials only in the role of tax collector or magistrate.[15]

The concepts of government and the practices of government administration commonly found in economically underdeveloped areas are not well suited to the task of introducing the basic changes needed for economic development. Development is not likely to burst forth spontaneously in isolated village economies. Yet the government official from outside the village is likely to be regarded with suspicion and distrust simply because he

15. Government tax revenues in underdeveloped countries come primarily from consumption taxes, customs and excise duties, license taxes, transactions taxes and levies on real property. The tax burden thus falls proportionately more on the poor than on the well-to-do. Few of the taxes commonly used in underdeveloped countries are incentive taxes in that they deliberately encourage economic activity and initiative; they tend to be repressive or, at best, neutral. Even more important, their imposition and collection frequently are capricious and inequitable; influence and even bribery often determine the levy. To the average person in underdeveloped areas, taxes are a staggering, if often hidden, burden that consumes much of his ingenuity and craft. From the point of view of the state, on the other hand, collection costs are high and the yields disappointing.

is an official. Moreover, the traditional government bureaucracy is usually unaccustomed to the kind of cooperative effort with the villager that is necessary to bring about changes in tillage methods, sanitary practices, land use and the like. Efforts to meet this difficulty by setting up new government agencies to undertake the new tasks of development have often been less successful than expected because of the obstructionist tactics of the old bureaucracy whose members stand to lose status and influence by the success of the new.[16]

Hence those who insist, as some do, that the absence of private entrepreneurs in most underdeveloped countries means that the government will have to perform these functions if development is to be achieved must perforce take full cognizance of what this means in terms of the conceptions of government and public administration that prevail in these countries. The substitution of government entrepreneurship for private entrepreneurs merely changes the administrative form, not the economic character, of the development undertaking; to assume that the government will necessarily be an efficient agency of administration is often unwarranted.[17]

## The Importance of the Legal System

The legal system—its conceptualization, its principles, interpretation and administration—is one of the most important of all institutions in its pervasive influence on economic activity. Cross-cultural comparison of laws and legal administration is of course an enormous subject. Broadly speaking, however, the underdeveloped countries either have a legal system which is based on principles of jurisprudence that are wholly different from those in the developed countries, as in the Orient and the Middle East, or, as in Latin America, a legal system with its roots in continental European jurisprudence but often lacking the elaborations and extensions necessary for an industrialized and urbanized society.[18] In either case, the legal

16. It will be recalled that President Franklin D. Roosevelt was of the opinion that the "old line agencies" in Washington were probably incapable of carrying out the bold program launched during his first administration and that he accordingly set up wholly new agencies to carry it forward.

17. A recent writer asserts that the reason why Adam Smith and his followers so strongly espoused laissez-faire policies, as against government direction and control, was that at the end of the eighteenth century so many of the then European governments were notoriously incompetent and corrupt. Consequently, these eighteenth-century writers sought "to confine the activities of government within the narrowest practicable limits, so as to minimize the damage that they might do." W. Arthur Lewis, *The Principles of Economic Planning*, Dobson, London, 1949, p. 121. The suggestion may be more plausible than historically defensible, however.

18. The intent here is not to suggest that the basis and theory of law are essentially similar in all Oriental countries but only to group them together in the negative sense that they have been largely untouched by the stream of thought which has shaped European and Anglo-Saxon law, that is, Roman law and customary law (common law) with a strong admixture of natural law concepts. There are also, of course, important differences between Anglo-American and continental European legal theory. For a brief historical introduction to the topic see Charles Grove Haines, *The Revival of Natural Law Concepts*, Harvard University Press, Cambridge, 1930, Part I.

The legal systems in Latin America are much closer to continental legal systems than those of Oriental countries. But because of the persistence of an agrarian type of society in many Latin American countries, their legal systems are probably more nearly similar to those of eighteenth-century Europe than to those of twentieth-century Europe.

systems in underdeveloped areas are probably less satisfactorily adapted to the promotion of economic activity than those in the economically more developed countries. In some instances it would appear to be the jurisprudence which is unconducive to the fostering of economic activity; in others the weakness, from the economic point of view, is centered more nearly in the actual functioning of legal administration through the judges and the courts.

In industrialized countries, especially since the eighteenth century, the legal system has to a remarkable degree developed along lines deliberately intended to foster economic activity.[19] The shift of Anglo-American and continental law away from a feudal-agrarian orientation has been going on for at least two centuries and still continues. There now exists a body of law which, while not nearly as simple as might be wished, is yet able to effect property transfers, to provide for a variety of equities of parties to contracts and, not least in importance, to litigate disputes effectively through a hierarchy of courts. The economic significance of this development is evidenced by the number of statutes, principles, doctrines and cases relating to the corporation and other business associations, the transfer of property, leases, mortgages, conveyances, trusts, agency, employer-employee relationships, etc. These are all concrete manifestations of the view now accepted in developed countries that the state should positively promote economic activity and provide the appropriate enabling rules and facilities.[20]

### Deficiencies of the Legal System in Underdeveloped Areas

The underdeveloped countries do not compare favorably with the developed countries in these respects: the arrangements for property transfers, contracts and the like are more cumbersome, more costly, less flexible and less well adapted to nurturing, promoting and giving free play to the economic interests of persons as individuals or in association.[21] The legal point of view toward economic affairs appears to be paternal and permissive rather than enabling and promotional. Insofar as this is true, the full potential of the existing factors of production to yield real incomes is not realized.

19. This is part and parcel of the shift in Western Europe away from mercantilism and toward laissez faire. To place the point in the text above in a broader setting: Most underdeveloped countries have not yet passed through a thorough revision of their age-old conceptions of the relation of the state or sovereign authority to economic activity such as occurred in Western society during the eighteenth century and later.

20. A friendly critic with wide experience in underdeveloped areas points out that one reason for their limited use of the corporate form of business enterprise is the virtual lack of protection afforded minority investors where the state does not require the filing and publication of certified balance sheets and income statements which must be transmitted to the shareholders. The minority investor invests in the dark and is kept in the dark concerning his company's affairs.

21. The leaders in some underdeveloped countries have stated repeatedly and forcefully that they distrust and dislike the "free play of economic forces" as against the alternative of comprehensive planning from above. This point is not here at issue and it probably cannot be answered wholly on economic considerations in any case. The only concern here is to point out the relation between the legal system and the flow of output from whatever economic resources a country possesses.

The rules governing the inheritance of land, land tenancy and land ownership are often among the most far-reaching legal institutions in their effects upon economic activity and initiative. The law or precedent that requires that even small pieces of land be subdivided among the children upon the death of the father often fragments the unit of tillage far beyond the limits of effective cultivation. Tenancy provides another example. In and of itself, tenancy is not necessarily an impediment to productivity; but if the tenant has no security or renewal rights he is not likely to improve his plot or husband its natural fertility. Similarly, if any increments in output are likely to accrue to the landowner, more or less regardless of the tenant's diligence or enterprise, then the tenant has little incentive to produce more.

Land titles, registration of land ownership, holdings in usufruct that are neither owned nor leased in the occidental sense, and various other hybrid forms of land "ownership"—all these, as they exist within the legal systems of many underdeveloped areas, seem to be such a quagmire of confusion, uncertainty and despair for all concerned that it is hard to believe that their effects on productivity are not strongly adverse. These difficulties are said to be particularly acute in the successor states to former parts of the Ottoman Empire. Concerning Iraq, for example, Sir Ernest Dowson says:

> Everyone directly or indirectly concerned with agriculture in el 'Iraq must know many individual cases in which the development and use of the land has been gravely obstructed by the widespread insecurity and confusion of rights. Indeed the most diligent inquiry would be unlikely to reveal anywhere any appreciable number of holdings, large or small, held in undisputed possession and free from hampering and conflicting claims.[22]

These obstacles to economic performance and development are deep rooted in the legal system. Until they are cleared away, economic measures are likely to be ineffectual.

### Institutional Aspects of Work Attitudes

The prevailing value systems in underdeveloped areas are often conducive to occupational and work attitudes that impede development. Sometimes this takes the form of contempt for anything that could be called "work," though more commonly only manual work is held in acute disdain.

Samuel P. Hayes, Jr., formerly of the Technical Co-operation Administration of the U.S. Department of State, has said:

> In a number of Near Eastern countries there are apparently plenty of technically competent personnel in the professions; what is lacking . . . is . . . the great

---

22. Sir Ernest Dowson, *An Inquiry into Land Tenure and Related Questions*, p. 33, as quoted by Doreen Warriner in *Land and Poverty in the Middle East*, Royal Institute of International Affairs, London, 1948, p. 103. The Warriner volume gives an excellent account of these problems in the Middle East. See also *Economic Survey Mission to the Philippines*, Report to the President of the United States, Washington, 1950, p. 56.

middle group of foremen, supervisors, etc. . . . . willing to get their hands dirty in actually getting a project under way. In a number of Latin-American countries the same general prejudice against work, especially manual work, exists. One gains prestige by delegating work to others. If one has been fortunate enough to get advanced training, especially abroad, one at once becomes too good for one's past job or for any job that takes one out of one's clean office.[23]

Professor P. T. Ellsworth draws attention to similar attitudes in Ceylon:

. . . such skilled workers as carpenters, blacksmiths come much lower down the scale [than cultivators], not to mention the still lower fishermen, potters, laundrymen, and the like.

Co-ordinate with the bias of the educational system and influence of caste in restricting the formation of a class of skilled and technical workers is the unusual prestige accorded government employment.[24]

Just why the value systems in many economically underdeveloped areas assign various occupations the prestige indexes they do is a problem for specialists in anthropology or sociology. Moreover, in drawing attention to such attitudes, the present writers do not mean to imply that they are "wrong" and "ought" to be changed. This is a question for the peoples in the economically underdeveloped areas to decide for themselves. What can be pointed out, however, is that such work attitudes are probably incompatible with a professed determination to achieve rapid material progress. For, among other reasons, a highly productive economic system is one that is characterized by a marked specialization of function and division of labor. This requires more than planners at the top and workers below. In between must be foremen, supervisors, technicians, minor bosses and a host of others whose jobs command respect and engender self-respect in those who perform them.

Economists are wont to emphasize cooperation as the reverse side of intensive specialization and division of labor. But this cooperative aspect of economic efficiency includes more than the organization of production through a price and market system that economists have often described. It involves the ability of people with different social, cultural, religious and political orientations to get along together well enough to avoid paralyzing wrangles, to engage in joint economic pursuits ignoring their differences of views on more fundamental matters. There is considerable evidence that this type of cooperation is less common in underdeveloped areas. It appears to be difficult to disentangle a person's abilities and capacities as a worker from his caste, religious beliefs, social or geographical origin or other at-

---

23. Samuel P. Hayes, Jr., "Personality and Culture Problems of Point IV," in Bert F. Hoselitz (Ed.), *The Progress of Underdeveloped Areas*, University of Chicago Press, Chicago, 1952, p. 211.

24. P. T. Ellsworth, "Factors in the Economic Development of Ceylon," *American Economic Review*, Papers and Proceedings, May 1953, p. 121.

tributes that have little to do with his potential contribution in production.[25] Consequently, efficiency suffers because special abilities go unused and job and worker are unlikely to be as well matched as they might be.

The capacity of a people to tolerate and compromise their differences, to distinguish between relevant and irrelevant considerations for the task in hand, to formulate decisions and then to execute these decisions in the spirit of the agreement has great economic significance. For, in the final analysis, economic resources such as labor, land and capital goods are brought together by human beings. What these resources can be made to yield for human welfare therefore depends a good deal upon how well the people can work together.

*Diverse Nature of the Institutional Problem*

Few, if any, of these general comments on the value systems and their accompanying institutional expressions that tend to be characteristic of the economically underdeveloped countries would be applicable to any particular underdeveloped country without substantial modification. The institutional structures of India and Pakistan, Brazil and Bolivia, Iran and Iraq, or of almost any two neighboring countries, differ greatly from one another in their implications for problems of economic development. Nevertheless, to assume, as is sometimes done, that one may proceed from a strictly economic analysis of the development problem to a prescription of a program for development without careful attention to the socio-cultural environment within which this program will have to be undertaken is to proceed in ignorance toward almost certain disillusionment and possibly outright disaster.

## APPROACHES TO THE PROBLEM OF CULTURAL CHANGE

Cultural change is not to be desired for its own sake. Insofar as certain features of the cultural environment stand in the way of material progress, however, they will need modification if the desire for development is to be realized.

The problem of cultural change can be approached in two ways. One approach would endeavor to achieve change directly by means which expose people to new ideas and techniques. This is essentially the Point IV concept, although the same results can be obtained by methods other than

25. Consider the following by a well-known anthropologist: "What I have said about the peasant society studied by the anthropologist is very much what the historian has described in other language for the economic life of the Middle Ages. One can translate this into various propositions. One may say that in such a peasant economy economic ties are personalized—that is, relationships as economic agents depend on the social status and relationships of the persons concerned. Put another way, labour is given as a social service, and not simply an economic service . . . . In primitive communities the individual as an economic factor is personalized, not anonymous. He tends to hold his economic position in virtue of his social position." Raymond Firth, *Elements of Social Organization*, Watts, London, 1951, p. 137.

those now used in technical assistance programs. The second approach is indirect and is based on the belief that if the economic foundations of the old culture, with its inhibiting institutions, can be destroyed, it will sink into insignificance. Some of those who favor the indirect approach insist that the economically underdeveloped areas will have to be "dynamited" into development; others believe that more gradual measures are not only possible but, in the long run, likely to be more effective.

For the economist, the question is summed up concretely and fully in the rate of capital accumulation required to effect the cultural changes necessary for development.

### DIRECT APPROACH TO CULTURAL CHANGE

The direct approach to cultural change relies essentially on an educational process. Like all education, knowledge of modes of living and working can be acquired by direct contact or by formal instruction. Historically, direct contact has been much the more important process, although, since the end of World War II, the other has been coming increasingly to the fore.

### Effects of Immigration and Migration

Social values and institutions are likely to be eroded and may give way altogether when a society is confronted with the necessity of accommodating new groups in large numbers. The rapid growth of a town or city, for instance, almost necessarily forces adaptations in the structure of values and in the accompanying social and economic institutions. The newcomers do not share the beliefs and attitudes of the old inhabitants and are likely to elbow them aside in introducing new activities, changing land uses, and so on.[26]

In recent times, migrations have commonly been associated with broad changes in the composition of demand, exploitation of new sources of raw materials, technical innovations, and the like. In earlier times, they appear to have been concomitants of invasions, wars, revolutions, religious persecutions and similar violent eruptions. But whatever their causes, sizable migrations usually have disrupted the established social and economic order. Frequently, the newcomers have brought superior techniques of production against which the traditional practices could not compete successfully; as a result, the old techniques were superseded.

The immediate prospects of international migration on a scale large enough to effect major cultural changes are quite unpromising. Internal migrations, on the other hand, could bring similar, if less rapid, results if communication and transport facilities were to be sufficiently well devel-

---

26. The north-south migration of many industries in the United States and the wartime mushroom growth of many towns in the Southwest and Far West afford many examples of this type of change.

oped. The opening of new industries in new places tends also to produce similar results.

Rural-urban movement is doubtless a peculiarly effective form of migration for breaking down old ways and creating a new elite group. The city-ward migrants will almost certainly acquire new value patterns, new ways of life and new attitudes. Rapidly growing cities usually bring a new elite group to the fore because the process of growth is likely to call for talents and abilities of a type that the old elite do not possess. The migrants from the country inevitably tend to absorb the values and attitudes of the new elite. Moreover, some of the migrants will not remain permanently in the city but in due course will return to their villages with urban ideas and new points of view that implicitly call into question the traditional ways of the village and its hierarchical structure. And the impact of the returned migrants upon village life will of course be greatly enhanced if they come with accumulated savings that give them affluence and influence well above their original status. The old forms are often helpless against these sub-versions.

### Education and Technical Assistance

An obvious alternative to internal migration or immigration, as a means of modifying deep-seated cultural values and institutions, is to attempt to expose the people to new and different ideas through education and demonstration. Reorientation of the educational system, agricultural extension services, sending students abroad, importing technicians, and the whole range of activities implied nowadays by the phrase "technical assistance" are examples that at once come to mind.

These methods operate more slowly and are probably less satisfactory because they can be more easily resisted. Exhortation accomplishes little, and the assumption that people need only to be shown in order to adopt new ways is usually ill-founded. Much "good advice" has been exported to the underdeveloped areas on the subject of taxation and fiscal policy, but most of it has had little effect on their management of financial affairs. The time-honored patterns of government remain unshaken. Disappointing results have also at times followed efforts to introduce better sanitary practices and techniques of cultivation or harvesting. Old customs are not easily dislodged.

If the culturally elite in the society reorient their values and drives, or if a new elite should rise to power and influence, the adjustments in the lower strata will be the more easily accomplished. The history of Japan following the Meiji restoration in 1867 (see Chapter 8) provides a good example of the first situation and Russia after the 1917 revolution illustrates the second, though, to be sure, with certain special features. A somewhat similar change appears to be currently under way in Mexico.[27] However, not much can be said, in general terms, concerning the factors that are primarily responsible for fundamental shifts in the value orientation of elite groups.

Barring abrupt shifts of this kind, the possibilities of modifying the cultural environment through patient education and instruction appear to vary widely according to the phase of the culture that is to be modified. Health and sanitary practices are perhaps the easiest to change because the beneficial results are so readily apparent, as for example with inoculation. Even here, however, a large trained staff is necessary and it must be willing to work at the grass roots level persistently and patiently. An effective program usually can only be undertaken by people native to the culture; it can be directed, but not carried out, by specialists from abroad.[28]

### INDIRECT APPROACH TO CULTURAL CHANGE

The indirect approach to cultural change is based on the belief that if the economic roots of the inhibiting values and institutions can be cut off they will lose their influence and wither away. Concretely, this usually means displacing the multitude of local and more or less isolated economies, with their personalized economic relationships and their largely static patterns of resource use and demand, by an expanding network of specialization and exchange with impersonal economic relationships. The approach is thus a dual one: static patterns of demand and resource utilization need to be disrupted; economic relationships need to be depersonalized.

The values and institutions that tend to debar material progress are supported from two sides. First, no competing possibilities exist for the utilization of productive factors, so that traditional uses are repeated decade after decade with little variation. Second, no new wants or tastes spring up to compete with the wants generated by the traditional value structure. In other words, so long as an underdeveloped country consists largely of village economies virtually isolated from one another, it is reasonably certain, first, that no new products or services will come into being to weaken the existing composition of demand for final products; second, that no

---

27. See, for example, Sanford A. Mosk, *Industrial Revolution in Mexico*, University of California Press, Berkeley, 1950, *passim*.

28. Dr. Sylvester M. Lambert, a physician with wide experience in the South Pacific, insisted, for example, that the concept of medical care as used in more developed countries had to be drastically modified before it could be applied in the South Pacific Islands. Western trained physicians, he argued, could never perform the task. Raymond B. Fosdick quotes his arguments as follows: " 'In the first place,' he said, 'their cost makes an adequate number prohibitive. Secondly, they fail to answer their full purpose from ignorance of the language and customs. Thirdly, they cannot and will not stand the hardships which medical work entails in these islands.' He had nothing but scorn for the average white doctor he met. 'He comes out to the islands often with no knowledge of tropical medicine,' he said, 'frequently an alcoholic, usually a medical cripple of some sort.' " Raymond B. Fosdick, *The Story of the Rockefeller Foundation*, Harper, New York, 1952, pp. 117–18.

changes will penetrate from outside to alter the way in which the village uses its productive resources. New wants and demands cannot appear as long as the isolation exists. And no alternative possibilities of resource utilization can arise. Consequently, one means of loosening the cultural ties is to introduce new wants competitive with the old and also to introduce new possibilities of using productive resources which compete with the old. In practice, of course, the two procedures are almost inevitably linked together.

Undoubtedly among the most powerful instruments for disrupting the settled pattern of consumers' tastes and demands in underdeveloped areas are radio and motion pictures. An entertainment film that incidentally portrays the level of material well-being and the mode of living in the more developed countries must be unsettling to ways of life in underdeveloped countries. The realization that not everywhere is life lived as it is in the local setting must create a desire for change, and perhaps even a determination to make changes. These disturbances tend to be reinforced by the speed with which ideas are communicated between and within countries by means of the radio. The greater frequency and intimacy of contact between national leaders that air travel permits also stimulates new ways of thinking. Consequently the demand structure in underdeveloped areas, even in the more remote regions, may be potentially much less inflexible and tradition bound than it was before mass communications were developed.

The depersonalization of economic relationships as a means of weakening cultural ties is perhaps more accurately regarded as a concomitant of the changes discussed than as an independent factor. Nevertheless, its importance needs to be underscored because, where the circumstances are such that economic relationships are strongly personalized, strictly economic considerations—for example, improvements in efficiency, acceptance of innovations, changes in the products grown or goods produced—are likely to be overridden by those of a socio-cultural nature. Thus, to depersonalize economic relationships is at once to weaken cultural bonds and beliefs and to promote efficiency.

### Two Routes of Indirect Economic Change

The indirect assault on the cultural barriers to economic development by depersonalizing economic relationships and by introducing new patterns of resource use and new demand structures may proceed by either of two routes. One method is the spread of the price-market system. The other is central economic planning. Both methods have been used in the past and are being used now. Moreover, the two methods can be combined, at least in part, by confining central planning to certain sectors of the economy and leaving the rest to be operated by the price-market system. The "mixed economy" as envisioned for India is a case in point.

Regardless of whether the market approach or the planning approach is used, their effects on the socio-cultural environment are likely to be felt through essentially similar channels. In either case, new possibilities of resource utilization are introduced and new demand structures appear in the many localized, self-sufficient village economies. From a broader point of view, there is increasing specialization and exchange among persons and regions and a growth of the stock of productive capital. In part, the first is the obverse of the second. But as already argued, it is the new patterns of resource use and demand that, by depersonalizing economic relationships, weaken the socio-cultural structure.

Nothing very useful can be said in general terms concerning the relative merits of the price-market system and central economic planning as means of effecting the economic changes necessary to undercut the cultural deadwood in underdeveloped areas. Either approach implicitly assumes that if new demand patterns and new ways of using productive resources are introduced, the necessary cultural changes will follow along. Economically, the only question is which approach will be the more effective. Invariably, however, far more than strictly economic considerations are at issue.

# 5. Demographic Factors in Development

IF WHAT ANY ECONOMY AFFORDS at any particular time as end product to its members depends largely upon the productive resources available to it and how effectively these resources are used within its particular socio-cultural environment, it is also true that how rapidly this end product will improve over time depends upon the rate of change in total output in relation to the rate of change in the numbers in the total population. Higher real incomes per capita in an area are contingent upon a more rapid rise in total output than in the numbers in the population. Since the vent of emigration is rarely available, this means that the rate of growth of output must exceed the rate of natural increase in the population. Unfortunately, the high growth potential of the populations in many underdeveloped areas, in relation to the prospective growth in national output in the near future, is sufficiently disquieting to raise, in some quarters, the fear that economic development is really a polite name for schemes designed merely to prevent a decline in the average level of material well-being.

Whether these fears are warranted or not depends largely upon whether the factors that account for this high population growth potential are likely to diminish in force over the near future. Can development itself be expected to react upon mortality and fertility in the underdeveloped areas in such a way that the end result will be higher levels of material well-being rather than larger populations at levels of well-being little different from those now prevailing? If the probable end result of economic development were simply larger numbers at about the same miserable level of existence, development schemes and programs would hold little appeal in many circles. Consequently, no discussion of the development problem can ignore the population factor without distorting the problem almost beyond recognition.

### POPULATION AND POPULATION GROWTH IN UNDERDEVELOPED AREAS

Roughly two thirds of the world's people live in the underdeveloped areas and, with few exceptions, the populations of these areas have increased substantially during the past century. The population of India in 1850 was almost certainly less than 190 million, according to one authority; in 1950 this area, including Pakistan, held more than 400 million people. The population of Egypt has grown from probably about 3 million in 1845

92

TABLE 5-1. APPROXIMATE POPULATION OF THE WORLD AND ITS
SUBDIVISIONS, 1700–1949

| Country or Region | 1700 | 1750 | 1800 | 1850 | 1900 | 1949 |
|---|---|---|---|---|---|---|
| Total | 617 | 749 | 919 | 1,163 | 1,555 | 2,368 |
| Europe | 115 | 140 | 188 | 266 | 401 | 548 |
| Asiatic Russia | 15 | 16 | 17 | 19 | 20 | 45 |
| Southwest Asia[a] | 31 | 32 | 33 | 34 | 35 | 74 |
| India | 100 | 130 | 157 | 190 | 290 | 439 |
| China major[b] | 205 | 270 | 345 | 430 | 430 | 503 |
| Japan | 27 | 32 | 28 | 33 | 44 | 82 |
| Southeast Asia, Oceania[c] | 24 | 28 | 32 | 37 | 71 | 158 |
| Africa | 90 | 90 | 90 | 95 | 120 | 198 |
| The Americas | 10 | 11 | 29 | 59 | 144 | 321 |

Sources: Merrill K. Bennett, "Population, Food, and Economic Progress," *The Rice Institute Pamphlet*, July 1952, pp. 13 and 68. Bennett says that his estimates for the period up to 1850 differ very little from the well-known figures published earlier by Walter F. Willcox (Ed.) in *Internation Migrations*, Vol. II, National Bureau of Economic Research, New York, 1931, or A. M. Carr-Saunders in *World Population: Past Growth and Present Trends*, Oxford University Press, London, 1936.

a. Afghanistan, Persia, all of Asia Minor, and the Arabian peninsula.

b. China proper plus Manchuria and Korea, Outer Mongolia, Chinese Turkestan or Sinkiang, and Formosa.

c. Siam, Indochina, the Malay States, Indonesia and other islands of the East Indies, the Philippines, Australia and New Zealand, and the Pacific Islands.

to more than 20 million in 1950. Ceylon's population—7.75 million in 1951 —is said to have trebled in the past seventy-five years.[1] Parts of Latin America, Africa, the Middle East and southeastern Europe have experienced similar large increases over the past century. A recent analysis of United Nations data on rates of natural increase in population shows that:

Of the 125 countries for which statistics for a recent postwar year (in most cases, 1950) are available, 43 report rates of natural increase of two per cent or more . . . More than half of these are Latin American countries. In this region, 25 of the 39 countries supplying vital data report rates of natural increase higher than two per cent and five a rate of more than three per cent. Seven of 17 Asian countries show rates of two per cent or more and five of the ten countries in Oceania report rates at this level. In contrast, 21 of the 39 European countries are increasing at a rate of less than one per cent per year.[2]

Estimates of the number of people in the main subdivisions of the world since 1700 show that the growth of population in the underdeveloped areas has occurred mostly in the past century and a half, and has been particu-

1. The present-day population figures are chiefly from United Nations, *Demographic Yearbook, 1952*, New York, 1953. Estimates for earlier years are from the following sources: for India, from Kingsley Davis, *The Population of India and Pakistan*, Princeton University Press, Princeton, 1951, pp. 26–27; for Egypt, from Charles Issawi, *Egypt: An Economic and Social Analysis*, Royal Institute of International Affairs, Oxford University Press, London, 1947, p. 48; for Ceylon, from International Bank for Reconstruction and Development, *The Economic Development of Ceylon*, Johns Hopkins Press, Baltimore, 1953, pp. 1 and 8.

2. Hope Tisdale Eldridge, "Population Growth and Economic Development," *Land Economics*, February 1952, p. 2. Eldridge points out that, especially in the underdeveloped areas, birth registration is probably less complete than death registration, so that the calculated rates of natural increase are probably understated.

larly rapid since 1900. The growth in Asia is particularly remarkable. Southeast Asia and Oceania, for example, gained only 8 million in population between 1700 and 1800, but the increase from 1900 to 1949 was 87 million. The population of the world as a whole increased by approximately one third from 1850 to 1900 and by more than half from 1900 to 1949, compared with an increase of roughly one fifth from 1700 to 1750. (See Table 5-1.)

Not all underdeveloped areas necessarily have unusually high *rates* of population increase. But even modest rates, compounded on an already large total, yield alarmingly large absolute increases in population in a few decades.

### Growth in the Nineteenth Century

The very fact that many underdeveloped areas have substantially increased their populations over the past century, and especially in recent decades, is evidence that "development" of a sort has occurred. If India, for example, now supports a population of 400 million as against less than half that many in 1850, then assuredly its consumable output must have increased. For somehow, by 1950, the combination of persons, natural resources and productive equipment was able to support more than twice as many people. Even if the average Indian in 1950 was no better off than his forefather in 1850, there was "development" at least in the sense that in later years certain persons survived who could not have been supported by the product of the economy in the earlier period. Apart from immigration, population will increase only if births exceed deaths. Hence, if, as the evidence strongly suggests, population growth in the underdeveloped areas is a phenomenon of the past century and a half, and if growth has been accelerating in recent decades, then certain changes must have lately appeared which disturbed the pre-existing relation between deaths and births.

Only three kinds of change are theoretically possible: (1) death rates remained the same while birth rates rose; (2) both death rates and birth rates rose, or both fell, but the excess of births over deaths increased; (3) death rates fell while birth rates remained at about their former level.

### ECONOMIC DEVELOPMENT AND MORTALITY

The remarkable growth of population in the underdeveloped areas in recent times is almost entirely attributable to a decline in death rates. While in many areas death rates are still high compared with the more highly developed countries, they have nonetheless fallen sufficiently in recent decades to cause the population substantially to increase. For example, in India crude death rates—the number of deaths per year per 1,000 persons in the population—fell from an average of 41.3 in the decade 1881–1891 to 31.2 in the decade 1931–1941. In Puerto Rico the death rate dropped from perhaps 24 at the turn of the century to 18.4 in 1940 and to 9.9 in 1950. By way of comparison, the United States death rate in 1940 was 11.5 and 9.6 in 1950.[3]

### DECLINE IN MORTALITY IN UNDERDEVELOPED AREAS IN MODERN TIMES

The drop in death rates in underdeveloped areas before 1940 is at first glance somewhat puzzling. It cannot be attributed to economic development in the popular present-day sense of the term since little of that occurred. The only plausible explanation seems to be that the increasing contacts of the Western world with the underdeveloped areas—the Orient, the Middle East, Africa, and Latin America—directly and indirectly brought about certain changes in these countries which resulted in lower death rates. Some of these changes were due to the spread of colonialism. Others were perhaps direct, though incidental, by-products of economic exploitation in the form of plantations or mining ventures. During the nineteenth century, the expansion of the European economy to overseas areas greatly intensified its contacts with the underdeveloped areas and many Europeans migrated to assist in the exploitation of overseas resources. While it is now fashionable to emphasize the more sordid aspects of this economic penetration, it seems nevertheless to have been primarily responsible for lowering mortality and thus disturbing the population equilibrium in these areas.

Doubtless, the precise causes of the fall in death rates in the underdeveloped areas were not everywhere identical. Yet, in retrospect, two broad types of changes seem to have been the principal causative factors.

*Order and Security*

First, economic penetration by the more advanced countries, either as colonial powers or as traders, usually led to greater internal stability and greater security for the people as a whole in these areas. Consequently, average usable output per worker rose as the people were freed from the more rampant forms of rapine, pillage and banditry. As a recent report on current conditions in the Far East put it:

There is little doubt that a period of peace and strong government, even one that merely improves the functioning of the economy along existing lines, would bring

3. In the period 1931–1935 no European country had a death rate greater than 20. The spread between the prevailing death rates in different countries in any year, or between the average rates in any one country at different historical periods, is usually greater than one might suppose. A death rate of 8.0 or even 9.0 is definitely low; in the Netherlands in 1950 the rate was 7.5. (Death rates in the neighborhood of 8–9 per 1,000 reported at times by some countries are not always to be relied upon.) In times of epidemic or acute famine a country's death rate may rise above 50 per 1,000. During the 1918 influenza epidemic in the United States the annual death rate rose only from 14 to 18, although the rate for the month of October 1918 was 44.1.

considerably more favorable conditions than have existed in the past two decades and would reduce death rates for at least some time.[4]

While India and the Netherlands Indies are probably the classic examples of improved internal security and stability resulting from overseas intervention, these are not isolated instances. They probably exemplify the kinds of changes which occurred elsewhere in the Orient, in Latin America, the Middle East and Africa during the nineteenth century and later.[5]

### Famines Less Frequent

Economic penetration, however, usually meant more than merely establishing a semblance of internal order. Transport was improved, partly to assist in the exploitation of resources, but partly, too, as in India, to ameliorate local famines. The same was true of irrigation. In the words of Kingsley Davis:

> In times of scarcity the same channels which ordinarily took food out of the country could bring food into it, and the breakdown of isolation inside India enabled areas of surplus to succor areas of deprivation . . . Some of the railways and hard-surfaced roads in India were undertaken precisely for the purpose of preventing famines.[6]

The promotion of commercial crops and the exploitation of mineral resources were also probably responsible for a sufficiently greater output per person to affect mortality. One may deplore some aspects of the "plantation system" as manifested in the production of sugar, coffee, tea, rubber, tobacco, bananas, cotton and other crops, or the paternalism of foreign capitalists in mining diamonds, tin, bauxite, etc., yet these outposts of the world economy probably more often lowered than raised death rates in the areas where they were established.[7] Population increased rather than decreased.

---

4. Marshall C. Balfour, Roger F. Evans, Frank W. Notestein and Irene B. Taeuber, *Public Health and Demography in the Far East*, Rockefeller Foundation, New York, 1950, p. 75. Issawi (*op. cit.*, p. 48) states that "the order and security introduced by Mohammed Ali" was a prime factor in Egypt's population growth in the nineteenth century.

5. The belief that most of those areas were serene and peaceful in their economic and political isolation before the great powers took an interest in them is a romantic delusion similar to Rousseau's well-known beliefs on the nature of primitive man before society corrupted him. Such views are still frequently encountered although historical and anthropological research give them little support. Whatever they may have been in some earlier millennium, few of the areas which attracted the interest of the European powers in the seventeenth century and later were then politically or economically secure.

6. Davis, *op. cit.*, p. 39.

7. The writers are not here concerned with the ultimate merit of these ventures from the point of view of the native populations or with their long-term international economic consequences. Such judgments involve far broader considerations than are now under discussion. The only concern is to point out that, whatever may have been their other effects, these enterprises probably reduced mortality in the areas where they were introduced.

*Health and Sanitation Measures*

A second, though probably less important, reason why mortality declined with increasing contacts between the more developed and less developed countries is that certain health and sanitation measures were introduced which struck directly at the high death rates. To be sure, the science of public health and sanitation as it is today was developed only in the very late nineteenth century and after. Nevertheless, even by 1850, medical knowledge and at least the rudiments of public health were better understood in the Western countries than in the rest of the world, and some of this experience was applied in the underdeveloped areas. Before 1900, such efforts were probably confined chiefly to the port cities and other centers where Westerners congregated and felt the need of self-protection. The control of smallpox in India and the Netherlands Indies is an instance.[8]

Against these advances, however, must be set the damage done by exposing the people in the underdeveloped areas to new diseases. Kingsley Davis points out that:

It seems clear, for example, that the invasion of India by tuberculosis began in the cities, and that at the present time, with the breakdown of the isolation of the rural villages, it is spreading rapidly and alarmingly to the countryside. Also, it is believed that India was not exposed to plague prior to 1896.[9]

As a result of contacts with the outside world, tuberculosis, syphilis and other diseases have at times nearly decimated the local populations, as for example in parts of the Pacific and Africa and among the Eskimos.

The net result of these opposing influences—purposive health measures as against the introduction of new diseases—cannot be estimated with any accuracy for, say, the period down to 1890. After 1900, the evidence suggests that public health measures, sanitation programs and medical care as transferred from the more developed countries outweighed the transplanted diseases in their effects upon mortality.

Thus, the remarkable growth in population in the underdeveloped areas from around 1850 down to the outbreak of World War II is perhaps largely attributable, on the one hand, to the rise in productivity resulting from outside contact and exploitation and, on the other, to direct attacks on some of the more patent causes of morbidity and mortality. The two factors are not entirely separable, of course. If, for example, improvements in well-being resulting from greater productivity take the form principally of more food and fewer famines, this in itself would increase resistance to disease and reduce mortality.

8. Cf. Davis, *op. cit.*, p. 47.
9. *Ibid.*, p. 42, citations omitted.

FUTURE MORTALITY PROBABILITIES IN UNDERDEVELOPED AREAS

The declines in mortality rates in underdeveloped areas during the nineteenth century, and in some of them even up to 1939, came mostly as byproducts of rising productivity rather than from direct assaults on the causes of morbidity and mortality. The fall in mortality was mostly a concomitant of other changes rather than an end directly pursued. Insofar as economic development does succeed over the near future in the underdeveloped areas, further declines in mortality must therefore be the expected consequence. At the same time, however, evidence is accumulating that the now underdeveloped countries can probably lower their mortality rates much more rapidly than the now developed countries did in the past, and,

TABLE 5-2. AVERAGE DEATH RATES IN 12 UNDERDEVELOPED COUNTRIES,
1936–1940 AND 1946–1950

*(Rate per 1,000 Population)*

| Country | 1936–1940 | 1946–1950 |
|---|---|---|
| Puerto Rico | 19.1 | 11.5 |
| Ceylon | 21.4 | 14.6 |
| Chile | 23.2 | 17.0 |
| Mexico | 23.4 | 17.4 |
| Greece | 14.1 | 10.6 |
| Japan | 17.3 | 13.4 |
| Jamaica | 16.1 | 12.9 |
| Poland[a] | 14.0 | 11.5 |
| Egypt | 26.7 | 22.2 |
| Malaya | 20.5 | 17.1 |
| Yugoslavia[b] | 15.7 | 13.4 |
| Guatemala | 26.0 | 23.2 |

*Source: Population Bulletin*, June 1952, p. 12.

a. Statistics for Poland are incomplete and the averages are for the years 1936–1938 and 1947–1950.

b. Averages shown are for 1936–1939 and 1948–1950.

furthermore, that some of this fall can be brought about without appreciable improvement in most of the usual economic indices of development. In other words, the *rate* of decline may be more rapid in the future and it may now be less dependent upon over-all economic progress.

The primary reason why further declines in mortality in the underdeveloped areas may soon be dramatically rapid is that certain infectious diseases, which are still major scourges in these areas, have been virtually eliminated in the developed countries by techniques that can be easily, and often cheaply, transferred to other parts of the world. These important scientific advances have been widely applied in the developed countries in the past two or three decades. The underdeveloped countries will not need to discover for themselves the causes of cholera, plague, typhus, smallpox, typhoid, malaria, etc. That knowledge exists and is freely available. The underdeveloped countries need only the material resources, the trained personnel, and, perhaps, the requisite administrative efficiency to apply this knowledge on an extensive scale. With some assistance from abroad, the underdeveloped areas could soon effect a sharp drop in their high mortality rates, even without much economic development in other directions. Mortality rates may now be much less closely tied to general economic development than they were in the nineteenth century.

Just how rapidly death rates may decline under modern conditions is shown by the declines that occurred in twelve underdeveloped countries between 1936–1940 and 1946–1950—a period too short to have permitted any comparable gain in general economic achievement. In half of these countries the death rate fell by one fifth or more in the ten-year interval. The declines ranged from nearly 40 per cent in Puerto Rico to about 11 per cent in Guatemala. (See Table 5-2.) If these data are approximately accurate, they suggest that mortality rates in the underdeveloped areas now can be reduced very rapidly and that, unless comparable declines in birth rates are to be expected, rates of population growth could be dangerously large.

### FERTILITY AND ECONOMIC DEVELOPMENT

All the evidence seems to indicate that in the Western world fertility[10] has declined with the spread of "modern civilization," which, on its material side, has been based on the economic developments after 1800. In the underdeveloped countries, fertility rates are now well above those in the developed countries—perhaps even above the rates prevailing in Western Europe before the Industrial Revolution. Granted the probability that mortality rates will fall as development proceeds in the poor countries, what is the likelihood that fertility rates will also decline? And how rapidly can the change be expected?

The usual approach to these questions is to try to discover what factors— either directly resulting from economic development or virtually certain to accompany it—have been primarily responsible for the drop in fertility in the Western world, and to what extent they can be expected to become operative where economic development is now in prospect of realization.

This type of causal analysis can be pursued at different levels. At the one extreme, for example, one might try to explain the decline in births by alleging—though there is little supporting evidence—that there has been a decline in "reproductive capacity" in a straightforward biological or

10. For an explanation of the methods of measuring fertility see Appendix 5-1.

physiological sense.[11] Only slightly removed from this level would be the generally accepted view that "the major part if not all of the decline in family size has been brought about by the practice of family limitation."[12] Statements so formulated, however, immediately pose the question why "the practice of family limitation" should have become so general in the Western world in the past century. What aspects of economic progress or modern civilization seem to make family limitation so widespread in contemporary Western society but so rare (apparently) in underdeveloped countries? This question can be approached by asking: (1) Why is fertility relatively low in developed countries? or (2) Why is it so high in underdeveloped countries? Presumably, the same types of factors are operative in either case. As might be expected, disagreements on these points arise less over the facts themselves than over their interpretation. Thus, there is agreement that urbanization and relatively low fertility are usually found together; but just *what* features in urban life tend to bring this about may be hotly debated.

SOME INTERRELATED FACTORS IN FERTILITY CHANGES

Perhaps the most generally accepted view of the decline in fertility in already developed countries is that it is

. . . due to a complex of inter-related causes acting upon one another and jointly bringing about the decline . . . the decline in fertility is closely connected with the changes which have fundamentally transformed European society in the last two centuries, but attempts to associate the decline exclusively with a particular aspect of these changes—such as urbanization—have not proved satisfactory.[13]

While conceding the complex interrelationships of the factors that have lowered fertility, we may still note the findings of a few studies which attempt to link fertility decline with something more specific than "the changes which have fundamentally transformed European society in the

11. Raymond Pearl lists six "direct" factors of this biological or physiological character that affect individual and group fertility—sexual desire, age-specific innate reproductive capacity, coitus rate, conception rate, contraceptive rate and reproductive wastage rate. But like other writers he also points out that these direct factors are not constant in their effects on fertility because they are modified by first and second order "indirect" factors. First order indirect factors would include economic circumstances, density of population, religious tenets, institutions of property, etc., which in turn fix the second order indirect factors—premarital fertility, age of marriage, education, occupation, personal values, physical and mental health, etc. See Raymond Pearl, "Biological Factors in Fertility," *Annals of the American Academy of Political and Social Science*, November 1936, pp. 24–25.

Pearl's classification suggests that efforts to influence fertility might be aimed at either the first or second order indirect factors or even at the direct factors. Probably most specialists in these matters would argue that efforts to influence fertility by modifying the direct factors, while leaving the indirect factors as they were, would be largely ineffective. In other words, fertility control will only be applied by populations whose value systems and economic and social conditions make people wish to control fertility.

12. United Nations, Economic and Social Council, "Economic and Social Factors Affecting Fertility," *Findings of Studies on the Relationships between Population Trends and Economic and Social Factors*, Chapter 2 of the final report, April 24, 1951, p. 34. The text discussion has drawn heavily on this document.

13. *Ibid.*, p. 55.

last two centuries." Urbanization, income and literacy are three factors considered here because they seem to be nearly inevitable concomitants of economic development and they are also partially measurable.

*Urban-Rural Differences*

Fertility in rural areas seems to have been higher than urban fertility even in the eighteenth century and this differential appears to have persisted up to the present in most countries, even though the margin has probably narrowed somewhat.[14] Frank Lorimer reports that in 1926–1928 in the U.S.S.R., rural birth rates held at 45 per 1,000 population, while urban rates moved down from 33.9 in 1926 to 28.3 in 1928. The gross reproduction rate in rural areas he calculated to be 2.87 as against 1.71 in the urban areas, though with marked differences between regions.[15] As to the regional differences he says:

. . . the difference in fertility between cities and rural districts overshadows all regional variations either among urban or among rural districts considered separately. In fact the most conspicuous regional differences are largely a function of degree of urbanization. In the U.S.S.R. as a whole, the gross reproduction ratio for the rural population is 68 percent higher and the net reproduction ratio 55 percent higher, than the corresponding ratios for the urban population.[16]

In Japan, between 1920 and 1935, urban gross reproduction rates fell from 1.8 to 1.6 and the rural rates from 2.8 to 2.6.[17] In Puerto Rico urban fertility rates also are lower than rural.[18] In India, the same generalization is applicable, with a further differential between smaller cities and larger cities.[19]

No useful purpose would be served by assembling all the illustrative cases. The general point is clear: with few exceptions, urban fertility rates

14. *Ibid.*, pp. 18–19. P. K. Whelpton has shown ("Industrial Development and Population Growth," *Social Forces*, March 1928, p. 462) that in the United States the number of children in the age range 0–4 years per 1,000 women aged 16–44 was consistently higher for each census year between 1800 and 1920 in agricultural states than in either semi-industrial or industrial states. The numbers fell in all three groups throughout the nineteenth century, though not with perfect consistency. Between 1800 and 1910 Whelpton's figures show a drop of 35 per cent in the agricultural states (from 1,043 children 0–4 years per 1,000 women to 678) as against a drop of 43 per cent (from 786 to 444) in the industrial states.

15. Frank Lorimer, *The Population of the Soviet Union: History and Prospects*, League of Nations, Geneva, 1946, pp. 87 and 90. Roughly, gross reproduction rates tell the number of females (potential mothers) born to the average woman in her lifetime, assuming she lives through the childbearing years, while net reproduction rates take into account the fact that not all women will survive through the reproductive years. Gross and net reproduction rates are described more fully in Appendix 5–1.

16. *Ibid.*, pp. 89–92.

17. Irene B. Taeuber and Edwin G. Beal, "The Dynamics of Population in Japan," in *Demographic Studies of Selected Areas of Rapid Growth*, Milbank Memorial Fund, New York, 1944, p. 28. Net rates fell less than gross rates because of reduced mortality among women in the reproductive years.

18. See Lydia J. Roberts, *Patterns of Living in Puerto Rican Families*, University of Puerto Rico, Rio Piedras, Puerto Rico, 1949, pp. 288–89.

19. Davis, *op. cit.*, pp. 70–73. Davis adds (p. 73): "In so far, then, as urbanization continues it will have slight effect in decreasing total fertility; but there is apparently no extra diffusion, no multiplier effect, that intensifies the influence of cities beyond their natural growth as time goes by. In short, the rural-urban and intra-urban differentials do not indicate an imminent decline of general fertility in India."

are below rural fertility rates even though the urban rates may differ substantially among countries. It should follow from past experience, therefore, that insofar as economic development induces urbanization, it should tend to cut fertility rates.

Explanations of *why* urbanization of a population tends to lower its fertility (by bringing it under conscious control) almost invariably stress the multiplicity of factors at work. As the United Nations report phrases it, the small-family system is not to be viewed as

. . . the result of a particular development, such as higher standards of living, but as a characteristic of a whole new way of life, of "civilization" in general, as it has sometimes been expressed. To describe the mentality accompanying family limitation, words such as "rational," "rationalization," "rationalist civilization" are often used. What constitutes this "rational mentality"? An element commonly stressed is freedom from tradition, the willingness to analyze institutions, values, patterns of behavior which were traditionally accepted without question . . . Economic rationalism has been particularly stressed.[20]

If the question is put the other way about—What kind of environment tends to make for *high* fertility?—the answer is probably similar: traditionalized ways of life, familial dominance, primacy of the male, ignorance and illiteracy, extreme poverty, and spatial, social and economic immobility. All these and related influences are likely to operate with diminished force in an urban environment. City life is more impersonal than rural life; the individual can be more anonymous and more free to fix his own social patterns. Consequently, it is not surprising that growing urbanization should be accompanied by new ways and new mores, including those affecting fertility.[21]

### Education and Fertility

These characteristics of urban living and urban points of view may partly explain the close correlations frequently found between education and fertility and income and fertility. That is to say, education may be indicative of the acceptance and adoption of urban points of view; higher incomes may imply modes of life patterned after those prevailing in the more highly developed urban centers, which often come to be almost axiomatically accepted as the standard of comparison. The American scene abounds in examples.

A recent study by Sven Moberg shows that among industrial workers in Swedish towns, the average number of live births per marriage fell as the income of the family rose. Among employers and officials, this held true

20. "Economic and Social Factors Affecting Fertility," p. 56.

21. Perhaps no change resulting from the shift from rural to urban living affects fertility more than the altered status of women. They cease to be regarded as inferiors fit only for *Kinder, Kuchen und Kirchen.*

for all successive income groups except the highest. Moreover, in the first two income categories among employers and officials, the average number of live births per marriage fell as the index of educational achievement rose. In the two highest income categories, however, the average increased as the index of educational attainment went higher. In other words, toward the top of the scale, fertility was positively, not negatively, correlated with income and education.[22]

For the United States, Bernard D. Karpinos and Clyde V. Kiser have shown that both net and gross reproduction rates in 1935 for urban populations, when classified by size of city and by income class, declined as the size of the city increased and as the average income rose. In cities of 100,000 and over, for example, gross reproduction rates for those in the $1,000–$1,499 income bracket were 0.81 as against only 0.42 for those with incomes over $3,000. For cities under 25,000, the gross reproduction rates in these income categories were 0.96 and 0.52 respectively.[23]

A Puerto Rican study in 1946 showed that more schooling for the women meant fewer children. Mothers with no schooling had had an average of 6.1 live births in comparison with an average of 2.4 live births for those with high school education or above; and the average moved steadily upward as the amount of schooling became less. Urban mothers with no schooling had fewer live births than rural mothers without schooling, 5.5 as compared with 6.3.[24] Studies in other areas tend to show similar results.

*Summary*

It is unnecessary to belabor the point: more education and diminished fertility seem usually to be associated; higher incomes and lower fertility tend to go together. And, perhaps, both incomes and education are not so inherently significant in themselves as for what they betoken of ways of life dominated by those mores and cultural values characteristic of modern, occidental, urban civilization—values which stress the importance of the individual and his well-being and so push more fertility per se far down the scale.[25]

Thus, some of the components of economic development and some of its direct consequences appear to evoke certain conscious attitudes toward

22. Sven Moberg, "Marital Status and Family Size among Matriculated Persons in Sweden," *Population Studies*, June 1950, p. 124.

23. Bernard D. Karpinos and Clyde V. Kiser, "The Differential Fertility and Potential Rates of Growth of Various Income and Educational Classes of Urban Populations in the United States," *Milbank Memorial Fund Quarterly*, October 1939, p. 383.

24. Roberts, *op. cit.*, pp. 288–89.

25. One of the most striking carry-overs of this kind is the differential between Oriental and Western Jews in Palestine. The Kurds and Yemenites are said to average about 8 children per woman, the Austrian Jews only about 1.3. The Austrians have the fertility patterns of contemporary, urbanized, Western groups while the Kurds and Yemenites have the fertility patterns of ancient, agricultural, Oriental groups. "Economic and Social Factors Affecting Fertility," pp. 75–76.

fertility which result in fewer births. Family limitation apparently tends to become a widespread practice.

Yet even were the evidence for this view overwhelming, one could not on that account casually drop the population problem from discussions of economic development. And this for two reasons. First, the decline in fertility that comes with development and progress is slow in getting started compared either with development itself or with the fall in mortality rates. Experience suggests that it does not occur simultaneously with development, but only after a lag. Second, even if fertility should decline as development moves forward, many of the now underdeveloped areas will start from such high plateaus of fertility that even an appreciable drop will still leave fertility rates dangerously high. Thus, on the one hand, there is a strong possibility of a time lag before fertility declines; on the other, even a sizable decline from present levels will not necessarily mean *low* fertility rates in many underdeveloped countries.

## THE DELAYED FALL IN FERTILITY AND ITS IMPLICATIONS

No one can forecast with any accuracy how rapidly fertility is likely to fall in consequence of economic development in the now poor countries. But more than a little is known as to when fertility began its steady decline in a number of already developed countries. This experience is not conclusive, of course; but it is suggestive for the question in hand.

### European Experience

For western and northern Europe as a whole, the average birth rate for the years 1841–1845 has been estimated at 31.8 per 1,000 population; it held close to this level up to 1891–1895, when it fell below 30 for the first time, dropping to 29.7.[26] Up to 1936, the average birth rate of this region never again climbed above 30. It dropped below 20 for the first time in 1924 and, according to Kuczynski's study, remained below 20 in every year from 1924 to 1936.

In a period of approximately 35 years, therefore, the birth rate in western and northern Europe dropped by about one third. This decline cannot, of course, be attributed entirely to development and urbanization. Some of it reflects the changing age composition of the population as a result of mortality changes and emigration. World War I also took a heavy toll in

---

26. R. R. Kuczynski, "The International Decline in Fertility," in Lancelot Hogben (Ed.), *Political Arithmetic*, Macmillan, New York, 1938, Table II, p. 50. Western and northern Europe for this calculation is said to include "Present [1938] territory of Belgium, Denmark (including Faroe Islands and Iceland), United Kingdom (including islands in the British Seas), Irish Free State, France, Germany, Holland, Luxembourg, Norway, Sweden, Switzerland."

dead and crippled, especially in France, Germany and the United Kingdom, and as a result more women remained unmarried.

For central and southern Europe, data are not available covering so long a time span.[27] Between 1922 and 1936, however, average birth rates for this area dropped from 32.0 to 24.6—a recorded drop of roughly 25 per cent in 13 years. Birth rates in central and southern Europe in 1936 were thus about where they were in western and northern Europe in 1911–1914. The period covered is possibly too short for safe inference and is subject to the influence of World War I. Moreover, the 1936 rate doubtless reflects the influence of the world depression of the 1930s as well as long-run factors.

Although these European data are averages for groups of countries, they nevertheless suggest two important points. The decline in birth rates began only after economic development had been in progress for some time. The decline in central and southern Europe began perhaps three decades later than in northern and western Europe; but once it did set in, birth rates fell rather more rapidly. Kuczynski says:

While it took France over seventy years to experience a drop in her birth-rate from 30 to 20, while this process lasted about forty years in Sweden and Switzerland and about thirty years in England and Denmark, in the last twelve years (from 1924 to 1936) the birth-rate has fallen in Bulgaria from 40 to 26, in Poland from 35 to 26, in Czechoslovakia from 26 to 17.[28]

*Gross Reproduction Rates*

Crude birth rates are a less satisfactory index of fertility than gross reproduction rates.[29] Kuczynski reports that about 1880 gross reproduction rates were over 3.2 in Russia; between 2.4 and 2.8 in Austria and Germany; between 2.2 and 2.4 in England, Denmark, Norway and Sweden; and between 1.6 and 1.8 in France. But by 1910, thirty years later, only two of these countries—Russia and Austria—had gross reproduction rates above 2.0. And by 1925, only Russia remained above 2.0—and her rate had fallen to about 2.7. The rates in some of these other countries in 1925 were: England and Wales, 1.086; Germany, 1.116; Sweden, 1.121; and France, 1.146.[30] (See Table 5-3.) It appears then, that in three of the principal coun-

27. Central and southern Europe for this purpose includes the 1938 territory of "Austria, Bulgaria, Czechoslovakia, Danzig, Estonia, Finland, Gibraltar, Greece, Hungary, Italy, Latvia, Lithuania, Maltese Islands, Poland, Portugal, Rumania, Spain, Yugoslavia." *Ibid.*
    Accurate data on birth rates in the United States are not available before 1915. The rate for the white population was 25.1 in 1915, as against 16–17 in the 1930s. *Historical Statistics of the United States, 1789–1945*, U.S. Bureau of the Census, 1949, p. 46.

28. Kuczynski, *loc. cit.*, p. 53. That these 1936 rates were partially influenced by depression conditions is shown by the fact that in Czechoslovakia in the period 1940–1948 the birth rate was above 20 most of the time; but the Bulgarian rate continued to fall. See United Nations, *Demographic Yearbook, 1949–50*, New York, 1950, pp. 292–93.

29. Net reproduction rates are not of particular interest in the present context since we are not here concerned with the combined effects of changes in fertility and mortality but only with the amount and timing of the changes in fertility. Kuczynski does, however, present estimates of net reproduction rates in his study.

30. *Ibid.*, p. 60.

TABLE 5-3. TREND OF GROSS REPRODUCTION RATES, 1880–1925

| Rate | About 1880 | About 1895 | About 1910 | About 1925 |
|---|---|---|---|---|
| Over 3.2 | Russia | Russia | | |
| 2.8–3.2 | | Poland | Bulgaria Russia | |
| 2.4–2.8 | Austria Germany | Austria | Croatia | Russia Japan |
| 2.2–2.4 | Denmark England Finland Norway | Finland Germany | Hungary | Bulgaria |
| 2.0–2.2 | Sweden | Denmark Norway | Austria | Poland |
| 1.8–2.0 | | Baltic Prov. England Sweden | Finland Germany Norway | |
| 1.6–1.8 | France | | Denmark Sweden Australia | Canada Union of South Africa |
| 1.4–1.6 | | France | England New Zealand | Czechoslavakia Finland Australia |
| 1.2–1.4 | | | France | Denmark Norway United States New Zealand |
| 1.1–1.2 | | | | France Germany Sweden |
| 1.0–1.1 | | | | England Estonia |

Source: R. R. Kuczynski, "The International Decline of Fertility," in Lancelot Hogben (Ed.), *Political Arithmetic*, Macmillan, New York, 1938, p. 60.

tries of Europe—England, Germany and Sweden—fertility, as measured by gross reproduction rates, fell fully 50 per cent between 1880 and 1925.[31]

31. How specialists in these matters analyze the reasons for the decline in fertility may be seen from a study by D. V. Glass, "Changes in Fertility in England and Wales, 1851–1931," in Hogben (Ed.), *op. cit.*, pp. 161–212. This is a careful study of changing fertility in England and Wales by counties. These counties showed considerable variation in the timing of their respective declines in fertility. Glass points out, too (pp. 165*ff.*), that for England and Wales as a whole, fertility increased slightly between 1841 and 1871, though when special circumstances are allowed for, the increase was probably concentrated between 1841 and 1851. Down to 1911, fertility differentials even increased somewhat. For this he offers the explanation that "regional differences in fertility are only marked in a period when industrial expansion has still not proceeded far enough to urbanize the whole community. In 1911 . . . large sections of the country still remained untouched by urban developments" (p. 193). But after 1911, developments in transport and communication destroyed the isolation of rural areas from the cities and so produced "a more universal pattern of life, a more generally accepted set of social *mores*" (p. 193). Glass tries to correlate the decline in fertility with marriage, employment of women, occupational type of the district and the employment of children but has to conclude that while these correlate quite well for any one year for which the statistics are available, the relationship breaks down "if we try to link up progressive changes in the operation of these social factors with the decline of fertility from one period to another" (p. 210). He says finally that the fall in fertility seems to have been caused by "less tangible factors which, so far, we have not been able to measure" (p. 211).

The drop in birth rates in northern and western Europe from about 30 to under 20 per 1,000, and the decline in gross reproduction rates from over 2.0 to slightly more than 1.0, thus extended over several decades. In central and southern Europe the change apparently went more rapidly; but the latest data show birth rates for most countries in this region still above those for northern and central Europe.

## Japanese Experience

Japanese experience scarcely justifies the assumption that development soon results in lower fertility as a matter of course. The birth rate in Japan fell from 34.6 per 1,000 population in 1921–1925 to 27.0 in 1938. However, the decline occurred largely in the younger age classes, because of fewer early marriages, and also among women over 30. Between 1920 and 1935, "the gross reproduction rate for all Japan declined from 2.6 to 2.2, for urban areas from 1.8 to 1.6, and for rural areas from 2.8 to 2.6."[32] But these reproduction rates were comparable to those in Bulgaria in 1925 or in England and the Scandinavian countries about 1895. Fertility declined in Japan, but up to World War II it was high compared with fertility in the West.

The changes in Japanese fertility after World War II were partly due to special factors, too complex to be described accurately here. After a temporary upsurge in 1947–1949, when birth rates averaged over 33 per 1,000, the birth rate declined again in 1950 to 28.3. The gross reproduction rate fell from 2.1 in 1940 to 1.8 in 1950.[33] The prewar trend toward lower fertility seems to be again in evidence.

## Demographic Patterns in Underdeveloped Countries

The demographic history just sketched might appear to justify the inference that high fertility rates in the underdeveloped areas, do not, perhaps, constitute as serious a problem as often alleged. Past experience suggests that fertility will probably decline as development moves forward. Yet one extremely important fact remains: almost all the underdeveloped areas *now* have fertility rates well above the corresponding Western European rates before a decline set in about 1880–1890.

Even if births should begin to decline at once in, say, India or Egypt or Ceylon, they would have to decline some 25 to 30 per cent, or more, before

32. Taeuber and Beal, *loc. cit.*, p. 28. The discussion of Japanese experience is largely based on this study.

33. See Irene B. Taeuber and Marshall C. Balfour, "The Control of Fertility in Japan," in *Approaches to Problems of High Fertility in Agrarian Societies*, Milbank Memorial Fund, New York, 1952, p. 102. Taeuber and Balfour discuss at length the effects of the war and changed social customs on postwar Japanese fertility. They comment (p. 109): "Fifty-six per cent of the women aged 20 to 24 are single. The proportion of the widowed and the separated rises steeply from five per cent at ages 25 to 29 to 15 per cent at ages 35 to 39 . . . Japanese women as a group [are] less married in 1950 than at any time in the recorded statistical history of Japan." Taeuber and Balfour feel, however, that the importance of these changes for future Japanese fertility patterns cannot yet be assessed with full confidence.

TABLE 5-4. CRUDE BIRTH RATES, CRUDE DEATH RATES, NATURAL RATES OF
POPULATION INCREASE IN UNDERDEVELOPED AREAS, 1946–1950

| Country | Crude Birth Rate | Crude Death Rate | Rate of Natural Increase |
|---|---|---|---|
| Africa | | | |
| Egypt | 42.5 | 22.2 | 20.3 |
| Mauritius (without dependencies) [U. K.] | 44.1 | 20.8 | 23.3 |
| Central America | | | |
| Costa Rica | 44.9 | 12.6 | 32.3 |
| Dominican Republic | 35.4 | 9.9 | 25.5 |
| El Salvador | 40.8 | 14.6 | 26.2 |
| Honduras[a] | 40.1 | 15.0 | 25.1 |
| Mexico | 45.1 | 17.4 | 27.7 |
| Nicaragua | 35.9 | 11.1 | 24.8 |
| Panama[a] (excluding tribal Indians) | 34.8 | 8.8 | 26.0 |
| Caribbean area | | | |
| Jamaica (without dependencies) [U. K.] | 31.9 | 12.9 | 19.0 |
| Puerto Rico [U. S.] | 40.5 | 11.5 | 29.0 |
| South America | | | |
| Argentina[a] | 24.8 | 9.5 | 15.3 |
| Bolivia | 30.1 | 12.2 | 17.9 |
| Chile | 33.1 | 17.0 | 16.1 |
| Colombia[a] | 34.4 | 14.6 | 19.8 |
| Peru (excluding jungle population) | 26.8 | 11.3 | 15.5 |
| Venezuela | 41.0 | 13.1 | 27.9 |
| British Guiana[a] | 39.9 | 14.7 | 25.2 |
| Surinam (excluding Bush Negroes and aborigines) | 34.5 | 11.7 | 22.8 |
| Asia | | | |
| Ceylon | 39.7 | 14.6 | 25.1 |
| India[a] | 26.9 | 17.9 | 9.0 |
| Indonesia (1940 only) | 28.5 | 20.3 | 8.2 |
| Thailand[a] | 24.8 | 12.5 | 12.3 |
| Federation of Malaya [U. K.] | 40.8 | 17.1 | 23.7 |
| Europe | | | |
| Greece (excluding Dodecanese) | 27.2 | 10.6 | 16.6 |
| Oceania | | | |
| New Zealand (excluding Maoris) | 25.3 | 9.3 | 16.0 |
| Maoris | 47.0 | 13.8 | 33.2 |

*Sources: Population Bulletin*, June 1952, p. 12, and United Nations, *Demographic Yearbook, 1951*, New York, 1951. Notes are omitted.
   a. 1946–1949 only.

they reached the level already prevailing in Western Europe about 1880.
Around 1881–1885, according to Kuczynski, only four European countries had crude birth rates above 40 per 1,000: Serbia (46.8), Hungary
(44.4), Rumania (42.2) and Poland (41.9).[34] But more than a dozen areas

34. Kuczynski, *loc. cit.*, p. 52.

reported birth rates above 40 per 1,000 during one or more years in the 1940s—some of them every year and some well above 40. (See Table 5-4.) Insofar as the data are imprecise, they are likely to have erred on the side of understating rather than overreporting the actual number of births.

## Mexico

Mexico illustrates the problem nicely. In no year from 1932 through 1948 was the crude birth rate in Mexico below 42.2 (1933), and the average for 1940–1948 was 44.9. The Mexican birth rate would thus have to drop by about one third before it reached 30. Between 1932 and 1948, the death rate dropped from 26.1 per 1,000 population to 16.8. This means that in 1948, with a birth rate of 44.6 and a death rate of 16.8 per 1,000, the "natural increase" was 27.8 per 1,000, or 2.78 per cent, a year.[35]

## Other Underdeveloped Areas

Mexico, however, is not an isolated or extreme case. If accurate and complete data were available, the Caribbean, much of Latin America, North Africa, the Middle East and perhaps most of Asia would probably show birth rates not much lower than Mexico's. Estimated annual rates of growth give some idea of the probable birth rates in these areas.

For nine Caribbean and Central American countries in 1940, the average annual rate of growth has been estimated at 21.3 per 1,000. In South America, rates of increase are believed to be similar to those in Central America and the Caribbean; only Argentina and Chile show much evidence of falling birth rates.[36] A recent writer reports that 25 Latin American countries have annual rates of increase of 20 or more per 1,000, according to the most recent data available.[37]

Kingsley Davis' calculations for India show an estimated birth rate of 45 per 1,000 rather than the much lower official figure shown in Table 5-4. In what is now Indonesia, the calculated annual increase for the period 1920–

---

35. Against this rate of "natural increase" of 27.8 per 1,000 per year in Mexico may be set the following careful estimates of annual rates of growth per 1,000 over long periods in four countries of northern Europe:

| Period | Sweden | Norway | Denmark | Finland |
|---|---|---|---|---|
| 1735–1800 | 5 | 7 | 3 | 12 |
| 1801–1900 | 7 | 9 | 9 | 11 |
| 1901–1940 | 6 | 7 | 11 | 9 |

See H. Gille, "The Demographic History of the Northern European Countries in the Eighteenth Century," *Population Studies*, June 1949, p. 28.

36. Most of these comments on rates of growth are drawn from United Nations, "Historical Outline of World Population Growth," in *Findings of Studies on the Relationships between Population Trends and Economic and Social Factors*, October 23, 1951, pp. 29ff. Since the calculations are at best rough indications, it is unnecessary to cite here all the various original sources, some of which were not available to the present writers.

37. Eldridge, *loc. cit.*, p. 3.

1930 was 17.3 per 1,000. Other estimates show Malaya (1948) at 24 and Ceylon (1948) at 27.4.

Although satisfactory data for the Middle East are virtually nonexistent, birth rates in this region are generally believed to be very high—ranging from perhaps as low as 27 in European Turkey to over 60, and to as high as 70 in some sparsely settled regions of Saudi Arabia. Birth rates below 50 are said to be "relatively low" for the Middle East.[38] Both here and in North Africa mortality rates are also high, however, so that the annual rates of increase are generally believed to be modest.

*The Prospects*

The implications of the foregoing for economic development are painfully obvious. The "natural" fall in fertility which results from the social and cultural changes incident to development may be "sure" but it is also discouragingly "slow." Perhaps fertility will decline appreciably in two decades as it did in parts of central and southeastern Europe, the U.S.S.R. and, to a lesser extent, in Japan; the longer time span necessary in Western Europe may not be directly relevant. Nevertheless, any assumption that fertility will automatically decline rapidly—in, say, five years coincident with the successful completion of a "five-year plan" for development—is unwarranted. Finally, even were fertility to decline more rapidly than in all previous demographic experience, birth rates are already so high in many underdeveloped areas that even a large percentage decline would leave these rates well above those in developed countries and probably far above the corresponding death rates. The danger of a rapid rise in population would remain.

POSITIVE MEASURES TO REDUCE FERTILITY

The gap between birth and death rates which looms ahead for many underdeveloped areas inevitably opens the question of the possibility of reducing fertility in these areas by deliberate efforts, instead of waiting for the slow workings of social change or for the grim alternative of a rise in mortality. The problem of bringing underdeveloped, agrarian societies to adopt the practice of birth prevention bristles with difficulties. These difficulties range all the way from unresolved problems in applied medical research to thorny questions of social anthropology and foreign policy. All that can be essayed here is to indicate briefly what some of these problems are and wherein their importance lies.

38. See Ernest Jurkat, "Prospects for Population Growth in the Near East," in *Demographic Studies of Selected Areas of Rapid Growth*, Milbank Memorial Fund, New York, 1944, pp. 85–87. Some demographers regard these high estimates for the Middle East with skepticism.

## Birth Prevention

Barring a rise in death rates, the only means of checking population growth is to make widespread the practice of "birth prevention."[39] All the evidence seems to show that the much lower fertility rates so common in already developed countries primarily result from the fact that their populations deliberately limit fertility while people in the underdeveloped countries do not. The broad problem, therefore, can be formulated in the following way: first, Are there contraceptive techniques which are suitable for the kind of living conditions which exist in most underdeveloped areas? second, If such techniques were readily available, would the people use them? third—assuming that a reliable answer can be given to the second question—What are the appropriate means of introducing these techniques and bringing about their widespread use among people in the underdeveloped areas?

These appear to be the essential questions implicit in any direct attempt to lower the dangerously high fertility rates now so characteristic of many underdeveloped areas. Such tentative answers as are available give little cause for jubilation.

## Cost Important

Competent medical opinion seems to be quite positive that *"We have no known harmless, simple, or low cost method today with which we can apply fertility control."* The most that can be said, evidently, is this: "We appear, though, to be nearing avenues of research that may lead to that goal. There is some indication for reasonable hope."[40]

The methods of contraception in use in already developed societies are said to be either poorly adapted for use in underdeveloped areas or too costly in relation to the real incomes of the people.[41] Insofar as the limit

39. This is the term used by David Glass to cover all practices, behavior patterns and techniques which have as their purpose the limitation of births. (See D. V. Glass, *Population*, Clarendon Press, Oxford, 1940, p. 28.) Besides contraception in the ordinary sense, the term therefore includes abortion and infanticide, the "rhythm method," moral restraint, etc. Presumably, moral restraint includes later age of marriage and celibacy.

40. Clair E. Folsome, "Progress in the Search for Methods of Family Limitation Suitable for Agrarian Societies," in *Approaches to Problems of High Fertility in Agrarian Societies*, Milbank Memorial Fund, New York, 1952, p. 130 (italics in original). To judge from this paper much additional work remains to be done on the physiology of human reproduction before the "goal" is likely to be reached. Folsome remarks (pp. 129–30) that "Far more knowledge about the reproductive processes of farm animals and race horses is available than of their owner, man himself . . . Large public funds can be used to promote research on reproductivity of stock or fur-bearing animals by the Department of Agriculture. No funds are available to study reproduction of mankind on a comparable scale." This paper gives a short summary of some of the medical approaches to fertility control in underdeveloped areas.

41. One writer with considerable firsthand experience with public health programs in underdeveloped countries in many parts of the world has said: "In general terms, a contraceptive method for use in underdeveloped countries should be effective in reducing pregnancies; not harmful physiologically; practical and acceptable from the point of view of custom, sanitation and hygiene and climate; and above all, it must be cheap . . . within the range of one to five cents per family per week." Marshall C. Balfour, "Administrative Problems in Connection with Aid to Underdeveloped Areas" in *ibid.*, pp. 168–69.

to use is one of cost, however, this might be removed by having the public health authorities assume the burden. The cost might be small in relation to the social benefits to be derived and in comparison with the costs of the development program as a whole.

## Cultural Acceptance of Birth Prevention

The question whether the great masses of the people in the underdeveloped areas *would* use contraceptives if they were available cannot be answered with assurance. In any case, opinion differs. Moreover, it is not known to what extent careful studies of the problem in one area provide even tentative answers for other and different areas. One can scarcely assume out of hand—nor have the investigators so pretended—that the findings of a study in Puerto Rico or Mexico show what attitudes toward family limitation prevail in the Middle East or Java and studies in this field have so far been confined to a very few countries and localities.[42]

Two officers of the Milbank Memorial Fund, summarizing the opinions of a conference of experts on problems of fertility control in underdeveloped areas, judged that:

Most of the participants believed that it would be erroneous and unwise to assume that the rank and file of the population in the underdeveloped countries are now ready for contraceptives, no matter how cheap, simple, and effective they may appear to be. They doubted that this attitude would change before public education becomes more generalized and before a more widespread inculcation of desires for higher levels of living occurs.[43]

Not all persons competent to judge would be equally pessimistic. Irene Taeuber seems to be among the more optimistic.[44] An unpublished manuscript by Kingsley Davis gives a similar impression of hopefulness. Recent press reports from India on the results of a sampling study of the acceptance of "family planning" by lower income groups in rural and urban areas are also encouraging.[45]

## Doctrinal Opposition

For some countries, the acceptability of family limitation among the people at large may be a less immediate question than the attitude of their leaders. The newly adopted official attitude of the government of India that

42. See, for example, Paul K. Hatt, "Some Social and Psychological Aspects of Human Fertility in Puerto Rico"; Millard Hansen, "The Family in Puerto Rico Research Project"; Wilbert E. Moore, "Attitudes of Mexican Factory Workers toward Fertility Control"—all three in *ibid.*

43. Foreword by Frank G. Boudreau and Clyde V. Kiser in *ibid.*, p. 7.

44. See Irene Taeuber, "The Reproductive Mores of the Asian Peasant," in G. F. Mair (Ed.), *Studies in Population*, Princeton University Press, Princeton, 1949.

45. See *New York Times*, November 28, 1952, p. 27.

population does constitute a problem for India, and a probable threat to its aspirations for improved welfare through development, is undoubtedly encouraging. This official view is very recent, however. It represents a complete reversal of Gandhi's firm, doctrinal opposition to contraception (though not to continence or moral restraint). Mr. Nehru's former position that "in the present scheme of political representation the use of biological propensity as a weapon of increase of political power is implicit"[46] is probably more nearly characteristic of official attitudes in many underdeveloped countries.

In other countries family limitation may run so counter to religious tenets that their governments are virtually estopped from officially encouraging proposals and programs for deliberately lowering fertility. Most Latin American governments would probably find themselves in this position.

Finally, the official Communist position—that fertility control is needless, that it merely demonstrates the determination of the "imperialist powers" to keep the underdeveloped countries subjugated by holding down their numbers—does not go entirely unheeded in the underdeveloped world.[47]

## International Complications

The pressure for diminished fertility comes at present, and will probably continue to come, from outside the high fertility countries themselves. Hence, even granted suitable techniques of control along with public and official acceptance of programs to generalize their application, two sets of problems still remain. First, too little is known concerning the principles of applied social psychology and cultural anthropology required to carry such a program through to successful realization.[48] Second, the international political connotations of a more developed country attempting deliberately to change fertility patterns on a large scale in other countries would require a plan formulated and executed with the utmost delicacy. The device of channeling the effort through international agencies is a partial, though probably not a sufficient, solution.

46. As quoted by N. V. Sovani, "The Problem of Fertility Control in India: Cultural Factors and Development of Policy," in *Approaches to Problems of High Fertility in Agrarian Societies*, p. 66.

47. Serious difficulties might also arise in the developed countries over giving official sponsorship to programs for lowering fertility in underdeveloped areas. From the days of Francis Place in early nineteenth-century England down to the present, proponents of birth control have often encountered strong opposition to their programs both from religious groups and from prevailing public opinion.

48. Persons experienced in public health programs to be carried on outside their own culture area have often stressed the intricate difficulties encountered in getting the local population to accept even the simplest remedies or to modify traditional practices ever so slightly. The readjustment of sexual mores and behavior is surely at least as difficult to achieve. As one writer put it, "Do cultural complexes travel as wholes, or can specific traits be spread faster than the complex as a whole?" Clarence Senior, "An Approach to Research in Overcoming Cultural Barriers to Family Limitation," in George F. Mair (Ed.), *op. cit.*, p. 149. Another question here is that of how separable sexual desire and the desire for progeny may be in the cultures prevailing in the several important underdeveloped areas that have serious population problems.

### DEVELOPMENT POTENTIAL AND POPULATION POTENTIAL IN UNDERDEVELOPED AREAS

If innovation, capital accumulation and cultural change are the three dynamic factors in the long-term growth of total output—and regardless of how they may be related to one another as cause and effect—the secular rise in real incomes per capita will depend upon the rate of change in total output relative to the rate of change in population.

Since about 1800 or 1850, the dynamic factors that make for progress have operated less powerfully in the underdeveloped areas than in the economies that are now more highly developed. At the same time, the dynamic factors making for population growth in the underdeveloped areas have been more powerfully operative than in the developed countries. Whatever potential for general betterment there might have been in the factors stimulating greater output and material progress—whether indigenous or imported—was largely nullified in the underdeveloped areas by the more powerful factors that stimulated population growth. Instead of any appreciable improvement in average material well-being, the result was mainly larger populations at about the same level of material welfare. Total output must have risen, because a larger population was supported; but the rise in total output was about matched by a proportionate rise in total numbers.[49]

From the social welfare point of view, the crux of the development problem obviously is to cause total output to grow faster than population. And the more the rate of growth in total output exceeds the rate of growth in population, the greater the welfare dividend per capita will be.

How rapidly total output can reasonably be expected to rise in a given period of time can scarcely be stated satisfactorily in general terms. The answer depends on the values assigned to certain variables. But, over a considerable range, various alternative values appear to be about equally plausible assumptions. For example, what average rates of saving should be assumed? Is 5 per cent of national income or 10 per cent the more plausible figure? What of marginal rates of saving? Theoretically, these might approach 100 per cent—almost all the increase in output might be poured back into further investment. In actuality, however, if the ratio of the increment in saving to the increment in income were to approach 30–40 per cent in any country this would be a remarkable achievement.

Again, what is a plausible figure to postulate for the capital-income or capital-output ratio with respect to increments in new investment? To put it another way: What is the relation between increments in capital investment and the increments in output or income consequent upon the new

---

49. It can be argued that this was because the innovations, capital accretions and cultural modifications—the factors tending to promote secular growth of total output—were nearly all superimposed from without the underdeveloped areas rather than generated from within; consequently the social conditions that accounted for the high birth rates lost none of their force or pervasiveness. If this is true, however, then it follows that until the factors making for economic development become truly indigenous to the underdeveloped areas not much change in fertility patterns and average material well-being is to be expected.

investment? In public utility undertakings and other capital-intensive investments a ratio of 5 to 1 or even 6 to 1 appears reasonable. But in agriculture or light industry the ratio is perhaps closer to 2 to 1 or even 1.5 to 1. What value to assign to this ratio for developmental investment as a whole cannot be specified with any confidence between, say, 2.5 to 1 and 4 to 1. But selecting 3 to 1 as against 4 to 1 makes an enormous difference in the derivative rate of growth in total output. And the same can be said for the savings percentages within the ranges mentioned above.[50]

Another important group of assumptions that must be made in order to calculate an estimated rate of growth in total output has to do with how rapidly, and by how much, productivity can be expected to increase from the productive resources already in hand as the development process gets under way. Reflection on the experience of countries that have already developed suggests that this question may be fully as important as the contribution to output from new investment. Yet is there any basis for a prognostication on this point?

The rate of growth in total output would of course be greater, and more soundly grounded as well, if there should be a revival of international investment and if the world economy should again move in the direction of greater international specialization and exchange. Yet it is almost anyone's guess how much capital investment and technical assistance can be expected to flow from the already developed countries into the underdeveloped areas over the proximate future. Similarly, a revival of the world trading system within a framework that would permit the underdeveloped areas increasingly to market abroad products requiring much labor and relatively little capital in their production would also raise total output and incomes appreciably in the underdeveloped areas.

In view of all the uncertainties—the possibility of major innovations is of course wholly unpredictable—it is difficult to arrive at a plausible potential rate of growth in total output. If the secular rate of growth in the past in now developed countries is any guide, a sustained rate as high as 3 to 5 per cent per year would not be surprising, though for short spurts 6 to 8 per cent might not be impossible.

Whatever the rate of growth in total output, however, it will have to be set against the potential rate of growth in population in order to determine the probable rise in average real income. The potential rates of population growth in the underdeveloped areas derive from projections of the trends of death rates and birth rates. Death rates have already declined appreciably and can be expected to fall further and perhaps quite rapidly. But no one can say how rapidly and how far fertility rates can be expected to decline with development, and how closely that decline will be linked with

50. For some interesting calculations on some of these points even under greatly simplified assumptions see H. W. Singer, "The Mechanics of Economic Development," *Indian Economic Review*, August 1952, pp. 1–18, and the "Comment" following by S. Sioma J. Kagan.

the rate of improvement in average well-being. Clearly, the more rapidly fertility does decline, the more rapidly will welfare improve.

The potential benefits from establishing new fertility patterns in the underdeveloped areas, simultaneously with programs for their economic development in the usual sense, are undoubtedly enormous. Indeed, perhaps no single change would be more effective in raising the general level of well-being. Hence, the most earnest attention, study and research deserve to be directed to overcoming some of the formidable difficulties which now seem to block the practical realization of this change. While it would be idle to pretend that real difficulties do not exist, it would be defeatist to conclude that they are insoluble. Yet the urgency of an early solution to the problem cannot be overstressed. As has been pointed out, the rates of annual increase in the populations of many underdeveloped areas are already high and their total numbers discouragingly large. The underdeveloped areas most in danger of experiencing acute population pressure are the greater part of the Orient, the Middle East and the Caribbean. Latin America appears to be in less immediate difficulties because the ratio of its population to resources is more favorable. Even if a thoroughly sound program for lowering fertility were now available and could be applied overnight, it would take nearly a generation before the total population would be appreciably affected.

All these considerations suggest a moderately pessimistic conclusion as to the probable relation between the output potential and the population potential in the underdeveloped areas over the near future. Most of the available facts give little ground for optimism. Nevertheless, the outlook is not entirely bleak. One ray of hope is this: While public health programs will doubtless cut mortality, they are also likely to increase productivity and output. Better health and sanitation, in other words, do not merely reduce mortality rates but also result in an improved factor of production— a better labor supply. Conceivably, this greater efficiency could keep pace with the growing numbers sufficiently well to prevent most of the dire consequences that the pessimists foresee. A second reassuring circumstance is that gloomy predictions of the same sort in the past have proved wrong. More than a century ago Malthus, too, saw no solution to the population problem for reasons remarkably similar to those adduced with respect to the underdeveloped areas today. As matters worked out, however, technical advance and the growth of the world economy with its complicated network of specialization and exchange prevented Malthus' predictions from being realized. Although no one can assert with confidence that further technical and scientific advances will soon obviate the present problem, there is little basis for contending that this is impossible. In the main, the optimists, not the pessimists, have the better record over past history. It may prove so again.

*Part II*

# ECONOMIC DEVELOPMENT AS
# RECORDED HISTORY

# 6. Introduction to Part Two:
## Progress in the Past and Present

No GENERAL "THEORY OF ECONOMIC DEVELOPMENT" is conveniently at hand to explain those complicated economic developments of the past two centuries that have brought a number of countries to comparatively high levels of material well-being. At least no theory sufficiently encompasses most of the major facts to command general acceptance. It is therefore possible only to summarize some of the more salient facts concerning the economic development of the present high-income countries.

### EMERGENCE OF THE MODERN WORLD VIEW IN THE WEST

It is often said that the quickened pace of economic development in England and parts of Western Europe during the late eighteenth and early nineteenth centuries occurred because "conditions were ripe for it." This merely emphasizes that the more rapid economic development would not have occurred had certain other changes not already gone before. Among these antecedent changes, the Renaissance and Reformation, the discovery of the New World, the rise of national states, the scientific revolution and the commercial revolution rank high. More narrowly economic in character, yet inseparable from these, were the inflow of precious metals and the ensuing "price revolution" of the late sixteenth century, the seventeenth-century growth of trade and commerce, and the growing numbers of commercially minded entrepreneurs who thought in terms of markets, prices and profits.

Of course no one can say with assurance that all these changes were indispensable prerequisites to the later developments in agriculture, transport, manufactures and foreign trade and investment. Yet it is hard to believe that the economic progress which did occur would have been realized if most of these important changes had not gone before.

### The Idea of Progress

Until the late seventeenth century in Western Europe, the very "idea of progress" in human affairs was notably absent.[1] Indeed, the conviction

1. This discussion of the development of this idea in Western Europe owes much to J. B. Bury, *The Idea of Progress* (American edition with an introduction by Charles A. Beard), Macmillan, New York, 1932. Also exceedingly valuable are the two large volumes by A. Wolf, *A History of Science, Technology and Philosophy in the XVIth and XVIIth Centuries*, Allen and Unwin, London, 1935, and *A History of Science, Technology and Philosophy in the XVIIIth Century*, Allen and Unwin, London, 1938. A convenient brief account is "The Origin of Modern Civilization," Appendix XVII, in Quincy Wright, *A Study of War*, Vol. I, University of Chicago Press, Chicago, 1942, pp. 598–614.

prevailed that history marked a steady retrogression from some earlier golden age. Moreover, this degeneration was expected to continue.

The golden age was variously placed in time according to the particular aspect of human affairs in immediate consideration. In moral or spiritual matters, the Garden of Eden or the days of Christ and the Twelve Apostles were obvious choices. In philosophical speculation, the tendency was to hold that no one was the equal of Plato and Aristotle. Even the physical prowess of the ancients was believed to be unmatchable by the best specimens of later generations.

Bury has summed it up as follows:

So long as men believed that the Greeks and Romans had attained, in the best days of their civilization, to an intellectual plane which posterity could never hope to reach, so long as the authority of their thinkers was set up as unimpeachable, a theory of degeneration held the field, which excluded a theory of Progress.[2]

### The Change from Pessimism to Optimism

This belief in human retrogression was in keeping with the general world view of the times. Throughout the Middle Ages and perhaps even up to the seventeenth century, many people believed that the world would "soon" come to an end; consequently, long-range views of progress and development lacked meaning or relevance. The impressive Roman ruins scattered all over Europe must also have suggested decay instead of progress to most people. During the Renaissance, those who could read or were privileged to listen to lectures must have felt that life in Imperial Rome or fifth-century Athens was a richer experience than what they themselves knew. Moreover, the dominance of a dark religious outlook in all phases of human existence tended to exalt the virtues of poverty, suffering and travail, and perhaps even to raise a question of the moral rectitude or social desirability of ameliorating man's lot. Man was born to suffer. The curse of Adam was upon him.

How these views changed with the birth of a new confidence and self-assurance among men is a fascinating story. The Renaissance led people to read about the past and also to look at the world about them. They read, they thought, they discussed, they wrote, they painted, they sculptured, they built, they went abroad and they discovered a new world. And as they looked about them, they became engrossed with their own world; it chal-

---

2. Bury, *op. cit.*, p. 66. Not least remarkable were the views held in the seventeenth century and even in the eighteenth century about the size of the population of the Greek and Roman world. Walter F. Willcox quotes Montesquieu as writing in 1721, "after a computation as careful as can be made in matters of this kind, I have found that there are on the earth scarcely one-tenth as many persons as there were in ancient times." Apparently people also completely accepted such statements as Herodotus' assertion that Xerxes had an army of 1.4 million men or Tacitus' claim that Rome had 6.9 million people under Claudius. See Walter F. Willcox, "Increase in the Population of the Earth and of the Continents since 1650," in Walter F. Willcox (Ed.), *International Migrations*, Vol. I, National Bureau of Economic Research, New York, 1931, p. 44.

lenged their imagination and ingenuity. Moreover, they had good reason to question the belief that all was retrogression and decay. Were the new thinkers not the equal of the old? Was Sir Francis Drake not as remarkable a mariner as those of classical times? Did the rise of the new national states of Holland, England, Portugal, Spain and France suggest decay or retrogression? Francis Bacon (1561–1626) boldly proclaimed that printing, gunpowder and the compass "have changed the appearance and state of the whole world; . . . no empire, sect or star appears to have exercised a greater power or influence on human affairs than these mechanical discoveries."[3] As a modern writer has expressed it:

Thus in the century between 1450 and 1550 Western civilization . . . lost the sense of being itself a universal civilization. It saw itself as but a small portion of a world of great variety . . . This realization gave the *coup de grâce* to the basic postulate of Western civilization—its own universality in a geocentric universe with an ecclesiocentric religion, an imperiocentric economy. The complete and rigid philosophy of Aquinas, expounded by ecclesiastically controlled universities, which had taught men how to adjust themselves to their closed world, perished before a vision of a great, varied, unexplored universe, presenting infinite opportunities.[4]

The idea of progress in human affairs thus displaced the age-old conviction of inevitable retrogression. This was a dramatic idea in the history of the Western world.

The idea that progress was natural and necessary, and that experience tended to demonstrate it so, was closely related to the opening up of the New World and the growth of the experimental sciences in the seventeenth century.[5] But it is doubtful whether it had penetrated far past the ranks of the intelligentsia even two centuries later when the classical economists were writing about progress. The common man might occasionally aspire to better his lot, but belief in material progress for the whole society was not widespread.

### IDEA OF PROGRESS IN UNDERDEVELOPED AREAS

The conviction that progress is possible is probably a necessary precondition to its realization. The idea of progress is still not a mass conviction in all countries, even in those that are officially announcing programs of economic development. Nevertheless, it does frequently approach a popular ideal in contrast to the narrow circle of believers perhaps even two centuries ago.

3. As quoted in Bury, *op. cit.*, p. 54.
4. Wright, *op. cit.*, Vol. I, p. 609.
5. George Hildebrand, *The Idea of Progress*, University of California Press, Berkeley, 1949, p. 12; also Carl Becker, "Progress," in *Encyclopedia of the Social Sciences*, Vol. 12, Macmillan, New York, 1934, p. 497.

The fact that progress is now often a popular ideal probably immediately underlies another contrast with the past. Economic development now has much more explicit political and ethical objectives than inhered in the old tradition of economic progress. The classical and neoclassical economists were disposed to regard the problems of increasing wealth and income as something rather generally apart from questions of morals and politics. Needless to say, the great drive toward economic development in most underdeveloped countries today either springs from or is intimately connected with movements of national independence and glory, internal political changes, and—generally speaking—equalitarian and social welfare sentiments. Ideological elements play a more conspicuous role in "development" than they did in the concept of "progress" a century ago. Paralleling this difference is a further one: nationalism imbues the current movement, whereas classical and neoclassical economics had, with some conspicuous exceptions, a strong international slant, especially in England.

Such contrasts as these characterize the idea of economic development as "forward looking," as planned or consciously directed action toward definite goals, as a break with the past. Older discussions, on the other hand, were marked by the idea of progress as a natural process of "growth," paralleling the biological concepts of inexorable continuity and unfolding. A kind of evolutionary "natural selection" in the economic realm was favored over the setting of goals or standards. The tempo of progress, subject in some degree to the influence of economic and political institutions, was thought to rest primarily upon deep-rooted and relatively stable habits and motives, such as saving and the individual's efforts to better his lot.

The planner of development today, however, often seems to have limitless faith in his ability to improve and quicken the process of evolutionary growth. This implies, of course, a far greater role for state initiative and control than the classical economists who wrote on progress would ever have thought justified. If capital is not forthcoming through saving, it is to be taken by forced levies, of which taxes are often merely the most polite form. If domestic compulsory and voluntary savings do not provide a sufficiently rapid pace of development, the gap is to be closed by foreign countries or international agencies. Direct action by governments moves capital in the international sphere, not the old-fashioned differences in rates of interest and profits. Little reliance seems to be placed upon the indigenous origination of new and highly productive techniques (unless, perhaps, through government research); here again, foreign governments or international organizations are vested with responsibility for supplying an essential element of development.

This is not to say that current development schemes all involve state socialism or totalitarian control. But they are a far cry from what was envisaged by Smith and Mill in terms of the reliance placed on the energy, saving, inventiveness and venturousness of the individual or the private firm.

## Similarities between the Past and the Present

On the other hand, there is also a profound similarity between the economic problems confronted by the older and the newer traditions of progress and development. Pressure upon productive resources now as then supplies a prime mover toward economic change; now as then, innovation, the creation of new productive resources, or the fuller exploitation of existing resources offer the chief available remedies. The supply of capital was and is a primary limitational factor. The means of transport and communication, along with costs and prices, have always been a chief element in the "extent of the market," and this in turn has always determined the possible division of labor and the feasibility of particular undertakings. From the very beginning of modern economics in the writings of the mercantilists, the "revenues of the sovereign" have effectively limited developmental projects—except by inflation, which is itself a time-honored institution. A surprising degree of continuity characterizes the problems of how much and in what ways to tax, how much to borrow, how much to spend, and similar fundamental questions.

Without something new, there would be no progress, but the new grows or springs out of the old. Just as biology supplies many examples of the gradual evolution of new forms of life and not a few cases of sports or mutations, so economic history supplies a wealth of evidence of continuity in development and some dramatic discontinuities. For this reason, one cannot pretend to foresee the course of development in the underdeveloped regions with any exactitude or to prescribe policy with any great degree of certainty. Perhaps, however, if some of the main causes of economic progress in past decades and centuries can be discerned, it will be possible to discover something worth while about the present and the future.

### PAST AND PRESENT SETTING OF THE DEVELOPMENT PROBLEM

The most obvious difference which distinguishes the contemporary from the past setting of the economic development problem is that the present underdeveloped countries appear to have a less favorable ratio of population to resources than did Western Europe, the British dominions and the United States in the nineteenth century. Many, though not all, underdeveloped countries are faced with a population problem—high annual rates of increase, overcrowding in rural and urban areas, almost no "free land" to be settled, little prospect of emigration, and an age composition of the population which assures a high fecundity. Moreover, tangible productive resources other than agricultural land—capital equipment, mineral deposits (insofar as they are known), internal transport and communication systems, etc.—are small in the aggregate and still smaller per capita.[6] This generally less favorable ratio of population to resources distinguishes the present development problem in numerous ways from nineteenth-century experience.

## Nineteenth-Century Progress

Economic progress of the western world in the nineteenth century originated in and derived much of its character from the agricultural and commercial revolutions of the seventeenth and eighteenth centuries. This circumstance greatly facilitated later industrial developments.

By the early eighteenth century, Western Europe and the American colonies had created a "middle class" which was able to recognize and create economic opportunities and to exploit them with vigor and ingenuity.[7] A management-entrepreneurial class was already on the scene before the industrial revolution began. The commercial revolution, moreover, had already accustomed these people to capital and they already had funds available when the new opportunities for investment first appeared.

The underdeveloped countries at present have no comparable pools of managerial skill and investible capital upon which to draw, while in most of them, commercial or other gainful employment still carries a stigma of long standing. In other words, the capital and the people to initiate development are not abundant and the socio-cultural environment may not favor their increase.[8]

Further, the centralized power and efficiency achieved by national governments in Western Europe and America in the eighteenth century probably made them better able to foster economic development than the governments in many underdeveloped areas today. While Adam Smith and others railed against the clumsiness, inefficiency and corruption of government and government administration in the eighteenth century, conditions

6. The skills, energy and literacy rates of these large populations are typically at a low average, so that even the limited nonhuman productive resources available are used ineffectively. A highly skilled, industrious population can sometimes extract a relatively high standard of living from quite poor natural resources, as Switzerland and Finland evidence.

7. Some writers attribute the new spirit of enterprise to the rise of Protestantism. One need not embrace this thesis to recognize the importance of the merchant classes in laying the grounds for the industrial revolution. Certainly these people were infused with new motives, new drives, new value scales and astounding energy and ingenuity regardless of whether the causes are to be found in Protestantism or in some other force. See R. H. Tawney, *Religion and the Rise of Capitalism*, John Murray, London, 1929, and Max Weber, *The Protestant Ethic and the Spirit of Modern Capitalism*, Scribner, New York, 1950. See also Karl F. Helleiner, "Moral Conditions of Economic Growth," *Journal of Economic History*, Spring 1951, pp. 97–116 and the literature there cited.

8. In some underdeveloped areas, parts of the Middle East for example, trade and commerce have been relegated to minority groups who suffer varying degrees of social ostracism. In parts of the Far East, the Chinese minorities living outside China hold a rather similar position. In Latin America the situation seems to be somewhat mixed. In Mexico, for example, quite striking changes have apparently occurred in recent years. See Sanford A. Mosk, *Industrial Revolution in Mexico*, University of California Press, Berkeley, 1950, Chapters 1 and 2 *passim*. In Europe the merchant and industrialist groups were accepted only very gradually. Traces of the earlier dominance of aristocratic values are still encountered today.

in many underdeveloped countries today are probably no less deplorable. Many of the ruling groups are new governments which have inherited authority but not an adequate civil service from the recently departed metropolitan powers. Others are dominated by long-outmoded conceptions of government functions or are riddled with corruption, sinecures and nepotism. Such conditions make administrative efficiency impossible, often negating the good intentions and imaginative undertakings of the national leaders. Some of the newer governments have not even been able to maintain satisfactory order.[9] A further difficulty is that, in some underdeveloped countries, the government is in the hands of groups that would lose personal power and influence if development were to occur. Hence they give it lip service but not genuine support.

*New Factors Which Facilitate Progress Today*

Although the underdeveloped countries may not possess some of the environmental factors which favored economic progress in earlier times, they have at least two significant advantages over their predecessors. In the first place, since economic development has already proceeded far in the rest of the world, they can borrow extensively from these achievements and need not repeat the whole life history of the already developed countries. Compared to Great Britain, Japan industrialized quite rapidly and Russia even more quickly. Thus, the underdeveloped countries have all the advantages of "a late start" in being able to profit by others' mistakes and to utilize their accomplishments. A country nowadays can develop hydroelectric power, for example, without first producing a Thomas Edison or developing a General Electric Company to make the equipment.

Second, the often burning determination of the poorer countries to develop economically—or perhaps more accurately the insistence of their leaders that they must develop—is quite unmatched in the earlier industrializations. Moreover, these leaders are dealing with populations accustomed to being ruled by fiat and edict. If the authority of the state can be combined with the requisite administrative skills, this enthusiastic determination may overcome many obstacles.

These and other peculiarities of the present situation seriously complicate any attempt to draw lessons from the past that might be helpful to countries now striving to achieve economic development. If the sights are not set too high, however, useful inferences may perhaps be drawn from past experience that have pertinence to the present problem.

9. See, for example, the report on conditions in Indonesia in early 1951 in *The Economist*, June 23, 1951, p. 1512, where it is stated: "Theft, indeed, is the order of the day: factories and estates have to count on losing regularly up to 25 per cent of their production—an almost incredible and ruinous figure . . . In the harbours nothing is safe. On the inter-island steamers, officers are not allowed to go into the holds and cargo is ransacked right and left. Indeed, one crew, seeing that they were carrying bales of textiles, sent one of their members ashore to fetch a sewing machine so that during the voyage what clothes they needed could be run up according to taste from the bales at hand."

# 7. Early Economic Development: England

THE GENERAL RISE IN PRODUCTIVITY which was the essence of economic development in the nineteenth century, and must also be its essence in the now underdeveloped areas, is bewilderingly complex both in its sequence and in its composition.

The current fashion is to measure economic achievement by national income data. Rising real incomes per person in the population presumably indicate rising productivity per person. Rising productivity per person, in turn, results from improved efficiency or technical progress in the use of economic resources already in hand and from the growing stock of real capital. Thus national income data, with due allowance for short-run cyclical variations, provide a general index of long-term changes in productivity.

No country, however, has reliable national income figures extending back more than a few decades.[1] Consequently, changes in productivity over longer periods can only be inferred from data for *certain* elements in the economy. But this deficiency in the data is not so serious as it might seem. For the sectors of the national economy that together make up the national product were far fewer in number in most countries from, say, 1750 down to 1850 than they are today or were even half a century ago. Thus coal, iron, textiles, transport and foreign commerce—for which some data exist—accounted for more nearly the whole of nonagricultural output than they do today. Consequently, the growth and development of these sectors of the economy, along with agriculture, more nearly portray economic development as a whole in the earlier periods. Furthermore, and for similar reasons, what technical progress and capital accumulation did occur was also largely centered in these industries. Hence, if the available data on economic development down to 1850 seem meager and fragmentary by present standards of national income reckoning, it is partly because in the earlier periods fewer industries existed as a source of national income or as a draft on current investment.

## AGRICULTURE AND AGRICULTURAL PRODUCTIVITY

The eighteenth-century improvements in agriculture, the most important single element of the economy at the time, are fundamental, for without

1. Simon Kuznets has prepared decennial estimates of national income in the United States back to the Civil War with as great accuracy as the available data permit. See, for example, his *National Product since 1869*, National Bureau of Economic Research, New York, 1946.

them advances in industry could hardly have proceeded as they did. In the middle of the twentieth century it is easy to forget that in 1700 by far the greatest proportion—probably more than 80 per cent—of the people in Western Europe were cultivators of the soil. Even in 1800, the typical European was a peasant. Moreover, his methods of cultivation were little different from those which his forefathers had been using for centuries past. What causes were responsible for initiating the agricultural revolution are less easily specified than what actually occurred. The economic improvements in agriculture of course did not occur all at once, nor did they quickly come into common use throughout Western Europe. The "revolution" in agriculture was less a few startling discoveries than the gradual accumulation of superior knowledge and its slow diffusion into accepted practice.

The changes in agriculture were basically similar throughout Europe, despite local differences in detail and timing. Three types of change appear to be distinguishable: the change from fragmented to larger units of land cultivation; changes in the techniques of agricultural production; changes in the outlook from which the peasants and larger landholders themselves approached their occupations and their problems of production.

## Enclosures

The gradual change from smaller to larger units of land cultivation in England and Western Europe in the eighteenth and nineteenth centuries was really a dual process.[2] On the one hand, the scattered arable strips of the medieval three-field system[3] tended to disappear in favor of larger enclosed plots. On the other hand, land that had been traditionally available for common use as pasture or woodland, or even not used at all, was also "enclosed." Enclosure thus involved both the disappearance of fragmented holdings and the extension of the area under cultivation.[4] Under

2. Most readers will be sufficiently familiar with the medieval system of landholdings and cultivation to make any discussion of it unnecessary here. Of course, the system was not the same in all important respects all over Western Europe, nor, except in a very broad way, was the process the same by which it disappeared through the enclosure movement.

3. The usual practice of cultivation in the three-field system has been well described as follows: "In the superior three-field system, rye, wheat, and winter barley would be planted in one-third of the arable land; oats, summer barley, drage and some beans, peas and vetches, in another part; and the remaining third of the arable land would lie fallow, though it would be ploughed two or three times in the course of the year so as to clean it and prepare it for the next year's crop." A. Wolf, *A History of Science, Technology and Philosophy in the XVIIIth Century*, Allen and Unwin, London, 1938, p. 502.

4. The kind of land enclosed and the use to which it was put varied considerably from period to period and from one part of England to another. Indeed, the variation is so considerable that it is difficult to generalize. Nevertheless, it appears that the later eighteenth-century enclosures mostly took in meadows and pastures and were used chiefly for pasturing sheep rather than growing grain. On the other hand, beginning with the scarcities and high wheat prices at the time of the Napoleonic wars and continuing well down to the middle of the nineteenth century, the tendency was much more to enclose wasteland and convert it to wheat production.

The later enclosures were thus not a factor in driving people off the land, since the land had not previously been used for wheat in any case, but they were an important factor in increasing food production. See A. Redford, *Labour Migration in England, 1800–1850*, The University Press, Manchester, 1926, pp. 60–62.

the strip system, the individual plots were not fenced but separated by untilled balks; no one could cultivate the common so long as it was literally the common. No less important than the enlargement of the area of cultivation was the fact that the enclosures opened the way to better methods of land use. Two authorities of the time, Arthur Young and Albrecht Thaer, were agreed that:

> . . . common rights were a standing obstacle to rational agriculture. Where holdings lay scattered in the fields and access to one was by right across another, where one cropping routine was enforced on a whole village, and where the right of stubble pasture prevailed, reforms were blocked at the start.[5]

## New Agricultural Techniques and Methods

The pressure to get on with the enclosures—so that "reforms were [not] blocked at the start"—was primarily due to the development of new methods of cultivation and husbandry which a new class of energetic landlords was anxious to put into practice. In other words, it was the profit possibilities of the new agricultural techniques that largely forced through the enclosure despite the opposition of tenants and peasants.[6]

The improved agricultural practices—which took hold first in England in the eighteenth century and subsequently spread over Western Europe—consisted, on the one hand, of more intensive methods of land use and, on the other, of better ways of doing such traditional farm work as plowing, sowing, harvesting and threshing. Selective breeding of livestock was also introduced.

The age-old parceling of land into arable, meadow, pasture and waste land was usually associated with the three-field system of cultivation which left fallow a third or even a half of the arable land each year. During the eighteenth century, the "Norfolk system" of crop rotation tended to displace the three-field system. Based on the sequence of clover, wheat, turnips, barley, the Norfolk system obviated the necessity of fallowing every third year. In a crude sense, this was equivalent to increasing the available arable land by 50 per cent, with the consequence that the poten-

---

5. J. H. Clapham, *The Economic Development of France and Germany, 1815–1914*, Cambridge University Press, Cambridge, 1921, p. 48. Albrecht Thaer (1752–1828), who founded the first Prussian school of agriculture in 1804, published a book on English agriculture in German in 1798. See *ibid.*, p. 47.

6. The rural village with its open fields and traditional three-field system of cultivation was fairly general, according to Clapham, "from the basin of the Seine and the Swiss Alps to the plains of the Slavonic northeast, and over the Danish peninsula to the lowlands of Scandinavia. The flats of western and northern Belgium, of Holland and of the marshy valley of the Ems in western Germany, were an exception, being in the main covered with hamlets and scattered farmsteads." *Ibid.*, p. 29. For an account of the enclosures (*skifte*) in Sweden see G. A. Montgomery, *The Rise of Modern Industry in Sweden*, P. S. King, London, 1939, pp. 50*ff.*

tial output in agriculture increased substantially.[7] As one writer has aptly put it, "The Agricultural Revolution was simply the use of root crops and clover—unlike so many technical improvements, it really merits the name of revolution, because it at one blow doubled the productivity of land and provided food for live-stock fattening."[8]

The output potential in agriculture was further raised in the eighteenth century by the discovery and introduction of better agricultural techniques in a narrower sense. For example, lighter and better plows were developed which could be drawn by two horses instead of six or eight oxen. By dibbling seeds in rows instead of broadcasting them by hand there was less waste and the shoots could be better cultivated as they grew. Other improvements occurred in harvesting and threshing.

The common-field system, according to Arthur Young, yielded 17–18 bushels of wheat per acre, the new system of large farms 26; the fleece of sheep pastured on common fields weighed only 3½ pounds as compared with 9 pounds on enclosures . . . the average size of cattle was greatly increased without any increase in expenditure.[9]

In general, however, these improved techniques required greater capital investments in agriculture, both as fixed investment and as working capital.

## Social Attitudes

These potential gains in agricultural productivity, of course, had not merely to be discovered and made known in order to be exploited in England and other countries. For example, although horse and dog breeding had long been practiced in Europe, no one thought to apply this knowledge systematically to cattle, sheep and poultry before Robert Bakewell of Leicestershire (1725–1790).[10] Nor could the common man be expected to take kindly to the new methods of cultivation that encouraged the more enterprising or rapacious squires and landlords to force through the enclosures. For if these changes had the over-all effect of increasing

7. The English are said to have borrowed the system from Flanders, where it is said to have been in use considerably earlier. See N. S. B. Gras, *A History of Agriculture in Europe and America*, 2d edition, Appleton-Century, New York, 1940, p. 209. Gras says also: "The agricultural revolution was made in England out of Continental materials: Spanish clover, Burgundian and French grasses, the Dutch plow, the horse-shoe of Languedoc, and the Flemish methods of cultivating turnips in fields . . . But . . . the important general background was native. England experienced the revolution herself rather than just learned it from abroad, though much of it might conceivably have been taken whole cloth from across the Channel." The introduction of clover and turnips as well as cabbages, carrots, parsnips and hops into England is usually credited to Sir Richard Weston (1591–1652) and Charles Townshend (1674–1738). Jethro Tull (1674–1741) showed the advantages of pulverizing soil as a restorative. The efforts of these men and others bore fruit only gradually, of course.

8. Doreen Warriner, *Economics of Peasant Farming*, Oxford University Press, London, 1939, p. 8.

9. Adna Ferrin Weber, *The Growth of Cities in the Nineteenth Century*, Columbia University Press, New York, 1899, p. 165, citing Gibbins and Prothero.

10. Perhaps, for one reason, because the practice of common pasture and common grazing, before land was fenced, made breeding hard to control.

agricultural productivity, they also initially brought misery and hardship to those directly forced off the land by these very changes. But the social conscience of the eighteenth century was not that of the middle of the twentieth century. Nevertheless, in England, had it not been for a group of enterprising landlords with an enthusiasm for agriculture and an eye to its profit possibilities from expanding markets, the agricultural revolution would doubtless have gone much more slowly than it did.[11]

*Superiority of English Agriculture*

By 1800, England was regarded as the agricultural leader of the Western world; people came from Germany, France, Flanders and America to learn English methods, which they then adapted to their own soils. British methods thus spread to the continent, where monarchs and governments lent their support.[12] In Prussia, Clapham reports:

Agricultural information was spread among eastern land-owners by methods now familiar—cattle shows, shows of implements, agricultural societies and agricultural colleges. The first cattle shows, in the early [eighteen] thirties, were wisely combined with race meetings. Get the squires together for what the most stupid of them appreciates and work from the known to the unknown, was the policy.[13]

But these were characteristically English ways, already developed in England toward the end of the eighteenth century, along with treatises, journals and magazines. The University of Edinburgh even established a chair in agriculture in 1790.

*Bases of the Agricultural Revolution*

In brief, then, the agricultural revolution consisted essentially in the larger units of cultivation, the improved methods and techniques of cultivation, and the rise of a more entrepreneurially minded and commercially oriented group of entrepreneurs who found a growing market for their output. Also important was the shift from grain production to an increasing output of animal products, fibers and other products not immediately suitable for human consumption.

Yet, though this was the nature of the agricultural revolution, it was the expansion of trade and commerce—foreign and domestic—that was its driving force. This increased demand tended to raise prices and profits in agriculture, and thus put pressure on existing forms and methods of production. The enthusiasm for agriculture would probably have soon spent

11. For a brief sketch of some of the leaders among this new group of landlords see Gras, *op. cit.*, pp. 211–20.

12. Gras reports that "Catherine II of Russia, Joseph II of Austria, Gustavus II of Sweden, Leopold II of Tuscany, Stanislaus II of Poland, and George III of Britain, lent their support to agriculture. Thinkers in France erected agriculture into an economic system." *Ibid.*, p. 217.

13. Clapham, *op. cit.*, pp. 51–52.

itself if the growing towns—which were growing partly because fewer people were needed on the land as a result of the agricultural innovations—had not created an insistent demand for agricultural products. In other words, agriculture tended to be profitable because markets for old products were expanding and because new markets for new products were opening up.

The process in England probably took nearly three quarters of a century, both because established economic and social institutions resist change and because people learn slowly even when they have for an example the evident success of their fellows. Even with the benefit of demonstrations, lectures and reading matter, the improved agricultural techniques only gradually became general practice over the decades. It took longer still for them to spread over Europe from England. The hard economic realities of cost, income and profit or the necessity of getting a living probably had as much to do with converting the average landlord, squire, worker or peasant to the new practices as friendly exhortation or the gracious patronage of royalty. Yet surely this is not a peculiarity of eighteenth- or nineteenth-century England or Europe. Do not people usually change and adapt their ways only under pressure?

## *The Underdeveloped Countries Today*

For the now underdeveloped areas, the question arises as to how to press toward rapid improvements in agriculture in order to achieve a larger output. There will be substantial obstacles and sullen resentments to be overcome. Some of these will be similar to the obstructions which earlier blocked agricultural progress in England and Western Europe. Will the growth of trade and commerce be the major solvent as it appears to have been in England? What other measures can be taken to clear the way—without recourse to tyranny and naked force? The success with which this problem is faced and handled may well be of cardinal importance for the already developed, but nonauthoritarian, countries in their dealings with the underdeveloped areas.

### IMPROVEMENTS IN TRANSPORT AND COMMUNICATIONS

Adam Smith once observed that "Good roads, canals, and navigable rivers, by diminishing the expense of carriage, put the remote parts of the country nearly on a level with those in the neighborhood of a town: they are, upon that account, the greatest of all improvements." The truth of this statement is apparent whether one is reviewing the economic development of already advanced countries or contemplating the development problems of low-income countries in our day. Unless his cargo is exceedingly valuable at its destination, a man with a pack will consume in a few days a sum equal to the full value of his load. The cost of transport in China today, for example, is said to double the price of wheat in fifty miles. Thus, how far division of labor between town and country, or between region and region, is feasible depends, fundamentally, on the efficiency of transport.

The historical development of transport and communication in modern times is a complicated story. A formidable literature exists on the improvement of transport and communication by road, river, coastal vessel, canals, railways, transoceanic shipping, postal service and telegraphy, together with the many mechanical inventions and technical advances which made these improvements possible. The general sequence of this development is familiar, however. Let us therefore inquire first into the nature of "improvements" in transport and communication and then try to outline some of the more important consequences of these improvements for economic development.

### *Nature of "Improvements"*

Improvements in transport and communications are usually recognizable even though the indirectness of their contribution to productivity and well-being makes them difficult to measure.[14] "Improvements"—whether in reference to a particular country or region at different times, or as between one country and another—may relate either to the coverage or extent of the facilities for transport and communications, or to their "efficiency" in some sense. The rate or degree of improvement to be recorded will differ according to whether the emphasis is upon the *spread* of the network or upon its "efficiency" either in its principal arteries or in general. Certainly from the middle of the eighteenth century onward transport and communication have improved greatly on both counts: the network has spread and it has gained in efficiency as well. Several criteria appear to be useful in judging the economic efficiency of a network of transport and communication.

### *Safety and Reliability*

First is the criterion of safety and reliability. To what degree may persons or goods move between various points on the network without danger of

14. Except where transport or communication are direct consumption goods, as in pleasure travel, they manifest their improvement either through changes in the costs of manufactures, agricultural products, etc., or through the greater accessibility or mobility of factors of production, the consequences of which are almost impossible to measure. For instance, how can one measure the full economic effects of the following: "In 1754 the journey between London and Edinburgh required ten days in summer and twelve days in winter. In the summer of 1776 the flying coach performed the same distance in four days. In 1818 the mail coach took only fifty-nine hours, and . . . in 1836 the mail coach was timed through in forty-five and one-half hours, at an average speed of nine and one-half miles an hour, exclusive of stoppages for meals and official work. Thus . . . the time required in 1836 was practically one-fifth of that required in 1754." W. T. Jackman, *The Development of Transportation in Modern England*, Vol. I, Cambridge University Press, Cambridge, 1916, p. 335 (notes omitted).

injury or loss? What degree of certainty is there that a journey begun will be completed? Although coaches had been introduced in England in the towns in Elizabeth's reign (1558–1603), a traveler in 1747 wrote:

In my journey to London, I travelled from Harborough to Northhampton, and well it was that I was in a light Berlin, and six good horses, or I might have been overlaid in that turnpike road. But for fear of life and limb, I walked several miles on foot, met twenty waggons tearing their goods to pieces, and the drivers cursing and swearing for being robbed on the highway by a turnpike, screened under an act of parliament.[15]

Even toward the end of the eighteenth century in England many highways were extremely hazardous in winter while the byways were often quite impassable. Small wonder that such roads were infested with footpads, robbers and highwaymen, who often connived with the innkeepers to the traveler's peril. French roads were probably somewhat better, while the canal traffic in Flanders must have been comparatively safe. As for Germany, Clapham says: "When Prussia took over the great Bishopric of Münster, 1803, a high official sent to open a meeting of magnates at the town of Hamm found it wiser to walk 4 and ¾ (German) miles [about 23 English miles] to the ceremony than to venture upon the local road in a wheeled conveyance." This, Clapham adds, is "an extreme case, no doubt, but instructive."[16]

The remarkable improvements in safety and reliability of travel and communication which came in the nineteenth century with better roads, canals and the railway were both cause and consequence of the contemporary changes in agriculture, commerce and industry.

## Cost

A second criterion of the efficiency of a system of transport and communication is the cost of the service performed. Absolute money figures, though often suggestive, are usually difficult to interpret unless the relative prices of other services and goods are also known, as often they are not. Nevertheless, costs of travel and of the carriage of goods undoubtedly declined enormously from 1750 to 1850. Jackman concludes, for example, that in England in the early nineteenth century "the cost of canal carriage normally did not exceed one-half, and in most cases was from one-fourth

15. As quoted in *ibid.*, p. 85.

16. Clapham, *op. cit.*, pp. 107–08. Another English writer records that in 1752 (or thereabouts) "a rich citizen in London who had relatives or friends in the west of England might hear of their welfare half a dozen times in his life, by post, 'he thinks no more of visiting them than of traversing the deserts of Nubia.' " Edwin A. Pratt, *A History of Inland Transport and Communication in England*, Kegan Paul, London, 1912, p. 94.

to one-third, of the cost of land carriage."[17] By the third quarter of the nineteenth century the railways were often able to cut below these canal charges by a third to a half, and frequently more.[18] But the canals by no means disappeared; for a long time they held their own in the haulage of heavy, bulky cargoes for which rapid transit was unimportant. The tonnage volume of canal-barge traffic in Europe is still very substantial.

*Speed*

Speed is a further criterion of the efficiency of a transport and communications network. Speed in the transport of goods is usually important only if storage costs are high or the cargo perishable. For some goods, storage costs, apart from interest on the investment, are often trifling. Sand, gravel, coal and ore are examples. For grains, flour, dry goods, etc., costs of storage are often great enough so that small inventories combined with rapid delivery from suppliers are more efficient than larger inventories combined with cheap but slow delivery.

While greater speed may occasionally be valuable for its own sake, its more pervasive effects are probably felt in two directions: first, it permits large national and international markets to develop out of a host of small, isolated markets; second, it tends to integrate a country politically and socially to a degree quite impossible when the horse is the fastest available means of locomotion. Both developments are likely to have profound economic consequences. One well-known, though often forgotten, consequence of the increased speed and lower cost of transport in nineteenth-century Europe was that local famines and gluts virtually disappeared because the transport system was sufficiently good to overcome a local crop failure or carry away a local surplus. Down to the end of the eighteenth century, famine was a real threat in most parts of Europe.

The broad consequences of increased speed of travel, transport and communication achieved during the nineteenth century cannot be fully appreciated by merely noting that, for example, the two hundred and ten miles from London to Liverpool took two days in summer and three in winter by coach in 1776, as against seven to eight hours by railway in 1900. Far more important than the mere fact of greater speed of movement and contact between major centers was the fact that, with rapid transit, the average merchant or businessman in these centers for the first time really came into touch with whole sections of the country, for example, Wales and

17. Jackman, *op. cit.*, Vol. I, p. 449. As partial explanation of this result he states (p. 448): "In the early years of the nineteenth century, a very careful historian referred to the fact that where, forty years before, a single horse toiled along the road from Knaresborough to Skipton, with a sack of wheat upon his back, now a horse would draw, with equal or greater ease, a canal boat loaded with forty tons of wheat."

18. *Ibid.*, Vol. II, Appendix 10, pp. 731*ff*.

the West Country. The railways truly "opened up" the country. For, as Usher has nicely put it, "Before the development of the railroad the world economy was in effect the maritime fringe of the great continents. The interiors were open only to the extent that some form of water transport was available."[19]

*Spread of the Network*

If improvement in transport and communication is essentially a matter of the greater spread of the network and of its increased efficiency in terms of speed, cost and reliability, then certainly there was steady improvement in Western Europe from the middle of the eighteenth century forward. At the beginning of the period, those few people who traveled by land found it costly, time-consuming and hazardous. Goods moved by packhorse or in lumbering wagons at a pace too slow for perishables and at a cost too high for hauling bulky raw materials more than short distances. Consequently, the inland towns depended for their sustenance mainly upon the immediately adjacent countryside, for which they, in turn, were almost the sole market outlet.

Sea transport was of course much better by comparison, with the result that the seaport towns had a more thriving commerce and a more diversified existence. Remarkable progress in sea navigation occurred in the seventeenth century. It was mainly in land transport that the major eighteenth-century improvements occurred. This is not to say that no further improvements were made in sea transport, but rather that before the use of steam and the appearance of the iron ship these improvements were mainly along already familiar lines.[20]

With the coming of the railways, the gap between seaports and inland towns narrowed greatly as the inland areas began a rapid development. As one writer has put it, "There was no longer the same necessity for each family to brew its own ale, to bake its own bread and make its own cloth, or to provide stores of salt beef and other supplies as if for a winter siege."[21] These changes, which occurred first in England, were little different from those that appeared later on the continent.[22]

---

19. Abbott Payson Usher, "Technical Change and Capital Formation," a paper submitted to the Conference on Capital Formation and Economic Growth, November 1953, sponsored by the National Bureau of Economic Research.

20. Melvin M. Knight, Harry Elmer Barnes and Felix Flügel, *Economic History of Europe*, Houghton Mifflin, Boston, 1928, pp. 298–99.

21. Pratt, *op. cit.*, p. 398.

22. The growth of railways on the European continent followed that in England by a lag that seems rather remarkable in retrospect. For example, while the United Kingdom had 10,500 kilometers of line open for traffic in 1850, the Austro-Hungarian Empire had only 1,500, and Russia only 500; Germany had 6,000 as against only 3,000 for France. Spain with twenty-eight kilometers and Switzerland with twenty-five had virtually no railways at all. See Clapham, *op. cit.*, pp. 339–40.

*Effects of Transport Improvements*

In relation to economic development, the primary effects of improved transport and communications are probably threefold. In the first place, improvements in transport and communications extend the area over which productive resources can be utilized in production. Arable land, even if distant from the centers of population, becomes usable because other factors of production can now be combined with it and because its product can move to market. Alternatively expressed, better transport widens the market and broadens the area over which specialization is feasible. Hence, output improves both in volume and variety because specialization per se raises productivity and because the natural advantages of each locality can be exploited. Moreover, the superior quality of product available in some regions will tend to force higher standards of performance upon producers in other regions, with the result that the general average tends to improve. Consequently, the widening of the market and the bringing into production of previously unused resources are likely to increase total output, enrich its variety and improve its quality.

Second, economic development is stimulated because, as transport and communication improve, the country's markets tend to change from a host of isolated centers of trading and exchange into a complex of closely inter-connected markets. This means more than the disappearance of local gluts and famines. It means also that any appreciable change, either on the side of supply or that of demand, will spread its effects over the whole country through the linkage of prices. But this very diffusion of effects tends to lessen the impact of the change at the point of origin and hence to ease the process of adaptation. Small adjustments over a large area are less trouble-some and more easily made than major shifts which must be worked out locally. On the more positive side, this economic linkage means that if economic development is proceeding apace at certain points, these centers can draw on the resources of the rest of the country to support this develop-ment and by so doing impart an impetus to development even in regions far removed. The nineteenth century is replete with examples of this type of diffusion of development both nationally and internationally.

Finally, ease of communication and transport also have the effect of forcing new ideas and methods of production into practice despite the "crust of custom" and the tenaciousness of outmoded techniques. This is not only because people move about more and are otherwise in touch with what is going on elsewhere. Even more important, probably, is the fact that better methods of production already in use elsewhere push down prices in the local markets to a point where the local producers must improve their methods or go out of business. Consequently, better methods of production are likely to be more quickly generalized throughout the country and so to raise the average level of efficiency.

In the nineteenth century these forced adaptations were often accompanied by great human hardship and suffering. Nevertheless, average efficiency rose enormously and the improvements of transport and communication did much to bring it about. Similar results would probably flow from improved transport in now underdeveloped areas.

### Conclusions Suggested by Transport History

The conclusion seems inescapable that improved transport played an enormous role in the rise in productivity and real incomes during the nineteenth century, although this role was less direct and less obvious than the effects of some of the great inventions of Watt or Arkwright now so familiar to every schoolboy.

Two other points emerge from the historical record that appear to have relevance to the problems of the now underdeveloped areas. First, the improvements in transport necessitated large capital investments which, though highly productive within the economy as a whole, frequently did not "pay off" for those who made them. Many private investors—for example in turnpikes, canals and railways in England and overseas—certainly lost heavily, notwithstanding the high economic productivity of their investments. The second point is quite different in character and less easily documented. At the time these improvements in transport and communication were being proposed and even introduced, few people realized how drastically they would change the economic organization of production. The possibilities of increased specialization and exchange, of bringing new resources into production, of the greater mobility of productive factors, and of generally improving agriculture, commerce and industry through better transport and communication were usually grossly underestimated by contemporary observers. Perhaps this was inevitable.

### GROWTH OF INDUSTRY AND MANUFACTURES

Although the phrase "industrial revolution" usually recalls the dramatic inventions in textiles or iron manufacture, the accelerated growth and expansion of industrialization after 1850 also saw the appearance and development of wholly new industries.[23] Historically, industrial development

---

23. Knight, Barnes and Flügel (*op. cit.*, pp. 368*ff*) use the phrase "new industrial revolution." The term "industrial revolution" apparently only came into popular use after 1837. *Ibid.*, p. 383. These writers emphasize that: "The Industrial Revolution did not burst upon a stereotyped and unsuspecting world in 1750, 1770, or at any other time. Professor Ashley's characterization of it as a 'rapid and irresistible evolution' is quite strong enough to suit the critical mind. Too much attention has been paid to a few textile inventions." *Ibid.*, p. 376.

was perhaps less a matter of improvements in existing industries than of the rise of industries theretofore almost unknown.

A comparative study by L. Rostas of the structure of manufacturing in the mid-1930s in the United Kingdom, Germany and the United States illustrates the point. Rostas breaks down manufacturing into 13 categories and shows their relative importance in net output and employment. His calculations, as shown in Table 7-1, demonstrate the latter-day dominance of the "engineering" industries, iron and steel and chemicals over textiles and clothing. Yet figures on industrial employment in England in 1851 and in Prussia in 1855, cited by Usher, show that about 35 per cent of industrial employment at that time was in textiles and clothing. (See Table 7-2.) For 1800 or 1750 the percentage of workers in clothing and textiles would be greater still. Moreover, if textiles and clothing are lumped together with mines and metals in Table 7-2, they together account for about one half of total industrial employment in England in 1851. Industrial development up to 1850 was heavily centered in textiles, coal and iron.

This fact points to an important difference between the spread of industrialism in the first half of the nineteenth century and the problem of underdeveloped countries bent on industrial development today. In the early nineteenth century, the choice of industries to be developed in following England's lead was obvious. But the many new industries which have since appeared and grown to importance offer countries that are now underdeveloped a wide range of selection. While textiles, for example, may still be a logical starting point for a country desiring to industrialize, this is by no means the only possible choice.

*Evidences of Industrial Growth*

The amazing improvements in industry during the nineteenth century are perhaps best illustrated by noting how output rose and prices fell for a few key products.

The five-year average centering on 1776 of cotton imports into England was 6.7 million pounds; for the year 1831, imports were 280.5 million pounds; and for 1861, 1,261 million pounds. In 1779, the selling price of Number 40 cotton yarn was 16s.; in 1830, 1s. 2½d.; and in 1860 only 11½d.[24] For coal, English production figures for the early period are apparently somewhat in dispute, although Clapham suggests perhaps 6.2 million tons in 1770 and possibly 6.4 million tons in 1780. He adds:

If an output of some 16,000,000 tons of Great Britain in 1816 be accepted as a starting point, some such progression as the following may be suggested as not

24. Figures as cited by Abbott Payson Usher, *The Industrial History of England*, Houghton Mifflin, Boston, 1920, pp. 305 and 310. During this period cotton textiles overtook wool in value terms, both in home consumption and exports. See *ibid.*, p. 308.

TABLE 7-1. STRUCTURE OF MANUFACTURING PRODUCTION IN THE UNITED KINGDOM, GERMANY AND THE UNITED STATES, MID-1930S

| | Percentage Share in: | | | | | | | |
|---|---|---|---|---|---|---|---|---|
| | Net Output | | | | Employment | | | |
| | United Kingdom | Germany | United States | | United Kingdom | Germany | United States | |
| Branch of Manufacturing | 1935 | 1936 | 1935 | 1937 | 1935 | 1936 | 1935 | 1937 |
| Total factory trades | 100.0 | 100.0 | 100.0 | 100.0 | 100.0 | 100.0 | 100.0 | 100.0 |
| Iron and steel | 9.9 | 16.5 | 11.2 | 13.6 | 10.6 | 16.1 | 12.2 | 13.6 |
| Engineering, shipbuilding and vehicles | 21.0 | 21.4 | 18.3 | 21.3 | 21.4 | 19.4 | 16.1 | 18.4 |
| Nonferrous metals | 2.5 | 2.4 | 3.1 | 3.4 | 2.4 | 1.8 | 3.0 | 3.2 |
| Chemicals | 7.4 | 9.9 | 9.8 | 9.5 | 3.8 | 5.0 | 5.2 | 4.9 |
| Textiles | 13.3 | 11.0 | 8.0 | 7.2 | 20.5 | 15.2 | 15.1 | 13.4 |
| Clothing | 6.9 | 4.0 | 7.7 | 6.3 | 10.4 | 5.6 | 11.5 | 10.5 |
| Leather | 0.9 | 1.0 | 1.4 | 1.1 | 0.9 | 1.5 | 1.5 | 1.4 |
| Rubber | 1.2 | 1.0 | 1.7 | 1.5 | 1.1 | 0.9 | 1.6 | 1.5 |
| Clay and stone | 4.5 | 6.7 | 3.2 | 3.5 | 4.8 | 9.5 | 3.2 | 3.5 |
| Timber | 3.2 | 4.0 | 4.7 | 5.0 | 3.8 | 6.1 | 8.0 | 8.1 |
| Paper and printing | 9.5 | 5.7 | 11.8 | 10.5 | 7.9 | 6.4 | 7.5 | 7.2 |
| Food, beverages and tobacco | 17.0 | 14.0 | 16.5 | 14.6 | 10.1 | 10.2 | 12.3 | 11.4 |
| Miscellaneous | 2.5 | 2.4 | 2.6 | 2.5 | 2.4 | 2.3 | 2.8 | 2.9 |

Source: L. Rostas, "Industrial Production, Productivity and Distribution in Britain, Germany and United States," *Economic Journal*, April 1943, p. 44.

TABLE 7-2. INDUSTRIAL OCCUPATIONAL GROUPINGS IN ENGLAND AND GERMANY, 1851 AND 1855[a]

| | England, 1851 | | Prussia, 1855 | |
|---|---|---|---|---|
| Occupational Group | Thousands of Persons | Percentage of Total | Thousands of Persons | Percentage of Total |
| Total | 4,808 | 100.00 | 1,212 | 100.00 |
| Textiles and clothing | 1,720 | 35.78 | 417 | 34.41 |
| Food[b] | 378 | 7.86 | 81 | 6.68 |
| Mines | 355 | 7.38 | .. | .. |
| Leather | 332 | 6.90 | 173 | 14.27 |
| Metals | 322 | 6.70 | 113 | 9.32 |
| Clay, stone, etc. (including building) | 287 | 5.97 | 113 | 9.32 |
| Woodworking | 166 | 3.45 | 191 | 15.77 |
| Paper and printing | 50 | 1.04 | .. | .. |
| Chemicals | 30 | .62 | .. | .. |
| All other occupations | 1,168 | 24.29 | 124 | 10.23 |

Source: Abbott Payson Usher, *The Industrial History of England*, Houghton Mifflin, Boston, 1920, p. 257.

a. The figures for England are from the Census for 1851, Population Tables, Vol. II, Part I, p. c. The figures for Prussia are from Dieterici, *Statistik das preussischen Staats*, Berlin, 1861, p. 400. The states covered by the enumeration are: Prussia, Posen, Brandenburg, Pomerania, Silesia, Saxony, Westphalia and the Rhine Province.

b. This heading refers to the preparation of food products, beverages and tobacco. It excludes all agricultural work.

unlikely: 1826, 21,000,000 tons; 1836, 30,000,000 tons; 1846, 44,000,000 tons; 1856, 65,000,000 tons.[25]

And these increases in the production of coal occurred *despite* enormous improvements in the efficiency with which coal was used in steam engines.[26] Prices—which varied considerably according to the means of transport available and proximity to the mines—also declined, particularly after 1825.[27]

Figures for pig iron tell a similar story. About 1800 the pig iron production in Great Britain was perhaps 200,000 tons, having risen from about 68,000 tons in 1788. By 1830, production had risen to 678,000 tons and by 1850 it was 2.5 million tons.[28]

The price of pig iron in England between 1800 and 1830 varied considerably and per ton was "upon two occasions as low as £3, but £7 to £9 was not an uncommon figure."[29] But by 1850 Scotch pig iron is said

---

25. J. H. Clapham, *An Economic History of Modern Britain*, 2d edition, Vol. I, Cambridge University Press, Cambridge, 1930, p. 431. Compare the following figures in *metric* tons for France:

| 1787 | 215,000 | 1840 | 3,003,000 |
| 1802 | 844,000 | 1850 | 4,433,000 |
| 1811 | 773,000 | 1860 | 8,309,000 |
| 1820 | 1,093,000 | 1865 | 11,652,000 |
| 1830 | 1,862,000 | 1870 | 13,179,000 |

From Witt Bowden, Michael Karpovich and Abbott Payson Usher, *An Economic History of Europe since 1750*, American Book Company, New York, 1937, p. 451 (citing F. E. Saward, *The Coal Trade*, Philadelphia, 1879, p. 47). Even in 1910, however, French coal production at 38.5 million tons was only 8.6 per cent of British coal production of 445.8 million tons. *Ibid.*, p. 452. For figures on coal production in other countries see pp. 162, 164, below.

26. W. Stanley Jevons cited figures to show that between 1769 and 1859 "the efficiency of the engine [was] increased at least ten-fold." *The Coal Question*, 2d edition, revised, Macmillan, London, 1866, p. 128.

27. A chart in L. H. Dupriez, *Des Mouvements Économiques Généraux*, Vol. II, Institut de Recherches Économiques et Sociales, Université de Louvain, Louvain, 1947, p. 38, shows a fall in the index of coal prices (1909–1912 average = 100) from about 160 in 1820 to about 100 after 1845, with of course frequent fluctuations. According to the Dupriez chart British coal prices down to 1910 did not decline substantially below the level already reached in 1845.

These calculations are confirmed in a more recent study by W. W. Rostow (which puts together data from Jevons, Mulhall, the Royal Statistical Society and an unfinished study by the late A. D. Gayer) using overlapping eleven-year averages. Rostow reports the following indexes of British coal prices (1840–1850 = 100):

| 1790–1800 | 170.5 | 1830–1840 | 114.1 |
| 1795–1805 | 159.8 | 1835–1845 | 111.5 |
| 1800–1810 | 172.5 | 1840–1850 | 100.0 |
| 1805–1815 | 180.8 | 1845–1855 | 97.2 |
| 1810–1820 | 168.4 | 1850–1860 | 97.5 |
| 1815–1825 | 149.1 | 1855–1865 | 97.9 |
| 1820–1830 | 139.8 | 1860–1870 | 97.7 |
| 1825–1835 | 120.0 | 1865–1875 | 111.1 |

W. W. Rostow, "The Historical Analysis of the Terms of Trade," *Economic History Review*, 2d Series, Vol. IV, No. 1, 1951, p. 72.

28. These figures probably are not precise but they appear to be the best available. They are taken from Sir Lowthian Bell, *The Iron Trade of the United Kingdom*, British Iron Trade Association, London, 1886, pp. 4–6. By the middle 1880s, production was around 7.5 million tons. *Ibid.*, p. 165.

29. *Ibid.*, p. 6. According to Usher the per capita consumption of pig iron in Great Britain was 15 pounds in 1735, 26 pounds in 1800, 77 pounds in 1830 and 303 pounds in 1890. See Usher, *loc. cit.*, p. 30.

to have averaged less than 45 shillings per ton.[30] Prices of bar iron at the forges in certain European countries in January 1825 are said to have compared unfavorably with English bar iron prices in 1825. Prices per ton were:[31]

| | |
|---|---|
| France | £26 10*s.* |
| Belgium and Germany | £16 14*s.* |
| Sweden (at Stockholm) | £13 13*s.* |
| Russia (at St. Petersburg) | £13 13*s.* |
| England (at Cardiff) | £10 |

## Late Growth of Manufactures

Despite this remarkable development of manufactures in the first half of the nineteenth century, by 1870 manufacturing was still *far* below the level it was to reach in the succeeding forty years. According to Folke Hilgerdt, taking an average for 1871–1875, the index of manufacturing (with 1913 as the base year at 100) stood at only 22.4 for the world as a whole, 49.0 for the United Kingdom, 20.5 for Germany, 14.8 for the United States and 11.1 for Sweden—the only countries for which such an estimate is possible. For the *year* 1870, Hilgerdt estimates that the indexes of manufacturing had probably attained the following percentages of their 1913 level:[32]

| | |
|---|---|
| United Kingdom | 44.0 |
| France | 31.7 |
| Germany | 16.3 |
| United States | 12.7 |
| Italy | 17.0 |
| Russia | 13.0 |
| Belgium | 27.4 |
| Canada | 9.1 |
| Sweden | 8.1 |

30. *Ibid.*, p. 8. This is a somewhat greater decline than that indicated by Dupriez's chart of the course of pig iron prices. Cf. Dupriez, *op. cit.*, Vol. II, p. 38. The Rostow study referred to above shows the behavior of British iron prices as follows (overlapping eleven-year averages, 1840–1850 = 100):

| | | | |
|---|---|---|---|
| 1790–1800 | 151.2 | 1830–1840 | 121.4 |
| 1795–1805 | 165.0 | 1835–1845 | 114.9 |
| 1800–1810 | 173.2 | 1840–1850 | 100.0 |
| 1805–1815 | 175.4 | 1845–1855 | 107.0 |
| 1810–1820 | 174.8 | 1850–1860 | 110.1 |
| 1815–1825 | 169.4 | 1855–1865 | 109.9 |
| 1820–1830 | 149.4 | 1860–1870 | 102.4 |
| 1825–1835 | 132.8 | 1865–1875 | 130.2 |

31. As reported in Harry Scrivenor, *History of the Iron Trade*, Longman, Brown, Green and Longmans, London, 1854, p. 270.

32. League of Nations, *Industrialization and Foreign Trade*, Geneva, 1945, Annex A, especially pp. 130–33.

Thus, the growth of manufacturing production for most countries came after, not before, 1870. Moreover, of what manufacturing there was in 1870, almost 70 per cent was in four countries: the United Kingdom, 31.8 per cent; the United States, 23.3 per cent; Germany, 13.2 per cent; and France, 10.3 per cent.[33]

*Means of Financing*

Where did the entrepreneurs come from to initiate these new industrial undertakings and what was the source of the capital that they used in financing them?[34] Apparently, the early industrial entrepreneurs came mostly from the merchant and trading classes and already had capital of their own to invest. The great growth of commerce in the seventeenth and early eighteenth century in England had produced a substantial number of prosperous merchants who had funds to invest and saw market outlets at home and abroad for manufactured products. As long as industry was a small-scale affair, the capital needs of the merchants to finance their inventories were greater than the investments needed for fixed plant in manufactures. When the fixed capital investments in industry did increase, however, it was the merchants who had the liquid capital and access to credit to finance them; they also had the entrepreneurial vision and skills to create and direct them. Thus, initially, the entrepreneurs and the capital both came out of the flourishing growth of commerce that preceded the industrial developments of the late eighteenth and early nineteenth century. The government supplied neither entrepreneurship nor capital.

*Social Results*

The remarkable changes in industrial production during the nineteenth century and the urbanization that accompanied them, had their sordid side and were often tainted with human suffering and misery. Only after industrialization had gone on apace for some time did the social conscience of the times belatedly recognize the dangers and evils of industrialism by enacting legislation affecting hours and conditions of work, safety precautions, urban living, etc. Unemployment, old age, sickness and other problems of economic insecurity were of course recognized as a social responsibility only at a very much later date. Perhaps the pace of industrial advance in the first half of the nineteenth century is therefore partly to be explained by the fact that these social costs of the transition to industrialism were not included in the reckoning. But they were none the less real, even though

33. *Ibid.*, p. 13.
34. On these questions see Bert F. Hoselitz, "Entrepreneurship and Capital Formation in France and Britain since 1700," a paper submitted to the Conference on Capital Formation and Economic Growth, November 1953, sponsored by the National Bureau of Economic Research.

they fell where they might rather than immediately upon those responsible for them or upon the economy as a whole.

Industrial development in the now underdeveloped countries is not likely to proceed with anything like so callous an attitude toward its social costs. To this extent, the process is likely to proceed more slowly, at a greater capital cost and more directly under the supervision of the state. Perhaps, too, the social evils of nineteenth-century industrial development that produced Manchester and the Manchester school of laissez-faire thinking partly account for the present distrust, in many underdeveloped areas, of allowing private enterprise any important role in their development plans. It is also a striking fact that present laws and regulations relating to industrial employment and social security in many underdeveloped areas, for example some Latin American countries, are often far more stringent— at least on paper—than those in the economically most developed countries. How far this may influence their pace of industrial development, in comparison with nineteenth-century development, is an interesting question.

### Changes in Foreign Commerce and Investment

The development of British foreign commerce and investment, which went hand in hand with the internal changes in the British economy, is not easily summarized nor interpreted. Changes in volume and prices of exports and imports inevitably reflect wars and revolutions, changing technology and efficiency at home and abroad, cyclical oscillations, changes in transport costs, tariff changes, shifts in demand preferences or sources of supply, capital movements and much else besides. The problem of interpretation is further complicated by recent researches that cast doubts on what were long considered to be the actual "facts" concerning the prices of British exports and imports in the first half of the nineteenth century.[35]

#### *Exports and Imports, 1800–1913*

In 1820—after the disturbances created by the French Revolution and the Napoleonic wars had subsided—the British export volume was only 6.7 per cent of the point to which it was to climb by 1880. The export price index, according to Albert Imlah, fell from 242 in 1820 to 100 in 1880, the base year. (See Table 7-3.) In other words, the physical volume of exports rose greatly while export prices fell.

---

35. The price statistics long used in studies of British exports and imports in the nineteenth century have been the "official values" reported in the *Parliamentary Papers*. But a recent study by Albert H. Imlah ("Real Values in British Foreign Trade, 1798–1853," *Journal of Economic History*, November 1948, pp. 133– 52), seems to prove that these "official values" are unreliable for the first half of the nineteenth century. Much of what follows here is based on Imlah's researches.

In total exports, cotton goods held a predominant place; they accounted for as much as 40 per cent of the value of British exports in 1816 and the same in 1850. Even in 1880, despite the fall in cotton goods prices and despite the more diversified export list, cotton goods still accounted for 34 per cent of the total value of exports.[36] The overseas markets to which these exports went were in America, Europe, the Orient and British overseas possessions like India and Ceylon.

TABLE 7-3. BRITISH EXPORTS AND IMPORTS, 1800–1910 AND 1913
*(Indexes Based on 1880 as 100)*

| | Exports | | | | Net Imports | | | |
|---|---|---|---|---|---|---|---|---|
| Year | Current (Declared) Value | Absolute Value 1880 Price | Export Price Index | Export Volume Index | Current Value | Absolute Value 1880 Price | Import Price Index | Import Volume Index |
| 1800 | 37.7 | 9.1 | 414.1 | 4.1 | 51.7 | 25.6 | 202.0 | 7.4 |
| 1810 | 48.4 | 13.4 | 362.6 | 6.0 | 77.3 | 37.0 | 208.9 | 10.6 |
| 1820 | 36.4 | 15.0 | 242.0 | 6.7 | 43.8 | 29.1 | 150.5 | 8.4 |
| 1830 | 38.3 | 24.0 | 159.6 | 10.8 | 50.3 | 45.9 | 109.6 | 13.2 |
| 1840 | 51.4 | 40.2 | 127.8 | 18.0 | 81.2 | 67.4 | 120.5 | 19.4 |
| 1850 | 71.4 | 69.9 | 102.2 | 31.3 | 91.0 | 100.0 | 91.0 | 28.7 |
| 1860 | 135.9 | 124.0 | 109.6 | 55.6 | 181.9 | 159.2 | 114.3 | 45.8 |
| 1870 | 199.6 | 168.1 | 118.7 | 75.3 | 258.8 | 224.0 | 115.5 | 64.4 |
| 1880 | 223.1 | 223.1 | 100.0 | 100.0 | 347.9 | 347.9 | 100.0 | 100.0 |
| 1890 | 263.5 | 304.1 | 86.6 | 136.3 | 356.0 | 450.1 | 79.1 | 129.4 |
| 1900 | 291.2 | 318.6 | 91.4 | 138.8 | 459.9 | 634.2 | 72.5 | 182.3 |
| 1910 | 430.4 | 478.6 | 89.9 | 208.4 | 574.5 | 737.7 | 79.4 | 208.0 |
| 1913 | 525.5 | 542.9 | 96.8 | 236.5 | 659.2 | 831.8 | 79.2 | 239.1 |

Source: Albert H. Imlah, "The Terms of Trade of the United Kingdom, 1798–1913," *Journal of Economic History*, November 1950, pp. 177–82.

On the import side, the volume index in 1820 was only 8.4 per cent of the 1880 level; only in 1866 did it first reach one half its 1880 level. But the import price index in 1820 at 150 was much nearer its 1880 level than the price index for exports (242). Indeed, the import price index between 1842 and 1854 was already generally *below* its 1880 level. The import price of cotton fell more rapidly than that of wool, while the prices of imports other than cotton and wool moved downward slowly, but more or less steadily: in only eight years between 1820 and 1880 did the price index for imports other than cotton and wool dip below the 1880 base.[37] Yet these imports, too, consisted predominantly of food and other primary products—sugar, tea, timber, coffee, silk, saltpeter, etc.

---

36. Albert H. Imlah, "The Terms of Trade of the United Kingdom, 1798–1913," *Journal of Economic History*, November 1950, p. 184n.

37. Imlah, "The Terms of Trade of the United Kingdom, 1798–1913," *loc. cit.*, Tables I and II.

*The Import Surplus*

More remarkable than the growth of British exports and imports and the fall in prices is the evidence, brought out by Imlah's studies, that Great Britain had a negative balance, a surplus of imports over exports, on "visible trade," or merchandise trade, in all but four years between 1798 and 1880. Contrary to general belief, the import surplus did *not* arise out of the free-trade policies of the 1840s—though of course free-trade policies made it larger than it would otherwise have been. It appeared much earlier. As Imlah has expressed it:

There seems to be no escape, therefore, from the conclusion that Britain's new industrial system did not create export surpluses, and that her phenomenal accumulation of overseas credits in the nineteenth century cannot be explained by this time-honored assumption . . . In this period, as later, Britain's invisible credits—the earnings of the merchant marine, the commercial commissions, the savings of her experts and technicians and colonial officials abroad, and the income from the investments already placed in other lands—made up the deficit on her visible trade and supplied whatever new capital was invested abroad.[38]

*Foreign Lending*

If this view, that the British trade balance showed an import surplus even as early as 1800, is accepted, it becomes all the more remarkable when considered in connection with the substantial British foreign investments in the same period. For foreign investment tends to stimulate exports relative to imports.

British foreign lending in this early period of capital export, however, followed no simple pattern. Immediately after the French wars, France, Russia, Austria and Prussia floated loans in the British market. In the 1820s there was a flurry of loans to Colombia, Chile, Peru, Mexico and Guatemala as well as a romantic but scandalously executed loan in aid of Greek independence.[39] In the 1830s many loans were made for ventures in the United States. British capital built railways on the continent of Europe in the 1840s; more than a decade later it was performing the same service in India and, later still, in Canada. More than £37 million was invested in Indian railways between 1858 and 1863, and more than another £32 million between 1864 and 1869.[40] Foreign governments alone borrowed more than

38. Imlah, "Real Values in British Foreign Trade, 1798–1853," *loc. cit.*, p. 149.

39. Leland Jenks says: "the migration of capital from Great Britain began as a function of the activity of a handful of merchant-bankers interested primarily in keeping alive the foreign connections which were the basis of their business life. Between 1815 and 1830 at least fifty million pounds had been invested more or less permanently in the securities of the most stable European governments, more than twenty millions had been invested in one form or another in Latin America, and five or six millions had very quietly found their way to the United States." Leland Hamilton Jenks, *The Migration of British Capital to 1875*, Knopf, New York, 1927, pp. 63–64.

40. *Ibid.*, Chapter 2.

£320 million in the London market between 1860 and 1879.[41] According to Jenks, British holdings of foreign investments in 1854 amounted to between £195 and £230 million, of which perhaps nearly one half were loans to governments.[42]

Statistics on British foreign investments in the whole period down to 1913 are unfortunately fragmentary and conjectural. The following, however, appear to be the best available estimates of the probable size of British foreign investment holdings in various years (in millions of pounds):[43]

| 1825–1830 | £  100 | 1895 | £1,600 |
|-----------|--------|------|--------|
| 1843      | 150    | 1905 | 2,025  |
| 1854      | 210    | 1909 | 2,332  |
| 1880      | 1,300  | 1913 | 3,763  |
| 1885      | 1,302  |      |        |

## Implications for Underdeveloped Countries

The bearing of all this on contemporary problems of economic development is more oblique than direct. Domestic economic development and expansion of overseas trade certainly went hand in hand in Great Britain, and they were intimately linked from at least the late sixteenth century onward. But the important point is that expansion of foreign commerce and the profits to be made from that trade were of the greatest importance, along with transport improvements, in inducing changes in the composition of output and the deployment of productive resources within the domestic economy. The highly profitable foreign trade and its expanding volume put pressure on the older methods of production and, to a considerable extent, the merchant and trading groups directly exerted that pressure. Commerce with overseas markets quickened domestic trade, and a livelier domestic trade forced changes in methods of production and in the kinds of goods produced. As a means of bringing about internal economic changes foreign commerce was highly effective. May it not also be true that foreign trade is still one of the most effective means of reorienting a traditionalized, static and unprogressive economy?

In view of the marked degree to which eighteenth- and early nineteenth-century industrial development in England was concentrated in cotton textiles, it is worth noting that cotton was an imported raw material. Although wool and woolens had long been traditional English specialties, the industrial advance did not appear there first but rather in cottons, which soon rose to a position of primary importance in British exports—

41. *Ibid.*, p. 280.

42. *Ibid.*, p. 413.

43. Royal Institute of International Affairs, *The Problem of International Investment*, Oxford University Press, London, 1937, p. 115. These estimates are not from any single source but have been consolidated from several. Cf. *ibid.*, pp. 113*ff*.

accounting for 40 per cent of the total even in 1850. From this, it might be urged that industrial development does not necessarily require domestic sources of supply unless one starts with autarchic preconceptions. Perhaps a less obvious inference is that long-established trades do not offer the most hospitable environment for innovations and rapid technological advance.

Viewed from the present, it might seem that the rapid industrial development in England would have made England a net borrower on international account. But the exact opposite seems to have occurred: England was probably a net exporter of capital during the nineteenth century. In contrast to what has happened in many now underdeveloped countries, industrial development in England did not, apparently, cause her to experience a shortage of foreign exchange. The explanation is doubtless that the machinery and other capital goods needed for industrial development simply could not be imported because other countries were even less industrially advanced than England. Hence, there was no foreign exchange drain from this source. Rather, what England had to do was to import more raw materials and more food as people were drawn into industry, and in order to get these flowing she had often to make sizable foreign investments. It is noteworthy that England was able to provide for herself all the capital needed for her domestic industrial development and to invest considerable sums abroad as well.

*Trade Linked with Investment*

Thus, England's industrial development was from the first intimately linked with her international commerce. Around this nucleus, moreover, gradually evolved the familiar "network of world trade" based on the principle of international specialization, which, from one point of view, was perhaps the most distinctive economic achievement of the whole nineteenth century. As the center of this development, England not only provided the capital for her own industrial advance, but also supplied productive investments to other points in the network in substantial amounts. This was a unique accomplishment.

### CAPITAL ACCUMULATION AND INDUSTRIALIZATION IN ENGLAND

Capital accumulation in England during the early phases of the industrial revolution cannot be separated from the amazing commercial expansion of the seventeenth and early eighteenth centuries which preceded it. This commercial expansion yielded substantial profits, which, for the most part, were reinvested rather than consumed; real capital accumulated. Even more important, however, the growth of commerce greatly fostered the idea of investment for profit and its concrete manifestations such as government stock, trading companies, banks, bourses, bills of exchange, etc. While these developments were often heavily charged with the fever of speculation and a quick profit, as with John Law or the South Sea Bubble, other enterprises, like the East India Company or the Hudson's Bay Company, represented more solid undertakings using substantial amounts of capital goods. Also, as previously emphasized, the commercial expansion developed a group of merchants, traders and adventurers who had a quick eye for profitable undertakings and had resources in hand with which to exploit them. Consequently, with trade profitable and with a group of people eager to invest for further profit, total consumption in England rather consistently lagged behind the total value of output. Capital accumulated.

So far as can be determined, this same process of financing capital accumulation out of current production continued throughout the early phases of English industrial development. Productivity rose. Profits increased. The profits were reinvested. Productivity increased still further. In other words, capital accumulation went hand in hand with rising productivity. The "Protestant ethic" may have led people to work harder or may have constrained them from dissipating their profits in luxurious consumption. The inflation of the Napoleonic period probably fostered capital accumulation at the expense of consumption. Yet, all in all, it was the rising productivity in many branches of agriculture, commerce and industry that made possible the simultaneous growth of consumption and real capital per person in the population.

## THE ROLE OF THE STATE

The role of the state in British economic development during its most vigorous advance was largely permissive and passive, rather than directive and promotive. Nowadays, schemes for economic development are likely to assign the state a dominant influence in the whole plan. But in the late eighteenth and early nineteenth century, the emphasis in political thought and discussion was to get the state out of economic affairs, not to draw it in further. Adam Smith, for one, stressed "the obvious and simple system of natural liberty" as against, in his view, the paternalistic, obstructionist and bumbling activities of the state in economic affairs. In England, the state was in no sense considered the ideal entrepreneur, nor did it have any plan for economic development in the modern meaning of that phrase. In the laissez-faire mood which prevailed in the early stages of British economic development, the role of the state was to keep out of the way of private initiative. The state did not try to guide development, set its pace, or decide what form it should take.

Where the state did intervene in economic affairs, it usually did so in belated recognition of blatant evils or clear and present dangers. Thus, the conditions of employment of women and children in mine and factory were shown to be so scandalous that they threatened the future vigor of the English population. Sanitary conditions in the early industrial towns made plague and epidemic an ever-present danger. Housing conditions not only created a bad moral environment but constituted a real fire hazard. Only when these conditions were recognized as a threat to the general welfare, or when it was seen that they would not be corrected by people acting in pursuit of their own self-interest, did the state intervene. Yet state intervention was contrary to the political philosophy of the times and often only grudgingly undertaken. Nor did the social conscience of the day view the inevitable dislocations which accompany rapid economic change as social costs to be borne by society at large: they were regarded as misfortunes which befell people in the normal course of events and were to be suffered accordingly.

Thus the role of the state in early English economic development was both reluctant and timorous. In the main, economic events ran ahead of state action. Yet, despite the hardships which this laissez-faire attitude often engendered, the fact remains that industrial development did take place and took place rapidly.

### Conclusions from English Development

From the point of view of the now underdeveloped areas, with their strong desire to lift themselves from economic stagnation on to the road of progress, it would be helpful to have a clear-cut answer as to whether it was historically first agriculture that changed, and then industry, or the other way about in English economic development. Was it, broadly speaking, the improvements in agricultural productivity that drove people off the land and so made possible the development of manufacturing? Or did manufacturing pull people out of agriculture and so pave the way for improvements and readjustments in agriculture? Perhaps the more logical view is that improvements in agriculture came first. But if the agricultural improvements tended to push people out of agriculture, the newly developing manufactures also pulled people into industry and commerce.

As to the economic developments in agriculture, it is noteworthy that progress was not dramatically rapid nor did it proceed without opposition or hardships. Moreover, to a remarkable degree, eighteenth-century agriculture in England and Western Europe displayed many of the bad features of present-day agriculture in underdeveloped areas—traditionalized methods of production, fragmented holdings and systems of land use which checked production and inhibited its improvement. Yet these obstacles were overcome; productivity rose; total output increased.

*Importance of Transport Development*

The role of improvements in transport and communication in making possible and quickening late eighteenth- and early nineteenth-century economic development in England was probably of fundamental importance. Because the effects of improvements in transport and communication are so diffused and indirect their significance is easily underrated. But by widening the market—and so extending the area over which specialization and exchange are possible—better transport increases and improves the output from resources already in use and brings previously idle resources into production. Perhaps of all the improvements that facilitate economic development those in transport and communication—because they foster trade, specialization, innovation—are at once the most certain to yield results and the most widespread in their consequences.

*Effects of War*

The rapid pace of English economic development might not have been achieved had the French Revolution and the Napoleonic wars not isolated England from the European continent during much of the period 1789–1815. This was plainly a fortuitous circumstance; but the consequences were no less on that account. When the French Revolution broke out England had made some promising beginnings in industrial development. When Napoleon was defeated at Waterloo, England was the world's most advanced country economically with a substantial lead over the others.

The reasons for this spurt ahead seem to center around two factors. First, the war created an inflationary environment—"too much money chasing too few goods"—which strongly stimulated the production of goods of all kinds including foods. This put existing methods of production under pressure. Improvements were therefore more readily adopted. Consequently, too, the usual obstacles to such changes which might have prevailed in more tranquil times were the more easily and often harshly brushed aside. Second, wars and disturbances by breaking customary relations with the outside world are likely to open up new economic opportunities internally and allow them to be developed through the early stages without their being checked by counterdevelopments in the outside world. Recent history abounds in examples of this phenomenon of wartime economic isolation jolting an economy onto a new plane of economic development. The Napoleonic period seems to have given England just such a timely forward propulsion.

*Population Shifts and Food*

Out of the bewildering complexity of Britain's economic development two consequences emerged which may prove important to the now underdeveloped areas. First, England's economic development was accompanied by an important geographical shift in the centers of concentration of her population. An agricultural economy and an industrial economy deploy their populations differently. In England, as probably also in most such cases, the shift in population was accomplished by "short distance" migration: the expanding urban areas drew most of their increased numbers from the immediately surrounding countryside which, in turn, drew from the adjacent territory, and so on. Few people moved great distances; but the net result was a major shift in the centers of population.[44] Moreover, probably because of the great differential in real wages and the low cost of transport by water, considerable numbers immigrated from Ireland to man the factories in the Manchester-Merseyside area. Important population shifts such as these break up long-established social and cultural patterns that tend to inhibit economic change because they destroy the economic foundations on which these patterns rest.

Second, industrialization made England dependent upon foreign food. In her heyday England was able to exchange manufactures for inexpensive food from abroad with comparative ease because of the opening of new lands overseas. How other countries would make a comparable adjustment in the twentieth century—particularly if industrial development proceeds rapidly in a number of countries simultaneously—is far from clear.

It is currently fashionable to stress the sordidness, the ugliness, the vulgarity or the suffering which the rapid industrial development of England brought in its turbulent wake. But this emphasis is often so highlighted as to obscure the fact that the average Englishman lived less than an idyllic existence in his rural hamlet before industrialization got under way. All the evidence indicates that, before industry developed, his life span was shorter, he ate less well, he was more poorly clothed and housed, and that he usually had to struggle harder with nature to eke out a humble living. In the Epilogue to his classic work, *The Economic Development of France and Germany, 1815-1914*, J. H. Clapham has written the following:

That the land reforms had been accompanied by a certain crushing of men down in the social scale, and that the peasant of the east in 1914 was often miserable enough, judged by absolute standards, must not be allowed to hide the far more miserable position from which he had been raised. The "hapless missing link between a beast of burden and a man" had become at least human. It was no longer likely that a traveller in the east would see a woman in the fields, in October, working in an old open coat, a skirt, and nothing else, a sight possible in the years before emancipation.[45]

Such miserable conditions were not exceptional; indeed, they were pretty much the common lot before industrial development began.

44. See Redford, *op. cit.*, Chapter 11.
45. Clapham, *op. cit.*, p. 403.

# 8. Early Economic Development in Western Europe and Europe Overseas

JUST AS IN A FAMILY the younger children never develop in quite the same environment as the first-born, so countries that developed economically during the nineteenth century were bound to be affected by the plain fact that England had gone before. English experience and English achievements were an inescapable part of the background from which other countries approached their own development problems and aspirations. In a very real sense, there was no "problem" of initiating or accelerating economic development until England had first shown that a novel and higher level of economic performance was possible. Once England had done this, as it clearly had by, say, 1850, then other countries faced the question of how, and against what obstacles, they might bring their own economies to comparable achievements. Economic development came into existence as an objective and a "problem."

## INITIATING DEVELOPMENT

Economic development in Western Europe in the nineteenth century is of major interest here for the light it may shed on the important problem of "getting started" and picking up momentum. What changes appear to have been peculiarly effective in bringing the countries in Western Europe closer to England's new pattern in the use of economic resources? What factors tended to accelerate this transition and what factors tended to retard it?

### The General Setting

While historical parallels are always hazardous, nevertheless there were striking similarities between the economic, political and social setting in Western continental Europe after 1815 and that in many underdeveloped countries after 1945. In both cases, there seems to have been a mounting awareness that fundamental economic and social changes were imperative and past due, that economic development was neither inconceivable nor impossible. Neither in 1815 nor in 1945 did the average man comprehend the momentous character of the events through which he had recently lived; but he probably was aware that broad changes were afoot and felt— especially when told that he should—that some of the annoyances and

152

frustrations of his daily existence "ought" to be set right. Some of his leaders or rulers, whose lives were not circumscribed by the local village, doubtless saw certain implications in recent historical happenings and drew from them important conclusions for public policy and action.

The French Revolution and its aftermath could hardly have failed to leave a profound impression upon thoughtful men in Western European countries and upon their monarchs and ministers. Some of these confined themselves to bemoaning the passing of a social order long familiar; but others sensed or half-realized two important implications of the events of the period 1789–1815. The first was that feudalism in economic affairs would have to go. The second was that, in the end, England had been able to win out over France in the Napoleonic wars partly because English industry and commerce had outstripped that of France and the rest of Europe. The two principles were closely interwoven: England's industrial strength, for example, was partly due to the efficiency of agriculture under the English system. After Waterloo, no astute ruler was likely to overlook the political implications of these crude facts. Consequently, rulers and statesmen in post-Napoleonic Europe took more than a casual, if at times grudging, interest in the agricultural and industrial development of their particular countries.

Such concerns were by no means unknown before 1789; but after 1815 they took more concrete form in measures to modernize agriculture and to foster industry. Indeed, economic development in Western Europe seems to have been motivated primarily by considerations of political power and the threat of social unrest and only secondarily and at far remove by a desire to improve the general level of well-being of the people. Consequently, the state and considerations of national political power played a larger role than they did in England. In England, political power was a welcome consequence of economic development, but it was scarcely the impelling factor.

### CHANGES IN EUROPEAN AGRICULTURE AFTER 1815

The changes in European agriculture that occurred in the several decades following Napoleon appear to have their explanation in two sets of influences. On the one hand is the breakup of the feudal system of landholdings and land-utilization and its accompanying body of privileges and obligations. On the other are such more narrowly economic factors as new methods of cultivation, new crops, new markets and the general commercialization of agricultural activity. The two sets of influences operated conjointly; only in an analytical sense can they be separated. Moreover, the relative importance of each differs considerably from place to place and from time to time. Only a very broad, general view can overlook important local differences of timing and detail. For example, interest in agricultural improvement in France antedated the Revolution, but according to Herbert Heaton it is difficult to judge how far a desire for improvement was carried over into practice.[1]

## Agricultural Change in France

Feudalism in agricultural production crumbled away gradually in Western Europe. In France, most of the feudal dues, tithes and obligations were summarily abolished during the Revolution. In the next few decades large holdings seem to have diminished; however, French agriculture, except in the north, was not well suited to large units of cultivation and the principle of equal inheritance operated also to keep the units small. Perhaps the most important change wrought in agriculture in France by the Revolution was the sweeping away of the many restrictions on ownership and types of crops.[2] After the Revolution, anyone could own land or make a free contract for sharing the produce of land belonging to another. Many of the lands confiscated from the nobility and the Church were sold to members of the new aristocracy, who farmed them on shares or leased them at fixed money rentals. Commons were also broken up, though to a lesser extent than in England, and common pasturing after the harvest (*vaine pâture*) gradually disappeared. On the whole, the pattern of French agriculture was not dramatically and drastically changed by the Revolution, but the changes left no doubt that the *ancien régime* had passed and that the French peasant was a free man.[3]

## Agricultural Advances in Germany

In Germany, the post-Napoleonic period saw many important shifts from a feudal type of organization in agriculture to a freer peasantry and more rational methods of land use. Though Frederick the Great (1740–

1. Herbert Heaton, *Economic History of Europe*, revised edition, Harper, New York, 1948, p. 433.

2. In pre-Revolutionary France there were numerous rules which sought to assure an adequate grain supply in each district. See J. H. Clapham, *The Economic Development of France and Germany, 1815–1914*, Cambridge University Press, Cambridge, 1921, p. 10. One writer has summed up the matter as follows: "If the Revolution of 1789 was essentially a peasant revolution, it was not a revolution of landless men to divide between themselves the land of those in possession, but a revolution of small owners who wanted both to round off their properties and, above all, to shake off the yoke which weighed on them. The principal effect of the Revolution was not to cause any considerable increase in the division of ownership, which was already a characteristic feature of the French countryside, nor to augment the number of properties to enormous proportions, but to liberate peasant property." H. Hauser, "The Characteristic Features of French Economic History from the Middle of the Sixteenth to the Middle of the Eighteenth Century," *The Economic History Review*, October 1933, pp. 271–72.

3. Particularly in the south of France there was far less economic justification for any drastic changes in the kind and methods of cultivation in use at the time of the Revolution. The open-field system was found only in patches, but the crops raised—vines, fruits, olives, etc.—were usually not suited to such a system. Cf. Clapham, *op. cit.*, p. 7.

1786) had tried both to lighten the obligations of the peasants on his own estates and to foster improved methods of cultivation, the nobility and gentry gave him little support. Only after the disastrous defeat of the Prussians at Jena in 1806 did these privileged groups concede the necessity for reform. There followed the emancipation edicts of 1807–1808, which abolished personal serfdom, established freedom of choice of occupation and permitted land transfers between classes.[4] Adam Smith's doctrine of economic freedom was acknowledged to have merit as applied to agriculture; peasant protection and paternalism in economic affairs were in obvious decline. The edicts of 1807 were followed by others in 1811, 1816 and 1821.

One feature of the Prussian reforms was that the seigneurs were compensated in land for the loss of their rights to receive dues. At the same time, the Prussian peasants got rather more protection, on the whole, than did their English cousins when common pastures and wastelands were broken up. Agricultural reforms seem to have been conducted with much greater attention to the "general welfare" of the people as a whole than in either England or France.[5]

The implications of these changes were not identical for all of Prussia, because the way in which agriculture was conducted east of the Elbe River differed fully as much from that of the west as did the relations between the peasants and their betters in the two areas. Broadly speaking, the emancipation of the peasants had a shorter distance to go in west Prussia and western Germany than in the east, because more of the peasants were close to being freeholders and servitude was less onerous. Proximity to the Low Countries, where peasant ownership of land was customary well before 1789, had somewhat strengthened the position of the peasants in the west; the French, during their stay, removed other restrictions. But even after the edicts, the peasants did little to abolish the common pasture and woodland because "common use was congenial to peasant habits and on the whole not uneconomical."[6] The peasants were not innovators by temperament.

In the Prussian kingdom east of the Elbe—Brandenburg, Silesia, Pomerania and the province of Prussia—the landlord was more powerful and the emancipation tended to strengthen his economic position. Large units of operation were the rule well before the reforms. The estate owners had managed to bring much of the commons under their own control even before 1807. The reforms, however, increased the number of landless peasants in the east. As one writer put it,

4. Before the edicts Prussia had a kind of caste system which required townsmen, nobles and peasants not to venture outside occupations reserved for their particular group. See Heaton, *op. cit.*, p. 440.

5. See Witt Bowden, Michael Karpovich and Abbott Payson Usher, *An Economic History of Europe since 1750*, American Book Company, New York, 1937, pp. 271*ff*.

6. Clapham, *op. cit.*, p. 47.

. . . the losses in land and money which were the price of this emancipation left great masses of peasants either landless or with so little land as to leave them only the choice between labouring on the estates and more substantial peasant holdings or seeking the industrial labour market of the towns, chiefly in the West.[7]

Harsh as some of these developments were, they nevertheless opened the way to more efficient agricultural production. As it had done earlier in England, large-scale, commercialized farming grew in importance in eastern Prussia after the edicts of reform.[8]

*Feudalism Persisted Elsewhere*

The gradual disappearance of feudalism in agriculture in Europe after 1815 was mainly confined to France, Prussia and northwestern Europe. In Sweden also, however, agricultural modernization went forward along familiar lines after 1815: wastelands were reclaimed; some men grown rich in commerce became landlords and operated their lands commercially, using more capital and better techniques. In the kingdom of the Netherlands feudalism had disappeared long before.

In Russia, the Iberian peninsula, central and southern Europe, including southern Italy, reforms came much later. Despite the ostensible freeing of the peasants in Russia in 1861, that country was essentially feudalistic until 1905. In Spain, only the Spanish-American War seems to have brought a belated realization that the rest of Europe had changed during the preceding century. Romania abolished serfdom only in 1864, and in other parts of the Balkans some long-overdue land reforms occurred only after 1918. In terms of social outlook and agricultural practice Russia, central and southeastern Europe, Spain and southern Italy were underdeveloped areas until well toward the end of the nineteenth century.

*Innovations in Agricultural Practice*

The benign view that the European peasant, once freed from his feudal obligations and restrictions, rushed eagerly forward to adopt new ways and better practices of land utilization is palpably false. Peasants are cautious conservatives as a rule: their environment and outlook are hostile to change. If the changes in European agriculture after 1815 had had to draw their impetus directly from the emancipated peasants, the rate of progress would have been discouragingly slow. Other influences had to impinge from without to break down outmoded practices. It seems reasonable to suppose that similar generalizations are valid for Asiatic peasants or

7. Carl Brinkmann, "The Place of Germany in the Economic History of the Nineteenth Century," *The Economic History Review*, April 1933, p. 132.

8. Whether the long-term political consequences of strengthening the position of the east Prussian landlords more than outweighed the gain in other directions is not examined here. But see Alexander Gerschenkron, *Bread and Democracy in Germany*, University of California Press, Berkeley, 1943.

Middle Eastern peasants today. Merely to relieve them of the dominance of landlords or moneylenders is not to assure progress in agriculture. Probably lectures, demonstrations and exhortations will not suffice to do the job either, unless they are supplemented by the pressure of the market in combination with high rewards to a few aggressive innovators who serve as catalysts.

Broadly speaking, two influences were of dominant importance in modernizing European agriculture once the old restrictions and stifling restraints were lifted. The first of these was the compelling force of the changing markets for agricultural products joined with an insistence from certain quarters—outside the peasantry—that agriculture be modernized. The second was the introduction of new techniques and the appearance of certain previously unfamiliar crops, the cultivation of which required a fresh approach to production problems. These two influences of course acted and reacted on each other so as to be often indistinguishable. Nevertheless, they are separable analytically.

## New Crops and Methods

Between the appearance of new techniques and new crops and their general acceptance and use, there was typically an appreciable lag. For example, in France, Parmentier had tried unsuccessfully to introduce potatoes during the reign of Louis XVI. Potatoes were long regarded as poisonous and they were apparently considered an inferior food, as compared with rye and wheat, all through the Napoleonic period. But by 1850 their use was widespread, partly, it appears, because they were found suitable for cultivation along with turnips and grasses in land previously fallowed or left as waste. In Germany, perhaps because soils were more favorable and the people poorer, the potato was more quickly accepted as a basic food. "By 1815," Clapham says, "it was grown everywhere, east and west, by squire and peasant; and within a few years spirit was being distilled from it extensively."[9]

The continental blockade gave the impetus to the introduction of sugar beets in France, especially in Flanders, the Pas de Calais and Somme regions. In Germany the big extension of sugar beets came only in the 1830s, after the depressed period in agriculture following the defeat of Napoleon. From the point of view of agricultural progress, the sugar beet had salutary effects. Its cultivation demanded more careful planting than broadside sowing; the land had to be more deeply plowed; and after the sugar had been extracted, the pulp was good fodder. These advantages were most fully exploited in eastern Prussia where beet cultivation led to

9. Clapham, *op. cit.*, p. 51.

substantial improvements in agricultural implements and to a more scientific approach to agricultural problems.[10]

The new agricultural products were by no means limited to edible foods. Both in France and in Germany, the wool yield was improved by introducing merino sheep, although this had begun in France before 1789. The output of silk also expanded greatly in France under official stimulation between 1815 and 1850. In Germany linseed, rape and other oil seeds came into active production.

An adequate discussion of the progress of these newer crops and newer techniques in Western Europe would require many pages. From the economic point of view, they suggest more intensive and more careful land utilization, more variety and specialization in production, more skillful management and, not least in importance, a greater tendency to subject agriculture to the economic calculus of costs and returns. Before 1850, however, and before the coming of the railways, such practices did not become general among the peasants in Western Europe despite official sponsorship and some enthusiastic pioneers. How did these new attitudes come about and how were they infused into agricultural practice?

In both France and Germany, the government pushed vigorously for agricultural progress. In both countries, too, there were aggressive men who were ready to try better methods and anxious to secure better returns. But in Germany, the government's methods were generally more successful because, first, the east Prussian squires formed a more numerous group of ingenious, commercially minded men with whom to work, and, second, these men had large estates with hired laborers and so could experiment with new crops and methods. In France, and also in southwestern Germany, the small farms were owned and operated by peasants with a peasant outlook who were less easily converted to new crops or new methods. The French authorities thus found it harder to stimulate progress in agriculture, although, on the technical side, probably fewer changes were needed. From the point of view of the now underdeveloped areas, therefore, the German program carries greater interest.

### Roots of German Agricultural Change

The modernization of agriculture in Prussia in the nineteenth century had its roots in the efforts of Frederick the Great and the considerable interest in English farming methods generated during his reign—crop rotation, enclosures, more scientific methods of approach, and so on. But not until after the humiliating defeat of the Prussians at Jena in 1806 did the king

10. Beet sugar production in France up to 1850 is said to have rarely exceeded 50,000 tons annually. *Ibid.*, p. 26. Perhaps the production of cane sugar in the French colonies was partially responsible for this slow advance in France proper, compared with Germany, but the application of comparative cost principles was probably the main reason.

grant authority to the administrative departments to make substantive changes.[11] There then followed a whole series of legal changes extending to 1858.

Once the legal framework was modified, the economic factors could exert their influence. The high prices and expanded production that were characteristic of the Napoleonic period were followed by a severe slump in the 1820s. But recovery was not long delayed, as both home and foreign markets expanded for grain, wool, sugar and potatoes. All these products except grain were relatively new in the Prussian provinces east of the Elbe, and their production both increased and became more efficient. The number of sheep in the province of Prussia more than doubled between 1816 and 1837, according to Heaton. Wool exports to Great Britain rose from 5 million pounds in 1820 to 32 million in 1836.[12]

For the most part, it was the large, commercially minded landlords who tried the new crops and pushed their production. They formed agricultural societies; they held cattle shows; they patronized touring exhibits of farm implements and machinery; they learned about drainage and fertilizers; and they even studied bookkeeping. Moreover, they had capital with which to apply what they learned. In the 1830s and after, Liebig and Wöhler brought their researches in organic chemistry to bear upon the complex problems of plant growth. Though their findings were subsequently modified by further researches, it is significant that their work appeared in Germany during a period of feverish interest in agricultural progress.[13] But what kept this interest alive and vigorous was probably the fact that markets were good and that astute squires would be well repaid for being knowledgeable and efficient. By 1840, it is said, even the peasants east of the Elbe were beginning to comprehend scientific crop rotation.[14]

Thus, in Germany it would appear that the government helped to pave the way for agricultural progress by cutting away feudal restrictions and obligations; the larger estate owners saw the opportunities afforded by bigger markets, new crops and improved techniques and made the most of them; and these conditions together established a situation in which government officials, estate owners and university scientists collaborated to carry progress still further. All three factors appear to have been important

11. Frederick the Great had built up an efficient and enlightened administration. Some of the leaders and department heads had studied English farming methods and tried to relate them to the widely varying conditions throughout the Prussian kingdom. Consequently after Jena it was not necessary to start from the beginning and consider what was to be done and how it was to be put into effect. Much of this groundwork had already been done. What was needed mainly was the authority to proceed. This came with the recall of Baron von Stein as minister in 1807. The Edict of 1807 was published eight days after his recall on October 9. See Bowden, Karpovich and Usher, *op. cit.*, pp. 271*ff.*

12. Heaton, *op. cit.*, p. 443.

13. See Bowden, Karpovich and Usher, *op. cit.*, pp. 283–87. Ironically, Liebig did some of his early work in Paris and Wöhler in Sweden.

14. Clapham, *op. cit.*, p. 52.

in getting agricultural progress under way and keeping it moving forward. In a very real sense, it was a cooperative achievement. The *Landschaft* for making mortgage loans on land and the *Raiffeisen* cooperative credit banks were only material manifestations of a cooperative effort which was much broader and deeper.

## THE DEVELOPMENT IN INDUSTRY

Industry, as loosely contrasted with agriculture, was of course far from nonexistent in Europe before 1789, and it did not lack its advocates and sponsors in high authority. Frederick the Great not only continued the protective system begun by his father but fostered and subsidized the production of woolens, satins, leather goods and even iron and sugar. Peter the Great (1682–1725) tried to "Europeanize" Russia after he had seen for himself, in Holland, England, Austria and Italy, how backward industry was in his own country. In France, from Colbert to Turgot, many efforts were made to promote industry, but other policies were at times economically disastrous, as in the case of the expulsion of the enterprising Huguenots.

### European Industry before 1800

An emphasis on industry and a desire to see it flourish in Europe well antedated Napoleon. But what was implied by "industry," as against agriculture, in the seventeenth and eighteenth centuries was something rather different from what the term came to mean during the nineteenth century. Early industry was handicraft work, with some specialization and even with some persons who can only be called "capitalists." Essentially, it consisted in the production of wearing apparel of cloth or leather, the simple tools needed in agricultural production at the time, and all those activities necessary to provide the nobles and clergy with those amenities and appurtenances of living characteristic of a stratified society based on agriculture. And then finally there were those industries that could rightly be regarded as indispensable to the army or navy. All such "industry," however, differed appreciably from industry in the modern sense of the term: the workers were not factory laborers using machinery to make goods for a wide market. Until well into the nineteenth century in most of Western Europe industry meant workers in arts and crafts catering to the few or furnishing locally a few bare necessities to the poor and humble.

All this was to change in the course of the nineteenth century. The full story of that transition cannot be undertaken here, but some few of its salient features seem so pertinent to the present-day problem of development, from the point of view of holding back or moving forward the modernization of industry, that they must be mentioned.

### The State and Industrial Development

The state played a greater role in industrial progress in continental Europe than it had earlier in England. The reasons are many, but three particularly seem worthy of mention.

First, the governments and statesmen of Europe after 1815 were rarely able to separate the development of industry from problems of politics. Consequently, their concern for industry was usually linked with their determination to make their particular nations politically powerful. For some countries—France, for instance—this meant protecting and bolstering what strengths the country had already achieved. For others, like Germany, it meant trying to create what had not previously existed and weakening foreign industry if possible. Different countries followed different policies to try to reach closely similar ends.

Second, continental European countries tried to match quickly or surpass England's industrial success, without undergoing either the social upheavals or the weakening of domestic agriculture that England had experienced. The national state therefore had to bear some of the costs of moving ahead more rapidly than private initiative would have done and of protecting those interests that private enterprise would not have included in its reckoning.

Third—and this may be more questionable—most Western European countries in the early nineteenth century appear to have lacked entrepreneurs and capitalists in sufficient numbers and with sufficient energy and aggressiveness to achieve an "industrial revolution" on their own.[15] Consequently, government played the role of entrepreneur and capitalist more than in England.

### The Case of Germany

All these influences are apparent in the nineteenth-century economic history of Germany. The Zollverein (customs union), established under Prussian sponsorship in 1834, finally cleared away a tangle of trade restrictions, taxes and other regulations which inhibited commerce and choked industry. But it represented also the triumph of Prussian efforts since Stein to unify Germany under Prussian leadership. The customs union of 1834 was preceded by the important Prussian tariff act of 1818, which made customs and excise duties uniform throughout the Prussian kingdom and applied to transit trade as well. The political map of Germany at the time made these transit duties exceedingly burdensome for the smaller states

---

15. Holland was more nearly comparable to England in this respect than any other European country, but the nature of her resources as well as political developments afforded her relatively little opportunity to develop industrially in the early nineteenth century. What is now Belgium was separated from France in 1815 and given to Holland. Belgium did develop rapidly in industry after 1815, but in 1830 it became an independent country. Moreover, many Dutch migrated to Germany.

contiguous to Prussia and this was a powerful factor in bringing them to accept Prussian proposals.[16]

The Zollverein, however, according to Friedrich List (1789–1846), was a "Siamese twin" of the German railways. At any rate, in 1838 Prussia announced that it would willingly foster railroad construction by bond purchases and interest guarantees and by granting monopolies; in 1848, mainly for military reasons, the state itself began construction of a line from Berlin to the Russian border. Although the lines were often built cheaply and with little regard to providing really fast transport, "this service had far-reaching effects in tying town and country together, fostering interregional exchange of goods, stimulating industry, and encouraging commercial farming."[17] The preceding chapter has already analyzed and stressed the pervasive effects of improved transport upon development. In industry proper in the modern sense, German progress was slow and uncertain until after 1850. As late as 1871 Germany had only eight cities with more than one hundred thousand population and nearly two thirds of the German population was still engaged in agriculture.[18]

Some steps toward industrial development that antedated 1850 are of interest. In 1821, the Prussian government set up the Gewerbe Institut to make available knowledge of new processes and developments in technology and to encourage their adoption. In the early stages, German industry mainly applied methods that had already proved successful in England. The customs union and the tariff afforded a good home market for developing industries. Significantly, the cotton and silk industries—both of which used imported raw materials—were modernized more easily and rapidly than such traditional German industries as woolens and linens. By 1850, Germany supplied about half her own needs for cotton yarn for weaving.

Coal output was not large until after 1845, because it required the cheap transport provided by river steamers and railways. The iron industry was also unimportant until after 1850; steel, of course, came much later. Modern German industry, indeed, flowered to the full only after the establishment of the empire in 1864 and the annexation of Alsace-Lorraine in 1870. The advances in coal and iron before 1850 were striking in terms of percentage increases, although small in absolute quantities. In Prussia, for example, output of coal and lignite amounted to 1.7 million tons in 1831, 3.0 million in 1839 and 4.6 million in 1845; but in 1861 it reached 12.8 million tons. The period of greatest expansion was 1849–1857, when coal output increased at an average rate of approximately 11 per cent a year.[19]

16. For a brief account of the developments leading up to the Zollverein of 1834 see Bowden, Karpovich and Usher, *op. cit.*, pp. 331–40.

17. Heaton, *op. cit.*, p. 531, on which this account of German railway development is largely based.

18. See Melvin M. Knight, Harry Elmer Barnes and Felix Flügel, *Economic History of Europe*, Houghton Mifflin, Boston, 1928, p. 529.

19. See Bowden, Karpovich and Usher, *op. cit.*, pp. 470–71.

The important steps in development had been taken before 1864, however, with establishment of the Zollverein, removal of restrictions on choice of occupation, agricultural improvements, a start on railway construction, and the formulation of a government policy designed to stimulate and promote industry in many directions.[20] How important these positive efforts of the government directly to promote economic development were, in comparison with the significant emphasis on general and scientific education, is a matter of dispute. J. B. Condliffe, for example, has insisted that the fact that Germany provided "both general and technical education for the masses of the people, earlier and more adequately than did the governments of other countries," was more important in her industrial development than state aid and tariff protection.[21] In any case the combination appears to have been notably effective.

## *French Efforts at Industrialization*

The course of French economic progress outside agriculture after 1815 has features that puzzle anyone interested in development problems and policy. France is said to have been the leading industrial nation of Europe just before the 1789 revolution[22] and certainly many changes occurred between 1789 and 1815 which would seem to have been helpful to industry. Yet neither in comparison with the pace of development elsewhere nor in terms of relative efficiency in particular industries were France's industrial achievements down to 1850 impressive. In very general terms, and apart from the Revolution itself and its aftermath, the explanation may, perhaps, be a combination of the following factors: the humiliation of Waterloo; the severance of Belgium from France; the delay in commercialization of agriculture until after the construction of railways; a protectionism which tended to guard what already existed rather than to foster the new and promising; a dearth of aggressive entrepreneurs; and last, a national economic policy that wavered between conciliating conflicting sectional interests and trying to restore France's former greatness by giving her a strong industrial economy. These features were of varying importance in the several segments of the French economy outside agriculture; their interaction seems to have been responsible for the end result. A few illustrations

20. Friedrich List played an active part in the formulation of ideas bearing on the industrial development of Germany. He argued strongly in favor of the protectionist policy for German industry until it could compete on even terms with English industry. His American sojourn impressed upon him the great importance of good transport, especially railways, and he pressed vigorously for railway construction in Germany and mapped out many of the routes. Perhaps most important of all, he emphasized, as against the Manchester school of economists, the powerful role which wise government policy could play in accelerating sound economic development.

21. J. B. Condliffe, *The Commerce of Nations*, Norton, New York, 1950, p. 280; the argument is developed in *ibid.*, pp. 273–81.

22. See Bowden, Karpovich and Usher, *op. cit.*, pp. 477*ff.*

drawn from industry and transport lend support to these broad generalizations.

## Examples of French Policy

In textiles—wool, linen and silk—there had been a long tradition, dating from the time of Colbert, of rules and restrictions to promote stability and discourage innovation. But the new English processes and techniques were primarily in cottons, which afforded a cheaper product with a potential mass market. France had the choice of shifting over to cottons or protecting the textile industries she had already established. She chose to bolster what she had by imposing virtually prohibitive duties on imported textiles.

In iron manufactures, France, with no shortage of charcoal as in England, found no immediate need, for domestic reasons, to go over to the newer techniques which used coal. But the iron manufacturers demanded and got highly protective import duties against the cheaper English products. When the railways had to be built, the French iron industry was not equipped to supply the necessary rolled products and large castings. Again, protection did not promote technical progress, but merely preserved outmoded practices in established industry.

France also lagged behind her neighbors in coal production. In 1840, Great Britain produced ten times as much coal as France and both Belgium and Prussia produced more than France's 3 million tons.[23] Doubtless French coal production would have moved ahead more rapidly if France had not lost Belgium in 1815. However, the Belgian deposits in the Valenciennes field were extensively developed long before the French deposits—though, allegedly, the exploitation of the deposits on the French side of the border encountered certain technical obstacles not present on the Belgian side.

## French Railways

The industrial progress of France quickened with the coming of the railways, but they, too, were delayed in comparison with those of other countries. Partly, this seems to have been because French roads were better than most European roads and because France had done much to improve river navigation and canals. But there was another reason. Heaton puts it this way: "As ministries changed frequently, policy changed abruptly, and meanwhile the bureaucrats who were in charge of inland transportation were skeptics, quick to see problems and difficulties but slow to find solutions."[24]

23. Bowden, Karpovich and Usher, *op. cit.*, p. 451. The paragraphs immediately preceding have drawn heavily from Chapter 22 of this work.

24. Heaton, *op. cit.*, p. 529.

The Liverpool-Manchester railway was opened in 1830; yet only in 1842 did France pass an "organic law" for railways.[25] Although some lines of a few miles had been built earlier—for example, from Lyon to St. Étienne— the first important line was the Paris-Rouen railway, which was opened in 1843 and was extended to Le Havre in 1846. But this line was conceived, financed and built by Englishmen.[26] Despite the speculative aura which surrounded the undertaking, other lines might have been built with English capital had not the revolution of 1848 brought such schemes to an abrupt halt. As matters worked out, the basic plan of the 1842 law—which combined public and private enterprise in construction and finance with the principle of regional monopolies—was the policy actually followed. After 1850, French railway construction went ahead rapidly until a crisis developed in 1857. The financial difficulties then besetting the companies led the French government in 1859 to make new agreements with the companies, by which they were guaranteed interest charges on new construction costs, so that the railway network contemplated in the 1842 law could be constructed. By 1870, most of the principal lines of the French railway network were completed.[27]

### Industrialization Elsewhere in Europe

If space permitted, it would be useful to trace the economic development of the rest of Europe. Yet, apart from Belgium, which forged ahead rapidly after it was transferred from French to Dutch control in 1815 and even more rapidly after it became independent in 1830, these other European countries generally did not develop industrially until after 1870.

Belgium, after being joined with Holland, was fortunate in having Dutch capital and enterprise flow into manufacturing and commerce. Linens, cottons, woolens, leather, hardware and coal were among the important exports. After gaining her independence, Belgium began to build railways rapidly according to a plan formulated as early as 1834. Some of these were constructed and partly financed by English firms. At the same time, she used her roads and canals to serve western Germany and central Europe

25. Although there were proposals for railways in France as early as 1835, and others before 1842, the projects bogged down in debate over the issue of state ownership. The 1842 law was comprehensive and provided for a joint effort by the state and private companies: the state was to acquire the land and to construct the roadbed, together with tunnels and bridges; the companies were to provide the rolling stock, operate the trackage on a lease from the government and manage the undertaking. A later law of 1845, granting the charter for a line from Paris to Belgium, spelled out these policies in detail and became the pattern for later charters. See Bowden, Karpovich and Usher, *op. cit.*, pp. 528 *ff.*

26. For an account of this venture and subsequent efforts of British financiers in French railway construction see Leland Hamilton Jenks, *The Migration of British Capital to 1875*, Knopf, New York, 1927, pp. 140 *ff.*

27. On the financial side the principles of the law of 1842, and the further state assistance provided by the 1859 agreements, did not work out satisfactorily for the French government. After 1870 the state had to build lines at its own expense to round out the system, and in 1883 the state undertook to guarantee a return to bondholders and shareholders. In 1938 the government nationalized the system. See Heaton, *op. cit.*, p. 529.

commercially. In cotton textiles, Belgium early adopted English methods. To find out just why Belgium spurted ahead as it did after 1815 would require more analysis than is possible here. However, the presence of a powerful entrepreneurial class in a small country with relatively superior transport facilities, combined with enlightened government policy, appears to have had much to do with the country's rapid development.[28]

Each country possessed its own special characteristics—geographical, political and historical—and these helped shape its economic development. Generally speaking, modernization and industrialization came sooner to European countries that were close to the centers of development than to those that were more remote. Scandinavia, for example, went ahead more rapidly than did the Balkan portion of Austria-Hungary. Italy could make little progress until it was unified and better governed. Even then it was handicapped, as were other countries, by having no coal and iron. The Iberian peninsula remains economically backward even today. Yet, geographical remoteness or lack of coal and iron do not wholly explain the levels of economic achievement attained in the various European countries by, say, 1900. Past history, public policy, the "character" of the people, chance factors and much else appear to play a part in the development process.

Perhaps no single factor has been more important in breaking down isolation and planting the seeds of economic change than improvements in transport and communication. The effects of such improvements are so pervasive and their influence so fundamental that it is not easy to exaggerate their importance. Consequently, one way of getting a quick impression of the advances in the European economy during the last half of the nineteenth century is to compare railway maps of Europe in 1848 and in 1877.[29] (See Figure 4.) The results in terms of industrial production in France and Germany are shown graphically in Figure 5.

28. For a brief account of Belgian economic development after 1815 see Knight, Barnes and Flügel, *op. cit.*, pp. 673–76.

29. For those who find statistical tabulations easier to interpret than maps, the following figures may be useful:

*Railway Mileage*

|                   | 1840  | 1860   | 1880    |
|-------------------|-------|--------|---------|
| United Kingdom    | 840   | 10,430 | 17,930  |
| France            | 260   | 5,860  | 16,260  |
| Prussia           | 290   | 6,890  | 20,750  |
| Austria-Hungary   | 290   | 3,200  | 11,470  |
| European Russia   | 20    | 990    | 14,820  |
| Rest of Europe    | 230   | 4,870  | 23,350  |
| Total Europe      | 1,930 | 32,240 | 104,580 |
| United States     | 3,320 | 30,590 | 90,560  |

Adapted from Melvin M. Knight, *Introduction to Modern Economic History* (processed), Berkeley, 1940, p. 140.

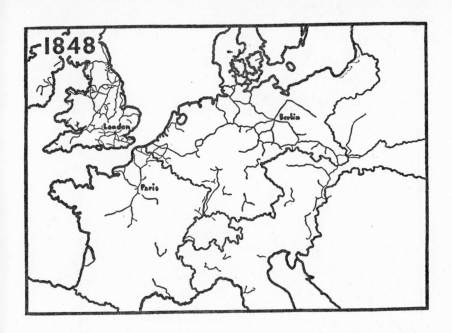

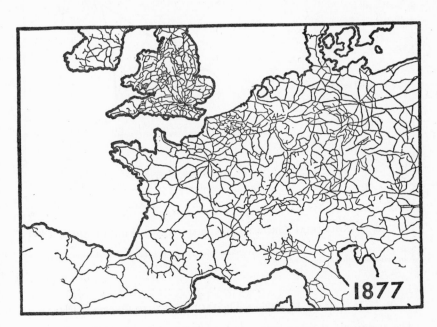

FIGURE 4. EUROPE'S RAILWAY NETWORK, 1848 AND 1877

Source: Varian Fry, *Bricks without Mortar* (Headline Series), Foreign Policy Association, 1938.

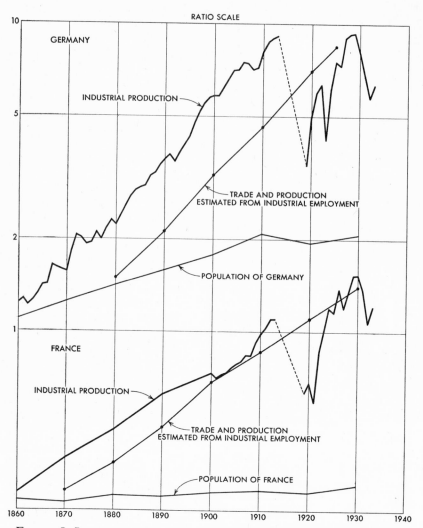

FIGURE 5. INDUSTRIAL GROWTH IN GERMANY AND FRANCE AFTER 1860

*Source:* Carl Snyder, "Measures of Industrial Growth and Their Significance," in *Beiträge zur Konjunkturlehre,* Hanseatische Verlagsanstalt, 1936.

## THE EXTENSION OF EUROPEAN DEVELOPMENT INTO OVERSEAS AREAS

The economic developments in England and Western Europe in the nineteenth century were accompanied by a remarkable growth in the economic relations of these countries with the rest of the world. This is not to play down the importance of overseas commerce by the English, Dutch, French, Spanish and Portuguese in the sixteenth, seventeenth and eighteenth centuries. But the twentyfold increase in the value of world trade between 1815 and 1914 was something unique. The new situation gave meaning to the term "world economy"—the phrase commonly used to describe it after its disintegration was far advanced. The main features of the development are so well known that attention need be given here to only one or two aspects of this "reaching out" of the developing European economy to less developed areas.

Technical progress was of fundamental importance to this expansion. The growing intimacy and variety of the economic relations between Europe and the outside world would have been quite impossible without the improvements in transport and communication achieved during the nineteenth century. Improved sailing vessels and the steamship dramatically cut the costs, time and risks of moving cargoes and passengers by sea. These advances in sea transport would have been much less far-reaching, however, if there had not also been improvements in port facilities and in land transport by railway and canal. The Argentine pampas and the plains of Kansas were no better suited climatically for wheat production in 1880 than they were in 1750; but by the late nineteenth century their wheat could be brought to Manchester or to Frankfurt at a cost that made it salable.

*Investment and Migration Abroad*

To achieve this result, the European economy, and Britain especially, had to invest heavily in transport and ancillary facilities in the overseas areas. The people of these areas lacked either the financial resources or the technical skills, or both, to develop transport and communication. The capital and technical assistance could come only from the more economically advanced European countries. As one writer has described it, "Everywhere it was the same story of the rail pushing over ground hitherto trodden only by hunters, explorers and nomadic savages, and carrying labour and capital to the exploitation of corn lands and pasture lands, wealth-yielding forests, and mining areas previously unworkable."[30] In all this, England, the first country to develop industrially, took the lead.[31] Her victory in the war against Napoleon "confirmed and extended the earlier imperial victories. Britain emerged with a special set of trade relations with India and most of the Western Hemisphere that were virtually monopolistic in their effect."[32]

30. James A. Williamson, *A Short History of British Expansion*, 2d edition, Vol. II, Macmillan, London, 1930, p. 167.

31. See Chapter 7, pp. 143–46.

32. W. W. Rostow, *The Process of Economic Growth*, Norton, New York, 1952, p. 159.

It would be wrong to suppose that these achievements were made possible by the mere investment of profit-seeking funds on private account. It took also a vast migration of people and the active, frequently forcible, intervention of the authority of the European nation-states.[33] Without both these factors the private capital doubtless would never have been committed or, if it had been, it would frequently have failed to achieve its purpose.

### Government Aid to Overseas Expansion

The role of European governments in the nineteenth century in opening up non-European areas and initiating changes in the use of their particular economic resources is a large subject.[34] To some people, the whole story is one of sordid exploitation of subject peoples, summed up in the scornful epithet "imperialism." To others, it is the record of how the miserable lot of most of mankind was made less wretched than before. Regardless of which of the many shades of these two opposing views one accepts, European governments undeniably played an indispensable role in making private investments both possible and productive in these overseas areas.

This role was apparently dual. On the one hand, the authority of these governments made entry into overseas areas possible and assured personal protection to their nationals in their economic pursuits. On the other, government funds supplied whatever capital was necessary as "social overhead," either to make the area habitable for Europeans or to assure the productivity of investments in mines, plantations, warehouses and other enterprises.

In the early stages, the contribution of government was preponderantly that of opening the way and establishing a semblance of internal order. Later on, the costs of health services, public works, public administration, etc., became more important. The essential point is that these were necessary outlays, for without them the private investments which did so much directly to bring about the astounding growth of production and trade in the nineteenth century would have been largely abortive. If they were often

33. Humanitarian sentiment and the missionary movement played an important part, especially after the ate eighteenth century. A hatred of oppression and a sense of duty to people less economically and politically developed were sincerely felt by men like William Wilberforce, who agitated for the abolition of the slave trade before the French Revolution broke out in 1789. The London Missionary Society was formed in 1795.

34. Many important non-European areas came under European influence only in the nineteenth century. In 1785 British rule in India was largely confined to Bengal and some hinterland of the ports of Bombay and Madras. British rule did not become fairly extensive until 1850 and it was threatened by revolt in 1857. Singapore came under British control in 1824. Although the British had traded with China at Canton in the late seventeenth century, the notorious "treaty ports" with their extraterritorial privileges for Europeans were opened only in 1842. Japan's connection with the West came mostly after 1860. France completed its efforts to control Cochin-China only in 1868.

If one remembers that the Monroe Doctrine was given formal expression only in 1823, that the partition of Africa by the European powers occurred after 1870, and that the Suez Canal was opened in 1869, one begins to realize how much of the world's surface came under European influence during the nineteenth century. For a fascinating account of the growth of the British Empire over the globe see Williamson, *op. cit.*

made as much in the vainglory of empire building as from a calculation of their prospective over-all economic returns, that is immaterial. They had to be made if the area was to have any economic significance. They were, in fact, made as public, not private, commitments. One of the most crucial problems in many underdeveloped areas today is how to finance the large capital investments in "social overhead" requisite to the achievement of their economic aspirations, now that the metropolitan powers have withdrawn.

*Migration of People*

Probably as important as the overseas investment of European public and private capital in bringing the outlying regions into a world economy centered in Western Europe was the actual migration of many Europeans to these regions. These people brought the technical knowledge and specialized skills that gave the investment funds their productivity potential. To be sure, the outsiders frequently assumed privileges that still rankle; but their services were indispensable to the growth of production and the flow of trade in these areas. The search for an alternative means of providing comparable specialized abilities in the underdeveloped areas continues today, notwithstanding technical assistance programs.

Thus the extension of the European economy into overseas areas in the nineteenth century involved more than the obvious and important growth of commerce and trade. This was the result. Beneath this obvious achievement lay a complex and shifting pattern of combined private and public investment in far-off places to which European specialists migrated in large numbers. That the whole episode benefited the average Western European is undeniable. As for the others at the fringes of the trade network—the people in those regions that now constitute some of the most important underdeveloped areas—there is room for question.

## CONCLUDING OBSERVATIONS ON EUROPEAN DEVELOPMENT

The course of economic progress in France and Germany—after England had pointed the way—is illuminating for the whole problem of economic development. The experience of the two countries suggests the difference between creating an environment which, in a negative sense, is conducive to development because it is relatively free from hampering restrictions and positively interjecting into such an environment factors which directly effectuate progress even though people in general are content to let well enough alone.[35]

35. While the present work is in press there comes to hand a valuable new study: W. O. Henderson, *Britain and Industrial Europe, 1750–1870*, University Press, Liverpool, 1954. Henderson stresses and vividly illustrates, by numerous specific examples, how large a role British entrepreneurs and skilled workmen played in Western European economic development in its early stages. This fact, we think, could have been more stressed in the text above than it was.

For example, both French agriculture after 1800 and Prussian agriculture after 1821 were no longer checked by confining regulations. But a peasantry freed from its shackles does not at once leap forward to adopt new techniques or to devise novel methods: more often than not, the peasant's attitude is one of husbandry and caution frosted over with rote and tradition. Rapid progress requires a catalyst. In Germany, the combination of entrepreneurially minded landlords and the introduction of such new crops as sugar beets and potatoes initiated an agricultural revolution, even though it also made hired laborers out of many peasants by making them landless. As improved transport opened wider markets at home and abroad, these agricultural changes picked up momentum and extended their scope. France apparently lacked an entrepreneurial class of comparable vigor, with the result that, even though the restrictions were removed earlier than in Germany, the farming methods and types of crops in French agriculture changed very little. Only with the coming of the railways in the 1850s and later did the peasant cultivators appreciably change their practices. The railways upset price relationships because they widened markets and thereby extended the area of competition. The peasants had change and improvement forced upon them. The evidence suggests, therefore, that merely abolishing hampering restrictions in a peasant economy will not in itself much affect agricultural practice or productivity.

## Stimulus of New Crops and Products

It would seem also that in both agriculture and industry, technical progress moves more rapidly with "new" crops, with products using "new" raw materials, and in "new" environments in the broadest sense. Well-established industries or crops long cultivated tend to impede progress because the people who labor in them gradually build up a complex of institutionalized practices, traditional beliefs and self-protective behavior patterns which repel innovation and resist change. It is a striking fact that in textiles the important technical advances and price declines came not in woolens or linens—traditionally important industries in England, France and Germany for centuries past—but in cottons, a minor industry using an imported raw material. Similarly, discovering the best way to cultivate sugar beets or potatoes could be considered as a practical problem in ways and means uncomplicated by pre-existing folklore.

The development process is also likely to proceed more rapidly if new groups can assume control, either through the entrance of migrants from outside the region or through shifts in economic or political power. The new bourgeoisie in France, for example, who acquired much of the land confiscated from the nobles, were scarcely more "market conscious" in their attitude toward their absentee holdings than the courtiers of Louis XVI from whom the lands had been taken. Thus agricultural progress lagged in France until after the railroads came and forced changes.

### Role of Government

The role of the state in stimulating and guiding economic progress, as exemplified by Germany and France in the first half of the nineteenth century, is decidedly varied. Certainly good will and good intentions are not enough. The Zollverein and railway development together apparently did much to forward economic development in Germany. Protectionism in France, however, seems to have fostered no new industries, but merely sheltered vested interests against the superior efficiency of industry abroad. In retrospect, this protectionism appears to have served as a delaying action in circumstances where delay was exceedingly costly in the longer run. Perhaps, also, France and Germany illustrate the pervasive and profound effectiveness of improved transport and communication in destroying isolationism and spreading new ideas and practices by making possible a national price system which links all of the parts of the economy together. Goods move. Ideas spread about. People migrate. And these factors combine to lift the level of economic achievement and keep it moving upward. Consequently, if it appears that no private groups are likely to modernize transport and communications—as they did in England, for example—then perhaps a wise government, intent upon developing the national economy, should concentrate first on transport and communications.

These impressions are offered in a tentative fashion. Drawing "lessons" from history is fraught with the danger of self-delusion, but the pastime will probably never lose its fascination since man is constantly forced to make choices between alternative policies affecting his uncertain future.

### Importance of Overseas Areas

How important the access to overseas areas was in the economic development of Western Europe is not easy to decide. Certainly, without the remarkable technical improvements in transport and ancillary facilities it would have been impossible for the raw materials and supplies from overseas to have been furnished to the expanding economies in Western Europe. Cotton textiles—in which so much early industrialization centered—depended on a raw material which was not produced in Europe. But it was not enough merely to "get in touch" with these distant areas; this had indeed already happened in the seventeenth century. Before raw material supplies could be drawn from them much capital had to be invested on private and public account and many people with the requisite technical and organizational skills had to migrate abroad. Capital and technical assistance came from without, and here the role of governments appears to have been much larger than casual observation might suggest. Whether these ventures into overseas areas "paid," in the sense that they yielded net returns to the metropolitan economies from which they came, is an open question. But at least the gross returns from overseas areas contributed appreciably to economic development in Western Europe and often gave particular national economies much of their individual form and content.

The foregoing discussion has no more than sketched the early stages of the development process in England and Western Europe, a limited geographical area. Yet it was the kind of process that seems to have been repeated, though not without important differences, by most of the countries that modernized their economies in the nineteenth century on the principles of the price system and predominantly private initiative. Japan and the U.S.S.R. have since joined the list of industrialized countries by converting their economies from a primarily agricultural base to one resting heavily on industry. Their development, however, followed different patterns, which now need to be examined.

# 9. The Economic Development of Japan: 1868-1914

JAPAN AND THE U.S.S.R. ARE OUTSTANDING examples of countries that have deliberately converted their economies from a predominantly agricultural base to a heavily industrial one. Because it has occurred so recently, the economic development of these two countries may throw more light on the problems of the underdeveloped areas than the earlier experiences of England and Western Europe.

Japan's drive toward industrialization did not get under way until after the middle of the nineteenth century. Historians usually divide Japanese history into three periods. The first is the period of autocracy from 660 B.C. to A.D. 1192. The second is the period of "feudalism" from 1192 to 1868. The latter part of the second period is frequently referred to as Tokugawa feudalism, after the Tokugawa family, which was the ruling feudal family from the beginning of the seventeenth century until 1868. The head of this family exercised full governing authority as the shogun, while the emperor lived in seclusion in Kyoto, apparently occupied officially with religious concerns. The third or "modern" period dates from the restoration of the emperor's power in 1868, known as the Meiji restoration.

Until Commodore Perry reached Japan in 1853 the country had been virtually isolated from the outside world for many centuries. The Portuguese are said to have introduced "tobacco, firearms and Christianity in its Roman Catholic form" in 1543, but they were excluded in 1638 because of their alleged complicity in an attempted revolution. The Dutch were licensed to trade with Japan in 1605 and thereafter maintained for a time a precarious trade monopoly. When Perry came in 1853 a representative of the shogun called upon him, though not without great reluctance. Perry's arrival marks the beginning of Western pressure upon Japan and the consequent internal turmoil which was climaxed by the shogun's formal surrender of power to the emperor. This consolidation of authority was, in effect, a restoration of the Meiji.[1]

It was with the Meiji restoration in 1868 that Japan began to develop economically. Understandably enough, not all scholars are agreed upon the relative importance of the factors involved in Japan's dramatic rise to industrial eminence, or upon the real costs of this rise for Japan and the world. Despite their differences, all authorities agree that in the forty-five

1. See Ernest Wilson Clement, *A Short History of Japan*, University of Chicago Press, Chicago, 1915, pp. 60 and 94*ff.*

years preceding 1914, Japan was transformed from a secluded preindustrial society into an industrialized nation-state commanding universal economic and political respect. E. Herbert Norman has described the transition in this way:

Japan skipped from feudalism into capitalism omitting the *laissez-faire* stage and its political counterpart, Victorian liberalism . . . [Her leaders] were so far in advance of the rest of their countrymen that they had to drag a complaining, half-awakened nation of merchants and peasants after them. The autocratic or paternalistic way seemed to the Meiji leaders the only possible method if Japan was not to sink into the ranks of a colonial country.[2]

The rapidity of Japan's economic transformation is seen at once in a few production indices. With the years 1921–1925 taken as 100, the index of primary production jumped from 15.7 in 1873 to 52.1 in 1900, and that of mineral production from 1.03 in 1874 to 28.15 in 1900. Rice output rose from 119.1 million bushels in 1873 to 205.6 million in 1900; in the same period the output of silk increased more than sixfold and the output of cotton yarn four hundred and thirty times. Railway mileage increased from only 18 miles in 1872 to 3,855 miles in 1900, while steamship tonnage grew from 15,500 tons in 1870 to 543,400 tons in 1900. Pig iron production increased sevenfold between 1874 and 1900 and the number of factories increased from 24 to 662 between 1868 and 1900.[3] These achievements appear all the more remarkable when it is considered that Japan's economic position in the eighteenth century probably compared unfavorably with England's in the sixteenth.[4]

The restoration of the Meiji in itself was of course not sufficient to put Japan on the road to economic progress.[5] It was the way in which this consolidation of power was applied that pointed the Japanese economy in a new direction. For purposes of discussion, it seems convenient to disentangle those changes that were essentially a sweeping away of outmoded forms, practices and institutions from those more positive changes that clearly promoted economic development. The second type of change is impossible without the first; the dead timber must be cleared out to make way for the new growth. But merely clearing away the clutter of the past does not produce development automatically. The postrestoration leaders of Japan seem to have been fully aware of this.

2. E. Herbert Norman, *Japan's Emergence as a Modern State,* Institute of Pacific Relations, New York, 1946, p. 47. This remarkably informative account of the development of modern Japan has used Japanese sources extensively. It contains also (pp. 211–22) an annotated bibliography of the principal works on the subject which the nonspecialist will find invaluable.

3. All figures are from Shigeto Tsuru, "Economic Fluctuations in Japan, 1863–1893," *Review of Economic Statistics,* November 1941, p. 187.

4. Norman, *op. cit.,* commenting on a comparison made by John E. Orchard.

5. The seeds of change were already germinating in the late Tokugawa period, so that "the Meiji Restoration was bound to come sooner or later, and the invasion on the part of foreign capitalism decisively accelerated its advent." Yasuzo Horie, "The Economic Significance of the Meiji Restoration," *Kyoto University Economic Review,* December 1937, p. 70.

### CLEARING THE GROUND FOR ECONOMIC DEVELOPMENT

By 1853, Japanese leaders realized that Japan would fall under the domination of one or more of the European powers unless she quickly acquired economic and military strength. This, rather than social reform for its own sake or the welfare of the people, was what motivated the new Japanese government after 1868. The leaders in the modernization of Japan, the samurai-bureaucrats, feared foreign encroachment above all else. They were therefore determined to "modernize" Japanese social and economic organization rapidly from above.[6]

In the economic sphere, the most far-reaching changes that were made were those intended to establish a competitive, market-type economy based on principles of private property. As one Japanese writer reports,

. . . under the category of the recognition of free competition fall the abolition of the system of *Kabunakama* (a guild system authorized by the Shogunate or by the feudal lords) in commerce and industry, in the first year of Meiji (1868) and the recognition of the freedom of occupation for four classes (samurai, farmers, craftsmen, and chonin) of people, in the fourth and fifth years of Meiji . . . the embargo on the permanent sales of land was lifted . . . restrictions on *Bunchi* (division of land among sons and daughters) were removed . . . Besides, the operation of commerce by prefectures or clans, which had been impeding the development of the commercial interests of merchants, was prohibited.[7]

### Land Titles and Taxes

In the middle of the nineteenth century the Japanese peasant typically cultivated rice on land which, by custom and long practice, was his to work as he saw fit subject to the superior rights of the warrior or samurai class. The Japanese "manor" of 1853 has been described as

an untidy conglomeration of irregular plots which, as far as the cultivated parts were concerned, were perpetually left under the individual possession and the personal exploitation of their holders. Subject only to the dues which he owed, the tenant enjoyed large freedom in the disposition of his plots and their profits, so that the communal life of the domain as a whole was extremely tenuous.[8]

Japanese agriculture had for centuries been characterized by small family plots intensively cultivated. There was no open-field system as in Europe and very little livestock. There were, however, common rights in forests and

6. See Norman, *op. cit.*, Chapter 3 and *passim*.

7. Horie, *loc. cit.*, p. 77. The samurai were the feudal warriors or knights, also called bushi; the chonin were originally commoners but during the Tokugawa period (and later) the term was applied to the merchant class. The feudal-type lords ranking above the knights (samurai) were the daimyo. For an account of agrarian organization in relation to the foregoing see Thomas C. Smith, "The Japanese Village in the Seventeenth Century," *Journal of Economic History*, Winter 1952, pp. 1–20.

8. K. Hsakawa, "Agriculture in Japanese History: a General Survey," *The Economic History Review*, January 1929, p. 87.

fishing grounds. The samurai tended to live in towns and not on the land, from which they collected revenues in kind.

In 1872 the ban on the sale of land was lifted and in 1873 a new land tax law was passed. This law substituted a money tax, based on the value of the land, for tax payments in kind, which were a customary fraction of the crops harvested. After the passage of the new tax law, the government undertook a land survey to assess land values. These assessments were based on the capitalization of the five-year average value of the product.[9] By making the owner of the land liable to the national central government for tax payments and by divorcing the amount of the tax from the yearly vagaries of the harvest, the state both blocked evasion and assured itself of a steady stream of tax revenues. Indeed, down to 1882, about 80 per cent of the government's revenue came from this land tax.

*Results of the New Land Laws*

Merely to require land titles and to impose a money tax calculated on assessed land values and payable to the central government—rather than let the cultivator render a portion of the harvest to the local overlord— would not, at first glance, be expected to initiate important changes or have profound consequences. Yet major changes followed. Moreover, the effectiveness of these changes, from the point of view of development, lay not in any increase in the tax levy, which was actually diminished slightly, but in the fact that they tended to commercialize agriculture.

This occurred in three ways. First, in requiring that land ownership be formalized by possession of legally recognized title certificates, the government gave force to the concept of private property in land. As might be expected, the process also caused many small cultivators to be, in effect, dispossessed because they could not establish their rights to title certificates. Tenancy therefore increased as the lands of some of the smaller cultivators passed legally out of their hands.[10] Second, the necessity of paying a fixed money tax, regardless of the size of the harvest, forced many farmers to borrow from moneylenders against their title certificates. When they failed to repay the debt they lost their land. Finally, the whole arrangement tended to force the cultivators to market their crops promptly for cash, so that they might pay the government or the landlords the amounts due them.

Thus an increasing commercialization of agriculture and growing tenancy seem to have been the net effects of the new land laws. This transformation did not come about overnight; but between 1873 and 1890 both

9. See Norman, *op. cit.*, pp. 138–44, on which the above draws heavily.

10. Some of the land formerly held in common in the rural areas was taken over by the central government and later (after 1876) sold to former feudal lords (daimyo) at attractive prices. See Norman, *op. cit.*, p. 99.

tenancy and commercialization of agriculture increased appreciably. Dispossession of the peasants did not lead to any increase in the unit of cultivation, however. This had long been small and remained so.[11]

## Effects of Commercialization of Agriculture

It is not at all clear how far the leaders of the new Japan foresaw that commercialized agriculture would follow from the changes they imposed for the purpose of increasing the power of the central government by assuring it a steady flow of tax revenues. According to Norman's account, action was taken only "After a patient, exhaustive review of all relevant memoranda, and after many deliberations of committees and assemblies."[12] The revenue aspect of the change seems to have been the primary consideration, however. Whatever the leaders' intentions, Japanese agriculture was able both to increase rice production by about 40 per cent between 1879 and 1903—just about enough to match the increase in population —and, through the migration of second and third children to cities, to provide labor for industry.[13] In addition, the agricultural areas became increasingly important suppliers of manufactures produced in the rural households.

In 1873, five years after the Meiji restoration, about 78 per cent of the employed Japanese population were engaged in agriculture. (Prior to the restoration the percentage was probably slightly larger.) By 1876 the proportion had decreased only slightly to 77 per cent, but it was down to 52 per cent by 1920. On the other hand, artisans and those engaged in commerce, who constituted about 11 per cent of the employed population in 1873 and 1876, jointly made up a much larger bloc of 32 per cent in 1920.[14]

Despite changes in forms of land tenure, agricultural practices continued much as before though cultivation increased in intensity and was extended to lands not previously worked. G. C. Allen puts the amount of new riceland brought under cultivation in the thirty years 1878–1908 at 343,000

11. See *ibid.*, pp. 144–48 and 153*ff.*

12. *Ibid.*, p. 140.

13. See G. C. Allen, *A Short Economic History of Modern Japan, 1868–1937*, Allen and Unwin, London, 1946, Tables, pp. 58 and 163. The connection between domestic consumption of rice and population growth is made closer by the fact that Japanese rice is apparently not acceptable as an export commodity and the Japanese regard foreign rice as a substitute for barley or wheat but *not* for rice. Cf. Tokutaro Yamanaka, "Japanese Small Industries during the Industrial Revolution," *Annals of the Hitotsubashi Academy*, October 1951, p. 33 and *passim*. For a "corrected" population Elizabeth Schumpeter finds a 43 per cent increase in Japan from 1871 to 1911, and one of 60 per cent for England and Wales. Hence, after the Meiji restoration, the Japanese population rose above the plateau which had existed from 1721 to 1846; but Japan did not overtake the English-Welsh rate of increase until 1911. See E. B. Schumpeter *et al.*, *The Industrialization of Japan and Manchukuo*, Macmillan, New York, 1940, pp. 49 and 53.

14. These figures are roughly adapted from Schumpeter, *op. cit.*, p. 64, n. 37, and Table 6, p. 76. The classification "artisans" was used in the earlier years and this was changed in 1920 to "manufacturing." Clearly the groups are not the same, but they roughly represent the nonagriculturally occupied.

cho (840,000 acres). Although the age-old method of rice production may not lend itself to further development,[15] Allen indicates an increase in production per cho from 11.6 koku to 17.0 koku from the "early eighties to . . . the years just before the Great War."[16]

Japanese agriculture did not undergo a revolution after the Meiji restoration: the economic position of the farmer remained practically unchanged; he still had to work hard to meet his taxes and provide a meager living for his family. The environment in which he worked altered, of course, chiefly in that he was increasingly exposed to the exigencies of the market and to the spreading system of private property and free contract. But, by preserving stability and maintaining output, all this facilitated rather than hampered economic development. Moreover, if the landlord-tenant relationships shifted income distributions and tax burdens in a way contrary to modern notions of "social justice," they also limited consumption in favor of investment. From a broader point of view, the truly remarkable fact was that a new government was able to impose drastic social and economic changes from above without throwing the country into hopeless confusion or economic collapse.

### Other Important Changes

Apart from the changes in agriculture, the samurai-bureaucrats who came to power with the Meiji restoration also cleared the way for economic development by abolishing the feudal tariffs and tolls on internal trade and commerce, by granting freedom of occupation, domicile or trade, and by lifting the bans on dealings with the outside world. These steps were important because they cleared away the debris that blocked initiative and enterprise and hampered the internal mobility of economic resources that is so necessary to specialization and greater productivity. As might be expected, the merchant class were the first ones to benefit from these new freedoms.

In setting the stage for more positive measures designed to promote economic development, the leaders of the new Japan displayed remarkable skill as policy-makers and administrators. There was no social upheaval comparable to the French Revolution. The government's policies were of course not entirely unopposed, but by autocratic measures and skillful political maneuvering the government succeeded in keeping its critics from seriously interfering with its plans, although it had to use force to put down some revolts in 1882–1884.[17]

15. See Yamanaka, *loc. cit.*
16. Allen, *op. cit.*, p. 57. (One koku is approximately 5.12 American bushels.)
17. See Norman, *op. cit.*, Chapter 5.

### POSITIVE MEASURES FOR ECONOMIC DEVELOPMENT

As already pointed out, the dominant drive in the economic modernization of Japan came from the fear of the samurai-bureaucrats that Japan, like China, might fall under the domination of a foreign power. The reshaping of the Japanese economy according to the principles of private property and free enterprise came about not because the leaders in the Meiji restoration were fired by the principles of the French Revolution or the liberalism of John Stuart Mill, but because they believed that, with proper guidance from the top, economic liberalism offered the most effective means of quickly building the military strength necessary to assure political security. As G. C. Allen has expressed it, the government's function was

. . . to set up certain economic objectives and to assist private enterprise to attain them. In other words, its aim has been to create the conditions which should lead the entrepreneur to direct and organize the economic resources of the country in the way believed to be desirable.[18]

The samurai-bureaucrats saw that a modernized economy could not be created merely by sweeping away feudal restrictions and replacing them with the principles of personal freedom, private property and free contract. Problems still remained, which they believed required positive action on the part of the government. There was no entrepreneurial class at hand with the drive and the investible capital resources necessary to launch a commercial and industrial revolution. Moreover, at the time of the restoration there were no financial institutions that could be expected to foster real capital formation and allocate it wisely in modernizing the economy. Finally, Japan would have to have capital equipment and technical assistance from abroad. Therefore, she needed imports, which would have to be paid for by exports. But her people, long isolated from the rest of the world, could not be expected to develop a vigorous foreign trade without guidance and assistance from her new leaders. In brief, the government believed it had to perform entrepreneurial functions, to foster capital formation and to fit Japan into the growing network of international trade and finance.[19] Although closely linked, these were three distinct areas in which the government felt it had to take positive action if it was to achieve political security through rapid development of the economy.

### Government Action to Develop Industry

The government used both direct and indirect means in attacking the problems of entrepreneurship and capital mobilization and allocation. On

18. G. C. Allen, "The Last Decade in Japan," *Economic History*, January 1933, p. 629.
19. See *ibid.*, pp. 629–34.

the one hand, the state itself at times acted as entrepreneur and capital supplier; on the other hand—and perhaps this was more important in generating a self-sustaining economic development—the state encouraged and fostered private enterprise and investment.

Directly following the Meiji restoration the government took the lead in developing industry.[20] It saw that, at least in the beginning, private groups would not build railways and telegraph lines or factories to manufacture wholly unfamiliar products even though these might be necessary to assure Japan's political independence. Consequently the government established railways and telegraph systems, constructed pilot plants or demonstration plants and saw to it that foreign experts and technicians were brought to Japan so that the people might learn. By 1880, government properties are said to have included "3 shipbuilding yards, 51 merchant ships, 5 munition works, 52 other factories, 10 mines, 75 miles of railways, and a telegraph system which linked all the chief towns."[21]

Even in 1880, however, shipping, telegraph systems, railways and munitions were widely regarded as undertakings appropriate to government, either on the grounds of strategic necessity or because the important indirect benefits that they conferred were so diffused that no private entrepreneur could turn them into collectible revenues. In other words, much of the state enterprise in Japan up to this time was in undertakings already sponsored by the state in other countries.[22] The rest were mainly manufacturing plants constructed at government expense to show what was possible. Following a change in policy in 1880, most of these were turned over to private firms, often, to be sure, at attractive prices. By then, however, industrial progress had picked up enough momentum from the government's efforts for private firms to carry on, aided, if necessary, by the government.[23]

*Financing*

The government financed these undertakings from tax revenues, from loans and by fiat currency issues. Between 1872 and 1877 the internal national debt rose from 23 million yen to 213 million yen; the external debt, however, rose only from 10 million yen to 27 million yen. The totals remained about the same in 1885: 223 million yen in internal debt as

20. Even before 1868, some of the more powerful clans had built works for the manufacture of arms and ships; a steamboat was built in 1857. These industries were taken over by the state in 1868. See Norman, *op. cit.*, pp. 118–21.

21. Allen, *A Short Economic History of Modern Japan*, p. 30.

22. The Yawata Iron Works, which was formed much later, in 1896, was established largely to supply military needs.

23. Joint-stock companies were inaugurated in Japan in 1869. Norman, *op. cit.*, p. 112.

against only 16 million yen in external debt.[24] Apparently, however, wholesale prices in Japan rose slightly less than 10 per cent between 1875 and 1880.[25]

*Indirect Promotion of Production*

The government's efforts to promote the modernization of the economy by indirect methods are less easily summarized. The way in which the government handled the financial side of the breakup of the feudal-type agrarian system provides one example. Before the Meiji restoration, the peasant paid dues in kind to his feudal lord, who in turn supported his knights. When in 1873 the government substituted a direct money tax on land values for these feudal dues, it placated the daimyo and samurai by paying them in money one half the value of their former annual revenues.[26] This was only a stopgap arrangement, however, for three years later, in 1876, the government capitalized its obligations to the daimyo and samurai and issued them bonds in satisfaction of their acknowledged claims. As Norman has neatly put it,

In Japan, the feudal lord ceased to be a *territorial* magnate drawing his income from the peasant and became instead, by virtue of the commutation of his pension, a *financial* magnate investing his freshly capitalized wealth in banks, stocks, industries, or landed estates, and so joined the small financial oligarchy.[27]

Actually the bond allotments going to the samurai, while large in total, were small per capita—not large enough, it is said, to support an individual for a year. Perhaps partly for this reason, the leaders in the Meiji restoration did all they could to absorb the former samurai into posts in the expanding government bureaucracy. In the main, the samurai were not wealthy following the abolition of the feudal-type agrarian system.

24. The Japanese national debt from 1872 to 1919 was as follows (in millions of yen):

| Year | Total | Internal | External |
|------|-------|----------|----------|
| 1872 | Y    33 | Y    23 | Y    10 |
| 1877 | 240 | 213 | 27 |
| 1885 | 239 | 223 | 16 |
| 1894 | 234 | 230 | 4 |
| 1903 | 539 | 441 | 98 |
| 1907 | 2,224 | 1,078 | 1,166 |
| 1914 | 2,561 | 1,036 | 1,525 |
| 1919 | 3,326 | 1,995 | 1,331 |

Allen, *A Short Economic History of Modern Japan*, p. 187. The Sino-Japanese war occurred in 1894–1895 and the Russo-Japanese war in 1904.

25. Harry T. Oshima, "Survey of Various Long-Term Estimates of Japanese National Income," paper presented at the Conference on Economic Growth in Brazil, India and Japan, 1952, Social Science Research Council, New York, Table 1. (Unpublished.)

26. The restoration government had agreed as early as 1869 to pay the daimyo one half their usual revenues if the feudal dues should be abolished. This concession to the daimyo was apparently necessary to enlist their support for the new regime. See Norman, *op. cit.*, p. 94.

27. *Ibid.*, p. 94. Italics in original.

At the time of the restoration the government also guaranteed the claims of the moneylenders—many of whom were landlords as well—and these, too, were paid off by the issuance of bonds. These claims were mostly debts contracted by the daimyo during the late Tokugawa period. The Meiji government did not, however, recognize the debts of the shogunate to some of the more powerful merchants; about 80 per cent of these were repudiated.[28] Presumably, the bonds issued to the daimyo in commutation of their former feudal rights were net of the indebtedness these daimyo owed to the moneylenders, although this point is not clear. Indeed, the details of the funding operation are too complex to be described here in full.[29] What was important politically was that the way these debts were recognized and funded enabled the new government to draw strong support from the moneylenders and many of the daimyo alike.

*Bonds, Paper Money and Banks*

The bonds issued to settle feudal dues and debts could be used as a reserve against national bank notes, and many of them were so used. Some one hundred and forty-eight national banks are said to have been organized on this basis. By handling the commutation of feudal dues as it did, the government funded sizable claims against itself, and, in effect, checked the holders of bonds from spending them; simultaneously, however, the government made the bonds a base for credit creation in the form of bank notes which could assist industrial financing and, through their contribution to inflation, "force" savings on the population at large.[30]

This was not all the government did in the sphere of banking and currency. Before the founding of the Bank of Japan in 1882 the government resorted to direct issues of paper money to such an extent that the period prior to 1880 has been called the "era of paper money." These paper money issues were gradually retired in favor of notes of the Bank of Japan.[31]

28. See Smith, *loc. cit.*, p. 3*n*.

29. See Norman, *op. cit.*, pp. 94–99.

30. The total bonds issued under this arrangement amounted to 190.8 million yen at interest rates ranging from 5 to 10 per cent. Since the total of national bank notes outstanding in 1881 is reported to be 34 million yen (Allen, *A Short Economic History of Modern Japan*, p. 46), it is obvious that many bonds were not used as backing for notes. The fraction actually so used cannot be expressed as a percentage because not all of the bonds issued were necessarily still outstanding in 1881.

Nonetheless, the classes that actually received these bonds were the same groups who owned most of the shares in the national banks. According to a Japanese study reported by Norman (*op. cit.*, p. 100), the former feudal lords (daimyo) and court nobles (kuge) together owned 44 per cent, the samurai 32 per cent and the merchants 15 per cent of the national bank shares outstanding in 1880—a total of 91 per cent in all. Thus, their influence in the banking system was not limited to their use of bonds as backing for bank notes.

31. The amount of paper money outstanding in various years was as follows (in millions of yen):

| End of Year | Government Paper Money | National Bank Notes | Bank of Japan Notes |
|---|---|---|---|
| 1881 | Y 118.9 | Y 34.0 | .. |
| 1885 | 93.4 | 30.2 | Y  4.0 |
| 1890 | 40.1 | 26.4 | 102.9 |
| 1895 | 15.7 | 22.3 | 110.5 |
| 1900 | 5.1 | 1.6 | 179.8 |

Allen, *op. cit.*, p. 46.

In order to help finance industry and agriculture, the government also established three special banks—the Hypothec Bank for agriculture, the Industrial Bank, and the Yokohama Specie Bank to assist in the financing of foreign trade. These banks were used primarily to provide long-term credits in much the same ways as the German banks and in contrast to the traditions of English and American banking.

## The Spirit of Enterprise

The relative importance of other indirect measures taken by the government to foster industry and propagate the entrepreneurial and capitalist spirit is hard to assess. After the state had pointed the way with pilot plants and demonstrations, individuals and private groups seem to have displayed a remarkable willingness to try new ventures and master new techniques and skills. According to one Japanese writer:

The section of the *samurai* class that did not take an active part in politics entered the business world. Many of these failed miserably in their new ventures, but the capitalist spirit which they displayed in trying their hands at company enterprises did much to arouse public interest in such enterprises. The general sentiment among the *samurai* in those days was that if new occupations must be chosen, they should turn to novel industries and undertakings not yet tried by *chonin* or farmers. Prince Iawakura was quite right when he declared that the *samurai* class alone had the capitalist spirit.[32]

Just how the samurai were brought to accept the fact that "new occupations must be chosen" and that they should try "novel industries and undertakings'" would be an interesting sociological study, the results of which might be applicable to many underdeveloped countries. The important point is that a traditionally "elite" group was drawn into the drive toward development, instead of becoming obstructionists or useless remnants of a bygone age.

## Household Industry, Education and Public Works

The development of household industry in Japan seems to have been the result of both deliberate encouragement by the government and tax pressure upon the small agricultural producer. This tax pressure forced the farming families to take on manufactures in the home, to limit their consumption to the traditionally meager level and to send off much of their produce, and their younger children as well, to the industrializing urban areas. Judged by the standards of a later age, the process doubtless had its ruthless aspects; as a means of transforming a feudal agricultural economy into an industrialized economy it was remarkably efficacious.

32. Yasuzo Horie, "An Outline of the Rise of Modern Capitalism in Japan," *Kyoto University Economic Review*, July 1936, p. 112.

The samurai-bureaucrats were not unmindful of the necessity of improving the educational system and of providing some local public works. Before the Meiji restoration, the masses of the people, as in many Oriental countries, were left illiterate and uneducated, except for the apprenticeship system, while the samurai, daimyo and kuge cultivated formal learning. Yet once the new leaders had settled on their ultimate objectives, they transplanted Western science and learning to Japan by bringing in foreign experts and sending students abroad. Primary and secondary schools were set up to combat illiteracy and ignorance, and technical schools and universities were established through grants-in-aid from the central government in order to give roots to the imported Western learning. One eminent specialist on Japan writes: "this system of general and technical education as it expanded was fundamental to Japan's industrial advance . . . No other enterprise of the State paid more handsome dividends to the nation."[33] The technique of grants-in-aid was also used to provide local public works, though in the main these were left to the ingenuity of the local authorities.

*Foreign Trade*

The industrial development of Japan would have been impossible without imports of capital goods. The samurai-bureaucrats seem to have recognized this early and to have encouraged associations of manufacturers and merchants in order to push export trade as a means of paying for the needed imports. At least one Japanese writer, however, contended that it was the flood of imports from the more developed countries that forced Japan to develop her own consumers' goods industries to supply the home market and, later on, to finance the import of those heavy goods especially desired by the government. Count Okuma wrote in 1900 that "Japan thus adopted a Free Trade policy neither voluntarily nor knowingly, but at the pleasure of the Treaty Powers. This was the external force which helped to bring about the industrial revolution . . ."[34]

Participation in the evolving system of multilateral trade was, fortunately, relatively easy at the time Japan needed it most. From 1880 to 1914, the world economy—built on the principles of multilateralism, the exchange of specialties, moderate tariffs and long-term trade treaties—was in its full vigor and strength. Any country willing to follow the accepted standards of commercial and financial conduct was readily admitted to the system. Japan qualified for full membership by her adoption of the gold

33. William W. Lockwood, "The State and Economic Enterprise in Modern Japan, 1868–1939," paper presented at the Conference on Economic Growth in Brazil, India and Japan, 1952, Social Science Research Council, New York, p. 11. (Unpublished.)

34. Count Okuma, "The Industrial Revolution in Japan," *North American Review*, November 1900, pp. 677–78.

standard in 1897, which was made possible partly by a gold indemnity collected from China.

Japanese foreign trade grew remarkably in volume between 1868 and 1914. Imports increased in annual average value from 23 million yen in 1868–1872 to 223 million yen in 1894–1898 and to 544 million yen in 1909–1913, just before World War I. Exports, averaged for the same years, rose from 16 million yen to 139 million yen to 496 million yen. (See Table 9-1.)

TABLE 9-1. JAPANESE FOREIGN TRADE, 1868–1920[a]
*(In Millions of Yen, Annual Averages)*

| Period | Imports | Exports |
|---|---|---|
| 1868–1872 | Y    23 | Y    16 |
| 1873–1877 | 27 | 22 |
| 1878–1882 | 33 | 30 |
| 1883–1887 | 33 | 42 |
| 1888–1893 | 73 | 77 |
| 1894–1898 | 223 | 139 |
| 1899–1903 | 270 | 244 |
| 1904–1908 | 442 | 377 |
| 1909–1913 | 544 | 496 |
| 1914–1920 | 1,300 | 2,434 |

*Source:* G. C. Allen, *A Short Economic History of Modern Japan, 1868–1937*, Allen and Unwin, London, 1946, p. 179.

a. Excludes trade between Japan and her colonies.

The composition of Japanese trade also changed. Imports of food and drink and finished goods diminished in importance relative to raw materials; in exports, semimanufactured goods and finished goods steadily gained over raw materials and food and drink. (See Table 9-2.)

TABLE 9-2. STRUCTURE OF JAPAN'S FOREIGN TRADE, 1868–1912

| | Value as Percentage of Total Exports | | | | |
|---|---|---|---|---|---|
| Period | Food and Beverages | Raw Materials | Semi-manufactured Goods | Finished Goods | Others |
| | Exports | | | | |
| 1868–1872 | 25.4 | 23.1 | 40.8 | 1.9 | 8.8 |
| 1878–1882 | 37.1 | 11.6 | 40.4 | 7.2 | 3.7 |
| 1893–1897 | 16.8 | 10.3 | 43.3 | 26.2 | 3.4 |
| 1903–1907 | 11.9 | 9.1 | 45.3 | 31.1 | 2.6 |
| 1908–1912 | 11.1 | 9.2 | 48.1 | 30.5 | 1.1 |
| | Imports | | | | |
| 1868–1872 | 29.0 | 4.1 | 20.2 | 44.5 | 2.2 |
| 1878–1882 | 14.8 | 33.5 | 29.9 | 48.6 | 3.2 |
| 1893–1897 | 20.8 | 22.7 | 19.1 | 35.1 | 2.3 |
| 1903–1907 | 23.5 | 33.0 | 16.7 | 25.5 | 1.3 |
| 1908–1912 | 12.0 | 44.3 | 18.9 | 24.1 | 0.7 |

*Source:* G. C. Allen, *A Short Economic History of Modern Japan, 1868–1937*, Allen and Unwin, London, 1946, p. 181.

CONCLUDING OBSERVATIONS ON JAPANESE ECONOMIC DEVELOPMENT

Once the development process has attained a certain momentum in a country, it is not difficult to understand why it is likely to generate its own power of forward propulsion. The early stages—in which "everything seems to depend on everything else" or in which "nothing can be done because everything needs to be done at once"—present the most stubborn difficulties. So it is these problems and the ways in which they were overcome in Japan that are of principal interest. What, then, does Japanese experience suggest on the crucial problem of initiating economic development?

*The Role of Government*

First, Japanese experience seems to underscore the importance of a strong central government with definite objectives and an ability to focus old traditions toward new ends. One of the most remarkable features of the Japanese achievement was the fact that, despite drastic changes in the old order, the economy as a whole never broke pace in confusion or disorder. Even though the social, political and economic orientation of agriculture was drastically altered, there was no agricultural revolution and no decline in output. The daimyo and samurai were shorn of their traditional privileges, but they quickly adapted themselves to the new points of view and to the new roles assigned to them. Most remarkable of all perhaps was the ability of the postrestoration leaders to set up a system of centralized administration which was able from the start to cope with the most difficult problems on a nationwide scale. There was revolution—in the sense of very rapid and drastic change—but not economic collapse. Neither in the French nor in the Russian Revolution did the new groups coming into power know how to administer the national economy once they had gained control.

*The Land Tax*

The second feature of Japan's economic development that bears on the problem of "getting started" is the amazing speed with which a few fundamental institutional changes created an economy founded on the price system out of a feudalistic economy based on rights and obligations. The stroke of genius here seems to have been to link private property in land with a money tax system based on assessed land values. When this was combined with the abolition of guild restrictions and, at least legally, with free choice of occupation for all, a price-market economy seems to have quickly emerged. All four factors were doubtless of great importance, but the tax device which forced the peasants to market their produce, instead of hoarding it or consuming it or investing it in livestock and the like, was perhaps the most powerful.

*Capital Formation*

Finally, Japan's experience in initiating the development process is significant because of the techniques used to effectuate real capital formation. Japan was a poor country in 1868, with a stock of real capital little different in amount or composition from that of other economies in which agriculture occupies most of the population. Yet by 1914 she had all the attributes of an emerging world power backed by an industrialized economy. How was the real capital created?

In the early stages, the major role fell to the government, which used taxation and inflationary finance to command the real resources needed to build at home and to import from abroad those real capital goods that were indispensable to industrial development. The government decided both the total amount that could be accumulated and how it should be allocated between possible alternative uses. Subsequently, it veered toward more orthodox finance, but it kept income distributed in such a way that total consumption was limited in favor of savings. There was no foreign borrowing until development was well under way. Japanese economic development was initiated and financed at home throughout the difficult early stages.

Factors other than the three touched upon here were of vital importance, too, in the sense that Japanese development would have followed different lines had they not been present. There were also chance factors and noneconomic events that proved to be favorable for development—the collapse of the European silk industry as a result of the silkworm disease, for example, and the stimulus of two important wars. It is likely, however, that influences such as these were of secondary rather than primary importance in the impressive development of the Japanese economy between 1868 and 1914.

# 10. Economic Development of the U.S.S.R.

THE TRANSFORMATION OF THE U.S.S.R. from an agricultural to an industrial economy is one of the most interesting and controversial chapters in recent economic history. The case is unique in many respects. In the first place, it was a "planned" development that made little use of the usual institutions of markets and prices so that other means had to be devised to organize output and allocate investment. Second, the drive toward industrialization was from the start permeated by the leaders' fears of foreign intervention; this fear gave the industrial development a special character which it has never lost. Of course this feature may only reflect the pervasive influence of Marxist-Socialist ideology in all economic and political questions in Russia since 1917. Finally, Russia's industrial development was remarkably swift. It began inauspiciously after a decade of internal strife and disastrous policies had virtually destroyed the national economy which the new leaders took over from the old. Before there could be industrial advance—at least as measured by the usual indices—the Russian economy had first to regain its previous level of achievement. This it did not do until early 1927. Consequently, the period of Russian industrial development of primary interest to countries yet to develop extends from 1927 to the outbreak of World War II in 1939. Russian development did not stop in 1939; but most of the worst problems had already been surmounted by that time.

## ECONOMIC DEVELOPMENT BEFORE 1913

Russia's economic development after 1927 was facilitated somewhat by the start made on industrialization between 1880 and 1913; some of the real capital resources then accumulated remained usable and did not have to be provided anew. In 1913, for example, Russia had more than 40,000 miles of railways, mostly built and financed by the state, a respectable inheritance for any country bent on industrialization.

While Russia was far from industrialized in 1913, she was still not wholly agricultural. Slightly less than 18 per cent of the population was urban.[1] Russia's coal production of 36 million long tons was only 7.4 per cent of Germany's output, on a per capita basis. The comparable figure for pig

1. Alexander Baykov, in *Bulletins on Soviet Economic Development*, Bulletin 1, Faculty of Commerce and Social Science, University of Birmingham, Birmingham, May 1949, p. 3.

iron was 8.3 per cent; for mechanical horsepower used in industry, 8.1 per cent.[2] Foreign capital—French, English, Belgian and German, in that order —dominated joint-stock enterprises, especially in mining, chemicals, iron and steel, and engineering. Even in textiles, 28 per cent of the capital is said to have been foreign capital.[3] Most of this foreign capital came in after 1890. According to Alexander Gerschenkron's estimates, industrial production in Russia doubled between 1898 and 1913 and, except for 1888, increased every year between 1885 and 1905.[4]

Russian foreign trade in 1913 also reflected her limited industrial development. In 1909–1913, 70 per cent of her exports were agricultural products and the remaining 30 per cent in industrial products were mainly raw materials. Imports in the same period were largely consumption goods (27 per cent), mostly manufactured, and manufactured production goods (33 per cent); the remainder was raw materials and semimanufactures used in production.

In 1913, Russian industry was developing along much the same lines as industry in other central European countries. If Russia's achievements at that time were not impressive compared with those of England, Germany or the United States, it nevertheless took ten years following the 1917 revolution for output again to reach its absolute 1913 level. In the interval, of course, other countries were not marking time.

*Agriculture before 1913*

Russian agriculture in 1913 was probably less efficient than German or English agriculture of a half century earlier. Serfdom had been abolished in 1861; the nobility are said to have lost about one third of their land, as well as their serfs, by the emancipation. In compensation for the serfs the landlords received payments totaling about one billion rubles. Agriculture did not quickly take on a commercial character as in Germany, however, nor did the landlords mainly shift their money capital to industrial under-

2. Calculated from data in *ibid.*
3. Alexander Baykov, *The Development of the Soviet Economic System*, Cambridge University Press, Cambridge, 1946, p. 3.
4. The rate of growth varied as follows:

|  | Average Annual Percentage Rate of Growth | Years Required to Double Output at This Rate |
|---|---|---|
| 1885–1889 | 6.10 | 11.7 |
| 1890–1899 | 8.03 | 9.0 |
| 1900–1906 | 1.43 | 49.0 |
| 1907–1913 | 6.25 | 11.4 |
| 1885–1913 | 5.72 | 12.5 |

Alexander Gerschenkron, "The Rate of Industrial Growth in Russia since 1885," *Journal of Economic History*, Supplement VII, 1947, pp. 145–46. For the period 1862–1882 Gerschenkron estimates the average annual rate of growth to have been 3.5 per cent.

takings as in Japan. In fact, the landlords were so anxious or so pressed to convert their securities into liquid form that they forced down the market value of the securities 30 per cent below par.[5] Unfortunately, too, the law required the serfs to cover part of the payments due to the landlords and, until they had done so, ownership was vested in the commune. Although this arrangement generated much discontent, the payments were not canceled until 1905, after revolutionary outbreaks among the peasants. The Stolypin reforms in that year enabled the peasants actually to claim land, and also to consolidate scattered strips into more efficient units of production.

## Productivity

Despite the 44-year delay between the freeing of the serfs and the enactment of the Stolypin reforms, the average annual yield of cereals on peasant holdings increased as much as 48 per cent between 1861–1870 and 1901–1910.[6] On "other" lands, the increase in cereal yields was 64 per cent. Thus agricultural productivity increased after the emancipation, but it increased more on the larger units than on the smaller peasant holdings. Moreover, the gap in average yield between the larger and the smaller units increased on the average from 4 poods to 11 poods.[7] Lyashchenko, a Russian economist, declares that "for a period of sixty years during the nineteenth century, our agriculture under serfdom was distinguished by an almost stationary yield."[8] In contrast to this stagnation of 1801–1870, agricultural productivity increased more than 50 per cent from 1870 to 1910. If this was not spectacular progress it was scarcely economic stagnation. Indeed, in the 24 years between 1909–1913 and 1933–1937 the average yield of grain crops

5. Witt Bowden, Michael Karpovich and Abbott Payson Usher, *An Economic History of Europe since 1750*, American Book Co., New York, 1937, p. 602. About 40 per cent of the amounts payable to the landlords for the loss of their land was withheld by the government against debts already owed on previous borrowing from state agencies. *Ibid.*, p. 601. The pressure of debts and the costs of their accustomed living patterns apparently forced the aristocracy to dispose of their bonds at a discount. See Peter Lyashchenko, *History of the National Economy of Russia*, Macmillan, New York, 1949, pp. 411–12.

6. The lot of the peasants during much of this period was often marked by great hardship and suffering. Tax burdens were heavy and discriminated against small holdings. According to Gerschenkron (*loc. cit.*, p. 149n), taxes on peasant land were close to seven times as high per acre as on estate lands. The tax burdens allowed the peasants little chance to accumulate any reserves, so that crop failures easily led to famines.

7. The average cereal yields on peasant holdings and "other" lands are calculated to have varied between 1861 and 1910 as follows:

|  | Peasant Holdings | | Other Lands | |
|---|---|---|---|---|
|  | Poods | Per Cent | Poods | Per Cent |
| 1861–1870 | 29 | 100 | 33 | 100 |
| 1871–1880 | 31 | 107 | 37 | 112 |
| 1881–1890 | 34 | 117 | 42 | 127 |
| 1891–1900 | 39 | 134 | 47 | 142 |
| 1901–1910 | 43 | 148 | 54 | 164 |

Alexis N. Antsiferov *et al.*, *Russian Agriculture during the War*, Yale University Press, New Haven, 1930, p. 55. One pood equals 36.1 pounds.

8. Lyashchenko, *op. cit.*, p. 324.

climbed only from 7.4 quintals per hectare to 9.1—a gain of not quite 23 per cent.[9]

By 1913, economic development in Russia had made some progress. Industrial growth was especially rapid during the 1890s, slowed down almost to a standstill during the disturbed years of 1900–1906, but resumed thereafter with renewed vigor. Most important, the country acquired a railway network. Agriculture also improved, though probably less rapidly than it would have if the Stolypin reforms had not been so long delayed. World War I intervened before these reforms had time to exert their full economic effects. Close on the heels of the war came the revolution of 1917.

### Economic Development under the Five-Year Plans, 1927–1939

Few events in world history have had more profound or more enduring consequences than the political and economic upheaval in Russia between 1917 and 1920. Nor can anyone say whether the consequences yet to appear will be more far-reaching or less than those already visible.

By 1920, three years after the revolution, the gross value of output in large-scale industry in Russia had fallen to 12.8 per cent of its 1913 level and in small industry to 20.4 per cent. The causes of these and other declines, according to Gerschenkron, lay in "sanguinary civil war, nationalization of industries coupled with syndicalist tendencies among the workers, other ill-advised industrial policies, inflation, and the transformation of basic property relationships in agriculture."[10]

The economic development that followed after 1920 can only be sketched.[11] The revival of output began with the New Economic Policy, but important as the N.E.P. was in restoring the economy to working efficiency, the deliberate industrialization under the five-year plans from 1927 to 1939 is more pertinent to the economic development problems of still underdeveloped countries. Primary attention will be directed to industrial development, leaving discussion of the changes in agriculture to the last. There are some reasons for believing that the Soviet leaders themselves considered their problem from this angle, that is, the primary decisions were those relating to industry, and agriculture had to be adapted accordingly, not the other way about.

---

9. *Bulletins on Soviet Economic Development*, Bulletin 2, December 1949. Around 1913, peasant agriculture in Russia, while probably less efficient than agriculture in Western Europe, seems not to have been as poverty-stricken as is sometimes assumed. Peasant farms "had at their disposal" 10.6 acres on the average. As for capital equipment, "34.8% of peasant farms had no horses, 45.2% had only one horse, 16.1% had two horses, 2.9% had 3 horses and only 2% had four horses." *Ibid.*, pp. 3–4.

10. Gerschenkron, *loc. cit.*, p. 158.

11. Perhaps the most readable and informative report on the subject is Maurice Dobb's *Soviet Economic Development since 1917*, International Publishers, New York, 1948.

*Basic Aims*

The overriding objective in all three of the five-year plans was the rapid development of industry, above all, heavy industry. The decision to move in this direction was reached only after bitter controversy. But in December 1925 the 14th Congress of the Russian Communist party voted:

. . . to convert our country from an agrarian into an industrial country able to produce all necessary equipment by its own means. To carry out such measures of industrialization as will secure the economic independence of the country, strengthen its defensive capacity and create the conditions necessary for the victory of Socialism in the U.S.S.R.[12]

During the period of the N.E.P., the issue of whether or not to industrialize was hotly disputed by the Soviet leaders. The decision to do so seems to have been prompted by the realization, or even fear, that without industrialization the power of the Communist party would be threatened. Baykov phrases it differently: "without a speedy reconstruction of the country's economy it would be impossible to solve those ideological problems for the sake of which the Revolution had been made."[13] The emphasis on defense and economic independence, and the necessity for establishing a particular kind of social and economic system, necessarily gave prominence to heavy industry and often dictated the means used to solve particular problems in the industrialization process.

*The Stress on Industry*

The stress on industry in the five-year plans is apparent from the allocation of investment by major economic fields. Industry accounted for a strikingly high proportion of investment, almost 40 per cent of the total in all three plans, while the commitments to communications and to trade and procurement were trifling by comparison. (See Table 10-1.) Moreover, the investments in industry were predominantly in capital goods industry (referred to as Group A in the Soviet scheme of classification), not in industry for the production of consumption goods (Group B). Between 1929 and 1932 the investments in Group A averaged 84.8 per cent of all investments *in industry;* in 1933–1937, the figure was 83.0 per cent, while the plan for 1938–1942 called for 84.1 per cent.[14] In other words, about 40 per cent of total investment was investment in industry, and of this amount more than four fifths was investment in capital goods industry and only about one fifth in consumption goods industry.

12. As quoted in *Bulletins on Soviet Economic Development*, Bulletin 1, p. 4. The dates for the first three five-year plans were as follows: I, 1928–1929 to 1932–1933; II, 1933–1937; III, 1938–1942.

13. Baykov, *The Development of the Soviet Economic System*, p. 158.

14. Norman M. Kaplan, *Soviet Capital Formation and Industrialization* (processed), Rand Corporation, Santa Monica, 1952, pp. 78–79 and 84. These percentages correspond closely with those which can be calculated from figures appearing in Baykov, *The Development of the Soviet Economic System*, p. 421.

Among the capital goods industries, those stressed were electric power, coal, petroleum, and ferrous and nonferrous metals. These five groups in the early years of the program got between 37.5 per cent and 42.7 per cent of the total investments in all industry, or roughly one half of the total capital goods investment. By contrast the textile industries, food industries and light industry usually got less than 20 per cent of all industrial investment, except in 1929, when they received 25 per cent.[15]

TABLE 10-1. PERCENTAGE DISTRIBUTION OF INVESTMENTS IN THE U.S.S.R. BY MAJOR ECONOMIC FIELDS, UNDER THREE FIVE-YEAR PLANS[a]

| Economic Field | 1928–1929 to 1932 | 1933–1937 | 1938–1942 |
|---|---|---|---|
| Total | 100.0 | 100.0 | 100.0 |
| Industry | 41.0 | 37.1 | 41.9 |
| Agriculture | 19.1 | 19.1 | 19.5 |
| Transport | 17.3 | 15.6 | 15.6 |
| Communications | 1.1 | 0.8 | 0.8 |
| Trade and procurement | 1.8 | 2.0 | 1.1 |
| Socio-cultural services and administration | 19.7 | 25.4 | 21.2 |
| Housing[b] | 9.2 | 9.1 | 8.2 |

*Source:* Norman M. Kaplan, *Soviet Capital Formation and Industrialization* (processed), Rand Corporation, Santa Monica, 1952, Table 7, p. 15.

a. "Nonproductive" investment by economic organizations eliminated from economic sectors and added to "Socio-cultural services and administration."

b. Housing is included in "Socio-cultural services and administration" but is given separately in order to facilitate comparison with other components of total investment.

This concentration on capital goods is also apparent from data on growth of output and employment by industrial classifications. Comparison of the physical output of different industries, both heavy and light, at various stages of industrialization shows that the gains in capital goods industry far exceeded those in consumer goods. The deliberate concentration on the capital goods sector is apparent from the striking increases in the output of iron and steel products, of coal, oil and cement, in sharp contrast to the slight increases in the output of cottons and woolens. (See Table 10-2.) On a per capita basis, less textile goods were available in 1937 than in 1929 or 1913.

*Geographical Distribution of Industry*

An additional feature of the industrial development of the U.S.S.R. was the planned geographical distribution of industry as a whole.[16]

15. Kaplan, *op. cit.*, p. 85.

16. A brief and easily accessible account of the purposes and accomplishments of the relocation of Russian industry will be found in Maurice Dobb, *Soviet Economy and the War*, International Publishers, New York, 1943, Chapter 6.

The heavy industrial investments were not altogether in areas that had already evidenced some industrial concentration prior to 1929. Mixed motives appear to have been at work—considerations of national security, a desire to economize in the use of very scarce transportation resources, the known existence of rich raw materials in nonindustrial areas, and probably the usual social and cultural arguments that are advanced for a dispersion

TABLE 10-2. PHYSICAL PRODUCTION IN RUSSIAN INDUSTRY, SELECTED YEARS

| Industry | Unit | 1913 | 1929 | 1933 | 1937 | 1938 |
|---|---|---|---|---|---|---|
| Engineering and metal industries | billion rubles, 1926–1927 value | 1,446 418 | 3,054 602 | 10,822 941 | 27,519 1,581 | 33,613 1,626 |
| Engines | | | | | | |
| Goods trucks | thousands | 14.8 | 15.9 | 18.2 | 66.1 | 49.1 |
| Motor cars | thousands | .. | 1.4 | 49.7 | 200.0 | 211.4 |
| Electric power | billion kw-h. | 1.9 | 6.2 | 16.4 | 36.4 | 39.6 |
| Coal | million tons | 29.1 | 40.1 | 76.3 | 127.9 | 132.9 |
| Oil | million tons | 9.2 | 13.8 | 22.5 | 30.5 | 32.2 |
| Iron ore | million tons | 9.2 | 8.0 | 14.4 | 27.7 | 26.5 |
| Manganese ore | thousand tons | 1,245 | 702 | 1,021 | 2,752 | 2,273 |
| Pig iron | million tons | 4.2 | 4.0 | 7.1 | 14.5 | 14.6 |
| Steel | million tons | 4.2 | 4.9 | 6.9 | 17.7 | 18.0 |
| Rolled steel | million tons | 3.5 | 3.9 | 5.1 | 13.0 | 13.3 |
| Copper | thousand tons | .. | 35.5 | 44.5 | 99.8 | 103.2 |
| Aluminum | thousand tons | .. | .. | 7.0 | 37.7 | 56.8 |
| Cement | million tons | 1.5 | 2.2 | 2.7 | 5.5 | 5.7 |
| Cotton textiles | million meters | 2,227 | 3,068 | 2,422 | 3,447 | 3,491 |
| Woolen textiles | million meters | 95 | 100.6 | 86.1 | 108.3 | 114.0 |
| Leather shoes | million pairs | .. | 48.8 | 80.3 | 164.2 | 213.0 |
| Raw sugar | thousand tons | 1,290 | 1,283 | 995 | 2,421 | 2,519 |

*Source:* Alexander Baykov, *The Development of the Soviet Economic System*, Cambridge University Press, Cambridge, 1946, p. 307.

of industry.[17] The areas specially marked for intensive industrial development appear to have been Siberia and the eastern portion of European Russia. Coal production shows a marked percentage increase in a number of new regions, but in 1937 the Donbas area still accounted for 60 per cent of the total, as against 77 per cent in 1927–1928. Electric generating installations were concentrated in the industrial areas, as one might expect. In pig iron, steel and rolled steel, the south still accounted for 53 to 63 per cent of total output in 1939, compared with the only slightly higher range of 59–73 per cent in 1927–1928, although the national output of these prod-

17. More attention seems to have been devoted to geographical dispersion of industry and to bringing industry nearer to raw material supplies in the third five-year plan than in the first two. The third plan also aimed to make the areas contiguous to the newer industrialized regions a source of food and other bulky materials for local consumption. See Baykov, *The Development of the Soviet Economic System*, p. 287. Transport congestion appears partly to have dictated this policy.

ucts increased roughly 400 per cent in the interval.[18] There is some evidence that geographical dispersion in the consumption of iron increased over the period, but this appears to have occasioned bottlenecks in transportation.

On the whole, the statistical data do not seem to evidence as much decentralization of industrial production as is popularly assumed to have occurred. The percentage increases in some regions are certainly startling, but their share in the total is often negligible. If at the start output is virtually zero, its percentage increase can be enormous and it can still be a trifling fraction of total output.

From the point of view of type of production as well as geography, only a planned and strictly controlled economic system could have followed this pattern of investment and output. In market economies, in which the price system organizes output and allocates investment, consumers' goods industries would have increased their output much more and would have bid capital for investment away from producers' goods industries. Thus, the extreme concentration on capital goods industries, one of the outstanding features of Russian development, would be impossible in a market economy if consumers and entrepreneurs held sway without interference. The authorities would have to direct the price system by a combination of taxes, subsidies and direct controls such as are usually reserved for time of war.

### *"Social Overhead" Investments*

Activities classed as "socio-cultural services and administration" claimed a large percentage of investment in Russia, being second only to industry. (See Table 10-1.) This group includes those investments imposed by growing urbanization incident to industrial development—"public works" in American usage; housing; education and public health; and, lastly, administration and military facilities and installations.[19]

A detailed breakdown of these investments, both as to kinds and types and in relation to productive investment in industry, would be of great interest, since in contemporary development programs such investments, which are ancillary to industrialization, present special financial difficulties and are of uncertain cost. There is usually the widest disagreement concerning the "indispensable minimum" in housing, public works, public health, education and similar facilities and services. All agree that investment for such purposes is unavoidable. But the question of how much and what kinds provokes much controversy. Unfortunately, however, such data are not available in detail for Russia.

---

18. Production data cited in this paragraph are from Birmingham Bureau of Research on Russian Economic Conditions, *Results of the Second Five-Year Plan and the Project of the Third Five-Year Plan* (Memorandum No. 12), Birmingham, 1939, p. 7.

19. See Kaplan, *op. cit.*, p. 13.

Lacking such a breakdown, it is possible only to note the percentage of total investment that went for housing. In view of the fact that some 23 million persons migrated from rural to urban areas between 1926 and 1939, it is astonishing to discover that the planned investment in housing for 1933–1937 was only 10.1 per cent of total investments and for 1938–1942 only 8.2 per cent. And the amounts actually invested fell below those planned by roughly one tenth. For every ruble invested in housing during the period 1933–1937, 4.06 rubles were apparently invested in industry.[20] Moreover, during the 1930s the proportion of housing within the omnibus category "socio-cultural services and administration" actually declined.[21]

The rapid expansion of Soviet industry must, therefore, have been made possible, in part, by limiting drastically the outlays on housing—that is, by urban crowding and by "making do" with what already existed. Presumably not all the housing construction was in urban areas but much the greatest proportion was probably concentrated there.

*Investments in Transport*

New investment in transport during the five-year plans accounted for a remarkably small fraction of total investment: 17.3 per cent from 1928–1929 to 1932 and 15.6 per cent in the following period. (See Table 10-1.) However, the U.S.S.R., unlike countries that industrialized in the nineteenth century, inherited a railway network from the old regime. Moreover, much of the fixed investment in railways is virtually indestructible, as wartime experience in many countries has shown; railways will continue to function for long periods despite substantial undermaintenance. Undermaintenance makes for inefficient operation, of course, and not all parts of the railway investment can be wholly neglected. The rolling stock will break down unless repairs and replacements are made. But the roadbed, stations and other installations are nearly permanent in their usefulness—barring competition from other types of transport—and require little upkeep. In the circumstances, if the U.S.S.R. was determined quickly to create heavy industries and was hard pressed to find the real resources to do so, the authorities may have been compelled to cut transport investment to the barest minimum. In other words, some of the new investment in industry may have been financed by deliberate disinvestment in the transport sector.

20. Figures on housing investments from *ibid.*, p. 83. Actual investments in housing in 1933–1937 amounted to 9.1 per cent of total investments. (See Table 10-1.) Ratio of housing investments to total investments in industry computed by the authors from data in *ibid.*, pp. 15 and 23.

21. According to Simon Kuznets' calculations, investments in housing in the United States averaged about 25 per cent of total investments until 1929 and even in the depression of 1930–1940 dropped only to 13.5 per cent. See *ibid.*, p. 23. It has recently been reported that, from the end of 1926 to the beginning of 1939, the urban population in Russia increased 112 per cent as against only a 50 per cent increase in urban living space. As a consequence the space per capita was reduced from 6 to 4 square meters, omitting halls, kitchens, lavatories, closets, etc. Gregory Grossman, "Some Current Trends in Soviet Capital Formation" (mimeographed; Conference on Capital Formation and Economic Growth, November 1953), National Bureau of Economic Research, New York, 1953, p. 25, citing a forthcoming study by Timothy Sosnovy.

Although there is no clear-cut evidence that this was, in fact, the logic of the allocation of investment to transport under the five-year plans, the decisions could have been defended on these grounds.

A recent writer puts the total "first main track" in the Soviet railway system in 1940 at 106,102 kilometers (66,300 miles), of which he estimates 67 per cent was inherited from the czars; 15 per cent acquired along with new territories annexed in 1939–1940; and 18 per cent was newly built. Thus the newly built lines are estimated at 18,798 kilometers.[22] Of the total mileage in 1940, about 23 per cent was double-track and about 8 per cent was equipped with automatic block signaling. Many of the new lines were apparently constructed in remote new areas or for suburban needs.

### The Pressure on the Railways

The allocation of investment between railways and other alternative uses seems to have put the railways under extreme pressure during most of the period 1928–1939. The volume of freight and passenger traffic increased greatly as the industrialization program got under way and more raw materials, finished goods and factory workers had to be moved. Colin Clark gives the following comparative figures on traffic density (in millions of ton-kilometers per kilometer of line per year):[23]

|  | 1913 | 1934 | 1934 or 1935 | 1935 | 1936 |
|---|---|---|---|---|---|
| U.S.S.R. | 1.13 | 2.47 | | 3.06 | 3.80 |
| Germany | | | 1.17 | | |
| France | | | .81 | | |
| Belgium | | | .98 | | |
| Sweden | | | .21 | | |
| Canada | | | .50 | | |
| Australia | | | .13 | | |
| United States | | | 1.08 | | |
| Great Britain | | | .83 | | |

This increased traffic density, combined with parsimonious capital expenditures on the railways, made for costly delays in shipment and for inevitable confusion. The backlog of unshipped freight is said to have amounted to 20 million tons at the end of 1932, and it increased during 1933. Despite exhortations to improve efficiency, the backlog was still about

22. Different authorities give rather different figures for the railway mileage of Russia in 1913 or 1917. So far as can be determined, these discrepancies arise from two sources: first, some writers give figures referring to European Russia alone and either omit entirely or report separately the lines in Asiatic Russia; second, the figures sometimes refer to the 1913 boundaries of Russia and sometimes to the boundaries of the U.S.S.R. in the interwar period. The figures given in the text above are from Holland Hunter, "Soviet Railroads since 1940," in *Bulletins on Soviet Economic Development*, Bulletin 4, 1950, pp. 10–11.

23. Colin Clark, *A Critique of Russian Statistics*, Macmillan, London, 1939, p. 66. Clark's figures for the U.S.S.R. are from the *Handbook of the Soviet Union*, and for other countries, where the year is either 1934 or 1935, from the official German *Statistical Yearbook*,

15 million tons at the end of 1934. Rationing and priority systems failed to solve the crisis, with the result that in 1935 the government was forced to double-track certain key lines and otherwise improve their efficiency under a reorganized Communications Commissariat. When, by 1937, the freight backlog was reduced to tolerable size, "the amount of iron and steel allocated to the railroads was cut back, and emphasis was again placed on other sectors of the economy."[24]

Thus, the investment allocations to transport during the five-year plans prior to 1939 were evidently deliberately small and may have been insufficient to maintain the system. This undermaintenance doubtless allowed investment in industry to proceed at a faster pace. At the same time, however, it produced difficulties on its own account, because efficient transport is a prerequisite to efficient industrial production.

In the middle 1930s the transport problem seems to have become so acute that the government had to reverse itself and assign greater resources to certain key railway lines in order to overcome the emergency. Whether, in retrospect, the Soviet authorities would conclude that their industrialization program would have gone more rapidly, as measured by the flow of final product, had they invested more in transport and less directly in industry is an open question. One rather suspects that they would.[25]

*Sources of Labor Supply*

The problem of labor supply is bound to be acute in any program of rapid industrialization. It is likely to present a congeries of problems rather than a single difficulty. In a traditionally agricultural country, the peasants —unless overcrowding is already acute—usually prefer the familiar routines of their villages to the uncertainties of factory employment and urban living. Yet to man factories people have to be drawn off the land by one means or another. An enclosure movement, a shift in the type of agriculture, or the pressure of taxes may serve this purpose—as they did in England, Prussia and Japan respectively. If the market mechanism with its wage and price differentials is unacceptable, other means must be used to draw labor out of agriculture and into industry.

24. Hunter, *loc. cit.*, p. 11. The above paragraph is little more than a paraphrase of Hunter's article. During the period of most acute pressure on the transport system, in 1931–1936, the number of accidents appears to have been appalling. An article in *Izvestia* (March 20, 1935) announced: "According to a statement of the State Commissar of Railways, in 1934, there were 62,000 accidents and disasters in which 7,000 engines were more or less seriously damaged . . . 4,500 coaches were destroyed and more than 60,000 damaged, hundreds of people were killed and thousands injured as a result of these accidents." This is reported in Birmingham Bureau of Research on Russian Economic Conditions, *Results of the Second Five-Year Plan and the Project of the Third Five-Year Plan.* Since the same report gives the figure of 19,400 as the total number of engines in 1934, the *Izvestia* article would imply that in one year more than 35 per cent of the engines were "more or less seriously damaged." This figure is so high that it suggests the new commissar was making a stern announcement in order to drive home to the workers the urgent need for improvement.

25. The foregoing discussion has related only to the railways. But according to Hunter, *loc. cit.*, p. 11, "Both in 1937 and 1940, the railroads accounted for 86% of domestic freight traffic, measured in ton-kilometers, the remainder being divided among river (7%), sea (5%), and road carriers (2%)."

Soviet policy concerning labor procurement for industry seems to have relied chiefly on the pull exerted by opportunities for industrial employment, and the push provided by agricultural mechanization. Frank Lorimer estimates that between 1926 and 1939 a net number of not less than 23 million persons shifted from rural to urban areas.[26] The decreases in rural population were greatest, he says, "in the fertile steppe zone across southern Russia, western Siberia, and Kazakhstan, i.e., in the regions most adapted to mechanized, large-scale farming." As Lorimer points out, "These are the areas where the reorganization and mechanization of agriculture could release the largest number of potential industrial workers, simultaneously with an extension of sown area and an increase in agricultural production."[27] These regions accounted for about three fourths of the total decrease in rural population, even though in 1926 they had only slightly more than half, 53 per cent, of the total rural population, according to Lorimer.

As would be expected, the urban areas of in-migration were the centers of industrial activity and the capital cities (the administrative centers) of the Soviet Socialist Republics. Moscow, for example, rose in population from 2.02 million in December 1926 to 4.13 million in January 1939; Leningrad, from 1.69 million to 3.19 million. Although Moscow and Leningrad thus had populations of over 4 million and 3 million respectively in 1939, the next largest city in Russia, Kiev, had only 846,000 inhabitants.[28] This drift to the cities and growing industrial areas was reinforced by the fact that industrial workers received much higher real wages than workers on the collective farms.[29] With the intense drive toward collectivization, independent peasants probably fared little, if any, better than the workers on the collective farms. Consequently, the countryside lost labor to the industrializing urban centers.

*Soviet Redeployment Policies*

"Planless" migrations prompted by general economic forces did not, apparently, solve the problem of labor supply and allocation completely. Lorimer quotes the following 1938 proclamation of the Communist party:

It is imperative for the planned development of our national economy that there be maximum utilization of the labor force and that it be so distributed, *both territorially and throughout the various branches of economy,* as to result in

26. Frank Lorimer, *The Population of the Soviet Union: History and Prospects,* League of Nations, Geneva, 1946, p. 149 and Chapter 10 *passim.* The urban migration was far from evenly distributed as between the individual years; in 1930 and 1931, the years of greatest net migration, the numbers were 2.6 million and 4.1 million respectively. The marked variations reported by Lorimer are puzzling. See *ibid.,* p. 150.

27. *Ibid.,* p. 161.

28. *Ibid.,* p. 250.

29. Maurice Dobb, certainly not an unfriendly critic, quotes figures which suggest that industrial workers in 1937 got incomes more than twice those of workers on the collective farms. See his *Soviet Economy and the War,* p. 73.

its most efficient use. The Soviet Government must immediately address itself to this problem.[30]

In other words, merely to draw workers from agriculture into the cities does not necessarily assure a labor force for the more distant regions or the less appealing occupations.

The Soviet solution to this difficulty appears to have proceeded along two lines. First, the government set up a recruitment program based on the principles of wage differentials, tax exemptions, subsidies and "fringe benefits" to entice workers into those branches of the economy where labor was in short supply. Second, it assigned labor battalions composed of "prisoners, deported kulaks, and those condemned for political deviations" to work at those tasks and in those areas that were unable to attract enough laborers. In 1940, after the outbreak of war in Europe, public control over migration and occupational changes was made much more stringent.[31]

On the whole, Russia apparently experienced less difficulty with the basic problem of labor supply than might have been expected. The number of "workers and employees"—which excludes farmers but includes workers on state-owned farms—increased between 1928 and 1938 as follows (figures in millions):[32]

| 1928 | 11.6 | 1934 | 23.7 |
|------|------|------|------|
| 1929 | 12.2 | 1935 | 24.8 |
| 1930 | 14.5 | 1936 | 25.8 |
| 1931 | 19.4 | 1937 | 27.0 |
| 1932 | 22.9 | 1938 | 27.8 |
| 1933 | 22.3 |      |      |

The primary means used to achieve this migration were differentials in real wages, mechanization of agriculture and a program of recruitment.

Unlike many underdeveloped countries today, Russia had the advantage of a labor force that already had a fairly high degree of literacy before the five-year plans began. As early as 1926, two thirds of the males in Russia nine years of age or over were able to "read or write," although for females the corresponding percentage was much lower, only 37.1 per cent. In fact, the proportion of literate males was above 70 per cent in three areas that included many of the most important sites chosen for industrial development. These were the Ukraine, Belorussia and the R.S.F.S.R.—the Russian Soviet Federated Socialist Republic, an administrative district comprising nineteen different regions.[33]

30. Lorimer, *op. cit.*, p. 173. Italics added.
31. See *ibid.*, pp. 172–75, for details.
32. See Baykov, *The Development of the Soviet Economic System*, p. 342.
33. See the map in Lorimer, *op. cit.*, p. 91.

During the five-year plans the concerted attack on illiteracy succeeded in raising the percentage of Russian males nine years of age and over able to read or write to 90.8 per cent in 1939 and that of females to 72.6 per cent. According to figures given by Lorimer, in the Tadzhik S.S.R. the literacy rate for males was only 6.2 per cent in 1926 but 77.7 per cent in 1939![34]

## Skilled Labor Needs

Apart from the mere numbers needed to man the new industrial plants, obviously one of the greatest difficulties in a program of rapid industrialization is to provide skilled laborers and technicians in adequate numbers. Machine technology is not something that an agricultural population can absorb overnight. In addition, a sizable body of administrative personnel is necessary to plan and operate a large-scale industrialization program. Plant foremen, engineers, supervisors, and a host of other specialized workers also seem to be indispensable.

The U.S.S.R. encountered serious shortages of all such workers. Even at the beginning of the third five-year plan (1938) the shortages seem to have been acute because insufficient numbers were being trained and recruitment and selection were not altogether satisfactory.[35] Foreign specialists were used in some of the earliest undertakings. Besides their specific assignments, they were to be used in such a way as to afford training to the Soviet specialists.[36] When the census of 1929 showed that 42 per cent of the industrial workers had had no industrial experience prior to the revolution, and that 43 per cent of those holding posts requiring technical training were without such training, it became clear that a thoroughgoing recruitment and education program was essential. The universities are said to have trained 170,000 specialists during the first five-year plan and 369,000 during the second; the technical schools, 291,000 and 623,000 respectively. Among the 106,000 graduates from the universities and technical schools in 1938, there were 25,000 engineers for industry and construction, and 35,000 teachers for secondary and workers' schools, besides nearly 6,000 lawyers

34. *Ibid.*, p. 199.

35. One major difficulty in the earliest years after the revolution was that Russian specialists were often suspect, because of their "class origins," and so were unwilling to accept responsibility for tasks that often they alone were able to perform. In this period, the press is reported to have carried many news items such as the following: "Every specialist is branded as a criminal in advance." "When it is deemed necessary to accuse or attack a specialist, more often than not the charge brought against him is that he persecutes Party men. And only those who are subjected to these accusations know how difficult it is under the circumstances to defend one's good name." "For instance, proceedings have been started 27 times in the course of a year (1928) against the director of the Shaitan works on various trifling charges. The director of the Bereznikov works in the course of 8 months has been called upon 28 times to defend himself." As reported by Baykov, *The Development of the Soviet Economic System*, p. 151.

36. Among the American firms which supplied technical assistance were Electric Auto-Lite Co., Ford Motor Co., Seiberling Rubber Co., Timken-Detroit Axle Co., and Brown-Lipe Gear Co. Some Japanese specialists were employed in improving the railway repairs industry. See *Handbook of the Soviet Union*, American-Russian Chamber of Commerce, New York, 1936, pp. 164–247.

and economists and almost 10,000 miscellaneous specialists.[37] Despite these numbers, shortages continued acute. Effective industrialization consists of something more than constructing buildings and installing machinery. What Veblen called the "state of the industrial arts" must also be cultivated.

Space does not permit discussion of the difficulties encountered in industrial management, labor incentives, differential wages, and a host of other matters important in the problem of labor procurement. There were difficulties with respect to all these and they were only gradually overcome.

### AGRICULTURE IN RUSSIAN ECONOMIC DEVELOPMENT

Few aspects of Russian economic development between 1928 and 1939 are more controversial than those pertaining to agriculture. Collectivization and mechanization are the dominant features of both official policy and the recorded facts. Stalin established these aims when he proclaimed before the 15th Congress of the Communist party in 1927:

> The way out is to unite the small and dwarf peasant farm gradually but surely, not by pressure, but by example and persuasion, into large farms based on common, co-operative, collective cultivation of the soil, with the use of agricultural machines and tractors and scientific methods of intensive agriculture. There is no other way out.[38]

Dobb calls this pronouncement "an act of great political courage as well as of genius." But others have contested this view—quite apart from the human costs suffered because collectivization was *not* carried through "gradually" and merely by "example and persuasion."[39]

Whether collectivization and mechanization succeeded or failed seems to depend largely upon the criteria used to assess them. By the test of maximizing agricultural output or improving agricultural efficiency, these policies were probably less effective than others that might have been followed. On the other hand, the overriding objective of the government of the U.S.S.R. was to develop heavy industry quickly, and this in a social environment that was badly disorganized and frequently hostile. Consequently, people and produce had to be drawn off the land into the industrializing urban centers. As a means toward this end the collective farm was a signal success. Moreover, the collective farm, especially when dominated by a few

---

37. Baykov, *The Development of the Soviet Economic System*, pp. 161, 217 and 353. Since there were some 22 million workers and employees in industry at the end of the first five-year plan in 1932, the half million (461,000) specialists and technical school graduates trained *during* the first five-year plan constituted around 2 per cent of those employed in industry. This is a small ratio for a country that, prior to 1928, was predominantly agricultural.

38. As quoted by Dobb, *Soviet Economy and the War*, p. 22.

39. For example, Naum Jasny, *The Socialized Agriculture of the USSR: Plans and Performance*, Stanford University Press, Stanford, 1939, and Lazar Volin, *A Survey of Soviet Russian Agriculture* (Monograph 5), U.S. Department of Agriculture, 1951.

Party members, offered a means of keeping the central administration informed of what was afoot in the hinterland so that it could crush incipient resistance before it became unmanageable. The Party was never more than a small fraction of the total population, and the policy of relentlessly steering the course of events must have presented acute problems at all times. In agriculture, collectivization offered a solution to this stubborn difficulty.

*Mechanization*

Collectivization went hand in hand with increased mechanization. Mechanization of agriculture was emphasized partly because it served to speed up the familiarity of the population at large with machine technology, and thereby to facilitate rapid industrial development. Moreover, farm machinery, especially the tractor, seems to have fascinated the early leaders of the new Russia. For example, Naum Jasny writes:

> Lenin thought, or at least said, in 1919 that "if we could only provide agriculture with 100,000 tractors the peasants would turn Communists." . . . Hubbard correctly stated: "The tractor is to the Russian Communist something more than a machine; in his heart of hearts he regards it as, in some way, a mystical symbol of the new faith."[40]

This enthusiasm for mechanization was apparently linked with the firm conviction that the economies of scale in agriculture were virtually unlimited.

The first machine-tractor station came into existence only in 1928. By 1940 there were nearly 7,000 such stations with 523,000 tractors. There were also 182,000 harvester combines in 1940, as against 1,700 as late as 1930. In 1938, the 153,000 harvester combines are said to have performed slightly less than half, 48 per cent, of the total harvesting, while mechanical threshers did 95 per cent of the total threshing. In the same year, 71 per cent of the plowing is said to have been done by tractor-drawn plows. The quantity of fertilizers supplied to agriculture is stated to have grown from 234,000 tons in 1928 to 3,216,000 tons ten years later in 1938. In 1913 only 188,000 tons of fertilizer were used, according to Baykov.[41]

*Changes in Output*

In view of the application of capitalistic methods—increased consumption of fertilizer and increased mechanization—the gains in agricultural production seem small. The area sown to crops in 1939 was 27 per cent greater than in 1913 according to the present "official" figure for 1913, which gives a more favorable comparison than the previous figure for that year. As compared with the 1928 acreage, the sown area in 1939 was up

40. Jasny, *op. cit.*, p. 27.
41. Baykov, *The Development of the Soviet Economic System*, *op. cit.*, p. 331.

18 per cent. With a reduction in the proportion of the sown area used for grain crops—from 90 per cent in 1913 to 82 per cent in 1928 and 74 per cent in 1939—gross production of cotton and sugar beets increased markedly. Between 1928 and 1939, cotton output showed almost a fourfold gain and output of sugar beets doubled. In contrast, production of grain increased 43 per cent in this interval, and the average yield of grain per hectare rose only from 7.5 quintals in 1928–1932 to 9.3 quintals in 1939. (See Table 10-3.)

There was, of course, a drain of population to the urban areas. In 1914, the urban population is estimated to have been 17.5 per cent of the total as against 33 per cent in 1939.[42] Since the total population increased from 142.3 to 170.5 million in these years, however, the absolute numbers in rural areas, those presumably primarily engaged in agricultural production, changed very little—from 117.4 million in 1914 to 114.5 million in 1939.[43] With nearly the same number of people in agriculture, using more capitalistic and larger-scale methods of production as well as about 18 per cent more land, it is surprising that production in 1939 was so little over the 1914 output—perhaps not more than 30–35 per cent.[44]

*Agriculture in Relation to Industrialization*

The role assigned to agriculture in Soviet industrialization appears to have been largely influenced by certain highly unique features of the industrialization process, as determined by the planning authorities. The industrialization program deliberately put almost its whole emphasis on capital goods. The plans did not call for any appreciable increase in the total flow of consumption goods, and certainly not for increased consumption per capita. The planning authorities must have foreseen that the peasants would not easily be enticed into shipping their produce to the towns and cities unless the industrial sector could furnish them consumption goods in exchange. But the plans did not contemplate more consumption goods output. Had the organization of agriculture been left unchanged, two difficulties might well have arisen to block the industrialization program. First, though total agricultural output would probably have risen, the farmers would have tended to expand their own consumption and to increase their

42. Alexander Baykov, "Note on the Trend of Population and the Labour Problems of the U.S.S.R.," *Journal of the Royal Statistical Society*, Part IV, 1943, p. 349.

43. Computed from figures in Lorimer, *op. cit.*, pp. 30–32 and 241.

44. As Table 10-3 shows, the increase in grain crops from 1913 to 1939 was 31 per cent, and grains accounted for about three quarters of the sown area. Further details, by types of crops and regions, are given by Volin, *op. cit.*, pp. 111–13. Also to be taken into account, perhaps, are the changes in livestock numbers. Between 1916 (which is usually considered about the same as 1913) and 1938, horses decreased about 50 per cent; cattle increased about 5 per cent; sheep and goats seem to have diminished about 15 per cent; while swine increased about 50 per cent. See *ibid.*, p. 153. Just what weights should be assigned to these various changes to reach an over-all figure for production increases is too technical a question to be discussed here. Around 30–35 per cent appears to be a reasonable estimate.

TABLE 10-3. SOWN AREA AND AGRICULTURAL PRODUCTION IN THE U.S.S.R., 1913–1939

| | 1913 | 1928 | 1930 | 1932 | 1934 | 1936 | 1937 | 1938 | 1939 | Percentage Increase | |
|---|---|---|---|---|---|---|---|---|---|---|---|
| | | | | | | | | | | 1939 over 1913 | 1939 over 1928 |
| **Sown Area (Millions of Hectares[a])** | | | | | | | | | | | |
| Total | 105 (116.7)[b] | 113 | 127.2 | 134.4 | 131.4 | 133.8 | 135.3 | 136.9 | 134.0 | 27 (15)[b] | 18 |
| Grain crops | 94.4 (102.7)[b] | 92.2 | 101.8 | 99.7 | 104.7 | 102.4 | 104.4 | 102.4 | 99.6 | 5 (−3)[b] | 8 |
| **Gross Production (Millions of Quintals)** | | | | | | | | | | | |
| Grain | 801 (816)[b] | 733 | 836 | 699 | 894 | 827 | 1,203 | 950 | 1,054.4 | 31 (29)[b] | 43 |
| Flax fiber | 5.1 | 3.2 | 4.4 | 5.0 | 5.3 | 5.8 | 5.7 | 5.5 | 6.4 | 25 | 100 |
| Cotton | 6.8 | 8.2 | 11.1 | 12.7 | 11.8 | 23.9 | 25.8 | 26.9 | 28.2 | 315 | 244 |
| Sugar beets | 99.2 | 101 | 140 | 66 | 114 | 168 | 219 | 167 | 210 | 112 | 107 |
| | | 1928–1932 | | 1933–1937 | 1938 | 1939 | | | | | |
| Average yield of grain crops (quintals per hectare) | | 7.5 | | 9.1 | 9.3 | 9.3 | | | | | |
| Average harvest of grain crops (millions of quintals) | | 735.9 | | 944.7 | 949.9 | 1,054.4 | | | | | |

Source: Adapted from Alexander Baykov, The Development of the Soviet Economic System, Cambridge University Press, Cambridge, 1946, p. 325.

a. One hectare equals 2.47 acres.
b. Figures in parentheses relate to earlier "official" estimates.

farm investments by building up their herds and improving their farms—in short they would have done what peasants have done for centuries.[45] Second, there would be little in this combination of circumstances to draw people off the land and into the cities; labor would be short, either to build the factories or to man them when finished. Consequently, either the industrialization program had to be substantially modified or agriculture had to be so reorganized that these difficulties did not arise. Collectivization and mechanization of agriculture offered a solution that would drive people into industry and assure their food supply once they got there and, at the same time, check increased consumption and investment on the part of those who remained on the land.

### An Over-All View of Russian Industrialization

The planned industrialization of the U.S.S.R. encountered problems and difficulties little different from those experienced by other countries. At the outset, the economy lacked the entrepreneurial skills, the capital and the labor force from which to create an industrial system. On the favorable side, however, was an inheritance of capital goods in the form of a railway network, some industrial plants, mines and other facilities, and a small, tightly knit group of zealots determined to achieve a special kind of industrial development regardless of cost, obstacles or opposition. This group supplied the entrepreneurship, fired not by profits but by the tenets of dialectical materialism as pronounced by Marx, Lenin and Stalin. It was entrepreneurship of a special type, but it was entrepreneurship nonetheless.

Apart from determining the basic aims of Russian industrialization—which were self-sufficiency in producers' goods and the development of a military potential adequate to the believed need—the task of the Communist entrepreneurs was to redeploy much of the labor force and inherited capital assets into building up heavy industry. The "real saving" necessary to this end was brought about by a combination of controls and organizational changes that severely limited total consumption of all kinds—food, clothing, housing and the like—and that allocated it among persons and groups so that the industrial program could be carried out. Probably some capital formation came from resources saved through undermaintenance of existing capital assets. Even if a rational accounting would show that railroads and housing, for example, were not actually undermaintained, these sectors of the economy will probably have to be assigned considerably more investment than they have received since 1928 if the industrial system is not to become so unbalanced as to reduce its efficiency.

45. Exactly the same problem arose in Western Europe during and immediately after World War II. The cities had nothing to offer the countryside, with the result that the peasants both ate better and increased their investments, instead of delivering their produce to the cities in exchange for paper money.

*Capital Goods versus Consumers' Goods*

The all-important fact is that the Soviets did transform an agricultural economy into an industrialized economy in little more than a decade. At any rate, the U.S.S.R. became an industrialized economy in the sense that it possessed a capital goods sector and a substantial fraction of its population was engaged in nonagricultural pursuits. It was not geared to the production of a large flow of consumption goods; but then this was not the objective sought.[46] The plans concentrated on the capital goods industries with the result that the consumers' goods industries were allotted relatively few resources. It is estimated that in both 1913 and 1928 the gross output of consumers' goods was double the output of producers' goods, but in 1937 and 1940 the gross output of consumers' goods had fallen to less than half, 46 per cent, of the gross output of all industry.[47]

Actually, in both the first and second five-year plans, the committed investment was only a little more than half the amount originally planned. In other words, as the program got under way it was found that the development of "key" or "basic" industries required more productive resources than was expected: consumers' goods industries had to go short because of the priorities established by the whole spirit of the program.

It is interesting to speculate on why the development of the consumption goods industries proceeded less rapidly than the planned schedule. While it is not easy to give a satisfactory answer, there is some evidence that two facts may have been mainly responsible. First, the training and development of adequate numbers of supervisors, technicians, specialists, operatives and other skilled workers proved to be more difficult than was anticipated. Since skilled labor was *generally* scarce, this meant a slowing down in the rate of progress over a wide front. In the circumstances consumption goods industries were sacrificed. Second, in planning the development of key industries, such as steel, coal and machinery, there was probably a tendency to concentrate on large undertakings, big production units, obvious deficiencies, and to overlook the statistically less important but still indispensable ancillary industries and production units that made the whole undertaking workable. Hence, in addition to the planned utilization of resources in the major undertakings, it was found that resources were needed for these ancillary activities, and so consumption goods had to be cut more than was planned.

Notwithstanding the frenzied pace of industrialization and the strict concentration on producers' goods, the U.S.S.R. in 1937 was still well below other industrial countries in per capita output of these goods and very

46. See p. 194. The expectation of life at birth for males rose in Russia from 41.0 years in 1926–1927 to an estimated 46.7 in 1938–1940. Thus well-being improved but even in 1940 was well below that in Western Europe. See Lorimer, *op. cit.*, p. 125.
47. A. Yugow, *Russia's Economic Front for War and Peace*, Harper, New York, 1942, p. 14.

much below in per capita output of consumers' goods. Per capita, the U.S.S.R. produced less pig iron, steel and coal in 1937 than the United States, Germany, England and France did in 1929. Its 1937 per capita output of electric power and cement was surpassed in 1929 by these countries and by Japan as well. In per capita production of such consumers' goods as cotton cloth, footwear, sugar and soap the U.S.S.R. in 1937 was appreciably behind the level these countries had reached in 1929, and the gap would probably be even more pronounced if data on more such goods was available. (See Table 10-4.)

TABLE 10-4. PER CAPITA PRODUCTION IN THE U.S.S.R. IN 1937 AND IN OTHER INDUSTRIAL COUNTRIES AROUND 1929

| Product | Unit | U.S.S.R. | United States | Germany | England | France | Japan |
|---|---|---|---|---|---|---|---|
| Electric power | kw-h. | 215 | 1,160 | 735 | 608 | 490 | 421 |
| Pig iron | kilo] | 86 | 292 | 234 | 183 | 189 | 30 |
| Steel | kilo | 105 | 397 | 291 | 279 | 188 | 62 |
| Coal | kilo ⌟ | 757 | 3,429 | 3,313 | 5,165 | 1,065 | 643 |
| Cement | kilo]{ | 32 | 156 | 173 | 154 | 86 | 60 |
| Cotton cloth | sq. me. | 16 | 58 | .. | 60 | 31 | 57 |
| Footwear | pair | 1 | 2.6 | 1.1 | 2.2 | .. | .. |
| Paper | kilo | 5 | 48 | 42 | 42 | 23 | 8 |
| Sugar | kilo | 14 | 12 | 29 | 8 | 21 | 17 |
| Soap | kilo | 3 | 12 | 7 | 11 | 10 | .. |

Source: A. Yugow, *Russia's Economic Front for War and Peace*, Harper, New York, 1942, p. 32.

### National Income

Between 1928 and 1937 the Soviets officially reckon that their net national income increased from 25.0 to 96.3 billion rubles of the base year 1926–1927. This is an increase of 3.85 times, or an annual average of 16 per cent. But most authorities agree that this reckoning overstates the increase, although by exactly how much depends upon the methods of computation. Probably the average annual rate of increase did not exceed 8.8 per cent and was not less than 5.1 per cent. Gregory Grossman seems to feel that 6.5 to 7 per cent is a reasonable approximation.[48] Whatever the "true" rate, if any such can be firmly established, the expansion was certainly a rapid one and one which has rarely, if ever, been matched by other countries even for short periods.[49]

### Basic Problems: Skilled Labor

The economic development of the U.S.S.R. illustrates some of the problems that might be encountered by other countries bent on development.

48. Gregory Grossman, "Soviet National Income and Product: Trends and Prospectives" (processed), Russian Research Center, Harvard University, Cambridge, 1952, pp. 7 and 8*ff*.

49. See Colin Clark, *The Conditions of Economic Progress*, 2d edition, Macmillan, London, 1951, Chapters 10 and 11.

It would appear that the most difficult problem of all was that of providing adequate numbers of skilled and trained workers capable of carrying through the construction program as planned, and capable also of operating the industrial facilities when they were completed. Planning steel mills and hydroelectric power plants is one thing. To bring a large rural population quickly to a degree of technical proficiency in industrial techniques and operations is something else again. Observation and reflection upon advanced industrial cultures suggest that, on the human side as well as in the more narrowly technical aspects, the process of industrialization is highly organic. It is not something that can be fabricated overnight.

In planning the industrialization of the U.S.S.R., a large educational program was recognized as an important part of the whole undertaking. Much training was planned and a good deal carried through. Nevertheless, shortages of skilled personnel appear to have been one of the main limitations in the effort to raise output. More resources used for labor training and less for plant construction might have been a wiser allocation. In formal planning for deliberate industrialization, there may be an almost inevitable tendency to concentrate on the more tangible undertakings such as plants, equipment, machinery and raw materials, and to allocate resources accordingly. A priorities system for the allocation of scarce resources is likely to be so administered that tangible rather than intangible undertakings get a high rating.[50] Consequently, when the scarce resource becomes even scarcer than was originally contemplated, it is the comparatively intangible undertakings that are most likely to suffer. It may not be so surprising, therefore, that the Russian five-year plans slighted worker-training programs in comparison with construction programs and output of "basic" materials. In retrospect, the wisdom of this policy is questionable. In the industrialization of other areas, special care might be exercised to prevent a similar development.

*Transportation*

More resources might also have been allocated to transportation. Efficient transportation is such an integral part of effective industrial production that it is perilous to jeopardize it by undermaintenance. Whether the U.S.S.R. actually did so is obviously difficult to judge. However, statements of the Soviet authorities themselves, as well as certain data already cited, suggest that transportation might have been allocated a greater share of investment with beneficial effects on total output.

50. There are some interesting parallels between the difficulties encountered in administering a priorities system of allocation, in contrast to allocation by the price system, in the American war economy and the Russian industrialization program.

*Large-Scale Undertakings*

There is, finally, some evidence that the planning authorities were overly impressed with the possible economies of large-scale undertakings and insufficiently appreciative of their limitations and handicaps. The result was that investment commitments were often a long time in coming into production, that transport facilities were strained, and, not least in importance, that management and control problems were multiplied out of proportion to the gain in productive capacity while, at the same time, there was a loss of flexibility in production.[51] The evidence is not conclusive, but there is more than a suggestion in the record that this was the case.

These comments on the industrialization of the U.S.S.R. are necessarily general and to a degree inconclusive. But the Russian experience does suggest how complicated a process industrialization is and how easily many of the most important factors may be overlooked or given insufficient weight. Industrialization is something more than the erection of factories in a rural wilderness. People, as well as the landscape, have to be industrialized.

51. In the early days of the war production program in the United States, there appears to have been a similar tendency to assume a direct relationship between size and efficiency and to construct production units that were too big for optimum efficiency. For example, if it were to be done over again, would the Willow Run plant be authorized?

# 11. The Pace of Material Progress in the Past

THE EXPECTED DIVIDEND OF ECONOMIC development nowadays is an improvement in average material well-being. If this dividend is to be realized, total output must grow more rapidly than population. Whether or not this objective will be achieved in the now underdeveloped countries remains an open question. It is worth examining the relationship between growth in output and growth in population in the developed countries, since this relationship must have determined the per capita gain in material well-being that they have realized. As their development programs get under way, the presently underdeveloped countries may do much better on both counts: real incomes per person may rise more rapidly than they have in the past. Nevertheless, the historical record of the already developed countries may provide a rough benchmark against which to check contemporary expectations.

In comparing rates of growth as between one country and another, at least two general considerations must be kept in mind. First, there is a strong presumption that the later in time a country develops the more rapid should be its progress. Since it comes late to the task, it can borrow from already developed countries their technical achievements with the certainty that the techniques will work—all the experimental, pilot-plant difficulties and costs have already been shouldered elsewhere. And, because technical progress is cumulative, the later in time the borrowing occurs, the more there will be to borrow. Hence, the latecomer can apply borrowed knowledge over a wider front. For example, Russian development after 1928 proceeded on a number of fronts simultaneously, in pig iron, steel, tractors and motor cars, etc. In 1900, it would have been impossible to borrow tractors or, in 1850, the advanced technology of steel production. By the same token, the longer a country delays before embarking on development, the greater will be the gap between its level of economic achievement and that of the technically advanced economies. To this extent, it may be harder to overcome the gap. Nevertheless, its rate of progress should be comparatively more rapid than that of the countries that developed earlier.

The second general comment on rates of development is that the actual rates in particular countries always reflect random influences as well as developmental factors. A war, fear of external aggression, social upheavals

213

and other social, psychological or political factors will accelerate or hold down a country's rate of economic development according to the timing and combination of circumstances that accompany them. The fact that Japan, for example, was able to pass from a quasi-feudal economy to an industrial economy without a violent social revolution was probably extremely favorable to its economic development. Similarly, the 1917 revolution in Russia put economic development in reverse for a time, while later on the fear of external aggression drove it rapidly forward. Thus, before development begins, the facts of a country's economic position, both internally and in relation to the rest of the world, do no more than fix its potential rate of growth. It will approximate or fall short of this potential according to how certain chance or circumstantial factors impinge upon it. In the future, as in the past, these factors are likely to be quite as important as the economic data.

### NATIONAL INCOME AND CAPITAL FORMATION

National income series are frequently used nowadays to portray a country's economic performance over a span of years, or to compare economic performance between countries as of a particular year. Provided the time span is moderate, or the degree of development in the countries compared is not widely disparate, such national income comparisons per capita are often highly revealing. Neither qualification can be met for the countries that developed economically between, say, 1800 and 1938. Even if national income calculations were available for England, Germany, France, Japan, Russia and the rest of these countries for the whole period 1800–1938—which of course they are not—most of the conclusions drawn from such data as to relative rates of development would still be dubious. If, for example, one had figures of per capita income for England in 1800 and 1900 and found that the 1900 income was some multiple, $x$, times that of 1800, one would find the utmost difficulty in interpreting what this meant because of the enormous changes in products consumed, in the way of life, the scale of values, and so on between these years. Let any reader old enough to remember the 1920s in the United States try to compare that decade with the 1950s and the difficulties will be readily apparent.

### The Long-Run Growth in Income

According to Simon Kuznets, "the rates of growth in per capita income (in constant prices) are quite high. On a per century basis, they are: USA, 1869–1938: 381 percent; Sweden, 1861–1938: 661 percent; UK, 1860–1938:

231 percent; France, 1950–1938 [*sic:* 1850?–1938]: 135 percent."[1] Reduced to a crude annual basis—that is, the total percentage gain divided by the years in the interval—these figures become: United States, 4.8 per cent; Sweden, 8.5 per cent; United Kingdom, 2.9 per cent; and France, 1.5 per cent. But such figures mask the important facts that the rate of growth was far from even over these long intervals; that the rate of growth in the United Kingdom was almost certainly higher before than after 1860; and that, as Kuznets points out, "for the economically advanced countries, we observe in all—provided the record is carried far enough back—a retardation, a decline in the percentage rates of growth of population, total national income, and income per capita."[2] In the case of Japan, the index of per capita national income in constant (1928–1932) prices is estimated to have moved as follows:[3]

| | |
|---|---|
| 1878–82 | 100 |
| 1888–92 | 137 |
| 1898–1902 | 189 |
| 1908–12 | 220 |
| 1918–22 | 270 |
| 1928–32 | 400 |
| 1938–42 | 526 |

Crudely reckoned as before, this gives an annual average, over the 60 years, of 7.1 per cent; but it will be observed again that the rate varied from decade to decade. For Russia the comparable per capita figure for the period 1928–1939 would probably be higher, though by how much is open to dispute.

## Capital Formation

Rates of capital formation might be compared among countries on several bases. Perhaps the most useful method would be to compare increases in the capital stock expressed as a percentage of the capital stock —in other words, the rate at which the capital stock was growing as economic development moved forward. Apart from the inherent theoretical difficulties, which are formidable, the data necessary for such calculations are simply not available over long periods for any of the countries that

1. Simon Kuznets, "Population, Income and Capital" (mimeographed), Round Table on Economic Progress, International Economic Association, Santa Margherita Ligure, Italy, 1953, p. 6.

2. *Ibid.*, p. 8.

3. Adapted from Shigeto Tsuru and Kazushi Ohkawa, "Long-Term Changes in the National Product of Japan since 1878," in Milton Gilbert (Ed.), *Income and Wealth, Series III*, International Association for Research in Income and Wealth, Bowes and Bowes, Cambridge, 1953, p. 39.

developed during the nineteenth century.[4] Furthermore, the absence of data on the capital stock in various European countries a century or more ago is not likely to be remedied in the near future, if ever.

Some crude estimates of the ratio of net capital formation to net national product have recently been compiled for a few countries. These show a wide variation—from a figure as high as 14.5 per cent in the United States in the decade 1889–1898 to one of less than 3.5 per cent for Sweden in 1861–1870. For the United Kingdom between 1870 and 1909, net capital formation seems to have been a fairly steady proportion of net national product at about 8.2 per cent. In France, the rate is believed to have been similar at 8.3 per cent for the period 1853–1878, but only 4.6 per cent for the period 1878–1903. The Swedish rate seems to have risen each decade from its initial 3.5 per cent in 1861–1870 to 13.5 per cent in 1911–1920.[5]

Other than their obviously considerable range, these figures do not reveal much. At best, they seem only to confirm, in a very crude fashion, what one would have supposed to have been true of capital formation from the figures given previously on the change in per capita income in constant prices.

## Difficulties of Partial Measurement

Lacking an over-all measure of economic achievement, as provided by national income, one must resort to partial measures. Because economic development is a many-sided process, individual statistical series can be only partially descriptive at best and sometimes downright misleading. For example, an index of manufacturing production or industrial production will almost certainly exaggerate economic progress as a whole simply because it probably portrays the very sector that is developing most rapidly. Similarly, to use the rates of increase in production of certain products as indicative of manufacturing as a whole—especially where these products were virtually nonexistent before the period of development—will usually exaggerate, by implication, the rate of increase in the whole manufacturing

4. Among the theoretical difficulties are such questions as, What is a suitable concept of capital and hence of capital formation? If capital growth is conceived as one of the primary causes of the growth in total output, then many items—for instance, houses and many consumers' durable goods—are scarcely relevant because they are more an expression of the fact that total output did grow than an explanation of why it grew. On the other hand, if the focus is on the growth rate of output as a whole, then there are reasons for believing that the capital stock will tend to grow in proportion to output, so that it may not give any additional information. A further difficulty is that the yield rate on capital investment may change substantially over long periods so that there is no uniform significance, in terms of income, to be attached to a given percentage increment to the capital stock. Finally, capital equipment may be, and almost certainly has been, of different degrees of durability over the past two centuries; the same gross capital formation means a different amount of net capital formation because the average depreciation rate properly to be applied to the existing capital stock keeps changing. All these are problems over and above those inherent in the question of how to value capital by a capitalization method or otherwise.

5. These figures are drawn from Simon Kuznets, "International Differences in Capital Formation and Financing" (mimeographed; Conference on Capital Formation and Economic Growth, November 1953), National Bureau of Economic Research, New York, 1953, Appendix A, Table I–3. Kuznets also gives figures on the ratio of gross capital formation to gross national product.

or industrial sector. To illustrate by an extreme example: Table 10-2 shows that the Soviet output of motor cars increased from 1,400 in 1929 to 200,000 in 1937. But this large increase is obviously far greater than the increase in industrial output as a whole, while this in turn was far greater in Russia than the rise in total output, which includes agriculture, industry and services. A small segment of an economy can grow at a very high percentage rate at the expense of, or in lieu of, growth elsewhere. In Russia, the very rapid growth of heavy-goods production was possible in part because consumers' goods production was deliberately held down.

### Coal Output as a Measure of Development

Apart from textiles, economic development in the past has been built heavily on coal and iron. Consequently, comparative rates of growth in output of coal and iron afford at least a rough indication of the pace of economic development. Because of the rise of electricity and oil as sources of power, however, coal is now less the primary source of power than it was in the nineteenth century. Hence, economic development in the future will be founded rather less on coal than it has been in the past. Moreover, many of the now underdeveloped countries have practically no coal and so will resort to hydroelectric power and oil instead.

The growth of coal production in the nineteenth century can be calculated for several countries. For England, coal output in 1826 was 31 per cent above that in 1816; 1836 was nearly 43 per cent above that of 1826; 1846 was 46 per cent above 1836; and 1856 was 43 per cent above 1846. In other words, between 1836 and 1856 in England, coal production increased on the average approximately 4 per cent a year. By 1836, England was, of course, well into the industrial revolution although the big period of railway construction was still ahead. For France, the comparable percentage increases in coal production beginning with the decade 1820–1830 and ending with that of 1860–1870 were as follows: 80, 66, 46, 88 and 36. These show much greater variation but also a higher average than the figures for England. Germany's coal production increased 100 per cent in the decade 1860–1870, but in the three succeeding decades to 1900 the increases were only 74, 50 and 67 per cent. In Belgium, coal production increased 70 per cent between 1831 and 1840, 40 per cent from 1840 to 1850, 65 per cent between 1850 and 1860, 41 per cent from 1860 to 1870, but only 24 per cent from 1870 to 1880. For Sweden—which produced no coal—the percentage increases in the consumption of coal and coke—using a five-year average, such as 1861–1865 compared with 1871–1875—by decades from the early 1860s to the early 1900s appear to be 82, 84, 66 and 23. In Russia between 1929 and 1938, coal production rose by 231 per cent. (See Table 11-1.)

Accepting Russia as a special case for several reasons, it is somewhat surprising to find that the variations between countries are no greater. Less than 50 per cent per decade seems to be a bit on the low side, while slightly more than 80 per cent seems to have been near the ceiling. Thus, in very rough terms, 5–8 per cent represents about the average annual rate of increase.

TABLE 11-1. COAL PRODUCTION IN SELECTED COUNTRIES, 1770–1938

(*Millions of Tons*)

| Year | England | United States | France | Germany | Belgium | Sweden[a] | Russia |
|------|---------|---------------|--------|---------|---------|-----------|--------|
| 1770 | 6.2 | | | | | | |
| 1787 | .. | | .2 | | | | |
| 1780 | 6.4 | | | | | | |
| 1811 | .. | | .7 | | | | |
| 1816 | 16.0 | | | | | | |
| 1820 | .. | | 1.0 | | | | |
| 1826 | 21.0 | | | | | | |
| 1830 | .. | | 1.8 | | 2.3 | | |
| 1836 | 30.0 | | | | | | |
| 1840 | .. | 2.1 | 3.0 | | 3.9 | | |
| 1846 | 44.0 | | | | | | |
| 1850 | .. | 7.0 | 4.4 | | 5.8 | | |
| 1856 | 65.0 | .. | .. | | .. | | |
| 1860 | 80.0 | 14.6 | 8.3 | 16.7 | 9.6 | .35 | |
| 1870 | 110.4 | 33.0 | 13.3 | 34.0 | 13.6 | .64 | |
| 1880 | 146.8 | 71.5 | 19.3 | 59.1 | 16.8 | 1.18 | |
| 1890 | 181.6 | 157.8 | 26.0 | 89.2 | 20.3 | 1.96 | |
| 1900 | 225.1 | 269.7 | 33.4 | 149.7 | 23.4 | 3.5 | |
| 1913 | 287.4 | 570.0 | 40.8 | 277.2 | 22.8 | 5.7 | 29.1 |
| 1923 | .. | 658.0 | .. | .. | .. | .. | 40.1[b] |
| 1933 | .. | .. | .. | .. | .. | .. | 76.3 |
| 1937 | | | | | | 9.1 | 127.9 |
| 1938 | .. | .. | .. | .. | .. | .. | 13.29 |

*Sources:* Figures for England are from J. H. Clapham, *An Economic History of Modern Britain*, 2d edition, Cambridge University Press, Cambridge, 1930, p. 431; for Sweden, from G. A. Montgomery, *The Rise of Modern Industry in Sweden*, King, London, 1939, pp. 136–37; for Russia, from A. Baykov, *The Development of the Soviet Economic System*, Cambridge University Press, Cambridge, 1946, p. 307; for other countries figures are from Simon Kuznets, *Secular Movements in Production and Prices*, Houghton Mifflin, Boston, 1930, Appendix, which has also been used to supplement some of the sources just cited. Certain relatively unimportant notes appearing in some of the sources have been omitted.

a. Data are for consumption of coal and coke and are based on five-year averages.
b. 1929.

If the percentage increases per decade for the various countries are converted to *compound* annual rates, however, the range is somewhat lower. The *compound* annual rates of growth seem to have been most frequently about 4–6 per cent—though with some lower and some higher rates. (See Table 11-2.)

## Output of Pig Iron

The comparable figures for pig iron show for most countries for which the data are available somewhat greater variations decade by decade and, on the whole, somewhat smaller rates of increase. For the United Kingdom, for example, after 1800 only once did the annual compound rate of increase go above 5.5 per cent; that was in 1830–1840, when the rate was 7.5 per

TABLE 11-2. AVERAGE ANNUAL PERCENTAGE RATE OF GROWTH IN COAL PRODUCTION IN SELECTED COUNTRIES, SELECTED PERIODS, 1770–1938

| Period | England | United States | France | Germany | Belgium | Sweden[a] | Russia |
|---|---|---|---|---|---|---|---|
| 1770–1780 | .3 | | | | | | |
| 1787–1811 | | | 5.4 | | | | |
| 1780–1816 | 2.6 | | .. | | | | |
| 1811–1820 | .. | | 3.6 | | | | |
| 1816–1826 | 2.8 | | .. | | | | |
| 1820–1830 | .. | | 6.0 | | | | |
| 1826–1836 | 3.6 | | .. | | | | |
| 1830–1840 | .. | | 5.2 | | | | |
| 1831–1840 | .. | .. | .. | | 6.0 | | |
| 1836–1846 | 3.9 | .. | .. | | .. | | |
| 1840–1850 | .. | 12.8 | 3.9 | .. | 4.1 | | |
| 1846–1856 | 4.0 | .. | .. | .. | .. | | |
| 1850–1860 | .. | 7.6 | 6.6 | .. | 5.2 | | |
| 1856–1860 | 5.3 | .. | .. | .. | .. | | |
| 1860–1870 | 3.3 | 8.5 | 2.4 | 7.4 | 3.5 | 6.2 | |
| 1870–1880 | 2.9 | 8.0 | 3.9 | 5.7 | 2.1 | 6.3 | |
| 1880–1890 | 2.1 | 8.2 | 3.0 | 4.2 | 1.9 | 5.2 | |
| 1890–1900 | 2.2 | 5.5 | 2.5 | 5.3 | 1.4 | 6.0 | |
| 1900–1913 | 1.9 | 5.9 | 1.6 | 4.9 | −.2 | 3.8 | |
| 1913–1923 | .. | 1.4 | .. | .. | .. | .. | .. |
| 1913–1929 | .. | .. | .. | .. | .. | .. | 2.0 |
| 1913–1937 | .. | .. | .. | .. | .. | 1.9 | .. |
| 1929–1933 | .. | .. | .. | .. | .. | .. | 17.5 |
| 1933–1937 | .. | .. | .. | .. | .. | .. | 13.8 |
| 1937–1938 | .. | .. | .. | .. | .. | .. | 3.9 |

*Source:* Calculated from Table 11–1.

a. Data are for consumption of coal and coke and are based on five-year averages.

cent. For France, the highest rate achieved was 5 per cent in 1840–1850; the other periods show rates of increase that are below 5 per cent more frequently than above. The German rate was apparently 9.0 per cent in 1840–1850, and above 7 per cent from 1860 to 1880. Belgium sustained the noteworthy rate of 7–8 per cent from 1830 to 1860. The rate of increase in the United States was above 9 per cent from the early 1870s to the mid-1890s. Canada's rate for 1891 to 1910 was higher, and the rate reached 24 per cent in the decade just before World War I.

## TABLE 11-3. PRODUCTION OF PIG IRON IN SELECTED COUNTRIES, 1500–1910

(Thousands of Tons[a])

| Year | World | United Kingdom | United States | France | Germany | Belgium | Austria | Russia | Sweden | Canada |
|------|-------|----------------|---------------|--------|---------|---------|---------|--------|--------|--------|
| 1500 | 60 | 6 | .. | 12 | 5 | .. | .. | .. | .. | .. |
| 1700 | 104 | 12 | .. | 22 | 10 | .. | .. | .. | .. | .. |
| 1740 | 157 | 20 | 1 | 26 | 18 | .. | .. | .. | .. | .. |
| 1790 | 278 | 68 | 30 | 40 | 30 | .. | .. | .. | .. | .. |
| 1800 | 460 | 190 | 40 | 60 | 40 | .. | .. | .. | .. | .. |
| 1810 | 616 | 250 | 55 | 85 | 46 | .. | .. | .. | .. | .. |
| 1820 | 1,010 | 400 | 110 | 140 | 90 | .. | .. | .. | .. | .. |
| 1830 | 1,585 | 680 | 180 | 220 | 120 | 35 | 80 | 103 | 105 | .. |
| 1840 | 2,774 | 1,396 | 290 | 350 | 170 | 73 | 140 | 185 | 130 | .. |
| 1850 | 4,468 | 2,250 | 564 | 570 | 402 | 144 | 140 | 228 | 130 | .. |
| 1860 | 7,300 | 3,827 | 821 | 898 | 530 | 320 | 310 | 335 | 185 | .. |
| 1870 | 11,900 | 5,964 | 1,665 | 1,178 | 1,391 | 565 | 400 | 360 | 300 | .. |
| 1880 | 17,950 | 7,749 | 3,835 | 1,725 | 2,729 | 609 | 464 | 448 | 406 | .. |
| 1890 | 27,157 | 7,904 | 9,203 | 1,970 | 4,685 | 782 | 856 | 926 | 456 | 19 |
| 1900 | 40,088 | 8,960 | 13,789 | 2,670 | 8,381 | 1,002 | 1,473 | 2,889 | 518 | 86 |
| 1910 | 66,211 | 10,217 | 27,304 | 4,038 | 14,793 | 1,852 | 2,010 | 3,042 | 604 | 740 |

*Source:* George H. Hull, *Industrial Depressions*, Codex Book Company, New York, 1926, Appendix M, pp. 296–301.

a. United States, United Kingdom and Canada in long tons; others in metric tons.

Broadly speaking, the countries that industrialized later had somewhat more rapid rates of increase in pig iron production than those that industrialized earlier, although there were exceptions. A compound annual rate of increase of under 5 per cent was not at all unusual in the nineteenth century, while rates of increase of above 7 per cent were rather out of the ordinary. (See Tables 11-3 and 11-4.)

### Manufacturing Production

Dr. Folke Hilgerdt has computed indexes of manufacturing for several countries back to 1870 and these also afford some indication of relative rates of growth at different periods in different countries. According to these figures, the compound annual rate of increase in manufacturing between 1871 and 1913 was more frequently below 3.5 per cent than above, especially in those countries that accounted for the largest proportion of total manufacturing output prior to 1913. The rate of increase in Sweden from the early 1880s to 1905 was notably high. (See Table 11-5.)

Figures for production of coal, pig iron and manufacturing undoubtedly show more rapid rates of increase than figures for output as a whole would show if complete data were available. Yet, in general, the compound annual rates of increase in these three areas were only 3 to 8 per cent or thereabouts. If the figures were corrected for population growth by reducing them to a per capita basis, the annual rate of increase would be smaller still. Thus, although the nineteenth century was a period of very rapid economic development, the rates of growth of even those indices that portray what was undoubtedly growing most rapidly seem to have been surprisingly small.

## THE GROWTH OF POPULATION

Contrary to an apparently popular view, secular growth in population has not been the "normal" state of affairs throughout human history. The population history of Western Europe during the past two centuries is quite unique. As one eminent scholar, R. R. Kuczynski, has written:

Practically nothing is known of the trend of the total population of Europe prior to the eighteenth century; there is no reason to assume that the population in 1700 was any larger than in 1600 or that the population in 1600 was much larger than in 1300. Although there is no doubt that the total population of Europe increased in the course of the eighteenth century, the size of the increase is not known. It amounted apparently to about 25 per cent in France, to about 50 per cent in England and Wales and to about 60 per cent in Sweden . . . It was probably much larger in Russia, where the population of the territory constituting the empire of Peter the Great is reported to have doubled between 1724 and 1796. From 1770 to 1800 the combined population of England, Denmark, Norway,

TABLE 11-4. AVERAGE ANNUAL PERCENTAGE RATE OF GROWTH IN PIG IRON PRODUCTION IN SELECTED COUNTRIES, SELECTED PERIODS, 1500–1910

| Period | World | United Kingdom | United States | France | Germany | Belgium | Austria | Russia | Sweden | Canada |
|---|---|---|---|---|---|---|---|---|---|---|
| 1500–1700 | .3 | .3 | .. | .3 | .3 | .. | .. | .. | .. | .. |
| 1700–1740 | 1.0 | 1.3 | .. | .4 | 1.5 | .. | .. | .. | .. | .. |
| 1740–1790 | 1.1 | 2.5 | 7.0 | .9 | 1.0 | .. | .. | .. | .. | .. |
| 1790–1800 | 5.2 | 10.8 | 2.9 | 4.1 | 2.9 | .. | .. | .. | .. | .. |
| 1800–1810 | 3.0 | 2.8 | 3.2 | 3.5 | 1.4 | .. | .. | .. | .. | .. |
| 1810–1820 | 5.1 | 4.8 | 7.2 | 5.1 | 6.9 | .. | .. | .. | .. | .. |
| 1820–1830 | 4.6 | 5.5 | 5.0 | 4.6 | 2.9 | .. | .. | .. | .. | .. |
| 1830–1840 | 5.8 | 7.5 | 4.9 | 4.7 | 3.5 | 7.5 | 5.8 | 6.0 | 2.2 | .. |
| 1840–1850 | 4.9 | 4.9 | 6.9 | 5.0 | 9.0 | 7.0 | 0.0 | 2.1 | 0.0 | .. |
| 1850–1860 | 5.0 | 5.5 | 3.8 | 4.6 | 2.8 | 8.3 | 8.3 | 3.9 | 3.6 | .. |
| 1860–1870 | 5.0 | 4.5 | 7.3 | 2.8 | 10.1 | 5.9 | 2.6 | 0.7 | 5.0 | .. |
| 1870–1880 | 4.2 | 2.7 | 8.7 | 3.9 | 7.0 | 0.8 | 1.5 | 2.2 | 3.1 | .. |
| 1880–1890 | 4.2 | 0.2 | 9.2 | 1.3 | 5.5 | 2.5 | 6.3 | 7.5 | 1.2 | .. |
| 1890–1900 | 4.0 | 1.3 | 4.1 | 3.1 | 6.0 | 2.5 | 5.5 | 12.0 | 1.3 | 16.3 |
| 1900–1910 | 5.1 | 1.3 | 7.1 | 4.2 | 5.8 | 6.3 | 3.2 | 0.5 | 1.6 | 24.3 |

Source: Computed from figures in George H. Hull, Industrial Depressions, Codex Book Company, New York, 1926, Appendix M, pp. 296–301.

TABLE 11-5. AVERAGE ANNUAL RATE OF GROWTH OF MANUFACTURING IN SELECTED COUNTRIES, SELECTED PERIODS, 1871–1913

| Period | World | United Kingdom | United States | France | Germany | Belgium | Russia | Sweden | Canada | Japan | India |
|---|---|---|---|---|---|---|---|---|---|---|---|
| 1871–1875 to 1881–1885 | 3.1 | 1.6 | 5.1 | .. | 2.7 | .. | .. | 4.7 | .. | .. | .. |
| 1881–1885 to 1891–1895 | 3.4 | 1.2 | 4.4 | 2.0 | 4.1 | 2.1 | 5.8 | 6.6 | 5.3 | .. | .. |
| 1891–1895 to 1901–1905 | 4.6 | 1.8 | 5.7 | 2.4 | 5.5 | 3.4 | 6.4 | 7.7 | 5.0 | 11.4 | .. |
| 1901–1905 to 1911–1913 | 3.5 | 1.9 | 3.4 | 4.3 | 3.5 | 4.4 | 4.4 | 3.1 | 7.2 | 7.8 | 3.5 |

*Source:* Folke Hilgerdt, *Industrialization and Foreign Trade*, League of Nations, Geneva, 1945, p. 130.

Sweden, Finland, France, Spain and Italy rose from 61,000,000 to 69,800,000, or by one seventh.[6]

Carr-Saunders reaches a similar conclusion: "there may have been some increase in the population of certain parts of Europe during the later years of the seventeenth century . . . On the whole it is more likely that the definitive increase in the population of Europe began after than before 1700."[7]

*Population Growth in the Nineteenth Century*

Whatever uncertainty attaches to the estimates of European population for the seventeenth and eighteenth centuries, those for the nineteenth century and later probably are reasonably accurate. The best available estimates show a notably high rate of population increase in the United Kingdom from 1800 to 1840 and again from 1860 to 1870; an even higher rate in Germany and Belgium from 1870 to 1910; and a still higher rate in the Netherlands from 1870 to 1920. Unusually high rates of increase in Sweden and Norway between 1840 and 1860, in contrast to appreciably lower rates both before and after, are puzzling unless they can be attributed to the rising prosperity from foreign commerce and shipping.[8] Low rates of increase in France, where total output undoubtedly improved, especially during the last half of the century, and a rise in Spain after 1880, where aggregate output probably increased only moderately, are contrary to the general pattern. In the main, the period 1820–1910 was characterized by rates of population growth in the several European countries that roughly parallel the timing of their accelerated economic development. (See Tables 11-6 and 11-7.)

*Decline in Mortality*

The growth of population in Western Europe in the late nineteenth century was almost entirely attributable to the fall in mortality rates that accompanied development.[9]

6. R. R. Kuczynski in *Encyclopaedia of the Social Sciences*, Vol. 12, Macmillan, New York, 1933, p. 243. While European population *as a whole* may not have increased between 1600 and 1700, the evidence seems to suggest that the population of some individual European countries increased appreciably during the seventeenth century. The population of England appears to be variously estimated at from 3.5 to 4.8 million about 1600 and at from 5.5 to 6.5 million about a century later. J. N. L. Baker, "England in the Seventeenth Century," in H. C. Darby (Ed.), *An Historical Geography of England before 1800*, 2d edition, Cambridge University Press, Cambridge, 1948, pp. 435*ff.* See also A. P. Usher, *The Industrial History of England*, Houghton Mifflin, Boston, 1920, p. 89.

7. A. M. Carr-Saunders, *World Population*, Oxford University Press, Oxford, 1936, p. 43.

8. See G. A. Montgomery, *The Rise of Modern Industry in Sweden*, King, London, 1939, pp. 115*ff.*

9. The decline in mortality rates and the resulting growth of population in nineteenth-century Europe would probably have been considerably greater had development not been accompanied by increasing agglomeration and urbanization of the population. Authorities seem to agree that the growing urban areas generally had higher mortality rates than the rural areas. Without migration from the countryside, the towns would probably have declined in population because their birth rates are usually believed to have been well below their death rates. On comparative rates of growth of cities and urban areas in different European countries during the nineteenth century see Adna Ferrin Weber, *The Growth of Cities in the Nineteenth Century*, Columbia University Press, New York, 1899, pp. 144–45 and *passim*.

TABLE 11-6. ESTIMATED POPULATION OF SELECTED INDUSTRIAL COUNTRIES, 1800–1949

(Millions)

| Country | 1800 | 1810 | 1820 | 1830 | 1840 | 1850 | 1860 | 1870 | 1880 | 1890 | 1900 | 1910 | 1920 | 1930 | 1940 | 1949 |
|---|---|---|---|---|---|---|---|---|---|---|---|---|---|---|---|---|
| Austria-Hungary | 24.3 | 25.5 | 27.0 | 29.8 | 31.4 | 32.5 | 34.8 | 37.5 | 39.2 | 42.9 | 47.1 | .. | .. | .. | .. | .. |
| Belgium[a] | 3.1 | .. | .. | 3.8 | 4.1 | 4.4 | 4.7 | 5.1 | 5.5 | 6.1 | 6.7 | 7.4 | 7.4 | 8.1 | 8.3 | 8.6 |
| Canada[b] | .4 | .. | .. | .6 | .. | 2.3 | 3.2 | 3.7 | 4.3 | 4.8 | 5.4 | 7.2 | 8.8 | 10.4 | 11.5 | 13.5 |
| Finland | .8 | .9 | 1.2 | 1.4 | 1.4 | 1.6 | 1.7 | 1.8 | 2.1 | 2.4 | 2.7 | 2.9 | 3.1 | 3.5 | 3.7 | 4.0 |
| France | 26.9 | 28.2 | 30.0 | 31.9 | 33.4 | 34.9 | 35.7 | 36.8 | 37.5 | 38.3 | 39.0 | 39.5 | 39.0 | 41.6 | 39.0 | 41.5 |
| Germany | 24.5 | 25.5 | 27.2 | 30.4 | 32.8 | 35.4 | 37.7 | 40.8 | 45.2 | 49.4 | 56.4 | 64.6 | 61.8 | 65.1 | 69.8 | 68.5 |
| Italy | 18.1 | 18.5 | 19.0 | 20.9 | 22.3 | 23.9 | 25.1 | 26.7 | 28.3 | 30.5 | 32.5 | 36.3 | .. | 41.2 | .. | 46.0 |
| Netherlands[c] | 2.2 | 2.3 | 2.4 | 2.6 | 2.9 | 3.1 | 3.3 | 3.6 | 4.1 | 4.6 | 5.2 | 5.9 | 6.9 | 7.9 | 8.9 | 10.0 |
| Norway[d] | .9 | .. | 1.1 | 1.2 | 1.3 | 1.5 | 1.7 | 1.8 | .. | 2.0 | 2.2 | 2.4 | 2.7 | 2.8 | .. | 3.2 |
| Russia | 38.0 | 42.0 | 46.0 | 51.2 | 55.6 | 60.0 | 65.0 | 73.0 | 83.5 | 95.9 | 109.7 | .. | .. | .. | .. | .. |
| Spain[e] | 10.5 | .. | .. | 14.6 | .. | .. | 15.6 | 16.2 | 16.6 | 17.6 | 18.6 | 20.0 | 21.3 | 23.9 | 25.9 | 28.0 |
| Sweden | 2.3 | 2.4 | 2.6 | 2.9 | 3.1 | 3.5 | 3.9 | 4.2 | 4.6 | 4.8 | 5.1 | 5.5 | 5.9 | 6.1 | 6.4 | 7.0 |
| United Kingdom[f] | 9.0 | .. | 15.5 | 17.8 | 20.2 | 22.3 | 24.5 | 27.4 | 31.0 | 34.3 | 38.2 | 42.0 | 44.0 | 46.0 | 48.2 | 50.4 |
| United States | 5.3 | 7.2 | 9.6 | 12.9 | 17.1 | 23.2 | 31.4 | 38.6 | 50.2 | 62.6 | 76.0 | 92.0 | 105.7 | 122.8 | 131.7 | 149.1 |

Sources: Figures for Austria-Hungary, France, Germany, Italy, the Netherlands, Russia, Sweden and the United States for years 1800–1900 are taken from Norman S. Buchanan and Friedrich A. Lutz, *Rebuilding the World Economy*, Twentieth Century Fund, New York, 1947, p. 318, which, in turn, were drawn mostly from Gustav Sundborg, *Aperçus statistiques internationaux*, Norstedt, Stockholm, 1906. Figures on population since 1900 have been taken from the statistical yearbooks of the respective countries or from publications of the League of Nations or the United Nations.

a. Figure in 1830 column is for 1831.
b. Figures in columns for 1850–1940 are for 1851–1941.
c. Figure in 1910 column is for 1909.
d. Figures in columns for 1820–1870 are for 1825–1875.
e. Figure given for 1880 is for 1877; the 1890 figure is for 1887.
f. From 1850 on the actual years are 1851, 1861, etc. Includes England, Wales, Scotland and Northern Ireland.

225

| Period[a] | Belgium | Canada | Finland | France | Germany | Italy | Nether-lands | Norway | Spain | Sweden | United Kingdom | United States |
|---|---|---|---|---|---|---|---|---|---|---|---|---|
| 1800–1810 | .. | 50 | 12 | 5 | 4 | 2 | 4 | 22 | 39 | 4 | 72 | 36 |
| 1810–1820 | .. |  | 33 | 6 | 7 | 3 | 4 |  |  | 8 |  | 33 |
| 1820–1830 | .. |  | 17 | 6 | 12 | 10 | 8 | 9 |  | 12 |  | 34 |
| 1830–1840 | 8 | 283 | 0 | 5 | 8 | 7 | 12 | 8 |  | 7 | 15 | 32 |
| 1840–1850 | 7 |  | 14 | 5 | 8 | 7 | 7 | 15 | 7 | 13 | 13 | 36 |
| 1850–1860 | 7 | 39 | 6 | 2 | 6 | 5 | 6 | 13 |  | 11 | 10 | 35 |
| 1860–1870 | 8 | 16 | 6 | 3 | 8 | 6 | 9 | 6 | 4 | 8 | 10 | 23 |
| 1870–1880 | 8 | 16 | 17 | 2 | 11 | 6 | 14 | 11 | 2 | 10 | 13 | 30 |
| 1880–1890 | 11 | 12 | 14 | 2 | 9 | 8 | 12 |  | 6 | 4 | 11 | 25 |
| 1890–1900 | 10 | 12 | 12 | 2 | 14 | 6 | 13 | 10 | 6 | 6 | 11 | 21 |
| 1900–1910 | 10 | 33 | 7 | 1 | 15 | 12 | 13 | 9 | 7 | 8 | 10 | 21 |
| 1910–1920 | 0 | 22 | 7 | −1 | −4 | 13 | 17 | 12 | 7 | 7 | 5 | 15 |
| 1920–1930 | 9 | 18 | 13 | 7 | 5 |  | 14 | 4 | 11 | 3 | 4 | 16 |
| 1930–1940 | 2 | 10 | 6 | −6 | 5 | 12 | 13 | 14 | 10 | 5 | 5 | 7 |
| 1940–1949 | 4 | 17 | 8 | 7 | −2 |  | 12 |  | 8 | 9 | 4 | 13 |

Source: Calculated from Table 11-6.

a. Decade limits vary slightly depending on census practice.

The primary reason why economic development tends to cut mortality appears to be twofold: first, greater output per capita permits greater consumption per capita, including better diets, clothing, housing, personal sanitation, all of which tend to lessen morbidity and mortality; second, because of its enhanced productivity, a more developed society can provide its people with the public health and sanitation measures (and the basic substructure of scientific knowledge on which these rest) which hold disease in check. A poor country can neither afford the health and sanitation measures necessary to lower mortality directly, nor does its economy afford the people a level of consumption high enough to enable them to resist disease.[10]

### Mortality Decline at Different Ages

In Western Europe the influence of economic development on mortality was typically not uniform in all age groups nor were its effects equally visible with respect to the various causes of death. In other words, to judge from the rather scanty data available, development appears to have lowered mortality much more at some ages than at others and to have reduced deaths from some causes much more than from others.[11]

As between different age classes, infant and child mortality seem to have shown the greatest decline. Between the first decade of the nineteenth century and the first decade of the twentieth, the over-all infant mortality rate for legitimate births in Sweden fell from 199 to 85. The rate in England and Wales at the beginning of the nineteenth century is apparently not known, but in 1841–1850 it was 167. This was higher than the Swedish rate at the time (153), but about 16 per cent below the Swedish rate at the beginning of the nineteenth century. After 1841–1850 the English-Welsh rate declined little until the end of the century.[12] The most suggestive information on mortality by age categories is provided by the Swedish data— said to be much the most complete for any country for the period since 1750. The greatest declines were achieved at the younger ages even though

10. Poverty and high death rates, moreover, are likely to be associated with, if not actually caused by, apathy and acceptance of the kind of conditions of filth, squalor and neglect which breed disease and facilitate its spread. A tidy slum, for example, is a contradiction in terms.
Even in countries with high average incomes per capita, economic status is inversely correlated with death rates. For example, in England and Wales, "The standardized mortality index for males was 90 for social class I (professional) compared to 111 for social class V (unskilled workers) . . . The standardized mortality index for married women, grouped according to the social class of the husband, shows a similar relationship, varying from 81 for class I to 113 for class V . . . Infant mortality varies more sharply with differences in socio-economic status than does general mortality. In England and Wales, for example, the legitimate mortality rate, in 1939, was more than twice as high in class V . . . as in class I . . . and rose with each step from class I to class V." United Nations, "Economic and Social Factors Affecting Mortality," *Findings of Studies on Relationships between Population Trends and Economic and Social Factors* (mimeographed), Chapter 1 of the final report, March 14, 1951, pp. 27–28.

11. While age of death and cause of death are often closely correlated, they are not necessarily so linked; for example, enteritis probably is age linked while cholera, typhoid and diphtheria are not.

12. Figures from S. Peller, "Mortality, Past and Future," *Population Studies*, March 1948, p. 409.

TABLE 11-8. PERCENTAGE DECLINE IN MORTALITY RATES IN SWEDEN, 1751-1945

| Age Group (Years) | 1751–1800 to 1801–1850 | 1801–1850 to 1851–1900 | 1851–1900 to 1901–1945 | 1751–1800 to 1901–1945 |
|---|---|---|---|---|
| Under 1 | 14.6 | 27.9 | 53.8 | 71.6 |
| 1–4 | 27.5 | 15.6 | 74.5 | 84.4 |
| 5–14 | 29.1 | 10.1 | 65.6 | 78.1 |
| 15–24 | 11.5 | 17.9 | 26.5 | 46.6 |
| 25–44 | 5.5 | 29.4 | 39.7 | 59.7 |
| 45–64 | −5.9 | 31.9 | 35.2 | 53.3 |
| 65 and over | −7.1 | 21.5 | 19.0 | 31.9 |

*Source:* United Nations, "Economic and Social Factors Affecting Mortality," *Findings of Studies on Relationships between Population Trends and Economic and Social Factors* (mimeographed), Chapter 1 of the final report, March 14, 1951, p. 16.

notable declines occurred also at the middle and later ages.[13] (See Table 11-8.)

These reductions in infant and child mortality doubtless were traceable to two factors: the general improvements in diet and physical comfort of mothers and young children in both the prenatal and postnatal period; and the striking advances in knowledge and practice concerning the control and treatment of infectious diseases and other childhood ailments. For example, it is reported that:

Infectious diseases which strike by preference during the ages of childhood and early maturity were by 87 per cent reduced in England and Wales from 1848–72 to 1947. Diarrhea and enteritis, a major cause of death for infants and children, was lowered 86 per cent; maternal mortality 80 per cent and pneumonia, 53 per cent.[14]

There is probably no way of determining to what extent the declines in infant and child mortality in developed countries are traceable to generally improved living conditions as against advances in the handling of particular sources of morbidity.

*Progress and Mortality*

Insofar as economic progress has entailed improved housing, shorter work periods, sanitation control and a generally better physical environment in which to work, especially in urban areas, it has brought truly

13. English and Swedish experiences were broadly similar but the sequence in which the different age groups showed a decline in their respective mortality rates was not quite the same. In England between 1850 and 1900 mortality fell somewhat more in the age group 5–14 years than in the group 0–4 years. See United Nations, "Economic and Social Factors Affecting Mortality," pp. 16–17 and references there cited.

14. *Ibid.*, p. 18. These percentages relate to the direct causes of death in a medical sense. Probably the accuracy of diagnosis has improved over the past century and, if so, this would make the percentage declines rather more striking than the "facts" might warrant.

remarkable declines in mortality. Better sanitation—through improved sewage disposal, water supply and facilities for personal cleanliness—has cut mortality sharply by drastically reducing the incidence of such "filth" diseases as typhus, cholera, plague, typhoid and dysentery. Some of these diseases have become almost clinical curiosities in the United States and most other developed countries.[15]

The virtual disappearance of many of these diseases from the developed countries could not have occurred of course without the great strides that have been made in scientific medicine and public health. And many of these are almost contemporary achievements. It was only in the last quarter of the nineteenth century that Pasteur and Koch established the microbic origin of infectious diseases. The implications of their discoveries were enormous for,

> As a consequence, the formerly vague consciousness of a relation between filth and infectious disease, coloured by the traditional Hippocratic doctrine of miasms, gave way to the scientific knowledge of the real causation of these diseases. Progress followed rapidly. Lister, inspired by the above events, made surgery safer and more effective through the application of antiseptic methods. Behring's antitoxin, which conveys immunity against diphtheria, was placed on the market in 1892. During the following fifty years, the death rate from diphtheria declined by over 90 per cent in the United States and several other countries.[16]

But these were merely the beginnings of modern medical science and of systematic efforts to establish comprehensive public health programs. Even since 1920, the progress made in both has been enormous. Recent advances in sanitation, inoculations, antibiotics and other developments less familiar to the layman have probably gone beyond even the most optimistic expectations.

### NINETEENTH-CENTURY DEVELOPMENT AND SOCIAL WELFARE

Considerations of social welfare played a distinctly minor role in the drive for economic development in the Western world after 1815. Nevertheless, the astounding gain in the average level of human well-being which accompanied this development is both its most important consequence and the primary source of its interest in the present day. To be sure, this gain

---

15. It is easy to forget that many of the sanitary practices which today are accepted as a matter of course in developed countries are of very recent origin. Only in 1865 did London provide a series of interconnected sewers which gradually displaced open ditches and cesspools. Filtered water for cities apparently did not become general in Europe until 1900; chlorination was introduced only after 1900. The fall in the price of soap and cotton goods apparently had much to do with making some pretense of personal cleanliness possible for most people. The more powerful cleansers which now find so many applications in factories and the home have only been available for a few decades or years. See *ibid.*, pp. 20–21.

16. *Ibid.*, p. 22.

was not everywhere the same nor did it cumulate at a steady rate from year to year. But taking the period from 1815 to 1914 as a whole, or more especially its latter half, the improvement in the lot of the average man was probably greater than during any comparable span in recorded history.

## Population Growth

Perhaps the most incontrovertible evidence of the improvement in the average level of human well-being in Europe during the nineteenth century is the fact that Europe's population more than doubled between 1800 and 1900. This growth in population was the end result of a complex of changes that profoundly altered the whole environment and context of human existence. The life expectancy of the average Western European in 1800 was probably little more than 33 or 34 years at birth, while his familial descendant in 1890 had an expectancy of about 44 years; a child born in 1890 could look forward to almost a 30 per cent longer life span on the average than one born in 1800.[17] The authors of a recent article go so far as to proclaim that "if the expectations derived from prehistoric skeletons and from ancient tombstones are even approximately correct, expectation of life has increased as much since 1800 as it did during the entire preceding 50,000 years."[18]

Moreover, the varying rates of growth of population by decades in particular European countries seem to conform fairly well to the uneven rates of economic progress as recorded by familiar indices. The relatively high rates of population growth in England between 1820 and 1840, and in Germany between 1870 and 1910, and the notably higher rates of growth in Belgium than in France between 1830 and 1900, all seem to suggest a close relation between economic development and improved well-being.

## Diet as an Example of Well-Being

The stuff and substance of this improved well-being is well illustrated by a few figures showing the changes in per capita consumption of some familiar articles in the English diet between 1840 and 1886:[19]

17. An addition of ten years to life expectancy may not appear at all noteworthy today, in view of the very remarkable improvements that have so raised life expectancy in advanced countries in recent decades. In the United States, for example, the life expectancy of white males at birth rose from about 49 years in 1900 to about 64 years in 1940. But this is a distinctly modern phenomenon, wholly untypical of the history of mankind.

18. Hornell Hart and Hilda Hertz, "Expectation of Life as an Index of Social Progress," *American Sociological Review*, December 1944, p. 621.

19. David A. Wells, *Recent Economic Changes*, Appleton, New York, 1889, p. 356. Since these commodities were either subject to excise tax or imported, there is a strong presumption that the figures are not far wide of the mark. The gains for wheat and wheat flour, however, are probably considerably exaggerated.

| Item | Unit | Annual Per Capita Consumption | |
|---|---|---|---|
| | | *1840* | *1886* |
| Bacon and ham | lb. | 0.01 | 11.95 |
| Butter | lb. | 1.05 | 7.17 |
| Cheese | lb. | 0.92 | 5.14 |
| Eggs | no. | 3.63 | 28.12 |
| Wheat and wheat flour | lb. | 42.47 | 185.76 |
| Raw sugar | lb. | 15.20 | 47.21 |
| Refined sugar | lb. | 0.00 | 18.75 |
| Tea | lb. | 1.22 | 4.87 |

Bacon, butter, flour, eggs and tea may not by themselves assure a longer life span but they doubtless increase resistance to disease as well as add to the satisfaction of the daily round. The remarkable increases in per capita consumption of these products provide homely examples of how the welfare of the English population improved in the last half of the nineteenth century. The fourfold increase in sugar, the more than fourfold increase in eggs and even greater increases in butter and cheese are striking illustrations of welfare gains.

## Real Wages

The behavior of real wages—money wages in terms of their command over goods and services at prevailing prices—affords another measure of improved well-being. A recent careful study by Phelps Brown and Sheila Hopkins compares average real wage rates in 1860 and 1913, and in 1919 and 1939 as well, in five countries.[20] According to these investigators, the money wage rate paid in employment in 1913 in France and Germany was such that it was able to buy at 1913 prices 60 per cent more than the average wage rate of 1860 would buy of goods and services at 1860 prices; in the United Kingdom, 90 per cent more; and in Sweden, three times as much. (See Table 11-9.)

These figures compare wage rates, *not* earnings, by means of a fixed-weight index; consequently, they make no allowance for the shortening of the working day, improved physical conditions under which people labored,

20. E. H. Phelps Brown and Sheila V. Hopkins, "The Course of Wage-Rates in Five Countries, 1860–1939," *Oxford Economic Papers* (New Series), June 1950, pp. 226–96. This detailed study evidences a prodigious amount of research into a variety of sources which the authors have weighed and sifted with apparently great care. They repeatedly emphasize that the raw data do not warrant drawing inferences of consequence from small differences in the ratios calculated.

social security benefits, shifts between occupations, or other changes.[21] Thus the gain in real incomes was probably greater. What a comparable study for the period 1815–1860 would show, were the data available, one can only guess. But that it would show a very appreciable gain can hardly be doubted.

The rise in real wage rates in the nineteenth century seems to have reached what the investigators call a "climacteric" in the late 1880s: a "turn towards a lower rate of rise in real wage-rates . . . occurred, in each of our countries except Sweden, at some time not earlier than 1886." In France and Germany, for example, real wage rates continued to advance after the late 1880s, but they advanced at a slower rate than they did between 1860 and, say, 1886.[22]

TABLE 11-9. APPROXIMATE RATIO OF AVERAGE REAL WAGE RATE AT END OF PERIOD TO ITS INITIAL VALUE, 1860–1913 AND 1919–1939

| Country | 1860–1913 | 1919–1939 | 1860–1939 |
|---|---|---|---|
| France | 1.6 | 1.9 | 3.0 |
| Germany | 1.6 | 1.1 | 1.8 |
| Sweden | 3.0 | 1.8 | 5.4 |
| United Kingdom | 1.9 | 1.3 | 2.5 |
| United States | 1.5 | 1.7 | 2.6 |

*Source:* E. H. Phelps Brown and Sheila V. Hopkins, "The Course of Wage-Rates in Five Countries, 1860–1939," *Oxford Economic Papers* (New Series), June 1950, p. 236.

## Social Legislation

The improved welfare position of Western European peoples during the nineteenth century was strengthened by laws governing conditions and hours of work, by social insurance schemes and by other social legislation. In part, these measures evidenced an awakened social conscience, but in part, too, they resulted from the persistent efforts of trade unions, socialist leaders and reformers to bring about a more equalitarian distribution of an enlarged total output. Public education was extended and illiteracy de-

21. As Phelps Brown and Hopkins explain (*loc. cit.*, p. 228), "the movements of the earnings of the average wage-earner are the outcome not only of changes in the rate of pay for a given job but also of the shift of wage-earners between one job and another . . . We should have liked to combine these wage-rates in a chain index whose weights changed with changes in the distribution of wage-earners between occupations and industries, but the evidence is not usually extensive enough for this, . . . where we are able to compare the movements of a fixed-weight index of wage-rates with those of the earnings of the average wage-earner, we generally find that the latter rises more, because of the continual upgrading of labour, the shifting of the centre of gravity of the wage-earners to higher levels of competence and pay." In other words, the study tends to underestimate rather than overestimate the improvement in the wage earner's position.

22. This illustrates the point that different indexes of improved well-being show different results. If well-being is measured by death rates, the period after 1886 does not show any less favorable rate of improvement than the period before. This does not mean, of course, that either one or the other measure must give a "wrong" inference. It is reasonable to believe that the purchasing power of money wage rates over food and other necessaries of life was increasing at a slower rate at the same time that the environmental circumstances in which people lived continued to improve sufficiently to lower death rates at, if necessary, an accelerated rate. An index of real wage rates, for example, would be unlikely to reflect a better system of sewage disposal.

clined.[23] Thus not only were there direct gains in real wages in the nineteenth century, but also, and especially from 1870 on, a number of supporting changes were introduced that improved the "quality and texture of life as end product" for the average European.

## The End Result of Development

The complex of changes that constituted economic development in the nineteenth century unquestionably improved the well-being of the average man. While betterment of the common lot can scarcely be said to have inspired the people who were most active in bringing about this development, it was nevertheless the result. Much of the improvement came from the simple fact that people on the average were better fed, better clothed and better housed because their productivity was greater. But much of it came, too, because this higher productivity made it possible for the economy to support a whole host of activities in science, government and community living which earlier societies had neither the knowledge nor the wealth to undertake. In retrospect, one can see how at various points the development might perhaps have been accompanied by less suffering and a more equitable division of its benefits. Yet, when all is said and done, the gain in well-being which *was* achieved appears truly remarkable.

23. Probably the most important factor making for the decline in illiteracy was the spreading realization of the close relationship between relevant information and economic rewards. The rise in Protestantism and the Sunday School movement—for example, in nineteenth-century England—were also influential. In 1839 in England, about one third of the adult males and about one half of the adult females are said to have been illiterate; but by 1893 a comparable estimate puts the proportion at 5 per cent, which would appear to be probably too low. In France, around 1827–1829, about 55 per cent of the population is alleged to have been illiterate. For other countries the following figures are reported: Italy, in 1872, 69 per cent; Portugal, in 1872, 82 per cent; and Russia, in 1897, 78 per cent. Figures from Helen Sullivan, "Literacy and Illiteracy," in *Encyclopaedia of the Social Sciences*, Vol. 9, Macmillan, New York, 1935, pp. 511–23. In England, school attendance was not required for children under twelve years of age until 1876, and the provision of elementary education out of public funds came only in 1890.

*Part III*

# ACHIEVING DEVELOPMENT IN THE CONTEMPORARY WORLD

# 12. Agricultural Development for Increased Welfare

POVERTY IN THE UNDERDEVELOPED REGIONS of the world is almost always associated with low incomes derived from agriculture. In Africa and Asia, which include most of the regions lowest in per capita income, 74 per cent and 70 per cent of the total population is rural; in Europe and North America, the areas of highest income, the percentages are 33 and 20.[1] Indeed, the close association of agriculture and low incomes has been regarded in some quarters as evidence of cause and effect. But some of the regions with the highest average incomes, such as Nevada in the United States, Australia, Denmark and Argentina, are also preponderantly agricultural. Thus a simple and exclusive explanation of poverty is hardly provided by its association with agriculture.

## Low Productivity in Agriculture

But *low productivity* in agriculture undeniably explains the low income level of the great underdeveloped regions. Of the world's population, 1.3 billion, or 60 per cent, depend upon agriculture; and of these, over one billion live in Asia, Africa, and Central and South America, where the yields of agriculture per person are the lowest of the six continents. A glance at Figure 6 reveals the close association of lack of economic development and low agricultural productivity. Output in metric tons per person in agriculture on the North American continent exceeds the world average by sixfold, the average of Asia by tenfold and of Africa by twentyfold![2] As a unit of productivity, the metric measure may seem rough and ready, since it reduces caviar and beans to the common denominator of weight. But for the broad masses, wheat, potatoes and rice are the great staples and comprise a very large fraction of the total food produced and consumed; hence the measure of product by weight alone is probably superior to any other single comparison.

Yields per hectare differ very much less than output per capita. The extremes are represented by the European average wheat production at 1,450 kilograms per hectare and the African, which is about half as much.[3] Greater equality of yield per hectare follows naturally from the lower popu-

1. United Nations, Food and Agriculture Organization, *Yearbook of Food and Agricultural Statistics, 1951*, Vol. V, Part 1, Rome, 1952, p. 15.

2. See *Point Four*, U.S. Department of State, Publication 3719, January 1950, p. 121.

3. United Nations, *Yearbook of Food and Agricultural Statistics, 1951*, p. 23.

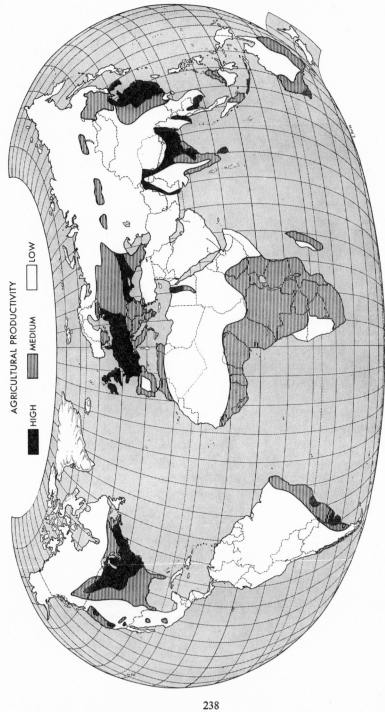

FIGURE 6. DISTRIBUTION OF LAND IN EACH CONTINENT BY AGRICULTURAL PRODUCTIVITY

Source: W. S. and E. S. Woytinsky, *World Population and Production*, Twentieth Century Fund, 1953.

AGRICULTURAL PRODUCTIVITY

HIGH   MEDIUM   LOW

lation density in the continents of high per capita output. Yet probably the most striking feature of such agricultural statistics is that output per hectare is lower on an *absolute* basis in the agricultural than in the industrial regions! Thus either when output is measured per capita or per unit of land, low productivity in agriculture underlies the low incomes of the underdeveloped world.

Differences in agricultural productivity are even more striking when the large total figures by continents are broken down into individual countries.[4] Among wheat-consuming nations, for example, the average yield per hectare in 1935–1939 varied from 730 kilograms in Israel and 760 in Brazil to 2,640 kilograms in the United Kingdom and 3,230 in the Netherlands. For rice-consuming nations, the Indian yield was 1,020 kilograms per hectare and the Indonesian, 2,290; but the yield in Japan—with no better inherent physical factors—amounted to 4,010.

*Factors in Low Productivity*

Disparities of such striking magnitude arise from a great variety of causes. Some of them, such as conditions of soil, climate, terrain and natural waterways, are relatively immutable; some, such as population densities, availability of capital, social mores and religious taboos, appear as relatively fixed from a short-run view but vary strikingly over the decades; others, such as production techniques, systems of land tenure, irrigation and drainage projects, can bring revolutionary changes in a single decade; while still others, such as monetary and credit policies, taxes, marketing channels, relative demands and prices, can produce large effects in the span of a year. Whether subject to fast or slow change, however, any of these and many other factors can become the *strategic* one, that is, the one (or ones) which seems most crucial in a given context of time and place, and which seems most urgently to demand remedy. Some remedies, such as the improvement of plant and animal breeds and strains, frequently promise large increases of output without vast projects of mechanization. Other remedies, particularly the provision of public utilities, are inevitably expensive. The combined effort of engineers, agricultural specialists, economists, anthropologists, population experts, political scientists, politicians and practical businessmen will generally be required to determine what factors are really strategic for the increase of agricultural productivity in a given situation.

Agricultural production in the world as a whole lagged seriously behind the population increase of 20 million annually in the immediate postwar years but has now begun to catch up. The world total of agricultural output is now 20 per cent over the prewar level; from mid-1950 to mid-1953 it increased by 2 per cent annually, while population grew by 1.4 per cent

4. See *ibid.*, pp. 24–25.

each year. But this general improvement masks the fact that the Far East has fallen far short of providing for its rapidly growing population. Agricultural output in the Far East is still only 80 to 85 per cent of the prewar level.[5] The better showing of other parts of the world also conceals the fact that output lags in particular countries. Even where agricultural production is increasing faster than population, many economies would gain from an increased efficiency of production coupled with a shift from starchy to more diversified diets, particularly those providing proteins. Thus the high incidence of tuberculosis in Japan could be reduced. Finally, increased productive efficiency in agriculture, even beyond the provision of physiologically adequate diets, is desirable wherever the factors of production it employs can be shifted to those other employments which higher standards of living imply.

## General Education and Technical Instruction in Agriculture

One of the most potent factors in economic progress is *motivation*. The masses of people must be imbued with a desire to better their material lot; in other words, the *standard* of living that is considered desirable for rearing a family must exceed the *level* of living actually attained.[6] Since the great masses in the underdeveloped areas live and work on the land, this means that the motivation of the agricultural laborer is basic. One well-qualified student of this problem says:

> It was my observation in East Africa that a great increase in agricultural output would physically be possible merely if those who worked with nothing but hoe and digging stick had an incentive to do more digging and weeding: capital was less prominently the lack than was sheer incentive to work. I do not know how to demonstrate that this shortage of incentive is prevalent in a wide range of underdeveloped countries, or that it may very well be a more important drag on economic advance than lack of capital; but I am convinced that it is.[7]

### Education and Incentives

Partly, no doubt, this lack of motivation may be traced to unfavorable political and economic settings—to corrupt governments, bad tax systems, racial discrimination and caste systems, inflations, poor systems of land tenure, and to poverty itself including physical debilities. Another contributing factor is that "Many cultures . . . have placed a low value on

---

5. Figures given by the World Food Council of the United Nations Food and Agriculture Organization, reported in the *New York Times*, July 1, 1953.

6. Joseph S. Davis, "Standards and Content of Living," *American Economic Review*, March 1945, pp. 1–15.

7. Comment by Merrill K. Bennett, Director of the Food Research Institute, Stanford University, in a private communication.

material advance and, indeed, some have regarded it as incompatible with more desirable objectives of society and of the individual."[8]

In part, however, weak motivation toward material improvement may be an aspect of ignorance, and ignorance and illiteracy, though by no means synonymous, are closely conjoined. The countries lowest in income are generally also lowest in literacy. Only one of the fifteen countries of the world having per capita incomes exceeding $200 on a prewar basis had an illiteracy rate above 5 per cent. But in a group of 28 countries (most of Africa being omitted) with average annual incomes less than $100, the proportion of illiteracy was rarely below 50 per cent, and in the most populous countries—Egypt, India, China and Indonesia, for example—it ran from 85 to 92 per cent.[9] High levels of illiteracy surely impair the quality of life as end product, both spiritually and materially.

Nowadays, of course, motion pictures and radio may contribute to the enlightenment of the completely illiterate, particularly in communicating higher standards of living. American films may have had a good deal to do with revolutionary movements in the economically underdeveloped world. But while motion pictures and radio can provide the impulse toward development, it would be difficult to imagine their sustaining the movement past a rather low level if the population remained illiterate.

*Technical Education*

In demonstrating simple industrial and agricultural techniques and rudimentary matters of public health, motion pictures and radio are highly effective. It has been said it would take 5,000 agricultural teachers to convey the elements of rational peasant farming to the population of Nigeria alone.[10] Modern methods of mass communication could greatly reduce this demand upon skilled manpower and finances.

The propagation of improved agricultural methods for the underdeveloped areas needs to be undertaken at a very modest level. Eloquent accounts have been given as to the necessary simplicity of instruction, and the high value of the teacher's living in close association with the peasant farmers. For example, to induce the farmers in the neighborhood of Mahewa, India, to plow under green legumes for the purpose of fertilizer, it was necessary to convince them that taking the life of a growing thing was warranted in the Vedic laws by the superior injunction to the household head to provide for his family.[11] In Nigeria, the introduction of goats to

8. International Bank for Reconstruction and Development, *Eighth Annual Report, 1952–53*, Washington, 1953, p. 9.

9. *Point Four*, Appendix C-3, pp. 117–18.

10. W. Arthur Lewis, "Developing Colonial Agriculture," *The Three Banks Review*, June 1949, pp. 6–8.

11. *Point Four Pioneers*, U.S. Department of State, Publication 4279, October 1951, p. 32.

provide milk had first to surmount the belief of the emirs that goat's milk causes smallpox.[12]

The skillful use of direct and simple methods of instruction may be attended by marked "multiplier effects" through imitation. The following is an illustration from Liberia:

> When Pinder first started making his expeditions into the countryside living with the people and making note of what was lacking in their diet, he was struck by the small, scrawny chickens which laid eggs not much larger than robins' eggs. At his recommendation, the Economic Mission and the Department of Agriculture imported from the United States several hundred large roosters of the best strains . . . Reports of big, healthy chickens and the size of the eggs they laid spread through the countryside. People traveled long distances on foot or by canoe to see them. A few of the new chicks were given to native farmers. They agreed to feed them strictly according to the rules laid down by the Mission, and later to distribute their offspring to neighbors . . . Large, fresh eggs are doing wonders in raising the Liberian standard of living and eating.[13]

For most countries in the early phases of development, scientific research in agriculture—on soils, fertilizers, insecticides, plant strains and animal breeds—will have to be limited to a very few centers, while a large part of the funds available for education will need to be spent to train teachers of elementary techniques. The native agricultural expert trained in European or American universities cannot always be used for this purpose because his ideas are often much too "fancy."[14]

### Appropriate Agricultural Techniques

Determining just what agricultural techniques are to be propagated may be a complex matter. On the one hand, Western methods may be too advanced in any one of several senses. Where labor is the cheap factor, labor-saving machinery is uneconomical: the cheapest method of production depends upon relative factor prices. The primitive nail-board plow may therefore prove to be the best type of equipment. Any particular improvement, moreover, must be appraised not only for its immediate effect on costs and output, but also in the general economic matrix of complementary industries. Are transportation, processing and marketing facilities adequate for the expansion of primary production? Finally, the saving of labor may encounter limits in the social cost and disruption entailed by technological unemployment.[15]

12. United Nations, *Proceedings of the Scientific Conference on the Conservation and Utilization of Resources, 1949*, Vol. I, *Plenary Meetings*, New York, 1950, p. 315.

13. *Point Four Pioneers*, pp. 7–8.

14. See the testimony to this effect of Professor Albert Rhoad of the Inter-American Institute of Agricultural Science (Costa Rica) in United Nations, *Proceedings of the Scientific Conference on the Conservation and Utilization of Resources, 1949*, Vol. I, p. 8.

15. On this general range of topics see James Baster, "A Second Look at Point Four," *American Economic Review, Proceedings*, May 1951, pp. 399–406.

On the other hand, the only way to break the vicious circle of surplus labor, low incomes and concealed unemployment in agriculture is to make the unemployment explicit, that is, to introduce progressive methods of production which will *raise wages* even at the cost of throwing people out of work. As the International Labor Office study of unemployment in less developed regions emphasizes, "extreme labour-intensive methods of cultivation . . . [are] the result of centuries of adaptation to growing pressure on the land."[16] Somewhere between enduring the full amount of unemployment that would follow from the most promising innovations and avoiding unemployment altogether by conforming to present prices and practices is a reasonable degree of progressiveness. What is reasonable depends, of course, on the availability of alternative industrial employments and provisions for the transitionally unemployed.

The risk that outside experts or native officials imbued with excessive enthusiasm for up-to-date techniques might proceed with too little regard for the factor endowment of less developed areas, or with too little concern for technological unemployment at the other extreme, has made some observers quite skeptical of the consequences of technical aid.[17] Several writers stress agricultural cooperatives as a hedge against the possible mistakes of imported techniques. In India the "pilot development projects," which are partly paternalistic enterprises of the central government and partly cooperative, seem to work effectively. In the United Provinces (Uttar Pradesh), for example, such projects have not only increased wheat yields per acre by 20 per cent in two years but have also introduced the villagers to more modern ways of living.[18]

It would be well to remember, too, that Western Europe and the Western world in general may not be the sole reservoirs of technical knowledge for improvement of agriculture in underdeveloped areas. Japanese methods, for example, have constantly improved the land and the forests, while supporting the highest recorded density of rural population, with a standard of living considerably superior to the rest of Asia. Japan would have much to offer in techniques applicable to India, Southeast Asia and other areas.

## LAND REFORM

From the time of Adam Smith's chapter "Of the Rent of Land" in Book I of *The Wealth of Nations*, through John Stuart Mill's successive chapters on "peasant proprietors, métayers, and cottiers," to Alfred Marshall's analysis

16. C. Hsieh, "The Special Problem of the Less Developed Areas," in *Action against Unemployment*, International Labor Office, Geneva, 1950, Chapter 7.

17. Baster, *loc. cit.;* see also Joseph E. Stepanek and Charles H. Prien, "The Role of Rural Industries in Underdeveloped Areas," *Pacific Affairs*, March 1950, p. 69.

18. Elizabeth Converse, "Pilot Development Projects in India," *Far Eastern Survey*, February 7, 1951, pp. 21–27.

in Chapter 10, Book VI of the *Principles*, economists have stressed the importance of systems of land tenure. These matters have receded somewhat into the background in the advanced industrial nations through legal reforms and the lessened importance of agriculture; but they stand in the forefront of the economic problems of underdeveloped areas. Agrarian reform—in the sense of redistribution of land ownership, and beginning with the Communist revolution in Russia—has swept through the satellite states of central and eastern Europe, through Manchuria, China, Indonesia, etc., and was carried through by the Far Eastern Command in Japan. To this vast movement it is possible to give only sporadic notice here. The present discussion will largely concentrate on other regions as yet untouched by the movement and will be concerned less with the problem of equalitarian ethics than with productive efficiency in terms of the two aspects of optimal size and economic incentive.

*Property Rights*

Let us begin with the "simple" matter of legal ownership. Clear title in any system of private property seems to be a matter of course to the average American or European. And yet this is far from the fact in many large areas, particularly where tribal community of land has recently disintegrated, as in Africa, or where property rights have never been well defined. In the Near East, for example, the Ottoman legal code of ownership was never really enforced, and mere customary possession often prevailed in conflict with the law. In Palestine, Transjordan and Syria a periodic three-year reallocation of land has discouraged permanent improvement. In Iraq the legal tenure system is said to be a "complete muddle."[19] Many underdeveloped countries have never had a complete land survey; in China, according to John Lossing Buck, as much as one third of the land in the late 1940s was not recorded in the deed offices.[20] Situations of this sort lack the definiteness of outright collectivism, tribal or modern communal tenure, feudalism or private property. Developing economies which rely on private enterprise must begin by an exhaustive registration of title; and uncertainty as to ownership and control would be inimical to productive efficiency under any system.

The separation of individual holdings into small parcels is another important problem. Over much of Europe this condition has survived from feudalism, and has been intensified by the principle of succession of the Napoleonic Code. In Asia, subdivision and separation result chiefly from

19. Doreen Warriner, *Land and Poverty in the Middle East*, Royal Institute of International Affairs, London, 1948, p. 22.

20. John Lossing Buck, *Some Basic Agricultural Problems of China* (Secretariat Paper No. 1 [mimeographed], Tenth Conference of the Institute of Pacific Relations, Stratford-on-Avon, September 1947), International Secretariat, Institute of Pacific Relations, New York, 1947, p. 21.

pressure of population. Fragmentation interferes with the use of agricultural machinery; even with primitive labor methods it reduces efficiency by a large fraction[21] through wasted effort in moving from one plot to another, sometimes far separated. The Monnet Plan in France, aided by Marshall Plan funds, has consolidated 1.3 million acres into larger plots and is aiming at an eventual goal of 25 million acres.[22] India is proceeding by means of a voluntary cooperative system inaugurated in the Punjab in 1921 and continued in other provinces under later legislation. By 1949 the number of plots in the United Provinces had been reduced from 4,250,000 to 646,000.[23] Consolidation of holdings is an obvious channel of improvement of the productive power of agriculture. In some areas, land yields have been increased by 50 to 100 per cent through this measure.[24]

A peculiar type of fragmentation or, alternatively, of uncertainty of title in the Near East has been the separation, under the Ottoman code, of water rights from title to land. Not only has this limited the full use of the cultivated land and delayed necessary irrigation projects, but it has in addition enabled the wealthy owner of water to rack-rent the poorer landowners. Generally, state control of these rights appears to have been the best solution.

*Tenancy*

Another set of problems has to do with tenancy. There is a predisposition in much popular discourse and even in some economic writings to couple tenancy with exploitation and low standards of living. But Buck's painstaking statistical investigations into land tenure and land utilization in China show that sweeping generalizations of this sort are fallacious.[25] In the first place, tenancy rates are as high or higher in some high-income countries. In England 75 per cent of the farmers are tenants, in the United States 42 per cent, and in Germany 25 per cent, as compared with 50 per cent in China and 27 per cent in Japan. True, the farmer's low income makes it difficult for him to mount the ladder from tenancy to ownership; but this is a matter of income and not of the institution of tenancy. Tenant farms in China approached closer to the minimum size for economic operation than owner farms because tenant and owner automatically pooled resources, the owner supplying the fixed capital and the tenant the operating capital. Yields per acre were found to be about equal for owner and tenant farms, though the tenant's living conditions were somewhat inferior to the

21. Estimated at 30 per cent for the Middle East by Warriner, *op. cit.*, p. 20.

22. W. S. and E. S. Woytinsky, *World Population and Production*, Twentieth Century Fund, New York, 1953, p. 494.

23. United Nations, *Land Reform—Defects in Agrarian Structure as Obstacles to Economic Development*, New York, 1951, pp. 11–14 and 67.

24. Woytinsky, *op. cit.*, p. 492.

25. Buck, *op. cit.*, pp. 24–48.

landlord's since the tenant depended on wage income alone. J. H. Boeke gives a favorable evaluation of sharecropping in Indonesia.[26]

Elsewhere in the underdeveloped regions the story is different. Syria, for example, illustrates nearly all of the sinister possibilities of tenant systems: absentee landlordism, rack-renting, arbitrary evictions, uncertainty of tenure, and chronic indebtedness of the peasants.[27] Evils of this sort are widespread and are too familiar to require detailed description of their mutations in various regions.[28] Insecurity of tenure has the universal consequence that tenants are loath to make improvements or even to maintain the land. Excessive rentals (exceeding the true economic rent) operate in the same direction. By engendering a general feeling of hopelessness, they discourage the tenant from efforts even to maximize current outputs and thereby contribute to his low income and his tendency to run into debt for consumption outlays, particularly in bad seasons. On the part of the owner, excessive rentals encourage laxity in administration of the property, a penchant toward purchasing more land without maintaining the soil, and finally idleness and absenteeism.

### Correcting Abuses of Tenancy

Since tenancy itself cannot be held to be the root of these evils, a direct attack on tenancy as such is indiscriminate and futile. Even the Draconian measure of equalization of landholdings, however much it may appear as retributive justice against the inequities and iniquities of landlordism in some countries, is not a final solution. Thus, following the "basic land reform" of the Mao regime in China, it appears that:

. . . the old class distinctions have been re-emerging. The investigators were surprised to find that 96 peasant families had sold land to pay for wedding and funeral expenses, an affront to the new social order. About 20 per cent of the peasants had become poor again; and an equal percentage "obviously wealthy." This was blamed on the fact that 99 family heads had increased their land holdings, causing prices to rise. They had even begun lending money at the usurious rate of 60 per cent per annum.[29]

What are the alternatives to an evolution of this sort, which implies a reversion to primitive systems of periodic equalization with their inevitable ruin of incentive and impoverishment of the populace?

26. J. H. Boeke, *The Structure of Netherlands Indian Economy*, Institute of Pacific Relations, New York, 1942, p. 42.

27. Warriner, *op. cit.*, pp. 84–85.

28. In addition to the sources already referred to, note especially Appendix III, "Survey of Land Tenure and Agricultural Labor Systems in Eastern and Southern Europe," in Wilbert E. Moore, *Economic Demography of Eastern and Southern Europe*, League of Nations, Geneva, 1945, pp. 210–67.

29. Robert Neville, "Rise of the Red Star," *Life*, December 31, 1951, p. 18.

In the first place, the "natural" tendencies toward inequality could be suppressed by totalitarian controls which would in effect abolish private property. Second, the land might simply be collectivized. Third, various milder forms of modified private ownership might be introduced under the concept of "cooperation." Finally, multiple reforms under private ownership could—as they generally *do* in Western Europe and the English-speaking countries—result in workable systems of land tenure.

### Collectivization

Collectivization of agriculture seems in recent history to be designed chiefly for two ends: to control the peasants politically, and to absorb from them a maximum of agricultural produce. These are the only plausible reasons why the U.S.S.R. has persisted in its course of collectivizing agriculture despite its notable failure to achieve much progress in food production.

The idea that "the small enterprise creates capitalism and the bourgeoisie permanently, hourly, daily, inescapably, and on a mass scale"[30] supplies one motive for the U.S.S.R.'s liquidation of 20 million peasant farmers in the collectivization drive of 1928. The other motive for the U.S.S.R.'s collectivization program, as Naum Jasny points out, is revealed by the trends of agricultural output and income. Though the annual output per person employed in agriculture *increased* by 15 to 20 per cent in the decade following collectivization, average agricultural income per capita *fell* by 10 per cent, and the income of the rank and file peasant fell by *20 per cent*.[31] Thus industrialization was literally squeezed out of the bodies of the poorest peasants. But from the standpoint of technical performance, collectivization was a failure. The 15 to 20 per cent increase in annual output per person falls considerably short of the 45 per cent increase in number of days worked annually, and this despite a considerable increase in mechanization. In Jasny's opinion, productivity per hour did not increase and may indeed have fallen.[32] Total income from agriculture regained the level prior to collectivization only by 1938, and the setback of World War II was probably only recouped by 1950.[33]

Jasny's general diagnosis has been seconded more recently by Lazar Volin, who characterizes the recent drive in Russia to merge agricultural collectives as "gigantomania." Volin believes that the main motives have

30. V. I. Lenin, *Works*, Vol. 25, p. 173; quoted by Joseph Stalin in *Foundations of Leninism*, 10th edition, International Publishers, New York, 1932, p. 48.

31. Naum Jasny, *The Socialized Agriculture of the USSR; Plans and Performance*, Stanford University Press, Stanford, 1949, pp. 75, 417 and 701.

32. *Ibid.*, p. 416. This conclusion takes account of the shortened work day.

33. *Ibid.*, pp. 68 and 70.

been to control the peasant's use of his time more strictly and to make sure that he remains merely a "residual claimant" on the produce of the farms.[34]

### Reforms within Private Enterprise

Contemplating this experience, free nations in the underdeveloped areas may well choose to remove the evils, or more accurately the abuses, of land ownership and tenancy by reliance upon reforms within a private enterprise system or by the elaboration of cooperative schemes. Some of the reforms within a system of private property and enterprise have directly to do with tenancy and ownership themselves and others with the general economic setting of these institutions.

Uncertainty of tenure, one of the most widespread curses of the tenant's status, can be alleviated by legal codes protecting tenants from arbitrary eviction and covering all matters generally relevant to the tenant-landlord relation, and by clearly drawn contracts for each individual case. Uncertainty of tenure is, however, largely a consequence of the tenant's slender financial position, a matter embracing nothing less than the whole problem of low incomes in the underdeveloped areas. Much the same general diagnosis must be made of chronic indebtedness, another evil associated with tenancy but not a necessary part of it. Improved agricultural credit facilities, discussed in Chapter 14, could relieve the uncertainty created by a single bad harvest and persistent indebtedness by reducing interest charges from usurious levels—sometimes 50 per cent or more a year—to manageable proportions.

Uncertainty of tenure and chronic indebtedness cannot be cured by *ad hoc* measures, however. They can be alleviated to some extent by the whole galaxy of measures to increase the general productivity of agriculture and industry. But, in part, these and other evils associated with tenancy emanate from corrupt and oppressive governments, from the lack of free elementary education, from regressive systems of taxation, from the absence of social security legislation, from social systems which reduce one race or class to inferior status, and from other characteristics of the political and social setting. In Latin America, the pernicious workings of the land system seem to have begun with outright expropriation of the traditional native owners and to have been perpetuated by general conditions of the sorts just described.[35]

A general parallel emerges from an analysis of the economic ills associated with land ownership. Here, too, *ad hoc* measures cannot suffice.

34. Lazar Volin, "The Turn of the Screw in Russian Agriculture," *Foreign Affairs*, January 1952, pp. 277–88. A similar view of collectivization of agriculture in North Korea has been expressed by Arthur Bunce, quoted by Isidor Lubin in "Hope of the Hungry Millions," *New York Times Magazine*, February 10, 1952, p. 49.

35. See Stanford A. Mosk, "Latin America versus the United States," *American Economic Review, Proceedings*, May 1951, pp. 367–83.

Certainty of title forms the bedrock of incentives in a private enterprise system of agriculture. Consolidation of scattered holdings, while it is a merely mechanical matter, also conditions productive efficiency. Water rights must be definite at least, but state operation of irrigation and drainage systems would in most cases seem to be necessary. Aside from certain specific conditions such as these, however, the efficiency and merit of private ownership of land depend upon the whole environment. This does not deny that the distribution of ownership and the way ownership rights are exercised may not in particular cases assume strategic importance in the character of the environment. Extreme concentration of land ownership seems eventually to lead to either peaceful or violent redistribution. But once a fresh start is made or before the concentration has progressed too far, a private enterprise society can prevent progressive concentration. The remedies, however, are not particularly different in the case of landholding from those designed to prevent too great inequality of wealth and income in *any* form. Underdeveloped countries have an opportunity not only to take some technological short cuts by adopting already known techniques of production, but also to take over some of the specific devices for reconciling capitalism and equality of opportunity.

### COMMERCIAL VERSUS PEASANT AGRICULTURE

The most interesting issue concerning the type of productive unit in agriculture pertains to the relative merits of plantation or commercial farms which produce cash crops for a local or international market as against peasant or "subsistence" farming.[36] The issue is a complex one, involving among other things the most economical size of agricultural unit, the availability of farm labor, profitability and welfare aspects of "commercial" crops (often export, compared to domestic food supplies), the subtle social and economic utilities or disutilities accompanying the status of "landless worker" compared to the small landowner, and the relative significance of equalitarian ideals compared to sheer productivity. In view of all these elements, which inevitably differ in relative importance in varying climates, with different crops, and with widely diverse political and social structures, it requires considerable hardihood to declare, as one close student of the problem does, that the plantation system is now finished because it is dependent on indentured labor.[37]

36. The association of plantation and commercial agriculture is usual but not invariable. Thus in the South of the United States, the plantation ownership unit included subsistence farmers and sharecroppers. See Thomas C. Blaisdell, Jr., in the *Proceedings of the International Conference on Agricultural and Cooperative Credit*, August 4–October 2, 1952, University of California Press, Berkeley, 1953, Vol. I, pp. 590–93.

37. Lewis, *loc. cit.*, p. 4.

*Advantages of Large-Scale Production*

The great strength of the plantation or commercial type of agriculture lies in the effectiveness of large-scale production.[38] The advantages include superior command of advanced techniques, adequate capital for machinery and improvements, skilled management, superior knowledge of world demands and fuller utilization of overhead. The per acre yield of sugar on the large plantation is said to be double that of small farms. But its very bigness and its specialization in particular products—bananas, sugar, coffee, beef, cacao, sisal, tea—make commercialized agriculture more vulnerable to cyclical and secular change than the small, diversified peasant economy. Even the generalization that higher yields accompany large scale is subject to some notable exceptions: the great grain estates of eastern Europe failed to rotate crops scientifically, and in Venezuela the large ranches, protected by the existing land tenure, occupy rich bottom lands which would produce more as truck gardens.[39]

Writers on the present theme often betray a certain naïveté in decrying large commercial agriculture based on a cheap and abundant labor supply. The labor supply would be cheap and abundant anyway, whether farms were large or small. The high ratio of labor to cultivated land results from relative factor prices. The large *size* of the farm derives basically from certain virtual indivisibilities, such as the manager or owner, machinery and the owner's resources. Mere size, resting on cheap labor, is only to be decried if the low wages rest on exploitation. Thus the apparent efficiency of the large plantations of the ante bellum South was partly spurious, depending partly at least upon the institution of slavery. In many South American countries, the great estates are built on a foundation of peonage fostered by various devices for keeping the laborer in bondage to his debts. As underdeveloped areas progress, it would be fair to assume that, insofar as such exploitative practices disappear, and insofar as wages rise simply from the fact of economic progress, the natural tendency would be for the size of the agricultural unit to decline.[40] But such a tendency must be relatively weak in view of the persistence of large farms and ranches even in the high-wage United States of today.

*Negative Factors in Commercial Systems*

As economic development proceeds, a force which may play a larger role in the future of commercial versus peasant farming may be the increasing

38. There is a certain irony in the fact that Communist Russia adopts collectivized agriculture for this ostensible reason, being willing to take into the bargain all of the supposed disadvantages to the common man ("landless laborer," "peon," etc.) which the political radicals of many other countries decry in the plantation system!

39. United Nations, *Land Reform*, pp. 20 and 71.

40. The presumption in economic theory is that the size of the productive unit varies directly as the manager's capacity to manage resources. As a given physical unit of resources grew more valuable—for example, as labor and land rose in price—optimum efficiency would imply the combination of a smaller physical quantity of these resources with an entrepreneur of given capacity.

competition of the native population for foodstuffs as their incomes rise.[41] One of the chief economic interests of Western Europe and America in the underdeveloped world—a quite legitimate interest requiring no apology— has always been the relatively abundant exports of textile fibers and food. The great commercial farms have been the source of this exportable surplus, but often this has meant for the indigenous population a lack of variety in diet or an actual deficiency of certain basic foods. Throughout Latin America, milk is in short supply because grazing lands are devoted to meat production; in Nyasaland, Kenya, Rhodesia and South Africa, food production is scarcely adequate because of the competition of commercial crops for labor.[42] A natural accompaniment of rising real incomes would be a certain growth in smaller-scale, diversified agriculture and in "subsistence" farming, both supplying more products and more diversified diets to the native population. But, as Sir Alan Pim points out, subsistence agriculture cannot support a very great advance in the standard of living.[43] Agricultural exports will be required to command the wherewithal for a larger flow of imported consumers' and producers' goods. Conceivably, peasant farming could itself reach a level of productivity high enough to supply the requisite exports; but experience in Europe and North America would point to the survival of much large-scale commercial agriculture.

Finally, developing economies may be considerably influenced by the lot of the "landless laborer." The implication of this term ought to be rejected if it means that laborers, even farm laborers, who do not own land are impoverished. Bank clerks in Manhattan or cowboys in Texas are not necessarily impoverished. In many primitive economies, however, the sole means of livelihood is a small plot of ground or free access to common hunting or fishing territory. The British in Uganda, the Belgians in the Congo, and the French in French Equatorial Africa discovered that the allocation of "unoccupied" lands to foreign concessionaires or even to natives left many people destitute. In most cases, some degree of restitution and protection has followed. But "landless laborers" have also presented problems in less primitive, but still underdeveloped, economies that have undertaken to redistribute the land. After 1945, many eastern European governments followed this course. But the results are often disappointing: in Poland the tracts range from 2.5 to 10 acres; in Hungary 7 out of 10 holdings amount to less than 7 acres; and in Rumania 12.5 acres is a maxi-

---

41. D. H. Robertson wrote pungently: "How strong and persistent are the forces making it progressively more difficult for the manufacturing populations of Western Europe, however correct their monetary arrangements, to earn from overseas the requisite fodder alike for their own fastidious stomachs and for their insatiable machines . . . We ought perhaps to have foreseen the emergence of the revolutionary notion that some day 1,000 million Asiatics would take it into their heads to expect to have enough to eat." "Britain and European Recovery," *Lloyds Bank Review*, July 1949, p. 3.

42. United Nations, *Land Reform*, pp. 20 and 31.

43. Sir Alan Pim, *Colonial Agricultural Production*, Oxford University Press, Oxford, 1946, p. 177.

mum. This kind of "reform" conforms to Churchill's description of Communism as equal sharing of misery. It is a "once-for-all measure," exhausted in one act; it generally results in *lowered* productive efficiency; and it does not afford the new "landed" peasant a decent, or even sometimes a subsistence, income.[44]

### Conclusions

In summary, then, neither tenancy nor a "landless" condition of agricultural labor is necessarily an evil or a handicap to advancing agricultural economies. Several particular evils of an institutional sort exist, however, which can be remedied with potentially great gains to productivity. So far as concerns peasant versus commercial agriculture, both have their merits and both will persist. As incomes rise, the larger resources of the typical farmer may bring about some increase in the proportion of owner-occupied farms. But unless the evolution of peasant farming is so favorable as to make it no longer "subsistence" farming, capitalistic farming or commercial agriculture will continue to be the main source of purchasing power for imports.

### OTHER FACTORS AFFECTING AGRICULTURAL PRODUCTIVITY

Economic development in countries dependent at present upon primary production, particularly upon agriculture, awaits the realization of further reforms and improvements, some of them directly pertaining to agriculture, and others relating to the national and international economies.

### Land Improvement and Reclamation

Improvement and reclamation of land through drainage, irrigation and other means offer the double advantage of extending productive capacity and, for the duration of the undertaking, also absorbing labor in those countries that suffer from surpluses of agricultural manpower. Many operations of this sort require relatively large amounts of labor and can be carried on without violence to relative factor prices in underdeveloped areas. Gigantic multipurpose developments, combining the reclamation of land for the plow with large-scale hydroelectric and possibly also water and navigation facilities, require large drafts on capital, engineering skills, construction laborers and technicians, all of which are usually scarce and expensive. On the other hand, the value of these projects, in introducing new techniques, alleviating shortages of land, power and water, and fostering a progressive spirit in the populace, may be immense. The large commitments which such projects entail imply a careful weighing of costs and

44. See Woytinsky, *op. cit.*, pp. 502–05; Moore, *op. cit.*, pp. 103*ff.*; United Nations, *Land Reform*, pp. 71–72.

advantages in advance. Beyond this warning the economist cannot offer many useful generalizations because of the diversity of regional conditions.

## Farm Machinery

Something of the same sort is true of investment in farm machinery: there is virtually no possibility of useful generalization. Heavy and expensive equipment may pay in some regions and not in others. John Lossing Buck has carried through some computations of the cost of plowing with a water buffalo and a tractor, and of threshing with a flail and a threshing machine, under farming conditions near Nanking. In the case of plowing, the water buffalo came out the winner, but the thresher was superior to the flail. Buck's eloquent platitude is worth repeating: "Farmers should not use power machinery only because it is considered 'modern.' Farmers cannot afford to gain 'face' by using machines if this means increasing expenses greater than the saving in labor costs. By doing this, the farmer will soon lose his farm."[45]

On the other hand, even within the past decade or so, the range over which expensive machinery can be used more economically than hand labor has been considerably extended. For some time, bulldozers have supplanted labor in most large-scale earth-moving operations, as in the building of dams and the leveling or contouring of land; and more recently mechanical pickers have been found economical for harvesting corn, cotton and other crops in some regions. Depending, of course, on wage levels and on the size of the agricultural unit (plantation, cooperative, etc.), "costly" machinery is increasingly applicable even in the less developed areas.

## Taxation Reform

In many primitive economies of Asia and the Middle East, the farmers are taxed on the units of products marketed. This would seem to be a fairly good tax in providing a rough-and-ready exemption for subsistence on the output not marketed, and in avoiding the expense of trying to collect on these small sums. Even the more "advanced" countries rely heavily on direct land taxation, the defects of which are sufficiently familiar to Europeans and Americans—its lack of progressive rates, the inequities of assessment, its too onerous weight in depression, and so on. In contrast to Europe and America, however, rural incomes elsewhere are often more heavily taxed than urban incomes. This circumstance is particularly perverse where the prospects of economic development depend chiefly upon agriculture. Brazil, Argentina and Chile apply income taxation to farmers and ranchers, but also tax the land directly. In Pakistan and India, movements are under way to introduce progressive income taxation in agriculture. The difficulty

45. Buck, *op. cit.*, p. 12; cf. Moore, *op. cit.*, pp. 108–09, to similar effect.

of successfully administering income taxation of farmers, particularly of illiterate peasants, is proverbial; but, otherwise, the merits of the tax are substantial from the angles of equity and of economic incentive.[46]

### Marketing and Other Institutions

The marketing of farm products offers a field in which much improvement is possible, particularly for the peasant producer whose knowledge of outlets, prices and desirable types of goods is limited and whose financial resources are equally slender. A report on Turkey states:

> No important agricultural progress is possible without provision of better marketing outlets than those which survive from ancient times and still characterize most of Turkey . . . The farmer, his wife, and perhaps his children, lay out their modest produce and wait for a buyer to appear. If the buyer is a merchant, the peasant is likely to be in debt to him and is in no position to bargain.[47]

Marketing facilities are so limited that the report concludes "it would be useless to attempt to increase agricultural output by improved methods." In China, it is said, it was easier in the late 1940s for a Shanghai merchant to purchase wheat by cable from Australia than to buy domestic wheat because the home product had to be acquired in small lots, and then cleaned, graded and stored.[48] Farmers' cooperatives occasionally can overcome these difficulties, but their generally limited resources and limited business abilities indicate the necessity of central government aid.

It will be apparent how intimately agricultural development depends upon good roads, rail connections or water transport for the marketing of farm produce. Of immediate importance, also, are the agricultural processing industries, which represent one of the most basic investment requirements for underdeveloped areas. Agriculture would benefit from increased storage facilities to even out seasonal and annual variations in production; from refrigerated transportation for perishable produce; and from standardized cleaning and grading practices.

Another specific need of considerable importance arises from the lack of lending agencies for agriculture at nonusurious rates of interest. But it will, perhaps, be better to consider this in the general context of capital problems in underdeveloped areas. (See Chapter 14.)

### Responsibility of the State

A deliberate development process probably implies a considerable role for the state in all cases, and for relatively primitive or illiterate peoples this may imply a sort of paternalism. W. Arthur Lewis goes so far as to suggest

---

46. United Nations, *Land Reform*, pp. 43–48.

47. Max W. Thornburg, Graham Spry and George Soule, *Turkey: An Economic Appraisal*, Twentieth Century Fund, New York, 1949, pp. 52–53.

48. Buck, *op. cit.*, p. 17.

that in order to avoid the rapid depletion of newly opened agricultural lands, the government should stipulate the actual cultivation practices, besides providing roads, water, capital for livestock, etc.[49] Elsewhere, government may dispense with prescription and own or manage pilot projects as in India, cooperative farms as in China, "proportional profit" farms as in Puerto Rico—enterprises which not only yield living wages to the participants but also demonstrate new techniques, provide some general education, disseminate the basic principles of sanitation and health, and instill a progressive spirit. Under some conditions, cooperatives successfully take over responsibility for agricultural credit, marketing and crop insurance. Sir Alan Pim describes these establishments for the colonial areas and Wilbert E. Moore for eastern and southern Europe.[50] Ownership and management of power machinery, particularly of tractors, seem also to be a promising activity for cooperatives or for the village or central government.

In short, the proportions of private, cooperative and government ownership and enterprise can be varied infinitely to fit the requirements of the particular society. Whatever the line of procedure, however, there is no substitute for honest and effective government. It may require a political revolution as it did in eighteenth-century France, to rid a country of corrupt government, landlordism, absenteeism, extreme inequality of wealth and opportunity, and grinding taxation of the peasant.

*A Stable World Economy*

Economic progress is fostered by reasonable stability of demand for exports and by free and expanding multilateral trade. Agricultural countries fare badly in depressions: they lose in their terms of trade with other countries and in volume of sales, and, possessing small reserves of gold and international balances, they face the alternatives of strong depreciation of their currencies or artificially high exchange rates supported by exchange control. Moreover, the rudimentary financial and fiscal organization of many of these countries makes impossible the application of contra-cyclical policies or "compensatory" monetary and fiscal policy for the time being. Undoubtedly, the best remedy against the vulnerability of primary producers would be the stabilization of domestic economic activity in the chief industrial nations. But until some measure of stability has actually been achieved, one need not be surprised if primary producing countries elect to follow a conscious policy of diversifying exports, purchasing some measure of stability by some sacrifice in export yields.[51] This policy, in turn, is sub-

49. Lewis, *loc. cit.*, p. 17.

50. Pim, *op. cit.*, pp. 41–42, 57–58, 68, 86, 105–06 and 145–47; Moore, *op. cit.*, pp. 111–14.

51. S. G. Triantis, "Cyclical Changes in the Balance of Trade," *American Economic Review*, March 1952, pp. 68–86.

ject to severe limitations, which cannot be pursued here.[52] But if no policy for stabilizing export yields succeeds, the agricultural exporting countries are likely to be thrown by depressions into devaluations, exchange controls, quotas and embargoes. If the agriculture of the underdeveloped world is to flourish and contribute to economic progress, the industrial nations will need to cooperate in stabilizing the markets for the great international primary products.

### POPULATION AND AGRICULTURE

Probably no one would deny that rational lines of economic development differ substantially as between regions of heavy or light pressure of population; but it is hard—if not impossible—to draw a logically neat dividing line between the two categories. The change-over from increasing to decreasing product per capita with increments to population might suggest itself; but this dividing line proves to be not only spuriously exact, for reasons yet to be explained, but also too rigorous. Rent in the sense of economic theory begins to arise at the "point of diminishing average product." By this criterion any land would be overpopulated if it bears rent, and this is surely too inclusive for any operational use of the term.

An inviting alternative would be to designate as underpopulated any region (with its given complement of natural resources) in which increments to population have not yet brought the productivity of labor below a wage affording the workers an "acceptable" standard of living. But economics is partly normative, and nothing in its character prevents an economist from declaring that a given standard of living is "too low," whereupon the definiteness of the line between underpopulated and overpopulated disappears.

But what is worse, many other economic factors besides the mere ratio of manpower to natural resources operate upon the marginal productivity of labor, such as variations in its skills, energies and age distribution. Beyond the economic factors are political and sociological forces of considerable importance. Finally, the size of a country's population is seldom evaluated from a purely economic standpoint unless there is an extreme deficiency or surfeit in numbers of human beings—and not always even then.

Nevertheless, it is the extreme cases which offer the most profitable employment of the terms, particularly in relation to economic development. Thus if numbers are so great that laborers could be removed from agriculture (or other genetic or extractive industries) without reducing—even possibly with the effect of increasing—the total product, there could be

52. See Chapter 18.

little objection to designating the region as overpopulated. And if numbers could be increased without serious reduction—permitting even an increase possibly—of per capita productivity, the region is clearly underpopulated. By restricting these terms to the extremes we are left with an "undistributed middle." In view, however, of the numerous economic factors other than mere numbers which determine productivity, and in view also of the political and social factors which inevitably enter into any judgment as to whether population is deficient, excessive or not conspicuously either, it is well to have an undesignated middle ground.

On the basis of these definitions, Japan, China, India, much of Southeast Asia, parts of the Middle and Near East, and much of southeastern Europe are overpopulated. Much of Africa, Australasia and Latin America are underpopulated. Other great areas, such as the United States and much of Western Europe, would not be meaningfully characterized by either condition.

## Misconceptions about Overpopulated Areas

From this discussion of terms it is possible to draw an important moral concerning development. Dense population does not necessarily mean overpopulation. Surely Western Germany, Belgium, the English Midlands and the northeastern seaboard of the United States are densely populated, but it would be difficult—except perhaps on aesthetic grounds—to hold that they are overpopulated. The element which intervenes to destroy the synonym is *trade*. From an economic angle, the export of products of the relatively abundant factor of production (say labor) can, within certain limits, act as a substitute for the outward migration of the abundant factor itself.[53] Thus the relationship of freedom of international trade and payments to the welfare of the underdeveloped but overpopulated world is evident.

Some people have held that excess population is a real *asset* for developing countries because the increase of national income cannot be impeded by a labor shortage.[54] Stated in this general way, the argument can just as easily be reversed to say that *underpopulation* is an asset since an increase of national income cannot be impeded by a shortage of land and natural resources. In fact, the excess or deficiency of *any* factor of production relative to others is an unmitigated nuisance. But this truth in no way denies the attractiveness of measures to absorb surplus agricultural labor

53. Paul A. Samuelson, "International Trade and the Equalization of Factor Prices," *Economic Journal*, June 1948, pp. 163–84, and "International Factor-Price Equalization Once Again," *ibid.*, June 1949, pp. 181–97. Samuelson's position, however, has been shown to be extreme.

54. Hans W. Singer, "Problems of Industrialization of Under-Developed Areas" (mimeographed), Round Table on Economic Progress, International Economic Association, Santa Margherita Ligure, Italy, 1953.

into other pursuits, its original surplus character being taken as a datum. Nor does it deny that, in exceptionally favorable circumstances, a surplus of labor can rapidly be absorbed by economic progress.[55]

Pressure of population has frequently been held accountable for certain undesirable features of agriculture in the underdeveloped areas: uneconomically small holdings of land, geographically fragmented units and extreme inequality in land ownership. But the connection, if real, is by no means direct or invariant. Population pressure may lead to too small holdings if inheritance customs dictate the distribution of a man's land to all his sons; but it may be prevented from doing so by primogeniture, by emigration, by alternative pursuits in trade and industry, and other means. Fragmentation of holdings can occur in a country like France, with no conspicuous overpopulation; or it can be present in sparsely settled regions, as in parts of Africa, if rules of inheritance and dowries are sufficiently complex. Finally, inequality of land ownership seems no less characteristic of Latin America, for example, than it is of, say, the Near East.

### Implications of the Land-Labor Ratio

There have, then, been a number of false leads for economic policy from conditions of overpopulation or underpopulation; but the contrast does form the bedrock of policies for development. It will, in general, suffice to draw some necessary inferences regarding overpopulated regions, since the policies appropriate to underpopulated areas will be apparent.

For the quite short run, during which the population in agriculture has to be regarded as fixed, the chief available remedies against overpopulation, aside from improved production techniques, are the utilization of surplus labor and the liberation of exports and imports from artificial impediments. Surplus labor, if it is genuinely surplus, can be advantageously absorbed into any use with a productivity above zero. This implies great emphasis on labor-using techniques in agriculture and industry—short of plain "make work"—and on public works requiring relatively small amounts of capital. As for the international field, measures to expand profitable exports or imports operate immediately to lessen the pressure of population on domestic resources alone.

In a somewhat longer run, the agricultural population becomes a variable while the total population of the country remains constant or changes too slowly to matter. The greater the degree of overpopulation and the closer the agriculture of the country already approaches optimum techniques, the more vital is the shift of surplus farm labor to industry.

---

55. It is said, for example, that Western Germany, having suffered in the immediate postwar years from the influx of ten million refugees from the east, has already largely utilized them in her rapid development. But it would be surprising to discover a parallel in a nonindustrial, and indeed in any, underdeveloped country.

In the truly long run, if these more immediate measures have not relieved the pressure of population, the only remedies remaining are the demographic ones—emigration and declining birth rates. The world today affords meager opportunities for emigration, least of all to the great masses of Asia. In the last analysis, therefore, the only solution to overpopulation in the underdeveloped world lies in the behavior of population itself.

Whether underdeveloped countries are overpopulated or underpopulated, they earn most of their livelihood now from primary production—agriculture, mining and, in a few cases, forestry. National income, therefore, cannot rise much without improvements in agricultural and kindred incomes; furthermore, most of the wherewithal for industrialization will have at the beginning to come from the yield of primary production. For these reasons, the discussion of agriculture in earlier parts of this chapter could largely dispense with the contrast between areas of greater or lesser pressure of population. The same may be said of increasing the level of low-income countries by measures to expand multilateral international commerce: its benefits extend equally to overpopulated and underpopulated areas.

### The Role of Agriculture in the Economy

Since underdeveloped regions are primarily agricultural, chief emphasis should be placed initially on increasing agricultural output in attempts to raise incomes. This is frequently not the conviction of national leaders in countries that are economically underdeveloped. Desire for self-sufficiency or military power, national pride, or a purely romantic association of manufacture with affluence—these and other noneconomic motivations frequently result in an almost contemptuous attitude toward farming and in the glorification of gigantic industrial or public utility projects. Attitudes of this sort, however irrational, have to be reckoned as part of the general setting of the problem of economic development.

#### Is Agriculture Inferior to Industry?

But what of the position, maintained with great vigor by several economists, that agriculture in a genuinely *economic* sense is somehow inferior to industry? While these economists would presumably not deny the desirability of efforts to raise the productivity of agriculture, they do not put much faith in such policies but, instead, lay chief emphasis on industry. At least, they say, the proportion of agricultural to industrial output should be reduced.

The plain fact is that economic analysis provides no basis whatsoever for inferring a general inferiority of primary production. As Jacob Viner says:

Misallocation of resources as between agriculture and manufactures is probably rarely a major cause of poverty and backwardness, except where government, through tariffs, discriminatory taxation and expenditure policies, and failure to provide, on a regionally non-discriminatory pattern, facilities for education, health promotion, and technical training, is itself responsible for this misallocation.[56]

Why then do some economists believe that agriculture is inherently inferior to industry in an economic sense?

Over two decades ago, Mihäil Manoïlesco, Minister of Industry and Trade of Rumania, attempted to demonstrate—by means of largely "unreliable and irrelevant" statistics, according to his critics—that industrial production is always more efficient than agriculture, and that David Ricardo's law of comparative costs did not apply to countries of low agricultural productivity. Protective tariffs offered the only solution. His position drew the attention of some of the most distinguished international-trade economists.[57]

More recently, Louis Bean, an economist then connected with the United States Department of Agriculture, offered a superficially much more sophisticated demonstration of a supposedly "universal need for occupational adjustments out of agriculture into other industries and services."[58] Bean presents statistics for the main countries of the world and for the states of the United States purporting to show that low proportions of the labor force engaged in primary (agricultural and extractive) industries and high proportions in secondary (manufacturing) and tertiary (service) industries are closely associated with high per capita incomes. The degree of association of the two variables is artificially enhanced by a purely arbitrary division of the statistical items into four or five groups.

But an even more serious error arises from implicitly ascribing low per capita incomes to the high *proportion* of labor in primary production. Bean once recognizes explicitly that other factors may be responsible for low incomes—"population density, per acre productivity in agriculture, industrial productivity, and the relative volume of power, mechanical equipment, and other capital resources available to rural and urban populations."[59] Thus although too low proportions of the population engaged in manufacture or in tertiary production may be a contributory cause, along

56. Jacob Viner, *International Trade and Economic Development*, The Free Press, Glencoe, Illinois, 1952, p. 71.

57. M. Manoïlesco, *Théorie du protectionnisme et de l'échange international*, Paris, 1929 (English translation: *Theory of Protection and International Trade*, King, London, 1931). The book was reviewed by Bertil Ohlin in *Weltwirtschaftliches Archiv*, January 1931, pp. 30–45, and by Jacob Viner in the *Journal of Political Economy*, February 1932, pp. 121–25, reprinted in his *International Economics*, The Free Press, Glencoe, Illinois, 1951, pp. 119–22. See also Wilhelm Röpke, *International Economic Disintegration*, Hodge, London, 1942, p. 167.

58. Louis Bean, "International Industrialization and Per Capita Income," in *Studies in Income and Wealth*, Vol. 8, National Bureau of Economic Research, New York, 1946, pp. 119–43.

59. *Ibid.*, pp. 126–27.

with many other factors, of low incomes, the main line of causation may be from low incomes to low proportions in these fields. As Jacob Viner has pungently remarked: "if the data were available it could be demonstrated that the positive correlation between percentages of the national populations who were *dentists or hairdressers* and the national per capita incomes was even higher than Bean's correlations."[60]

### The Prebisch Analysis

Another supporter of the idea of the generic inferiority of primary production compared to industry is Raul Prebisch, Governor of the Central Bank of Argentina from 1935 to 1943 and now Executive Secretary of the United Nations Commission for Latin America.[61] It is Prebisch's belief that the price ratio of primary to manufactured goods in international trade has fallen since the 1870s, and that this means that labor and entrepreneur incomes in the industrial countries have increased more than productivity, since otherwise prices would have *fallen* as productivity rose. By this reasoning, incomes in the "periphery" countries producing primary goods have increased less than productivity. The benefits of technical progress have thus gone disproportionately to the industrial countries, and will continue to do so until the underdeveloped areas are themselves industrialized. The essential fact accounting for these disparate movements of incomes in Prebisch's view is a ratcheting action upon money wages produced by labor unions in the advanced countries. During the prosperity phase of a business cycle, money wages rise along with prices; but in depression wages are inflexible downward. This resistance sustains aggregate incomes in the industrial countries, but the gain accrues at the cost of the "peripheral" or primary production countries where laborers are not generally organized.

It would readily be granted, in appraising Prebisch's position, that agricultural countries may suffer in depression by reason of the tendency of industrial prices to be maintained and of competitively produced primary goods to decline. Furthermore, primary producer countries are more likely to have one or two major exports and this may expose the economy to greater risks than a diversity of export commodities would.

### The Factor of Quality of Exports

It seems very questionable, however, whether the raw-material-producing country has undergone a progressive deterioration of its real terms of trade over the three quarters of a century (1876–1947) covered by the British Board of Trade price indexes used by Prebisch. The one great variable which eludes this price comparison is the *quality* of industrial exports.

60. Viner, *International Trade and Economic Development*, p. 64. Italics added.
61. United Nations Economic Commission for Latin America, *The Economic Development of Latin America and Its Principal Problems*, New York, 1950.

Technological advances have improved manufactured products enormously over this period, but the quality of wheat, tin, rubber and other
primary products must have remained practically constant. The real terms
of trade and real incomes of primary producers can scarcely have been impaired significantly as a long-term development. Any such loss as was
actually realized would shrink to complete insignificance as a cause of the
low incomes of underdeveloped areas in comparison with lack of capital,
inefficiency of agricultural methods, political conditions, feudal land systems, ill-conceived taxation, inflation and the like.[62]

*The Singer Analysis*

That agriculture is generically inferior to industry is also the view of
H. W. Singer, an economist of the United Nations in New York. Singer's
case for industrialization seems to embrace three elements: (1) a special
aspect of the "infant industry" argument; (2) an extended meaning of
"external economies" of industry; (3) a supposed progressive decline in the
terms of trade for primary producers.[63] With regard to the third of these,
Singer resembles Prebisch in one respect. Both apparently take it as axio-
matic that technological progress has always been (and always will be?)
much more prevalent in industry than in agriculture. But this fact should
turn the terms of trade progressively in favor of *agriculture*. Hence, both
writers shy away from the factor of technical cost of production altogether.
For Prebisch, agriculture finally gets the worst of the deal through monopoly exaction by labor unions in the manufacturing countries. Singer asserts
that technical progress in industry accrues to the *producers* in the form of
higher prices and incomes, but in agriculture it accrues to *consumers* in the
form of lower prices and higher real incomes. Instead of supporting this
argument by a reference to the greater frequency of administered prices in
manufacturing, Singer supposes that inelastic demand for foodstuffs would
explain a long-term decline in their prices. Equally implausibly, he argues
that "in the case of raw materials, technical progress in manufactures
*largely consists* of a reduction of the amounts of raw material used per unit
of output."[64] But the real weakness of the terms-of-trade basis of a supposed inferiority of primary production lies, as emphasized in the comments on Prebisch, in its failure to allow for the vast increase in the quality
of manufactured goods.

The infant-industry argument, in Singer's hands, takes on a form frequently encountered in discussions of developing areas: that the preoccupa-

62. Prebisch himself points out that inflation has been one of the chief factors which have seriously
limited economic progress in many Latin American countries. *Ibid.*, p. 41.

63. H. W. Singer, "The Distribution of Gains between Investing and Borrowing Countries," *American
Economic Review, Proceedings*, May 1950, pp. 472–94.

64. *Ibid.*, p. 479. Italics added.

tion of these areas with exporting raw materials interfered with the growth of potentially productive enterprise in other fields. This possibility cannot be altogether denied. But it is problematical to what degree a benevolent dictator of such a region would—in the past or in the present—wish to substitute merely *potentially* productive manufacture for *actually* profitable primary production. If industry may have suffered from relative neglect, so may also diversified agriculture and improved agricultural techniques in general. The "infant" may well have been or may well be something other than industry, particularly industry in the all too usual sense of big factories and large-scale capital ventures in general.

Finally there remains Singer's extension of the "external economies" idea of Marshall and Pigou. The most important contribution of industry, he hazards, may not be its immediate product, but rather "its effect on the general level of education, skill, way of life, inventiveness, habits, store of technology, creation of new demand, etc."[65] One may wonder, however, how exclusively these benefits accrue merely to *industrial* economies, and to what degree they may be the causes, accompanying circumstances and results of high average incomes, however earned. Consider Holland's position in the fifteenth and sixteenth centuries arising from its maritime *trade;* the affluence of a state like Iowa or Nevada, or a country like New Zealand, arising from *agriculture*. Furthermore, many or most of the indirect external economies of manufacture accrue to agricultural regions in the form of cheaper or better products and also in the form of techniques which can, with appropriate modifications, be applied to genetic and extractive industries.

Clearly, there are no generally valid reasons why countries that possess natural advantages in agriculture and other types of primary production should not expand and improve these outputs. This does not deny the benefits of industrialization or development of tertiary production when these bid fair to cover costs or, within a predictable future, to lay the foundation of profitable operation. The question of the future of agricultural prices still remains, however. Will prices of agricultural products (specifically, and not the products of fishing, forestry and mining) be subject to long-term decline in the future? Or is the prospect rather that foodstuffs and textile fibers will rise in value over the next half century relative to manufactures?

### Prices of Primary Products in the Future

Certain economists who have concentrated their attention on population trends favor the idea that agricultural prices will rise in value in the next half century. Best known among these is Colin Clark, formerly economic

65. *Ibid.*, p. 476.

adviser to the government of Queensland and presently professor at Oxford University, whose *Economics of 1960*, written in 1940–1941, boldly proclaimed the thesis of increasing scarcity.[66] Clark recently has reaffirmed his belief in the correctness of this prediction and has extended his statistical analysis through 1970.[67]

Clark points to the expectation that the population of the world will increase at about 1.125 per cent a year for the period 1950–1970 or by 25 per cent in total. The consensus of evidence, he believes, is that European countries and Japan can increase agricultural output at a rate of 1.5 per cent annually and the United States and Australasia by 2 per cent. But any increase of agricultural output in other regions is conditioned in his view on a painful process of raising the level of literacy and developing transportation and commerce. Conceivably, and from the technical side alone, average output over the world *might* rise by 1.5 per cent annually. But this ignores the long-run tendency of the rural labor force to decline and its increasing claim for a shorter working week. On balance, Clark believes that the prospect is for a 70 per cent advance of world food prices, relative to industrial products, to meet the demand for an increasing standard of living, and that it will require twenty or thirty years to achieve equilibrium.

Similar reflections lead W. Arthur Lewis of Manchester University to comparable conclusions. Lewis points to the fact that in the forty years before 1913, manufacturing and primary production grew at about the same rate. Since 1913, however, manufacturing has risen by 147 per cent and primary production by only 55 per cent; in other words, the annual growth rate of primary production (allowing for compounding) is only half that of manufactures. On the technical side, Lewis believes that nothing prevents an increase of agricultural production by 2 or 3 per cent annually, and this would equal or outstrip the annual rate of population increase. But the obstacles to achieving this increase of primary production are social, with the provision of adequate investment perhaps the chief factor. Britain's interest in overseas investment, in his opinion, is to protect her standard of living from a progressive scarcity of food and raw materials.[68]

Contrasting with the pessimistic or at least apprehensive views of such writers as Clark and Lewis, leading American agricultural economists such as Davis, Schultz and Black take more sanguine views of the future supply

66. Colin Clark, *The Economics of 1960*, Macmillan, London, 1942; 2d edition, 1951.

67. Colin Clark, "The Future of the Terms of Trade" (Proceedings of the International Economic Association, Monaco, September 1950), *International Social Science Bulletin*, Spring 1951, pp. 37–40. See also "World Resources and World Population," in United Nations, *Proceedings of the Scientific Conference on the Conservation and Utilization of Resources, 1949*, Vol. I, pp. 15–27.

68. W. Arthur Lewis, "Food and Raw Materials," *District Bank Review*, September 1951, pp. 1–11.

of foodstuffs and other agricultural products.[69] We need not concern our-
selves with the details of this position, which rests in general on the expectation of noteworthy technological advances in food production.

### Pitfalls in Analyzing Price Developments

In order to discover the significance of future price developments of
agricultural as against manufactured products for underdeveloped areas,
several pitfalls must be avoided. In the first place, population increase—
like the physiological "requirement" of the individual for calories—does
not in itself signify demand and an increase in the price of foodstuffs. As
Professor Davis sagely warns: "Demand is different from need or want, and
low individual productivity and purchasing power spell weak demand
despite urgent needs and wants."[70] Doubtless some relation obtains between mere numbers and demand, but a simple—or perhaps even any
definite—ratio cannot be assumed. Second, dealing with this matter in
global figures may mislead the unwary. Not all foodstuffs pass across world
markets. Wheat and rice conform to the classical requirements of a perfect
market reasonably well, though even here exchange controls, tariffs and
quotas interfere with the formation of a single world price. Potatoes, fish,
vegetables and many fruits, however, conform more to the character of
Roy Harrod's C-type or "purely domestic" goods. It is quite conceivable
therefore that agricultural products may rise in price relative to manufactured goods in one region while they fall in another region where other
supply conditions and food habits prevail.

Future development of these two sets of prices can bear intimately upon
the success of economic development in any country. But the possibility of
planning development for any significant number of years in advance with
reference specifically to the price ratio of food and manufactures would
seem to be quite limited. Differential rates of technical progress in the two
spheres are, in sober truth, simply not predictable. Furthermore, this relationship is subject to strong influences proceeding from national programs
of price support or protection, from employment conditions the world
over, from inflation or deflation, and from whether there is peace or war.
The failure of concerted attempts to stabilize the price of raw materials or
foodstuffs, such as the Stevenson rubber scheme and the world wheat
stabilization plan, reveals the vicissitudes to which these markets are exposed. For about a year following the outbreak of the Korean war, raw

69. Joseph S. Davis, "American Agriculture: Schultz' Analysis and Policy Proposals," *Review of Eco-
nomic Statistics*, May 1947, pp. 80–91; Theodore W. Schultz (Ed.), *Food for the World* (Harris Foundation
Lectures), University of Chicago Press, Chicago, 1945, pp. 306–20. For John D. Black's opinions see United
Nations, *Proceedings of the Scientific Conference on the Conservation and Utilization of Resources, 1949*,
Vol. 1, pp. 211–14.

70. Davis, *loc. cit.*, p. 83, n. 7.

materials supplied from south and southeast Asia commanded such favorable prices that the world dollar shortage vanished. One journal declared that if the favorable swing in the terms of trade were to persist for five or six years, the Colombo Plan, except for India, could be financed without external aid.[71] This is unlikely, but who can say with certainty?

*Conclusions from Analysis of Price Developments*

For underdeveloped countries the moral would seem to be clear: the future of prices several decades hence cannot be foretold. Furthermore, assuming that governments do not withhold from private enterprisers the statistical and other information which they and the international agencies possess, there is no reason to believe that government planning will be any more successful than the planning of individual producers in exploiting favorable market prospects.

All of this, however, need not be particularly disturbing. The die need not be cast for decades ahead; new investment year by year can be adapted to the changing relative demands in world and local markets. Particularly for agriculture, where investment is less specific and more flexible than in industry, this is reassuring, especially for underdeveloped areas, where agriculture predominates. Fundamentally, the divergence of convictions among food supply experts as to the future course of prices does not affect the basic requirement for increasing the income levels of the less developed nations; agricultural production must in any case be raised by strenuous and persistent effort.

71. "Recovery in South-East Asia," *The Eastern Economist*, April 27, 1951, pp. 679–80.

# 13. Commerce and Industry in Economic Development

THE FORMS, MEANS, AND GOALS of industrialization are often vague in the mixture of reason, rationalizing and sentiment accompanying the clamor for it. Occasionally, no doubt, an almost childish admiration for complicated machinery underlies an agrarian nation's attitude toward industrialization. Perhaps the driving force has often been a blind emulation of the opulent industrial nations of the Western world, particularly England and more lately the United States, in the belief that monstrous factories are the "open sesame" to wealth and prestige. National pride, the desire for "economic independence"—however much "independence" may cost in terms of real income—plays a role. Certainly autarchy, nationalism and the desire to create offensive or defensive armaments are, in conspicuous cases today, the driving forces. On a more nearly economic plane, it is often said that primary producers cannot escape the devastation of recurrent depressions originating in America or Europe except by lessening their dependence on the markets of the industrial West.

Whether rational or not, most of these urges have a surprising force which it would be folly to ignore. Analysis on a purely economic level does not suffice either for diagnosis or prescription. Thus it would seem wise to point out that better remedies for cyclical depression and unemployment are available than a retreat into autarchy—if it is a remedy. But other aims of industrialization, such as "defense," will have to be taken into account by each country according to its own circumstances. In this discussion, the raising of levels and standards of living is regarded as the *economic* motive par excellence; and it is chiefly with this welfare objective in mind that the subject of industrialization is approached.

### THE BEGINNINGS OF INDUSTRIALIZATION

The first "industrialization" is scarcely distinguishable from improved agriculture. In the broadest sense of the term, it includes the building of highways and access roads and railways to help in the marketing of farm products; it would include the development of electrical or other sources of power for rural industries and the securing of wood, coal or oil to supplant animal droppings as fuel in some countries; in very many cases, it would mean the development of agricultural processing plants to prevent spoilage or to permit more diversified farming.

267

Wherever low incomes are associated with surplus population on the land another very potent reason exists for investing in industries which can successfully operate in rural areas. Human resources are utilized where they naturally occur, without the delay, social disruption and capital costs entailed by the movement of population into cities.

Finally, where the majority of the inhabitants are peasants with very low incomes, many manufactures are precluded by the limited size of the domestic market. Mass production cannot be introduced to achieve low unit costs and thus to offer competition to imported items. It would, indeed, be difficult to exaggerate the obstacle to the growth of industry created by the sheer incapacity of most of the population to buy. A striking example is given in the International Bank study of Colombia: for the production of electric light bulbs, "the smallest mechanized plant is such that three months' operation would fulfill Colombia's present demands for a year. The smallness of the domestic market is primarily due to the extremely low purchasing power of the mass of the people."[1] From similar facts, Sanford Mosk in his illuminating study of the economic development of Mexico concludes that higher agricultural productivity is a prime requisite for industrialization. "The Mexican farmer," he says, "will not be a better buyer until he is a better producer."[2]

*Developing Industry Based on Agriculture*

To sum up, the same logic which recommends first emphasis on direct measures to improve *agricultural* techniques and implements in regions preponderantly agricultural also counsels the orientation of a large share of early investment *in industry* toward processes intimately associated with agriculture. First, this is necessary because of the sheer magnitude of agriculture in the gross national output. Second, the scarcity of capital, skilled labor and trained management makes preferable those uses of resources belonging to a "stage of production" close to the great producer in the backward economies—the land. Among those uses, the provision of transportation and marketing facilities is very important. Third, where too many people are on the farms, plantations or paddies, Mahomet should move to the mountain; industry should generally move to labor. Thus the heavy costs of urbanization can be postponed until incomes have risen. Finally, industries based on farm production and farm population afford a direct means of increasing mass purchasing power, expanding the domestic market and laying the base for thriving domestic manufactures of varied sorts. True, large-scale urban industry is an indispensable complement to the

1. International Bank for Reconstruction and Development, *The Basis of a Development Program for Colombia* (Report of a Mission Headed by Lauchlin Currie), Washington, 1950, p. 93.

2. Sanford A. Mosk, *Industrial Revolution in Mexico*, University of California Press, Berkeley, 1950, p. 209.

small-scale dispersed production of the villages and farms. But there is a significant contrast in emphasis as between step-by-step improvement in many localities at once and the concentration of investment in a few large undertakings.

## VILLAGE AND RURAL INDUSTRY: PROCESSING FARM PRODUCTS

In India, small-scale or cottage industries account for 85 per cent of all industrial employment; in China, small units produce 85 per cent of the sugar, half the paper and half the cotton cloth; in Japan, 75 per cent of the textile workers are engaged in plants with fewer than 50 employees and 50 per cent in plants with fewer than 14.[3] Some of these small plants, of course, are to be found in the cities, but many are scattered throughout the country in small villages and towns. In Indonesia, pursuant to the welfare program or "ethical policy" adopted by the Dutch in 1900, the old native handloom industry was revived. "The success of this policy," one writer reports, "is indicated by the increase in the number of mechanical looms between 1930 and 1941 from almost none to about 10,000, while the number of modern hand looms perfected by the government's Textile Institute increased from around 500 to 49,000."[4] In India, several thousand demonstration centers have been established to develop the so-called cottage industries.

### Advantages of Village-Rural Industry

The case for village and rural industries as the chief carriers of industrialization in the Orient rests not only on the four general economic factors previously mentioned, but also on two further and somewhat special considerations. The first is the relief from want attending seasonal unemployment in agriculture. In Japan, it was estimated in 1938, 54 per cent of the peasants were engaged in supplementary jobs.[5] The International Labor Office has urged that governments consider the possibility of "dovetailing of public works with seasonal variations in the excess supply of agricultural labour."[6] Highway, irrigation and drainage projects could thus create highly necessary capital out of waste manpower and eliminate the misery of seasonal unemployment as well.

Another potential gain from the village and rural industries would be their appeal to local savers and investors. Large imports of gold and silver bullion into the Orient over many decades suggest that substantial private

---

3. Henry G. Aubrey, "Small Industry in Economic Development," *Social Research*, September 1951, p. 276; Joseph E. Stepanek and Charles H. Prien, "The Role of Rural Industries in Underdeveloped Areas," *Pacific Affairs*, March 1950, pp. 68–69.

4. Aubrey, *loc. cit.*, p. 279.

5. *Ibid.*, p. 290.

6. International Labor Office, *Action against Unemployment*, Geneva, 1950, p. 138.

investment could come from hoards scattered throughout the broad masses.[7] The main emphasis, however, should doubtless be put on *current* saving and investing. In relatively primitive economies lacking banking facilities, especially in rural areas, the visual appeal of the small village industry may be important.[8]

### Raising Efficiency of Peasant Industry

If all these substantial social and economic gains are to be realized from peasant industry, why has it not laid the basis of significant advances in incomes? The answer lies in the inefficiency of traditional production. The small gains made in the past have not sufficed to alter standards of living; much of the increase has been swallowed up in population growth. But if, as may be possible, a 5 to 10 per cent annual increase in the productivity of rural industry can be achieved, this large and cumulative advance might conduce to lower birth rates. What steps are necessary to raise efficiency?

As previously noted, the first industrialization is scarcely distinguishable from improved agriculture, and high in the list of priorities should stand the provision of simple, improved tools and instruments. The development of an improved metal plowshare costing about 60 cents by the Agricultural Department of Burma before World War II resulted in sales of 5,000 annually and a noticeable increase in crop yields.[9] The introduction into India of the fly-shuttle, which ushered in the industrial revolution in England, increased output in typical households by 30 per cent; and a 40-spindle foot-powered cotton-spinning machine amortized its cost in a month if operated full time.[10]

Another high priority for improving peasant industry is the opening up of roads, highways and other facilities for transportation, both for obtaining raw materials and for marketing produce. Over the past decade there has been a decided shift in emphasis in many development plans from blast furnaces to roads. The opportunity to create transportation facilities with seasonally slack agricultural labor is worthy of note.

The industrial revolution in Western Europe and America was based on steam as the motive power; power-driven machinery was consequently heavy and expensive. But the advent of internal combustion engines and of electric motors driven from central generators has made possible the decentralized use of power machinery. Japan, with its highly developed electric

7. See Stepanek and Prien, *loc. cit.*, p. 66. The simple creation of money by the government or banking system could supply the same funds, but the difference for central banking reserves and international trade is obvious.

8. Morton Solomon, "The Structure of the Market in Underdeveloped Economies," *Quarterly Journal of Economics*, August 1948, p. 532.

9. H. Belshaw, "Observations on Industrialization for Higher Incomes," *Economic Journal*, September 1947, p. 383, n. 3.

10. Aubrey, *loc. cit.*, p. 280.

grid, has brought cheap electric power to every hamlet and within reach of every farmstead. This achievement goes far to explain the efficiency of the small-scale industry of that country, including its notable gains in wool-weaving output.[11]

Other channels of improvement await exploitation. Government investigations into the most promising lines of future development for peasant industry may be desirable as complements to private initiative, especially where the populace is generally illiterate, apathetic or ridden by disease and poverty. The encouragement of producing or marketing cooperatives for peasant manufactures is recommended in many quarters; they have attained modest success in India, Pakistan, Burma, Indochina and China. The availability of credit at reasonable rates is often stressed.

Further argument and documentation could be presented, but probably enough has been said to indicate the promise and necessity of improving the rural and village industries.

### Processing Farm Products

Another phase of industrialization which often should be accorded high investment priority on much the same grounds as peasant industry is the processing of agricultural produce. Processing in a broad sense includes not only simple operations such as the milling of rice, ginning of cotton, grinding of sugar and molasses production for domestic or export markets, but also grading, standardizing, packaging and storing. The primitiveness of many poorer economies is painfully evident in these latter activities, which often, indeed, are almost completely absent. Thus in China, as in much of the underdeveloped world, refrigeration facilities are limited to the foreign sectors of the port cities, and refrigeration for food in transit is simply not available. The effect of this on the market values for primary producers of perishable goods requires no explanation.

An increasing emphasis appears in development programs on industries using the raw materials of domestic agriculture. Mosk regards these as "foremost among the industries which should be expanded at once" in the economy of Mexico.[12] He includes "the processing of cereals; the preparation of edible oils from various seeds and nuts; the production of sugar and sugar by-products such as alcohol; the fabrication of articles made from fibres, such as cotton, silk, wool, henequen, ixtle, and lechu-guilla; production of raw rubber." Similar emphasis is put on processing industries, with appropriate changes in the list of products, by the Economic Survey Mission to the Philippines (the Bell Mission) and the Joint Brazil–U.S. Tech-

11. *Ibid.*, p. 286.
12. Mosk, *op. cit.*, p. 36.

nical Commission.[13] A recent economic survey of Cuba recommends, as the chief measure to ensure the island's comparative advantage in sugar export in the future, the provision of supplementary income for sugar workers in the off-season through processing such by-products as molasses, sirups, alcohols, rum and cane spirits. Aside from this, Cuba could raise agricultural incomes significantly by producing candies, preserves and marmalades from her abundant fruit and sugar.[14] But enough examples have been given to underscore the importance of "industrialization" in the processing of foods and other farm products.

*Monopoly in Processing*

Unfortunately, the inadequacy of processing and marketing facilities for the peasant or small farmer is not the end of his troubles, for often when the facilities are available they are the object of monopolistic restriction. W. Arthur Lewis declares flatly that "we are compelled to write off private enterprise in processing as a social failure."[15] Some colonial experts incline to the view that cooperative storage, finance and marketing are the only guarantee that the native producer shall not receive a price so low as to preclude him from any gain in the level of living.[16] Others are inclined to believe that cooperatives have in general not yet demonstrated their viability.[17] However this may be, it seems very likely that government action, whether in fostering cooperatives, in providing agricultural credit, in negotiating with strong monopolists—as the government of Jamaica did with the United Fruit Company on the price paid for bananas—may prove necessary at times.

### THE SEQUENCE OF INDUSTRIALIZATION

The most urgent and most profitable lines of first development in processes closely linked with the produce of the land have usually been food processing, transportation and marketing facilities, and home and village manufactures, in which of course textiles bulk large. Beyond this, what is the probable sequence of industrial growth?

*Eliminating Obsolete Methods*

One fairly safe generalization is that any process carried on by obsolete methods should come under scrutiny. Many underdeveloped regions are

13. M. J. Deutsch (adviser to the Bell Mission), *Technical Memorandum on Industrial Development and Utilities* (mimeographed, no date), pp. 8–23. *Report of the Joint Brazil–U.S. Technical Commission*, Publication 3487, U.S. Department of State, June 1949, pp. 80 and 208–12.

14. Stacy May, *Economic Development in Cuba* (a report for the Chase National Bank), International Basic Economy Technical Services Corporation, New York, 1948, pp. ii, iii, 46–47 and 51–54.

15. W. Arthur Lewis, "Developing Colonial Agriculture," *The Three Banks Review*, June 1949, pp. 14–15.

16. Erich H. Jacoby, *Agrarian Unrest in Southeast Asia*, Columbia University Press, New York, 1949, p. 51.

17. Sir Alan Pim, *Colonial Agricultural Production*, Oxford University Press, London, 1946, pp. 10–11.

indeed "rampant with technological slack";[18] here may lie a prospect of getting something for nothing, or for very little. Without doubt, this consideration explains the complete reorientation of President Truman's Point Four, which was originally interpreted in some quarters as a plan for billions of capital investment, to the more realistic and compassable present program of technical aid in terms of millions.

When improvement begins to *cost*, however, many criteria present themselves, and their proper evaluation will vary greatly from one country to another. Often, the criteria will prove in greater or lesser degree mutually incompatible; as in all genuinely economic problems, opportunity costs make themselves felt. Whether industrialization is carried on by governments with civil servants making the decisions, or by private enterprises under the guidance of corporation managers and technical experts, much the same general kinds of problems, with the necessity of resolving competing or conflicting objectives, will be involved.

### Basic Industries

Among the industries stressed in recent studies of particular economies have been chemicals, power, fertilizers, machine tools, and such industrial equipment as pumps, filters, centrifugals, mixers, heat exchangers and compressors.[19] In some cases, the list continues with electrical goods, motor vehicles, paper and pulp, and even steel. Apparently, the criterion here is the generality of the industry or its lack of specificity; multitudes of products depend upon it for raw materials. There can be little doubt that this criterion is important—at least until it runs afoul of such other considerations as scarcity of capital and of skilled labor and management.

One possible solution to the dilemma created by the need for basic industries which are often highly capitalistic and the limited resources from which they must be bought or produced lies in concentrating the industrialization in limited regions within countries, particularly in large and populous countries.[20] From these more highly developed regions, industry can then be spread into the provinces as a result of the increased income generated at the centers.

### The Productivity Test

A rule for determining the sequence of investment among industries, and undoubtedly the most basic single consideration, is the test of productivity:

18. Warren Wilhelm, "Soviet Central Asia: Development of a Backward Area," *Foreign Policy Reports*, February 1, 1950, p. 225. Obsolete *equipment*, however, may not be uneconomical; see below, p. 277.

19. See Mosk, *op. cit.*, pp. 36–37; *Report to the President of the United States by the Economic Survey Mission to the Philippines*, U.S. Department of State, October 9, 1950, p. 62, hereafter called the Bell Report; Deutsch, *op. cit.*, p. 6; *Report of the Joint Brazil–U.S. Technical Commission*, pp. 96–101.

20. H. W. Singer, "Development Projects as Part of National Development Programmes," in United Nations, *Formulation and Economic Appraisal of Development Projects* (Major Course Lectures Delivered at the Asian Centre on Agriculture and Allied Projects, Lahore, Pakistan, October–December 1950), Lahore, 1951, Book I, p. 29.

as more funds are accumulated, the normal progression would be from the higher to the lower productivity. Indeed, it has been argued that this is the sole legitimate test, and that the admission of other elements leads to unwarranted conservatism.[21] In a world in which unlimited capital was available, provided the going interest charges could be met, in which economic fluctuations and the risk of withdrawal of foreign loans were absent, and in which the articulation of economic processes was perfectly adjusted so that the flow of output in one line would never be impaired by hitches in another, the productivity rule might suffice.

But loan capital is always limited for any one borrower (capital is "rationed" in the technical parlance); national reserves of foreign exchange are always more or less limited and more or less exposed to unpredictable hazards; domestic markets undergo depression. And it is no part of false conservatism if the order or sequence of industrialization takes account, at private or public hand alike, of these risks.

### Factors Determining Priority

Thus, because sufficient capital cannot be saved or borrowed, a given country may assign lower priority to a continuous-production steel mill. Because foreign capital may in some cases be had only at short term, or because governments, in investing domestic capital, may have to make a quick showing for political reasons, priority in the sequence of industrialization may have to go to industries with short gestation periods. Because domestic or foreign depressions may threaten currency reserves and national currency values, the time-shape of export yields and of imports induced by higher incomes may assume great importance. Because plant operation at a loss in depression is frequently less costly than a complete shutdown, industries involving relatively low capital intensity may take preference in the industrialization process. The removal of bottlenecks of production may assume a significance not measured by the profitability or productivity of the particular operation in any normal sense of the term.[22] Finally, of course, in many types of investment—for public health, education and the like—productivity can scarcely be measured in quantitative terms. Other things being equal, the guide of productivity is not being called into question here, but there are other criteria.

New planned or socialist economies must, in general, face the same facts and the same mutually exclusive choices as private enterprise. Even booms and slack times occur in socialist as well as in private enterprise economies,

21. Alfred E. Kahn, "Investment Criteria in Development Programs," *Quarterly Journal of Economics,* February 1951, pp. 38–61.

22. See E. De Vries, "Financial Aspects of Economic Development," in United Nations, Economic Commission for Asia and the Far East, *Cottage and Small Scale Industries* (mimeographed), E/EC–11/I & T/30, pp. 337–42.

if from no other cause than wars, defense activities and change-overs to peace. The basic conditions of industrialization probably show greater diversity from such factors as population pressure, natural resources, literacy and technological practices than from political organization.

So far as generalization is possible, industrialization has commonly and rationally begun with processes close to agriculture, including food processing and the manufacture of textiles. The next stage would seem rationally to include such basic and general industries as chemicals, power, fertilizer, electrical equipment, machine tools, and standard and common industrial equipment. Further stages can be predicted only in a specific situation.

### PROBLEMS OF CAPITAL INTENSITY, SIZE AND TEMPO

Aside from the *time sequence* of industries to be established in the process of economic development, there are far-reaching questions regarding the desirable *proportions* of capital and labor, that is, capital intensity, the appropriate *size* of industrial projects, and the *rapidity* with which the whole evolution should proceed. These three issues are involved and controversial; furthermore, they lead immediately into questions of the state's role in the whole process of development.

#### CAPITAL INTENSITY

There is a philosophy of economic development which stresses the importance of tools, equipment and projects relatively economical of capital; of modest beginnings in light industry and small-scale operations; and of a close association of industry—at least initially—with agriculture. It tends to stress the many pitfalls in the path of rapid development and to raise doubts about the capacity of governments to force the process successfully past certain limits. On the other hand, an eloquent case can be pleaded for capital-intensive projects, for large units to realize the economies of scale, for pushing hard upon industry (as opposed to agriculture) for the sake of the gains of complementarity, "external economies," or "increasing returns," and for operating the engine of development under forced draft through extensive state controls and compulsions.

General issues of this sort can seldom be resolved categorically, for much depends upon the particular time and place. Yet it is a striking circumstance that the second of these two philosophies permeated the earlier and more abstract treatments of economic development, while the first has gained ground steadily in empirical studies of particular economies.

A general common sense presumption exists for using the scarce and expensive factor of capital sparingly relative to labor; the theoretical counterpart of this common sense is the productivity test examined in the previous section. Capital-intensive investment should grow out of abundant capital supplies and low interest rates. Historically, industrialization has typically progressed from light to heavy forms, a dramatic example being afforded by the industrialization of Japan.[23] Critics of the light-industry position accept this as the traditional progression, but they would hold with Maurice Dobb that "this is a purely static argument. It starts from a *given* endowment of capital in each country; whereas the crucial question at issue in discussing policies of economic development concerns *change* in the capital endowment of a country and how rapidly this capital endowment should be changed."[24] With Evgeni Preobrazhenski—apparently a leader in theoretical discussions in the U.S.S.R. of the 1920s—the argument takes the form that "highly capitalistic technology" on a large scale greatly expands output by using surplus farm labor.[25]

Both these lines of argument play fast and loose with two quite separate phenomena. Doubtless, as Dobb implies, the rate of increasing "capital endowment" can be greatly accelerated by government compulsions; but nothing in a rapid *rate of saving and investment* dictates the practical use of capital in combination with labor at a higher *ratio* than would minimize costs on the basis of current interest and wage rates. Any departure from this test, even though the interest rate were not a form of actual payment to private persons but only an approximate market-clearing rate for government cost-accounting purposes, would be as wasteful to a planned or socialist economy as to the capitalistic private entrepreneur. Precisely the same criticism applies to Preobrazhenski's argument proceeding from the use of surplus labor to capital-intensive forms of investment. On any sensible calculus, surplus labor requires the opposite—high ratios of labor to capital! The argument is not about *what* is made, whether capital goods or consumers' goods, but *how*. Even if the pace of capital accumulation is rapid, the appropriate instruments for a developing country may be light; and if accumulation proceeds against odds, as frequently happens, a high ratio of labor to capital is appropriate.

*Studies of Particular Countries*

An overwhelming proportion of recent studies of particular countries emphasize this position; but a few examples must suffice for illustration. With respect to Turkey, William Nicholls complains of inattention to the scarcity of managerial skills, capital and foreign exchange requirements;

23. Tokutaro Yamanaka, "Japanese Small Industries during the Industrial Revolution," *Annals of the Hitotsubashi Academy*, October 1951, pp. 15–36.

24. Maurice Dobb, *Some Aspects of Economic Development* (Three Lectures at the Delhi School of Economics), Ranjit Printers, Delhi, 1951, p. 54. Author's italics. Dobb's views on this matter are apparently shared by K. Mandelbaum, *The Industrialization of Backward Areas* (Oxford Institute of Statistics, Monograph No. 2), Blackwell, Oxford, 1945, pp. 14–15.

25. Alexander Erlich, "Preobrazhenski and the Economics of Soviet Industrialization," *Quarterly Journal of Economics*, February 1950, pp. 64–65.

"the result has been an undue emphasis upon inefficient, capital intensive producer-goods industries."[26] Lewis says of colonial agriculture generally that the farmer needs spades instead of wooden digging sticks—not tractors.[27] The Economic Commission for Latin America complains that many machines imported by the less developed economies are too saving of labor, thus causing unemployment and wasting capital.[28] "Even in this machine age," says the Brazil–U.S. Technical Commission, "Brazil might more profitably direct its efforts first toward improvements in animal traction with simple implements, and not toward extensive power mechanization."[29] Using data of the Central Planning Bureau of the Netherlands which show value added by labor and by capital for twenty industries, De Vries emphasizes the necessity for Asian countries to concentrate on labor-intensive industries.[30]

### The Factor of Obsolete Equipment

An interesting aspect of the general presumption in favor of light, or labor-intensive, industry is the matter of technically obsolete equipment. The Latin American Commission observes perceptively that the relative scarcity of capital makes it economical to continue obsolete equipment in operation; and Aubrey remarks that if equipment is simple, the problem of obsolescence as such is less serious.[31] It would be consistent with these conclusions to say that an all-round saving for both more mature and less developed countries could be effected by the importation into underdeveloped countries of technologically obsolete equipment—such, for example, as outmoded coach or Pullman cars.

#### SIZE OF PROJECTS

Separate from the question of light or heavy industry (the choice between labor- and capital-intensive production) is the question of *scale* or *size* of producing unit. Planners for underdeveloped countries often betray a Marxian fascination with mere size and an implicit faith in the economies of large-scale production. Of course, no hard and fast generalizations can be laid down: occasionally these economies may be quite real. Capital-intensive producer goods are likely to be associated with large scale, however, and in all such cases the evidence already cited for light industry and for peasant and village industry makes a powerful argument for relatively small-scale ventures.

26. William H. Nicholls, "Trade in an Underdeveloped Country—Turkey," *Journal of Political Economy*, December 1951, p. 465.

27. Lewis, *loc. cit.*, p. 13.

28. United Nations, Economic and Social Council, *Theoretical and Practical Problems of Economic Growth*, Economic Commission for Latin America, Fourth Session, Mexico, May 28, 1950, pp. 14 and 51.

29. *Report of the Joint Brazil–U.S. Technical Commission*, p. 202.

30. De Vries, *loc. cit.*, p. 338.

31. *Theoretical and Practical Problems of Economic Growth*, p. 57; Aubrey, *loc. cit.*, p. 294.

*Disadvantages of Large Projects*

Beyond the ever-present problem of scarcity of capital, several further considerations point to the wisdom of conservatism in the matter of size. For one thing, large projects come slowly into fruition; meanwhile, ancillary projects may be delayed, or consumers may chafe under the postponement of services. None other than Molotov complained in a speech in 1939 of a "megalomania in construction . . . There are many instances of cases," he said, "where we embarked upon construction of gigantic projects, sank a lot of money into these schemes, but their completion dragged out interminably." He gave as illustration the Frunze heat and power station in Moscow, which was still unfinished after seven years of construction though two or three smaller plants could have been completed in the same period.[32]

Much of the success of industrial development, as everyone recognizes, depends upon the proper articulation of the several parts of the economy. If investment is committed to huge projects, the danger of wrongly estimating optimum outputs and optimum locations for plants is augmented. A further risk lies in the exhaustion of financial resources before the project can be completed. Finally, the risk of technical obsolescence also mounts.

*Modern Technology and Small Plants*

A further significant fact is that modern mechanical engineering, particularly as aided by electrical motive power, is able to reduce the size of plant required for the full realization of economies of scale. Aubrey points to the accomplishments of the Agricultural Industry Service of UNRRA in this respect. Cement factories, brick kilns, sulphuric acid plants and spinning and weaving equipment are a few examples among many.

It is well to recall the large role played in the development of Japan—and even in its present economy—by small-scale industries. They prevail not only in more or less indigenous commodities such as various types of brushes, paper lanterns, paper umbrellas and dolls (for all of which there is a very lively home market), but also in "Western" goods—fountain pens, bicycles and rubber shoes, boots and tires, for example, In some industries, such as wool-weaving, the large-scale producer has even lost ground within the past few decades to smaller units.[33] Widespread availability of electric power, in contrast to the earlier concentration induced by steam-driven machinery, helps to account for this. Japan's experience provides an instructive example of how possession of a large sector of small-scale enter-

---

32. Reported in *Pravda* in 1939, according to the Birmingham Bureau of Research on Russian Economic Conditions, *Results of the Second Five-Year Plan and the Project of the Third Five-Year Plan* (Memorandum No. 12), Birmingham, 1939, pp. 6–7.

33. See Aubrey, *loc. cit.*, pp. 282–86.

prise may give initial impulse to industrialization as well as sustain its viability.

THE TEMPO OF INDUSTRIALIZATION

Countries embarking on economic development programs must settle, besides the questions of the correct degree of capital-intensity and of suitable scale, the difficult problem of the *tempo* of industrialization. Some noteworthy students of economic development have written rhapsodic accounts of the potentialities of rapid progress. This conviction rests in part on factors already mentioned—enthusiasm for heavy industry and belief in nearly limitless economies of scale. But it also involves some new elements of expectation: the gains of complementarity among the many industries, "external economies," increasing returns of industry as opposed to agriculture, and kindred ideas, all of them closely related and often not clearly distinguishable. To appraise this fabric, it is necessary to disentangle the many threads and to test their tensile strength. One thing, of course, is clear: so far as the economic aspect of development is concerned and aside from sociological, moral and political issues, a maximum tempo of increase in income is the objective.[34] The practical issue is whether haste is better made precipitately or slowly.

*Complementarity and "External Economies"*

Complementarity and "external economies" may profitably be considered together. Complementarity refers to the fact that virtually all the industries of an economy are interdependent: each furnishes a market for the others and each determines the prices of productive factors and raw materials used by the others. In an expanding economy each industry, provided its growth is gauged correctly to the growth of others, should develop economies of production or improve its product; and the benefits of each to the others are augmented by their very interdependence. External economies refers essentially to the same phenomenon except that the viewpoint is shifted from all industries to a particular one. Even if a plant or industry has already realized all internal economies (perfectly exploiting its overhead or fixed factors), its expansion may induce other related and contributory services or industries to better their products or to realize lower costs, and these improvements in turn lower the costs of the first industry.

A number of writers have seized upon the fact of complementarity and the potentiality of external economies as prima-facie evidence that industrialization of underdeveloped areas must proceed rapidly, on a large scale

34. Mere aggregate or average income may increase without an increase of welfare if inequality grows, or if the average increase is ground out of some luckless class, such as the bourgeoisie or the peasants.

and under the auspices of the state. According to Rosenstein-Rodan, "complementarity of different industries provides the most important set of arguments in favour of large-scale planned industrialization."[35] Much the same conviction is expressed by Preobrazhenski: "to secure the development of the whole complex of the state economy and not only of its particular parts," the state must provide for rapid expansion of its capital equipment "because the chain connection in the movement of the whole complex makes an isolated advance entirely impossible."[36] Similar views are set forth by Mandelbaum and Dobb.[37]

Whether or not these arguments support extensive state intervention,[38] one thing is certain: external economies and complementarity have a completely neutral relation to the tempo of industrialization. External economies cannot banish the scarcity of capital and of skilled labor from the scene nor annihilate illiteracy, poor health and apathy, bad systems of land tenure and other real limits to progress. As for complementarity, if panegyrics can be written on the great possibilities of development through the successful dovetailing of industries, volumes can also be written on the complexity of the problem and the infinity of chances to go wrong, whether the investment process is controlled privately or by the state.

## Technological Improvements in Industry and Agriculture

Is the rate of industrialization to be pressed hard because, in the terms of English classical and neoclassical economics, "industry is subject to increasing but agriculture to diminishing returns"? Modern economics rejects this quaint language because both industrial and agricultural units of production are characterized by decreasing, optimal and increasing phases of costs. What the contrast usually means, even with the classical economists, is that technological improvements are more numerous in industry than in agriculture; and this seems to be the conviction of many of the proponents of rapid and heavy industrialization already named. But this generalization is categorically rejected by outstanding agricultural economists. John D. Black, for example, asserts that "agricultural revolution has accompanied industrial revolution and has kept pace with it."[39]

Recently, indeed, the number and variety of inventions and their practical application in agriculture have been striking. Mechanization, improved varieties of crops that reduce the hazards of weather by shortening the maturing periods, liming, fertilizers, control of insects and diseases and

35. P. N. Rosenstein-Rodan, "Problems of Industrialization of Eastern and South-eastern Europe," *Economic Journal*, June–September 1943, p. 205.

36. Erlich, *loc. cit.*, p. 67, quoting from Preobrazhenski's *Novaia Ekonomika* (p. 92).

37. Mandelbaum, *op. cit.*, p. 4; Dobb, *op. cit.*, pp. 58–59.

38. See pp. 290*ff.*

39. John D. Black in United Nations, *Proceedings of the Scientific Conference on the Conservation and Utilization of Resources, 1949*, Vol. I, *Plenary Meetings*, New York, 1950, p. 213.

land conservation have produced near miracles since the late 1930s. In comparison with averages over the years 1920–1939, wheat, corn and hay yields were, respectively, one quarter, one third and one tenth higher in the United States in 1945–1949; and livestock productivity per animal unit rose by 15 to 20 per cent, largely as a result of the development of high-protein legume hays.[40] The consumption of liming materials increased by 400 per cent from 1935 to 1947; of fertilizer, from 1936 to 1948, by 300 per cent; egg production per layer rose over the years 1909 to 1948 by 60 per cent.[41]

The technological knowledge is already available to allow even more remarkable increases in production, and means of further expanding such knowledge are promising.[42] This seems to be the general opinion of agricultural experts today. Of course, the future of technical discovery and of its practical application cannot be scientifically predicted. But unless perverse intervention on the part of governments interferes too sorely, the incentive for invention and the elaboration of improved agricultural techniques will be very strong.

Should the character of investment in underdeveloped areas be guided to any significant degree, however, simply by guesses as to lines of production which the future may bless by rapid technological advance? The really relevant test would seem to be *present productivity*. From this standpoint the tempo of industrialization might well be held somewhat in restraint in order to exploit first the more widespread and less costly opportunities for increasing incomes from the farms, paddies, ranches and plantations.

*Technical Aid from Abroad*

The availability of advanced productive techniques from the industrialized nations has led some people to the belief, shared by some persons in the underdeveloped areas themselves, that these areas can attain to the levels of per capita income of the West in as many decades as the process originally required in centuries. At the other extreme stands the view that cultural differences are so great that Western techniques are quite inappropriate or that they almost inevitably lead to such social disruption as to make any material gains in output too costly in cultural and other intangible values.

Surely there must be a middle way. In some degree even techniques must be indigenous, and it is well that cautions have been sounded against the

40. *A Water Policy for the American People*, Report of the President's Water Resources Policy Commission, December 1950, Vol. I, p. 155.

41. Sherman E. Johnson, *Changes in American Farming* (Miscellaneous Publication No. 707), U.S. Department of Agriculture, December 1949, pp. 26, 27 and 49.

42. *A Water Policy for the American People*, p. 163; see also Reuben W. Hecht and Glenn T. Barton, *Gains in Productivity of Farm Labor* (Technical Bulletin No. 1020), U.S. Department of Agriculture, December 1950, p. 3; and John A. Hopkins, *Changing Technology and Employment in Agriculture*, U.S. Department of Agriculture, May 1941.

absurd assumption that techniques can be transplanted bodily, and transplanted without vast complementary changes in the whole society. As
Herbert Frankel complains, there has been too great a tendency "to speak
of 'the social consequences of technical change,' and not of 'technical
change as a social consequence.' "[43] It may even be true, as Simon Kuznets
suggests, that, instead of trying to transfer techniques, "it is more a matter
of finding within the country whatever groups among its population are
aware of the need for and the ways in which elements of the industrial
system can be adopted; and of mobilizing support behind these groups in
the difficult effort which they will necessarily face."[44]

Yet the fact remains that the history of Western Europe and even of non-
European countries shows numerous examples of the transfer of techniques, including industrial techniques, to the great advantage of the receiving economy.[45] They have not, it is true, been transferred without
modification, without a laborious refitting of other economic elements
complementary to them, or without substantial social costs. But all progress
entails adaptation and costs. When all is said and done, it would appear
that the advanced techniques of the industrial nations offer, with proper
modifications, one of the most promising channels for raising the levels of
living and the quality of life as end product of the less developed areas. But
it may be that the greatest danger to desirable changes within the native
cultures is the very speed of industrialization to which these areas themselves aspire.

FACTORS AFFECTING THE TEMPO OF INDUSTRIALIZATION

Neither the mechanical wonders of heavy industry nor the potentialities
of external economies and of technical complementarity nor future possible inventions establish any presumption favorable or unfavorable to
rapid industrialization. What then are the real factors determining its rate?
Probably the chief limiting factors are the supply of raw materials, capital,
skilled labor, trained managers and able entrepreneurs, the general economic organization of the society, and access to foreign markets. To these
may be added a host of economic and noneconomic elements: production
techniques, public health, life expectancy, general literacy and education,
morals and morale, religious taboos, etc., to many of which attention is
devoted elsewhere. Here the main concern is with the scarce factors of
production and their organization.

43. S. Herbert Frankel, *The Economic Impact on Under-Developed Societies*, Blackwell, Oxford, 1953,
p. 18.

44. Simon Kuznets, "International Differences in Income Levels: Some Reflections on Their Causes,"
*Economic Development and Cultural Change*, April 1953, p. 25.

45. See Chapters 6–11.

*Capital Formation*

Progress and accumulation are not quite synonymous, as Ricardo seemed disposed to assume. And yet the generalization is valid that investment without inflation cannot exceed "voluntary" saving and foreign borrowing. A later chapter inquires into these sources of capital in some detail. Briefly, how formidable or how easy is the problem of accumulation for underdeveloped areas?

Some writers on economics apparently consider the matter to be relatively simple: create capital from surplus agricultural labor. One writer goes so far as to suggest that this surplus obviates the necessity of saving.[46] Of course, to the degree that the surplus labor is successfully employed, national income increases by just so much. If this increase is saved either privately or by the government, the saving involves no *deprivation* compared to the original state of affairs. But to say that *no* saving is necessary is to forget that added income *can* be consumed.[47] In poor economies, excluding for the moment fairly ruthless totalitarian regimes, the pressure in both private and government sectors to devote increments of income to consumption will be very great. Indeed, in view of the poor health and low energy of the populace, considerations of human welfare and efficiency alike may recommend precisely this use of increased income for a certain range.[48] Past this point the public clamor for bread and circuses may, however, merely impair saving and investment.

*Monetary Expansion; State Appropriation*

Keynesian methods—or more precisely monetary expansion—for absorbing unemployment do not ordinarily hold forth much promise for underdeveloped areas.[49] On the contrary, the typical prevalence of fear of inflation or actual inflation in these economies would counsel a considerable degree of monetary orthodoxy. The use of monetary expansion as a remedy for unemployment depends upon the existence of a plethora of idle plant and equipment. Where capital goods are scarce, pressures on capacity with consequent rising costs will quickly cause a cheap money policy to blow off in inflationary steam. Furthermore, in "underpopulated" areas, an additional obstacle presents itself to increasing output through mere credit creation in the scarcity of labor, particularly of certain kinds.

46. By way of flat assertion, Dobb (*op. cit.*, p. 39) says merely that *prior* savings are not necessary. But he discredits the view that a "savings fund" limits accumulation (p. 36) and even says (p. 43) that saving may put out of use equipment specialized for producing consumers' goods, at least "immediately."

47. Except, perhaps, in those cases in which the saving is done "in kind," e.g., where surplus labor is devoted to road-building and the like.

48. See Joseph J. Spengler, "Economic Factors in the Development of Densely Populated Areas," *Proceedings* of the American Philosophical Society, February 1951, pp. 20–53; see especially p. 36.

49. The contrary view seems to be represented by Mandelbaum, *op. cit.*, pp. 4–11.

Totalitarian economies can theoretically appropriate all income in excess of bare subsistence for capital formation, and capital formation rates realized by the U.S.S.R. have been high.[50] But even Dobb, who bases his recommendations for underdeveloped countries quite forthrightly on the Russian example, apparently recognizes limits to the completeness with which the "marketable surplus" product of agriculture can be diverted to industrialization.[51] In passing, it may be worth noting that, while surplus agricultural *labor* may be an asset to a totalitarian state undertaking industrial expansion, the same is not necessarily true in a free economy in which these people, along with others, will naturally consume all or virtually all of their increased disposable income, up to a considerable point at least.[52] Examination of policies which have increased productive saving in the less advanced economies is postponed to a later chapter. Aside from direct compulsion, it is clear that the chief measures lie along the well-worn route of monetary and political stability, effective savings institutions and the general encouragement and reward of thrift.

## Skills and Techniques

It would be gratuitous to attempt to assign any order of rank to the various shortages or bottlenecks which condition the speed of industrialization; but the paucity of skilled laborers and managers, and the general level of enterprise, literacy and energy among ordinary laborers would stand high in any list. Russia has suffered perennial limitations on these scores. In 1929, more than 40 per cent of persons holding posts requiring technical training lacked it completely; administrative personnel has been scarce, partly because of exposure to accusations and reprisals.[53]

Some writers believe that industrialization creates its own skills, but students of particular countries in the early stages of development speak otherwise. Concerning Mexico's "human resources for industrialization, industrial wage earners, industrial technicians, and industrial managers," Mosk writes: "In time the shortages will be overcome from within Mexico, but this will be a long-drawn-out process because it involves a complex

---

50. Norman M. Kaplan, *Soviet Capital Formation and Industry* (processed), Rand Corporation, Santa Monica, 1952, p. 12, gives the following figures:

|                          | Investment as Per Cent of Beginning Capital | Investment as Per Cent of Average Capital |
|--------------------------|---------------------------------------------|-------------------------------------------|
| July 1, 1928–July 1, 1935 | 23.3                                        | 12.8                                      |
| July 1, 1928–Jan. 1, 1938 | 28.3                                        | 12.1                                      |
| Jan. 1, 1931–Jan. 1, 1936 | 22.7                                        | 14.5                                      |
| Jan. 1, 1933–Jan. 1, 1938 | 19.7                                        | 13.2                                      |

51. Dobb, *op. cit.*, pp. 34 and 45–48.

52. Part of the additional consumption takes the form of durable consumers' goods. These goods may be considered as capital, though scarcely in the sense of an addition to the apparatus turning out further goods.

53. See Chapter 10.

social readjustment for large numbers of people."[54] The shortage of technicians in some countries is appalling. Paraguay, with a population of 1,406,000 chiefly dependent on agriculture, is reported to have only nine native graduates of an agricultural college.[55] In Indonesia with 60 million people, where doctors are numbered in the hundreds, and where there are ten persons holding Ph.D. degrees in economics, the "crowning lack" is teachers for general and vocational training. The problem is made more serious, if not desperate, by poor communication and transport facilities, a shortage or complete lack of textbooks and paper, and a bewildering variety of dialects.[56]

## Quality of the Labor Force

However important basic education and special training, the availability and quality of labor are based on certain physiological facts and are intimately bound up with a host of psychological and cultural elements. Most of the factors bearing on the general rate of development impinge even more sharply on the tempo of industrialization. Work in modern factories may be more exacting of physical and nervous energy than the pace of the plantation; it probably requires a higher level of discipline; and it depends for its effectiveness in large degree upon the incentive of money wages.

The transition to industrialism involves formidable questions of labor motivation, frequently complicated by industrial relations problems which have been imported along with the technology of more advanced economies.[57] Thus Currie remarks that in Colombia "the provision of three good meals a day within the plant enabled workers to handle heavy work which they previously had been incapable of performing."[58] In the Caribbean, as an economist has written in a letter to one of the authors, "it seems to be an established fact . . . that if wages are raised, as they have been for example on public works projects, there will be less work offered . . . in these areas elasticity of effort with respect to income is negative at all points —even at a level which we would consider way below subsistence or at

54. Mosk, *op. cit.*, p. 272; Chapter 13, on "Labor, Technicians, and Management," supplies many examples supporting this conclusion.

55. Harold B. Hinton, "Point Four Methods in Use Ten Years," *New York Times*, February 4, 1952, p. 49.

56. Lawrence S. Finkelstine, "Education in Indonesia," *Far Eastern Survey*, August 22, 1951, pp. 149–53.

57. Guatemala presents a specific example. "Money wages have barely kept pace with the rise of the price level. Working standards appear to have declined and higher wages, even though often they have been largely nominal, seem to have given rise to greater irregularity in working habits. Resistance to modernization and mechanization of factories, as well as legal provisions which make it extremely difficult to release unsatisfactory workers, have naturally raised manufacturing costs and impeded development." The Labor Code of 1947 is "frequently described as being so partial as to impose unjustified, and at times almost ruinous, requirements upon the employer." G. E. Britnell, "Problems of Economic and Social Change in Guatemala," *Canadian Journal of Economics and Political Science*, November 1951, pp. 477–78.

58. International Bank for Reconstruction and Development, *The Basis of a Development Program for Colombia*, p. 92.

least below minimum health." Many factors beyond mere indolence help to explain this phenomenon, but they would form the subject matter for a separate treatise.[59]

Finally, it is quite evident that, where industrialization depends upon private initiative, it will be effectively conditioned by the supply of able entrepreneurs and the conditions under which they operate. This is a matter so intimately involved with the role of the state that it is treated in that connection in a later section.

### Historical Examples: The West

How much can be learned about the probable rate of industrialization of underdeveloped areas from historical examples? The review of industrialization in Western Europe, Japan and the U.S.S.R. in Part II has revealed a wide range of underlying conditions and accomplishments. While the industrial revolution in England doubtless serves as a prototype in much thinking about this process, it probably would be generally agreed that the succession of technological discoveries supplying the main drive of this transformation, the wide areas of unexploited colonial territories that existed then and the singularly favorable context of domestic and international politics are scarcely to be paralleled in the future. The industrialization of a country such as Norway, which came relatively late, beginning about the middle of the nineteenth century and reaching relative maturity by the time of the first world war, benefited at least indirectly from these same highly favorable conditions.[60] The still later and more spectacular industrialization of Germany between the unification in 1873 and World War I took place in the same general setting, now so greatly changed. Furthermore, these and all other European industrial nations and North America took as a point of departure a level of average income, of general health, of education, of business and financial conditions and of social institutions favorable to industrialism so far in advance of most of the present economically underdeveloped world that analogy breaks down completely.

### Japan and Russia

Japan and Russia doubtless supply much closer analogies to the present underdeveloped world. And yet there are notable differences. Japanese industrialization was certainly forwarded, particularly in the concentrated development of heavy industry in the interwar period, by the fact that

---

59. See Wilbert E. Moore's articles on "Primitives and Peasants in Industry," and "Theoretical Aspects of Industrialization," in *Social Research*, March 1948, pp. 44–81, and September 1948, pp. 277–303; his book *Industrialization and Labor: Social Aspects of Economic Development*, Cornell University Press, Ithaca, 1951; and the extensive bibliographies given in these three sources.

60. Allan Lyle, *Die Industrialisierung Norwegens, Probleme der Weltwirtschaft*, Schriften des Instituts für Weltwirtschaft an der Universität Kiel, No. 65, Gustav Fischer, Jena, 1939.

Japan had a free hand in Manchuria and a dominant position in China. Russia, it is true, has never been a colonial power; but economically Asiatic Russia can in many ways be regarded as a region of colonial expansion for western Russia. The great difference between both these countries and most of the nations now entering upon industrialization is the "monolithic" character of the state and society—the absolute power of the central government, the presence of able and dedicated leaders devoted to a few overwhelmingly strong objectives such as "defense" and national economic strength, and the subservience of the populace and their institutions to these objectives.[61] China *may* now be moving in this direction and other countries may swing into the totalitarian drift. But most of the underdeveloped world shows a weakness of government and a diffusion of purpose which, though they may have their merits in certain respects, certainly do not make for a maximum tempo of industrialization.

### Contemporary Conditions

Whether contemporary conditions favor a more rapid rate than has characteristically been attained in the past can be argued both ways. The one most powerfully favorable factor would seem to be the existence of superior production techniques, both simple and more advanced, which are available for application. Furthermore, transplanting and adapting these superior methods of production is now probably easier. Communication is technically faster and more widespread, as is physical transportation of persons and goods. Governments, and even private firms, of the industrial nations seem favorably disposed toward the export of scientific and practical knowledge; the United States leads with its technical aid policy; and the international agencies carry on a widely ramified program of similar nature, beginning with elementary steps in public health and education. Another powerful and favorable factor is the availability of government and international loans for development.[62] In part, of course, this merely takes the place of the flow of private funds which was so important in the nineteenth century; and it is far from certain that, for the developing areas, the place has been taken in equal measure.

The progressive breakdown of colonial empires, the ferment of nationalism in Asia, the general political and social unrest throughout the under-

61. For the somewhat less well known case of Japan, see D. H. Buchanan, "Japan versus 'Asia,' " *American Economic Review, Proceedings*, May 1951, pp. 359–66; Shigeto Tsuru, "Economic Fluctuations in Japan, 1868–1893," *Review of Economic Statistics*, November 1941, pp. 176–89; G. E. Hubbard, *Eastern Industrialization and Its Effect on the West*, Oxford University Press, London, 1935, pp. 45–63; and for the immediate prewar period, E. B. Schumpeter and others, *The Industrialization of Japan and Manchukuo, 1930–1940*, Macmillan, New York, 1940, pp. 789–864.

62. United States foreign aid in the postwar period to March 31, 1951, was $31.4 billion (*New York Times*, September 19, 1951). This amounted to more than the sum total of all outstanding foreign investment by *all* countries of the world in 1947. However, a substantial part of this aid merely offset war damage to productive plant and sustained consumption. See Chapter 20.

developed world and the spread of Communism outside the U.S.S.R.—all of these furnish a powerful drive toward increasing incomes and industrialization, but also they give rise to some formidable obstacles. The disturbed international scene, actual domestic strife in some countries and the turbulent state of political and social affairs in others create legal and psychological barriers to saving, investment and enterprise. In much of Southeast Asia, production falls below prewar levels in significant parts of the economy.

### Negative Factors Today

Indeed, among the distinctly negative or adverse forces not present in earlier periods is the general reduction of labor and capital mobility and the growth of sensitiveness to uncertainty. This takes several forms. Private capital moves with difficulty against exchange controls and the danger of discriminatory taxation, to say nothing of nationalization and expropriation. International trade moves against quotas and other direct limitations unknown to an earlier age, and the international movement of labor has become sporadic and exceptional. Equalitarian redistributions of wealth, while they may in some ways have improved the lot of the common man somewhat, have reduced the flow of private saving and have thrown the responsibility for accumulation upon governments, which sometimes respond successfully and sometimes not. Finally, the growth of social security legislation, of labor union power and of labor laws, however they may be judged on humanitarian and ethical grounds, involves heavy budgetary burdens and costs for private business, which weigh against industrial expansion.

On balance, the component of forces at work may favor a more rapid tempo of industrialization than in the past. But the rate will certainly be less than many countries expect. In successive annual reports, the International Bank for Reconstruction and Development has emphasized the paucity of really promising projects.[63] The head of the Joint Brazil-U.S. Technical Commission, Mr. John Abbink, observed: "few of these countries are ready for the degree of industrialization to which they seem to aspire . . . industrialization may easily create more problems than it solves."[64] Population growth alone will require large increases of output in many countries even to maintain present levels of living. It is an open question whether population or output will win the race. But in the early stages of the race the most crucial part of output is food, fuel and raiment;

---

63. International Bank for Reconstruction and Development, *Second Annual Report, 1946–47*, Washington, 1947, p. 5; *Third Annual Report, 1947–48*, Washington, 1948, pp. 5 and 15–16; see also *New York Times*, December 11, 1951, "World Bank Head Rejects U.N. Plan."

64. United Nations, *Proceedings of the Scientific Conference on the Conservation and Utilization of Resources, 1949*, Vol. I, p. 476.

that is the reason why improvements in agriculture and the industries most directly related to it are so fundamental.

### INDUSTRIAL DEVELOPMENT AND THE STATE

Although the world is being shaken today by the ideological conflict between government and private conduct of economic activity, a more fundamental issue for the rate of economic progress is the contrast between *good* and *bad* government. This issue affects every phase of economic life, from fundamental legal and political institutions such as land tenure systems, water rights and the security of life and property, through such elements of the social structure as health and literacy, to more complex levels involving saving and investment institutions, taxation and monetary systems and foreign exchange controls.

"Government-generated insecurity"—the fear of ruinous taxes, inflation, expropriation and political reprisals—goes far toward explaining some of the most formidable obstacles to industrial development. The English classical economists laid great stress on this fact. In the contemporary scene it is reflected in hoarding, the flight of capital abroad, investment in land instead of equipment, price policies designed "to amortize plants in as little as three years to assure recovery of . . . capital before some unexpected blow falls," and the like.[65] Indeed, there is little doubt that the "necessity" of government undertakings in finance and production often appears as the direct consequence of "government-generated insecurity" for private enterprise. The circle is closed in a curious fashion when state enterprises function badly and the demand arises for a return to private operation. The Bell Report on the Philippines characterized the twenty-four government corporations, organized for the most part after 1938, as "inefficient, wastefully operated, and in some instances . . . misused," and called for a house cleaning of the corporations and a return of most of their functions to private initiative in order to "assure a management with a basic interest in efficient and economical production."[66]

By contrast, one may contemplate the case of El Salvador, which, despite the highest population density and the poorest natural resources, has achieved distinction as one of the most prosperous of Central American countries. This record is ascribed to "political ability and sound administration of the Government," including efforts to reduce inequality and raise the income level of the masses of agricultural laborers.[67] Good government is the cornerstone of all efforts to improve the economic lot of underdeveloped countries.

65. See Solomon, *loc. cit.*, p. 537; Britnell, *loc. cit.*, p. 476.

66. Bell Report, p. 67; see also Deutsch, *op. cit.*, p. 5.

67. C. H. Calhoun, "Central America Betters Economy," *New York Times*, January 4, 1952, pp. 41 and 43.

*Where State Intervention Is Needed*

Generally speaking, government action will be called for in those fields in which private profit-making—particularly competitive enterprise—is precluded in the nature of the case, where profits would be too low or the risks too large, or where private enterprise produces unsatisfactory results in decisive respects. Elementary and sometimes also more advanced education, public health undertakings and large segments of the transportation and communications industries have proved themselves particularly suitable for public initiative and operation in the industrially more mature countries, and thus presumably for the industrially younger countries as well. But scarcity of capital establishes a further argument for state enterprise in several fields where private undertakings have been quite adequate in the richer nations—in banking and other businesses concerned with the flow of accumulation and investment, and in large "developmental" projects such as hydroelectric plants for which the capital requirements are so large and the returns often so low or uncertain that they do not attract private resources.

*Present Trends*

Aside from its frequently extended role in supplying capital and in the normal public utilities and services, government activity in underdeveloped areas has, of course, varied widely from country to country, and there is no compelling reason for believing that the future will be otherwise. Partly as a consequence of the chaotic condition of property rights after World War II, and partly, if not chiefly, as a political tactic, nationalization has absorbed most of the industry of the satellite nations of eastern Europe.[68] Latin America, Egypt and most of the Near East base their plans for industrialization chiefly on private entrepreneurship, while India follows a middle way. The course of events in Africa and Southeast Asia is problematic; but there is a fair chance that it will be dictated more by political events than by a purely rational economic point of view.

Of one thing, however, one may, unfortunately, be fairly certain: governments of underdeveloped areas will make extensive use of the "infant industry" argument, and of tariff, quota and exchange control devices to put this argument into effect. Many countries, particularly in Latin America, regard this as the state's most important role in industrialization; and they have not hesitated to proclaim this conviction at international assemblies such as the Chapultepec Conference in 1945 and the London, Geneva

68. A good factual account, written, however, at a relatively early stage, can be had from Samuel L. Sharp, *Nationalization of Key Industries in Eastern Europe*, Foundation for Foreign Affairs, Washington, 1946.

and Havana negotiations (1946–1948) which led to the proposed International Trade Organization charter.

Efforts on the part of the United States to limit these protectionist urges in the interest of expanding international trade encounter at least two embarrassing obstacles. In the first place, there is the abstract case for sheltering infant industries, the pure logic of which, assuming a superior knowledge of future development on the part of legislative chambers over private entrepreneurs and the eventual weaning of the infant from the protectionist pap, has always been admitted. In the second place, the underdeveloped countries can always discount the concrete evidences of economic disarmament by the more mature countries—the Hull program, G.A.T.T. and the reductions of quotas in Europe under the O.E.E.C.—by saying that, having once attained their strong position, the industrial nations now want to deny to potential competitors an essential condition for the growth of young industries. Although the United States and Western European countries cannot completely be exonerated from this motivation, their general recognition of the peculiar position of the underdeveloped countries is clearly embodied in exemptions and escape clauses from the general principle of free multilateral trade in both the statutes of the International Monetary Fund and the proposed charter for an International Trade Organization.

*Dangers of Protecting Infant Industries*

The real perils of infant industry protection in any objective view, however, are not its threat to the older countries but the potential losses for the underdeveloped areas themselves. How long are these countries prepared to deny to their domestic consumers the gains of cheaper or better imports? Is it certain that protection may not have exactly the wrong effect in perpetuating technical backwardness?[69] Are the import quotas and tariffs imposed only on those lines of production which careful scientific study—and not the pressure of vested interests—recommends for what amounts to concealed subsidies?[70]

Perhaps still more important is the danger that the hue and cry for protection diverts attention from more important factors in development. As Clair Wilcox writes:

The basic importance of natural resources, of agriculture, and other extractive industries, and of power, transportation, and communications is lost from sight; attention is centered on manufacturing. The dependence of manufactures on raw materials, skilled labor, managerial talent, wide markets, and marketing facilities

69. This seems clearly to have been true of protection in France; see Chapter 8.

70. Mosk, *op. cit.*, pp. 71 and 73. Apparently no such study has been given to the sheltered industries in Mexico where protective tariffs are high and numerous.

is forgotten; factories are wanted whether or not they can ultimately face competition on the basis of comparative costs . . . The obstacles to industrialization inherent in social and religious patterns, in lack of health and education, and in political instability and corruption are never mentioned; the fact that increasing population may cancel increasing output is ignored.[71]

This does not signify that infant industry protection can never be successful; but it indicates the relative unimportance of the whole effort and the strong chance of its eventual miscarriage.

### Industrial Monopolies

Not far removed from the question of infant industries is the problem of industrial monopolies in the early stages of development. Commercial and sometimes other types of monopoly characterized much of the economic expansion of Western Europe in the colonial areas from the seventeenth century onward. In part, this is explicable in terms of cost and risk. Only by the assurance of high profit rates could the East India or Hudson's Bay companies assemble sufficient capital for "developmental" types of investment, currently so strongly emphasized, which were entailed by their more directly profitable operations; these investments in relatively unknown lands were fraught with risk. Another reason for the frequency of monopoly—particularly aside from these cases of exclusive charters—is, as Adam Smith pointed out and George Stigler has recently re-emphasized, that the division of labor is limited by the extent of the market.[72] Until the whole market has grown to a certain size, potential economies within the single firm prevent it from specializing and afford it a monopoly for the time being. Finally, of course, many purely institutional and adventitious factors may enter.

This reasoning may lead to conclusions almost diametrically opposed to the Marxian tenet of increasing monopoly under capitalism; and one economist, who bases his conclusions on experience in the Middle East but is convinced of the wide applicability of his analysis, finds that in the majority of market-type cases, monopoly is more prevalent in the less than in the more developed world.[73] However this may be, and however "natural" monopoly may be in early phases of development, the possible or actual abuses of monopoly power inevitably require public control.

### Intervention to Induce External Economies

Another factor considered to support the necessity of state intervention is external economies. These are economies that occur in contributory or

---

71. Clair Wilcox, *A Charter for World Trade*, Macmillan, New York, 1949, p. 143.

72. George J. Stigler, "The Division of Labor Is Limited by the Extent of the Market," *Journal of Political Economy*, June 1951, pp. 185–94.

73. Solomon, *loc. cit.*, pp. 519–41.

"feeder" industries when they are enabled to expand output and thus to realize *internal* economies, as a result of increased output in the *key* industry. The internal economies of ancillary or feeder industries are *external* to the *key* industry, but its costs and also its prices, if it is not a monopoly, can effectively be lowered by these external economies. But all of this is contingent upon an initial expansion of output in the key industry, and this expansion may not be forthcoming because the indirect savings to the key industry are uncertain and are furthermore spread over the several ancillary industries. A case can thus be made under certain circumstances for government subsidy to induce the original expansion.[74]

Certain socialist or interventionist writers have seized upon this argument of orthodox economics as a proof that the state must manage industrialization in underdeveloped countries in order to realize the benefits of external economies and complementarity.[75] But the case for subsidy or government support of "external economy" industries is conditioned in the first place by all the limitations upon the typical "infant industry" defense of protecting young industries. It has to be assumed that experts hired by the government can make better guesses about the future development of industry than can the experts hired by private business. It has to be clear also that the subsidizing does not need to be perpetual and, finally, that when the need is past, the subsidy will in fact be withdrawn—all of which has rarely occurred.

To this line of reasoning the interventionists might respond that they are not necessarily contemplating a process of industrialization through subsidy, that in a developing economy, wherein *all* industries may be assumed to be expanding, it is not necessary to induce expansion in the key industry by subsidies since the feeder or ancillary industries will likewise be growing. This response shifts the argument from external economies to general complementarity. But if one assumes that feeder or ancillary industries are expanding anyway *without* subsidy to the key industry (*not* the assumption of the orthodox economists), then the special case favorable to government intervention for industries of decreasing cost from external economies collapses along with the disappearance of the case for subsidy.[76] The argument loses its special sanction from economic theory and narrows down to

---

74. The case for subsidies for industries of decreasing costs from external economies was stated by Marshall, Pigou and F. D. Graham. They failed to distinguish two cases: one in which, if the subsidy is removed, output lapses to its original size and the external economies disappear; and another—more interesting from the angle of economic development—in which the subsidy can be transitional without causing output to lapse by its eventual removal. The second case is essentially analogous to the "infant industry" defense of protective tariffs. See Howard S. Ellis and William Fellner, "External Economies and Diseconomies," *American Economic Review*, September 1943, pp. 503–11.

75. See the authors cited in notes 35, 36 and 37.

76. Marshall and Pigou, assuming that other industries do *not* expand, would scarcely have ventured to generalize their argument for subsidy in case all industries are expanding, since this would amount to offering a *rigorous quantitative* proof that economies can grow only by universal subsidy or nationalization of all industries.

the bare assertion that government can manage industrialization better than private enterprise.

## Kinds of State Intervention

The very liveliness of such issues as protection for infant industry, regulation of monopoly, subsidizing or "planning" the expansion of "external economy" or complementary industries illustrates a broad principle of great importance. Government participation in industrial development is by no means identical with state ownership and operation; on the contrary, it may assume a wide variety of forms, of which some are quite compatible with freedom of the market and others are designed even to increase the scope and effectiveness of private enterprise.

The industrialization of Japan from the Meiji restoration in 1868 to the second world war is an instructive example. The central government itself imported machinery from Europe; trained laborers, managers and technical experts; built and operated factories; and marketed produce at home and abroad. But one industry after another, once brought to a certain level of development, was sold or leased to private hands. In addition, a panoply of policies—subsidies, tariffs, banking, taxation—marshaled the flow of savings and forced the tempo of industrialization. It seems generally to be agreed that the animating purpose was "to create the conditions which should lead the entrepreneur to direct and organize the economic resources of the country in the way believed to be desirable. Only in this sense can Japan be said to possess a 'planned economy.' "[77]

Taking as a point of departure the proposition that deliberate industrialization requires "planning," some persons have regarded government planning and state socialism as synonymous. But there are many kinds and degrees of intervention. At the opposite pole from economic totalitarianism would stand a completely laissez-faire policy such as characterized the great industrial revolution in England. Nowadays, however, with the obvious necessity of making productivity outstrip population increases, the practicable antithesis to socialism involves the concept of "planning" described by the International Bank:

The technique of development-programming consists in essence of making an inventory of the sum total of resources available to each economy, and then deciding the order in which various development projects should be undertaken within the limits of available resources . . . The main instrument of all development is accelerated capital formation.[78]

77. G. C. Allen, quoted by G. E. Hubbard, *op. cit.*, p. 67. See also, in the same sense, the sources on Japan cited in note 61.

78. International Bank for Reconstruction and Development, *Sixth Annual Report, 1950–51*, Washington, 1951, p. 12.

Planned industrialization thus involves three main elements at a minimum: a survey of resources; the establishment of a schedule of priorities; and measures to promote capital formation. None of these necessarily involves the state as entrepreneur.

### Minimum Requirements of the State

What is implied, aside from the essential preliminary stocktaking of the economy, is that at a minimum the state create "favourable conditions for private enterprise and . . . the indispensable incentives which will enable it to fulfill the planned goals."[79] Public health and education, economic stability and political security certainly belong to the "favourable conditions"; but the incentives may be the ordinary individual's economic motives, influenced in the direction of the schedule of priorities only by taxation and public expenditure policies. Thus the International Bank's report on Colombia contemplates a program which "has the great merit of avoiding the use of a wide variety of restraints and orders which the use of direct control requires. It also dispenses with much of the policing and the necessity for building up a large bureaucracy to administer the controls."[80]

In addition to providing incentives for private undertakings the state will, of course, engage in some or many development projects which surely ought to be "planned" in the sense of resting on a careful appraisal of resources, of being mutually consistent and of proceeding according to rational priorities. Even in government projects, however, the widest imaginable latitude obtains for the state's own activity: it can build, own and operate or confine itself to one of these three; it can do all three and, after a period, sell or lease to private entrepreneurs; it can leave all three to private initiative and regulate operation; it can build and operate "pilot projects" and leave the bulk of production to imitation by private producers; or it may seek to realize its schedule of priorities solely by taxes and subsidies. Any of these procedures can be called "planning"; any one may be best for a given country or region; and probably only the first of the long list would be clearly recognized as socialism.

"Planning," even in the limited sense of a schedule of investment priorities to be encouraged by government policies, has constantly to be revised. Just as in the case of planning by private corporations, it must make wide use of trial and error; and there is no magic in five-year intervals. "*La carga se arregla andando*," says an Argentine proverb: the load settles itself on the way.

79. United Nations, *Theoretical and Practical Problems of Economic Growth*, p. 22.

80. International Bank for Reconstruction and Development, *The Basis of a Development Program for Colombia*, p. 609.

## PROBLEMS ARISING FROM INDUSTRIALIZATION

In a program of deliberate industrialization for higher incomes, the actual formulation of policy will encounter certain important choices involving gains and losses of *unlike kind*. It is tempting to designate these as "dilemmas," but since nearly every economic choice for the individual, and much of life itself, involves rule-of-thumb resolution, perhaps these should be regarded simply as difficult marginal decisions.

### Technological Unemployment

Among them is a possible conflict between employment and progress, at least in the short run. A United Nations group of experts, commissioned to report on unemployment in underdeveloped areas, takes the position that unemployment is basically to be remedied by increased productivity.[81] And *basically* the position cannot be questioned. In the short run, however, the factor of technological unemployment, of workers thrown out of jobs by improved methods of production, cannot be ignored. Measures may be introduced to increase labor mobility; and the encouragement of village and cottage industries may soften the impact of change. Yet a certain residuum of technological unemployment will persist. Theoretically, the cost of unemployment relief could be balanced against the increase of social output; but this ignores the human costs of idleness and uselessness. Decision about technological innovation will at best be difficult and uncertain.

### Technical Equipment

Another difficulty pertains to the optimum technical equipment in a society which progresses rapidly. Here the choice may involve a simpler machine which is correct for present relative factor prices but will be wrong if labor incomes rise and interest rates fall. Or the choice may concern, not the labor-capital ratio, but the size of the venture: optimum size now may presently be uneconomically small. Yet if rates of growth in population and income are estimated and allowed to influence choice of industrial equipment in the direction of large, expensive and labor-saving machines, the risks of misdirected investment and technological obsolescence increase. All these problems beset any progressing economy; but the general poverty of underdeveloped areas makes the cost of errors more burdensome for them.

### Social Effects of Industrialization

Finally, many dilemmas beset deliberate industrialization as a result of the disruptive effect of the sheer material gains of higher incomes on tradi-

81. United Nations, Department of Economic Affairs, *Measures for the Economic Development of Underdeveloped Countries*, New York, May 1951, pp. 7–9.

tional ways of life, the human and material costs of big industrial cities, the rise of new labor-management problems—involving the whole fabric of society.

Complications such as these do not destroy the case for industrialization nor do they prove that it must move at a snail's pace. But they do reinforce the growing conviction that headlong introduction of European and American techniques and machinery does not in itself improve life in the relatively primitive economies nor even necessarily eventuate in increased productivity. The mere fact that Western Europe and the United States are the objects of widespread emulation constitutes a real danger that the full implications of industrial society will not be recognized.

# 14. Domestic Financing of Development:
## Private Saving

THE ORIGINAL ANNOUNCEMENT of the Point Four Program in President Truman's Inaugural Address on January 20, 1949 produced in many quarters the expectation of massive capital exports by the United States to the underdeveloped areas. Earlier discussions of the economic problems of these areas had, however, aroused some skepticism concerning such a program.[1] What seemed essential, in this view, was an initial "grubstake" of international investment, the yeast to leaven the mass, rather than utopian schemes of international gifts or even vast loans, which could complicate the future for lender and creditor alike. Probably a much greater number, however, adhered to the view that international and national loans and grants to the economically less developed countries should be both large and extended in time; arguments of both political and economic nature, they believed, supported this conviction.

### MERITS OF FOREIGN CAPITAL

On the political side there was—and is—the rationale of the European Recovery Program, that low incomes without prospect or hope of improvement offer fertile soil for Communist infiltration. An additional argument of political and ethical character has, however, recently won some adherents. Three decades ago Alfred Marshall wrote:

. . . it is becoming clear that this [England] and every other western country can now afford to make increased sacrifices of material wealth for the purpose of raising the quality of life throughout their whole populations. A time may come when such matters will be treated as of cosmopolitan rather than national obligation; but that time is not in sight.[2]

That time is now in sight, though it would be rash to herald its actual advent. One committee of the United Nations has indeed gone so far as to express the hope that private investors will be moved to invest in underdeveloped areas "in the interests of world economic development, of the promotion of world peace, and of the achievement of the objectives of the

1. Norman S. Buchanan, *International Investment and Domestic Welfare*, Holt, New York, 1945; Norman S. Buchanan and Friedrich A. Lutz, *Rebuilding the World Economy*, Twentieth Century Fund, New York, 1947.

2. Alfred Marshall, *Industry and Trade*, 4th edition, Macmillan, London, 1923, p. 5.

United Nations."[3] Somewhat less utopian is the idea that governments or international agencies should regard loans or grants to underdeveloped areas as a logical extension of the principle of progressive taxation, long since accepted within the national economies of the West. Even this is quite premature as a rigorous principle. But there is no denying that humanitarian sentiments played a considerable role during the past few years in the international loans coming directly and indirectly from the United States, Canada, England and other countries.

### Economic Reasons for Loans

On an ostensibly economic plane it is frequently argued that development *must* come through foreign grants or loans, since living levels in the underdeveloped world are so low that they cannot be trenched upon by either voluntary or compulsory savings. But in the first place, the increase in population of many underdeveloped areas not long after the beginnings of trading relations with Europe and North America must have been made possible by increased income, which afforded a *potential* choice between some capital accumulation and a mere increase of population. This potential choice still exists. Aside from this, as many commentators have emphasized, the great inequality of wealth in many of these countries points toward a source of capital in progressive taxation. Furthermore, many countries with marked potentials for further development are currently achieving quite satisfactory rates of capital formation; in a large number of Latin American countries the rates exceed 12 per cent. Finally, even in economies where the *average* per capita income is very low, the utilization of surplus agricultural labor offers possibilities of increasing capital, particularly of the basic social or community-use variety. The experiences of Japan and Russia in financing their development almost entirely at home seem to show that "minimum" standards of living are somewhat elastic.

The basic *economic* justification of loans and grants to underdeveloped areas—quite apart from political and moral considerations—depends upon a positive yield differential as between lending and borrowing countries. This justification is not one which derives solely from the interests of the private capitalist. The Charter of the United Nations contemplated as one of its objectives equality of access to the natural resources of the world. Free international migration of labor would go far toward accomplishing this end, but can scarcely be seriously contemplated in fact. Free international movement of goods and services can, within limits, substitute for labor mobility.[4] In default of significant labor mobility and with freedom

3. United Nations, Sub-Commission on Economic Development, *Methods of Financing Economic Development in Underdeveloped Areas*, New York, 1949, p. 126.

4. Paul A. Samuelson, "International Trade and the Equalization of Factor Prices," *Economic Journal*, June 1948, pp. 163–84.

of trade and payments seriously impaired in the present day, capital movements in the direction of higher productivity can work powerfully toward reducing the inequalities and inequities in the lot of the common man as among the rich and poor countries.[5]

No really fundamental doubt can be raised as to the presumptive benefits of a capital flow from lower to higher productivity areas. These benefits, such as "making development possible," "speeding up capital formation," "longer range for development programs," "maintaining consumption," "reducing inflationary pressure," "reducing balance-of-payments pressure," "increasing the international division of labor"—all these are real economic advantages *if* the capital moves from lower to higher productivity regions.[6] Otherwise, it scarcely needs to be said, the capital movement can be justified only on political or ethical grounds.

### Change in Emphasis on Economic Aid

With the lapse of time the emphasis on massive foreign loans and grants has declined. Equal or greater attention has come to be given to the transfer of *techniques*, to *public health* and *education*, to the necessity of inducing *effective public administration*, and so on. American private investors have clearly shown their judgment that, allowing for risks, the realizable yields of capital are *lower* in underdeveloped areas than at home. And the directors of international and national lending agencies have emphasized the fact that capital alone cannot produce miracles: social, economic and political organization conditions its effective use.

MERITS OF DOMESTIC CAPITAL

Corresponding to this change, the emphasis has been moving from foreign to domestic finance. For certain countries, as for example Indonesia, Iran and Egypt, this change may parallel a revival of the old suspicion of imperialism or a new xenophobia. For other countries, it may spring from the conviction that sufficient foreign capital will not be forthcoming, and from apprehensions of cyclical variation in the flow of international capital. But the conviction of experts in such international organs as the

5. Productivity is the basic fact in the case for the foreign financing of underdeveloped areas. It is a basic common-sense fact which stands independently of any supposed tendency of "mature" capitalist economies to drop into a Keynesian trap of equilibrium with less than full employment, or to founder in the Hansen morass of economic stagnation. It is a fact which also stands despite the Marxian belief that investment or loans from the capitalistic West fasten imperialistic exploitation upon the capital receiver and artificially prolong the throes of a dying capitalist system. Increased productivity through foreign capital is a basic fact which can also contribute to offsetting autarchic developments, furthering the international division of labor and articulating all areas into a world economy. See P. N. Rosenstein-Rodan, "The International Development of Economically Backward Areas," *International Affairs*, April 1944, p. 162.

6. United Nations, *Formulation and Economic Appraisal of Development Projects*, Vol. I, New York, 1951, pp. 102–07. This enumeration of the advantages of foreign finance was set forth by H. W. Singer, but without the proviso given above regarding higher productivity.

United Nations and the International Bank that "the role of foreign finance in economic development can therefore only be of a subordinate character" derives from a more fundamental reflection.[7] Unless the habits of consumption and saving, the institutions and legal framework for accumulation, lending and investing can be adapted to the building and maintenance of capital, foreign aid can bring only transitory benefits. A permanent basis for higher living standards must be created *within* the society; indeed, this is the very meaning of economic development. Unless the chief nurture of growth is indigenous, the society is constantly exposed to retrogression.

In certain senses foreign and domestic finance are complementary. For one thing, with present rates of population increase, most countries will find it necessary to exploit both sources of capital to the utmost in the attempt to achieve a sufficiently strong forward surge in productivity to break the vicious circle of poverty and high birth rates. It is also true that foreign investment is most likely to be attracted to those countries in which domestic saving and investing thrive best. Conversely, but in a quite limited and transitory sense, an inflow of foreign capital may induce domestic capital formation. But it is parsimony on the part of the indigenous population, their willingness to venture capital in new investment and their wise use of capital which will finally prove to be the more basic foundations of progress.

## FOSTERING VOLUNTARY SAVING

Throughout the economically underdeveloped world, with only rare exceptions, the typical peasant, fellah, coolie or peon saves little or nothing. A middle class, composed of comfortable farmers after the American prototype and the members of the "tertiary" or service industries, is so limited in number that it does not contribute much to the meager flow of nonbusiness saving. Prosperous landowners, merchants and industrialists save; but their savings frequently do not go into forms which increase the productivity of the economy.

### OBSTACLES TO VOLUNTARY SAVING

Very low per capita incomes make saving difficult and the dearth of saving holds incomes at low levels. In the lowest-income countries, hopeless poverty, illiteracy and poor health would smother the spark of economic motivation to save even if age-old cultural patterns had not long since allowed it to flicker out. In agricultural pursuits, systems of land

7. United Nations, *Methods of Financing Economic Development in Underdeveloped Areas*, p. 94.

tenure frequently discourage the improvement or, indeed, even the maintenance of the soil, and alternative lines of investment may scarcely exist; rack-renting and usurious rates on loans similarly balk "the effective desire of accumulation." When average incomes are somewhat higher, spendthrift habits often prevail; or ceremonial consumption in ostentatious weddings, funerals and religious celebrations may claim any surplus over daily needs. When incomes rise still further, the populace may attempt to emulate Western, and more specifically American, standards of living. While progressive taxation may garner a certain amount of compulsory saving, equalitarian redistribution may have a preponderantly adverse effect on aggregate saving, particularly at modest average per capita income levels, stimulating wage and personal consumption demands and excessive social security and other forms of communal consumption.[8] In Africa and Asia, even the most rudimentary forms of saving and investment institutions may be lacking. Chronic inflation often deals the final blow.

### Fruitless Saving

Individual voluntary saving, even such as there is, may fail to come to fruition in productive investment. In many of the less developed countries, capital owners seek to transfer their wealth into more solid currencies, and embargoes on the export of capital are by no means easy to enforce. It is often said also that the hoarding of money causes much saving to be lost to the society. This would be true if governments, particularly in the newer republics, permitted hoarding to have a general deflationary effect on prices and incomes. In point of fact, however, inflation appears to be so endemic in Latin America and other developing regions that hoarding renders a public service in offsetting inflation as much as it does.

Investing in the title to land may be a wasteful use of "savings" if the recipients of the appreciation of land values dissipate the "savings" in luxury consumption. On balance in such circumstances there has been very little saving.

### The Problem of Interest Rates

High rates of interest, which obtain in so much of the world outside of Western Europe and other Western countries, are unwelcome to the borrowing investor; but simply to impose legal maximum rates would be a perverse way of encouraging development. The combination of circumstances just reviewed results in capital being in short supply; and it is

---

8. The International Bank reports social security taxes of 13 to 15 per cent of wages in Turkey, which is judged to be "excessive for a country in Turkey's stage of economic development." International Bank for Reconstruction and Development, *The Economy of Turkey*, Johns Hopkins Press, Baltimore, 1951, p. 224.

usually this fact, rather than a high productivity of capital, which explains the high rates of interest. To depress this price by legal measures might somewhat lessen the supply; but—more important—it would certainly impair the desirable selection of profitable uses on the side of demand.

### Living Levels and Saving

Economic progress in the underdeveloped world requires, not that levels of consumption should generally fall, but merely that a part of the rise be devoted to capital formation. But even this milder requirement may be extraordinarily difficult to attain. Evidence to this effect appears with dramatic force in the use made of the large gains in export values to much of the underdeveloped world in the twelvemonth following the outbreak of war in Korea. The *World Economic Report* of the United Nations finds that only a tenth of the increase of export yields between the first half of 1950 and of 1951 went into imports of machinery, metals, manufactures and trucks. India devoted all of the increase to food, raw cotton and jute; indeed, imports of capital goods actually fell![9] This was also the case for Indonesia and the Philippines during 1950 and to the midyear of 1951, as compared with 1949. Between the first half of 1950 and of 1951, passenger car imports increased by 100 per cent or more in the Middle East and Latin America.[10] Accumulation of capital is a thorny path.

Many writers quite properly stress the cumulative effect of increased saving, which can increase national income and permit larger absolute and relative saving quotas and so on in a spiral, without incursions on living standards. Thus, taking the recent 12 per cent net capital formation rate attained by many countries in Latin America as a point of departure, John H. Adler assumes that this addition to capital adds about thirty times its own magnitude to net national product, which equals a 4 per cent annual increase thereof, or 2 per cent if population increases even as much as 2 per cent a year. But if the *marginal* rate of saving (the proportion of *additional* output which is saved) could be raised to 25 per cent, the *average* proportion of income saved would rise to 13.2 per cent in five years, 14.3 per cent in ten years and 16.3 in twenty years.[11]

The crucial problem of economic progress at the outset is to prevent the dissipation of the *whole* of increased output by population increases or advances of consumption. How can the scene be set favorably for beginning and maintaining the cumulative process of saving and investment?

9. The short crop in India in that year and the dispute with Pakistan over jute were probably partly responsible.

10. United Nations, *World Economic Report, 1950–51*, New York, 1952, *passim*.

11. John H. Adler, "The Fiscal and Monetary Implementation of Development Programs," *American Economic Review, Proceedings*, May 1952, pp. 597–98.

METHODS OF FOSTERING VOLUNTARY SAVING

Frugality, thrift and good economic management are scarcely to be expected in a setting of endemic disease, ignorance and hopeless poverty. Hence, the route to national material prosperity must begin with instruction and measures for public health, with general education and with the introduction of simple and easily available improvements in productive techniques. Security of persons and property stands high in the list of requirements. Preventing inflation would also seem to belong in an equally conspicuous place, although the advocacy of inflation as a method of extracting forced saving is not unknown. But forced saving must occur at the expense of voluntary saving on this particular score; and the fruits of saving of any sort are wasted by inflationary distortions in the use of real resources.

## Local Projects

A simple and direct method of capital formation which seems to hold much promise for relatively primitive economies is offered by the so-called self-help local work projects. They swell the stream of national *savings* if they elicit the donation of spare-time labor or the services of the unemployed, if these workers are supported by their families or if they work for less than market wage rates, or if the benefits of the improvement to the locality induce the people of the region to restrict consumption in order to provide the wherewithal for the undertaking. In Greece, a program called "Community Development Employment for the Utilization of Idle Manpower" has successfully engaged in road building, irrigation, flood control, water supply and sewer projects, small incentive payments being supplied to the workers by the national government.[12] The International Bank has recommended for Iraq a system by which the *sarifa* dwellers would build their own mud houses with some help from the government.[13] The government would supply sewer and water systems and a few essential structural materials.[14] Volunteer labor is to supply the basis of the new National Extension Service of India, which is eventually to reach 120,000 villages with a population of 80 million. The new plan represents an enlargement of the present program of rural and community development by voluntary labor which has been partly financed by $100 million in grants from the United States Technical Cooperation Administration.[15]

12. *United Nations Bulletin*, March 1, 1951, pp. 235–37.

13. The *sarifa* dwellers of Baghdad and Basra, numbering 60,000 and 20,000, are unemployed people from rural areas who have settled in great squalor in the empty lots and on the periphery of the cities.

14. International Bank for Reconstruction and Development, *The Economic Development of Iraq*, Washington, 1952, pp. 55, 59, 60.

15. *New York Times*, May 1, 1953, p. 4.

Local work projects of a second category are designed, not to utilize idle manpower, but to evoke savings from a local clientele by establishing small industries with which the populace is familiar and which they would trust more than a plant in a faraway city. A United Nations survey indicates considerable success with the device in Mexico and Chile; but elsewhere, as in India and the United Kingdom colonies, it seems to have met with difficulties.[16]

### Savings Institutions

Savings institutions, especially for the small man, who is typically a farmer in the underdeveloped areas, are relatively few and far between. Banking systems in these regions have generally been oriented to the needs of the large estates, plantations or other primary production units. But in some regions cooperative agricultural credit societies have achieved a considerable measure of success—in the Caribbean countries, Cyprus, Egypt, Turkey, Ceylon and latterly in India. In Burma and Indonesia, the credit cooperatives collapsed in the depression of the 1930s. More recently, however, the movement has revived in Indonesia; the credit groups have accumulated a capital of $3 million with only slight aid from the government.[17] Mexico and Puerto Rico have had only limited success with cooperatives. But in Ceylon there were 897 cooperative credit societies as early as 1934. In Egypt one fifth, and in Turkey one sixth, of the rural population is included in the membership of cooperatives; and in India the cooperatives are estimated to provide 15 per cent of the total financial requirements of agriculture.[18] While the contribution of these associations to the flow of capital has been modest, they have also frequently served as vehicles of education and technological improvement.

With rather rare exceptions, countries now in the early stages of economic development have not exploited the potentialities of savings banking. In Brazil, it is said, the major part of the savings of the middle and working classes flows into the federal savings banks.[19] In Colombia, savings banking is virtually a legal monopoly of the state-owned Caja Colombiana de Ahorros, but the annual supply of funds from this source is small.[20] In Mexico, savings banking is a recent development. As in the United States,

16. United Nations, Department of Economic Affairs, *Domestic Financing of Economic Development*, New York, 1950, pp. 20–22.

17. *New York Times*, October 10, 1951, p. 5.

18. Sir Alan Pim, *Colonial Agricultural Production*, Oxford University Press, London, 1946, pp. 68–69; United Nations, Department of Economic Affairs, *Land Reform—Defects in Agrarian Structure as Obstacles to Economic Development*, New York, 1951, pp. 37–43 and 74–77.

19. They also have a monopoly of pawnbroking and of discounting the salaries of public servants and bank employees, U.S. Department of State, *Report of the Joint Brazil–U.S. Technical Commission*, Publication 3487, June 1949, pp. 159–60.

20. International Bank for Reconstruction and Development, *The Basis of a Development Program for Colombia*, Washington, 1950, pp. 52–53.

it is generally conjoined with commercial banking; but the Mexican savings banks make short-term commercial loans and do not invest extensively in industrial or government bonds.[21]

Surveying the entire scene, a United Nations inquiry recommends the extension of savings banks to small communities, economizing on overhead and personnel by utilizing the post offices or any existing system of federal local offices. The study also recommends that higher rates be paid on savings deposits, partly, no doubt, to evoke more capital for public lending agencies and thus to break the monopoly of the local moneylender in certain primitive economies.[22] The report notes several further measures especially designed for the small saver: government sponsorship of building societies, of industrial risk and old-age insurance schemes and of lotteries, which curiously enough have successfully been operated in conjunction with savings banking in Mexico, Israel and India.

### Commercial Banks and Securities Exchanges

Commercial banking has thus far played a role in the underdeveloped area largely limited to the financing of exports and imports and, to a somewhat less important extent, domestic trade. Its significance in gathering up funds for long-term investment has been correspondingly slight. Mention will be made of commercial banking, however, in a later context, since by their very nature commercial banking operations are not primarily concerned with savings.

At some stage in its history, a developing economy will find an organized securities exchange to be a necessary institution for the process of evoking savings and allocating capital among competing uses. Most of the underdeveloped world lacks any semblance of capital markets, and in many regions there would be no purpose in stock exchanges. Where they exist already, their significance is usually very limited, as in Mexico, Chile, Colombia, the Philippines and Brazil. This is usually less the fault of the exchange organization than a result of lack of confidence of the public in, or their complete unfamiliarity with, corporate securities, the close holding of stock by wealthy families, and a preference for investment in real estate. Furthermore, various tax and other impediments to the corporate form of organization in some countries account for a dearth of security offerings to attract savings. Nevertheless, in some of the more advanced commercial and industrial centers, an effort to promote the functioning of existing exchanges seems to be in order. India has under way legislation to provide government supervision of the stock exchanges, which are private organ-

---

21. Sanford A. Mosk, *Industrial Revolution in Mexico*, University of California Press, Berkeley, 1950, pp. 241–42.
22. United Nations, *Domestic Financing of Economic Development*, pp. 16–20.

izations. For Brazil, the first Joint Technical Commission recommended a supervisory authority similar to the United States Securities and Exchange Commission, the overhauling of corporation law and also the examination of certain taxes which inhibit security trading.[23]

*Government Securities*

For any government, but especially for the governments of rapidly developing countries, a broad and receptive market for government bonds with the saving public affords an invaluable, indeed an almost indispensable, basis for domestic finance without inflation. In this respect, countries vary between the extremes of India and Egypt, where the Treasury can tap the savings of the public, to the case of several Latin American countries where the prospects of borrowing from the public are negligible. The typical situation, unfortunately, is closer to the latter: the native population distrusts the bonds of its own government. Partly, this distrust emanates directly from misgivings as to the stability of the government itself; partly, it is the inevitable consequence of past inflations and the fear of inflation; sometimes it is explained by defaults or postponements of interest or principal payments; finally, even without these catastrophes, if there exists no organized market for government securities, the individual hesitates to sacrifice liquidity by buying bonds. The remedies for several of these major obstacles require no comment—save that, if there were any doubt as to the generally pernicious effects of inflation on other scores, its effect on the government bond market should be conclusive. Conversely, as will appear in a subsequent connection, a well-developed government securities market is essential to central bank open-market operations for monetary control purposes, and to Treasury debt management for monetary and fiscal purposes.

What measures can a government take to increase the breadth of its securities market, assuming other matters to be in order? Compulsory bond purchases, such as those once imposed on Brazilian exporters, tend to undermine receptiveness for other bond issues and in other quarters. Generally speaking, the issuance of securities by other divisions or agencies of the government than the Treasury comes under suspicion. A variety of Treasury issues, suited to the varying needs of different sectors of the market, increases marketability. Propaganda to acquaint the public with the advantages of government securities and of regular saving habits may have a place. Needless to say, the rate structure must be competitive with private issues.

23. *Report of the Joint Brazil–U.S. Technical Commission*, pp. 152–54; United Nations, *Domestic Financing of Economic Development*, pp. 70–73; Mosk, *op. cit.*, pp. 229–30; International Bank, *The Basis of a Development Program for Colombia*, pp. 55–56; *Report to the President of the United States by the Economic Survey Mission to the Philippines*, U.S. Department of State, October 9, 1950, p. 75 (the Bell Report).

The investment portfolios of commercial banks offer a promising field for the placement of government securities which has been imperfectly recognized in many developing countries. In some cases, the traditional orientation of commercial banking in colonial areas exclusively to the financing of foreign and domestic trade has to be overcome. Mosk reports that in Mexico the commercial bankers refuse to absorb government bonds because of their hostility to the social program of the revolution.[24] It is difficult to believe, however, that the *banking* community would long withstand the attractions of government securities if the basic requirements for making these issues *generally* acceptable were fulfilled. Another field for government issues is to be found with insurance companies.[25]

Commercial bank purchases of government bonds, just like purchases of private securities or notes, may involve the creation of additional purchasing power. They are inflationary only if the purchases (i.e., loans) are a net addition to securities already held by the banking system as a whole, and if the additional purchasing power increases faster than the flow of available commodities. Government agency purchase of government securities avoids a *deflationary* alternative, the holding of idle cash; but ordinarily the agency is not endowed with the power of creating demand deposits. Hence, the government agency, like the individual purchaser, cannot have an inflationary effect unless—in both cases—a commercial bank or the central bank makes additional loans to cover the security purchases. Central bank purchases of government securities create reserves for the commercial banking system and are therefore inflationary if the banks expand credit on the increased base, and if the bank credit creation outstrips production. One writer, observing the proliferation of central banks during the past decade, states:

> This inability of government to sell securities to its own people is the primary reason for the establishment of national central banks in virtually all of the underdeveloped economies, for it is only from this source that governments can obtain credits.[26]

Credit from this source, as we have just observed, does not necessarily mean inflation; but there is danger that it may. Inflation is, indeed, a constant threat to developing economies.

### COMPULSORY SAVING: THE PROBLEM OF INFLATION

The less developed areas are even more vulnerable to inflation than the older industrialized nations. Prices rose fourfold in Mexico from 1932 to 1948 and between three- and fourfold in Brazil from 1939 to 1948, although

---

24. Mosk, *op. cit.*, pp. 233–34.

25. But it is doubtful how far governments should go to *compel* insurance companies to invest in government securities. See International Bank for Reconstruction and Development, *The Economic Development of Guatemala*, Washington, 1951, p. 277.

26. Morton Solomon, "The Structure of the Market in Underdeveloped Economies," *Quarterly Journal of Economics*, August 1948, p. 536.

neither country was deeply involved in the war. For Brazil, this was merely a short segment of a century of rising prices. Prices have risen continuously in Chile since 1870 and by five and one half times from 1937 to 1950.[27] Inflation is, of course, lamentably common in the settled economies of the West, generally in consequence of wars. But in time of war and peace alike, countries in process of development show the same inveterate tendency with only rare exceptions.

For one thing, excess capacity scarcely exists in plant and equipment because, being generally designed for processing agricultural raw material, the units are small and simple. Outputs are thus fairly rigid, and increases of money income quickly force up prices. The propensity to consume is characteristically high; and the facilities for moving savings into new investment are limited, so that monetary expansion may simply bid up the prices of existing assets. An economy in the midst of development encounters many bottlenecks in production, and the lag between launching an investment project and its fruition in actual production leaves the economy vulnerable to inflationary impacts. Even the use of surplus agricultural labor produces inflation unless food supplies are elastic, or unless taxes are increased. But the fiscal and monetary devices for coping with inflation may still be rudimentary. Confidence in the financial probity of the national government may be lacking, and long experience with inflations often produces a persistent inflationary pressure to consume or to transfer savings abroad. Older industrial countries may experience any and all of these, but less constantly and forcefully.

## DOMESTIC INFLATIONARY FINANCE

### Deliberate Inflation

As a method of extracting the wherewithal for economic development in countries without good fiscal and financial institutions, inflation has not lacked apologists. One writer apparently would recommend mild inflation "when inducements are necessary for large-scale movements of labor and for increased supplies of foodstuffs and raw materials to be made available by the village for the towns."[28] In South America, particularly in Chile, government officials have frankly been ready to countenance the redistributive effect of inflation in favor of the more well-to-do classes, on the grounds that they save and invest more than the poor.[29] A number of

27. Mosk, *op. cit.*, p. 274; *Report of the Joint Brazil–U.S. Technical Commission*, p. 12; H. W. Spiegel, *The Brazilian Economy, Chronic Inflation and Sporadic Industrialization*, Blakiston, Philadelphia, 1949, pp. 52–54; David L. Grove, "The Role of the Banking System in the Chilean Inflation," International Monetary Fund, *Staff Papers*, September 1951, pp. 33–59.

28. Maurice Dobb, *Some Aspects of Economic Development*, Ranjit Printers, Delhi, 1951, p. 48.

29. David L. Grove, *Objectives and Potentialities of Monetary Policy in Underdeveloped Countries* (unpublished study), p. 17; H. C. Wallich, "Underdeveloped Countries and the International Monetary Mechanism," in *Money, Trade, and Economic Growth*, Macmillan, New York, 1951, p. 29.

American economists, contemplating the war and postwar boom in the prices of raw materials, emphasize the fact that an attempt to preserve stability of the general price level in the primary producing countries would have required that rising export prices be compensated by a fall in the prices of purely domestic goods. And this, they believe, would lead to depression and interrupt the process of development.[30]

But there are overriding objections. Mobility of factors can be furthered by direct measures without the high social costs of inflation. Of course, Dobb's "mild inflation" would have only mild disadvantages; but a deliberate *policy* of mild inflation in this best of all possible worlds usually gathers momentum into a substantial inflation, particularly in an inflation-sensitive age. Few champions of forced saving through the deliberate increase of inequality of wealth and income would be found in most of the young republics now bent on progress. As for allowing the inflation of international commodities to be paralleled by inflation at home, there are better alternatives at hand.

### Is Inflation Inevitable?

At least passing attention should be given to the thesis that developing economies *inevitably* run inflations, accompanied by deficits in their foreign balances. Charles Kindleberger divides countries into four quasi-historical categories: primitive undeveloped countries, and economically senescent countries, both of which types have balanced international accounts and domestic stagnation; early development countries, which run deficits and internal inflations; and countries in the later stages of development, which show tendencies toward deflation and capital export. After repeating several of the more commonplace reasons for expecting inflation in the early development stage, Kindleberger adds that borrowing is itself inflationary according to all theories of international economic adjustment; that planning may be more inflationary than private enterprise; and that technical assistance plus direct private investment as in the Point Four program is also inflationary because it fails to cover the necessary fundamental investment in highways and other utilities, thus swelling the budgetary deficit of the state.[31]

---

30. International Bank, *The Basis of a Development Program for Colombia*, p. 293; Spiegel, *op. cit.*, pp. 51–52; Grove, *Objectives and Potentialities of Monetary Policy in Underdeveloped Countries*, pp. 36–37.

31. Charles P. Kindleberger, *The Dollar Shortage*, Wiley, New York, 1950, Chapter 6, especially pp. 127, 129, 130, 133, 142 and 143. Like the Hansen stagnation thesis and the Balogh-Kindleberger idea of a "chronic" dollar shortage, this position is imbued with an atmosphere of inevitability: development *means* inflation. This idea may not seem categorically different from the common observation that the effort to achieve rapid development results in "an inflationary bias at home and a persistent tendency towards disequilibrium in the balance of payments" (Ragnar Nurkse, "Some International Aspects of the Problem of Economic Development," *American Economic Review, Proceedings*, May 1952, p. 580). But the difference may be quite significant. If an inflation wastes most of the forced saving which it is supposed to create and besides inhibits domestic saving and foreign investment, the development may fail to materialize. Those who speak of a "persistent tendency" toward inflation probably imply that it *impairs* development by just so much, rather than *characterizes* it.

## Costs of Inflation

With rare exceptions, the consensus prevails that the economic, political and social costs of inflation are such that public policy should be designed to achieve development without it. Inflation discourages voluntary saving and induces conspicuous consumption by those who benefit from it. To achieve a certain amount of forced saving, several multiples of that sum must be transferred to higher income brackets, because the propensity to save is only a fraction of income. Income distribution is distorted from the results either of a price system or a rational interventionist system. Windfalls from inflation go less into industrial investment than into land values, ostentatious apartment and office buildings, hoards of foreign exchange and inventories, and speculative ventures. With any substantial degree of inflation the number of people engaged merely in trade grows out of all proportion. The natural process of selection among firms is held in abeyance—all firms including the most inefficient survive. Cost and price relations are distorted, resources are misapplied and business and government planning becomes impossible. Continuous inflation induces a flight of capital abroad and repels foreign capital. Imports are subsidized and exports are penalized; pressure develops on the balance of payments, necessitating devaluation, direct controls or exchange control. The small man loses—small farmers, petty tradesmen, unorganized industrial labor and the civil servant class. Inflation creates social antagonisms, undermines the individual's sense of responsibility, reduces incentives for honest work and entrepreneurial effort, creates labor unrest and occasions government interventions which are inimical to private initiative.

Aside from all this social disruption and economic waste, inflation increases saving slightly if at all, according to a recent staff study of the International Monetary Fund.[32] This conclusion seems to be borne out by the following figures on investment rates in Brazil, Chile and Colombia during years of very large expansion of bank credit:[33]

*Gross Private Investment as Percentage of*
*Gross National Product*

|          | 1946  | 1947  | 1948  |
|----------|-------|-------|-------|
| Brazil   | 10.22 | 11.22 | 8.39  |
| Chile    | 12.2  | 11.2  | 10.5  |
| Colombia | 12.1  | 12.8  | 12.1  |

Whatever stimulus may have been given to investment, it declined as the inflation progressed. With less inflation, private investment in the United

32. E. M. Bernstein and I. G. Patel, "Inflation in Relation to Economic Development," *International Monetary Fund, Staff Papers*, November 1952, pp. 363–98.

33. *Ibid.*, p. 377.

States during the same three years formed higher proportions of gross national product—13.1, 12.9 and 16.1 per cent.

The monetary authority of a developing country has an almost categoric duty to avoid inflation; but it should be emphasized that its obligation extends equally to offsetting deflationary forces. In the present context, an important part of this activity is to make certain that all voluntary saving goes into investment. As previously pointed out, if people hoard or if they set afoot a deflationary force upon other prices by bidding up the prices of existing assets such as land or urban real estate, the central bank could extend credits to the government for development purposes without inflating the price of current output. The same is true of monetary expansion to parallel population increases and increases in national product.[34] Furthermore, inducements or compulsions to prevent the conversion of domestic savings into foreign investment would be justified to avoid the deflationary or contractive effect of capital exports.

It scarcely needs to be said that without an "anti-inflationary" government budget, monetary control alone cannot be effective. Not every budget deficit need be inflationary, because a certain expansion of the money supply is required in a developing economy to parallel the increase of domestic trade and the increasing number of people who wish to hold money balances. The combination of fiscal and monetary policy which does not allow the increase of money to exceed these limits may be called "anti-inflationary." Dollar for dollar, money created through budget deficits is likely to be more inflationary than money created through the loans of commercial banks because it increases the reserves of commercial banks and because it is less likely to give rise to an equal flow of marketable product.[35] Thus the importance of budget policy for effective monetary control is apparent.

### The Need for Monetary Controls

The history of economically developing countries has been bedeviled by inflation because, on the one hand, certain peculiarities of these economies, already noted, make them vulnerable and because, on the other hand, monetary controls have been weak or nonexistent. Commercial banking has characteristically grown up on the basis of the "commercial loan" theory of banking—that the quantity of credit cares for itself automatically if banks confine their loans to first-class commercial paper. The prevalence of this philosophy of banking, which is bound to lead to inflation, is the

34. See H. C. Wallich, *Monetary Problems of an Export Economy: The Cuban Experience*, Harvard University Press, Cambridge, 1950, p. 295. The central bank must take account of velocity; see Grove, *Objectives and Potentialities of Monetary Policy in Underdeveloped Countries*, p. 38.

35. See V. K. R. V. Rao, "Deficit Financing, Capital Formation, and Price Behaviour in an Under-Developed Country," *Indian Economic Review*, February 1953, pp. 55–91.

more readily understandable when it is recognized that it imbued even the Federal Reserve Act of 1913 in the United States, and that it still dominates official theory and practice in Russia.[36]

The unregulated creation of credit has often proceeded in complete absence of central banks, as in Puerto Rico, Egypt, the United Kingdom dependent territories and in many other places until the recent wave of creating central banks. In other countries, as in Cuba, Mexico and Brazil, a central bank has existed for a longer period, functioning, however, "not so much as a mechanism for monetary regulation, but as an engine for credit creation."[37] Even if these institutions had been animated by a strong desire to combat inflation, in the absence of an organized market for government securities they would have been unable to utilize what is commonly regarded in Europe and North America as the most potent monetary restraint upon inflation—the sale of government securities.

The potentiality of monetary control is, however, rapidly being created in the numerous central banks founded in underdeveloped areas during the past decade.[38] India and Egypt already enjoy fairly adequate markets for government securities, and this complement to central banking will follow in other quarters as development proceeds. Meanwhile, central banks, where they exist and desire to combat inflation, can make use of the other chief weapons: the availability and cost of rediscounting, and—armed with the necessary legal authority—varying the reserve requirements for commercial banks. Or, if the commercial banking system has not yet progressed far, the central bank may need to establish its authority by direct lending to the public or to the various development organizations of the government. In the latter event, central bank decision as to the availability and cost of credit must prevail if monetary control is to prevail.

## INFLATION INDUCED BY EXPORTS

By all odds the one most formidable obstacle to the effective control of inflation in those underdeveloped countries that are heavy producers of primary products for export—in "export economies," to employ Wallich's descriptive term—is that the share of national income generated by exports exceeds the shares generated by government expenditures or by investment from domestic and foreign sources. Primary products are notoriously unstable in both price and demand, and the resulting variations expose the export economies to uncontrollable variations of the total yield of exports,

---

36. This is the finding of Raymond P. Powell in *Soviet Monetary Policy* (doctoral dissertation deposited in the Library of the University of California, Berkeley, 1952).

37. Wallich, *Monetary Problems of an Export Economy*, p. 284; see also United Nations, *Domestic Financing of Economic Development*, pp. 67–70; Mosk, *op. cit.*, p. 252: *Report of the Joint Brazil–U.S. Technical Commission*, pp. 49 and 163.

38. Cf. p. 338 below, n. 18.

and through this channel to enormous variations of domestic incomes, prices and employment.[39] It is, of course, true that even economically developed countries such as New Zealand and Australia experience these difficulties as primary producers. The emphasis in the present context, however, is on fluctuations of export yield in their bearing upon economic development. This subject will be considered more fully in Chapter 18; for the present, a single example will suffice:

> From 1938 to 1947 total exports of Latin America increased from 1,936 to 6,622 million dollars, or more than a three-fold increase in value. Responding to this primary stimulus and to domestic private investment and official development programs, monetary income has expanded more than fourfold, and despite restrictions imports have increased from 1,925 million dollars in 1938 to 6,668 million dollars in 1947. Prices and costs of living have risen sharply but real income probably has increased by 30 to 40 per cent.[40]

Economic development under these circumstances is sorely impaired by the alternating profligacy of inflation and devastation of recession; the situation obviously requires intervention. Those economists who advocate a domestic monetary policy of allowing the home price of exports to parallel the rise on international markets implicitly accept the full impact of the inflation. What are the alternatives to this policy, not by way of permanent *insulation* of these economies from the outside world, but by way of *compensating for* or reducing the impact of cyclical or episodic booms and depressions coming from abroad?

ALTERNATIVES TO EXPORT-INDUCED INFLATION

*Stabilizing a General Price Index*

One alternative to inflation of prices would be a policy, implemented by domestic monetary and fiscal measures, of stabilizing a general index of product prices. Import prices, presumably being unaffected by the upward movement of export prices, would probably remain at about their old level. The prices of purely domestic goods would have to be contracted to offset a certain rise in export prices. In the absence of direct controls, the decline of domestic prices and the rise of export prices relative to one another would be determined by the relative magnitude of these two segments in the domestic economy and hence in the composition of the index. The absolute level of all prices taken together—export, import and domestic—is determined by domestic monetary and fiscal policy.

39. See Robert Triffin, "Central Banking and Monetary Management in Latin America," Chapter 4 in Seymour Harris (Ed.), *Economic Problems of Latin America*, McGraw-Hill, New York, 1944. See also: Joseph A. Kershaw, "Postwar Brazilian Economic Problems," *American Economic Review*, June 1948, pp. 328–40; and Felipe Pazos, "Inflation and Exchange Stability in Latin America," *American Economic Review, Proceedings*, May 1949, pp. 396–405; United Nations, Department of Economic Affairs, *Instability in Export Markets of Under-Developed Countries*, New York, 1952, p. 41; plus the publications by Wallich and by Grove already cited.

40. Pazos, *loc. cit.*, p. 398.

But since export prices are only one component of the three, stabilizing a general index would mean that exports would not rise in domestic currency as far as in foreign currencies. The country would develop a favorable balance and feel a certain stimulus through the higher incomes of exporters. But this stimulus would be confined to the direct and indirect impact of the foreign balance; it would not be augmented by a further factor as would be the case if the prices of domestic goods, instead of falling within the stabilized price level, were also allowed to rise sympathetically with export prices. Under the policy of price-level stabilization, any desired degree of offsetting of the export boom by restriction in the domestic sphere could be achieved by the rigor with which it was applied. Thus a tendency toward general contraction could be offset by permitting a mild upward movement of the general index.

If the export segment of the economy is a large part of the whole, this would probably be unnecessary. Prices, it is true, would not rise as high in that sector as they would in the absence of a general price-level stabilization policy. But money incomes from exports would be high, and in an export economy their sustaining influence on the rest of the economy would be very great and thus would probably offset the influence of lower domestic prices on output as a whole.

An obstacle to the successful prosecution of this variety of anti-inflation policy might be the resistance of labor unions and other "price-administering" units to a reduction of prices of domestic goods. In the underdeveloped world, however, this limitation is not widespread.[41]

### Exchange Appreciation

A second alternative to which countries threatened by inflation through a favorable balance-of-payments position have resorted is appreciation of the exchange rate.[42] Presumably, the price *differentials* between exports and purely domestic goods would be the same as in the first alternative, which rested on the old rate of exchange. But an appreciation of exchange would remove the necessity of a decline in the prices of domestic goods. It would thus offer less resistance to an inflation induced by the income increases in the export sector, but might recommend itself over the first alternative in those countries in which labor unions and industrial and agricultural monopolies resist a reduction in money income. The history of the International Monetary Fund would seem to give evidence of the desirability— not of *free* rates of exchange—but of considerably greater mobility of rates

41. See Wallich, in *Money, Trade, and Economic Growth*, pp. 20–21.

42. Illustrated recently in the case of a primary producer by New Zealand, which allowed its exchange to appreciate in August 1948 from N.Z. £125= U.K. £100 to parity in order to combat inflation. See C. G. F. Simkin, "New Zealand and International Economic Equilibrium," *Economia Internazionale*, February 1951, p. 128.

at least than was contemplated at its initiation. But it is doubtful whether many countries will, as a matter of fact, resort to exchange appreciation in order to curb excessive booms, because this implies devaluation to meet depressions. Whether rightly or wrongly, most countries reject this degree of instability in their foreign exchange rates.

### Export Taxes

A third alternative to foreign-induced price inflations and a particularly promising one for the economically underdeveloped countries is presented by export taxes. Alternatives one and two, involving the stabilization of a general commodity index and of an index of purely domestic commodities respectively, imply effective monetary-fiscal control of the flow of expenditures. But many underdeveloped countries lack a sufficiently inclusive and flexible tax system or a sufficiently strong central bank to carry on what is in effect "compensatory finance." In these situations, export taxes recommend themselves on the basis of ability to pay, ease of administration, flexibility and the absorption of inflationary purchasing power at its source. Furthermore, they can be applied by one country without the necessity of international consultation and without damage to the economic position of other countries.

Export taxes have been utilized extensively in primary producing countries for general revenue purposes and, in some instances, to offset inflation.[43] A variant of the export tax appeared in the compulsory purchase of government bonds imposed on Brazilian exporters, an effective anti-inflationary device but one ill designed to further the marketability of government securities and consequently poorly suited to developing economies. Still another variant is the government monopoly of a particularly important export or exports or the government-producer stabilization agency. The rice export monopoly of Thailand has as its objective "to insulate internal rice prices from the inflationary influence of the world market, but at the same time to provide growers with a return sufficient to stimulate production." Moreover, its operations in 1948 and 1949 provided 10 and 17 per cent, respectively, of total budgetary revenues for the Treasury. The West African Marketing Boards represent a somewhat similar effort for cacao, palm oil, palm nuts, peanuts and cotton.[44]

Through various devices, it is apparent that primary producers can very substantially mitigate the severity of inflationary—and, to a lesser degree,

---

43. Australia has made use of stabilization funds financed by levies on exports of wool and wheat and a voluntary price stabilization system for dairy products. See Douglas B. Copland, "Australia and International Economic Equilibrium," *Economia Internazionale*, February 1951, pp. 49–50. Mexico introduced a 15 per cent export tax in 1948. For a systematic review of countries, see International Monetary Fund, *Exchange Restrictions*, Second Annual Report, Washington, 1951.

44. See P. T. Bauer and F. W. Paish, "The Reduction of Fluctuations in the Incomes of Primary Producers," *Economic Journal*, December 1952, pp. 750–80, and comment on same by P. Ady, *ibid.*, September 1953, pp. 594–607.

deflationary—impacts from world markets. But it would be overly sanguine to imagine that the action of individual countries will result in general stability. It would carry the discussion too far afield to attempt to assess the merits and weaknesses of international commodity agreements. With the proper safeguards of the consumer interest, they could take over part of the burden of adjustment from the shoulders of the primary producers.

In concluding this discussion of inflation as a device for financing development, it may be well to add that the "large-project approach" to economic development augments the forces making for inflation. The deprivation of consumers has to be protracted and may pass the bounds of political tolerance in any but authoritarian regimes; and the risks of misapplication of investment also grow the longer a plan has to be projected into the future. This does not, of course, mean that all large projects are necessarily mistaken, but it does imply caution. The opportunity costs must be carefully assessed.[45]

### DIRECT COMPULSORY MEASURES TO INCREASE SAVING

Direct measures to deflect expenditure from consumption into capital formation include selective import controls; the rationing of consumer goods; domestic licensing systems which discriminate against consumer goods or particular consumer goods such as luxury apartments and amusement facilities; allocation priorities for labor and materials; and—in socialist economies—the direct conduct of production by the state. Perhaps one might add to this list the collectivization of agriculture as a method of extracting the "surplus" output of farms for general fiscal purposes or for providing the wherewithal for industrialization.

For developing countries, great significance has traditionally been attached to selective import controls. Other kinds of direct measures involve about the same pros and cons for the underdeveloped as for the more advanced economic regions. The less developed countries undoubtedly encounter greater difficulty in obtaining capital by alternative means—domestic saving, taxation and foreign borrowing—than do the more highly capitalistic economies. But they also find greater difficulty than the advanced economies in extracting capital by direct measures. It is, of course, possible that the comparative disadvantage of this route to capital formation will appear less. Much will depend upon the values set on the workings of the price system and on individual freedom of choice, on the actual and potential efficacy of financial and fiscal institutions and on many other factors, including cultural traits. Generalization does not seem to be possible. Most of these considerations also permeate the problem of *import*

45. Cf. Hesmat Ala'i, "How Not to Develop a Backward Country," *Fortune*, August 1948, p. 76.

controls; and the background of actual experience and theoretical discussion is much more extensive for these controls.

Since the present chapter is concerned with the domestic financing of economic development, the focus here is chiefly on selective import controls, that is, the imposition of controls on certain chosen items, because they can be used to reduce or exclude consumers' goods or luxury consumers' goods and to favor the importation of producers' goods or necessities. Disposable income within the country is thus forced into capital formation or "productive consumption." It will contribute substantially to clarity of thought if this objective is sharply distinguished from general import controls designed to reduce deficits in the balance of payments. There are several reasons for differentiating these purposes, even though a given set of import controls could conceivably partly serve both. The ideal *selectivity* differs for the two purposes; the *policy alternatives* to import control are only in part the same for the two purposes; but, most important, closing a balance-of-payments deficit is not a source of *domestic finance* for development. In another connection, the problem of balance-of-payments deficits for developing economies will require attention.

*The Rationale for Import Controls*

Ultimately, as in most matters of policy, the merits and demerits of import controls to secure savings depend not only upon the abstract rationale but also upon the probable working out of the device in practice. There is some advantage in beginning with the theoretical case in order first to see the question in the large. On this plane, then, the logic would be simple: if intervention by government is accepted as appropriate to secure savings, then the taxation of consumption, including the taxation of imported articles of consumption or of luxury consumption, is appropriate. Furthermore, the same degree of restriction on the consumption of imports can be achieved by appropriate import tariffs, by direct import controls such as licensing and quota systems, by exchange control and the allocation of foreign exchange and by multiple exchange rates on the various categories of imports. These devices differ among themselves considerably from the administrative point of view and in their various economic repercussions. For the time being, these differences must be overlooked in order to concentrate on the main objective of all of them, the furthering of capital accumulation for economic development. Provisionally, then, in this argument a system of import taxes discriminating against luxury consumption or against consumption as a whole represents all selective import controls.[46]

46. The taxes could be levied on exchange devoted to certain imports (foreign exchange tax), on the goods themselves (excise tax on imports) or by charging discriminatory exchange rates (multiple exchange rates).

Let us first contrast, for clarification rather than argument, such a system of *import* taxes with the *export* taxes discussed earlier. Export taxes, it was said, can absorb an inflationary impact from abroad. The occasion for introducing such taxes was the war and postwar boom in raw materials, but they would be equally appropriate normally to absorb the inflationary effect of sales of petroleum or other natural assets. The important thing to observe is that their primary reason for being is to take advantage of a large differential, temporary or permanent, between domestic costs and the world selling price, that is, to absorb excess profits. If the rate does not exceed this limit, exports are not reduced; any taxation of exports beyond this limit has no distinct merit over the taxation of normal business profits.

But the purpose of import taxes *is* to decrease imports, at least in the categories that are taxed. Export taxes are levied on *different* items from import taxes; the *criteria* of discrimination are quite different—excess or monopoly profit being the criterion for exports, lack of "essential" character for imports; the primary purposes are absolutely distinct; and the alternative policies are only partly the same.[47] Acceptance of export taxes as a useful measure against inflation carries with it no justification of import taxes as a measure to secure compulsory savings.[48] The case must be considered quite separately. The general positive argument has already been stated.

*Objections to Import Controls*

On the plane of theory still, import controls by whatever device are subject to two major objections. First, unless accompanied by equally severe taxes or quantitative limitations in the domestic economy, they encourage the domestic production and consumption of the imported items discriminated against, and they discourage the domestic production and consumption of the items favored by the import discrimination. To the degree this happens, they fail to achieve their purpose of compulsory saving. How important this negative offset may be depends, of course, upon the commodity and the country. Jamaica would probably not soon produce its own Rolls Royces even with a high import tax, and the absence of the protection afforded by an import tax will probably not do much to discourage the beginning of a domestic automobile-truck industry. But the latter could

47. Both taxes yield revenue and are thus, other things being equal, deflationary, and if the government uses the proceeds for investment, they may be regarded as sources of savings.

48. Hence it is misleading, and partly incorrect, to say that "Multiple rates are, in fact, selective devaluations, which at the same time operate as export-import taxes and raise badly needed government revenue." (Pazos, *loc. cit.*, p. 402.) An export tax does not take the place of *devaluation* but of *appreciation* of the exchange rate. Furthermore, there is no such thing as an "export-import tax"; and Pazos' identification of a *uniform* surcharge on the import rate plus devaluation with a *general* export tax—in itself correct—misses the point that to the degree that either tax is *uniform* it loses its character as a tax and its suitability for its purposes. Discrimination, on different bases, makes these *mean something* as taxes which the merely nominal exchange surcharge plus devaluation completely lacks. Pazos' passage is roughly paralleled by Wallich, *Monetary Problems of an Export Economy*, p. 268, n. 9.

conceivably be a wrong guess for India. Furthermore, even for Jamaica, if luxury consumption is cut off in one direction by import controls, it may take a quite new direction.

The second major objection to import controls as a means of enforcing saving is that its objective would be better served by domestic sumptuary taxes. Frequently, import controls against luxuries or against consumers' goods in general are defended on the grounds that the local tax system in underdeveloped countries is not equal to providing a substitute. But consumption taxes are among the most easy to collect, whether on minor luxuries by revenue stamps on cigarettes and alcoholic beverages, or by license fees on automobiles or use taxes on apartments and office space. Furthermore, sumptuary taxes can be imposed on nonimported consumption items, some of which would spring up as substitutes for the taxed imported goods. On the plane of generality, it would scarcely seem that the tax authority would be less efficient, more corruptible or less flexible than the foreign trade and exchange organization.

### The Record of Experience

On the score of actual experience, the record for import controls has not been reassuring. The Bell report on the Philippines, despite its conclusion that for the immediate future import controls cannot be dispensed with, finds them

needlessly complex, costly, and dilatory. To the difficulties caused by inefficiency are added those attributable to favoritism and even corruption, the inevitable accompaniments of a detailed system of controls in countries with inadequate, inexperienced, and underpaid staff.[49]

In Colombia, according to the Currie report, the complexities are illustrated by the six laborious stages of processing through which each application must pass; in addition, evasion has been widespread.[50]

Still more damaging is the evidence in recent detailed studies of several countries that import controls have affected the composition of imports very little. Thus in Colombia the categories especially significant for economic development, "metallic manufactures" and "machinery and apparatus," accounted for about the same fraction of imports in 1945–1947 as in 1937–1940, after a decade of controls.[51] In Brazil, capital goods declined from 33.2 to 31.5 per cent of imports from the 1937–1939 average to 1947, while consumption goods rose from 15.1 to 23.1 per cent.[52] The Joint Com-

49. The Bell Report, pp. 41–42.
50. International Bank, *The Basis of a Development Program for Colombia*, pp. 327 and 333.
51. *Ibid.*, p. 330.
52. *Report of the Joint Brazil–U.S. Technical Commission*, pp. 26–27 and 34–35.

mission observes: "The severity of the import restrictions suggested by this analysis would handicap efforts to make early progress in the economic development of Brazil. Consequently, every means of solving the balance-of-payments problem in other ways must be explored." Ellsworth believes that, for the entire period of exchange control in Chile until 1945, when he completed his study, the importance of articles in the workingman's budget, supposedly favored by the multiple import exchange rates, was minor; the disadvantages of exchange control were "unquestionable and considerable."[53] The International Bank study on Guatemala, however, recommends luxury import taxes, though the head of the mission, writing in an economic journal, charges the import restrictions with having reduced competition and impaired incentives.[54] Mosk looks favorably on import controls for Mexico; but Wallich merely mentions them as a possibility for Cuba, and in general hesitates to recommend exchange control.[55] Thus, despite the enthusiasm of some theoretical treatments of the subject, few of the studies of specific countries are able to give import controls more than a highly qualified recommendation.

MULTIPLE IMPORT EXCHANGE RATES

Among the various specific devices of selective import control designed to promote saving and investment for development there can be little doubt that multiple import exchange rates or discriminatory import tariffs (which can be devised to have identical results) are superior to the quantitative controls such as prohibitions, licenses and quotas.[56] The main points are that multiple rates and tariffs, being cost devices instead of restrictions based on absolute quantity, disrupt the price system less; and that they transfer to the government the windfall gains of import restriction, in place of leaving them in the hands of possessors of quotas and licenses. This transfer might be accomplished—at least theoretically—by auctioning the exchange bills for imports that are under quota restriction to the highest bidders.[57] Alternatively, the exchange authority can fix import exchange rates which would approximate the same results. Multiple import rates, being set administratively, show greater flexibility than tariffs or quotas;

53. P. T. Ellsworth, *Chile, An Economy in Transition*, Macmillan, New York, 1945, pp. 69–71.

54. International Bank, *The Economic Development of Guatemala*, p. 271; G. E. Britnell, "Problems of Economic and Social Change in Guatemala," *Canadian Journal of Economics and Political Science*, November 1951, p. 477.

55. Mosk, *op. cit.*, pp. 292–93; Wallich, *Monetary Problems of an Export Economy*, Chapter 14.

56. The case has been set forth most judiciously and exhaustively by Schlesinger, though earlier treatments made some of the same points. See E. R. Schlesinger, *Multiple Exchange Rates and Economic Development* (Princeton Studies in International Finance, No. 2), Princeton University Press, Princeton, 1952; John S. de Beers, "Some Aspects of Latin America's Trade and Balance of Payments," *American Economic Review, Proceedings*, May 1949, pp. 384–95; Pazos, *loc. cit.*, pp. 396–405; Triffin, *loc. cit.*, and Wallich, in *Money, Trade, and Economic Growth*, p. 31.

57. In fact, the danger would seem to be that the bids would cease to be competitive in the course of time as importers adopted a "live and let live" policy.

but to the foreign seller this is a risk and a disadvantage. The main advantages as compared to quotas are, as stated, their compatibility with a price system and their absorption of the windfall profit of protection. Although they capture this profit, or the larger part of it, they still protect by raising the prices of foreign goods to the consumer without raising the domestic cost of production of the good in question. It is to be feared that this fact, rather than the public gains described above, accounts for the adoption of the multiple exchange rate device in eleven or twelve Latin American countries, and in Greece, Indonesia, Israel, Spain and Thailand, among others.

### Conclusions Regarding Private Saving

The upshot of the foregoing analysis is that, outside of taxes, direct compulsory measures to increase private saving do not seem well designed to further economic development. One of the main preoccupations of governments in countries aspiring to development must therefore be the encouragement of voluntary saving, but the requirements for success are manifold and their attainment is uncertain. The following statement would apparently be valid for the whole of the underdeveloped world:

> The task of mobilizing savings in Asia and the Far East is difficult even when there is security of life and property, political stability, freedom from fear of external aggression, and confidence in the solvency of the government and in stability of the local currency . . . Moreover, many factors including low levels of income, growth of population, its density and age composition, with attendant pressure on resources, social factors, the limited number of persons interested in and able to develop concrete plans for capital investment, and relatively low levels of production and foreign trade, have added to the limitation on savings and investment.[58]

Monetary institutions to encourage and mobilize savings have to be perfected and expanded in the directions that have been indicated. But in addition the political atmosphere must be favorable to the private accumulation of savings, and adverse folkways and religious beliefs, such as the Islamic objection to interest, must be modified or compensated for. All of this is, however, a laborious and uncertain process. Meanwhile much of the wherewithal for economic development will have to be provided from government revenues.

58. United Nations, Economic Commission for Asia and the Far East, *Mobilization of Domestic Capital in Certain Countries of Asia and the Far East*, Bangkok, 1951, p. 224.

# 15. Domestic Financing of Development: Government Sources and the Application of Funds

## FISCAL SYSTEMS AND ECONOMIC DEVELOPMENT

A LOW LEVEL OF INCOME PER CAPITA is so generally characteristic of the economically underdeveloped world that the first has often been used to define the second. But the definition might be made almost as accurately in terms of government expenditures per unit of population. The contrast between the "haves" and the "have-nots" is enormous. The United States through its various units of government spent 168 times as much on its average citizen in a representative recent year as did the government of Haiti. But to make matters worse, so far as inequalities go, the government of New Zealand spent over a hundred times as much per capita on *economic development* as did Haiti. These are extreme cases, but the contrast between the economically advanced and retarded nations is as general as it is appalling. The hopeful side of the picture is the large *percentage* of total expenditure devoted to economic development in some countries. But let us not forget the *absolute* levels of per capita income nor the *absolute* amounts of the governments' contribution to development. Decided improvement may still mean near starvation. Some countries cannot spend much on the relief of poverty because their citizens are so poor.

## CHIEF SOURCES OF REVENUE: PROS AND CONS

### Direct Taxation

The relevance of poverty to revenue problems in underdeveloped areas is nowhere more striking than in the case of income taxes or, more generally, direct taxation. Direct taxes include taxes levied on personal and business income, undivided profits, excess profits, capital gains, gifts and bequests, some property taxes, and capitation taxes such as poll and hut taxes.

In India, where the income tax was introduced as early as 1860, though its effective use dates from 1936, and despite the inclusion not only of personal incomes but of all forms of business profits, only 500,000 to 600,000 persons pay this tax out of a population of 358 million—one fifth of one per cent![1] In addition to the fact that any reasonable exemption level excludes millions of persons in so poor an economy, income taxes are difficult to levy on peasants who are generally illiterate or, if literate, seldom keep records. Another major difficulty is that so much of income in such economies is income in kind, the value of which is difficult to fix. Some countries in the underdeveloped category, for example India and the United Kingdom colonies, have apparently reached the practical limit of direct taxation, and have in the past few years turned more extensively to the alternative of indirect taxes.

Nevertheless, underdeveloped countries at somewhat higher levels are able to derive considerable amounts of revenue from direct taxation, although the differences among them are great. Direct taxation of wealth and income accounts for about a third of tax revenue at the upper limit, and usually for much less. (See Table 15-1.) By comparison, in 1950 these taxes constituted 78 per cent of federal and 68 per cent of federal plus state tax revenue in the United States and 57 per cent in the United Kingdom.

While capitation taxes—head taxes and fixed levies on each hut or dwelling—are a rather crude form of direct taxation and are not progressively related to income as other direct taxation usually is, they cannot readily be dispensed with in primitive societies. If they are coupled with the opportunity to "work the tax off" on roads, land improvement and the like, they afford a desirable fiscal device for increasing the social capital, frequently out of seasonally unemployed or other forms of surplus labor.

When income taxation is possible, and when the political and social structure favors it, the introduction of social security taxation may induce saving. During an initial period, particularly, income from social security taxes may exceed outlay and thus result in considerable net saving on balance.[2] One particular advantage of these savings, which accrue to a

---

1. United Nations, Department of Economic Affairs, *Public Finance Surveys: India* (by Ursula K. Hicks), New York, November 1951, pp. 39–43. This study and the following are the sources of all fiscal data for the relevant countries in the present section unless specific reference is otherwise made. United Nations, Department of Economic Affairs, *Public Finance Surveys: Venezuela*, New York, January 1951; *Public Finance Information Papers*, No. 1: *Egypt*, New York, January 1950; No. 2: *Colombia*, New York, March 1950; No. 3: *Italy*, New York, June 1950; No. 4: *Iran*, New York, March 1951; No. 5: *Iraq*, New York, April 1951; No. 6: *Peru*, New York, October 1951. International Bank for Reconstruction and Development, *The Basis of a Development Program for Colombia*, Washington, 1950; *The Economic Development of Guatemala*, Washington, 1951; *The Economic Development of Iraq*, Washington, 1952; *The Economy of Turkey*, The Johns Hopkins Press, Baltimore, 1951; *Report on Cuba*, Washington, 1951; *Report of the Joint Brazil–U.S. Technical Commission* (Publication 3487), U.S. Department of State, June 1949; *Report to the President of the United States by the Economic Survey Mission to the Philippines*, U.S. Department of State, October 9, 1950 (the Bell Report); P. T. Ellsworth, *Chile, An Economy in Transition*, Macmillan, New York, 1945; Sanford A. Mosk, *Industrial Revolution in Mexico*, University of California Press, Berkeley, 1950; Harvey S. Perloff, *Puerto Rico's Economic Future, A Study in Planned Development*, University of Chicago Press, Chicago, 1950; H. W. Spiegel, *The Brazilian Economy, Chronic Inflation and Sporadic Industrialization*, Blakiston, Philadelphia, 1949; Henry C. Wallich and John H. Adler, *Public Finance in a Developing Country—El Salvador: A Case Study*, Harvard University Press, Cambridge, 1951.

2. In the United States, the social security system accounted for $27 billion in saving from 1936 to 1952. See E. M. Bernstein and I. G. Patel, "Inflation in Relation to Economic Development," International Monetary Fund, *Staff Papers*, November 1952.

TABLE 15-1. TAXES ON INCOME AND WEALTH IN SELECTED COUNTRIES, FISCAL OR CALENDAR YEAR 1950[a]

| Country | Tax Yield in Local Currency Units | | | |
| | On Income | On Wealth | On Wealth or Income (Undifferentiated) | Percentage of Total Tax Revenue |
| --- | --- | --- | --- | --- |
| | | (Millions) | | |
| Asia | | | | |
| Burma | .. | .. | 48 | 22 |
| India | .. | .. | 1,154 | 37 |
| Indonesia | .. | .. | 612 | 28 |
| Malaya | .. | .. | 45 | 13 |
| North Borneo | .. | .. | .5 | 5 |
| Pakistan | .. | .. | 90 | 15 |
| Philippines | .. | .. | 61 | 18 |
| Singapore | .. | .. | 25 | 32 |
| Thailand | .. | .. | 77 | 6 |
| | | | | |
| Middle East | | | | |
| Egypt | 15 | 7 | .. | 22 |
| Iran | 17 | .. | .. | 17 |
| Iraq | 10 | 3 | .. | 13 |
| Israel | 31 | 6 | .. | 37 |
| Jordan | 16 | 4 | .. | 20 |
| | | | | |
| Europe | | | | |
| Italy[b] | .. | .. | .. | 25 |
| | | | | |
| Latin America | | | | |
| Peru | .. | .. | .. | 22 |
| Cuba | .. | .. | .. | 26 |
| Guatemala[c] | .. | .. | .. | 10 |
| Haiti[c] | .. | .. | .. | 13 |

*Sources:* Publications of the United Nations as follows: Department of Economic Affairs, *Economic Survey of Asia and the Far East, 1950,* New York, July 13, 1951, Table 127, p. 437; *Review of Economic Conditions in the Middle East,* Supplement to *World Economic Report, 1949–50,* New York, March 1951, Table 49, p. 82; *Public Finance Information Papers* (ST/ECA/SER.A), No. 3, *Italy,* New York, June 1950, Table 10, p. 25; No. 6, *Peru,* New York, October 1951, Table 14, p. 27. Also John H. Adler, Eugene R. Schlesinger and Ernest C. Olson, *Public Finance and Economic Development in Guatemala,* Stanford University Press, Stanford, 1952, Table 18, p. 59; International Bank for Reconstruction and Development, *Report on Cuba,* Washington, 1951, Table 129, p. 669.

a. Fiscal year 1950 is August 15, 1949 to March 31, 1950. Figures are regarded as estimates only by the relevant sources except for Malaya, Philippines, Israel, Jordan, Peru, Italy, Cuba. Data here are rounded.
b. Includes direct but nonrecurrent taxes on capital levies and other emergency taxes.
c. Figures are for fiscal year 1948, the latest data available.

government fund, is that they may be invested in enterprises of basic significance to economic development, such as public utilities, electric power and communications.

So long as the specific obstacles to effective and equitable direct taxation persist, it cannot be pressed by underdeveloped countries. Thus one of the chief merits commonly ascribed to income taxation in the industrial West— its progressiveness—is lacking in Iran and Iraq, for example, where it falls heavily, on the salaried classes because agriculture is excluded. But its potential merits in progressiveness, collection at the source, withholding and the possibility of offsetting losses against gains for net income calculation would recommend continuation of the present general movement in underdeveloped areas toward adopting income taxation or improving its operation. Colombia, for example, moved from a situation in 1937 in which customs duties provided one half and direct taxes one fourth of total revenue, to a reversal of these proportions in 1948.

## *Criteria of Taxes*

From the particular angle of economic development, taxes may be appraised by three further criteria. One is simply their productiveness or yield, since much development requires government outlay; and on this basis the income tax is, of course, potentially the best. Another criterion is the economic repercussions of the taxes—whether they are favorable to saving, to investment, to productive use, etc. Income taxes, generally speaking, are probably neutral in most of these respects but avoid the adverse effects of some alternative sources of revenue. However, income tax rates can of course be so high as to discourage saving. Ursula Hicks reports in her public finance survey for the United Nations that this consideration, along with an increased emphasis on private enterprise, accounts for India's decision to reduce income taxes and make them less progressive. Finally, some taxes and some features of taxes are designed particularly to further economic development, but this is not true of direct taxes.

## *Indirect Taxation: Foreign Trade*

Whatever deficiencies in tax revenue remain after direct taxes must, of course, be made up by indirect taxes. In the economically underdeveloped countries a large share of this remaining burden falls to taxes on foreign trade. The proportions of tax returns obtained from foreign trade in these countries show a wide dispersion, but in those for which adequate data are available the range is from 30 to 80 per cent. (See Table 15-2.) Customs duties for the United Kingdom lie somewhat below the lower extreme of this range, at 22 per cent (1950), and in the United States the share of federal and state tax revenue obtained from this source is 0.9 per cent.

The division of taxes on foreign trade as between import tariffs and export taxes has in recent years shown a decided preponderance of the former, both in number of countries levying them and in yield in most countries.[3] Both types of taxes can be made to yield substantial revenues;

3. For 1946 figures see Wallich and Adler, *op. cit.*, p. 84. In 1950 the percentages of total revenue coming from import and export taxes were, respectively, 16.6 and 0 for Venezuela, 14.1 and 32.4 for Peru, 35.7 and 9.9 for Cuba; and in 1948, 57.6 and 19.6 for Haiti, and 41.9 and 8.5 for Guatemala.

TABLE 15-2. TAXES ON FOREIGN TRADE IN SELECTED COUNTRIES, FISCAL OR
CALENDAR YEAR 1950[a]

| | Tax Yield in Local Currency Units | | | |
|---|---|---|---|---|
| Country | On Imports | On Exports | On Imports or Exports (Undifferentiated) | Percentage of Total Tax Revenue |
| | (Millions) | | | |
| Asia | | | | |
| Burma | .. | .. | 113 | 52 |
| India | .. | .. | 1,247[b] | 40 |
| Indonesia | .. | .. | 727 | 33 |
| Malaya | .. | .. | 269 | 80 |
| North Borneo | .. | .. | 7 | 80 |
| Pakistan | .. | .. | 348[b] | 33 |
| Middle East | | | | |
| Egypt | .. | .. | .. | 34 |
| Iran | .. | .. | .. | 31 |
| Iraq | .. | .. | .. | 34 |
| Israel | .. | .. | .. | 28 |
| Jordan | .. | .. | .. | 56 |
| Latin America | | | | |
| Peru | 14[c] | 32[c] | .. | 46 |
| Venezuela | 17[d] | .. | .. | 17 |
| Cuba | 36[e] | 10[e] | .. | 46 |
| Haiti | 58[f] | 20[f] | .. | 78 |
| Guatemala | 42[f] | 8[f] | .. | 50 |

*Sources:* Publications of the United Nations as follows: Department of Economic Affairs, *Economic Survey of Asia and the Far East, 1950*, New York, July 13, 1951, Table 127, p. 437; *Review of Economic Conditions in the Middle East*, Supplement to *World Economic Report, 1949–50*, New York, March 1951, Table 49, p. 82; *Public Finance Information Papers: Peru* (ST/ECA/SER.A/6), New York, October 1951, Table 14, p. 27; *Public Finance Surveys: Venezuela*, New York, January 1951, p. 38. Also International Bank for Reconstruction and Development, *Report on Cuba*, Washington, 1951, Table 129, p. 669; John H. Adler, Eugene R. Schlesinger and Ernest C. Olson, *Public Finance and Economic Development in Guatemala*, Stanford University Press, Stanford, 1952, Table 18, p. 59.

a. Fiscal year 1950 is August 15, 1949 to March 31, 1950. Figures for Burma, India, Indonesia, North Borneo, Iran and Iraq are regarded as estimates only by the relevant sources. Data here are rounded.
b. Customs are shown net of refunds.
c. The column labeled "Imports" is actually entitled "Customs Duties" (largely imports) in the original. Export duties on agriculture and mineral products.
d. Figure does not include stamped paper, postal, harbor, consular fees in per cent of 9.4 and alcohol 4.1, cigarettes 2.8, and taxes on matches, petroleum consumption and telecommunications in amount of 0.6.
e. Cuba technically has no export taxes. Taxes on sugar production have been listed as export taxes here.
f. Figures are for fiscal year 1948.

and they have in common the disadvantage that revenue varies greatly with the ups and downs of world trade. But further appraisal must distinguish sharply between import and export taxes.

*Import Levies*

In general, import tariffs are regressive; but this unwelcome feature can be considerably reduced by levying high duties on articles of luxury consumption and admitting the necessities of life on the free list or at low rates.

This remedy, however, may involve a considerable loss of revenue. If the main purpose were to reduce luxury consumption or consumption as a whole, domestic sumptuary taxes—as we have argued in the case of multiple import exchange rates—would be less subject to tax evasion and to tax avoidance through the use of substitutes, without sacrifice of ease of administration. But the aim of protection to domestic producers in most cases must be assumed to be paramount. Little can be added to the age-old pros and cons of the infant industry argument for protection, which has already been touched upon.[4]

## Export Levies

The taxation of exports avoids most of the objections to import taxes. It appropriates the excess profits or rents arising from differentials between domestic costs and the international market, whether this excess be caused by conscious monopoly restriction, by lags in the international adjustment mechanism or by the existence of valuable soil or mineral properties in their natural state.[5] By appropriating monopoly or windfall profits, export levies, in contrast to import tariffs, are progressive in their effect. If export tariffs are not raised beyond the cost-price differential, they yield revenue without reducing sales and without impairing the international division of labor. They represent, in the case of irreplaceable natural assets, a reimbursement to the nation for the exhaustion of these resources. In particular cases, they are fantastically profitable and may, if properly managed, be sufficient to finance economic development.[6] Finally, export tariffs can be raised in boom times and lowered in depressions, thus maximizing revenue and contributing to domestic stability. Export taxes are well suited to the fiscal and economic needs of "export economies," particularly primary producers; and most, though not all, underdeveloped countries fall into these categories.[7]

## Fiscal Monopolies

Fiscal monopolies represent, in effect, a combination of domestic excise and export taxation. This is true especially of the Thailand rice monopoly because substantial quantities of its sales are domestic.[8] Occasionally, the major emphasis is on domestic sales, as with the Iranian fiscal monopoly of tobacco, opium, cotton piece-goods, sugar, tea and matches, which

4. See pp. 290–92, above.

5. It must be in this sense that Wallich and Adler (*op. cit.*, p. 107) argue that export taxes are borne by producers.

6. In Venezuela, royalties on petroleum exports contribute 34.2 per cent of government revenues; income and other taxes included, the industry supplies 60 per cent of total revenues; and petroleum exports supply 80 per cent of the country's available foreign exchange.

7. Only a small fraction of India's production is for export.

8. This monopoly provided 10 and 17 per cent of total government revenues in 1948 and 1949.

provides about one third of total government revenues. In the case of oil royalties in Iraq, Iran, Venezuela, etc., the foreign market is overwhelmingly more important. The economic appraisal of fiscal monopolies will depend upon the preponderance of the export tax element relative to the excise tax element, that is, upon the preponderance of foreign or domestic sales, taking into account any price discrimination which may exist. This weighting is not necessary to arrive at the conclusion that fiscal monopolies are suitable instruments of taxation for underdeveloped areas, for both the export tax and excise tax elements offer distinct advantages. But the nature of the advantages differs as between the two.

*Consumption Taxes*

In the fiscal systems of most undeveloped areas domestic consumption taxes are among the three or four leading sources of revenue. In a sample of eleven countries the portion of total tax revenue from this source in 1950 ran from one fifth to one third with only two exceptions. (See Table 15-3.) In the United States in 1950, consumption taxes yielded one quarter of total federal and state tax revenue, and in the United Kingdom about one fifth. Because it is a staunch producer of revenue and not easily evaded, taxation of consumption plays a considerable role in most countries. But the less advanced fiscal systems, as the percentages in the table illustrate, rely on it heavily as the counterpart to the limited use of income and other direct taxes.

Sumptuary taxation can be made mildly progressive if, as is commonly the case, it is confined to liquors, tobacco and other luxuries; if levied on articles of common consumption such as salt, matches, and even food and raiment, it becomes regressive. But the case of India seems to show dramatically how the combination of high excises on expensive luxuries and low rates on minor luxuries, if they are consumed by millions of persons, can tap levels of income—perhaps those somewhat above the lowest levels —which income taxation cannot exploit.

*Taxes on Capital and Property*

A number of observers recommend the capital gains tax to appropriate part of the windfall which may come with rapid development.[9] As in a good share of the "advanced" countries, the taxation of real property seems to leave ample latitude for improvement, and this is particularly true of taxes on agriculture in the Far East. A besetting defect of rural land taxation is the inequitable assessment of values, sometimes the result of cadastral surveys long since outdated, sometimes the outgrowth of official corruption or inertia.

9. Its use in India is said to have been not very successful.

TABLE 15-3. TAXES ON CONSUMPTION, IN SELECTED COUNTRIES, FISCAL OR
CALENDAR YEAR 1950[a]

| Country | Tax Yield in Local Currency Units | Percentage of Total Tax Revenue |
|---|---|---|
| | *(Millions)* | |
| Asia | | |
| Burma[b] | 46 | 21 |
| Indonesia[b] | 733 | 35 |
| Pakistan[b] | 123 | 21 |
| India[c] | 65 | 28 |
| Middle East | | |
| Iraq[d] | 7 | 31 |
| Iran[e] | 550 | 10 |
| Turkey[f] | 406 | 32 |
| Europe | | |
| Italy[g] | 483,150 | 52 |
| Latin America | | |
| Peru[h] | 290 | 19 |
| Cuba[i] | .. | 21 |
| Guatemala[j] | .. | 27 |
| Haiti[j] | .. | 3 |

*Sources:* Publications of the United Nations as follows: Department of Economic Affairs, *Economic Survey of Asia and the Far East, 1950,* New York, July 13, 1951, Table 127, p. 437; *Public Finance Surveys: India,* November 1951, Table 6, p. 48; *Public Finance Information Papers* (ST/ECA/SER.A), No. 5, *Iraq,* New York, April 1951, Table 3, p. 39; No. 4, *Iran,* New York, March 1951, Table 4 (a), p. 31; No. 3, *Italy,* New York, June 1950, Table 6, p. 70; No. 6, *Peru,* New York, October 1951, Table 13, p. 27. Also *Overseas Economic Surveys: Turkey,* April 1950, H.M.S.O., London, 1951, Appendix II, p. 128. International Bank for Reconstruction and Development, *Report on Cuba,* Washington, 1951, Table 129, p. 669; John H. Adler, Eugene R. Schlesinger and Ernest C. Olson, *Public Finance and Economic Development in Guatemala,* Stanford University Press, Stanford, 1952, Table 18, p. 59.

a. Fiscal year 1950 is August 15, 1949 to March 15, 1950. Figures for Burma, Indonesia, Pakistan and Peru are regarded as estimates only by relevant sources. Data here are rounded.

b. In some instances, license taxes, stamp duties and "other" taxes have been included in consumption taxes. However, only those countries for which such amounts are very minor have been included in this table.

c. States of Indian Union only. Consumption taxes include sales and excise.

d. Excise, animal and Istihlak taxes. Istihlak is a tax on agricultural produce collected at the time of sale.

e. Excise tax only.

f. Transaction and consumption (including petrol tax).

g. General turnover tax and excise tax.

h. Figure here refers to excise and transaction. (Transaction tax [60] *includes* stamp duties.)

i. Refers only to consumption taxes.

j. Figures are for fiscal 1948.

One alternative to taxes based on land values is the levying of taxes on agricultural produce as it is brought to market. This has the merit of certainty, but the trouble is that the peasant comes to bear a heavier tax load than the city dweller, whose product is less visible to the tax collector. So it has seemed in Japan and parts of India.[10] Moreover, the taxing of farm produce as it reaches the market is expensive and subject to considerable

10. United Nations, Economic and Social Council, *Land Reform—Defects in Agrarian Structure as Obstacles to Economic Development,* New York, 1951, pp. 43–48.

evasion. During the fiscal years 1943/44 and 1944/45, Iran tried another alternative in the form of a special agricultural income tax, but without success; it reverted to taxing the land. The Indian provinces are in the process of revising the agricultural income tax, which forms the chief source of provincial revenue.

The opinion has often been voiced that improved property taxes may work better in relatively primitive economies than the attempt to apply income taxes to the land.[11] First and foremost, the improvement would imply full and equitable assessment and the adjustment of rates to equality with the tax burden in other parts of the economy. As a part of a general reform of agricultural taxation, attention might well be given to numerous suggestions for a special tax on uncultivated land. In virtually no country do property taxes form an important part of central government revenue; but their improvement would substantially aid the various units of local government. However, bad systems of land tenure have probably been a greater obstacle to progress than have defective systems of taxation.

### SPECIAL FISCAL DEVICES TO FURTHER DEVELOPMENT

Certain fiscal measures, in contradistinction to types of taxes, have been designed specifically to further economic development. A number of countries, including Colombia, El Salvador, Guatemala, Mexico and Puerto Rico, have granted more or less complete immunity from taxation to new industries in certain stipulated categories for various periods, ten years being fairly typical. In Guatemala the results are said to be moderately successful; but in commenting on tax exemption in both Guatemala and Colombia, reports of the International Bank warn that it is no less important to discourage uneconomic and speculative investment than to encourage new productive ventures. In Mexico, tax immunity was first applied in 1926 to a very few new industries for short periods; but since then, the number of industries and the period of exemption have grown, the granting of exemptions has been made partly a matter of administrative discretion, and a number of states have joined in the fun. Sanford Mosk, who devotes careful study to this phenomenon in Mexico, discovers that small firms have not been especially favored, that the concept of "new" industry has been interpreted with increasing generosity, and that vested interests have been created in perpetuating the exemptions. Despite these drawbacks, it is said, tax exemption has successfully stimulated industrial expansion.

11. John H. Adler, "The Fiscal and Monetary Implementation of Development Programs," *American Economic Review, Proceedings*, May 1952, p. 594.

## Tax Exemption versus Subsidies

Against this background it would seem that direct subsidies or loans would be preferable to tax exemptions on the same grounds that subsidies are frequently advocated by economists in preference to tariffs. The overt nature of the subsidy and the fact that it must be subjected to comparison with other demands on the budget argue in its favor. Problems might of course arise since specialized government institutions would probably be entrusted with the detailed allocation of subsidies or loans.[12]

## Tax Discrimination: Earmarking

Tax discrimination favorable to the reinvestment of profits offers a milder form of persuasion in regard to which there can be only minor misgivings. In the United States, tax discrimination in the opposite sense has been supported frequently by argument and occasionally in practice by special penalties on undivided profits. In this country the danger is that several factors, including tax considerations and mere self-esteem, may induce a firm to excessive reinvestment in its own venture. But in the underdeveloped world, the temptations to export capital, to venture into speculative activities and to consume may justify some tax discrimination to induce reinvestment.

A substantial number of countries have sought to guarantee the financing of economic development by earmarking certain sources of revenue for specific development projects. This procedure has been rather persuasively supported by the argument that revenue derived from the sale to foreign countries of irreplaceable natural assets should be devoted to an equal upbuilding of the home country's productive equipment. But, of course, this desirable result can be achieved through the effective investment of government revenue from *any* source or, quite possibly, through private investment. The aggregate amount and the direction of investment matter, but the source is secondary. A more important purpose of earmarking has been to protect funds for development from incursions by corrupt governments or pressure groups. Where this precaution is not necessary, it would be better to avoid earmarking because of the budgetary rigidity it entails.

More important to economic development than the inventive novelty of devices such as these is a soundly conceived, effectively organized and honestly administered revenue system. Most commentators, both official and unofficial, complain of the needless proliferation of taxes, particularly in the Orient. The five or six taxes reviewed here usually produce nine tenths of the tax revenue even as matters stand. Unproductive nuisance taxes should be abolished and the main taxes should be simplified and

12. United Nations, Department of Economic Affairs, *Domestic Financing of Economic Development*, New York, 1950, pp. 44–45.

codified. Still more important, methods of administration in many cases require a general overhauling to prevent laxity on the one hand and whole-sale evasion on the other. In some cases the elimination of corrupt officials is the prime requisite. The Bell report on the Philippines was able to suggest improvements in the revenue system which would increase its yield by over one third; the Abbink report on Brazil, by one tenth; the Britnell report on Guatemala, by about one fourth. These reports would accomplish increases of these amounts despite a general shifting of the tax systems toward greater progressiveness through increased use of personal and business income taxes, capital gains and excess profits taxes, etc. While neither ideal equity nor optimum yield may be expected of tax systems in many coun-tries, the improvement of revenue systems throughout the underdeveloped world offers one of the greatest unexploited instruments of economic progress.

### GOVERNMENT BORROWING FOR DEVELOPMENT

Insofar as government outlays for development go into well-conceived long-term investments, there is nothing adverse to borrowing. Indeed, in Sweden and a number of other countries this logic has led to a dual budget system, one budget being devoted to current and another to capital out-lays. In Sweden, the system seems to be more the immediate outgrowth of the idea of deficit financing in depressions than related to economic de-velopment; but the ultimate rationale is the same.

### Chief Problems of Borrowing

In the present context of domestic finance, the chief problems of borrow-ing for the governments in underdeveloped areas are the absence in some cultures of any habit of saving, the lack of organized markets for govern-ment securities and of demand on the part of commercial banks and insur-ance companies, together with the leaning of the governments themselves toward inflationary finance and the public fears of inflation.[13] Most of these matters have been touched on already, but one important aspect must be mentioned. Compared to the capitalistic nations of the West, countries in the rest of the world usually have much smaller national debts relative to their national income. Belgium's national debt in 1950 was equal to nearly 94 per cent of her national income, Canada's to 117 per cent, while in Brazil (1949) and India the percentages were 18 and 28. (See Table 15-4.) This better debt position is somewhat offset by higher interest rates. Never-theless, relative freedom from debt is in itself an advantage from both

---

13. Thus in Turkey less than 10 per cent of the public debt has been purchased by the public out of savings; see International Bank, *The Economy of Turkey*, p. 211.

fiscal and monetary angles. If the *increase* of debt can be managed without inflation, economic development can be partly financed without bearing too heavily on the poor man.

TABLE 15-4. NATIONAL DEBT AS PERCENTAGE OF NATIONAL INCOME IN
SELECTED COUNTRIES, 1950

| Relatively Developed Economies | | Relatively Underdeveloped Economies | |
|---|---|---|---|
| Belgium | 93.7 | Argentina[a] | 59.0 |
| Canada | 117.1 | Bolivia[a] | 51.0 |
| France | 55.9 | Brazil[a] | 18.0 |
| Norway | 35.2 | Burma | 35.1 |
| Sweden | 40.6 | Ceylon[b] | 15.2 |
| United Kingdom | 232.1 | Chile | 6.8 |
| United States | 109.2 | India | 28.4 |
| | | Mexico[a] | 10.0 |
| | | Peru[a] | 21.0 |
| | | Uruguay[a] | 53.0 |

*Sources:* Computed from United Nations, *Statistical Yearbook*, New York, 1952, except 1949 data, which are from United Nations, Economic and Social Council, *Public Finance Developments in Latin America*, Mexico City, 1951.

a. Debt and national income for 1949.
b. Gross national product instead of national income.

GOVERNMENT EXPENDITURES

Some of the most important aspects of government expenditures have already been examined: the roles of private and of state expenditures in development, priorities in government spending for this purpose, and the problem of inflation.[14] But certain aggregative aspects of public spending are quite significant, and none more so than the enormous disparities obtaining among the underdeveloped countries in *per capita* government expenditure for all purposes. In 1949–1950 the United States spent $282 per capita while India spent $2; even Venezuela, despite the fabulous yields of petroleum in royalties and income and other taxes, spent only 34 per cent as much on each inhabitant as the government of the United States. (See Table 15-5.)

Data on per capita government expenditure for development are difficult to secure and still more difficult to evaluate. The gap between the poorer and richer underdeveloped countries in dollar outlays by government for development is abysmal. Per capita, India spent $0.12 for this purpose in 1949–1950 and Venezuela $33. (See Table 15-5.) When government expenditures are broken down into their major components, as in Table 15-6, "investment" presumably represents the chief development item, though not all investment is necessarily developmental. Unknown parts of "loans and advances" and "social services" should probably also be allocated to

14. See pp. 289–95 and 308–13.

development. It is evident that "national defense" cuts into development heavily in India and Pakistan; and "other current"—mostly the overhead cost of government—takes a startlingly heavy proportion in Iran, Iraq and Jordan. Perhaps the best indicator of the proportion of government outlay devoted to development in a broad sense is the combined total of social

TABLE 15-5. TOTAL AND PER CAPITA GOVERNMENT EXPENDITURES IN SELECTED COUNTRIES, 1949-1950

| Country | Total Budget Expenditure | Total Development Budget Expenditure | Total Budget Expenditure | Total Development Budget Expenditure | Total Expenditure Per Capita | Development Expenditure Per Capita |
|---|---|---|---|---|---|---|
| | (*Millions, National Currency*) | (*Millions, National Currency*) | (*Millions of Dollars*) | (*Millions of Dollars*) | (*Dollars*) | (*Dollars*) |
| India[a] | 3,280 | 196 | 692 | 41 | 2 | 0.12[b] |
| Philippines | 486 | 75 | 243 | 37 | 12 | 2 |
| Egypt[c] | 188[d] | 63[e] | 538 | 170 | 28 | 9 |
| Iran[f] | 11,117 | 1,638[g] | 342 | 51 | 19 | 3 |
| Italy[h] | 1,336,915 | 252,096 | 2,674 | 504 | 58 | 11 |
| Venezuela[i] | 1,602 | 550 | 478 | 164 | 96 | 33 |
| Peru | 1,500[j] | 255 | 231 | 39 | 28 | 5 |
| United States | | | | | 282 | |

*Sources:* Calculated from following publications of the United Nations: Department of Economic Affairs, *Public Finance Surveys: India,* New York, November 1951, Table 1, p. 33; *Venezuela,* New York, January 1951, Table 1, p. 81 and Table 2, p. 82; *Public Finance Information Papers* (ST/ECA/SER.A), No. 1, *Egypt,* New York, January 1950, p. 5; No. 4, *Iran,* New York, March 1951, Table 3 (a), p. 25; No. 3, *Italy,* New York, June 1950, Table 3, pp. 61–63; No. 6, *Peru,* New York, October 1951, Table 5, p. 13; Philippines, *Economic Survey of Asia and the Far East, 1950,* New York, July 13, 1951, Table 125, p. 420; conversion based on *Federal Reserve Bulletin,* exchange rates for December 1949.
a. Singapore not included.
b. State development expenditure in 1949–1950 was 1,065 million rupees, so that per capita expenditure on development by federal and state units would amount to roughly $0.77. This, of course, ignores the interstate variations both in expenditure and population.
c. Financial year ending February 28, 1950.
d. Figure is for "total expenditure (including gross expenditure of public undertakings)."
e. Figure includes "public works" and "new works (including five-year plan)." Item "gross expenditure of public undertakings" is not included since "renewal of railways" is included as a five-year plan expenditure.
f. Arithmetic mean of buying and selling rate was used in converting to dollars.
g. Figure includes "capital and development expenditure," which "includes 910 million rials as a part of the expenditure of the Seven-year Development projects."
h. Conversion based on mean daily exchange rate.
i. Includes expenditures of Department of Economic Development; contributions of capital to autonomous institutions by the Department of Agriculture; expenditures by the Department of Public Works; and capital contributions by the Department of Labor and Communications.
j. Estimate for 1950.

services, investment and loans. Again the dispersion is very marked; and high proportions going to development purposes bear no definable relation to development "needs," at least so far as these are measurable by the usual criteria of income, health, housing and the like.

Government expenditures of certain sorts, as for example on public health, are generally made directly. But investment outlays may involve a

TABLE 15-6. MAJOR COMPONENTS OF GOVERNMENT EXPENDITURE AS PERCENTAGE OF TOTAL, SELECTED COUNTRIES, FISCAL OR CALENDAR YEAR 1950[a]

| Country | Defense | Social Services | Interest on Public Debt | Other Current | Invest-ment | Loans and Advances | Total of Social Services, Investment, Loans and Advances |
|---|---|---|---|---|---|---|---|
| **Asia** | | | | | | | |
| Burma[b,c] | 26 | 5 | 1 | 41 | 22 | 5 | 32 |
| Ceylon[b] | · 1 | 37 | 5 | 38 | 19 | .. | 56 |
| India[b,d] | 38 | 1 | 8 | 27 | 13 | 13 | 27 |
| Pakistan[b] | 57 | 1 | 3 | 14 | 10 | 15 | 26 |
| Malaya[b] | 4 | 10 | 5 | 65 | 16 | .. | 26 |
| Philippines[b] | 14 | 34 | 2 | 29 | 20 | 1 | 56 |
| **Middle East** | | | | | | | |
| Egypt[e] | 27 | 17 | 3 | 38 | 15 | .. | 32 |
| Iran[e] | 22 | 11 | 4 | 49 | 14 | .. | 25 |
| Iraq[e] | 22 | 13 | .. | 56 | 9 | .. | 22 |
| Jordan[e] | 32 | 4 | .. | 53 | 11 | .. | 15 |
| **Europe** | | | | | | | |
| Italy[f] | 26 | 14 | 6 | 28 | 25 | | 39 |
| **Latin America** | | | | | | | |
| Cuba | 17 | 40 | 3 | 28 | 12 | | 52 |
| Peru[g] | 23 | 26 | 8 | 26 | 13 | 4 | 43 |

*Sources:* All United Nations sources with exception of Cuba: Department of Economic Affairs, *Economic Survey of Asia and the Far East, 1950*, July 13, 1951, Table 126; *Review of Economic Conditions in the Middle East*, Supplement to *World Economic Report, 1949–50*, New York, March 1951, Table 48, p. 81; *Public Finance Information Papers* (ST/ECA/SER.A), No. 3, *Italy*, New York, June 1950, Table 5, p. 17; No. 6, *Peru*, New York, October 1951, Table 6; International Bank for Reconstruction and Development, *Report on Cuba*, Washington, 1951, Table 131, p. 679.

a. Figures are estimates of varying degrees of accuracy. All figures are rounded.

b. *Defense:* expenditure of military department plus capital outlay for defense purposes. *Social Services:* education, public health and public assistance (in some countries those services provided primarily by local government). *Investment:* public works expenditure on a gross basis, capital outlays of government enterprise and grants to local authorities. *Loans and Advances:* net basis and granted mainly to provinces for capital expenditure.

c. Burma current expenditure includes the net results of government sales and purchase of supplies.

d. Interest on public debt is given on a net basis, e.g., after deduction of interest received from public undertakings.

e. Data refer to expenditure of central governments, the net results (loss) of public undertakings. The distribution of expenditure among the different categories is somewhat arbitrary because of the nature of available data. *Defense:* capital outlays for military purposes as well as current expenditure. *Social Services:* includes education, public health and social welfare. *Public Works:* ascertainable expenditures of capital nature. *Public Debt:* includes interest and redemption payments. *Other Current:* civil administration, such as outlays to various ministries and departments and transfer payments.

f. *Other Current:* the classifications "other," "general administration" and subsidies. Subsidies refer to grants to state enterprises to meet current deficits, including wheat subsidy. *Defense:* defense and expenditures arising from war and peace treaty. *Investment and Loans:* classified as capital expenditure (other than defense).

g. *Social Services:* pensions are included in amount of 4.1. *Interest on Public Debt:* debt service and amortization. *Other Current:* deficit of public enterprise and food subsidies. *Investment and Loans:* includes public works and capital contribution to government-controlled banks.

variety of intermediaries, as is true also of private investment. Indeed, the quality of these intermediaries forms an important element in the financing of economic development.

## APPLICATION OF CAPITAL FUNDS TO DEVELOPMENT

Capital funds may at times be applied directly, without intermediaries, by the economic agents who originate them as capital, to the purchase or fabrication of capital goods. This may be the case with the maintenance and improvement of farms, shops and business property, with the reinvestment of corporate earnings and with projects carried on directly by the state. But generally, financial and administrative organs intervene, whether the capital funds originate in taxation, domestic saving, foreign borrowing or credit creation. Economic development depends heavily upon the functioning of these intermediaries, which are sometimes also creators of capital funds.

### COMMERCIAL AND CENTRAL BANKS

Aside from the usurious village moneylender, commercial banks are the oldest of these intermediaries. Historically, they made their appearance in the port or capital cities of the underdeveloped countries and were devoted to financing the exports and imports of primary producers, generally with funds supplied by foreigners. Since the principal traders were often few and concentrated in the largest towns or cities, commercial banks dealt with a restricted and favored clientele, rarely having contact with industrial producers or the agricultural back country.

Even today in parts of Southeast Asia, the Near East and Africa, commercial banking answers to this description. In other parts of these regions and in numbers of Latin American countries where commercial banking has developed and spread to the smaller cities, it nevertheless still bears the marks of these early origins; and these characteristics limit its role in economic development.

### *Limitations of Commercial Banks*

But other considerations signify that the commercial banks should *not* finance economic development past a certain limit. In the first place, commercial banks are custodians of demand deposits, and if they become heavily committed in their loan portfolios or investments to long-term industrial or agricultural requirements, their solvency, and hence the financial liquidity of the country, is put in jeopardy.[15]

Nevertheless, it is clear that commercial banking should play an integral role in development. The financing of trade and of the short-term inventory needs of industry and agriculture is *itself* important. Furthermore, there seems to be considerable agreement that, if the regulatory authority speci-

15. See United Nations, *Domestic Financing of Economic Development*, pp. 60–63.

fies limits, a certain proportion of the banks' assets can safely go into medium- and long-term financing of industry.[16] Again, if commercial banks do not absorb government bonds to an inflationary extent, they can, as Mosk points out, contribute to the establishment of an effective government bond market.[17] And such a market is highly desirable for the provision of "social capital" undertakings by the state and as a prerequisite of monetary control, at least through central bank open-market operations. The ancillary activities of commercial banks in maintaining savings accounts and time deposits and in the clearing of checks, although these services can be supplied by other means, also justify their existence and geographic expansion. Finally, organized domestic capital markets are almost inconceivable without commercial banks; only completely controlled economies can advance far without them.

## The Growth of Central Banks

Central banks, on the other hand, are a relatively recent phenomenon even in some of the modern industrialized nations of the West. Their number has grown in two great waves, one following the first world war and the recommendation of the Geneva conference in 1922, and the other during and after the second world war. In the less developed regions, the first wave included South Africa (1920), Colombia (1923), Australia (1924), New Zealand (1933), India (1935), Costa Rica (1937) and Venezuela (1939). The second wave has been even larger and has left practically no country without either a central bank or a dominant commercial bank carrying on central bank functions.[18]

## Relationship of Commercial and Central Banks

In relatively primitive financial communities, it is perhaps natural for commercial and central banking to be undifferentiated; moreover, an orthodox central bank can scarcely antedate the emergence of a domestic capital market.[19] Often the central bank has evolved from a commercial bank, but in this evolution the bank usually allowed its commercial opera-

16. *Ibid.*, p. 63; *Report of the Joint Brazil–U.S. Technical Commission*, p. 573; International Bank, *The Basis of a Development Program for Colombia*, p. 165.

17. Mosk, *op. cit.*, p. 233.

18. Other central banks include those of Argentina, Chile, Cuba, Bolivia, El Salvador, Ecuador, Korea, Mexico, Turkey and China. The central bank of Afghanistan was established early in World War II (1941). Others followed in Ceylon (1942), Paraguay (1944), Albania (1945), Guatemala (1946), the Dominican Republic (1947), Pakistan (1948), the Philippine Republic (1948), the Belgian Congo and Ruanda-Urundi (1951), Egypt (1950), Honduras (1950), Indochina (including the states of Laos, Cambodia and Viet Nam) (1952), Israel (1952), Libya (1951) and Peru (1951). Banks have been proposed for the following: Brazil, Haiti, Indonesia, Nicaragua, Southern Rhodesia and Surinam. Data from International Monetary Fund, *International Financial Statistics*, various issues.

19. In Saudi Arabia the lack of a central bank and of conditions auspicious for establishing one led to the creation of the Saudi-Arabian Monetary Authority on April 10, 1952. See International Monetary Fund, *International Financial News Survey*, May 30, 1952.

tions to fall into desuetude, since it appeared improper to risk compromising public functions by private profit activities. This process of divorcement was vastly accelerated by another postwar wave, the spate of nationalizations of central banks, which still continues.[20] Nevertheless, the central banks of Australia, Finland, Egypt, Brazil, and even the Banque de France carry on commercial banking, though in some of these cases there is a movement afoot toward reform. In Chile, of recent years, the central bank has not been permitted to deal with the public.

### Chief Functions of Central Banks

The main argument against allowing the central bank itself to participate directly in financing economic development is that this would deflect its attention from and undermine its devotion to the primary responsibility it has for credit control and economic stability.[21] This is essential if economic development is not to undergo disastrous cyclical reversals. During the 1930s and the early 1940s, central banking suffered an eclipse in both theory and practice relative to this function, first because of the preponderant importance of fiscal measures to combat depression and subsequently because of the sacrifice of monetary stability to the maintenance of government bond markets. But in Western Europe and to some degree in the United States and England the past two or three years have witnessed a return to monetary orthodoxy which may in some measure be reflected in the economically less developed countries. Whether nationalized or not, it would be valuable if central banks preserved intact the reputation which Wallich believes they have acquired in many countries "as the defender of long-time viewpoints *vis-a-vis* the frequently short-time viewpoints espoused by the government."[22]

In addition to its responsibility for avoiding inflation and deflation, the central bank of a developing economy has two further major duties: maintaining equilibrium in the international balance of payments (discussed in Chapter 18); and purchasing—or, preferably, through the provision of loans or rediscounts, enabling the commercial banks to purchase—government bonds or the paper of government development agencies, in amounts compatible with the objective of stability. In terms of the division of labor and functional responsibility, it seems best for central banks to concern themselves with the daily administration of domestic and external stability,

20. See M. A. Kriz, "Central Banks and the State Today," *American Economic Review*, September 1948, pp. 565–81; A. F. W. Plumptre, *Central Banking in the British Dominions*, University of Toronto Press, Toronto, 1940.

21. United Nations, *Domestic Financing of Economic Development*, p. 67; International Bank, *The Basis of a Development Program for Colombia*, pp. 571–73; *Report of the Joint Brazil–U.S. Technical Commission*, pp. 163–65.

22. Henry C. Wallich, *Monetary Problems of an Export Economy, The Cuban Experience*, Harvard University Press, Cambridge, 1950, p. 283.

leaving the financing of economic development to commercial banks and to the specialized credit institutions which have sprung up in all developing countries.

### AUTONOMOUS CREDIT INSTITUTIONS

Specialized credit institutions supported by government funds boast several conspicuous advantages. Unless a country has progressed rather far in the process of development, the brunt of financing will probably have to be borne by the state. An impossible administrative load would be put on the conventional central government departments if the detailed administration of development projects, loans and grants were not delegated. The specialized bank or authority may foster professional expertness and *esprit de corps*. Furthermore, it is often able to cut across the conventional lines of government jurisdiction to expedite action; this was said to be one of the chief gains of the Damodar River Development Authority in India. On the other hand, though a certain degree of autonomy is desirable for these industrial banks, rural banks, development corporations, and the like, the central bank or national treasury must retain general control over their loans, investments and grants, not only through the power to refuse rediscounts or funds, but also through specific policy directives.[23] Moreover, the proliferation of special government corporations can lead to confusion and inefficiency; and they can become ridden with corruption.

### Experience with Special Credit Agencies

No point would be served by a lengthy review of these institutions. It will suffice to point out that experience with them has not always been fortunate. The Bell report on the Philippines found that the twenty-four government corporations had reached a sad state of ineffectiveness and proposed a reduction in their number and the establishment of a Philippine Development Corporation to hold the stock of all government corporations and to carry through a general housecleaning.[24] The widely known Nacional Financiera (National Finance Institution) of Mexico has been the largest source of funds for industrialization in that country, according to Mosk, but has failed to care for the needs of small firms and furthermore has not succeeded in educating the public to invest in industrial securities.[25] But the Nacional Financiera operates to better effect than do the hundreds of private Mexican *financiera*, which form an approximate analogue to United States investment banking houses. In the case of Iraq, the Interna-

---

23. Wallich (*op. cit.*, p. 298) recommends the establishment of these institutions for Cuba, only with this proviso.
24. The Bell Report, p. 67.
25. Mosk, *op. cit.*, pp. 253–55.

tional Bank has proposed extending the operations of the Industrial Bank by a substantial increase of its capital. In Brazil and Turkey similar institutions have already been established, and for Ceylon, the Bank has recommended that one be created.

The merits of the government-supported specialized corporation differ from country to country, relative to both central government lending and private underwriting. The case for the government-financed bank is probably strongest in agriculture, because of the tenuous financial resources of the small farmer or peasant; and most of the less developed countries have established such institutions.[26] There can be little doubt that, despite occasional weakness and failures, autonomous government corporations are destined to play a large role in future economic development of the less advanced countries. Some of these corporations are the outgrowth of recommendations by international advisory commissions and have drawn upon their well-informed personnel.[27]

CONCLUDING OBSERVATIONS

Financial measures taken by the state to promote economic development range from steps designed to further private enterprise in certain especially desirable lines of production to direct operation by the government. Development banks, even in the most liberal economies, will exercise some selection in the purposes of their loans, or in the types of loans which they underwrite. It is no far cry from this to the laying down and rationing of maximums on commercial bank loans for purposes regarded by the state as unessential, to discriminatory reserve requirements and to other sorts of selective credit controls. Tax exemption would seem to be more far reaching as a measure of favoring certain types of production because of its protracted duration. From this point, the range of variation to some form of socialism includes direct controls, such as material allocations and the rationing of finished products, state undertakings in the field of public utilities, the launching of new industries by the government itself, collectivization of agriculture and the nationalization of existing industries. All of these may, of course, exist side by side in the same economy, together with private enterprise.[28]

This inquiry into the domestic sources of capital for economic development has led through many complex matters: numerous institutions to

26. United Nations, *Land Reform—Defects in Agrarian Structure as Obstacles to Economic Development*, pp. 37–43 and 74–77.

27. This appears to be the case with the newly created National Bank for Economic Development in Brazil. See *New York Times*, July 11, 1952.

28. In connection with the present theme of financing, it may be worth while to observe that the sale of industries once they are established, following the pattern of Japanese industrialization, sets free the capital resources of the state, though not of the economy, for new projects.

increase voluntary saving; various direct compulsions; the gamut of tax and other revenue sources for capital formation by the state; and an array of institutions to transmit accumulated capital funds to actual use. In all of these problems of detail there are examples enough of superior and inferior ways of doing things.

It must be amply evident that there is no royal road to economic progress. The salvation of the millions whose lives are "poor, nasty, brutish and short" by reason of low incomes will not be achieved by a few brilliant insights or miraculous policies. If at all, it will come through the patient improvement of human institutions, including, in a prominent place, the domestic institutions of finance. Among the royal roads which have proved to be only detours is inflation. As the British economist Joan Robinson has pointed out, monetary expansion offers little or nothing to underdeveloped economies in which idle plant and equipment scarcely exist. Finally, a scrutiny of the problems of domestic finance suggests strongly that "technical assistance" should not be conceived solely in physical terms. Native intuition will no more supply good fiscal and financial practices than good strains of cattle or well-designed machines. The several "joint technical commissions" of creditor and borrower membership have supplied essential elements from both sides for good economic government in countries aspiring to development. This fact should be given wide recognition, as wide as the more obvious contributions of the physical sciences.

# 16. Financing Economic Development from Foreign Private Capital

DURING THE SEVEN AND A HALF YEARS from mid-1945 to the end of 1952, the United States government transferred nearly $41 billion in capital abroad, while private investment totaled about $5.5 billion. The combined total of $46.5 billion amounts to $6.2 billion annually, which represents in some ways a notable achievement.[1] But in the decade preceding the first world war, Great Britain made foreign investments at an annual rate of £150 million, which, as Sir Arthur Salter has pointed out, would equal $2 billion annually at price levels in the United States after World War II.[2] Had the United States sent capital abroad after 1945 at a comparable rate, it would have transferred annually $8 billion (allowing for the difference in populations) instead of $6.2 billion. And the $6.2 billion was, of course, reached only by an extraordinary effort at postwar reconstruction, the launching of international lending agencies and economic aid, whereas the British investment was largely private and spontaneous.

What has changed the scene so vastly? For a variety of reasons, much of the spirit has gone out of private international investment.

## OBSTACLES TO PRIVATE FOREIGN INVESTMENT

In part this decline of private foreign investment results simply from inadequate rates of return; but it has been due also to hostile ideas and ideologies, including Marxian doctrines, in the capital-poor nations. Thus the Colombo Plan is roundly condemned because it "deliberately" devotes so large a portion of planned expenditures to agriculture and a small portion to industries which, it is said, could compete with the output of the lenders. "It proves once again the Marxist contention that finance capital dominates the world."[3] Suspicion of foreign capital, particularly of direct investments, is sometimes linked with the conviction that developing countries need have no worries concerning a sufficiency of funds from abroad because the United States *must* export capital to prevent wholesale unem-

---

1. A substantial part of this sum merely replaced war damages to foreign productive capacity or sustained consumption during the reconstruction.

2. Sir Arthur Salter, *Foreign Investment* (Essays in International Finance, No. 12), Princeton University Press, Princeton, February 1951, p. 3. Conversion based on pound-dollar rate prevailing before 1914.

3. N. M. Perera, "Some Observations on the Colombo Plan," *Ceylon Economist*, February 1951, pp. 289-93.

ployment at home.[4] Xenophobia in economic matters sometimes keeps foreign investment out of such basic national projects as the utilities, railways and harbors, exactly where capital needs are most vital.[5] If private foreign capital is encouraged by the government of the borrowing country, the young nationalists accuse it and the foreign investors of being the stooges of colonialism and repression.[6] Among the peasants of the Near East, foreign investment in agricultural facilities may merely stiffen resistance to progress, because they believe the benefits accrue only to the landlords.[7] The political atmosphere of Guatemala currently is hostile to foreign capital and enterprise.

But a substantial number of cases could be cited of countries that welcome foreign private capital without any substantial reservations. The government of India has taken this position lately and its recent agreement with the Standard Vacuum Oil Company concerning the erection of refineries bears out its declarations.[8] Where American private investment in the underdeveloped world is greatest, the opposition seems to be least, that is, through most of Latin America. For example, it was reported to the United Nations Economic Commission for Latin America with respect to Venezuela that "in spite of the fact that it operates with foreign capital, the oil industry is national, not only in a geographic sense, but also by virtue of its economic effects on the country."[9] Thus ideological obstacles to foreign capital are by no means universal, but distinct impediments do exist in certain Latin American countries and in some of the newer republics of Southeast Asia.

The chief impediments to the flow of international investment, however, are to be found not on the demand but on the supply side. Of these, the greatest are the fear of expropriation of direct investments or default on bonds,[10] and fear of the suspension or delay of profit or interest remittances through moratoria or exchange controls. Misgivings as to the stability of governments pertain fundamentally to these two contingencies, which are

4. The present writer has observed that this attitude is widely held in Japan. H. C. Wallich's similar impressions in Cuba are reported in *Monetary Problems of an Export Economy: The Cuban Experience*, Harvard University Press, Cambridge, 1950, p. 26.

5. H. J. Dernburg, "Prospects for Long-Term Foreign Investment," *Harvard Business Review*, July 1950, p. 45.

6. V. L. Horoth, "Can Africa Replace Asia as a Source of Raw Materials?" *Magazine of Wall Street*, June 30, 1951, pp. 351–53 and 377–78.

7. Doreen Warriner, *Land and Poverty in the Middle East*, Royal Institute of International Affairs, London, 1948, p. 139.

8. "Government and Business—Agreement with the U.S. Oil Company," *Indian Finance*, December 15, 1951, p. 1025.

9. "The Boom That Never Burst," *The Economist*, June 28, 1952, pp. 901–06.

10. The defaults eventually proved to be less serious than sometimes imagined. Of the bonds issued by countries in the underdeveloped areas from 1920 to 1931, 40 per cent were not defaulted on; 45 per cent, though defaulted, have been refunded and are now serviced; and 15 per cent are still in default. See *Report to the President on Foreign Economic Policies*, Washington, November 10, 1950, p. 62 (hereafter called the Gray Report). But the psychological shock outlasts the defaults.

fatal to foreign investment, whether of the direct or portfolio kind. Furthermore, in contrast to the golden age of private investment before the first world war, the controlling stockholding interests cannot always be relied on to conduct the affairs of the firm equitably for foreign bondholders. Geographic proximity to the U.S.S.R. and its spheres of influence is a factor that makes a region unattractive to the private investor. In the creditor countries much capital is concentrated in institutions such as life insurance companies, investment trusts and savings banks, which cannot appropriately or cannot legally take the risks of foreign investment. One of the great potential capital-exporting countries, the United States, is still itself undergoing rapid development, and returns on domestic investment are very attractive.

In addition, *direct* investment in plant and equipment is subject to certain further risks, among which export and import quotas, multiple exchange rates and exchange controls, and extensive government regulation probably head the list. Foreign owners of plant may be the object of discrimination or of special requirements: to pay special taxes, to hire a certain quota of native employees, to reinvest certain proportions of profits, etc. Foreign participation in ownership may at times be limited to a minority share.[11] Finally, there may be general factors in the economic setting which are unfavorable—such as a shortage of trained personnel, inadequacy of the basic utilities, uncongenial business laws or business ethics, high taxation, inflation and the like.

Because most of these risks arise fundamentally out of the absence of international government or at least of an enforced code of international law, they are nothing new. But by contrast with the era of international investment extending over the half century preceding the first world war, they appeared with sudden intensity in the Great Depression and its aftermath. The results have been to eliminate portfolio investment almost completely and to reduce the total volume of private investment.

Moreover, the protective tariff policy of the United States has worked indirectly but powerfully against her overseas private investment. High protection in one of the world's greatest markets has made it more difficult for other countries to earn dollars. And this, in turn, has led to legal limitations on the transfer of profits and to inconvertibility of currencies, both of which deter investment from abroad.

RELATIVE POSITIONS OF PORTFOLIO AND DIRECT INVESTMENT

The virtual disappearance of portfolio investment is not explicable on the basis of greater risk than direct investment. Typically, the reverse is

11. See League of Nations, Economic and Financial Organization, *Conditions of Private Foreign Investment*, Columbia University Press, New York, 1946; and United Nations, Economic and Social Council, *Survey of Policies Affecting Private Foreign Investment* (mimeographed), New York, February 1950.

true, for foreign manufacture is exposed to all the hazards of investment in bonds together with a whole set of additional risks. But the bond buyer usually wants safety, and this quality melted away rapidly in the 1930s and has not yet been restored. Foreign investment was left to the professional risk-bearer—the entrepreneur—who for sufficiently high profits takes a calculated risk in establishing foreign plants. Furthermore, direct investment abroad has several distinct advantages over producing within the United

TABLE 16-1. NET MOVEMENTS OF PRIVATE LONG-TERM UNITED STATES CAPITAL, 1946–1952

(*Millions*)

| Year | Total Capital Outflow[a] | Direct | Portfolio | Reinvested Earnings | Net Additions in Underdeveloped Areas[b] |
|------|------|------|------|------|------|
| 1946 | $   59 | $183 | −$124 | $303 | $266 |
| 1947 | 810 | 724 | 86 | 387 | 845 |
| 1948 | 748 | 684 | 64 | 581 | 832 |
| 1949 | 796 | 786 | 10 | 436 | 818 |
| 1950 | 1,168 | 702 | 466 | 443 | 504 |
| 1951 | 963 | 604 | 359 | 703 | 629 |
| 1952 | 973 | 830 | 143 | 750[c] | d |

Sources: *Survey of Current Business*, December 1951, p. 12; June 1952, p. 21; September 1952, p. 8; and June 1953, p. 4.

a. Includes direct and indirect investment but not reinvested earnings.
b. Includes reinvested earnings.
c. Estimated from information in National Advisory Council on International Monetary and Financial Problems, *Semiannual Report to the President and to the Congress*, March 31, 1953, p. 5.
d. Not available.

States for export. Firms are able to escape the import duties, quotas and licenses which repress their markets as exporters, to manufacture under local brand names and thus to build up "good will," and frequently to produce more cheaply. These considerations apply to direct investment which caters to the foreign *domestic* market. For the foreign direct investor in *export* industries, the prime consideration is and always has been the availability of a natural resource, a consideration which seems likely to increase greatly in importance for the United States.[12]

### Implications of Shift to Direct Investment

Over the seven-year period 1946–1952 United States portfolio investment averaged $143.4 million annually as against $644.7 million for direct investment. (See Table 16-1.) Over the decade 1919–1929, by contrast, portfolio investment averaged $650 million and direct investment $350 million.[13]

12. See The President's Materials Policy Commission, *Resources for Freedom*, Vol. I, *Foundations for Growth and Security*, June 1952.
13. Milton Abelson, "Private United States Direct Investments Abroad," *Survey of Current Business*, November 1949, pp. 18–23.

What will this reversal of the roles of portfolio and direct investment, if it continues, mean for underdeveloped countries? Since public utilities have sometimes been financed by private or state bond issues but seldom by direct investment, capital from either domestic or foreign government or international agencies must now assume the burden of supplying the wherewithal for these basic prerequisites of development.[14] Another disadvantage of private direct investment is its current tendency to concentrate on petroleum. In the past, this concentration was less conspicuous. In 1945, for example, petroleum accounted for considerably less private direct investment abroad than did manufacturing industries and for not very much more than public utilities or mining and smelting. By 1950, however, petroleum investment nearly equaled manufacturing investment and had far outstripped public utilities and mining and smelting. (See Table 16-2.)

In terms of its distribution among industries, American business investment has by no means shown the "exploitative" nature which has sometimes been ascribed to it. In 1945, extractive industries formed only 31 per cent of the total investment; and manufacturing, public utilities and agriculture, presumably the backbone of economic progress for the borrowing economy, absorbed 54 per cent. This type of investment was heavily concentrated in North and South America. But from 1946 to 1950, the petroleum industry took just under 49 per cent of private American direct investments and reinvestments in foreign countries. An intensifying of geographic concentration in specific countries has accompanied this recent tendency of petroleum to dominate direct investment.

Against these drawbacks of direct investment relative to portfolio investment stand several noteworthy advantages for underdeveloped regions. Direct investment induces the reinvestment of earnings, while portfolio investment probably has a negligible influence in this direction. Reinvested earnings were equivalent to 80 per cent of the net outflow of private direct investment in the years 1946–1952 and made up approximately 42 per cent of the net addition to United States direct investments abroad during 1946–1950. Of course, a large part of this reinvestment might not take place if the withdrawal of earnings were not so widely subject to severe exchange controls. Direct investment undoubtedly also helps further the transfer of techniques, particularly business and managerial techniques, to underdeveloped countries. Finally, since the economic return to direct investment occurs in the form of profits instead of fixed interest charges on bonds or dividends on stocks, which corporations usually attempt to maintain despite adversities, it helps the primary producing countries to weather depressions.

14. Indeed, the net movement of foreign private direct investment into public utilities has recently been negative. See Table 16-2.

*Approaches to Economic Development*

TABLE 16-2. NET ADDITIONS TO PRIVATE UNITED STATES DIRECT
INVESTMENTS ABROAD, 1946–1950[a]

(*Millions*)

| Area or Industry | Total Value as of December 31, 1945 | Net Additions During | | | | | Total Value as of December 31, 1950 |
|---|---|---|---|---|---|---|---|
| | | 1946 | 1947 | 1948 | 1949 | 1950 | |
| | | | By Area | | | | |
| Total | $8,369 | $485 | $1,111 | $1,241 | $1,212 | $1,132 | $13,550 |
| Canada | 2,527 | 136 | 143 | 290 | 263 | 491 | 3,850 |
| American republics | 2,999 | 147 | 559 | 528 | 565 | 267 | 5,065 |
| ERP countries | 1,689 | 79 | 119 | 132 | 114 | 139 | 2,272 |
| ERP dependencies | 264 | 27 | 101 | 107 | 65 | −3 | 561 |
| Other Europe | 329 | 4 | 4 | −13 | 17 | 8 | 349 |
| All other countries | 561 | 92 | 185 | 197 | 188 | 230 | 1,453 |
| | | | By Industry | | | | |
| Total | $8,369 | $485 | $1,111 | $1,241 | $1,212 | $1,132 | $13,550 |
| Petroleum | 1,538 | 231 | 577 | 635 | 683 | 408 | 4,072 |
| Manufacturing[b] | 2,671 | 183 | 317 | 380 | 280 | 411 | 4,242 |
| Distribution | 671 | 69 | 78 | 103 | 56 | 88 | 1,065 |
| Mining and smelting | 1,064 | −2 | 47 | 31 | 78 | 106 | 1,324 |
| Agriculture[c] | 518 | 27 | 40 | 56 | 10 | 3 | 654 |
| Public utilities | 1,357 | −80 | −9 | 20 | 20 | 30 | 1,338 |
| Miscellaneous | 550 | 57 | 61 | 16 | 85 | 86 | 855 |

Sources: *Survey of Current Business*, January 1951, p. 22, and December 1951, p. 13, as reported by Gardner Patterson and Jack N. Behrman, *Survey of United States International Finance, 1951*, Princeton University Press, Princeton, 1952, p. 116.

a. The small differences between "net additions" and the sum of "net outflows" plus "reinvested earnings," as given elsewhere in the *Survey, 1951*, is due to "other factors," including some allowance for revaluation of assets due to changes in exchange rates.

b. Includes paper and pulp enterprises.

c. Includes fishing enterprises.

## Net Decline in Private Capital

Weighing the gains against the adverse aspects would be difficult indeed if the shift to direct investment had involved merely a change of proportions in a constant total. Unfortunately, however, the shift has actually meant the disappearance of portfolio investment without a sufficient increase in direct investment to maintain earlier levels of American foreign private investment. The annual average of total private investment of $788.1 million for 1946–1952 falls sadly below the annual average of

$1 billion for 1919–1929.[15] If the figure for 1919–1929 is adjusted to the price level of 1948, the annual average becomes $1.62 billion,[16] which is twice the rate for the later years of 1946–1952.

But is the decline in private international investment really to be lamented, in view of the many charges which have been leveled against "finance capitalism" in the underdeveloped regions, and in view also of the present-day alternatives of loans and investments originating with governments and international organizations? One particularly insistent complaint is that private capital involves excessive costs. There can be no doubt that, relative to its earnings in the United States, foreign private capital brings high returns in the underdeveloped areas. Direct investment in such areas yielded considerably higher returns in nearly all sectors in1945–1948. (See Table 16-3.) But high rates of return do not necessarily mean excessive profits, as shown by the reluctance of private capital to enter the international investment field. The risks of such investment are not simply the product of morbid capitalist fantasy. And if the risks are not assumed by private capitalists but by a national government or international lending agency, they devolve ultimately upon the taxpayers of creditor countries.

Private capital probably encounters more formidable problems in certain countries because of legal and *de facto* complications for the ownership and management of foreign firms than does capital from foreign government or international sources. Sometimes the native population is less suspicious of foreign governments than of private firms; but more often it is the other way around since government loans usually have political implications. Private capital has betrayed a notorious penchant to follow the waves of prosperity and depression of the creditor countries, a fact set forth lucidly a decade ago.[17] The sensitivity of primary producing countries is already great because of their export-based economies; they can ill afford to become still more vulnerable to foreign-induced booms and depressions by an intensifying movement in capital accounts.

Finally, because private capital naturally seeks the optimum combination of safety and yields, it has a perverse tendency, from the viewpoint of countries standing low in the scale of economic advancement, to move first into the stronger regions and the more solid and lucrative industries. At the end of 1945, Canada had the lion's share proportionally to population; Latin America came next; and the entire Asian and African continents drew less than 10 per cent of American private direct investments.[18] By the end of 1950, this share had risen to 15 per cent; but this gave cold comfort to

15. Both figures refer to new transfers, i.e., they exclude reinvested profits.

16. See Dernburg, *loc. cit.*, p. 48.

17. Hal B. Lary, *The United States in the World Economy* (Economic Series No. 23), U.S. Department of Commerce, Bureau of Foreign and Domestic Economy, 1943.

18. See Table 16-2. The addition of portfolio investment would make these disparities still more marked.

## TABLE 16-3. RATIO OF EARNINGS TO BOOK VALUE OF PRIVATE U.S. FOREIGN DIRECT INVESTMENTS IN DEVELOPED AND UNDERDEVELOPED AREAS AND IN THE UNITED STATES, 1945–1948

(Per Cent)

| Year | Total Investment | Manufacturing | Distribution | Agriculture | Mining and Smelting | Petroleum | Public Utilities | Miscellaneous |
|---|---|---|---|---|---|---|---|---|
| Underdeveloped Areas | | | | | | | | |
| 1945 | 11.5 | 12.1 | 12.3 | 15.0 | 8.3 | 19.5 | 3.8 | 12.9 |
| 1946 | 14.3 | 14.7 | 21.1 | 15.5 | 9.5 | 23.8 | 3.6 | 19.8 |
| 1947 | 18.1 | 16.8 | 16.8 | 17.3 | 12.9 | 31.5 | 3.8 | 21.0 |
| 1948 | 17.8 | 19.7 | 20.1 | 12.9 | 17.8 | 32.2 | 1.8 | 16.5 |
| Developed Areas | | | | | | | | |
| 1945 | 7.2 | 10.0 | 9.2 | 2.0 | 5.5 | 2.0 | 4.6 | 4.7 |
| 1946 | 10.1 | 13.7 | 14.2 | 1.8 | 7.4 | 5.4 | 3.9 | 5.1 |
| 1947 | 12.4 | 17.0 | 12.5 | 8.9 | 9.8 | 8.3 | 4.6 | 6.5 |
| 1948 | 14.2 | 20.4 | 14.9 | .. | 6.5 | 11.0 | 3.7 | 7.1 |
| United States | | | | | | | | |
| 1945 | 7.7 | 9.6 | 11.0 | .. | 8.0 | 8.9 | 5.0 | 8.0 |
| 1946 | 9.1 | 12.3 | 22.0 | .. | 9.6 | 10.8 | 4.8 | 7.7 |
| 1947 | 12.0 | 17.3 | 18.8 | .. | 15.9 | 16.0 | 5.6 | 7.5 |
| 1948 | 13.8 | 18.1 | 17.9 | .. | 15.6 | 22.7 | 6.7 | 8.8 |

*Source:* H. J. Dernburg, "Prospects for Long-Term Foreign Investment," *Harvard Business Review*, July 1950, pp. 41–51.
Note: Those investments in which the earnings could not be transferred because of foreign exchange restrictions were excluded.

most of the underdeveloped world, since a substantial part of the new capital and reinvested earnings poured into the four or five chief petroleum-producing countries. Public utilities and agriculture, the foundations of development in the most needy economies, claimed only 22 per cent of American private direct investment in 1945 and had receded still further to less than 15 per cent by the end of 1950.

### Advantages of Private Investment

Private capital has its merits, however. For one thing, and this probably supplies the chief motive of the original proclamation of the Point Four program in terms of private capital, it takes some of the burden from the taxpayers' shoulders—no small consideration in view of present defense expenditures. If private capital shies away from some of the basic fields for development, it nevertheless exploits the immediately productive lines of investment and it would be difficult to dispense with these contributions to the current product of underdeveloped economies. Private capital investment, being nowadays in the foreign field almost altogether direct investment, brings with it managerial and technical talents not adhering to public capital. The significance of what has been called "private Point Four" has not been adequately recognized in most discussions.[19] Most importantly, private capital moves on a sound business basis of mutual profit—without involving moral problems concerning the duty of a creditor country to supply capital. It therefore provides a firmer foundation for long-run economic relations than does public capital. Last but not least, despite its decline from the heyday of the 1920s, new private American capital plus reinvested earnings has shown a surprisingly large ratio to the principal allocations of public moneys to the underdeveloped areas. In short, private capital is indispensable.

The tendency of private capital to seek the best profit opportunities can be compensated for only by general measures to raise the productivity of the most underdeveloped countries and the most ailing departments of production. But this therapy may require many years to show pronounced effects; meanwhile, the poorest economies may require a blood transfusion in the form of grants and loans of foreign public funds. Another of the characteristics of private international investment—that it flourishes in prosperity and withers in depression when most needed by the borrowing countries—can be mastered only by preconcerted schemes, national and international, to stabilize economic activity. In this the United States bears a heavy weight of responsibility. It would be difficult to believe that this perversity cannot be successfully compensated or eliminated.

19. See Jerome B. Cohen, "Private Point Four in Japan," *Fortune*, April 1953, pp. 148–49.

### MEASURES TO PROMOTE PRIVATE INVESTMENT

Because the supply of capital is sometimes among the immediate factors limiting development, and because it will remain so despite national government and international agency loans, policies designed to stimulate private investment in the underdeveloped areas are urgently needed.

#### TAX INCENTIVES FOR FOREIGN INVESTMENT[20]

Tax measures to stimulate private investment from abroad fall into two categories according to whether they aim merely to eliminate adverse discrimination against foreign (mostly direct) investment income, or seek to secure positive favorable discrimination through lower tax rates. The chief creditor countries have already progressed far toward realizing the first objective through eliminating double taxation on foreign income. Some countries simply ignore income from this source, while others, including the United States, give credit for taxes paid abroad. To prevent complete evasion of taxes through the crediting device requires, however, a tax convention between the two governments concerned. Since 1939, the executive branch of the United States government has pressed forward the negotiation of these conventions, though Congress has often long delayed ratification.[21] In addition to the tax credit, foreign investment earnings of subsidiaries are taxed only when remitted to the United States, so that reinvestment abroad incurs no liability for United States taxes; and net losses are deductible. Furthermore, American citizens resident abroad are exempt from the federal personal income tax.[22]

The administration of tax credits could be made more liberal by allowing foreign losses to be offset against domestic profits, applying the credit to cases in which the American corporation owns less than a majority share of the stock, extending the same tax privileges to foreign branches as to foreign subsidiaries, and—for personal taxation—allowing for foreign death duties and shortening the period required to establish foreign residence.[23] But such measures have only a marginal influence on the decision

---

20. For the special privileges extended to United States foreign investors in the Western Hemisphere, see United Nations, Department of Economic Affairs, *United States Income Taxation of Private United States Investment in Latin America*, New York, 1953.

21. Tax exemption conventions existed with eleven countries up to July 1, 1953—Canada, Denmark, France, Ireland, the Netherlands, New Zealand, Norway, Sweden, Switzerland, the Union of South Africa and the United Kingdom. Negotiations with Colombia, Israel and Uruguay have not yet resulted in the signing of conventions, and these negotiations have not been mentioned in the State Department *Bulletin* for at least a year. Conventions with Finland and Greece have been ratified but not yet entered into force. Ratification of a convention with Belgium is pending. See Gardner Patterson and Jack N. Behrman, *Survey of United States International Finance, 1951*, Princeton University Press, Princeton, 1952, pp. 86, 87 and Appendix, Table IX; Gardner Patterson and J. M. Gunn, *Survey of United States International Finance, 1952*, Princeton University Press, Princeton, 1953, pp. 119–20.

22. U.S. Department of State, *Point Four*, Publication 3719, January 1950, pp. 69–71.

23. *Ibid.*, pp. 70–71; "Point Four: A Re-examination of Ways and Means," *Yale Law Journal*, June 1950, p. 1294. Some of these measures were recommended to Congress by President Truman.

whether or not to invest abroad, or to live abroad, possibly as a technical consultant in an underdeveloped country.

Going much further than the elimination of adverse discrimination, the National Foreign Trade Council has recommended the complete exemption of foreign-earned income from American taxation.[24] This proposal is somewhat less extreme than the words may suggest because the United States already gives credit for taxes paid abroad. The proposal means specifically that the Treasury would lose the revenue it now derives from the *difference* in business taxes abroad, where rates are generally lower, and the tax in the United States. But the proposal has generally met with strenuous objections on the score of equity, that it would favor first the American firm which invests abroad, and second the large corporation, which more probably possesses foreign branches than the small concern. In order to avoid discrimination, moreover, already existing investment abroad would have to be included, but this exemption from taxes would serve no useful purpose. Along with the proposal that the government guarantee foreign investments against certain significant risks, this measure raises the general issue concerning overt or concealed subsidies. Tax exemption is a particularly distasteful form of subsidy and it is not likely to evoke the enthusiasm of national legislatures.

### INVESTMENT TREATIES

The possibility of double taxation in some cases or of unfavorable tax discrimination pales into relative insignificance as a deterrent to foreign private investment compared with the various direct restrictions frequently imposed on businesses by foreign governments. The *risk* of imposition may be as constraining as the actual fact. These restrictions are numerous, but they can be put in six main categories.[25] (1) Foreign firms may be denied entry into certain lines of production because they are "strategic" or regarded as especially suitable for domestic enterprise; or foreign ownership may be restricted to a minority share. (2) The conduct of business may be subjected to stipulations that a certain number of the employees be nationals, and that all employment be subject to the local minimum-wage laws and other types of welfare legislation. These benefits to employees sometimes appear to be excessive. (3) Maximum rates of earnings are occasionally set for foreign businesses, and steeply progressive taxes on profits or excess profits seem sometimes chiefly designed to catch the foreign concern. (4) Still more deadly to foreign investment are the limits imposed by exchange controls on the transfer of earnings or of capital

24. National Foreign Trade Council, *Private Enterprise and the Point Four Program*, New York, May 1949.

25. The sixfold division follows that of the article in the *Yale Law Journal* cited above, pp. 1304–11, with some amplification.

sums. (5) Equally serious is the threat of nationalization, expropriation or the establishment of directly competitive undertakings by the state. (6) Finally come a number of involved questions pertaining to the jurisdiction of the local courts and the status of the foreign investor before the law.

It has several times been proposed to deal with these restrictions, at least so far as they seem discriminatory, by international multilateral agreements.[26] But the complexities of multilateral negotiation have thus far prevented action. Meanwhile, since the end of World War II, the United States has proceeded with bilateral negotiations in order to modernize its treaties of Friendship, Commerce and Navigation, some of which originated a century or more ago, and to establish them where none existed previously. As the Princeton survey points out, however, progress on this program has been retarded by the growth of nationalism, particularly in the newly developing countries; by the lack of any assurance for the foreign country that it would obtain capital from the United States even after the conclusion of a treaty; and by the general realization abroad that foreign capital enjoys nondiscriminatory treatment in this country even without a treaty.[27]

The treaty with Uruguay[28] has frequently been regarded as a model. Nationals and companies of the United States are accorded free entry into and equal treatment in practically all lines of production with few exceptions, several of which, such as resource exploration and air transport, can be ascribed to the inability of the United States to grant reciprocal rights. In certain other cases which preclude equal treatment, most-favored-nation treatment is granted. American companies are not limited in the hiring of personnel, may not be subjected to higher taxes than local businesses, and have the same access to the courts and the same property rights. The treaty contains a "development clause" stipulating that neither party shall be impeded in obtaining "on equitable terms the capital, skills, modern technology and equipment it needs for economic development." In case of nationalization, a business is to be given prompt and just compensation; and the transfer of earnings and capital in dollars is assured save for the emergency imposition of exchange control by either party to give priority to "goods and services essential to the health and welfare of its people."

26. For example, the Havana Charter for an International Trade Organization, April 1948; Ninth International Conference of American States, Bogota, Colombia, May 1948; code proposed by the International Chamber of Commerce, cited below, in footnote 29.

27. Gardner Patterson and Jack N. Behrman, *Survey of United States International Finance, 1950*, Princeton University Press, Princeton, 1951, p. 114, and *Survey, 1951*, p. 87. See *Survey, 1951*, p. 309 for a convenient list of Friendship, Commerce and Navigation treaties by date of their becoming effective, including two in 1948, two in 1949, but none in 1950 or 1951. Others have been signed but not yet ratified by the legislatures. The only major negotiations in 1952 were with Japan, and the only new agreement signed was a protocol to the 1934 treaty with Finland. Treaties with Poland and Hungary were terminated. Patterson and Gunn, *Survey, 1952*, pp. 119 and 173.

28. As of September 1954 not yet ratified by the Uruguayan General Assembly.

More inclusive rights than those embodied in the proposed Uruguayan treaty have sometimes been demanded, as for example: complete freedom of entry for foreign capital into any industry; an unqualified commitment to transfer in dollars earnings, capital and compensation for nationalization; or at the least a qualification only for exchange priority for food, shelter and medical supplies; reimbursement for adverse effects of government competition and the like.[29] But the wisdom of these demands is questionable.

While it is doubtless in the interest of developing countries to admit foreign capital to most spheres of economic activity, preclusive regulations in favor of domestic capital may in some cases be warranted. Whether they are or not, it would be difficult or impossible to deny this prerogative to foreign governments. Unqualified, or virtually first-priority, commitments to transfer foreign earnings and capital in hard currencies may be next to impossible to fulfill in certain adverse circumstances; they could entail setbacks to economic development in underdeveloped areas incompatible with the proclaimed purposes of United States policy. For the same reason, American business abroad cannot expect immunity from steeply progressive taxation, social service charges or government competition; indeed, it cannot be assured of such immunities even in the United States.

It is reasonable to expect the American government to seek to gain as broad a field of entry for American capital as possible, and to insist on national and nondiscriminatory treatment once it is admitted. It is unreasonable to expect that underdeveloped countries will admit foreign capital to all fields, or accord it better than national treatment. It is reasonable to obtain pledges of transferability of capital, but not without reservation for emergency periods if they are not chronically protracted. Finally, it is reasonable to seek the negotiation of investment treaties with potential debtor countries but unreasonable to prescribe by law that no United States aid will be forthcoming until such a treaty is consummated, as the Herter Bill proposed. To employ the power of the purse as a bargaining weapon, even in defense of commercial principles of the highest type, would engender resentment and increase the likelihood that the treaty would be circumvented. It has been very wisely stated that "such treaties are invaluable if they reflect an already formed intention on the part of underdeveloped countries to welcome the aid of American private capital. . . . They are the second and not the first step in the creation of a favorable climate."[30]

29. See the "Herter Bill," H.R. 6026, introduced by Representative Herter on August 17, 1949; International Chamber of Commerce, *International Code of Fair Treatment for Foreign Investments* (Brochure 129), New York, 1949; National Foreign Trade Council, *op. cit.*

30. William A. Brown, "Treaty, Guaranty, and Tax Inducements for Foreign Investments," *American Economic Review, Proceedings*, May 1950, p. 492.

## GOVERNMENT GUARANTEES OF FOREIGN INVESTMENTS

In the past, private investment from abroad has been nurtured by government guarantees against default of individual firms. But nowadays the default of *firms* has declined in significance as portfolio investment has assumed a constantly smaller role; and as direct investment has increased, so have the risks peculiar to it. The latter-day risks for foreign businesses are, perhaps not surprisingly, the risks of foreign *government* action which may adversely affect the situation. When the disturbing factor shifts from the foreign firm to the foreign government, the latter inevitably loses caste as a guarantor; the American investor then looks to his own government for help. What he most fears are, first, the nationalization, expropriation or extensive regulation of his business and, second, the inconvertibility of his earnings or capital into his own currency. Ordinary business risks, including even the default of foreign firms, do not nowadays enter into the discussion of guarantees. Times have changed.

If the foreign investor could be relieved of these two great risks of expropriation and inconvertibility, private foreign investment might again assume an importance comparable to the days before the first world war. Indeed, in view of the great movement toward economic development, there might be prospects of an even greater field for investment abroad.

The government of the United States has taken a few hesitant steps toward foreign investment guarantees; but obstacles and complications are nearly endless.[31] The Economic Cooperation Administration (later the Foreign Operations Administration) was given authority to extend guarantees to stipulated total amounts. But until 1951 the guarantees pertained only to new investments in countries participating in the Organization for European Economic Cooperation and they still do not include devaluation risks.[32] These limitations and the relative novelty of the measure have prevented its use to any significant extent. The Administration sought, both in 1949 and 1950, to secure congressional authorization of guarantee powers for the Export-Import Bank specifically for the "improvement and growth

31. Yuan-li Wu, "Government Guarantees and Private Foreign Investment," *American Economic Review*, March 1950, pp. 61–73; Raymond F. Mikesell, *United States Economic Policy and International Relations*, McGraw-Hill, New York, 1952; "Point Four: A Re-examination of Ways and Means," *Yale Law Journal*, June 1950; Brown, *loc. cit.*; Salter, *op. cit.*

32. The maximum figures were $300 million, $150 million and $200 million in the E.C.A. acts of 1948, 1949 and 1950. The Mutual Security acts of 1951 and 1952 continued the $200 million maximum but opened the way to guarantees for underdeveloped countries by extending the geographic limits to include any area in which assistance was authorized by the Mutual Security Program.

During 1952 there were only eight new guarantees, totaling $5.9 million. As of March 31, 1953, 46 industrial investment guarantees, totaling $39.6 million, had been issued. Of this sum, $38 million was insurance against inconvertibility of foreign receipts and $1.6 million insurance against loss from expropriation or confiscation. All countries for whom aid is authorized under the Mutual Security Act of 1951, as amended, are eligible, but so far Turkey is the only non-European recipient. As of March 31, 1953, there had been no disbursements and $696,000 had been collected in fees. Cf. Patterson and Behrman, *Survey, 1950*, pp. 107–09; and *Survey, 1951*, pp. 84–86; Patterson and Gunn, *Survey, 1952*, pp. 118–19; National Advisory Council on International Monetary and Financial Problems, *Semiannual Report to the President and to the Congress*, March 31, 1953, p. 16.

of underdeveloped areas"; but no legislation appeared and in 1951 the President omitted mention of investment guarantees.[33]

The International Bank also has the power to guarantee private loans and investments; but the requirement of a guarantee by the government of the capital-importing country, the expense of the operation to the borrower and other barriers have thus far prevented its use.[34]

### Problems Inherent in Guarantees

Guarantees by national governments hold forth considerable promise but a number of objections on principle cannot be ignored. No practical purpose would be served by including already existing investments in the underwriting, and yet they would encounter a type of unfair competition from the new guaranteed ventures. American business interests have shown faint enthusiasm for guarantees, possibly because the government would require access to corporation records and possibly because the guarantees might involve extensive regulation of overseas operations. From a more general viewpoint, misgivings have been expressed, even in a United Nations report, that guarantees by creditor countries might lead to an atrophy of incentive on the part of the borrowing countries to establish conditions in their own economies favorable to foreign investment.[35]

Other difficulties may arise from the fact that creditor countries will scarcely be inclined to underwrite private foreign investments unless guarantees are forthcoming from the capital-importing countries. Thus concern for future flows of private capital for development did not prevent the Second Committee of the United Nations General Assembly from adopting, with the United States casting the sole opposing vote, the Uruguay resolution calling upon member states "to respect the right of each country to nationalize and freely exploit its natural wealth." An amendment to provide just compensation in case of nationalization was rejected.[36]

In order to make the execution of a guarantee manageable if occasion should arise, the debtor country may take a precautionary measure in simply excluding foreign private capital from certain domestic fields; and this works counter to the real aim of guarantees. Fulfillment of convertibility guarantees may impose sudden distortions of trade for underdeveloped countries if the guarantee extends to capital withdrawal (in contrast to gradual amortization). And, as Yuan-li Wu also points out as a representative of the borrowers' viewpoint, guarantees may invite interfer-

33. Detailed provisions under present legislation appear in the *Investment Guaranty Manual*, Mutual Security Administration, June 1952.

34. Salter, *op. cit.*, p. 43.

35. United Nations, Department of Economic Affairs, *Methods of Financing Economic Development in Under-developed Countries*, New York, 1949, p. 34.

36. Patterson and Gunn, *Survey, 1952*, pp. 122–23.

ence by creditor countries in the domestic affairs of the capital-importing country.[37]

Quite aside from matters of principle, however, vexing problems of definition complicate the question of investment guarantees. If, for example, firms are to be protected against expropriation, at what point do high tax rates amount to confiscation? Does a government-owned or government-subsidized competitive undertaking virtually mean expropriation sometimes? If the guarantee is made good in a particular case, how shall the business be valued as a going concern for the purpose of reimbursement? Does the guarantee of investment imply a right to withdraw the capital even if the foreign government has imposed no adverse measures; and if so, does it mean immediate liquidation or only gradual withdrawal? Should guarantees apply only to the original foreign-exchange investment or extend also to subsequent increases of capital through reinvested earnings?

Equally as many difficulties surround the problem of conversion of funds into the home currency of the lender or investor. At what rate of exchange shall the reimbursement be calculated? If the foreign country has devalued after much of the investment has been made, marked windfalls or losses could accrue to the foreign owner depending upon the relation of the devaluation to the behavior of the price of capital equipment in the devalued currency. Multiple export and import rates present further complexities. Finally, if the creditor country comes into possession of large amounts of a soft currency from the operation of its guarantee system, how can it utilize them to avoid "bear" movements on this currency, use them effectively for its own purposes, and expend them without favoritism among foreign suppliers of exports?

An important question relates to the inclusiveness of the guarantee as to type of investment. Shall the United States underwrite, for example, an American-owned amusement concession or a luxury hotel, or shall only "developmental" or "productive" investments be covered? It is clear also that a line must be drawn on the recency of investment, since otherwise the guaranteeing government would find itself underwriting mere current trade credits. The setting of the guarantee fee would surely present difficulties because of the unpredictability of many risks, some of them arising from the downfall of governments, depressions and wars.

The manifold complications of investment guarantees by national governments or international agencies need not mean that the idea is ill-conceived. They do, however, imply that any system must be elaborated with great care, and that experimentation is desirable at the beginning. It is necessary also to bear in mind that wisdom cannot consist merely in

37. Yuan-li Wu, *loc. cit.*, pp. 65–68.

limiting the coverage of guarantees, for the more limited the guarantee, the less it will influence the private investor to commit his capital abroad, particularly to new and underdeveloped countries. It must not be forgotten either that these guarantees do not eliminate the risks of investment but merely transfer their cost from the investor to the general taxpayer. Guarantees are not an open sesame enabling underdeveloped nations to draw upon the vast yearly capital accumulation of such a country as the United States; but they can play a useful role in conjunction with tax measures and treaties designed to reduce adverse discrimination against foreign capital.

## Maffry's Proposals

In a recent official report, August Maffry offers a long list of extraordinary measures and radical inducements to increase the flow of private capital.[38] He believes that great emphasis should be put on promoting American portfolio investment in Europe and Japan as areas much better understood than others by our private capitalists; Europeans and Japanese would then send venture capital to Asia, Africa and Latin America.

Mr. Maffry would press vigorously the program of bilateral treaties for the fair treatment of American foreign investors. He advances a large number of proposals for reorganizing federal government activities in Washington and in the consular and diplomatic service to encourage private investment. In addition he offers several specific financial inducements: (1) The Export-Import Bank should "aggressively extend its activities" by making loans on attractive terms to domestic corporations for their foreign operations, and lending to foreign corporations *without guarantees* by their governments. (2) "Tangible inducements" should be offered to secure the establishment of private international mutual investment trusts and to induce the purchase of foreign securities by investment trusts and insurance companies in this country. (3) Congress should extend the coverage of the investment guarantees to include losses from wars and civil disorders; and it should drastically reduce the cost of the guarantees. (4) The Treasury and the executive branch should explore the possibility of tax exemptions for qualified corporations operating anywhere in the free world, possibly after the pattern of present exemptions granted to Western Hemisphere trade corporations. Tax exemptions could be offered to private and institutional purchasers of foreign securities.

Mr. Maffry's proposal for seeking to make of Western Europe and Japan a kind of financial entrepôt of American private capital on its way to the underdeveloped countries has attractive qualities. Likewise his ideas seem promising with regard to more effective coordination and more vigorous

38. August Maffry, *Program for Increasing Private Investment in Foreign Countries* (mimeographed), report prepared for Technical Cooperation Administration (Department of State), Department of Commerce, and Mutual Security Agency, December 18, 1952.

activity in departments of government concerned with gathering and disseminating information about foreign investment opportunities.

But many of his proposals involving especially attractive lending, "tangible inducements" and tax exemptions to promote private foreign investment run into the overriding objection against most "incentive taxation."
If corporations making new investments abroad are to be the objects of
favorable discriminations, why not also give tax relief in varying degrees
for corporations that maintain "full" employment through depressions, or
show excellent records of labor relations or of public service, or refrain
from monopolistic practices, and so on? Once begun, discrimination can
endanger equity and objectivity in tax matters; it can corrupt politics; and
it is no friend of a market-controlled free enterprise economy. Fortunately
the principal tax adviser to the Secretary of the Treasury has said that
expectations of a tremendous outflow of American private capital associated with hopes of extensive tax exemptions will prove to be illusory.[39]

*Conclusions*

Tax, treaty and guarantee methods of encouraging private investment for
development offer promising channels, but they cannot be carried much
further and their quantitative effect is probably not large. Several of
Maffry's proposals deserve further exploration. In addition, codes of fair
business practice and the limitation of monopoly power in the international
sphere, such as contemplated in the proposal for an International Trade
Organization, would seem to be a desirable complement. The proposal for
an International Finance Corporation, closely linked with the International
Bank for Reconstruction and Development, also merits attention for its
possibilities in furthering private foreign investment.

Meanwhile, the encouragement of private sources of capital by the
underdeveloped world depends in large measure upon how these countries
govern their own affairs. It may well be that specific measures in the fields
of taxes, treaties and guarantees are less important means of attracting
foreign private capital than more fundamental measures to improve the
general climate for private enterprise. An economist sympathetic to underdeveloped nations, not an American, has written:

> The establishment of the rule of law in the economic field and the pursuit of a
> stable and intelligent policy of promoting competitive enterprise in the true sense
> would probably do more in encouraging the inflow of foreign capital than any
> initiative on the part of the investor countries.[40]

The applicability of such a point of view to unilateral devaluations, complex and arbitrary exchange controls and inflations is at once apparent.

---

39. Dan Throop Smith, speaking before the Fiscal Commission of the United Nations Economic and
Social Council; see *New York Times*, April 29, 1953.

40. Yuan-li Wu, *loc. cit.*, p. 71.

# 17. Public Loans and Grants
# to Underdeveloped Countries

APART FROM THE GENERAL INSUFFICIENCY of private funds, there are other specific reasons for assigning to public sources of foreign capital a crucial role. Chapter 13 has explained why the fields of public health and education, public communications and public utilities in underdeveloped economies are peculiarly the bailiwick of public investment, although they are not exclusively so.

## THE ROLE OF PUBLIC FOREIGN FINANCING

Conceivably, of course, while the undertaking might be public in the capital-receiving country, the source of funds might be private in the lending country. Indeed, prior to the first world war and even as late as the onset of the Great Depression, the great bulk of British investment, belying the Marxian idea that private capital is mainly interested in stripping a primitive economy of its mineral and soil resources or exploiting the native labor in these activities, was devoted to roads, railways, power plants and harbors.[1] But these social upheavals gave rise to political and economic risks which, as previously emphasized, have very nearly eliminated private portfolio investment and have limited private direct investment to the highest-profit fields—which do not include public services and public utilities.[2] Thus either the home government or a foreign public authority becomes the residual legatee for the bulk of investment in these undertakings.

So large are the capital requirements in these fields and so low their prospective earnings relative to the risks, that they have repeatedly been declared better suited to outright gifts than to investment in any true sense.[3] This position is probably more warranted for public health and education than for power and transport. Be that as it may, a large share of United States government grants to underdeveloped countries undoubtedly went for these purposes. Practical expediency, as well as the wisdom of main-

1. See Sir Arthur Salter, *Foreign Investment* (Essays in International Finance, No. 12), Princeton University Press, Princeton, February 1951, p. 18.

2. See pp. 345–48, 350, above.

3. For example, W. Arthur Lewis, "Food and Raw Materials," *District Bank Review*, September 1951, pp. 1–11; United Nations, Department of Economic Affairs, *Methods of Financing Economic Development in Under-developed Countries*, New York, 1949, pp. 100–01; United Nations, Department of Economic Affairs, *Measures for the Economic Development of Under-developed Countries*, New York, 1951, p. 84.

taining the integrity of genuinely productive investments, probably make it advisable simply to transfer certain funds from the "gift loan" category to the more honest category of gifts. In any case, "social capital" or "social overhead capital" is the chief type of development capital which must come largely from public sources abroad.

From the point of view of the capital-supplying economies, the chief economic argument for *public* investment in the underdeveloped world— aside from ideological and political factors—is the threat of food and raw material shortages. The meagerness of private foreign investment in agriculture appears both in the relative value to which it had arrived by 1945— not more than 6 per cent of the total of U.S. private capital abroad—and in the small increments since then.[4] Even mining and smelting, which in 1945 accounted for twice as much of the existing U.S. private investment as agriculture, has also declined in *new* investments relative to nonextractive production. The direction of international private investment reflects the basic fact that primary production on a global basis has fallen from 3 per cent to 1.2 per cent of total production since 1913.[5]

Until fairly recently, economists regarded this evolution as a natural and not unwelcome outgrowth of higher standards of living; but since the second world war the shortage of food has been an acute problem in Asia and by no means unknown to the United Kingdom and other European countries. The United States has in the past remained relatively untouched by such shortages, but the progressive reduction of certain domestic mineral resources has recently caused apprehension and even alarm.[6] It is possible, of course, that private capital might move into foreign primary production, especially in the underdeveloped countries, in great volume if acute shortages of food and raw materials in the Western world should make it sufficiently profitable to do so. Unless political and economic risks were to be notably reduced, however, the costs would be high to the consumer; and the military defense of the West might be exposed to unwelcome limits and uncertainties.

The needs of the underdeveloped world for capital in the public services and utilities and the needs of the developed economies for raw materials thus constitute a strong positive case for foreign public loans to the countries in the early phases of development.

MAGNITUDE AND CHARACTER OF PUBLIC FOREIGN FINANCING

The provision of capital for development, insofar as it depends upon sources outside the less developed countries themselves, has chiefly fallen to

4. See Table 16-2.

5. Lewis, *loc. cit.*

6. The President's Materials Policy Commission, *Resources for Freedom*, Vol. I, *Foundations for Growth and Security*, June 1952.

the United States, either directly or through the International Bank for Reconstruction and Development.

Over the five years following the announcement of Point Four, the flow of funds for development from the United States and from the International Bank doubled.[7] It is, unfortunately, impossible to obtain data for United States grants and loans to underdeveloped areas on the same basis for 1952 and 1953 as for 1949–1951. Comparing commitments, United States *grants* alone (without loans) exceeded International Bank loans in 1949 and 1950 but fell to one half in 1951. Comparing disbursements,

TABLE 17-1. LOANS BY THE INTERNATIONAL BANK FOR RECONSTRUCTION AND DEVELOPMENT TO UNDERDEVELOPED AREAS, FISCAL YEARS, 1948–1953

(*Millions*)

|  | Total 1948–1953 | 1948 | 1949 | 1950 | 1951 | 1952 | 1953 |
|---|---|---|---|---|---|---|---|
| Commitments | $980 | none | $125 | $152 | $297 | $227 | $179 |
| Disbursements | 521 |  | 20 | 77 | 72 | 169 | 183 |

*Source:* International Bank for Reconstruction and Development, *Annual Reports.*

TABLE 17-2. GRANTS AND LOANS BY THE UNITED STATES GOVERNMENT TO UNDERDEVELOPED AREAS, FISCAL YEARS, 1949–1953

(*Millions*)

|  | Commitments | | | Disbursements | |
|---|---|---|---|---|---|
|  | 1949 | 1950 | 1951 | 1952 | 1953 |
| Total | $338 | $520 | $690 | $814 | $731 |
| Grants | 291 | 184 | 142 | 504 | 480 |
| Loans | 47 | 336 | 548 | 310 | 251 |

*Sources: Survey of Current Business,* October 1953, pp. 16–17; *The Economic Report of the President,* January 1952, p. 127. The totals of U.S. grant and loan disbursements for 1952 and 1953 are given in the *Survey;* the division as between these two categories for these years is estimated from information in this source.

United States grants (without loans) greatly exceeded International Bank loans in 1952 and 1953. With respect to United States *loans* alone (without grants), commitments greatly exceeded those of the International Bank in 1950 and 1951; and United States loans disbursed in 1952 and 1953 also greatly exceeded International Bank disbursements. Taking United States loans and grants together, they have exceeded by several multiples the loan commitments or disbursements of the International Bank in each year. (See Tables 17-1 and 17-2.)

7. The analysis of United States foreign investment both private and government in the present chapter is largely confined to the postwar period since, by the latter part of 1944, the net amount was probably negative. See Robert L. Sammons, "International Investment Position of the United States," *Foreign Commerce Weekly,* January 27, 1945, pp. 5*ff.*

TABLE 17-3. FOREIGN AID PROGRAMS OF THE UNITED STATES GOVERNMENT: GRANTS AND CREDITS UTILIZED IN THE POSTWAR PERIOD AND UNUTILIZED AS OF DECEMBER 31, 1952[a]

(Millions)

| Program | Total Utilized | July–December 1945 | 1946 | 1947 | 1948 | 1949 | 1950 | 1951 | 1952 | Unutilized, December 31, 1952[b] |
|---|---|---|---|---|---|---|---|---|---|---|
| Total, all programs | $40,973 | $2,140 | $5,681 | $6,225 | $5,714 | $6,122 | $4,601 | $5,006 | $5,484 | $16,746 |
| Total, grants | 29,141 | 1,267 | 2,592 | 2,099 | 4,303 | 5,430 | 4,155 | 4,593 | 4,702 | 14,641 |
| Military | 5,581 | 105 | 15 | 74 | 420 | 214 | 531 | 1,490 | 2,732 | 12,114 |
| Mutual Security[c] | 4,677 | .. | .. | .. | .. | .. | 467 | 1,478 | 2,732[d] | 12,114 |
| Greek-Turkish aid | 660 | .. | .. | 74 | 348 | 170 | 59 | 9 | .. | .. |
| Chinese aid | 244 | 105 | 15 | .. | 72 | 44 | 5 | 3 | .. | .. |
| Economic and relief[e] | 23,560 | 1,161 | 2,576 | 2,025 | 3,883 | 5,216 | 3,626 | 3,103 | 1,970 | 2,527 |
| Mutual Security[f] | 12,547 | .. | .. | .. | 1,490 | 3,812 | 2,824 | 2,619 | 1,802 | 2,492 |
| (European Recovery Program) | .. | .. | .. | .. | (1,394) | (3,713) | (2,731) | (2,309) | .. | .. |
| Lend-lease and civilian supplies[g] | 6,328 | 670 | 1,055 | 991 | 1,505 | 1,081 | 506 | 366 | 154 | 34 |
| Philippine rehabilitation | 634 | .. | 33 | 86 | 130 | 203 | 166 | 12 | 4 | .. |
| Donations of agricultural surplus | 82 | .. | .. | .. | .. | .. | 36 | 46 | .. | .. |
| Yugoslav aid | 38 | .. | .. | .. | .. | .. | .. | 38 | .. | .. |
| International refugee assistance | 241 | .. | 2 | 19 | 89 | 71 | 52 | 8 | .. | .. |
| Inter-American aid and technical assistance | 148 | 7 | 11 | 46 | 16 | 30 | 27 | 8 | 3 | [d] |
| International Children's Emergency Fund | 88 | .. | .. | 15 | 27 | 18 | 15 | 6 | 7 | .. |
| UNRRA, post-UNRRA and interim aid | 3,444 | 479 | 1,470 | 868 | 626 | 1 | [d] | .. | .. | .. |
| American Red Cross | 10 | 5 | 5 | .. | .. | .. | .. | .. | .. | .. |

| | | | | | | | | | |
|---|---|---|---|---|---|---|---|---|---|
| Total, credits | 11,832 | 873 | 3,089 | 4,126 | 1,411 | 692 | 446 | 413 | 782 | 2,105 |
| Export-Import Bank | 3,415 | 58 | 1,037 | 824 | 429 | 185 | 200 | 204 | 478 | 2,008 |
| Mutual Security[h] | 1,545 | .. | .. | .. | 476 | 428 | 157 | 193 | 291 | 54 |
| Lend-lease and surplus property[i] | 2,663 | 815 | 1,314 | 296 | 197 | 32 | 5 | 2 | 2 | .. |
| Philippine funding | 35 | .. | .. | .. | .. | .. | 35 | .. | .. | .. |
| United Nations loan | 65 | .. | .. | .. | 3 | 20 | 22 | 13 | 7 | .. |
| British loan | 3,750 | .. | 600 | 2,850 | 300 | .. | .. | .. | .. | .. |
| Occupied-areas commodity credits | 284 | .. | 137 | 86 | 7 | 27 | 27 | d | .. | .. |
| Miscellaneous | 75 | d | d | 70 | d | d | .. | .. | 4 | 49 |

Sources: National Advisory Council on International Monetary and Financial Problems, *Semiannual Report to the President and to the Congress*, October 1, 1952–March 31, 1953, pp. 51 and 57.

a. Figures are rounded.

b. Unutilized grants are estimates based on appropriations and transfer authorizations available December 31, 1952, and thus show the possible limit of additional grants without further legislative action.

c. Includes aid under the former Mutual Defense Assistance Program.

d. Less than $500,000.

e. Includes also technical assistance.

f. Includes Point Four technical assistance and aid under the former Economic Cooperation Programs. Contributions to international organizations for Palestine relief and Korean reconstruction are also included.

g. Net after deducting $1,256 million of credits mostly for lend-lease and in part for civilian-supply aid that was extended in the war period (prior to mid-1945) and in the early postwar period.

h. Includes aid under the former Economic Cooperation Programs; included are the deficiency material development financing and the special loans to India and Spain.

i. Includes war account settlement credits.

*Where U.S. Postwar Aid Went*

In fiscal 1949, 1950 and 1951 the total of U.S. economic assistance available to underdeveloped areas represented only 5.7, 11.5 and 15.4 per cent of total U.S. foreign aid; and net utilizations of U.S. aid to underdeveloped areas amounted to 17.7 per cent of total foreign aid in 1952 and 11.5 per cent in 1953. The brutal fact is that no sooner had the United States come reasonably close to dealing with the economic aftermath of World War II than it was overtaken with the necessity of providing the wherewithal for rearmament.

During the years 1948–1951, the European Recovery Program absorbed nearly 50 per cent of foreign aid, while a multiplicity of kindred undertakings elsewhere—Greek-Turkish aid, Philippine rehabilitation, refugee assistance, etc.—absorbed a further significant share. By the end of 1951, when the Economic Cooperation Administration expired administratively, Mutual Defense assistance already claimed one third of the annual grants, and the proportion going for this purpose amounted to 58 per cent during 1952. (See Table 17-3.)

If the sums available for strictly economic development seem small, the total assistance of nearly $41 billion over the seven and a half years following the war represents a draft upon the resources of one nation for the benefit of others unparalleled in history—at least in its absolute magnitude. Grants of $29.1 billion were nearly two and a half times the loans of $11.8 billion. The utilized portion of total loans and grants as of December 31, 1952 considerably exceeded the portion unutilized ($41 billion utilized to $16.7 billion unutilized). Of Export-Import Bank credits, 37 per cent were as yet not utilized at the end of 1952.

The preoccupation of the United States with European economic recovery, political allegiances and rearmament resulted in its giving to Europe 77.2 per cent of net postwar aid, though Europe's share in grants amounted to somewhat less (74.0 per cent) and its share in credits to somewhat more (81.3 per cent). Of total utilized Export-Import Bank credits, a somewhat smaller proportion (66.3 per cent) went to Europe, partly because, during the period of E.R.P. aid when the International Bank suspended operations in that area, the Export-Import Bank continued to make loans to Latin America. Almost the same ratio of European aid to total credits obtained in the loan disbursements of the International Bank (59.0 per cent), its inactivity in Europe during the Marshall Plan aid having been compensated by its initial loans for European reconstruction. Recently, as revealed by its loan *commitments*, the International Bank has turned its attention more extensively to non-European countries.[8] (See Table 17-4.)

8. For more detailed statistics showing the allocation of United States government grants and credits by individual countries, see National Advisory Council on International Monetary and Financial Problems, *Semiannual Report to the President and to the Congress*, October 1, 1952–March 31, 1953, pp. 48–50.

By far the largest part (64.6 per cent) of utilized grants and loans to Asia in the postwar period, which amounted to $7.5 billion, has to be almost completely excluded or discounted as "investment" in underdeveloped areas. The largest share (30.3 per cent) went to Japan, a country not usually regarded as underdeveloped; and the funds which had gone into China (14.2 per cent), the Philippines (10.7 per cent) and Korea (9.4 per cent) by the end of 1952 can scarcely be imagined to have contributed much to the productive equipment of these countries.

TABLE 17-4. UNITED STATES GOVERNMENT FOREIGN GRANTS AND CREDITS, 1945–1952, AND LOANS BY THE INTERNATIONAL BANK FOR RECONSTRUCTION AND DEVELOPMENT, 1947–1953

*(Millions)*

| | United States Government July 1, 1945–December 31, 1952 | | | | | International Bank March 1, 1947– November 31, 1953 | |
| | | Utilized | | | | | |
| | | | | | Credits | | |
| Areas | Net Postwar Aid | Total | Grants | Total | Export-Import Bank | Disbursements | Loan Commitments |
|---|---|---|---|---|---|---|---|
| Total, all areas | $37,847 | $40,805 | $28,825 | $11,980 | $3,667 | $1,053 | $1,557 |
| Europe | 29,229 | 21,072 | 21,328 | 9,744 | 2,430 | 621 | 773 |
| Canada | 7 | 150 | .. | 150 | 148 | .. | .. |
| Oceania | 8 | 32 | 19 | 13 | .. | 89ᵃ | 150ᵃ |
| Latin America | 644 | 952 | 289 | 663 | 628 | 209 | 355 |
| Asia | 6,979 | 7,509 | 6,243 | 1,267 | 412 | 78 | 178 |
| Africa | −25 | 84 | 6 | 78 | 77 | 57 | 100 |
| International organizations | 687 | 689 | 623 | 65 | .. | .. | .. |
| Unspecified, all areas | 316 | 316 | 316 | .. | .. | .. | .. |

*Source:* National Advisory Council on International Monetary and Fiscal Problems, *Semiannual Report to the President and to the Congress*, October 1, 1952–March 31, 1953; for U.S. government, pp. 48–50; for International Bank, p. 31.

  a. Australia.

## Proportion of U.S. Aid Going to Underdeveloped Areas

The direction of the larger part of United States postwar foreign aid to Europe and the probable waste of nearly half of the portion going to Asia together account for the relatively small sums shown in Table 17-2 as having been made available for real economic investment in underdeveloped areas. Total commitments to these areas from 1949 through 1951, according to the Economic Report of the President (January 1952), amounted to $1.548 billion. This represents only 8.7 per cent of total net U.S. foreign aid utilized ($17.68 billion) during 1949, 1950 and 1951,[9] but in 1951 and 1952 the amounts actually utilized were 17.7 and 11.5 per cent of total net aid. In the aggregate for the years 1949–1953, U.S. foreign aid in grants and loans utilized amounted to 2.0 per cent of national income in the United States. The funds made available during 1949–1951 and the funds utilized during 1952–1953 for economic development of underdeveloped areas amounted to 0.24 per cent of U.S. national income. Although these percentages may not seem large, unutilized aid at the end of 1952 was nevertheless nearly half as large as the amount utilized.

How much capital has been supplied to or withdrawn from underdeveloped areas by other countries than the United States is unknown, though with laborious research an estimate might be derived from the scattered statistics of the various creditor countries. The United Nations hazards the *guess* that for the period 1946–1950 the flow of net capital for investment—after allowance for the service on old debt—from all countries in the aggregate was *negative*, for most underdeveloped countries.[10]

Only about one tenth of United States government foreign aid had been extended in the postwar period to the end of 1952 in the form of loans by the Export-Import Bank. This fact is explained primarily by the large amount of outright grants and of loans made directly by Congress. But despite their small share in the total of United States foreign aid, Export-Import Bank loans to underdeveloped areas were more than double those of the International Bank from mid-1945 to March 31, 1953, as the following figures (in millions) indicate:[11]

|  | Export-Import Bank | International Bank |
|---|---|---|
| Total net authorizations, all areas | $4,194 | $1,557 |
| Total net authorizations, underdeveloped areas | 1,910 | 933 |
| Utilizations, underdeveloped areas | 1,252 | 475 |

Thus, while the Export-Import Bank authorized nearly 46 per cent of its loans in these years for underdeveloped areas, the International Bank authorized 60 per cent for these areas. This rather surprising ratio for the International Bank, which is nowadays generally regarded as a development institution, is explained by its preoccupation with reconstruction in 1947, the first year of its operation, when nearly $500 million was lent to

9. The ratio of aid to underdeveloped areas to total aid in these years would be even smaller if, in place of the $1.548 billion "made available" for the former, the amount actually utilized during these three years were to be used. This figure does not appear to be obtainable.

10. United Nations, Department of Economic Affairs, *Instability in Export Markets of Under-developed Countries*, New York, 1952, pp. 7 and 67–73.

11. National Advisory Council, *Semiannual Report*, March 31, 1953, pp. 21, 31 and 57.

France, the Netherlands, Denmark and Luxembourg. But in subsequent years loans to developed countries have been greatly attenuated: 1948, $12 million; 1949, $24.8 million; 1950, $100 million; 1951, nothing; 1952, $7 million (to Belgium). This decline has been attended, of course, by a rapidly increasing proportion of loans to the newly developing regions.

## The Export-Import Bank

Since its inception in 1934, the Export-Import Bank has, at the convenience of United States domestic and foreign economic policy, served a number of unrelated ends.[12] Initially, no doubt, the Bank's operations were gauged rather narrowly to export promotion as a part of New Deal employment expansion policy. But as American involvement in war became increasingly inevitable, Congress in 1940 increased the lending authority of the institution from $200 million to $700 million to develop the strategic resources of Latin America and strengthen its economy generally. When the end of the war approached, Congress again increased the lending authority, this time to $3.5 billion, primarily for the purpose of postwar reconstruction loans of an emergency character pending the launching of the International Bank for Reconstruction and Development. Since 1947, as already noted, the two institutions have devoted increasingly large proportions of their resources to economic development. In the most recent phase, again reflecting its role as the primary foreign economic organization of the United States government, the Export-Import Bank has extended many loans to augment the supplies of imported strategic materials. Virtually all of the purposes of its operations acquired over its two decades of history still persist; and their multiple importance persuaded Congress to increase the Bank's resources again on October 3, 1951 to $4.5 billion.

Of net credits authorized by the Export-Import Bank from July 1, 1945 to June 30, 1953, Europe accounted for 54 per cent, Latin America for 27 per cent and the entire continents of Asia and Africa for 15 per cent. For Europe, wartime and postwar drafts on the Bank's resources formed two thirds of the total, and development loans only 13 per cent. But for Latin America and for Asia and Africa together, development loans made up 63 and 72 per cent of the continental totals. These higher proportions result primarily from emphasis placed on economic development in the acts of 1945 and 1951 to increase the Bank's lending authority. Nevertheless, the relative shares going to individual countries indicate that political considerations still play an important role. (See Table 17-5.)

Export-Import Bank loans during the fiscal year 1953 covered a wide range of economic activities in underdeveloped countries: Brazil, liquida-

12. On the historical evolution of both the Export-Import Bank and the International Bank for Reconstruction and Development, see the excellent accounts in Raymond F. Mikesell, *United States Economic Policy and International Relations*, McGraw-Hill, New York, 1952, Chapter 12.

TABLE 17-5. NET CREDITS AUTHORIZED BY THE EXPORT-IMPORT BANK, BY AREA AND COUNTRY, JULY 1, 1945 TO JUNE 30, 1953[a]

(Millions)

| Area and Country | Net Authorized [a] | Development | Reconstruction | Lend-Lease Requisitions | Cotton Purchases | Other |
|---|---|---|---|---|---|---|
| Total, all areas | $4,439.7 | $1,704.1 | $1,007.7 | $655.0 | $402.8 | $670.1 |
| Total, Europe | 2,410.8 | 314.6 | 971.8 | 655.0 | 229.6 | 239.8 |
| France | 1,445.0 | .. | 650.0 | 550.0 | 45.0 | 200.0 |
| Netherlands | 205.3 | 3.1 | 152.2 | 50.0 | .. | .. |
| Belgium | 138.8 | 32.0 | 45.0 | 55.0 | .. | 6.8 |
| Italy | 136.1 | 106.6 | .. | .. | 24.6 | 4.9[b] |
| Finland | 100.2 | 73.2 | .. | .. | 17.0 | 10.0[c] |
| Yugoslavia | 55.0 | 49.6 | .. | .. | .. | 5.4[c] |
| Germany (Western) | 64.6 | .. | .. | .. | 54.6 | 10.0[b] |
| Norway | 50.2 | .. | 50.0 | .. | .. | .2 |
| Poland | 40.0 | .. | 40.0 | .. | .. | .. |
| Turkey | 35.3 | 35.3 | .. | .. | .. | .. |
| Czechoslovakia | 22.0 | .. | .. | .. | 20.0 | 2.0[b] |
| Denmark | 20.0 | .. | 20.0 | .. | .. | .. |
| Greece | 14.6 | .. | 14.6 | .. | .. | .. |
| Austria | 19.1 | 12.6 | .. | .. | 6.0 | .5 |
| Spain | 24.0 | .. | .. | .. | 24.0 | .. |
| Sweden | 2.2 | 2.2 | .. | .. | .. | .. |
| Unallotted cotton credits | 38.4 | .. | .. | .. | 38.4 | .. |
| Total, Latin America | 1,201.3 | 754.6 | .. | .. | 20.0 | 426.7 |
| Mexico | 223.5 | 223.5 | .. | .. | .. | .. |
| Brazil | 579.2 | 279.2 | .. | .. | .. | 300.0 |
| Argentina | 130.2 | 5.0 | .. | .. | .. | 125.2 |
| Chile | 109.0 | 109.0 | .. | .. | .. | .. |
| Colombia | 44.9 | 29.4 | .. | .. | 20.0 | .. |
| Bolivia | 21.9 | 21.9 | .. | .. | .. | .. |

| | | | | | |
|---|---|---|---|---|---|
| Peru | 21.5 | 21.5 | ... | ... | ... |
| Venezuela | 14.4 | 14.4 | ... | ... | ... |
| Haiti | 14.0 | 14.0 | ... | ... | ... |
| Ecuador | 13.1 | 13.1 | ... | ... | ... |
| Cuba | 12.0 | 12.0 | ... | ... | ... |
| Panama | 4.0 | 2.5 | ... | ... | 1.5 |
| Uruguay | 3.0 | 3.0 | ... | ... | ... |
| Nicaragua | .6 | .6 | ... | ... | ... |
| Other Latin America | 5.4 | 5.4 | ... | ... | ... |
| Total, Asia and Africa | 668.5 | 478.4 | 35.9 | 153.2 | 1.0 |
| Israel | 135.0 | 135.0 | ... | ... | ... |
| Indonesia | 100.0 | 100.0 | ... | ... | ... |
| Japan | 120.2 | ... | ... | 120.2 | ... |
| China | 66.2 | ... | 33.2 | 33.0 | ... |
| Union of South Africa | 111.5 | 111.5 | ... | ... | ... |
| Saudi Arabia | 25.0 | 25.0 | ... | ... | ... |
| Iran | 25.0 | 25.0 | ... | ... | ... |
| Afghanistan | 21.0 | 21.0 | ... | ... | ... |
| Philippines | 25.3 | 25.3 | ... | ... | ... |
| Portuguese Africa | 17.9 | 17.9 | ... | ... | ... |
| Liberia | 10.4 | 10.4 | ... | ... | ... |
| Egypt | 7.3 | 7.3 | ... | ... | ... |
| Ethiopia | 2.7 | ... | 2.7 | ... | ... |
| Thailand | 1.0 | ... | ... | ... | 1 0 |
| Canada | 150.7 | 150.7 | ... | ... | ... |
| Miscellaneous | 8.4 | 5.8 | ... | ... | 2.6 |

Source: National Advisory Council on International Monetary and Fiscal Problems, *Semiannual Report to the President and to the Congress*, October 1, 1951–March 31, 1952, supplemented by data given on p. 21, *ibid.*, March 31, 1953.

a. Credits authorized less cancellations and expirations, and participations by other banks.

b. For financing tobacco purchases.

c. For financing food purchases.

371

tion of dollar debts, plastics plant, rayon and cotton textile machinery, farm equipment, railroad equipment, cast-iron pipe production; Colombia, flood control; Mexico, manganese, steel and sulphur production, shipping facilities, mining development; the Philippines, small-business development; Portuguese Africa, railroad and port improvement.[13] In recent years, the heaviest allocations have accrued to Latin America and, there and elsewhere, have gone preponderantly into the public utilities and extractive industries. Faithful to its name, the Bank strongly emphasized the promotion of certain important imports and exports of the United States.

The Export-Import Bank does not operate under several limitations written into the charter of the International Bank: the "specific project" specification; the requirement of foreign government guarantees; and the exclusion of "local currency expenditures." Furthermore, *any* country, whether or not a member of an international organization, may be given a loan. But against the greater latitude enjoyed by the Export-Import Bank in these respects is to be set its practice—not imposed, however, in its enabling legislation—of requiring the expenditure of its loans for United States products.[14] The Export-Import Bank seems always to have enjoyed the confidence of the American business and financial communities, and Administration requests for expansion of its capital have met with practically no resistance. Recently there have been indications that Export-Import Bank lending activities to underdeveloped countries are at a standstill and that in the future only short-term credit for United States products might be available.[15] The drastic reduction or termination of Point Four in the sense of direct loans for development would involve for the United States a loss of prestige and confidence throughout the economically underdeveloped world quite out of proportion to the budgetary economy which it achieves. United States aid (of much smaller magnitude) now being extended through the United Nations might continue, but it is subject to interference from Soviet and satellite objections or vetoes.

*The International Bank for Reconstruction and Development*

To many representatives of the relatively less developed countries, the International Bank has been disappointing. In the first place, its original capitalization at $8.35 billion was probably only one half or one third of the magnitude thought suitable in some quarters. Actually, the Bank's operations at the outset lay well within the original United States subscription plus the relatively small 2 per cent gold subscription of other members, totaling $734 million. Meanwhile, chiefly through the sale of the

13. Export-Import Bank, *Semiannual Reports.*
14. See Mikesell, *op. cit.,* p. 215.
15. See *New York Times,* July 25, 1953, p. 18; September 15, p. 45; September 16, p. 49; September 30, p. 47.

Bank's own bonds and, in smaller amounts, through the accumulation of profits and availabilities on nondollar subscriptions, the total of disposable funds has nearly doubled, to $1,454.5 million in 1952. But this sum, however impressive in absolute terms, falls far below the expectations which preceded or accompanied the launching of the institution.

Even within these confines, the Bank seemed to some critics to move with unwarrantable conservatism—"as limited in its operations as . . . private investment," in the words of the Food and Agriculture Organization.[16] In part, this impression was founded on an erroneous interpretation of the rules and usages of the Bank; in part, the impression was correct for earlier practices which were subsequently somewhat modified; and in part, the conservatism is real and unavoidable in the nature of the institution itself.

The charter of the International Bank requires that its loans and guarantees, except in special circumstances, "be for the purpose of specific projects of reconstruction and development." (Art. III, Sec. 9.) Some critics assumed that the Bank was thus constrained to apply ordinary commercial tests of productivity and soundness to a given project—that it had to be profitable in the ordinary sense of a private investment. To this the Bank replied that, while it must consider a loan on the merits of a specific project and not merely for some vague and undefined developmental purpose, it has always judged the merit of a specific project on the broad basis of its contribution to the productivity of the economy, not its profitability in isolation.[17] On this score, the Bank's position may have been definite from the beginning, although it was rather tardily made explicit to the public.

But there seems also to be fairly clear evidence that on this same score, and in the matter of the so-called "local currency expenditures," the Bank has gradually moved to a somewhat less conservative position. During 1950 the Bank made several small loans to foreign banks for relending to private borrowers for development purposes, certainly not a "specific project" basis so far as the Bank was concerned; and at the same time it stated that it would "go farther" in considering the merits of a particular project in the light of general development needs. As for the "local currency expenditures," in the strict sense as well as in the extended sense of the foreign exchange needed because a given investment from abroad may lead *indirectly* to additional import demands, the Bank's charter prohibits their inclusion in loans save in exceptional cases. (Art. IV, Sec. 3c.) The Bank quite correctly insisted that the general inclusion of these derivative needs would lead in a spiral process to inflation and a demand for more loans;

16. United Nations, *Methods of Financing Economic Development in Under-developed Countries*, p. 78.
17. International Bank for Reconstruction and Development, *Fifth Annual Report, 1949–1950*, Washington, 1950, pp. 8–10.

and it laid down specific criteria of cases where an exception would not be dangerous.[18] In 1951–1952, apparently satisfied that these tests had been met, the Bank made a loan to Italy to include, for the first time, certain sums for "local currency costs," and a loan to Belgium to cover certain costs arising indirectly from the Bank loan to the Congo.[19]

Allowing for these changes, however, a basic conservatism remains; and so long as the institution preserves the character of a *bank*, this is quite necessary. In terms of its loans or its guarantees, its operations rest on repayment of the principal, and accordingly must rest on informed judgments of the prospect of amortization of the loan by the borrower out of a presumptive increase of productivity, direct or indirect, made possible by the investment in question. Otherwise, the Bank's resources, instead of serving as a revolving fund, would become a dwindling source of subsidies or "gift loans." A strong case can be made for outright grants to impoverished countries in the beginning phases of development for the basic "public services," and the United States government has itself responded to this need. But there would seem to be every reason for keeping separate the institutions and operations concerned with lending and with making grants.

For the less impoverished countries and for projects which directly or indirectly bid fair to yield a specific product, the capital-receiving country can, without jeopardizing its present or future welfare, undertake the investment from a loan at interest. This, it seems, has been the province of the Bank, beginning appropriately with the most basic categories. Thus in the fiscal year 1953 its loans were made for the following purposes: Brazil, highway improvement; Colombia, railroad development; Finland, wood products; Iceland, fertilizer plant; India, iron and steel production, electric power, flood control and irrigation; Northern Rhodesia, railway development; Peru, agricultural equipment; Yugoslavia, power, mining, transport, iron and steel.[20] In emphasizing large public service investments, "the Bank has been working toward the objective of developing conditions under which private capital could find profitable investment in other activities."[21]

Failure to distinguish between circumstances suitable for loans and those requiring grants, as well as the obvious inadequacy of International Bank resources for "loans" bordering on the second category, may account for some of the criticism of its policies and the demand for new development capital agencies. Thus V. K. R. V. Rao, in proposing a United Nations Economic Development Agency (UNEDA), defined its field as the financ-

18. *Ibid.*, pp. 10–11.

19. See Gardner Patterson and Jack N. Behrman, *Survey of United States International Finance, 1951*, Princeton University Press, Princeton, 1952, pp. 123–25.

20. International Bank for Reconstruction and Development, *Eighth Annual Report, 1952–53*, Washington, 1953.

21. National Advisory Council on International Monetary and Financial Problems, *Third Special Report*, June 1952, p. 7.

ing of projects "not financially productive in a banking sense," though the financing would be through "loans" on very liberal terms and at nominal interest rates.[22] Such an institution would compromise the merits of outright gifts and the merits of self-liquidating loans by a vague amalgam of both.

### Proposal to Supplement the International Bank

On the other hand, the International Development Advisory Board, appointed by President Truman under the chairmanship of Nelson Rockefeller, recommended the establishment of an International Development Authority for the explicit purpose of making outright *grants*.[23] The rationale of such an institution would be the need for grants on the part of impoverished countries for "public service" capital requirements, and the political arguments for international management and participation in the donation of such funds. Coupled with this, the Rockefeller group recommended also the establishment of an International Finance Corporation which would make loans; but—unlike the International Bank—it would lend directly to private industries without the requirement of a government guarantee in the receiving country, which has thus far proved to be a stumbling block for the Bank.[24] The International Finance Corporation would also be given the important power to make equity investments.

The proposals of the International Development Advisory Board have special merit in that they contemplate supplementing the International Bank rather than disrupting this effective going concern. The International Finance Corporation would be an affiliate of the Bank, and the international grant authority would operate under a management contract with the Bank. Thus one set of technical experts could be called upon in several contexts, effecting an economy in the number of skilled international servants and utilizing their powers fully. An institutional division of labor along the lines contemplated would cover the field more adequately without disturbing the role which the Bank has evolved for itself in its years of experience.[25]

22. United Nations, *Methods of Financing Economic Development in Under-developed Countries*, pp. 129–32.

23. International Development Advisory Board, *Partners in Progress*, Washington, March 1951, pp. 73–75. The proposed capital was $500 million, of which the United States would give $200 million.

24. Sir Arthur Salter believes that the chief reason for the International Bank's inability to elicit private capital through guarantees is its requirement of uniform credit conditions and uniform interest rates for all borrowers. He recommends that the Bank pattern its loan operations after the successful League of Nations loans in the 1920s to Austria, Hungary, etc. See Salter, *op. cit.*, pp. 46–51.

25. An apparently favorable exposition of the possible role of an International Finance Corporation was presented to the United Nations Economic and Social Council by the president of the International Bank, Eugene Black, on June 16, 1952. But the United States was reported as opposed to an "international development fund" for "grants-in-aid, low-interest and long term loans to underdeveloped countries." See *New York Times*, June 17 and 21, 1952. The Rockefeller Committee proposals of two such institutions had meanwhile been endorsed by the group of economists reporting to the United Nations in *Measures for the Economic Development of Under-developed Countries;* see pp. 82, 84–87.

This role has included, in the first place, a high degree of technical expertness, objectivity and impartiality in the granting of loans which has already earned for it a considerable degree of confidence, as evidenced by requests for missions and economic advisers by various countries aspiring to economic development. The Bank's studies of national economies are, in general, distinct contributions to the statistical and other information concerning less-known areas; and in nearly all cases they are models of common sense and economic analysis. Finally, the insistence of the Bank on careful schemes of national investment priorities, its emphasis on other than financial aspects of the economic problem and its repeated warnings against extravagant expectations have formed a consistent rationale of economic development. Hence, the significance of the International Bank for the underdeveloped world transcends by far the magnitude of its loans.

## PRESENT PROSPECTS FOR DEVELOPMENTAL CAPITAL

Marked differences of conviction underlie the current discussions of economic development in underdeveloped areas.[26] The older industrial nations of the West view the process in the framework of an international economy resting on specialization or division of labor in which underdeveloped areas will, for some time to come, continue chiefly as primary producers. Economic progress will unfold gradually for these countries and will—or should—follow the lines of maximum productivity as indicated by the price system. Only as industrial skills accumulate and as literacy, public health, monetary-fiscal systems, commercial codes, etc., reach higher levels can these growing economies hope for significant increases in real incomes per capita. And only after this increase has attained a considerable height and momentum can the state and the individual escape the necessity of plowing back a very large part of the increment to income into investment for further development.

To these tenets, generally speaking, the attitudes of the underdeveloped areas form direct antitheses; the details can readily be supplied in the imagination. But on no point, perhaps, is the divergence of conviction more overt than on the score of the appropriate magnitude, sources and conditions of capital supply. The relatively underdeveloped countries aspire to speedy change, to all or most of the trappings of modern industrialism, to "welfare" and social security, to national self-sufficiency or a "balanced" economy—all of which require vast sums of capital. Much of this money, they believe, must come from abroad, to avoid pressure on domestic living standards or even to permit some increase in per capita consumption. If the

---

26. See the general analysis of these broad issues by Norman S. Buchanan in Bernard F. Haley (Ed.), *A Survey of Contemporary Economics*, Vol. II, Richard D. Irwin, Homewood, Illinois, 1952, pp. 307–50.

capital is to be borrowed from abroad, the loans must run at low rates and on long term. But grants are economically more appropriate for much of the investment in underdeveloped countries; and it is argued that both conscience and political expediency would counsel greater liberality on the part of Western creditor nations, particularly the United States. Capital flows amounting to several multiples of their present magnitudes are a "necessity," they believe.

The probability is great that neither of these opposing sets of views will entirely prevail, and that individual countries will follow widely divergent patterns. With respect specifically to the financing of development, several generalizations seem to be possible concerning the outlook for the next several years.

*Prospective Flow of Private Capital*

In the first place, the flow of private foreign capital, largely originating in the United States, does not promise to exceed by far the level of $800 million achieved annually in the years 1947–1949. Some underdeveloped countries can hardly expect foreign private capital to enter the arena so long as domestic capital takes refuge from the risks of expropriation, high taxes, inflation and political upheavals by flight abroad. For other under-developed countries, where adverse discrimination against foreign capital has been the conspicuous obstacle, favorable effects would follow from progress in negotiating investment treaties, removing tax discrimination and extending the field of government guarantees on private loans. Each of these, however, even in the most sanguine view, has only marginal significance in encouraging private investment. An international setting in which these measures could make substantial progress would also be a setting favorable to the relaxation of foreign exchange control, including the limitations imposed on transfer of profits. A fair share of the substantial reinvestment of American earnings abroad must be ascribed to this compulsion. Investment treaties, tax reform and guarantees would indeed seem preferable to the compulsions of exchange control. But if the international economic policy of the United States succeeds in promoting the one and attenuating the other, thereby substituting the incentives of free choice for force, the net outcome may leave the flow of direct investment unchanged.

Over the long run, no doubt, foreign capital can only be had by attraction, and as compulsions, such as a capital export embargo, lose their force. Meanwhile, however, political revolutions and violence exercised on foreign investments, such as the seizure of British oil properties by Iran and the treatment of the United Fruit Company by Guatemala, are likely to reduce the interest of private investors in the foreign field strongly and categorically. A decade or more might elapse during which progress along the front of investment treaties, tax incentives, guarantees and other devices to encourage private investment would merely compensate for political and economic cataclysms. On balance, the Gray report's assumption of a flow of private investment to underdeveloped areas equaling its recent magnitude of $500–$800 million annually does not seem far afield.[27]

Grounds for a more optimistic prognosis for private investment would be provided by a combination of political stability, absence of expropriation and inflation, etc., with the gradual creation of a basis of public services and public utilities—from domestic resources or foreign public loans or grants. But the very rationale of these public undertakings, it must be remembered, lies in their long-run character; and private investment in a world of great uncertainties will rather await than anticipate the completion of most of these large-scale projects.

*Public Loans and Grants*

The Gray report also contemplates a continuation of United States government loans and grants (including Export-Import Bank credits) and International Bank loans to underdeveloped regions at a rate of $600–$800 million annually, and $500 million in United States government grants and contributions to technical aid.[28] The expansion of International Bank disposable funds by the sale of its own bonds has indeed, over the seven years of its history, brought a $500 million addition to its originally available $734 million in dollars and gold. Currently, this process has gathered more momentum, for during the 1951–1952 fiscal year it augmented the Bank's resources by $175 million.[29] This sum increases the annual flow of capital to underdeveloped areas by about one tenth. Further small additions to the Bank's disposable funds are made through the liberation of the original 18 per cent local currency subscriptions by the respective members. Hence, the chief methods of increasing the International Bank's resources are confined to rather narrow limits.

As to the magnitude of United States government loans and grants, it would be difficult to discover grounds in the present setting of defense budgets and public opinion for expecting a substantial *increase* of capital for development from this source. Even the proposal made in 1949 by a group of United Nations experts that the United States commit itself over

27. *Report to the President on Foreign Economic Policies*, Washington, November 10, 1950, p. 72. (Generally called the Gray Report.)

28. *Ibid.*

29. Each of the following groups holds about one fifth of the Bank's bonds: mutual savings banks; life insurance companies; pension and trust funds; commercial banks and other investors—all in the United States; and fifth, foreign investors. International Bank for Reconstruction and Development, *Seventh Annual Report*, Washington, 1952, p. 39.

a period of five years to a *constant* annual sum of long-term foreign loans[30] met with flat rejection by the United States delegation and with generally adverse comment by American economists.[31]

A fairly convincing case can be established for increasing the *proportion* of United States aid to developing countries in the form of grants and decreasing the proportion of loans. The movement has in fact been in this direction. But it is more than doubtful whether a convincing case can be made even abstractly, quite aside from the political mood of the country, for a vast extension of gifts. As Jacob Viner has observed, the principle of sharing the wealth internationally does not carry conviction when it is conspicuously absent within many of the countries most vocal in espousing it for the United States. Gifts do not generally have very favorable effects on the morale of the recipient, and the tax systems of some countries seem to show that nations are no exception to the rule. On the donor's side, it is difficult not to cast shame upon the receiver and to refrain from imposing conditions or implicitly attaching obligations which would really convert the gift into a bribe.[32] These considerations and the political actualities indicate that the total of American gifts and loans will not and probably should not be expected to increase greatly.

### Total Investment Probabilities

In attempting to estimate the future annual capital flow to underdeveloped territories, it is probably wise not to count on other sources than those just reviewed. Contributions by countries other than the United States to colonial territories and to the Colombo Plan may for some years be largely offset by the repatriation of private capital to metropolitan areas in Europe from Southeastern Asia, India and the Near East. Thus the total amount estimated here is from $1.6 to $2.1 billion annually for the proximate future,[33] paralleling the conclusions of the Gray report. This estimate combines $500–$800 million in private capital (including reinvested earnings), largely from the United States; $600–$800 million from the Inter-

30. United Nations, *National and International Measures for Full Employment*, New York, December 1949.

31. See C. P. Kindleberger, "International Disequilibrium," *Canadian Journal of Economics and Political Science*, November 1950, pp. 529–37; W. W. Rostow, "The United Nations' Report on Full Employment," *Economic Journal*, June 1950, pp. 323–50; Jacob Viner, "Full Employment at Whatever Cost," *Quarterly Journal of Economics*, August 1950, pp. 385–407; H. C. Wallich, "United Nations Report on Full Employment," *American Economic Review*, December 1950, pp. 876–83; and J. H. Williams, "International Trade Theory and Policy—Some Current Issues," *American Economic Review*, May 1951, pp. 418–30.

32. See Jacob Viner, *Rearmament and International Commercial Policies*, Foreign Service Institute, U.S. Department of State, 1951, pp. 20–21.

33. This falls far short of the $4 billion annual average which the Food and Agriculture Organization in 1949 gave as the flow of funds to underdeveloped areas which had prevailed since 1945. See United Nations, *Methods of Financing Economic Development in Under-developed Countries*, pp. 65 and 81. The figure of $4 billion, however, includes not only funds for economic development but all other sums going to underdeveloped areas, such as lend-lease, U.S. Army civilian supply, U.N. International Children's Fund and U.N.R.R.A. rehabilitation programs, etc.

national Bank and the Export-Import Bank; and $500 million in United States grants and technical aid. Applied to the 1.4 billion inhabitants of the underdeveloped world outside the areas dominated by the U.S.S.R., these sums amount to $1.14 and $1.50 per capita per year.

A vast and indiscriminate aggregate of this sort must, of course, be treated cautiously. Nevertheless, it makes one prospect dramatically clear. An increase of the annual investment of international capital by several multiples would still leave most of the burden of providing the wherewithal for economic progress to the underdeveloped countries themselves.

But this conclusion in no wise negates the strategic importance of present supplies of capital from overseas. It is the marginal increments from abroad which may provide the upward fillip to production to lift standards of living to the point of inducing family limitation. The loans and grants of foreign public agencies, moreover, are possessed of an importance quite beyond their mathematical share in the aggregate of national investment. These funds go chiefly into basic services and utilities which private capital finds too extensive, too slow in coming to fruition and too risky in their prospective yields; they supply the *sine qua non* of progress past the most rudimentary level and pave the way for profitable private investment, both foreign and domestic. Finally, a major theme of much of the recent discussion of technical assistance has been the promise held forth by improved but inexpensive agricultural implements and simple equipment for the handicrafts and village industries. Precisely because a little capital goes a long way, that little is crucial.

*Differences in Borrowing Countries*

Naturally, the capacity of individual countries to absorb and effectively utilize capital varies markedly. India, for example, enjoys several outstanding advantages in this respect—most notably a universal language (English) for the intellectual and civil servant classes and well-established commercial and mercantile organizations in the larger population centers. In other quarters, particularly in Southeastern Asia and the Near East and occasionally in Latin America, these elements may be lacking. And by the common irony of human affairs, absorptive capacity and available capital often occur in inverse relation. The Sheik of Qatar is to receive from the foreign petroleum companies an annual royalty of $11.2 to $14.0 million,[34] which within less than five years would exceed the $57 million of United States loans and grants extended to the entire continent of Africa in the postwar period 1945 through 1951. Oil royalties for Iraq will suffice for its development program as planned through 1957,[35] and Venezuela's position is

34. *New York Times*, September 3, 1952.
35. International Bank for Reconstruction and Development, *The Economic Development of Iraq*, Washington, 1952, p. 76.

scarcely less strong. It does not seem unreasonable to inquire whether these highly favored countries should not themselves make contributions by gift or loan to the economic development of their less fortunate neighbors.

There is nothing paradoxical, but on the contrary a solid basis in common sense and observation, in the position that, however essential the present flow of foreign resources may be to the progress of underdeveloped regions, a vastly increased flow would not in present circumstances be warranted. A subcommittee of the United Nations has declared that "In practice, it is by no means always true that finance is the major limiting factor,"[36] a view repeatedly affirmed by the International Bank. The Executive Secretary of the Economic Commission for Asia and the Far East has recently estimated that from $8 to $10 billion of foreign capital would be required *annually* even to maintain present standards of living in Asia; but, he adds, "Even if this vast sum of money were available, it could not, under present circumstances, be effectively utilized. To do this Asia would need more technicians, scientists, machines, etc., and above all, sound administrative machinery."[37]

Economic development proceeds, if at all, along a very broad front which extends from the relatively rudimentary matters of public health and literacy, through the introduction of improved techniques and organization in agriculture, industry, commerce and finance, to commercial morality and the wisdom, energy and probity of government officials. It does not appear that the supply of capital lags conspicuously behind wherever these other forces are advancing vigorously.

36. United Nations, *Methods of Financing Economic Development in Under-developed Countries*, pp. 9 and 141.

37. P. S. Lokanathan, "The Economy of the ECAFE Region—The Measure of Capital Requirements," *Far Eastern Economist*, February 8, 1952, p. 207.

# 18. Underdeveloped Countries in International Trade

DEFICITS IN THE INTERNATIONAL BALANCE outside the dollar area have been so nearly universal since World War II that they cannot be considered peculiar to countries in the early stages of economic development. Indeed, some of the main causes of foreign deficits in these economies, such as inflation and overvalued exchange rates, are all too familiar in the experience of the older economies as well. Some older economies are also under certain special handicaps in attempting to achieve international balance, from paying off unfunded foreign debts, maintaining overseas armies and adjusting to the severance of colonial markets and sources of supply. These difficulties in the present age appear to be as troublesome as those of the newer regions.

Any country that earns a substantial portion of its total income from exports is exposed to the vicissitudes of international trade and finance. The United Kingdom, Denmark, Holland and Switzerland are just as much "export economies" as many of the less advanced Latin American countries. By contrast, among relatively "self-sufficient" countries, there are almost as many highly developed nations, such as the United States and France, as there are underdeveloped nations, such as China, El Salvador[1] and numerous primitive economies in Africa and Micronesia. But between two countries that are export economies to the same degree, the less developed country will probably encounter greater difficulty in compensating for a decline in export income by increasing domestic government expenditures, because these expenditures are likely to form a smaller proportion of the national income.

## BALANCE-OF-PAYMENTS PROBLEMS OF UNDERDEVELOPED AREAS

Although no single cause of balance-of-payments difficulties is unique with underdeveloped areas, four causes seem most common or most powerful. First, underdeveloped regions are usually primary producers and as such are exposed to *large fluctuations* in their markets and to consequent disequilibrating effects on their balances of payments. Second, underdeveloped regions generally have *low incomes*, and low incomes are associated with several specific causes of difficulties with the foreign balance.

1. H. C. Wallich and John H. Adler, *Public Finance in a Developing Country—El Salvador: A Case Study*, Harvard University Press, Cambridge, 1951, p. 3.

Third, developing economies are usually *borrowers;* the very receiving of funds, the character of the investment, and the service of the debt may all produce complications.[2] Fourth, inflation springing from budget deficits is widespread in the less developed countries.

### VARIABILITY OF DEMAND FOR EXPORTS

The disruptive effect of fluctuations in the export markets of primary producers has long been recognized, and a recent and notable statistical study of the United Nations reveals the violence of these movements.[3] The statistics, which cover eighteen important commodities and a large share of the export trade of the underdeveloped world from 1901 to 1950, show that the *average* year-to-year variation of export yield in foreign exchange was 22.6 per cent, while the average *cyclical* variation, covering a four-year period or slightly more, was 37.2 per cent.[4] Many individual commodities, of course, showed much larger variations than average; for some the average *annual* variation was 37 per cent. Contrary to the widespread belief that agriculture tends to compensate in some measure for price declines by increased volume of sales, the report proves that price declines generally accounted for a smaller portion of the shrinkage in total export proceeds than did reduced volume. It was the frequent repetition of price declines of 18–19 per cent annually for two, three and even more years, *coupled* with a falling volume of sales, which produced the violent cyclical contractions of export yields.

### The Case of the Primary Producers

If countries are divided into three large categories—economies that are relatively self-sufficient, export economies dependent upon industrial exports, and export economies dependent upon the sale of primary products—it is the last category that is far and away most subject to annual and cyclical variations in the total real value of exports. Most of the underdeveloped countries are in this category.

In times of prosperity, industrial countries tend to develop heavy imports of industrial raw materials and unfavorable balances of trade. The loss of gold or foreign currency reserves that these unfavorable balances involve has, if anything, a braking or restraining influence on the prosperity. But for the primary producer countries, prosperity does not have this effect; rather the contrary, for export yields increase strongly and gold

2. Countries receiving large revenues from oil royalties probably escape most of the first and the third kinds of difficulty.

3. United Nations, Department of Economic Affairs, *Instability in Export Markets of Under-developed Countries,* New York, 1952.

4. *Ibid.,* pp. 6, 43, 45 and 46.

or foreign balances pour in.[5] Incomes rise, bank loans are expanded, and the "prosperity" receives a further impulse. In these circumstances, many underdeveloped countries, such as Cuba, reveal a propensity to bid up the prices of existing assets in a speculative fever rather than add to their real capital equipment.[6] The ultimate destiny of these funds may thus be sumptuary or even luxury imports and a prodigal waste of prosperity.

To cap the climax, the variations in the trade balances of primary producers are accompanied, in general, by variations in lending by foreigners which intensify boom and depression. Prosperity in the maturer industrial countries results not only in large export yields for primary producers but also in a stimulating inflow of foreign capital. Depression abroad reduces export yields and induces foreign creditors to cease further lending or even to seek to withdraw their outstanding loans.[7]

### Export Changes Due to Demand Changes

The United Nations study of export markets makes an important contribution to intelligent policy formation in providing virtually conclusive statistical proof for the belief, long held on the basis of general observation, that conditions of demand, and not supply, are the principal explanation of the variations in the export yields of the primary producing countries. If the variations were generated on the supply side, lower prices would, through the increase of quantity demanded, *expand* sales. The finding of the study is, however, to the contrary: lower prices and *smaller* volumes of exports were associated together.

### Factors in Ills of Primary Producers

Variability of export proceeds plays so large a role in the economic ills of primary producers, most of them underdeveloped countries, that it may be well to restate the case. In the first place, the severity of these fluctuations is augmented in real terms by the lesser variability of the prices of imported industrial commodities. Second, primary producers tend to gain reserves of gold or foreign currencies in good times and to lose them in depressions, and this monetary factor increases both the upswing and the downswing of incomes and employment. Third, capital flows from overseas serve still further to increase the amplitude of these variations since foreigners lend in prosperity and cease to lend or even demand repayment in depression. The rigidity of interest and amortization charges on foreign loans, causing them to absorb as much as 40 per cent or more of the yield

5. H. C. Wallich, "Underdeveloped Countries in the International Monetary Mechanism," in *Money, Trade, and Economic Growth*, Macmillan, New York, 1951, p. 25.

6. H. C. Wallich, *Monetary Problems of an Export Economy—the Cuban Experience*, Harvard University Press, Cambridge, 1950, pp. 209–16.

7. United Nations, *op. cit.*, pp. 7 and 63–67.

of exports in depression in extreme cases, vastly complicates matters for the primary producers. Finally, because so large a part of its total income is earned from exports, the primary producing country may find it much more difficult to achieve stability by domestic measures than does the more developed manufacturing country.

In the depression of the 1930s, the general collapse of currency standards and default on foreign bonds in Latin America revealed the violence of this complex set óf forces. These same forces seem to be no less violent and wasteful in prosperity. Except in a few Latin American countries such as Colombia, El Salvador and Nicaragua, and possibly also in India, the raw-materials boom of 1950 and early 1951 made virtually no contribution to the economic development of the primary producers. The gains went only to a negligible extent into imports of machinery, metals and manufactures, and were instead dissipated in imports of consumption goods, often of ostentatious types.[8]

While the most primitive parts of the underdeveloped world, including the areas of "subsistence agriculture," are relatively immune to the fluctuations, they fall with concentrated fury on the export sectors. Much of the otherwise irrational drive for self-sufficiency, exchange controls and even controlled economies springs from the desire to escape these fluctuations. Until they are substantially curbed by appropriate national and international policies, much of the hard-won wherewithal for economic improvement will continue to be wasted.

### LOW PER CAPITA INCOMES

*Imitative Consumption*

Low incomes can contribute to the balance-of-payments difficulties of underdeveloped regions in several ways, though of course poverty does not necessarily or automatically produce foreign deficits. Imitation of standards of living of wealthier economies increases consumption expenditures, and the increase may result in domestic inflation and thus indirectly induce foreign deficits, or it may impinge upon the trade balance directly through the importation of those goods that particularly symbolize the higher standards of living abroad.[9] Indigenous populations have probably always tried to imitate the well-to-do foreign merchants, planters and governors in their midst. But since the political upheavals of the last decade, extravagant ideas of consumption, "social security" and economic equality have figured among the most formidable problems of countries launching development programs. Since this tendency toward imitative consumption does not de-

8. United Nations, *World Economic Report, 1950–51*, New York, 1952, *passim*.

9. Ragnar Nurkse has emphasized this factor strongly. See "Some International Aspects of the Problem of Economic Development," *American Economic Review, Proceedings*, May 1952, pp. 571–83; and *Problems of Capital Formation in Underdeveloped Countries*, Blackwell, Oxford, 1953, p. 63 and *passim*.

pend upon the absolute height of incomes but upon their slower rise in underdeveloped countries as compared with more advanced economies, it may play a perennial role in contributing to foreign deficits and foreign currency shortages.[10]

If the upward revision of standards of consumption were an isolated episode, the deficit in the balance of trade would gradually be rectified through the many channels of international adjustment.[11] But when the impacts are continually repeated in the same direction, the adjustment mechanism may prove less powerful than the disturbing forces. It is the persistent lag of adjustment that explains the "chronic" tendency of underdeveloped countries to show deficits, and the "chronic" shortage of dollars. These tendencies are not chronic in the sense of being inevitable; they would cease if the disturbing impacts ceased or if the automatic correctives were reinforced in the deficit countries by tight money policies and increased taxation. They are chronic only in the sense of being persistent and not being sufficiently offset by appropriate policy.[12]

### Influence of Foreign Technological Progress

The question arises whether the rapid rate of technological progress in some Western nations, particularly in the United States, may not be a cause contributing to the foreign deficits of underdeveloped areas in the same manner as the high consumption levels in Western nations. A technological lag tends to result in deficits if it weakens the power of a country's exports in world markets, or if it causes the home population to substitute imports for domestic products. Many of the raw material and cheap-labor exports of underdeveloped areas do not have to meet the competition of industrial countries. However, technological advance in the production of consumers' goods may lead the less developed countries into extravagant consumption and thus into foreign deficits. So far as the import of producers' goods is concerned, a more rapid pace of technological advance in the developed countries cannot impair the foreign balance of the underdeveloped countries if they already derive most of their specialized machinery from abroad. If a rapid rate of technical improvement causes the

10. An early expositor of this factor was Charles P. Kindleberger in his essay on "International Monetary Stabilization," in Seymour E. Harris (Ed.), *Postwar Economic Problems*, McGraw-Hill, New York, 1943, pp. 375–98. In *The Dollar Shortage* (The Technology Press, Massachusetts Institute of Technology, Cambridge, 1950, and Wiley, New York, 1951), Kindleberger has expanded on both the consumption factor and the technological factor.

11. A deficit country would be expected to show the following changes, each of which works toward the elimination of the deficit: a reduction of incomes, employment and the general level of prices; a rise in the prices of international relative to purely domestic goods; a movement of resources from domestic to international goods (exports or import substitutes); an inflow of private capital; and, if it is free to move, a fall in its rate of exchange. Opposite changes in the surplus country, of course, tend to reduce its one-sided balance.

12. This view is presented in Howard S. Ellis, "The Dollar Shortage in Theory and Fact," *Canadian Journal of Economic and Political Science*, August 1948, pp. 358–73, and more lately in Jacob Viner, *International Trade and Economic Development*, The Free Press, Glencoe, Illinois, 1952, pp. 77*ff*.

developed countries to increase their demands for raw materials, primary producers stand to gain.

What the net outcome of all these factors may be is hard to predict. It would scarcely be adverse to primary producers in all cases.

*Meager Reserves*

A further factor associated with low per capita incomes is the small amount of international currency reserves (gold and foreign balances) that poorer countries hold as a buffer against variations in export yields. Whether these reserves are large or small is not a matter of their absolute size but of their size relative to the swings of the country's trade balance. Underdeveloped areas, being subject to great variations in export proceeds, should require larger international currency reserves relative to the volume of their foreign trade than do the maturer economies exporting manufactured products. Yet most of the primary producing countries have very small international reserves.

This fact can be attributed largely to their reluctance, as low-income countries, to forego much-needed imports, as they would have to do to build reserves.[13] But this "reluctance" is not a matter of the choices of private income recipients, a factor very frequently difficult for governments to ignore, but a matter of government policy itself. Furthermore, international currency reserves do not usually tie up a very large fraction of a country's capital, even if they are adequate to meet most normal contingencies—and it is futile to expect to provide for every contingency in the balance of payments. By taking thought, most governments could provide reserves for normal contingencies even in relatively poor countries. The abnormal contingency, such as a severe world-wide depression or a sudden disaster to a particular country's exports, has to be faced by measures of international cooperation: currency reserves held by individual countries are not, in isolation, appropriate for meeting these adversities.

Even international cooperation in the form of stabilization loans by international agencies or loans by an individual country will not cure the shortage of reserves of underdeveloped countries if these reserves simply disappear in every cyclical depression. Domestic measures to control inflation are essential if the period of prosperity is, through the accumulation of reserves, to provide for the rainy days of recession.

### CAPITAL MOVEMENTS

Long-term loans and investments from abroad, if applied productively, eventually result in an increased flow of output, including exports and im-

13. See League of Nations, Economic, Financial and Transit Department, *International Currency Experience*, Geneva, 1944, pp. 88–94.

port substitutes. Foreign capital thus helps a developing country to prevent inflation, to maintain equilibrium in its foreign balance and to avoid depreciation of its currency. This fundamental fact must not be forgotten in considering certain inflationary potentialities of an inflow of foreign capital in the short run.

### How Inflation Arises

If the government of an underdeveloped country utilizes the proceeds of foreign borrowing for imported tools or other capital goods and then sells these to domestic companies, and if the domestic companies make the purchases from previously idle funds or from new bank loans, domestic inflation equal to the foreign loan will result. Over the course of a year, other things being equal, money incomes will rise by the amount of the foreign loan multiplied by the "income velocity" of the possibly augmented stock of money. Only if the private purchasers substitute the outlay for other purchases which they had been making—thus making new savings equal to the foreign loan, which seems unlikely—would the inflation be avoided. Otherwise, the government must tax its citizens, or the central bank must induce banks to contract credit, or the treasury must set aside, as "counterpart funds" in the language of the Economic Cooperation Administration, sums equal to the foreign loan, to prevent inflation.

The same generalizations hold for foreign borrowing by governments or private parties if the loan proceeds are used, not for imports, but for hiring or buying domestic resources to construct capital equipment. They hold also for expenditures of foreign capital by foreign companies within the underdeveloped country, whether for imports or for domestic resources. In all these cases, deflation by taxation or credit policy is necessary if the inflationary effect of the foreign funds is to be countered.[14] The inflationary impact of foreign capital, it should be noted, does not depend upon a possible multiple expansion of credit by domestic banks on the basis of an inflow of gold or foreign balances.[15]

When eventually the capital equipment begins to turn out products, the amount of money can safely be increased, provided, of course, the product is vendible. Alternatively, if the underdeveloped economy receives foreign loans in a more or less even flow, it can—after the earlier loans have begun to yield a flow of product—offset the inflationary effects of the new loans by the deflationary effects of the new production. A preponderance of one

---

14. Domestic inflation is not engendered, at least not independently, by a foreign loan to a government that uses the proceeds to buy foreign equipment which it then continues to hold and "operate" and does not sell. Reinvested profits by foreign companies are similarly noninflationary, since the disbursements proceed from new savings made in domestic money.

15. Foreign loans have been assumed to be "lines of credit" utilized only for the command of imports; or, if the loan was made for or included outlays on domestic resources, it has been assumed that imports were immediately made necessary in order to release these domestic resources for capital purposes.

over the other can be met by appropriate increases or decreases in the stock of money.

It may safely be assumed that the entire proceeds of a foreign loan are devoted to imports, either directly in the purchase of foreign capital equipment or indirectly, if the loan is spent first on domestic resources, in purchasing imported food and consumers' goods to permit the diversion of labor from necessary consumers' goods to the production of plant and equipment. But the original outlay of loan proceeds may not exhaust the demand for imports flowing from the loan. Income receivers presumably spend a part of their expendable funds on imports, and these "induced imports" are additional to the primary import demand arising from the foreign loan.

### How to Prevent Inflation

Consequently, a country financing part of its development by means of foreign capital must limit its expansion of domestic money incomes to what the primary plus the induced demand for imports will permit, with the basic consideration of the country's export capacity and any inflow of new loans as the limiting factors. But the same rule also applies to internally financed development, since purely domestic investment also may give rise to both primary and induced import demands. It is not the *source* of capital which may cause excessive imports but the rise of domestic incomes and prices relative to those abroad.

Induced imports are not a peculiarity of foreign loans, and least of all are they a peculiarity of foreign private loans and foreign private investment.[16] A foreign capitalist takes no account of how his investment may affect imports; the problem must be solved by appropriate monetary and fiscal policy. But the very same measures must be taken in order to hold within bounds the induced imports from foreign *public* loans and investments, as indeed from *domestic* investment, both public and private.

Furthermore, induced imports constitute no case against a "project basis" for development loans of the kind the International Bank has generally insisted upon. The total import demand from a given investment project will not exceed the original loans if the monetary-fiscal authorities in the receiving country do not allow money incomes to rise excessively. Obviously, no amount of supplementary foreign loans designed to "cover induced imports" will suffice if incomes in the borrowing country are progressively inflated.

### Questions of Policy

There is no given proportion of total domestic investment that must be financed at home by an underdeveloped country, or any other country, in

16. Contrary to what Kindleberger seems to imply in *The Dollar Shortage*, pp. 33–34.

order to avoid balance-of-payments deficits, so long as the investment is financed by voluntary saving or by the several forms of compulsory saving other than inflation. Even more obviously, there is no given proportion of domestic factors other than capital, such as labor, managerial services and materials, that must be employed in order to avoid deficits in the foreign balance.[17]

What is required to steer clear of balance-of-payments difficulties if developing countries borrow from abroad is a monetary and fiscal policy that offsets the inflationary impact of the original expenditures on capital equipment as well as that of the imports induced by subsequent expenditures of the additional income. Import and investment controls are *not* necessary to achieve these ends. Certain countries have shown a decided predilection for direct controls, and for such countries the inflationary potential of foreign borrowing offers a welcome excuse for more "planning" and more interference in trade. If the basic cause of balance-of-payments difficulties is inflation, however, these direct controls are likely to be mere palliatives. The pressure on the country's exchange rates is not removed but only restrained; and the restraints of direct controls on the deficit tend to contribute to an all-around shrinkage of international trade.

*Stipulations by Foreign Lenders*

Countries that are underdeveloped economically are often—perhaps even generally—underdeveloped also in institutions of monetary and fiscal control. It may therefore be necessary for foreign lending authorities to refuse to lend without stipulations concerning the achievement of balanced budgets, restraint of credit, and so on, unless they are prepared to see the economic fruition of their loans blighted by inflation and adverse foreign balances in the borrowing countries. The Bell Mission recommended this procedure in any further United States aid to the Philippines. In the 1930s, the League of Nations secured stable financial policies in countries receiving the League loans through a system of financial advisers. Arrangements of this sort have been made quite informally in connection with some of the International Bank's more recent loans. The practice might well be given wider recognition and use.

### PRINCIPLES OF INVESTMENT IN DEVELOPING ECONOMIES

As with the more mature economies, so also for the younger ones the avoidance of inflation by proper credit and budgetary measures is the primary prescription against foreign deficits. The "necessity" for extensive controls then disappears, as well as the "necessity" of observing largely

17. Alfred E. Kahn in his article "Investment Criteria in Development Programs," *Quarterly Journal of Economics*, February 1951, pp. 45–46, is correct in his criticisms.

self-evident rules, such as taking account of induced imports, or quite spurious ones, such as gauging the proper extent of foreign borrowing by the import content of capital improvements.

With regard to the appropriate character of investment in a developing country a simple prescription also suffices: investment that seems best from the standpoint of the country's domestic economy is also best from the standpoint of its balance of payments with the outside world. Unfortunately, this simple rule would be regarded as anything but self-evident in some quarters.

### Infant Industries

The proposition must be modified, of course, for genuine cases of "infant industries" that can be built up eventually to a position of effective import substitutes or competitive exports only by virtue of state subsidies or tariff protection. But the number of such industries is limited. For the validity of the "infant industries" argument rests on two conditions: first, that the legislatures which impose the tariffs have superior knowledge or insight regarding future economic development, as compared to private capitalists and their experts; second, that the subsidy or protection will be withdrawn once a period of not indecently prolonged infancy has elapsed. If these conditions are met, as they probably rarely are, there is then an instance of an investment that will eventually prove wise for both the national productivity and the balance of payments though not immediately optimal for either.

### Productivity as the Criterion

The proposition that investment which maximizes domestic productivity also makes the maximum contribution to balance-of-payments equilibrium is a direct corollary to the principle of free trade and the principle of maximizing total returns through the allocation of capital so as always to secure a rate of return as good as or better than what it might secure elsewhere. But the proposition, applied to developing economies, or others, requires two qualifications.

First, some investments, particularly those in the public services and utilities, have a productivity *not directly* revealed by the market value of their vendible product. If "productivity" is measured by *direct* product, the general principle of maximum return becomes subject to corresponding qualification. If productivity is measured broadly, the qualification is slight: public services of the sort here envisaged usually make important indirect contributions to export capacity.

Second, expenditures for consumption out of foreign loans are not usually regarded either as investment or as increasing the capacity to produce goods for home consumption or export. Thus the use of a foreign loan for foodstuffs or housing falls outside the principle except to the limited degree to which these outlays can really be regarded as productive investment. To this limited degree, however, they increase both domestic productivity and export capacity.

Productivity thus asserts itself as the criterion of correct investment for capital derived from abroad, just as it is for capital from domestic sources. In Polak's words, "foreign exchange troubles are not created by the fact that expenditure for 'unproductive' purposes is financed from abroad, but by the fact such expenditure is made at all."[18]

The general rule that, for regions of capital scarcity and abundant labor, investment should be "capital-economizing" represents neither a modification of nor an addition to the productivity rule. Costs are minimized and profits are maximized; that is, capital instruments are most productive when they employ the most economical combination of factors in view of their prices; this procedure also maximizes national income. The same rule of investment will make the largest contribution toward eliminating a deficit in the trade balance.[19]

### Special Types of Projects

Balance-of-payments deficits can be caused by investment in projects that take excessively long periods for completion. No productive facility yields a flow of goods, an addition to national income, until it is completed. It is the function of the saved-up purchasing power of the investment capital to provide the necessary real resources that come to be embodied in the final machine or improvement. If the capital provision is adequate for the undertaking, its gestation period, the period required to complete it, will not be excessive. This is true whether the project is financed locally or from abroad. In general, the high rates of interest and low rates of wages in underdeveloped regions will dictate an economical use of capital, and gestation periods will be correspondingly short. But, more specifically, it is only necessary, in order to avoid balance-of-payments difficulties, that the person or government undertaking a project be assured that enough domestic or foreign capital is available, or during the gestation period will become available, to complete the undertaking.

Observation of substantially the same principles will prevent underdeveloped areas from committing their capital to forms which have a too slow turnover, that is, a too low ratio of annual gross receipts ("sales") to

18. J. J. Polak, "Balance of Payments Problems of Countries Reconstructing with the Help of Foreign Loans," *Quarterly Journal of Economics*, February 1943, p. 228.

19. In other words, as Ohlin explained, a country gains most by exporting products in which its relatively cheapest resources form a large component. See Bertil Ohlin, *Interregional and International Trade*, Harvard University Press, Cambridge, 1933.

investment. If the capital is invested with due regard to the general rules of productivity, the *net* returns to capital will cover interest charges. In general, in a capital-poor economy, the most economical ratio of capital to labor will be a low ratio, and this means a high turnover or *gross* return rate in the sense that replacement charges are high in relation to interest charges. However, if the person or government undertaking the project constructs it in a sufficiently capital-economizing fashion to be able to meet the schedule of debt amortization agreed upon in the loan contract, there will be no reason for balance-of-payments difficulties. Naturally, however, the foregoing rule of financial prudence will have to be observed for domestic as well as for foreign borrowing, if any of the actual investment involves imports.

Some techniques admit of few or no variations in the size of investment or in the proportion of capital and labor utilized. There may be types of investment *unavoidably* entailing excessively long periods of gestation, projects involving a larger capital provision than the developing economy has at its disposal from prospective domestic or foreign sources. In this situation, the authorities cannot avoid the uncomfortable choice between not launching the project at all and going ahead with the hope of securing the necessary additional funds as the work proceeds. Purely technical requirements may also impose the necessity for a capital instrument of greater durability than would seem warranted in a cheap-labor country. Here again the choice is between foregoing the project and constructing an instrument that requires heavy initial capital outlay with subsequent low outlays for maintenance labor in a capital-poor, labor-abundant economy. There is no general solution to these dilemmas. But the great changes occurring in a rapidly developing economy make investment risks correspondingly great, and caution in launching large-scale capital-intensive projects would seem to be the better part of valor.[20]

### Timing and Size of Projects

Thus several of the hazards to which the balance of payments of a developing country has been considered to be exposed are avoidable by observing the ordinary principle of investment according to productivity and ordinary financial prudence. But, it may be asked, even if a particular investment meets the test of competitive productivity—that is, if the present discounted value of the total foreseeable future income from a particular project equals or exceeds the present cost of production of the projected instrument—cannot foreign deficits arise from a lack of coincidence in the *time* of the receipts and the schedule of interest and amortization? If a country intent on development were to launch simultaneously a substantial

20. See pp. 277–79, above.

number of heavy investment projects, foreign deficits could undoubtedly appear even though the investment were highly productive and domestic or foreign finance were adequate to cover the cost of the projects. Returns might still not *at times* cover the service of the debt. The very function of a foreign loan, if it suffices for the total construction cost, is to accommodate the *total* foreign deficits during the unproductive period from inception to completion of the project.

The danger of deficits from the lack of coincidence of the "time-shape" of returns with the schedule of the debt service is great only (1) if a large portion of the total foreign borrowing is committed to one particular project; (2) if, with a large number of projects, all or most of them have similar "time-shapes" of returns *and* if they are launched simultaneously or in rapid succession; or (3) if—often a serious possibility—there are long delays in the execution of construction plans. The probabilities are somewhat against the first two of these contingencies. A large succession of foreign borrowings together with an equally large succession of relatively small investments tends to produce an even flow of both amortization and investment yields. Furthermore, the developing country may possess monetary reserves sufficient to bridge over temporary deficits. But if not, and if the productivity of the investment has been clearly established, it would appear to be one of the primary responsibilities of the International Monetary Fund to care for these purely temporary deficits. To sacrifice the productivity of investment and hence its *aggregate* benefits in real income and in the balance of payments because of *temporary* sources of deficits would be an act of desperation.

### Loans versus Grants

A borrowing economy invites disaster for its balance of payments if it utilizes a foreign loan in such a way that the direct or indirect increment to real income resulting from it is smaller than the interest charge, that is, if the productivity of the capital is less than interest. For this reason, the use of foreign capital for consumption or for low-productivity purposes requires outright grants or low-interest loans. And the international agencies, including the International Bank, and governments, chiefly the United States, have in recent years recognized this need of capital for the establishment of low-yield basic utilities for welfare purposes.

### Overborrowing

If interest and amortization charges do not exceed the long-run productivity of the projects, developing countries may still run afoul of balance-of-payments difficulties because of autonomous variations in the balance of trade—in the relation of exports to imports independent of loans. It is from this angle that "overborrowing" assumes real meaning, for there is otherwise no definable proportion of the total foreign exchange receipts of the borrowing country that must not be exceeded by the foreign debt service. Overborrowing does not consist in a possible interest or profits slavery to exploitative foreign capitalists, for typically these sums, computed as a per capita charge per year, have been very small. It consists, rather, in so large a charge on the balance of payments—and dividends, while not a *fixed* charge, are nevertheless a charge—that cyclical or episodic *variations* in export yields may leave an insufficient margin for necessary imports. In Australia, for example, the "investment service ratio," defined as the "proportion of foreign exchange receipts absorbed by the service of foreign investments," having ranged from 14.8 to 26.0 per cent from 1904 to 1929, suddenly rose from 26.0 to 43.8 per cent from 1929 to 1931.[21]

For primary producers, whose export yields characteristically fluctuate in a wide arc, the investment service ratio is occasionally dangerously high. In 1949 the countries with the highest values for investment service in Latin America were Costa Rica and Venezuela, at 22.4 and 26.0 per cent of foreign exchange receipts; in Asia, Iran and Iraq, at 53.1 and 17.7 per cent; and in Africa, Northern Rhodesia, at 34.3 per cent. But 1949 was a year of recession in the developed industrial countries and hence the figures stood at high levels even for them. In that year the countries with the lowest investment service ratios were, in Latin America, Ecuador, Puerto Rico and El Salvador, at 5.6, 3.8 and 2.3 per cent; in Asia, India, the Philippine Republic and Ceylon, at 5.0, 5.0 and 3.2 per cent; and in Africa, Southern Rhodesia and Egypt, at 8.1 and 6.5 per cent. Most countries lay closer to the lower than to the higher limits.[22] Thus, with notable exceptions, the investment service ratios of underdeveloped countries are not in general perilously high. Where they are, the danger exists chiefly because of the variability of export yields.

*Capital Flight*

Many problems are involved for underdeveloped countries in the inflow of foreign capital, the utilization of these funds, and the service of the debt. But an *outflow* of funds, usually called a "flight of capital," is a still more serious matter. The repercussions of foreign borrowing may occasionally be adverse; but for a capital-poor country the *fact* of borrowing is generally favorable. By the same token, for a capital-poor country, a capital outflow is itself an unfavorable fact. The complications of borrowing belong to what mathematicians call the "second order of smalls," whereas the loss of capital to foreign countries is a first-order evil.

21. David Finch, "Investment Service Ratios of Underdeveloped Countries," International Monetary Fund, *Staff Papers*, September 1951, pp. 60–85.

22. *Ibid.*, p. 84.

Guatemalan private deposits in the United States amounted to 14 million quetzals (1 quetzal = $1 U.S.) in 1950, a sum almost equivalent to the annual volume of private capital formation.[23] In three months prior to the national elections of July 6, 1952, Mexican businessmen and investors sent $50 million to the United States for safekeeping or speculation,[24] an amount equal to one half the unfavorable balance of that country for January–June 1952. The abrogation of the Anglo-Egyptian treaty in October 1951 led to the establishment of several banks in Beirut that specialized in the transfer of capital from Cairo to the West at 12 to 15 per cent discount.[25] In the first six months of 1951, foreign private capital was withdrawn from Ceylon to a total of 33.9 million rupees, whereas new private foreign investments in Ceylon amounted to 14.9 million rupees during the same period.[26]

Clandestine capital exports on private account largely elude official estimate. It may be partly the lack of anything more than sporadic figures, such as those just cited, that has deterred economists from giving more attention to the problem of capital flight from the less highly developed economies. But it seems fairly certain that in some cases a large part of the new capital funds coming in from abroad is lost to domestic development in this reverse flow. Little has been said about this possibility in the various financial studies of the United Nations or in the International Bank's reports on countries.

## COPING WITH BALANCE-OF-PAYMENTS PROBLEMS

The foreign deficit of an underdeveloped country in large measure merely reflects its domestic deficit—it parallels the excess of domestic investment over domestic saving, voluntary and forced. In other words, inflation—either absolute or relative to the trading partners—is perhaps the most common cause of the balance-of-payments difficulties of underdeveloped countries, just as it is with the more mature industrial economies. Basically, inflation can be prevented, rather than merely concealed or suppressed, only by monetary and fiscal policies. If developing countries possess only rudimentary monetary controls or inadequate tax systems, they have the choice of improving these institutions or resigning themselves to open or suppressed inflation. The widespread need for such improvement as well as the most basic remedies against uncovered foreign deficits arising from inflation have already been discussed in Chapter 15.

23. International Bank for Reconstruction and Development, *The Economic Development of Guatemala*, Washington, 1951, pp. 290–91.

24. *New York Times*, August 11, 1952.

25. *The Economist*, May 3, 1952, pp. 299–300.

26. *Economic Weekly*, April 26, 1952, p. 428.

Other factors, besides inflation, that may cause deficits or make them hard to manage for the less developed economies include: large swings in export yields; imitation of foreign standards of living, and the small provision of international monetary reserves, both of which are closely associated with low per capita incomes; the troubles that may develop from a foreign capital inflow, from specific forms of investment, and from the payment of interest and repayment of principal; and finally, the flight of capital. What are the means for coping with these problems?

## Capital Flight

The flight of capital, to begin at the end of the list, is one of the least tractable of modern economic ills; to effect a cure, treatment must be directed toward the whole constitution of the suffering economy. However severe the penalties for evasion, the history of exchange control reveals a general lack of success in enforcing prohibitions of capital export. Even in the case of the United Kingdom, which enjoys a high level of civic responsibility and commercial ethics, capital export—either by way of "avoidance" or violation of the regulations—has at times played a predominant role in the development of payments deficits.[27] All of the countries cited previously as illustrations of recent severe flights impose embargoes on capital export. Not only do these prohibitions frequently fail in their purpose, but they also have the perverse effect of deterring new capital from entering the country.[28]

The phenomenon of capital flight from underdeveloped economies reinforces more powerfully than almost any other evidence the contention that domestic conditions favorable to the saving and investment of home capital are absolute prerequisites if foreign capital is to be attracted, and, if obtained, not then offset by a reverse flow of funds.

It is unnecessary to embroider on the necessity of political stability and freedom from political reprisals against savers and capital suppliers. But it may be desirable to add that taxation cuts two ways: while high taxes combat inflation and thus contribute to the safety of the home currency, they also drive capital abroad. In developing economies, *monetary* methods of avoiding inflation thus take on an added significance. The historical record, particularly in the more rapidly developing nations of Latin America, shows that the avoidance of inflation is one of the most difficult achievements.

27. See Lionel Robbins, "Inquest on the Crisis," *Lloyds Bank Review*, October 1947, pp. 1–27; Roy F. Harrod, *The Pound Sterling* (Essays in International Finance, No. 13), International Finance Section, Princeton University, February 1952.

28. The easing of exchange controls by Colombia during 1951 was immediately followed by an increased inflow of foreign capital. See *New York Times*, January 4, 1952, pp. 41 and 59.

*Capital Inflow*

To escape the inflation and the foreign deficits that may attend an *inflow* of foreign capital, on the other hand, should be feasible. For, fundamentally, the importation of long-term capital is disinflationary and favorable to the borrower's exchange rate. But the utilization of foreign loans, except for certain cases previously pointed out, sets inflation afoot.[29] It may be counterbalanced by credit contraction or an increase of taxation equal to the loan. Or, alternatively, sums equal to the sales of imported goods or the purchases of domestic resources from the loan may be rendered inactive by deposit in a "counterpart funds" account maintained by the government.

If foreign loans are used in consumption or for low-productivity projects without correspondingly low interest and amortization charges, the developing country's balance will deteriorate. To maximize the disinflationary effect of foreign long-term capital and its improvements of the balance of payments, high-productivity lines of investment must be placed first. Foreign and domestic private investors will certainly strive to achieve maximum returns, and their investments will maximize the balance of payments unless the state (that is to say, its civil servants) should possess superior knowledge or information concerning better lines of investment.

No departure from the rule of productivity, and therefore no further complication for the developing economy, is involved in selecting such investments as do not have excessively long gestation periods or excessively long turnover periods. Ordinary financial prudence on the part of the state or the private investor will preclude ventures that cannot be finished with the available domestic and foreign capital and ventures yielding returns at an average rate that lags behind the contractual rate of debt service. Complications may arise, it is true, even with high-productivity investments if their returns at times fall short of the debt service. But this difficulty may be avoided by launching a large number of smaller ventures so that their yields overlap and thus produce an approximately even flow in the aggregate. Or, alternatively, if a single large capital venture is the most productive, the government may accumulate reserves or borrow on short term to bridge the gap. The government will be loath to forego productivity in order to avoid the possibility of a temporary adverse balance, and foreign public lenders should presumably take the same position.

From the standpoint of the borrower's capacity to service the debt, foreign borrowing is, of course, excessive for any and all sums that are not invested in such a way as to yield the contemplated interest and amortization payments. Even with the successful investment, it may also be excessive at times in terms of yield over the lifetime of the venture, if the total

---

29. See n. 14. Naturally, also, so long as a loan stands merely as an unutilized line of credit in favor of the underdeveloped country, it has no inflationary force. The magnitude of these unutilized credits—possibly through no "fault" of the borrowing countries—is large. See Table 17–3.

of debt service charges forms a large proportion of the foreign exchange yields of exports and if these yields from exports are highly variable. Some underdeveloped countries appear to be in this unfortunate situation, but their number is not large.

Thus examination of the pitfalls that may await developing countries as a result of the transfer of foreign capital into their economies for investment purposes and the consequent servicing of foreign debts does not reveal much danger that cannot be avoided by good private and public management. And most of the good management consists in following ordinary rules of maximizing returns from investment, in exercising ordinary financial prudence, and in pursuing fiscal and monetary policies that will promote stability of prices and employment.

## Low Incomes

The situation is different with the causes of balance-of-payments difficulties that are associated with low average incomes—most notably the imitation of the levels of personal or family outlay of the more prosperous nations. A sufficient degree of austerity can, of course, be imposed by taxation, exchange controls or direct limitation of imports. But the developing country may face something of a dilemma in that, for a populace sufficiently sophisticated to know and to wish to imitate foreign consumption standards, one of the chief psychological drives toward economic progress may be withdrawn if the impulse remains unsatisfied. Some degree of compromise that induces or forces a certain amount of domestic capital formation for future higher incomes and still permits some increased consumption would seem to be the necessary solution for any but totalitarian states.

Also associated with low incomes is the tendency of underdeveloped countries to hold too small reserves of gold and foreign balances to protect their currencies from collapse with each major downswing in export markets. This difficulty is largely unsurmountable except by measures directed toward the stabilization of world commodity markets. In the absence of such a basic improvement, stabilization loans from foreign sources are likely to be dissipated at the first whiff of adversity.

## Swings in Export Demand

Economic development probably carries with it some tendency toward diversification of exports and self-sufficiency on the side of imports. But this tendency is altogether too slight to affect trade problems significantly. For a long time to come, the less developed countries will continue to be primary producers so far as concerns export markets; and they will continue to suffer from periodic crises in their foreign accounts unless world commodity markets become more stable.

Thus an early theme of this chapter recurs—the vulnerability of export economies to swings in export yields. It is difficult to believe that any other factor has a stronger *disruptive* effect on the foreign balances of underdeveloped countries. The pressure of the younger economies toward higher consumption levels is probably fairly constant; the operation is secular rather than cyclical. And while this unremitting pressure complicates the attainment of balance in their international accounts, it does not present a crisis phenomenon. Partly for this reason and partly for others, it should be amenable to control. Even capital flights would be less serious if the currencies of the underdeveloped countries were not undermined in each major depression by unfavorable trade balances.

### Diversification

An idea that has found rather wide support in underdeveloped countries and has been championed by an occasional economist is that diversification of the primary producer's economy is desirable as a defense against fluctuations in international markets.[30] In order to make a conscious policy of diversification effective, it would have to involve a readiness to sacrifice productivity in favor of security, since otherwise no issue of diversification versus concentration would arise. The solution, in any event, must be one of degree. Proponents of diversification would rarely advocate the policy to its extreme, that is, no exports or imports; and opponents would rarely deny that reduction of risk is properly a part of economic arithmetic for individuals and nations alike. However, diversification that is not automatically the outcome of economic progress along lines of maximum productivity entails a loss of efficiency, of output and of the rate of progress itself.

### The Basis of Stabilization

The responsibility for bringing about a tolerable degree of stability in the international markets for primary products rests chiefly where the demand for these products arises—with the economically advanced nations. To come to the root of the trouble, *domestic* production and employment must be stabilized in the principal industrial and commercial countries. In default of this, what can be accomplished by international commodity stabilization schemes would seem to be doubtful, despite the judicious support given them in the Angell report to the United Nations.[31] In any event, it is

30. See, for example, S. G. Triantis, "Cyclical Changes in the Balance of Trade," *American Economic Review*, March 1952, pp. 69–86.

31. United Nations, Department of Economic Affairs, *Measures for International Economic Stability* (report by a group of experts appointed by the Secretary-General), New York, 1951. An earlier report, by a different group of experts, under the title *National and International Measures for Full Employment* (United Nations, New York, 1949), encountered much adverse criticism because of the "automatic," i.e., non-discretionary, obligations it would impose, particularly on creditor countries.

clear that the Western nations, especially the United States, have, through the alternations of hectic prosperity and deep depressions which their markets have induced in other nations, wasted a good deal of the substance of their well-meant loans and grants. Greater stability of international demand is a primary requisite for economic development, even aside from the requirement that defense policies shall not injure the actual or potential friends of the North Atlantic Pact.

Responsibility for restraining popular demands for higher levels of living, for maintaining adequate international reserves, for offsetting the initial inflationary effect of foreign loans, for the productive use of capital and for the service of foreign debt—all these responsibilities rest primarily on the countries aspiring to development. Advice, expert assistance, and even the attaching of conditions to loans by the other countries have their place; but they cannot supplant responsible management in the receiving economy. Adequate taxation and monetary controls are the first requirements of this responsible management. Inflation fosters excesses of consumption and foreign deficits; it wastes away reserves of foreign exchange; it thwarts the allocation of scarce capital to maximum-productivity ventures; and it undermines the maintenance of foreign debt service. How far direct controls and exchange controls may be substituted for monetary and fiscal measures is the next question to be considered.

### EXCHANGE CONTROL AND ECONOMIC DEVELOPMENT

The main purposes of exchange control are (1) to obtain protection from foreign competition; (2) to encourage or compel saving; (3) to obtain more favorable terms of trade; (4) to prevent capital flight; and (5) to obtain protection from foreign depressions. The term "exchange control," as used here, means, at the very least, a government monopoly of all dealings in foreign exchange, an embargo on the export of capital, and an official price on foreign exchange that usually but not invariably overvalues the domestic currency.

A decade ago exchange control was rather widely regarded as an especially powerful instrument of economic development. On the whole, there has been a retreat from this position, though it still has adherents. Exchange controls are in effect, to be sure, in nearly all of the less developed countries; but they are almost universal in the other countries as well. What are the gains that have been expected specifically by underdeveloped countries from exchange controls, and to what degree are these hopes likely to be realized? Perhaps a careful scrutiny of the five purposes of exchange controls will answer these questions.

*Protection from Foreign Competition*

An overvalued rate on the home currency maintained by means of exchange control automatically affords domestic industry some shelter from foreign competition, though this fact may not be immediately apparent. An overvalued rate discourages exports but, on its initial impact, *encourages* imports. How then can it be protective? The answer lies in the plain fact that a country cannot long continue to buy without delivering goods in payment; imports usually decline to the reduced level of exports imposed by the overvaluation. By appropriate adjustments, the same degree of protection may be secured by import quotas and by import taxes or import license fees as by exchange control with overvalued rates—both in the aggregate for all commodities or for one good separately.

Part of the political appeal, and part of the danger, of the exchange control type of protection is its covertness. The risks of protecting "infant industries" by tariffs are great enough. But if the original decision to protect is *concealed* and is imposed, not by legislation, but *administratively*, as it is under exchange control, clearly, additional risks are involved over tariff protection.

Whether protection comes by one way or another, its dangers are great. Writing with particular reference to Latin America, John S. de Beers of the United States Treasury Department says:

Drastic direct import controls have cut the trade deficit, but they do not automatically bring into play self-corrective processes which would eventually correct the basic maladjustments and make possible removal of the controls. On the contrary, their influence appears to be in the opposite direction. Import quotas, for example, reduce customs revenues without reducing total consumer demand or limiting the increase of prices, and thereby tend to intensify inflation, making it progressively more difficult to administer the direct controls unless anti-inflationary measures are taken. Furthermore, they may produce an "aspirin effect"; i.e., by taking care of immediate balance-of-payments headaches, they may divert attention from the basic maladies. Reform in matters such as tax and fiscal policy, central banking policy, and government policies affecting private capital formation may then be postponed, with resulting further deterioration in underlying economic and financial conditions.[32]

Each of these dangers is inherent in protection through exchange control, to which other dangers are peculiar because of its administrative and covert nature.

*Inducement or Compulsion to Save*

A state wishing to limit individual consumption in order to obtain desirable rates of economic progress may accomplish something toward this

32. John S. de Beers, "Some Aspects of Latin America's Trade and Balance of Payments," *American Economic Review, Proceedings,* May 1949, p. 390.

objective through selective import controls directed against consumption in general or luxury consumption, whether by means of tight import quotas, reduced exchange allocations, discriminating and high exchange rates or high tariffs. All such selective import controls, however, leave two problems untouched. Domestic consumers may simply deflect their sumptuary or luxury expenditures to other domestic goods. Domestic producers may begin to turn out substitutes for the foreign import, but at a cost equal to or greater than the original import, with a corresponding drain on domestic resources. Income, sumptuary or luxury taxes would thus appear superior to selective import controls of all varieties since taxes reduce *all* consumption expenditure and not merely expenditure on imports.[33]

*Favorable Terms of Trade*

As one of several devices, including state trading, exchange control can, under favorable circumstances, secure to a given country an extra margin of gain in international trade by reason of monopolistic selling or monopsonistic buying, with or without discrimination among sellers or buyers. The less developed economies probably cannot appreciably affect the prices of their imports, mostly of an industrial character, because each country accounts for too small a portion of the international demand. On the export side, however, as primary producers, these countries may occasionally control a large enough portion of the world supply to make monopoly exaction possible. In a sellers' market, such as followed World War II and the aggression in Korea, primary producers can raise prices even without monopoly power.

This securing of more favorable terms in times of cyclical or episodic sellers' markets for such staples as tin, rubber and wool has a general stabilizing effect—provided the price to the foreign buyer is abated in downturns—and it yields the primary producers substantial revenues on their exhaustible resources. Favorable arguments have already been presented for export taxes on these grounds.[34] Export taxes appear superior to differential export exchange rates in avoiding the necessity of an exchange control apparatus and the breaching of a uniform exchange rate.

How far primary producers could go beyond securing the full benefits of a sellers' market, in attempting a more or less consistent and persistent monopoly levy is, perhaps, questionable. By these tactics one seller invites undercutting from other sellers. And monopoly exaction by one or more sellers may invite retaliation on the part of the buyers. Occasionally, buyers among the advanced industrial nations have large shares of the market (e.g., the United Kingdom) and can meet monopoly with monopsony.

33. But if the primary objective were to close a balance-of-payments gap, the best measure would be devaluation, which bears on *all* foreign expenditures and not merely on "necessities."
34. See pp. 316, 328.

They are, furthermore, the lenders, whose good will is not to be too lightly set aside.[35]

*Prevention of Capital Flight*

If the political or economic conditions of a developing economy cause a flight of capital into foreign currencies, a capital export embargo may be the only recourse. This move usually entails full-fledged exchange control— the checking over of every individual export transaction and every individual outward payment, as well as inspection of the mails and of persons. Even if completely enforced upon a country's own nationals, exchange control cannot eliminate inequalities in the balance of payments caused by an uneven flow, generally cyclical, of new investment by foreigners. Furthermore, the very existence of exchange control undoubtedly reduces the *inflow* of foreign private capital on the average over a term of years.

Despite these serious disadvantages, a country with an overvalued exchange rate cannot usually escape a capital export prohibition, because such capital movements intensify the overvaluation and the motive for flight. The only escape from the unhealthy necessity of policing capital exports is to bring to an end the fundamental causes of disequilibrium— inflation, overvalued exchange rates, excessive consumption and the like.

*Protection from Foreign Depressions*

As primary producers, the less developed regions are highly vulnerable to cyclical or episodic reductions by the industrial countries in their demand for raw materials and, to a lesser degree, foodstuffs. Quotas, import licenses, exchange allocation and other barriers to imports can, if applied with sufficient severity, prevent the appearance of adverse trade balances and currency depreciation for the primary producers. But even if they were to allow their reserves of international currencies to ebb away, and even if they were to accept large declines in the foreign value of their own currency, the mere restriction of imports might not in extreme depressions counteract the shrinkage of domestic *income* from falling export yields. Fundamentally, their currency and income can be stabilized only by the stabilization of domestic economies in the rest of the world.

In conclusion, exchange control and direct quantitative controls afford the most feeble kind of support to economic development. Potentially, the protection of infant industries could make a positive contribution; but the risk of protecting infants that prove not to be viable or to be viable only

35. It may be remarked that nothing in the situation of a monopolistic seller justifies—even from the standpoint of self-interest—the maintenance of an overvalued exchange rate. The contrary may be implied by Wallich, in "Underdeveloped Countries in the International Monetary Mechanism," *loc. cit.*, p. 30. If, by whatever device, a government has advanced the prices of exports in terms of foreign currency to yield the maximum monopoly returns, overvaluation cannot be said to exist, unless an explicit comparison is being made to equilibrium under competition.

with continued cost to consumers and the risk of political logrolling with protective measures may put the contribution on the negative side. In the furthering of economic development by forced saving, such fiscal devices as income, sumptuary and luxury taxes are superior to import controls because these taxes cannot be evaded by a transfer of consumer and producer expenditure to domestic goods. And export taxes can be used in place of exchange control—avoiding the costs of a separate administration —to capture the windfalls of booming export markets as fiscal income. Exchange control has seldom coped very successfully with pressures toward capital flight; security of life and property, freedom from inflation and expropriatory taxation, and favorable treatment of home savers and investors are not only the general prerequisites of economic development itself but also the specific remedy—and the only true remedy—against capital flight. Finally, exchange control cannot ward off depressions of any significant strength if they are the result of collapsing export markets.

### Disadvantages of Exchange Controls

Not only do exchange controls and similarly oriented direct controls generally fail to secure the benefits to economic development expected of them, but they often entail actual losses or handicaps. Against any gains, in the first place, must be offset not only the sizable direct costs of operating the system, but also the costs to business firms of filling forms and arguing their cases, and the adverse effects on private enterprise of arbitrariness, discrimination, complexity, delay and uncertainty in administration.[36] By interfering with purchasing in the cheapest foreign markets and selling in the dearest, exchange control produces an allocation of consumption and production that is generally inferior to the allocation secured by prices without these controls. Its adverse effect on private capital inflows has already been emphasized.[37] By supporting overvalued rates on the home currency, exchange control limits exports and perpetuates the balance-of-payments disequilibrium.[38] Finally, the bilateral clearings, that is, the settling of accounts by direct dealings of one nation with another, that usually accompany exchange control inevitably produce further distortions of trade, both in terms of commodities and of regions, and a shrinkage of its aggregate value; thus they impose a corresponding toll on development.[39]

36. See P. T. Ellsworth, *Chile: An Economy in Transition*, Macmillan, New York, 1946, pp. 71–73; International Bank for Reconstruction and Development, *The Basis of a Development Program for Colombia*, Washington, 1950, pp. 328–31.

37. See Ellsworth, *op. cit.*; *Report of the Joint Brazil–U.S. Technical Commission*, Publication 3487, U.S. Department of State, June 1949, p. 297; *Report to the President of the United States by the Economic Survey Mission to the Philippines*, U.S. Department of State, October 9, 1950, p. 77.

38. G. E. Britnell, "Problems of Economic and Social Change in Guatemala," *Canadian Journal of Economics and Political Science*, November 1951, p. 477; de Beers, *loc. cit.*, p. 390.

39. International Bank for Reconstruction and Development, *The Economy of Turkey*, Johns Hopkins Press, Baltimore, 1951, pp. 240 and 242; Ellsworth, *op. cit.*, p. 73; *Report of the Joint Brazil–U.S. Technical Commission*, pp. 580–81.

# 19. A General View of Economic Development

BY DEFINITION, an underdeveloped country affords its inhabitants a poor end product from its economic system. At any point in time, the quality and texture of the end product is a function of the productive resources available to the country, how efficiently these are used in production, and the whole socio-cultural environment within which all economic activity is carried on. But more significant than the currently poor end product of the economic systems of underdeveloped areas is the fact that, in contrast to the developed countries, the product has continued to be poor over long intervals. In other words, the distinguishing feature of underdeveloped areas, even more than their current poverty, is the persistence of this poverty over time. This persistent poverty implies that whatever growth in aggregate output has occurred has been matched, or more than matched, by a growth of numbers in the population. Yet if one asks why total output has not grown more rapidly than population the basic answers seem to be outside the economic sphere. In an important sense, then, the really fundamental problems of economic development are noneconomic.

## THE DYNAMIC FACTORS IN ECONOMIC GROWTH

The remarkable growth of total output in the developed countries since, say, 1800 seems attributable to four basic factors that have operated powerfully and persistently: entrepreneurship; innovations and technical change; capital accumulation; and increasing specialization and exchange between persons and regions nationally and internationally. All four were of course linked together in complex patterns rather than in a simple, linear cause-and-effect relationship. Without innovation and technical change, certainly capital accumulation would have been far less than it was. Without entrepreneurs actively to mobilize, recombine and reorient existing productive resources, innovation and capital accumulation would not have augmented total output as they did. Indeed, they might not have occurred at all. Without the spread of the market that permitted specialization and exchange, the effects on output of the other three factors would have been much diminished. Finally, even the fact that population growth tapered off in the developed economies seems to be explainable only in terms of complex socio-cultural factors that induced a fall in birth rates.

## Cultural Barriers in Underdeveloped Areas

Just why, in the now underdeveloped countries, the basic factors that elsewhere have made for a secular rise in total output have operated with so little force, or why birth rates have not appreciably declined, must presumably be explained by the dominant socio-cultural values, with their accompanying institutions, that still predominate in those countries. Why Indian or Arabic mathematicians, for example, have so rarely applied their talents toward raising the material well-being of their own people; why entrepreneurs are scarce in the underdeveloped countries; or why productive real capital formation has been so trifling—all such questions seem answerable only in terms of the value scales that guide and motivate people in those societies.

If this is true, merely providing more capital equipment from abroad or demonstrating superior techniques of production will not create an environment from which innovations are bound to appear, or in which the entrepreneurial spirit and point of view are certain to flourish. If these could be assured, internal productive capital formation would almost certainly follow. Only in a very limited and comparatively trifling sense can economic development be "imported." In nearly all its important essentials it must be generated from within. A people whose standard of living is not above its level of living is not likely to achieve much material progress. There must be a desire for economic progress coupled with a determination to achieve it.

To contend that the really substantive barriers to development are mainly noneconomic is not to deny, however, that these barriers are most surely and easily crumbled from the economic side. Historically, the most powerful factor in reorienting and reshaping the socio-cultural environment seems to have been the spread of trade and commerce.

### TRADE AND THE SOCIO-CULTURAL ENVIRONMENT

A predominantly agricultural economy with numerous local village markets that are largely self-sufficient and have few trade relations with one another or with the world abroad offers little scope for entrepreneurship and little likelihood of generating innovations from within. Furthermore, it has few channels through which innovations might filter in from the outside. Consequently, its value patterns tend to be impermeable and its institutional structure unvarying. Such was the situation of many now developed countries a century or more ago, and such is the position of many underdeveloped areas today.

The growth of trade relations within such an economy and between it and the outside world has a dual effect: first, it offers other outlets for local products and nontraditional uses for human and nonhuman productive resources; second, trade by its very nature filters in new products, new techniques, new ways of doing things and new points of view. In short, trade disrupts traditional relations between products and productive factors because it introduces new outlets for products, and hence new demands for productive factors. But, equally important, the economy is no longer insulated from ideas and techniques that are common currency in the outside world.

The merchant-trader, who has usually been the active agent in the expansion of trade and commerce, becomes the initial source of innovations, and he provides the first visible manifestations of the entrepreneurial spirit in the villages and the countryside. By offering new market outlets, and thus a reason for new patterns of resource use, he weakens the economic base that supports the old values and the traditional social structure. Because he is widely imitated, the merchant-trader tends to spread the entrepreneurial attitude far beyond his immediate contacts. He fosters the commercialization of agriculture, for example; by extending the range of products he deals in, and perhaps also by advancing the necessary working capital from his own funds, he promotes the development of local handicrafts and local manufactures.

An oft-repeated sequence in economic development has been the growth of trade with increased interconnections between markets, an increasing shift to a money nexus within the economy, greater capital accumulation, growth of credit and banking facilities, expansion of nonagricultural production and general economic development. Development becomes an ongoing process.[1] Throughout this sequence—which of course has often been spread over several decades or even longer—the shift has been toward values that rate economic accomplishment more highly and toward a social environment that expects, accommodates and perhaps even welcomes change and innovation. The noneconomic blocks to development are pushed aside or submerged.[2]

## Transport and Foreign Trade

Historically, no two factors have done more to promote internal trade—with the social and cultural changes favorable to economic development

1. Historians now seem inclined to believe that the economically important inventions of the agricultural and industrial revolutions in the eighteenth and nineteenth centuries probably resulted more from the acute pressure on existing means and methods of production than from the timely, if unexplainable, appearance of ingenious inventors. This position tends to accord with contemporary experience, as witness the remarkable technical progress that wartime conditions seem to have produced under the pressure for greater output.

2. The process whereby commercial development undermines the peasant-type, static economy with its heavy overlay of aristocratic values has, however, sometimes come to a halt or even been partially reversed. Gerschenkron mentions the case of Russia after the emancipation of the serfs in 1861 as an example. According to his account, despite considerable vigorous commercial development, the nobility, the intelligentsia and the peasants so despised the traders and heaped such abuse upon them that the old value systems held firm. See Alexander Gerschenkron, "Social Attitudes, Entrepreneurship and Economic Development" (mimeographed), Round Table on Economic Progress, International Economic Association, Santa Margherita Ligure, Italy, 1953, pp. 8–10.

that expanding internal trade brings in its train—than improved transport and communications and intimate contact with foreign markets. During the nineteenth century, these two went hand in hand: drastic declines in the "cost of distance" greatly stimulated foreign trade; cheaper and better internal transport gave the hinterland access to tidewater and fostered internal trade as well. If the last half of the nineteenth century may be called, with pardonable exaggeration, a gigantic boom chiefly built around the steam engine and the steamship, perhaps the most far-reaching consequence of this boom was the astounding growth of internal trade and commerce in many countries. Manufacturing and industrial development subsequently followed along, if not at equal remove or to the same degree in all countries, nevertheless perceptibly and at an increasing pace down to 1914.[3]

If this telescoped analysis is reasonably accurate, and if it points up some of the more important difficulties that the underdeveloped countries now face, then it suggests that a country that would push its economic development within a price-market economy should also push its participation in foreign trade and commerce. It will not, then, adopt a policy of economic isolation, of avoiding external influences, or of government monopoly of those international exchanges into which it feels itself reluctantly driven. On all counts, its policy will be just the reverse.

Full participation in the international economy, as a means of stimulating domestic trade and commerce with all their desirable consequences, however, is only part of a sound approach to development. No less important is improvement of internal transport and communication facilities. Historically, these came slowly in the now developed countries, and in part they had to await technical advances. But this is no longer true. The road, the canal, the railway and the airplane, along with the telegraph, the telephone and the wireless, are accomplished facts. By deliberately widening the coverage and improving the efficiency of transport and communication facilities, a developing country can greatly hasten and extend the spread of specialization and internal trade with all their concomitant contributions to development.

To summarize: the chief barriers to economic development in a dynamic sense appear to be a cultural environment that is inhospitable to change; that lacks entrepreneurs; that does not generate innovations from within or borrow them from without; and that makes use of far too little specialization for high productivity. An effective way to overcome these difficulties is to increase the flow of domestic trade because it will force new value relations, new patterns of resource use, greater specialization and efficiency in

3. The economic development of the Scandinavian countries during the late nineteenth century seems to illustrate well the closely knit sequence of expanding foreign trade impinging upon domestic trade, improvements in internal transport, further growth in domestic and foreign trade, followed, in turn, by industrial development.

production, more commercialization of production and other important changes. To promote internal trade a country needs to link its economic life to the world market and simultaneously to improve the facilities for internal transport and communication.

To stress the importance of the commercialization of economic activity and the spread of specialization and exchange within the price system is not to contend that nothing more can or need be done to foster and achieve development. Neither historical experience nor good judgment supports this view. Everything need not be left to the gradual spread of the price system. The development process can be stimulated in other ways.

The government can promote development by deliberately modifying the socio-political environment, both by permissive legislation and by more positive measures.[4] Historical examples of the first are the abolition of serfdom, removal of restrictions on choice of occupation and elimination of nuisance taxes and tolls in Prussia and Japan; of the second, the requirement by Japan that land titles be established and that taxes be paid in money. Property rights, especially land titles, are often not of a kind to foster development because they hamper, rather than facilitate, new combinations of productive factors. The government could also reform the monetary and fiscal system in many underdeveloped areas with good effect. Only the state, moreover, can promote literacy and general education. In Germany, Japan and Russia, government efforts in the educational field paid large returns. The state may also take more than a passive attitude toward labor mobility, both geographical and occupational, not only by abolishing restrictive rules concerning entry to trades and occupations but also by fostering trade schools and technical education.

If a country is impatient for the development of private industry, the government can help directly to foster it in various ways, even though it puts its primary emphasis on specialization and exchange within the price system. The government may underwrite many of the costs of borrowing technology from abroad, of pilot plants and similar experimentation, of industrial and agricultural research. Both Germany and Japan offer many examples of successful government efforts of this type. Government credit can be employed where projects are too large or too risky to be undertaken by private enterprise unaided. Railway construction is an obvious case in point; other examples are communication facilities, roads and harbors.

For much of this "social overhead capital" the government will probably have to supply the necessary financing, that is, the purchasing power neces-

---

4. Obviously, development will not go forward in a country torn by civil strife or lacking a stable government; but a stable government by itself does not assure development.

sary to command productive factors. But this does not mean that the state itself must build the highways or railways or telephone system. The state may provide the funds, but private contracting firms may do most of the actual construction. Although highways are a public responsibility in the United States, most of them are built by private construction firms under a system of contract bidding. An underdeveloped country that proceeded in this way would multiply the number of its entrepreneurs, managers, supervisors and foremen, and generally foster development in a manner that would give it its own generative power in new directions.

Greater specialization and exchange between persons and regions with their salutary effects on output, technical progress and socio-cultural institutions need not of course be effected through the institution of the price system with its emphasis on the money calculus. As in Russia, the degree and types of personal and regional specialization may be prescribed and integrated by a central planning authority. In such a system the planning authorities determine the composition of output; they introduce the innovations and prescribe the form they must take; they devise the financial and fiscal arrangements necessary to carry out their plans; and they substitute other drives for productive activity than those of personal gain. But many of the necessary developmental changes are essentially the same: people must be shifted about, new productive activities requiring new skills must be introduced, capital must be accumulated. Despite the contrasts between development through central planning and development through the price system, the similarities are more than superficial.

### Labor Mobility

A striking feature of economic development in nearly all countries is the necessary occupational and geographical redistribution of the labor force. In an underdeveloped country most of the labor force is in agriculture; development involves new tasks outside agriculture, new concentrations of population in urban areas and, almost invariably, important changes in the relative economic importance of the various geographical regions of the country. The shift of the center of population northward in England, with the appalling growth of Birmingham, Manchester, Liverpool and other cities, illustrates one of the most important concomitants of development wherever it has occurred. Similar shifts took place in Germany, France, Belgium, the Netherlands, Japan, Russia and elsewhere.[5]

5. The rapid rise of new urban areas has usually been the major cause of the human misery and suffering which have so frequently accompanied the growth of industry in development. Usually the growth of cities was so rapid that overcrowding, bad sanitation and a generally unhealthy environment were inevitable. Moreover, during much of the nineteenth century, governments had no previous experience with such urban concentrations and the social costs they entailed, and therefore had no knowledge of how to deal with them. Social conditions in the new towns and cities growing up with the spread of industrialism usually have been strikingly similar in the early stages in all countries.

The means by which people were "drawn into" industry and the towns or "driven out" of agriculture in different countries are perhaps more remarkable for their similarities than for their differences. In price-market economies, it was the changed relationship of agricultural and industrial prices—in turn, mostly resulting from better transport and technical changes—that displaced workers in agriculture and opened up jobs for them in industry. Whether it was the agricultural revolution, as in England with its later enclosure movements, or new crops and growing commercialism in agriculture, as in eastern Germany, the result was much the same: people moved off the land into urban industrial employment. In Japan, the substitution of a highly regressive tax system requiring money payments in place of arrangements requiring payments in kind forced the small farmers to accept piece work on manufactures in their households and to send their daughters to take jobs in factories in the towns. In Russia, collectivization and mechanization of agriculture, requiring greater specialization and greater use of capital, freed workers for industrial employment, although the drift to the towns was already appreciable before this policy was introduced. In Russia, however, better rations and amenities, that is, higher real wages, also pulled people off the land.

Thus the redistribution of the labor force in economic development seems to have been accomplished by factors that "pushed" and "pulled" toward the same result. Both pushing and pulling were necessary in the past and both presumably will be equally necessary in the future. Little good will come from driving people out of agriculture if there is no industrial or other development to absorb them. Similarly, forcing industrial development without also revamping agriculture so that people are driven from the land into industry will probably be ineffective. Both are necessary because one complements and reinforces the other.

The somewhat delayed industrial development of France in the nineteenth century before the railroads broke down the traditional farm practices and types of crops seems to illustrate this idea, at least in part. Peasant agriculture is likely to follow tradition indefinitely unless forced to change by outside factors, such as significant changes in relative prices or the dictates of the central planners. Until the railways came in France, there was little to push people out of agriculture and efforts to stimulate industry were only moderately successful. Admittedly, other factors also contributed to the slow development of industry in France.

Perhaps the slow pace of industrial development in Latin America—despite government support through Fomento corporations, subsidies, highly protective tariffs and similar measures—can be partly explained by the fact that agriculture has never had to undergo a drastic reorganization that would disgorge workers and give them little choice but to accept industrial employment. Cities have grown in Latin America, but not mainly because of rising industrial employment; for reasons that are not clear, too many in the urban population seem to be engaged in service industries and too few in manufactures.

## The Acquisition of Skills

Both the increased specialization and the growth of industry which are inherent in economic development make it necessary for the labor force to acquire new skills. An agricultural population is usually made up of persons who have essentially similar skills and economic capacities, most of which can be acquired by trial and error or by imitation. But development requires many skills and many of these have to be formally learned. The labor force of a developed country, with its variety of technical skills, analytical abilities, scientific knowledge and specialized experience, differs markedly from that of an underdeveloped country.

The rank and file of the labor force acquired their new knowledge and new skills by "on-the-job" training and little else during the early phases of economic development in all countries. Agricultural laborers became factory operatives in much the same way in England or Germany as they did in Japan or Russia: they learned by doing. In the beginning, they were inept and often illiterate; but the factory broke down handicraft skills into a succession of simple operations, each of which could be easily mastered. Moreover, price-market economies tend to give a free rein to the ambitious and to bring those with initiative to the fore. Many workers saw clearly the personal rewards of literacy and special knowledge and trained themselves accordingly. The self-made, self-educated man is a familiar figure in nineteenth-century history and fiction. His example stimulated others to do likewise, with the result that skills and abilities were diffused throughout the labor force. Compulsory, rudimentary education for all was a late development; it came only long after economic development had made its most important strides forward. The bulk of the labor force in most countries got its necessary skills more or less automatically as economic development progressed. They were neither ready to hand nor planned for in advance.

### ENTREPRENEURSHIP, INNOVATION AND CAPITAL ACCUMULATION

The crucial problem with respect to entrepreneurship, innovation and capital accumulation in development is to determine their most probable and logical sequence. This is obviously a large and difficult topic on which only a few tentative comments can be essayed here. Yet economic experience seems to suggest several related points that are worthy of mention.

*Capital Accumulation and Increased Income*

The rate of growth of total output and real income per person is not determined by the rate of capital accretion alone. Mere increments to the capital stock do not suffice as an explanation of the growth of output in the Western world. Specialists believe that the rate of increase in total output in the developed countries over long periods has probably averaged about 2 to 3 per cent a year. Yet a calculation based on plausible (even generous) assumptions, first, concerning the probable yield on increments to the capital stock, say, 5 to 10 per cent a year, and, second, concerning the proportion of total income that goes to capital formation, say, 10 to 15 per cent, yields a rate of increase in total output well below the 2 to 3 per cent increase that in fact seems to have occurred.[6] In and of itself, therefore, capital accumulation cannot account for the realized secular growth in aggregate income. Moreover, the fraction of the national income that is not consumed, the part that goes into capital formation, includes certain types of capital that are more a manifestation of a higher income than an explanation of why the national income secularly increased. Among these, houses and many public buildings are only the "leading species of a large genus."

Consequently, the secular rise in national incomes in the developed countries (the rise per person will, of course, depend upon the population changes occurring simultaneously) must be *partly* attributable to other factors. Of those that are conceivably pertinent, none seems equal in importance to technical progress.

*Requirements for Technical Progress*

Observation and economic history alike suggest that, in order for technical progress to take concrete form in capital goods of improved productivity, some link is necessary between the possibilities of more productive capital equipment, on the one hand, and their actual realization, on the other. In price-market economies this link has been the entrepreneur and/or business manager. In his quest for greater profits, he was able to bring superior capital goods into existence and new combinations of productive factors into use because he had access to funds that enabled him to redirect the uses to which existing labor, capital equipment, land and other resources were put. Thus, in market economies, entrepreneurs, with access to credit to carry out their plans, have been the most important activators of technical progress. Through them, advances in technology have been applied in such a way that greater output could be realized. In this fashion, capital formation has been combined with technical progress.

6. For example, if total income were 100 and if 10 per cent of this were capital goods output on which the average yield was 10 per cent, then the increase per period in total output would be 1 per cent. With a yield rate of 15 per cent the figure would be 1.5 per cent. With capital formation 15 per cent of output and an average yield rate of 15 per cent, a figure which is almost certainly too high, the resulting increase in total output would be only 2.25 per cent.

As used here, technical progress is, of course, a broader concept than invention. It includes all those improvements, small and large, which make it possible to produce the same product with fewer productive resources or an improved product with the same resources. Inventions, in the ordinary sense of the term, are only a small part of the process. What fosters the appearance of these "improvements" and, more important, their application in practice? No very satisfactory answer seems to be available to this question. Adam Smith was certainly correct in emphasizing that specialization increased the likelihood of their occurring because it broke complex operations into their simpler components. Pressure on existing facilities of production also seems to have been a frequently powerful spur to their improvement. In recent times and in advanced countries, scientific research and applied science have been consciously directed toward the search for improvements. Nowadays, the translation of scientific progress into productive plant and equipment is a business undertaking with entrepreneurs in charge.

Viewed from this range of considerations, the problem of economic progress in underdeveloped areas is essentially one of overcoming an unfortunate combination of deficiencies. Their cultural patterns and institutional arrangements are not productive of technical progress. They lack entrepreneurs who might borrow and apply the technical progress that has already occurred elsewhere. Moreover, the entrepreneurs who are to be found there are not generally held in high esteem, nor have they access to the funds necessary to command factors of production into the formation of productive capital or new patterns of resource use. To remedy these deficiencies will inevitably take time.

## Problems of Capital Formation

The main inference to be drawn from the foregoing is that, at least over the near future, the underdeveloped areas must expect to improve their aggregate output mostly by means of additions to their productive capital stock and only to a negligible degree by means of technical progress that they generate from within their own socio-cultural environment. Since, however, the gap between the technology generally in use in the more developed countries and that generally found in the underdeveloped countries is so large, the latter can, for some time to come, raise their productivity performance appreciably simply by technological borrowing—provided they can devise ways and means to effect it. All the same, technological borrowing necessitates some solution to the problems of capital formation peculiar to the underdeveloped areas.

Productive capital formation in these areas need not necessarily be at the expense of consumption, in the sense that consumption must decline if capital formation occurs. If idle resources can be utilized or if resources can be diverted from nonproductive uses—from ceremonial activities, from nonproductive capital formation or from the maintenance of nonproductive capital goods—then productive capital formation can go forward without appreciably affecting consumption.[7] In order to achieve these results, however, the institutional arrangements in the developing society must solve two problems: first, provide means by which productive resources can be drawn into capital goods production; second, assure that those engaged in producing capital goods will share in the current flow of consumption goods. What appear to be the institutional means by which these problems were solved in the economies that developed earlier, and what bearing has this experience on the capital accumulation problems of the now underdeveloped areas?[8]

### Past Solutions

In a centrally planned, authoritarian society such as Russia, resources can be compelled to enter capital goods production. Once the Party decided, as it did, to concentrate on capital goods production, the authorities used a battery of direct economic controls to make certain that these goods would be produced and that others would not. They also established differentials in real wages to pull workers into the industries they were determined to expand.

Higher *real* wages, as against higher money wages, however, necessitated effective arrangements to bring food and other consumption goods to those workers who were thrust into the capital goods industries. This was accomplished primarily by the collectivization and mechanization of agriculture. Collectivization—combined with direct levies even on output not produced collectively—assured food supplies for those who were no longer producing food because they were making capital goods instead. Thus the established policy was not to allow the rural population to consume as much as it wished nor to permit it to invest in herds, farm structures, fences and so on as it saw fit. If the capital formation program in heavy industry was to succeed, the proclivities of the peasants to consume or to improve their plots through investment had to be checked by siphoning off a substantial part of the total agricultural output. Another variant was to force some of the land and labor into the production of crops that the peasants could not directly consume, such as flax and cotton. Moreover, after the very earliest stages, it was possible to feed back some of the output of the capital goods

7. The necessity for inserting the qualifier "appreciably" is that the ceremonial activities and nonproductive capital goods yield a flow of services that can only be reckoned as consumption. But they are services that do not affect the material welfare of the population or services that are supplied only to a favored few.

8. Historical literature may not throw these two problems to the forefront of the discussion, certainly not in so bald a form. Nevertheless, analytically, them seem to be problems that must have arisen and, somehow or other, must have been solved.

industries into the mechanization of agriculture and so sustain or increase food production while releasing still more labor for industry.[9]

How were these two problems solved in England, Western Europe, Japan and other countries where economic development was not centrally planned but moved forward within the institutions of a price-market economy? Either private entrepreneurs motivated by profits, or the state, for reasons of national policy, drew factors of production into the production of capital goods. What was done in either case was simply to bid for them in the market by offering a money price for their services. If, for example, private entrepreneurs believed that railroads would be profitable or the state proclaimed that they must be built, then a money economy with credit institutions could provide, through a variety of means, the purchasing power necessary to bid factors of production into the construction of railroads.[10] Credit creation, either through the state or through the banking system, played a major role in real capital formation; without it, there was no means by which labor and other productive resources could be brought together initially to make capital goods. The fact that important technical changes in agriculture and other trades were also driving people from the land and from other customary occupations made it all the easier.

The problem of ensuring a food supply for workers shifted to capital goods production seems to have raised no real difficulty in England, Western Europe and Japan. In contrast to Russia, where the emphasis was so much on heavy industry as opposed to consumers' goods industries, the capital goods produced in the market economies soon yielded a flow of consumption goods or of such intermediate goods as textiles, iron and coal. These goods were exchanged for food and other supplies from the rural areas and from overseas. The market mechanism sufficed to keep the towns supplied without resort to direct levies or collectivization. In Japan, heavy money taxes forced the small farmers to sell some of their produce. As transport improved, the market area over which this exchange was practicable steadily widened at home and extended into overseas areas. In all the market economies, increased capital formation and increased consump-

9. Undoubtedly the changes in agriculture combined with the stimulus to heavy industry made it easier to absorb much underemployed labor in agriculture. In other words, the arrangement was not entirely a transfer mechanism but also a means of using previously idle resources. While disguised unemployment on a big scale is not impossible in industry or in collective farming, it is probably easier to identify and correct.

10. The means actually employed differed from industry to industry and from country to country. This is essentially a financial problem of ways and means. In England, banks, credit institutions, speculators, stock-jobbers and the like were adequate in combination to create purchasing power and to draw it from those who already had it so that the promoters of the railways were able to bid factors of production into railway construction. In other countries, the state used its own credit. In Japan, as already noted, a rather ingenious means was used to finance industrial development. If a country has the rudiments of a banking and credit system, little difficulty should arise in providing the purchasing power necessary to bid factors of production into capital goods production. For an interesting recent discussion of the importance of the banks in nineteenth-century European economic development, see Alexander Gerschenkron, "Economic Backwardness in Historical Perspective," in Bert F. Hoselitz (Ed.), *The Progress of Underdeveloped Areas*, University of Chicago Press, Chicago, 1952, pp. 9–14.

tion went hand in hand. Each reinforced the other. And technical progress, especially better and cheaper transport, combined with greater specialization and exchange, were causal and permissive factors in both.[11]

## Basic Problems

What had to be solved in past instances of capital formation in development, then, was the twofold problem of devising means for getting factors of production, mostly labor, into the production of capital goods and of making certain that people would not starve while they were so engaged. Russian experience exhibits the problem in its most naked form: get some people off the land and into making capital goods and prevent those who remain from consuming any more than they did before so that those in the industrial towns can keep on making capital goods. Given the determination to push industry, the direct assignment of labor and the mechanization of agriculture solved the first problem of getting labor and resources into capital goods production. The collectivization of agriculture solved the second problem of ensuring a food supply for that labor. In the price-market economies, entrepreneurs or the government used credit to solve the first problem; the market-exchange system solved the second in that the towns had consumers' goods to give the agricultural producers in exchange. The fact that an agricultural revolution had gone before was enormously helpful, as were the technical advances in industry. But in its crudest form the economic problem was not essentially different from that facing the Russian planners or the government of an underdeveloped country today.

### THE USE OF REAL RESOURCES

Economic history seems to show that progress turns chiefly on the operation of three major forces—technological innovation that improves productive efficiency, the breaking up of the traditional economic and social mold by the impact of innovations, and the opening of new and broader markets inside and outside the country. Do the problems of countries aspiring to rapid economic development today lie in the same areas? If so, what measures and policies appear to be favorable to economic progress?

## Transfer of Techniques

The future of genuine innovation cannot be foretold, and there would be little to say about it if we were concerned with the broad theme of

11. Economic development in Russia after 1927 and in underdeveloped areas today has differed from early nineteenth-century development in that modern technology could be imported from abroad. Hence, there was no doubt that if factors of production were used to produce certain types of capital goods these would be highly effective; they had already been tried and proved. This was not true in, say, 1850. In those days capital formation, in part, had to await technical advances.

economic progress in general. However, what is needed today in the under-developed areas of the world is for the most part not genuinely new innovations but rather transfers of known techniques—with appropriate modification—from the countries with high per capita incomes. Thus we do not move in the dark regions of undiscovered methods of production, but on the familiar terrain of techniques already in use in the industrial nations of the West.

The less developed areas could establish a firm foundation for the introduction of techniques from abroad if they initiate the process of development by utilizing the real resources they *now possess*, by using them *well*, and, so far as possible, using *all* of them. Since the existing endowments of underdeveloped countries are chiefly in resources for primary production, including the manpower adapted to this end, it follows that agriculture and other primary pursuits should be the objects of the first transfers of improved techniques.

Utilizing resources which underdeveloped countries *now possess* is important in giving an *immediate* impetus to higher incomes without the hazards and delays that would result from concentrating on industrialization, particularly on heavy industry. The use of existing resources is important also in increasing exports of primary products and thus supplying the purchasing power for imports of capital equipment from the industrial West, which are an essential ingredient of progress.

Utilizing resources *well* means producing with the relatively abundant factors. Development begins, and indeed must for some time continue, on the basis of large masses of unskilled labor, with a paucity of managerial and technical skills, and with a general scarcity of capital and entrepreneurship. Agriculture and the extractive industries make relatively modest drafts on these scarce factors.

But in those vast regions of the underdeveloped world where population is so great that manpower is not merely relatively abundant but chronically unemployed or in surplus, the necessity of using *all* available resources to achieve development is a pressing one. To some degree and in certain senses, the utilization of surplus agricultural labor involves "industrialization"; but it is not necessarily, and most frequently necessarily *not*, industrialization similar to that of the Western nations.

*Utilizing Surplus Agricultural Labor*

The evils of urban congestion, nowhere more appalling than in the great cities of the Orient, the loss of social values when native populations are uprooted, and the pecuniary costs of new or larger cities may well incline the newly developing countries to try to provide profitable employment for surplus agricultural labor without extensive urbanization.

To some degree, the introduction of new techniques may permit more intensive agriculture and thus absorb labor directly. Colin Clark points out that, with its highly intensive agriculture, Denmark can export 45 per cent of its net product, using ten men per square kilometer, the "highest product at the highest density of settlement."[12] Improved fertilizers, irrigation, drainage, new crops and rotations, as well as new strains of plants and farm animals may greatly enhance the productivity and labor absorption of primitive agriculture. This source of demand for labor is distinct from that which may be occasioned by various forms of land reclamation. Public health projects, community improvements, roads, waterways, and the back-and-brawn jobs connected with many other local utilities may draw on the same pool of manpower.

Finally there is the whole congeries of cottage industries, rural cooperatives, self-help projects, and local industries processing food and other agricultural products, which do not entail the moving of laborers "off the land." Only as incomes rise considerably does there appear a definite necessity of reducing the proportion of persons engaged in agriculture (as in the United States), and within certain limits this may proceed without involving an absolute reduction in the number of farm workers.

In some countries, such as Brazil and India, with coal and iron deposits and with extensive domestic or regional markets, heavy industry naturally appears early in the growth of national income. But this is by no means either the eventual or necessary solution to effective utilization of the surplus agricultural labor for economic progress.

*Land Reform and Other Improvements in Agriculture*

When "innovation" is assigned a crucial role in the development process, it correctly conveys a considerable emphasis on new products and new methods of physical production. But improvements in the use of real resources, indeed, some of the most crucial innovations, need not pertain to physical processes at all but to management, organization, marketing and the like. In most of the underdeveloped world, increased efficiency in agriculture depends upon improvement in the conditions surrounding land ownership and tenancy. Frequently, ancient tribal practices or traditional religious-social structures have disintegrated, leaving property rights in chaos. Economic motivation cannot be effectively directed toward increased production until rewards are reasonably certain, and this means that the title to land, water rights, and the tenure, obligations and privileges of tenants must be clear. Furthermore, where the fragmentation of holdings into small and often widely separated plots has gone far, the consolidation of holdings is a necessary prelude to the use of modern techniques.

12. Colin Clark, "Population Growth and Living Standards," *International Labor Review*, August 1953.

In some countries, land ownership amounts to an entrenched political system and economic reforms await a gradual or violent displacement of the landlord class. Similarly, rack-renting, absentee landlordism, and the virtual peonage of agricultural labor may rest basically on political factors. Tenancy itself, which is more common in Europe and the United States than in many underdeveloped countries, cannot be categorically condemned. Cataclysmic change, such as the collectivization of land, carries with it certain risks, as for example that a ruthless central government may exploit it to appropriate "surplus" to the point of starvation. The history of Western Europe and North America shows many examples of successful economic change by a gradual process of correcting the evils besetting agriculture, carried on within the framework of private enterprise. Besides land reforms, these measures include improvements in the taxation of agriculture, in credit institutions and in marketing, and measures to stabilize the international demand for primary products.

A flourishing state of agriculture or other primary production can carry development far, as the position of Australia and New Zealand testifies. Private producers and government officials need have no fear that primary production is generically inferior to other economic activities. Nor should misgivings concerning the secular drift of agricultural prices relative to the prices of manufactures deter action for immediate improvements on farms and plantations; for expert opinion is about evenly divided on these prospects. Here, as elsewhere, resources must be committed with only the assurance that changes in demand can be countered by varying the current allocations of resources as the future unfolds.

## Sequence of Industrialization

Certain useful generalizations as to how real resources are most effectively marshaled for economic progress through industrial production can readily be inferred from the analysis of the similar problem in agriculture. Making the optimum use of what they already have, the underdeveloped areas would be expected to inaugurate industries, such as textile production, which require light capital equipment relative to labor; to prefer small-scale operations involving small risks and equipment; to exploit the existing primary production through processing industries intimately related to food and raw materials; and, finally, to encourage village handicrafts and local industries, provided efficiency is not too low and no better alternative employments exist. Heavy industry would appear only with exceptionally fortunate combinations of coal and iron resources and large domestic or regional markets. Otherwise, from food and raw material processing and local handicrafts, the normal progression in industry would be to the less highly differentiated types of industrial and agricultural instruments and materials—fertilizers, standard varieties of machine tools, pumps, mixers, certain basic chemicals and the like.

Meanwhile, much effort will necessarily be channeled into enterprises which constitute the indispensable underpinning of development: general utilities—railways, highways, harbors, electric power, multipurpose water developments and so on—and, not least, public health programs and general facilities. The indirect character of the benefits accruing from them, the sheer magnitude of the necessary investment, or the extent of the risks involved make these undertakings the natural bailiwick of government. But the role of government in these projects, as indeed in industry generally, can vary from mere general planning to loans to private enterprisers, to subventions, to construction with subsequent lease or sale into private hands, to outright ownership and operation. It is by no means clear that even rapid industrialization entails state socialism.

## Tempo of Industrialization

Except in outright totalitarian regimes, the growth of industry depends far more than is commonly recognized upon the first factor stressed in the historical analysis of progress—the number and vigor of genuine innovators and entrepreneurs. But it depends almost as intimately upon the availability and quality of managers, businessmen and foremen. People with these various capacities are perhaps scarcer even than skilled labor, which in a modern economy can be rapidly trained, and scarcer also than capital resources. As a strategic factor in economic development this scarcity of genuine entrepreneurial and managerial talent is probably equaled only by the complex of cultural factors and the extent of the market.

Abstract arguments can provide little or no guidance as to the desirable or achievable tempo of industrialization in underdeveloped countries. Countries differ markedly, and even for a single country the factors involved are numerous and complex. Technical assistance from the industrial West should vastly augment the purely physical efficiency of production, but the effect of this on the rate of growth of the economy may be partly or wholly offset by imitation of Western standards of consumption and "social welfare" which impede capital accumulation. External economies and the complementarity of industries may argue for the possibility of rapid growth, but the interdependence of parts also creates vast risks of incorrect plans or forecasts by governments and businesses. Cultural factors may limit the advance of industry more than purely economic factors.

All in all, the tempo of industrialization will probably fall far short of the aspirations voiced in many regions during the past decade. And this leaves aside the questions of the fate of per capita income as conditioned by population growth, and of human welfare as distinct from per capita income.

## FINANCING ECONOMIC INNOVATION

If the innovating entrepreneur is the prime mover in economic progress, it is equally true that it is the provision of capital for the innovator, without inflation, which sustains development once it has begun. Mere frugality and accumulation on the part of the general public is not likely to break through traditional ways of producing and consuming. But once a wave of wanting to do things in new and better ways has begun to swell, savings must be forthcoming if the potential force of innovation is not to be dissipated in consumption and inflation.

It is extremely unlikely that foreign governments or international agencies will ever supply a substantial part of the capital required for development in the underdeveloped world. They have not done so in the past; and with the current emphasis on "welfare" legislation in the Western world—even if the burden of military outlays should ever be lightened—the governments of one third of the world's population can scarcely tax their electorates heavily enough to supply the requisite capital for the other two thirds. Capital supplied by metropolitan powers, such as England, France and Belgium, or by the United States, or by the International Bank for Reconstruction and Development may indeed have quite powerful effects in providing *examples* of improved facilities and superior techniques. Reckoned as a capital investment per capita, however, the annual sums available to the underdeveloped world from these sources are quite paltry. They are quite insufficient, in themselves, to make appreciable differences in income levels.

This leaves foreign private investment and domestic sources of capital—both public and private—as the bearers of progress. In the nineteenth century, foreign private investment sometimes provided a foundation for development. But whether this foundation was built on or not depended upon many factors in the receiving economy. Large British investments did not result in rising levels of living for the masses in India, but they did in North America, in Australia and New Zealand. Unless the receiving economy generated indigenous forces which raised per capita income, foreign private capital—while it may have earned attractive profits—did not eventuate in development.

But the twentieth century differs from the nineteenth in a critical respect: private capital—in some measure following the first world war, increasingly after the Great Depression, and markedly after another world war—has not found the profits of foreign investment commensurate with the risks, except perhaps in the oil industry.

Thus, from any angle, domestic sources of capital are indispensable for development. Foreign private investment cannot be evoked unless the risks peculiar to the twentieth century (at least since 1931) can be eliminated. But even if they are eliminated and private capital does enter from abroad, it is unlikely to raise average incomes appreciably unless the receiving economy itself saves and invests substantial fractions of its own income. Perhaps a sufficient concentration of foreign capital on a limited area might produce an exception, as it has in Israel. A comparison of Israel's population with that of the underdeveloped world will show arithmetically its necessarily favored and unusual position.

Once a country is well advanced in the process of development, it can make large drafts on foreign private capital, as Canada does. Private capital will flow as the political instabilities and economic handicaps characteristic of young republics and beginners in development are overcome. But this signifies that these countries are demonstrating their viability by good economic performance. Foreign government and international loans may be the wet nurse of infancy; foreign private loans become available as adolescence proves its powers, and they are easily had by a healthy adult breadwinner. For the process of development itself, past the faint beginning stages, the finance is provided by domestic government revenues and private saving. And it would scarcely require much argument to establish that voluntary private saving in most instances cannot become significant in volume until a groundwork has been laid by domestic public investment. Tax systems are thus the ultimate foundation of development finance. They are essential to the curbing of inflation, for only with the prospect of a reasonably stable currency will domestic and foreign private savers entrust their capital to a country aspiring to development.

### Government Provision of Development Capital

Since a large and critical fraction of the substance of development comes from state revenues, tax systems in the underdeveloped countries must be enormously improved from their present state, which varies from rudimentary and unproductive to complex and ineffective. The ordinary canons of taxation—productivity, simplicity, certainty of enforcement, and equity —provide the natural starting point of improvement. But cultural and economic differences among countries will inevitably necessitate large differences in the practical application of intelligent fiscal policy.

Illiteracy and poverty undoubtedly mean that income taxation will generally play a less important role in the underdeveloped areas than in Europe and America. Hut and other simple capitation taxes are unavoidable at the beginning, and consumption excises, while only approximating proportional taxation at best, may long be indispensable. The limits to direct taxation of income may partly be compensated for by property taxes, especially by improved forms of land taxes. Much is to be said for levies on exports by primary producers, as a means of appropriating some of the yield of wasting natural resources for purposes of national development, and—no less important—as a flexible device for stabilizing the net return to domestic producers of raw materials which suffer from the instability of international markets.

National differences make it impossible to go into much more detail concerning desirable revenue systems, but certain negative indications may be equally useful. Excises on imports, in order to screen out items of luxury consumption or to reduce consumption in general, may fail because they encourage substitution from domestic sources. Tax exemptions, or favorable tax discrimination to encourage investment in certain industries considered essential to national development, enjoy a considerable vogue in Latin American countries. But the standard objections to these procedures as inequitable, prolific of official corruption and demoralizing for the taxpaying public are not easily answerable.

In addition to tax income, governments may obtain funds for development projects by domestic borrowing. Here the chief problem is to avoid the use of central and commercial banks as mere money factories and instead to cultivate a solid market for government securities in private and business saving. Banking systems can contribute development capital to the degree to which they absorb government securities and create credit without inflationary consequences. In the more advanced phases of economic development, an active government security market also provides the central bank with the opportunity of exercising monetary control through open-market operations. But effective monetary policy need not await this juncture, since bank lending can be regulated effectively through reserve requirements.

Official inquiries into the revenue systems of underdeveloped countries generally show that improvements in tax structures and—above all—in the efficiency and honesty of tax administration can substantially increase government income without added hardship to the population. Effective fiscal systems assume significance not only for the revenue they yield for development; they are essential in combating inflation, for encouraging private saving and investment, for attracting foreign capital and for permitting the relaxation of foreign exchange controls.

*Development Capital from Domestic Private Saving*

Voluntary saving on the part of the broad masses seldom if ever supplies a dynamic driving force in economic development, particularly in its early phases. It is the foreign trader or, perhaps as frequently in the contemporary scene, the local government that introduces technical innovations, opens up new lines of production and consumption, and supplies most of the capital. But even if ignorance, inertia or sheer poverty sorely limit the amount of capital formation which can be financed by it, domestic personal saving plays a very essential role, at least as a passive, permissive or background factor. Throughout the early and arduous phases of development, small increases per capita in consumption can easily wipe out the material basis of further progress. Alternatively, with given monetary outlays by firms and governments on capital equipment, small individual increases in consumer outlays may produce considerable inflation and undermine the results achieved.

The means of encouraging voluntary individual saving are probably not greatly different for underdeveloped and developed countries. Perhaps the advantages the individual may expect as the fruits of saving need to be propagandized more in societies where personal saving is something of a novelty. But for the rest the course would follow familiar lines: political stability, security of property, monetary stability, the spread of savings institutions, government regulation of banking, development of investment institutions, avoidance of expropriatory taxation, and the like. There are few if any short cuts in this route.

### Development Capital from Abroad

The great examples of rapid economic development—England during the industrial revolution, Japan after the Meiji restoration, Russia under the Soviet regime—have been cases of almost complete self-financing from domestic resources from the beginning on. Western Europe in general conformed to this pattern, but notable cases can be brought to mind of particular industries in which the capital, particularly the original investment, came from the outside. In still larger measure, North America, Australia, New Zealand and the Union of South Africa, to consider only areas now regarded as "developed" made drafts on foreign capital throughout their economic evolution. But even in these cases, domestic sources of capital rapidly overtook the inflow from abroad.

Aside from England, where the combination of resources, geographic position, cultural traits and technological advances was exceptionally favorable, it is probably safe to say that most countries that have recorded striking periods of economic progress have borrowed from abroad if they have preserved liberal institutions. This may be one of the more important lessons of history for nations concerned with the economic progress of underdeveloped areas today. It signifies that the nations of Western culture have a *political* interest in the economic development of low-income countries only if this development is accompanied by the growth or preservation of political and economic freedom. An inflow of foreign capital may help these countries avoid resort to the direct controls and compulsions which are characteristic of totalitarian regimes and their particular version of "progress."

The onus of inducing this fructifying inflow of foreign capital rests, however, with the developing nations themselves. Partly this is a matter of morale, but it is also partly a matter of simple arithmetic and simple economics. As for morale, it has repeatedly been said within these pages and elsewhere that, unless progressiveness becomes part of the very character of a nation, any forward movement in average incomes comes to a standstill as soon as foreign aid ceases. And among the more important elements of progressiveness is the habit of accumulation, investing, and thus providing the wherewithal of development.

The simple arithmetic embraces two fundamental facts. First, foreign government grants and loans, and international agency credits, when divided out over the vast populations of Asia, Africa and Latin America, cannot do more than provide occasional examples of modern techniques and isolated pieces of capital equipment. Second, foreign private capitalists, engaging in the simple arithmetic of profit and loss, do not now find conditions sufficiently attractive for investment in most of the underdeveloped world.

This brings us then to the economics, which are also relatively simple and straightforward. Governments of the higher-income countries cannot induce a much larger flow of private investment for development abroad except by inequitable discriminations or by guarantees and subsidies which would in effect convert private loans into public loans and grants. Something may indeed be accomplished by treaties, guarantees and tax measures; but the consensus is clearly that these measures make only marginal contributions to the flow of private investment.

Fundamentally, it is not the conditions within the chief potential lending countries but the conditions within the borrowing economies that need to be reformed. It is not the relatively high productivity of capital within the United States, for example, that should be attacked, but the low yields and high risks of investment abroad that require remedy. Marginal contributions of capital by outright gifts or by low-interest loans have their place in enlightened foreign policy of the Western nations, but these are—as they are correctly labeled—*aid* and not the *substance* of development.

## Opening up Markets

The last great impelling force in economic development, in addition to entrepreneurship, technical innovations and the breaking down of ancient traditions in the ordinary processes of earning and spending, is the widening of markets both within the national boundaries and outside them. The division of labor, economic efficiency, the receptiveness of the economy to change and its capacity to adapt itself to alterations in demand depend in large measure on the extent of the market. The continental free-trade area of the United States seems to illustrate these qualities quite clearly.

So far as concerns the domestic market within each of the relatively underdeveloped nations, this is peculiarly its own problem, to be solved in some measure with the help of foreign capital. Important factors are fostering the construction of rail, water and air transport facilities; improving communication, increasing literacy, disseminating information; and furthering the internal mobility of labor and capital and the diffusion of particular skills.

So far as concerns the international markets for the great staples of the primary producers and the quantitatively less important fabricated goods, a large measure of responsibility rests on the leading commercial nations. This responsibility consists in ensuring that the world trading system *expands* and thus affords the developing areas the opportunity to earn their way by increasing exports; that the direction of their development is *not distorted* by trade barriers, exchange controls and preferences; and that these economies enjoy a tolerable degree of *stability* in the demand for their exports. Economic progress in the underdeveloped world over the long pull depends more heavily upon a favorable international setting for ordinary production, sale and purchase than upon such initiating factors as the transfer of techniques and capital from foreign shores.

# 20. Interests and Responsibilities of the United States

THE UNITED STATES HAS VITAL INTERESTS at stake in the course of events in those vast areas now stirring with social unrest and resentment of their impoverished material state. First and foremost in the present international scene comes its *political* interest. The United States cannot stand idly by and witness the recruitment of the populous countries of Asia and perhaps even of Africa and Latin America to Communism. Not that the United States can purchase friendship or political allies by its loans, grants or technical aid; for the gratitude of the recipient countries may be strongly tinged with injured pride or suspicion, and at best will be only transitory. Rather, the guiding fact is that a country of satisfactory material well-being is rarely, if ever, a voluntary convert to the ranks of Communism. Even if the level of living is painfully low, if there is a reasonable chance of betterment, if the way to economic progress seems to lie open, if, in short, there is hope of satisfying national and personal feelings of worth and dignity, it is unlikely that these cravings will impel a country to sacrifice its independence to a foreign monster. It is vitally necessary to the United States to offset the "quick and easy" remedies of Communism through violence and expropriation by creating the external conditions under which an impoverished people may, by its own efforts, raise its levels and standards of living and yet maintain its political independence.

In addition to this political interest in the present international scene, the United States has strong *economic* interests in the development of nations comprising two thirds of the world's population. Many of the members of the North Atlantic Alliance, most conspicuously perhaps Great Britain and Western Germany, and in addition Japan, as a potential political ally in the Orient, require expanding markets for their industrial output and expanding sources of supply for foodstuffs and industrial raw materials. As allies, their economic interest is that of the United States; their economic weakness or vulnerability throws upon the United States a heavier share of the burden of military defense.

Other economic interests of the United States in economic progress in Southeast and South Asia, in Africa and in Latin America are, however, more direct. These regions have traditionally supplied the United States with some of its most indispensable imports, such as sugar, wool, tin and nonferrous metals; but within the past decade, certain great industrial raw materials, among them copper, lead and petroleum, have passed from the export to the import category, and the prospects are that iron ore and other indispensable elements of industrial civilization in the United States will make the same shift.[1] Moreover, foreign markets have always constituted an important part of the demand for American food and raw material exports, and at present they account for a significant part of the demand for many manufactures. Higher incomes in the developing areas may well come to be the critical factor in the prosperity of these exporting industries of the United States.

Finally, it cannot be denied that the United States has a purely humanitarian interest in the relief of starvation, disease and ignorance in other parts of the world. This concern was one of the animating forces of the American missionary movement; and it seems inevitable that the wealthiest nation of the world should continue to feel some measure of moral responsibility for the way the "other half"—in fact by far the larger portion—lives and thinks.

### THE NUMEROUS INTERNATIONAL INTERESTS OF THE UNITED STATES

Any realistic analysis of the interests of the United States for raising the economic level of the less advanced nations must recognize at the outset that these interests are not all in one direction. The existence of the United Nations and the North Atlantic Treaty Organization has not relieved the United States of an individual national responsibility for peace and war which parallels the role of the United Kingdom in the nineteenth century as custodian of the Pax Britannica. It is not national conceit but a chorus of voices from Western Europe and elsewhere which insists that the United States must be the chief defender today of parliamentary government, individual civil liberties and other heritages from the Magna Charta. For two decades the United States has been told by English and continental friends that its primary duty in the international scene is to preserve full employment at home, and by its enemies that the next great depression will sweep capitalism into justly deserved oblivion. Since World War II, and particularly since the Korean conflict, the United States has been charged with bringing disaster upon Europe by raising the international prices of raw materials through its military procurements: the United States must beware of inflationary pressures. But this country must at the same time import in large volume to relieve the world shortage of dollars. It is the responsibility of the United States, it is said, to shape the international scene in such a way as to permit other countries to achieve stable and convertible currencies and to relax or abandon their exchange controls.

1. The President's Materials Policy Commission, *Resources for Freedom*, Vol. I, *Foundations for Growth and Security*, June 1952, *passim*.

These are all genuine and grave responsibilities and interests. Although other nations may sometimes be too ready to permit their share of the burden to rest on American shoulders, the size and affluence of its economy make the United States inevitably the Atlas holding up the modern firmament. If, in one quarter of the earth, Japan, with the potential industrial might of 90 million frugal and hardworking people, feels the pull of trading eastward, who is to offset this attraction aside from the United States with its vitalizing military procurements and its shipments of coal and foodstuffs? If, in another quarter, Berlin is threatened as a bastion of the West, who is to provision it by means of a fantastically expensive airlift? If Pakistan experiences a famine, who can make up the deficit? And so one might continue, for the Near East, Indochina and other points of jeopardy.

Economic development in all low-income countries seems to be firmly established among the great ideals of the present age, and rapid improvement in those regions most exposed to Communist inroads is most urgent. But the United States has many other urgent responsibilities and interests, and meanwhile it must preserve the health and vigor of its own economy. As in all economic problems, therefore, alternative needs and opportunity costs have to enter the final calculation.

## How Can These Interests Be Made Compatible?

An expanding system of free international trade affords the one really great means of reconciling the numerous and potent interests of the United States which compete in the sphere of international economic affairs. Moreover, such a system provides the only reliable guide for United States policy toward the developing countries.

Economic progress is fundamentally a native product. But, it has been argued in previous chapters, an economy based on primitive subsistence agriculture has seldom, in isolation from other countries, generated the driving forces necessary for economic advancement. It requires the presence of the foreign trader to introduce entrepreneurship, to generate innovation, to break the crust of the traditional pattern of resource use, and—through the impact of economic change—to weaken those elements in the cultural environment which inhibit progress. Foreign traders furnish a modicum of capital also; but, more important, once a process of development has begun, the entrepreneurs and the innovations in both production and consumption begin to evoke capital from the domestic economy itself. Thus development usually has its beginnings in the first articulation of the country in the world trading system.

There are good reasons for believing that integration into this system is continuously necessary if all the various efforts at development in the various countries are to eventuate in a workable pattern. For one thing, the young developing economy will need to earn its imports of essential capital goods through its exports to the industrial countries. Its economy must be linked with the world economy so that, as change occurs in the world pattern of resource use and flow of products, it can adapt itself to these changes. The most effective and, indeed, almost the only means by which these changes can be known, their magnitude assessed and their devious influences appreciated is the operation of the price system. While it may theoretically be possible to plan development for a completely closed economy, it would seem to be both futile and a contradiction in ideas to lay autarchic plans for a country that hopes to accelerate its development by drawing in from the outside the techniques, the impulse toward genuine entrepreneurship and the capital equipment which its exports can command. The United States should neither implicitly nor explicitly encourage autarchic plans which run counter to the spread of a network of world trade based on a high degree of international specialization and exchange. Countries that plan to pattern their economies in greater or lesser degree on the Russian or other authoritarian models are, by that choice and to that degree, turning their backs on a rational international division of labor.

Beyond the imports of equipment and materials necessary to economic development which its exports can command, the young developing country will want to draw in additional capital through foreign investments. But it is only within the framework of a favorable world trading system that foreign investments will flow in the volume and kind most needed in the process of development. Public loans and grants will not be available in the foreseeable future in sufficient volume to finance the development of the low-income areas. A healthy system of multilateral trade and currency convertibility would most certainly lead to a revival of private international investment which carries with it technical and business know-how and an intimate knowledge of costs and market outlets in the world at large. Even at its best, foreign public investment cannot be expected to carry along these advantages.

On three major grounds, then, the arguments seem particularly strong for linking economic development with a vigorous international trading system. Commercial contacts nurture the beginnings of economic progress in breaking traditional techniques and patterns of resource use, in introducing an aggressive class of entrepreneurs, and in inducing social change and a weakening of the noneconomic barriers to higher productivity. Second, it is foreign trade which enables the developing countries to purchase with their exports the material basis of further progress through imports of essential capital equipment. Finally, only a flourishing state of international trade will encourage the financing of development in underdeveloped countries by foreign private capital.

Thus it appears that the interests of the United States in the under-developed world rest largely on the same foundation which the United States has proclaimed for its foreign economic policy in general: that improvement in levels and standards of living everywhere in the world depends upon the removal of barriers to trade, upon opening the United States market, as the most important part of the world market, to international supply and demand, upon currency convertibility and nondiscriminatory commercial policy, upon stability in world commodity markets and upon the revival of private international investment.

## Loans, Grants and Technical Aid

These should be the lodestones of United States policy concerning the economic development of the low-income countries. To them should be added the significant contributions which the United States can make through government loans, grants and technical aid. But these should be regarded as marginal contributions of a strategic character, and not as the core of the responsibility. Foreign loans, grants and technical aid are rather in the nature of catalysts: they may activate and temporarily sustain the prime movers of progress, but the process must get its continuing force from the developing economy itself. The basic contribution of United States policy, however, lies in trying to provide an auspicious international setting in which the developing economies can make their own way.

### PRIMARY PRODUCTION OR BALANCED DEVELOPMENT?

As part of this pattern of policy, should the United States seek to build up the underdeveloped countries as sources of supply for its consumers and industries? Or should it subordinate such interests to a policy of helping these countries attain a broad and diversified basis of development? Is this a clear choice between selfish and altruistic motives? Does primary production serve the interests of the industrial West but retard the economic growth of the other three quarters of the earth? These are real issues, and their reality is perhaps most vivid to the inhabitants of those countries and areas that are not yet very far advanced in the economic scale. As one writer has stated:

The Middle Easterner observes the continuing tendency of some Western enterprises and even governments to "use" the Middle East as a source of raw materials, a market for manufactured products or a place for profitable investment, instead of working with the countries of the area as co-equals.[2]

2. Peter Franck, "Economic Nationalism in the Middle East," *Middle East Journal*, Autumn 1952, pp. 429–54.

*Is Primary Production Exploitative?*

The revolt of peoples in the underdeveloped world against imperialism, colonialism, and Western paternalism is, of course, in large measure justified. But also in large measure the onslaught was misdirected, particularly at the hands of Marxists. Exploiting natural resources and other business opportunities does not necessarily involve exploiting people, and it can scarcely be taken as evidence of moral turpitude if European and American "capitalists" and business ventures in foreign lands paid no more than the market rates of wages and sold their products for what the market would bring. Moral guilt and the crime of exploitation lay rather at the door of metropolitan governments, usually with the strong support of privileged cliques in the underdeveloped areas, in denying to the people of their colonies the same political and economic freedom and equality which they proclaimed at home as universal principles. The evils of imperialism did not inhere in the type of production carried on in the colonies, but in the undemocratic social and political institutions which surrounded economic activity.

Oppression and exploitation are not inventions of Western civilization. Indeed, the European powers were responsible for introducing ideals of equality, human rights and democracy into many regions. But they undoubtedly failed to nurture ideals of national self-determination. Even in the case of the United States in the Philippines, where independence was long contemplated as the eventual outcome, local government was not sufficiently encouraged in preparation for this event.

The pursuit of the profit motive by foreign corporations and foreign nationals is now coming to be recognized in the new republics of the Near East and Asia as potentially very useful in economic development. Capitalism need not be conjoined with exploitative political and social institutions, and least of all need the extraction of minerals and the production of foodstuffs and industrial crops be exploitative. The bases of mutually profitable economic exchange in nonexploitative political and social institutions are now being haltingly and laboriously worked out by the former colonial powers and the newly developing countries.

*Elements of Mutually Satisfactory Exchange*

What the configuration of the new institutions and usages will be is difficult indeed to discern in the midst of the turmoil of their creation. Eventual political independence supplies the necessary cornerstone, though independence for some colonial areas without the prior development of a trained civil servant class and without prior schooling of the people themselves in political responsibility has in some cases produced national disaster. The accomplishment of some political revolutions was rather less the riddance of nefarious foreigners and rather more the deposing of oppressive native castes or classes which colonial powers, as a matter of convenience or necessity, had used to make their own positions secure. Another cornerstone of peaceful economic relations has been laid in the United Nations and its many specialized agencies, in the International Bank for Reconstruction and Development and other institutions for international cooperation.

On the plane of day-to-day economic affairs, one of the main elements of workable economic interchange appears to be the right of the newly developing country to deny foreign enterprise access to some types of production considered appropriate for nationalization or suitable only for entry by nationals because of military considerations. Stipulation of majority ownership by nationals and requirements as to the employment of nationals are more questionable prerogatives, and may indeed discourage foreign investment completely. If these countries desire to attain economic equality with the West, they will have to learn to make the conditions for the private foreign investor equally attractive with the opportunities he enjoys at home. No doubt some part of the earlier "exploitation" by colonial powers represented an effort to secure by force this sort of equality for the European investor and entrepreneur.

## *Reasons for Compatibility of Interests*

Once the political conditions for dealings between foreigners and natives have been reasonably well elaborated, there is no reason why the "procurement" motive of the Western nations and the development motive of Asia, Africa and Latin America should not be compatible. And the same applies to the export interest of the West and the desire of the rest of the world to progress economically. This is true for several reasons.

For one thing, the wherewithal for development, including also eventually heavy industries, will have to come for a long time into the future from exports of raw materials. Mexico is a particularly illuminating case because it has already developed to the point where a larger share of the national income comes from industry than from agriculture, and still it must depend upon its raw material exports in order to command the necessary imports of machines and heavy-industry products from abroad. These exports are necessary despite extensive foreign investments, which amounted in 1951 to 70 per cent of all investment in new industry in the country. Exports of lead, zinc, copper, petroleum and, in lesser measure, silver and cotton furnish the material basis for domestic expansion.[3] Thus the foreign procurement and marketing interests further the domestic development

3. "Mexico's Industrial Drive," *Financial Times*, October 20, 1952, pp. 4 and 6.

interest, and the situation is paralleled in most of the underdeveloped world.[4]

This generalization holds also for the vital sphere of foodstuffs. Although the less developed nations are net exporters of most industrial raw materials and will advisedly remain so during a protracted phase of their evolution, the situation with foodstuffs is more complex. Argentina, Brazil, certain other Latin American countries and New Zealand and Australia will probably continue to be exporters of foodstuffs in the aggregate; and some other less developed countries will, for the discernible future, continue to be exporters of certain foodstuffs. But some regions with poor, overcrowded or insufficiently developed agricultural resources may change quickly from net exporters to net importers of food, if indeed—like Egypt—they have not already lived on foreign supplies. The shift may be caused by war and political upheavals, as in parts of Southeast Asia; or it may result from the mere increase of population.

But net import of foods may also be a natural accompaniment of development. When highways, dams, factories and the like cannot be constructed by mobilizing *surplus* agricultural labor, men and resources must be diverted from food production. Thus the more highly developed primary producers, and even such industrial nations as the United States and Canada, may contribute their "surplus" grains and other foodstuffs to foreign development. If present pricing policies stand in the way of such a movement, this does not necessarily signify that, with the requisite internal adjustments in the producing countries, this fundamentally rational international exchange cannot take place on a profitable basis.

The question of the relative merits of peasant and plantation agriculture in the economies of the underdeveloped nations should yield to similar solution. Again internal political, economic and social reforms may first be necessary: the dethronement of governments resting on an oligarchy of landowners, clarification of land titles, reforms of tenure systems and of water rights, and so on. All of this, however, would still leave unresolved the main economic issues between small peasant holdings and large commercial farms—the merits of more diversified food production, presumably for domestic consumption, as against a few staples for export, and the question of small versus large units. On precisely these central economic issues, the answers in the main may be left to the arbitrament of the market. Whether farms should be large or small, and whether they should produce for foreign or for home consumption, should depend mainly upon which method of production has the lower costs and which brings the higher incomes.[5]

---

4. Densely populated countries like India and China will, of course, be the first in the course of their economic development to reduce the proportion of raw materials in their exports in favor of their use in domestic manufactures.

5. See Chapter 12.

*U.S. Policy and Balanced Development*

The upshot of these considerations for the foreign economic policy of the United States is that, so long as private businesses or government procurement agencies are conducting their purchases in an open and reasonably competitive market, the material wherewithal for economic development is being supplied to primary producers. Monopoly practices on the part of buyers and sharp fluctuations in demand can reduce or obliterate the possible gain to suppliers. But the fact of this demand, aside from such drawbacks, is favorable. So long as the underdeveloped countries are predominantly raw material producers, their *balanced development*—which has been stressed so much in recent discussions—requires that they earn the means for economic progress by large exports of primary products. The United States is not confronted with a choice between furthering the development of foreign sources of supply or foreign markets for its own exports and furthering the development of the economic potential of low-income countries.

For the rest, the United States—through its technical aid advisers, the direction of its grants and loans, and through its substantial influence in the United Nations and the International Bank—can help developing countries to maintain balance in their investment programs. This task is much less formidable today than it was in the first flush of enthusiasm for "industrialization." Ceylon, India, Pakistan and the United Kingdom territories in Asia, containing together half the population of Asia outside China, have formulated programs within the general framework of the Colombo Plan which reflect a major revision of views since the ill-conceived Bombay Plan was broached a decade ago for the rapid industrialization of India.[6] The new programs rest on the conviction, voiced by a former president of the United Nations Economic and Social Council, that the development of agriculture "would show quicker results than any other field," and that investing in industry "can only be done economically if small and simple units of machinery are installed in villages throughout the East."[7]

### PROVISION OF CAPITAL BY THE UNITED STATES

A decade ago, there can be little doubt, discussion of conditions for economic development in the low-income countries overstressed the role to be played by the provision of capital. It overestimated the amount forthcoming from the international agencies and the United States; and it un-

6. The current allocation of the projected costs in the Colombo Plan involves one third for agriculture, another third for transport and communication, 6 per cent for fuel and power, 10 per cent for mining and industry, and 18 per cent for social services.

7. S. Amjad Ali, in the *Summary of Discussions* (Pacific Coast Conference on Private Investment in International Development, International Development Advisory Board), Publication 4795, U.S. Department of State, December 1952, pp. 16–17.

duly depreciated the potentialities of creating the conditions for capital accumulation in a rising crescendo within the developing countries themselves. Capital was assigned too prominent a role relative to other economic factors, such as skilled laborers and managers; and all the economic factors took on an excessive emphasis relative to good government and favorable cultural elements.

Nevertheless, the flow of investment funds to the underdeveloped countries is insufficient today. In the words of the president of the International Bank for Reconstruction and Development:

> Granted that the underdeveloped areas do not yet have the capacity to make productive use of any huge inflow of resources, we must still admit that the present magnitude of international investment for development is clearly inadequate.[8]

How can that flow of capital be augmented? And what responsibilities, interests and opportunities does the United States have in the provision of funds for economic development?

### Outlook for U.S. Grants and Loans

Chapter 17 concurred in the general conclusions of the Gray report concerning grants and loans of the United States government to underdeveloped areas. These sources of capital cannot be expected under present conditions to exceed the level, attained in the recent past, of $500 million annually in grants and technical aid, and $600 to $800 million in loans through the Export-Import Bank and the International Bank. These sums must be viewed in the light of the categorical imperatives of present and future United States military expenditures, both direct and indirect through aid to Europe and other regions. If, for the time being, this country is obliged to pour resources into preparations against military aggression, a time may come when it can devote a larger proportion of its budget to the war against want and misery in the less fortunate countries.

### U.S. Private Investment

The flow of American private investment into the underdeveloped parts of the world has been running within the limits of $500 to $800 million annually. The United States can help lay the groundwork for a larger volume of private investment in foreign countries, including the low-income areas, by working toward the reduction of tariffs, exchange controls, quota restrictions and other barriers to the operation of the price and profit system in international trade. Something more, but probably only a mar-

---

8. International Bank for Reconstruction and Development, *Proceedings*, Seventh Annual Meeting (held at Mexico City), Washington, 1952, p. 11.

ginal contribution, can be achieved by this country through its commercial treaties, its information services, its guarantees, and the elimination of double taxation on foreign investment. In considerable measure, however, it depends upon the developing countries whether sufficiently attractive conditions will prevail to equal the opportunities open to the private investor in the United States. When these countries come to regard foreign private capital as important, the attractions will not be long in materializing.

What proportion of capital from the United States should be supplied privately and what proportion through public agencies is probably not subject to generalization; but the *complementary* nature of the two sources should not be ignored. Public loans and grants can best provide basic services such as public health projects and large ventures with uncertain and indirect benefits over long periods into which private capital might not be attracted. Private capital, on the other hand, is probably superior in those ventures in which technical know-how, skilled managers and supervisors, and the spirit of innovation count heavily.[9] Too frequently private and public loans from the United States have been thought of as alternatives rather than complements.

### National or International Auspices?

Regarded abstractly, international agencies offer many advantages for public investment in developing countries. The receiving countries are less likely to regard these investments suspiciously as the bribes of capitalistic imperialism. In addition to relieving the United States of these charges, international loans and investments may evoke contributions from other creditor countries, such as Switzerland, Belgium and Canada; and it is not inconceivable that the more affluent governments in the underdeveloped world might be persuaded to join in helping the lowest-income countries. The joint-guarantee aspect is also attractive. International organizations, such as the International Bank, can draw on the personnel and experience of many countries besides the United States; some of these have a long background of experience in Asia and Africa, for example. There are imponderable gains in the promotion of international cooperation in concrete working matters.

International agencies can impose conditions of domestic reform as a requirement for loans or grants more successfully than national agencies. Political pressure is less likely to be brought to bear on international agencies than on national agencies. Action through international bodies, moreover, insulates the United States from ill will when loans must be refused or when more aid is given to one country than to another.

9. See John M. Hunter, "Long-Term Foreign Investment and Underdeveloped Countries," *Journal of Political Economy*, February 1953, pp. 15-24.

These abstract merits are, however, attenuated by some contemporary facts: first, the United States supplies most of the finance whether the agency is national or international; second, the international political situation may require some *Realpolitik* on the part of the United States. The bland internationalism of the Economic Commission for Europe on the subject of East-West trade may not correspond to what the government of the United States regards as the essential conditions for guarding supplies of strategic goods. Some United States loans may have to be strategically placed; and when it comes to outright grants—for which much can be said even on purely economic grounds—the same consideration applies with stronger reason.

Both national and international organizations have their place. August Maffry and others would be glad to see the Export-Import Bank expand into the field of loans to American corporations which have extensive direct investments abroad and into equity investments and loans to foreign corporations without government guarantees. Others have envisaged similar functions as the basis of a new International Finance Corporation, to operate in spheres closed to the International Bank.[10] Just where to draw the line on principle is hard to say. Particular decisions will probably be determined by varying degrees of confidence in or mistrust of international agencies on the part of Congress. At any rate, there seem to be no grounds for a sharp revision of recent American policies.

### Attaching Conditions to Loans

"Give, hoping for nothing in return" cannot be the rule for the United States in making grants or loans to underdeveloped areas. It is legitimate for this country to choose to aid its friends or potential friends in a world of bipolar power where the possibility of peaceful survival is doubtful. Moreover, the funds granted or loaned must actually serve the purpose of economic development and serve it well, since all such allocations of capital must be compared with other intensely competitive claims in the federal budget or in the calculations of private firms or persons. Government loans or grants should therefore be made contingent upon clear evidence concerning not only the useful employment of the funds but also the satisfaction of essential conditions for healthy development, such as a workable fiscal system and reasonably effective monetary control, and upon the assurance that the funds will not be dissipated by political corruption.

Where overvalued exchange rates, exchange controls and quotas can be reduced, the objectives of United States policy and the developing country's

10. See August Maffry, *Program for Increasing Private Investment in Foreign Countries* (mimeographed), report prepared for Technical Cooperation Administration (Department of State), U.S. Department of Commerce and Mutual Security Agency, December 18, 1952, pp. 16–21.

welfare can be furthered by making these reforms a necessary condition of financial aid. Some of these stipulations have been made, either implicitly or explicitly, by the International Bank, which enjoys the advantage of being able to put financial consultants into semiofficial positions, after the pattern of the very successful League of Nations advisers, to see that the required reforms are worked out in detail.

At any rate it is clear, as the *Economist* writes, that "the idea that all poor countries have a natural and inalienable right to its [Point Four's] benefits needs to be corrected."[11] On the political side, the *Economist* continues, there must be the assurance that "development plans [will] not be nullified by revolution, disorder, corruption, or incompetence." On the economic side, the country seeking aid should produce a practicable plan and show that it can mobilize domestic capital to finance a good part of the plan. A further essential part of the sound financing of development is the "project" basis, which the International Bank has insisted upon. Whether a loan or grant is justified depends upon its particular use or, in the language of economic theory, its marginal productivity, not merely on some vaguely expressed need. However, the project and its productivity have to be broadly conceived, and indirect and intangible benefits have also to be considered.

Making loans or grants conditional upon sound economic and financial policies and upon effective use of the funds need not and should not imply interference with political "self-determination" in the countries to which capital is supplied. The record of Marshall Plan aid in Europe is enviable on this score, and the International Bank has earned an equally good reputation.[12] These examples should be emulated in United States foreign loan policy generally.

### Other Types of Contributions

The importance of United States capital for economic progress in the underdeveloped world must be assessed in a perspective which includes all the manifold elements involved in the great problem of development. Within this broad scene, noneconomic forces—cultural, political and demographic—may play a more crucial part than purely economic forces. Of these in turn, labor and entrepreneurial skills often limit expansion more narrowly than does the supply of capital.

The economic assistance which the United States can extend to low-income countries, moreover, goes far beyond supplying capital. The judgment has been expressed that the value of the technical aid program alone

---

11. "Self-help for Developing Nations," *Economist*, January 31, 1953, pp. 261–62.

12. According to the testimony of Ramon Betata concerning Mexico; see International Bank for Reconstruction and Development, *Proceedings*, Seventh Annual Meeting, *loc. cit.*, p. 14.

outweighs that of loans and grants. Whether this is so or not, the United States can make valuable contributions to foreign development by stabilizing its own economy, by reducing its import barriers, by promoting free multilateral trade throughout the free world, by helping to stabilize the incomes of raw material export lands, and—not least—by supplying expert guidance for the investment programs and the fiscal and monetary systems of developing countries. The creditor role is important, but it does not merit the exclusive emphasis it once received.

## TECHNICAL AID

In his inaugural address on January 20, 1949, President Truman said: "I believe we should make available to peace-loving peoples the benefits of our store of technical knowledge in order to help them realize their aspirations for a better life." Although this statement puts the matter of technical aid on a high plane of altruism, and although altruism may be a particularly appropriate motive in view of the nonpecuniary benefits and immeasurable material gains which accrue from it, the rationale of technical aid includes no less than the whole gamut of political, economic and humanitarian interests which this country has in the general material progress of low-income countries.

Whenever a more efficient technique can be substituted for a less efficient one, something is being got "for nothing";[13] and this fact supplies the compelling reason for a technical aid program.

Yet, if a nation divulges its superior techniques for political or other purposes, does it not run the risk that these very techniques will eventually be used to undercut its products in world markets? The theoretical possibility cannot be denied that in given lines of production a given country may feel precisely this effect. In practice, however, the United States would seem to have nothing to fear. Technical aid under Point Four is mostly concerned with the simple fundamentals of public health and the humblest sorts of agricultural methods, with which the competitive capacity of the United States in foreign markets is most remotely connected. Even where techniques are more advanced, the underdeveloped countries have at present so great a handicap that their competition is distant. In time, nearly any technical process can be imitated by other lands; but meanwhile the United States presumably will have advanced further and created new techniques. The ultimate defense against competition is not secrecy but progressive excellence. Fear of losing out to foreigners should be the least

13. Aside, that is, from obsolescence costs and the costs of transferring the new technique to the user. However, the paucity and primitiveness of capital instruments in the case of newly developing countries make obsolescence costs relatively unimportant. The costs of supplying the superior methods from the technically more advanced nation are also presumably small compared to the eventual returns.

of all deterrents to the furthering of present United States interests in aiding development.

## U.S. Technical Assistance Activities

In 1953 it was estimated that by the end of the 1954 fiscal year the United States would have expended approximately $400 million on technical cooperation and that this sum would have been more than matched in contributions of $490 million by the beneficiary countries themselves.[14] In addition, the United States contributed to the Technical Assistance Administration of the United Nations in fiscal 1951, 1952 and 1953, $13 million, $12.4 million and $9.2 million, respectively. Total outlays on technical assistance have never exceeded 0.2 per cent of the federal budget or slightly over 2 per cent of the annual foreign aid appropriations. At the close of the 1953 fiscal year it was estimated that, of the total United States technical cooperation program, about 49 per cent had been devoted to Asia and the Pacific, 37 per cent to the Near East and Africa, and 14 per cent to Latin America. Over this period (1951–1953) the allocation of funds by principal categories was as follows: 37.2 per cent to agriculture, forestry and fisheries; 15.7 per cent to industry, handicrafts and housing; 15.6 to natural resources and public utilities; and 13.5 per cent to health and sanitation.[15]

The matching contributions of the receiving countries demonstrate that technical aid has, on principle, not been conducted as a "give away" program. Another sound principle has been its emphasis on agriculture, small industries and handicrafts, and on public health. It has also apparently been conducted on the basis of a tapering off of the United States share and a complementary increase of the local contributions.

## Future Directions of Technical Assistance

The broad aggregate outlays cover a myriad of activities and accomplishments ranging from the marked reduction of deaths by malaria and other endemic diseases and dramatic declines in infant mortality to improved strains of agricultural stock and grains and technical advice on such varied matters as educational systems and multipurpose development of waterways. There have undoubtedly been occasional cases of obvious waste and other cases of misconceived means and ends. Generally speaking, however, Point Four, in the present sense of technical aid, has stood as a symbol of hope throughout the impoverished areas of the world and as concrete evidence of the benevolent intentions of the United States. Its cost has been relatively small in budgetary terms and the returns—though difficult to evaluate precisely—have apparently been large. It should continue, without

14. *New York Times*, September 26, 1953.
15. Hearings on Mutual Security appropriations for 1953, U.S. House of Representatives.

serious impairment of financial resources or skilled personnel. Any marked curtailment of technical assistance, it has been said, "would leave the world from Indonesia to Libya strewn with unfinished projects, each a monument to the broken promises of the West."[16]

In the future, more attention could profitably be given to the use of third countries as bearers of technical aid. Experts from Japan, for example, could probably introduce improved methods of rice culture into Southeast Asia better than experts from the West. The dissemination of superior but relatively inexpensive industrial methods and equipment is another field in which other countries could be of assistance.

As a matter of principle, the United States should maintain its own technical aid program but continue also to participate in the United Nations Technical Assistance Administration. Its own program ensures it against sabotage by unfriendly nations, while participation in the United Nations program ensures that the beneficial work can proceed even in countries that might be sensitive to the presence of agents from the United States.

### STABILITY AND PROGRESS

The furtherance of economic progress in the underdeveloped countries is by no means limited to grants, loans and technical aid. The United States might make an even greater contribution by helping to create an international economic setting in which the newly developing countries could earn the wherewithal for their own development. But progress requires stability.

Variations in the foreign-exchange yield of exports by primary producers, according to evidence presented in Chapter 18, have been extreme for a half century at least. These alternations of good and bad times are inimical to economic progress for several reasons. In the first place, income earned from exports frequently bulks large in the national income of primary producers; the population usually holds small cash balances, and hence increased income immediately boosts expenditures, and decreased income cannot be cushioned by drawing on balances. These forces cannot readily be offset in the less developed countries by contracyclical fiscal and monetary measures. In the second place, the high incomes of the lush years are likely to be squandered on consumption, and in the lean years the wherewithal for development is simply lacking. Third, the knowledge of their vulnerability to depressions in world markets leads the underdeveloped countries to try to insulate their economies by protectionist devices—

16. Hamilton Fish Armstrong, "The Grand Alliance Hesitates," *Foreign Affairs*, October 1953, pp. 48–49, quoting a United Nations official.

quotas, exchange controls and tariffs—all of which reduce the strength they might derive for development from the industrial nations.

## Possibilities of Self-Help for Primary Producers

Against the vicissitudes of demand in international markets, the primary producers have some recourse, though even their best efforts would still leave them exposed to excessive instability. Export taxes offer one avenue. When foreign exchange yields of exports are abnormally favorable, export taxes can be used to divert income into inactive funds to be held by the government against the day of sagging demand and falling prices.

The accumulation of foreign-exchange reserves through export taxes is a particularly useful device, but any device to appropriate part of the high incomes of boom years, even if only in domestic currency, and to pay them out in years of dearth, works in the right direction. Two English economists, Bauer and Paish, have presented a plausible scheme for reducing instability for primary producers through compensatory withholdings of part of the sales price or extra payments over the price, depending on the state of the market.[17] By employing a floating-average price index as the basis of operations, such schemes could avoid chronic divergence of the prices they pay to producers from the international level. Stabilizing operations of this sort require a government export monopoly, exchange control or drastic tax powers.

The shortcomings of efforts by individual primary producing countries will readily be apparent. The government may itself not be able to resist the temptation to spend the levies on exports in boom times—perhaps on developmental activities—hence the restraint on inflation is lost. Other countries exporting similar products, by *not* levying a charge on exports in boom times, can divert a portion of the demand to themselves, thus undercutting the system. Finally, no amount of alternate taxing and subsidizing of exporters in the producing countries can remove the variations of demand in international markets. A primary producer could conceivably keep its balance of payments in *equilibrium* by severe enough measures, but the impact of varying foreign demand on the domestic economy would still be a problem. It is this fundamental source of disturbance that requires remedy.

The stabilizing efforts of the producer nation can, however, form a valuable counterpart to other, more inclusive, schemes. And since a particular country may suffer from ups and downs peculiar to its chief export or exports, national commodity stabilization systems—if they do not lose

---

17. P. T. Bauer and F. W. Paish, "The Reduction of Fluctuations in the Incomes of Primary Producers," *Economic Journal*, December 1952, pp. 750–81.

their *compensatory* character to ulterior objectives—can play a role which general international systems cannot assume.

## "Charity Begins at Home"

The economic, political and humane interests of Western nations in the progress of the underdeveloped world should impress these countries with the truth that stability of domestic employment in the great industrial countries is the *first* ingredient of stability elsewhere. Economists have harped on this theme for a decade or more,[18] and its truth has not diminished with time. Other approaches to the problem are at best palliatives.

In its own interest, in the first place, the United States could demonstrate its capacity to stabilize output and prices at home. From the standpoint of international politics and ideologies it is a practical necessity for this country to prove that capitalism need not fall into suicidal swings between depression and inflation. In so doing it would remove one of the chief barriers to currency convertibility by allaying the fears of other countries, including the developing areas, of recurrent deficits in their foreign balances. To this end, the philosophy of compensatory public finance and monetary policy—long since the common property of the professional economists and that part of the business community represented by the Committee for Economic Development—must permeate to the electorates and legislators throughout the country. To this end, also, the exigencies of Treasury finance must not be allowed to prevail over monetary control; the Federal Reserve must not again on some future occasion engender inflation by its support of the government security markets.

Having set its own house in order to far greater degree than it has during the postwar years, the United States could then demand that other countries refrain from inflation if they are to receive grants or loans from it or from the international agencies. Two of Britain's leading economists have recently come to the conclusion that "The first desideratum for all countries affected with difficulties with their balance of payments is to stop inflation."[19]

## International Measures for Stability

But since the countries of Western Europe and North America so imperfectly achieve the objective of domestic stability, other remedies against international instability command attention. Within the past decade in-

18. Perhaps its most notable exposition is to be found in Hal B. Lary, *The United States in the World Economy* (Economic Series No. 23), U.S. Department of Commerce, Bureau of Foreign and Domestic Economy, 1943.

19. The words are Lionel Robbins'; see "The International Economic Problem," *Lloyds Bank Review*, January 1953, pp. 1–25; but James E. Meade also places the avoidance of inflation as the *first* of eight prerequisites for a viable international economy; see *The Three Banks Review*, December 1952, pp. 1–22.

numerable articles, books and reports of government inquiries, and the publications of three major international commissions have embodied the best efforts of economists and statesmen to describe how nations can co-operate to promote economic stability, including the more limited objective of stability in the markets for primary products. Only a brief reference can be made to some of these plans here.

One proposal, which was advanced in a League of Nations study and has weathered time and much criticism, is to establish international buffer stocks of industrial and agricultural staple commodities.[20] Another League proposal involved contracyclical lending by creditor nations. Both pro-posals, with modifications in detail, have been revived in the Angell report by five economists for the United Nations.[21] In addition to buffer stocks of important international staples and contracyclical lending to primary pro-ducers, nearly all recommendations include extension of the magnitude and availability of centrally managed funds of international means of payment to be used for countries experiencing temporary balance-of-payments dif-ficulties.

All these proposals involve formidable problems of application. But the dangers of economic instability for the underdeveloped and the industrial nations alike are still more formidable. Properly conceived systems of com-modity stabilization should be able to avoid both rigidity of relative prices and resource use and monopolistic tendencies toward restriction of supply.

## REDUCTION OF U.S. BARRIERS TO IMPORTS

Although the liberation of international trade from its trammels in all quarters of the earth would bring advantages to countries aspiring to development, these countries would realize particularly conspicuous gains from the sharp reduction of protection by the United States. Each of the gains accruing to them would be accompanied by gains and not losses to the American economy and to the position of the United States in interna-tional politics. These mutual interests in the reduction of this country's import barriers arise from five sources.

1. As the greatest creditor of underdeveloped and economically more advanced countries alike, the United States must accept imports if the bor-rowers are to be given the opportunity to behave as honest debtors and to

20. League of Nations, *Economic Stability in the Post-War World*, Geneva, 1945, pp. 265–71, 313. Indi-vidual proposals of this general sort have been made by Keynes, Hayek, and by Benjamin Graham supported by Frank D. Graham. See, however, the analysis of Graham's plan in M. K. Bennett and Associates, *International Stockpiling as an Economic Stabilizer*, Stanford University Press, Stanford, 1949.

21. United Nations, Department of Economic Affairs, *Measures for International Economic Stability*, New York, 1951. An earlier international report on this subject was also made to the United Nations, *viz.*, *National and International Measures for Full Employment*, New York, 1949; its proposals for automatic com-pulsory action by creditor countries aroused much opposition, particularly in the United States.

maintain the schedules of amortization and interest on their loans. American interest in imports from this angle is that loans shall not turn out to be donations. Imports into the United States condition the debtors' ability to pay and the ability of the United States to receive, whether the loan or investment has been made on government or private account, and whether it has come from the United States government or an international agency, since in the latter case also this country is ultimately the chief creditor.

2. As the largest importer of many primary products—and the list is bound to grow with the further depletion of domestic resources—the United States supplies underdeveloped countries with the purchasing power for essential equipment which they cannot, or cannot as cheaply, produce at home or purchase elsewhere. This is an aspect of the "trade not aid" avenue to higher incomes for the underdeveloped areas. The interest of American manufacturers in raw material supplies needs no elaboration.

3. As the chief producer within the North Atlantic Treaty Organization, the United States requires imports in general, and imports of strategic goods in particular. The same economic interests are involved here for American manufacturers and for foreign suppliers of materials as in 2 above.

4. As the chief exporter of industrial equipment to developing countries, the United States must import to the degree to which these exports are not financed by American loans, grants or private investment abroad. The interest of underdeveloped areas in United States imports from this standpoint (the obverse side of 2) is to have available a sufficient supply of dollar exchange to meet demand at current prices and exchange rates. The interest of the American manufacturer in export markets again needs no explanation.

5. As an importer of raw materials, the United States forms one side of a triangle of international trade which affects the interest, not merely of exporters of raw materials in the underdeveloped areas, but of European exporters of manufactured goods. Part of the dollar proceeds of United States imports of primary products has in the past been used by the newly developing countries to cover their purchases of European manufactures.[22] Again this is an import interest of the United States, and it corresponds to export interests in Europe and both export and import interests in developing countries.

### Special Interests and the National Interest

From these several standpoints, a strong case can be made for this country's departing, perhaps completely, from its traditional protectionist position. Many free-traders will delight in the fact that the case can now be

22. Bank for International Settlements, *Twenty-Second Annual Report*, Basle, 1952, pp. 148–49.

argued in "hard-headed" terms of the special economic interests of American creditors, exporters and importers. It is true, of course, that the virtually unanimous conviction of economists since the time of Adam Smith in the *general* welfare gains of free trade has not overwhelmed the Congress of the United States, or the legislatures of most other countries. The economic interest of the protected group of domestic producers has very often been more convincing, partly because its spokesmen—the tariff lobbyists—have been well paid, vociferous and armed with specific "hardship" cases, and partly because the costs of protection have been diffused, concealed and not even comprehended. Nowadays, however, the shoe is on the other foot: the strongest vested interests are rapidly changing from the protected manufacturers for the home market to the producers for export and the manufacturers requiring imported raw materials.

Nevertheless, good causes have to beware of some of their friends, or at least to recognize that friendship is sometimes disingenuous. It must be granted that lowering tariffs and other import barriers is bound to *injure* some agricultural producers, some manufacturers and some other domestic interests, such as maritime shipping. Some gain, some lose. In the end, the issue has to be resolved in the good old-fashioned way of Adam Smith, in terms of the general welfare.[23] It is gratifying, therefore, to find the Public Advisory Board for Mutual Security taking the position that United States trade and tariff policy should be "based on the national interest, rather than the interest of particular industries or groups."[24]

If, then, the creditor, export or import interests of the United States argue for an abandonment of its protectionist position, it is because the gain of these sectors would not be canceled by losses in other sectors of the economy. American producers in the aggregate and American consumers in the aggregate would gain, just as they now gain in domestic commerce from the large free-trade area of the United States itself.

Liberalization of imports by the United States would necessitate some internal readjustments. But one of the outstanding traits of the tariff-free domestic economy of this country is its flexibility. It has taken in its stride such revolutions as the change from horses to automobiles and tractors, from bulk to package retailing, from household drudgery to the mechanical conveniences of the modern home. One commentator believes that gradual tariff reduction would cause less dislocation than the ordinary processes of

23. By stressing the possible effects on the distribution of income, "welfare economics" has worked itself into a virtually nihilistic position on the free-trade issue. What seems to be needed is a careful quantitative analysis to see whether these income effects may really be large enough to offset the gains in productive efficiency and the lower costs to consumers with given incomes. This would seem to be highly improbable, just as it is improbable that net gains would accrue to any one region in the United States by its being walled off by tariffs from the rest of the country.

24. Public Advisory Board for Mutual Security, *A Trade Policy and Tariff Policy in the National Interest*, February 1953.

technical innovation.[25] Another has estimated that the "abolition of all tariffs would not displace more than 300,000 U.S. workers and none of the liberalizations proposed could displace more than 90,000 at the most."[26] Adjustments of this or even greater order are a small price to pay—and it is a "one-time" or nonrecurring price—for the achievement of the national interest in enabling people to buy what they want from abroad without let or hindrance.

## The National Interest and the International Interest

Even more significantly the national interest of the United States to admit imports without artificial impediments conforms to the economic requirements of other countries, whether they are the Western European nations, hoping for "recovery" or "progress," or the low-income nations elsewhere, hoping for "development." To achieve this concord of interest, the wise policy for the United States is to increase American imports and thus increase exports, rather than to stifle imports and thus stifle exports.

International organizations such as the United Nations, the Organization for European Economic Cooperation and the Economic Commission for Europe have, of course, repeatedly proclaimed the importance of United States imports for the survival of the free world. The ostensible policy of the Roosevelt, Truman and Eisenhower administrations has accorded with this position. But there are two policy-making branches of government in the United States—the executive and the legislative—particularly on foreign affairs.[27] While the Administration may favor "trade not aid," Congress may only falteringly extend the Reciprocal Trade Agreements Act for one more year.

The free-trade cause in the United States has been notably advanced in recent times in public pronouncements by Lewis Douglas, Eugene R. Black, Henry Ford, the Chamber of Commerce of the United States, speakers at the Chicago World Trade Conference, the president of the Elgin Watch Company and the Committee for Economic Development. *Fortune* magazine in its March 1953 issue asserted that "Free trade is inevitable." These are not declarations of special vested interests within the national interest, but of the general welfare; and they are also not declarations of national versus international interest. They recognize that the alternatives to exporting to the United States by which other countries can command imports vital for their economic survival or progress are either inadequate or undesirable. American private foreign investment does not

25. Meyer Kestnbaum, president of Hart, Schaffner and Marx, quoted in *Time*, November 9, 1953, p. 95.

26. Boris Shishkin, Research Chief, American Federation of Labor, in *Time, loc. cit.*

27. Harry D. Gideonse, *The Economic Foreign Policy of the United States* (Fiftieth Anniversary Commemoration Lectures), National Bank of Egypt, Cairo, 1953, pp. 6–13.

cover this need, and government grants and loans in anything like the amounts thought desirable by foreign governments would certainly not be desirable from the viewpoint of the American taxpayer.

## What the United States Should Do

Mr. Ford's statement of the necessary steps is direct and explicit.[28] The law providing for drastic unilateral reductions of tariff duties should have no exceptions or loopholes, although it should make provision for gradual reductions in some "hardship cases." The United States should abandon the quota system and the Buy America Act which compels the federal and some state and local governments to give first preference in their procurements to domestic sources. American customs procedures should be immediately simplified.[29]

These steps are clearer and bolder than those recommended in the report of the Public Advisory Board for Mutual Security. The time has passed for the mild procedures of the Reciprocal Trade Agreements Act. What American national and international interest requires is a unilateral, incisive and unambiguous abandonment of protection in all its forms, whether explicit or concealed.

The significance of a bold free-trade policy on the part of the United States would not be limited to its direct effect on the "dollar gap," that is, the excess of demand over supply in international trade for New York balances aside from United States foreign aid. It has been estimated that abolishing all barriers to imports would, in itself, reduce that gap by only one third or one fifth, depending upon certain assumptions. But the indirect influence of this policy would be much greater. If the United States were free of protectionist blemishes, it could firmly insist that other countries reduce exchange controls, quota restrictions and similar barriers as a condition of foreign aid. This reduction, in conjunction with vigorous monetary-fiscal policies to stabilize the American economy, would lay the foundations of an open international standard, in contrast to the closed-nation standards of the present scene. Parallel action in other countries would of course be equally important. Import liberalization by the United States is not a panacea, but it is an indispensable step toward creating the kind of international setting in which the underdeveloped nations can finance their own development.

## Currency Convertibility

In an international system which is conducive to economic development, freely convertible currencies play a particularly strategic role. As Chapter 16

28. *New York Times*, February 18, 1953.
29. Legislation to this end has already been enacted, but it is limited in scope.

has pointed out, private capital will not flow into exchange control countries except perhaps to exploit exceptionally profitable opportunities for *direct* investment. Even this exception has a somewhat limited significance for general domestic development, because—as recent history has demonstrated—investment of this sort is concentrated heavily in extractive industry (chiefly in petroleum), where profits can be withdrawn merely by exporting the raw material. If underdeveloped countries are to obtain direct private investments for production for the *domestic* market and private portfolio investment for *general* development purposes, currencies have to be convertible on current account and for the withdrawal of profits by foreigners.

Probably the best initial steps toward achieving currency convertibility in the underdeveloped countries themselves would be indirect: policies directed toward the convertibility of the key European currencies. If the pound sterling were convertible, the problem would be immeasurably simplified for all members of the sterling area; and the same would hold for the Belgian and French franc and for these spheres of economic and political influence in the underdeveloped world.

All measures initiated by the United States to liberalize its own imports or to break down quota and other trade barriers elsewhere contribute toward convertibility. But measures directed specifically toward convertibility are essential. Perhaps the best initial move might be a series of *ad hoc* stabilization loans by the United States to support the actual introduction of convertibility, once a particular country had set its domestic finances in order and had achieved general balance-of-payments equilibrium. Currently this goal appears to be within striking distance for the United Kingdom, Belgium and Western Germany, and to be within the realm of possibility for France and Italy. As one currency after another became convertible, the task would become simpler—and more imperative—for the remaining countries. Once currency convertibility was achieved in Western Europe—and this means, of course, conversion into gold or dollars—the commercially peripheral countries of the world would no longer find justification for exchange controls in the "dollar shortage." In place of this general categoric reason or excuse for exchange controls, there would remain, as there should, only the temporary balance-of-payments difficulties of a particular country at a specific time.

As an alternative to direct Treasury loans for convertibility, the United States could act through the International Monetary Fund. There would in any case seem to be little point in protracting for long such intermediate steps toward convertibility as the European Payments Union, or in creating new ones such as a North Atlantic Payments Union. Only if no further progress toward general convertibility were possible would such institutions have any particular reason for existence.

## Unitary Character of International Economic Problems

The United States acts in its own self-interest if it helps to develop primary producers as sources of industrial raw materials and strategic military supplies, and as markets for its industrial and other exports. This interest, it has been shown, corresponds to the interests of the developing areas themselves, though purely economic measures must be complemented by cultural change and political and social reforms. It corresponds also to the intense need of the United Kingdom, Western Germany and Japan—countries the United States prizes or hopes to win as friends—for overseas supplies and markets. Indeed, it is difficult to see any long-term hope for the economic viability of these countries, dependent as they are on international trade, except in a setting of sustained economic development in Asia, Africa and Latin America.[30] For these objectives to be realized, however, international trade must be vastly expanded. This implies its liberation from such barriers as prohibitive tariffs, quotas, exchange controls and inconvertible currencies.

Free multilateral trade is extolled by nearly all nations and practiced by few. Is this divergence between professed aims and deeds mere hypocrisy? It would be difficult to draw this conclusion for other countries without putting the shoe on our own foot, for the United States is scarcely without shortcomings, such as its subsidy of agricultural exports and the special favoring of American shipping. A more plausible interpretation would be the bewildering interdependence of all phases of the problem of achieving freer and more abundant trade and movements of capital. Each country would be pleased to expand its trade, but none knows where to begin.

Currency convertibility can scarcely be realized without relief from the shortage of dollars, but private American capital will not move into exchange control countries in any noteworthy volume. Foreign quotas and tariffs keep out dollar imports, but these imports may be necessary to build up the productive power of developing countries and reduce the balance-of-payments deficits which gave rise to the protective devices. Fluctuations in the foreign exchange yields of exports impel primary producers toward a goal of self-sufficiency; but true self-sufficiency would halt economic progress in these areas in its tracks. Everything depends upon everything else.

---

30. Howard S. Ellis, *The Economics of Freedom: the Progress and Future of Aid to Europe*, Harper, New York, 1950, Chapter 20 and pp. 518–28.

To the fatalist, this realization may readily bring despair; but, in fact, the endless interdependence of all parts of the international problem may as legitimately be given an optimistic reading. Each part holds forth an opportunity for improvement. And while one of them, as for example currency convertibility, cannot be pressed indefinitely and in isolation, it can nevertheless be carried forward somewhat, while forces are being marshaled for an advance in another salient.

The United States can encourage economic progress in underdeveloped areas by continuing its technical aid and by making marginal contributions of funds. A more basic kind of help, both now and in the long run, would be the creation of an expanding system of international trade based on comparative prices and profits. In such a world, the newly developing countries would be able to work out their own salvation.

# APPENDICES

# APPENDIX 1-1. ESTIMATED PROPORTION OF PER CAPITA CALORIE INTAKE DERIVED FROM VARIOUS SOURCES, SELECTED COUNTRIES, PREWAR YEARS

| Country | Calories per Day[a] | Percentage of Calories from Cereals and Potatoes | Percentage of Calories Crops | Percentage of Calories Livestock |
|---|---|---|---|---|
| **Group I** | | | | |
| United States | 3,249 | 30–40 | 60–65 | 35–40 |
| Germany | 2,921 | 40–50 | 75–80 | 20–25 |
| United Kingdom | 3,005 | 30–40 | 55–60 | 40–45 |
| Sweden | 3,036 | 30–40 | 60–65 | 35–40 |
| Australia | 3,128 | 30–40 | 55–60 | 40–45 |
| New Zealand | 3,281 | 30–40 | 50–55 | 45–50 |
| Canada | 3,109 | 30–40 | 60–65 | 35–40 |
| Denmark | 3,215 | 30–40 | 60–65 | 35–40 |
| France | 2,714 | 50–60 | 70–75 | 25–30 |
| Norway | 3,117 | 40–50 | 60–65 | 35–40 |
| Eire | 3,155 | 40–50 | 65–70 | 30–35 |
| Argentina | 3,164 | 40–50 | 65–70 | 30–35 |
| **Group II** | | | | |
| Union of South Africa | 2,300 | 70–80 | 75–80 | 20–25 |
| Chile | 2,353 | 50–60 | 80–85 | 15–20 |
| U.S.S.R. | 2,827 | 70–80 | .. | .. |
| Italy | 2,471 | 60–70 | 85–90 | 10–15 |
| Greece | 2,437 | 50–60 | 85–90 | 10–15 |
| Bulgaria | 2,788 | 70–80 | 85–90 | 10–15 |
| **Group III** | | | | |
| Japan | 2,268 | 70–80 | 85–90 | 10–15 |
| Egypt | 2,199 | 70–80 | 90–95 | 5–10 |
| Palestine | 2,570 | 60–70 | 80–85 | 15–20 |
| Uruguay | 2,845 | 30–40 | 60–65 | 35–40 |
| Brazil, etc.[b] | 2,300 | 50–60 | 70–75 | 25–30 |
| India | 2,021 | 60–70 | 90–95 | 5–10 |
| China | 2,201 | 70–80 | 95–100 | 1–5 |
| Turkey | 2,619 | 60–70 | 85–90 | 10–15 |
| Spain | 2,678 | 50–60 | 85–90 | 10–15 |

Source: John D. Black and Maxine E. Kiefer, *Future Food and Agriculture Policy*, McGraw-Hill, New York, 1948, p. 42.

a. Excluding wine, beer, etc.

b. Includes Central America, Caribbean, Venezuela, Colombia, Ecuador and Peru.

| Country | Period | Land Area | Agricultural Area | | | Unused but Potentially Productive | Hectares per Capita of Agricultural Population | | Hectares per Capita of Agricultural Labor Force | | Agricultural Labor Force per 1,000 Agricultural Population |
|---|---|---|---|---|---|---|---|---|---|---|---|
| | | | Total | Arable Land (Including Fallow) and Orchards | Permanent Meadow and Pastures | | Total Agri-cultural Area | Arable Land | Total Agri-cultural Area | Arable Land | |
| | | | (Thousands of Hectares) | | | | | | | | |
| **Northern Europe** | | | | | | | | | | | |
| Germany | 1948 | 34,734 | 20,673 | 13,686 | 6,987 | 141 | 1.68 | 1.11 | .. | .. | .. |
| United Kingdom | 1948 | 24,098 | 19,534 | 7,552 | 11,982 | b | 7.81 | 3.02 | 15.40 | 5.96 | 507 |
| Switzerland | 1948 | 3,999 | 2,189 | 489 | 1,700 | .. | 2.52 | 0.56 | 5.49 | 1.22 | 460 |
| Sweden | 1947 | 41,048 | 4,659 | 3,717 | 942 | 3,047 | 3.24 | 2.59 | 7.58 | 6.04 | 428 |
| Netherlands | 1948 | 3,310 | 2,401 | 1,179 | 1,222 | .. | 1.66 | 0.81 | 3.85 | 1.89 | 429 |
| Denmark | 1948 | 4,233 | 3,121 | 2,688 | 433 | .. | 3.09 | 2.66 | 5.79 | 4.99 | 534 |
| France | 1948 | .. | 33,276 | 20,976 | 12,302 | .. | 3.25 | 2.04 | 4.45 | 2.80 | 730 |
| Norway | 1948 | 30,923 | 1,038 | 805 | 233 | 272 | 1.34 | 1.04 | 3.41 | 2.65 | 394 |
| Belgium | 1948 | 3,051 | 1,728 | 1,008 | 720 | .. | 1.44 | 0.84 | 2.74 | 1.60 | 525 |
| Eire | 1948 | 6,889 | 4,684 | 1,615 | 3,069 | .. | .. | .. | 7.69 | 2.65 | .. |
| Finland | 1947 | 30,538 | 2,836 | 2,427 | 409 | .. | 1.52 | 1.30 | 2.48 | 2.12 | 612 |
| Austria | 1948 | 8,166 | 4,156 | 1,840 | 2,316 | .. | 2.19 | 0.97 | 4.26 | 1.88 | 514 |
| Czechoslovakia | 1948 | 12,517 | 7,539 | 5,512 | 2,027 | .. | 2.22 | 1.62 | 3.45 | 2.52 | 643 |
| **Southern and Eastern Europe** | | | | | | | | | | | |
| Italy | 1948 | 29,376 | 22,140 | 16,986 | 5,154 | .. | 1.17 | 0.90 | 2.53 | 1.94 | 463 |
| Spain | 1945 | 50,276 | 42,062 | 18,600 | 23,462 | .. | 3.549 | 1.57 | 8.995 | 3.977 | 394 |
| Portugal | 1939 | 8,862 | 3,380 | .. | .. | 2,675 | 1.104 | .. | 2.38 | .. | 464 |
| Greece | 1948 | 13,000 | 8,482 | 3,389 | 5,093 | 100 | 2.20 | 0.88 | 5.91 | 2.36 | 373 |
| Hungary | 1946 | .. | 7,561 | 5,950 | 1,611 | .. | 1.67 | 1.31 | 3.53 | 2.77 | 473 |
| Bulgaria | 1947 | .. | 4,537 | 4,286 | 251 | .. | 1.02 | 0.96 | 1.65 | 1.56 | 617 |
| Rumania | 1947 | .. | 12,700 | 9,300 | 3,400 | .. | 1.305 | 0.956 | 1.554 | 1.138 | 840 |
| Yugoslavia | 1935–1938 | .. | 14,470 | 8,261 | 6,209 | .. | 1.36 | 0.78 | 2.85 | 1.63 | 478 |
| Poland | prewar | .. | 20,864 | 16,824 | 4,040 | .. | 1.08 | 0.87 | 2.16 | 1.74 | 500 |
| Albania | 1938 | 2,620 | 1,160 | 310 | 850 | 300 | 1.45 | 0.387 | .. | .. | .. |
| U.S.S.R. | 1947 | .. | 349,000 | 225,000 | 124,000 | 12,000 | 3.59 | 2.31 | 4.86 | 3.14 | 739 |

| | Year | | | | | | | | | | |
|---|---|---|---|---|---|---|---|---|---|---|---|
| **Oceania** | | | | | | | | | | | |
| Australia | 1947–1948 | .. | 369,017 | 12,963 | 356,054 | 8,094 | .. | .. | 832.99 | 29.26 | 270.9 |
| New Zealand | 1948 | .. | 13,286 | 546 | 12,740 | .. | .. | .. | 111.64 | 4.59 | 376.0 |
| **North America** | | | | | | | | | | | |
| United States | 1947 | 771,061 | 452,915 | 177,178 | 275,737 | 32,374 | 16.47 | 6.44 | 60.81 | 23.79 | .. |
| Canada | 1941 | 896,684 | 58,282 | 33,644 | 24,638 | 83,632 | 18.49 | 10.67 | 49.14 | 28.37 | .. |
| **Caribbean and Central America** | | | | | | | | | | | |
| Cuba | 1946 | .. | 5,867 | 1,970 | 3,897 | 25 | .. | .. | 9.36 | 3.14 | .. |
| Costa Rica | 1946 | .. | 980 | 760 | 220 | .. | .. | .. | .. | .. | .. |
| Panama | 1947 | .. | .. | 140[b] | .. | .. | .. | .. | .. | 1.28 | .. |
| Mexico | 1946 | .. | 120,000 | 20,000 | 100,000 | .. | .. | .. | 31.55 | 5.26 | .. |
| Dominican Republic | 1946 | .. | 1,260 | 680 | 580 | .. | .. | .. | 3.40 | 1.83 | .. |
| Haiti | 1947 | .. | .. | 460[b] | .. | 3,890 | .. | .. | .. | .. | .. |
| Nicaragua | 1946 | 13,900 | 750 | 470 | 280 | .. | .. | .. | 2.91 | 1.82 | .. |
| Guatemala | 1947 | 10,889 | 3,600 | 3,000 | 600 | .. | .. | .. | 4.63 | 3.86 | .. |
| Honduras | 1947 | .. | 770 | 550[b] | 220[b] | .. | .. | .. | .. | .. | .. |
| El Salvador | 1947 | 3,413 | 590 | 430 | 160 | .. | .. | .. | 1.78 | 1.29 | .. |
| Puerto Rico | 1947–1948 | .. | 596 | 354 | 242 | 94 | .. | .. | 2.43 | 1.44 | .. |
| **South America** | | | | | | | | | | | |
| Argentina | 1946 | 278,334 | 145,153 | 30,000 | 115,153 | .. | .. | .. | 20.48 | 9.53 | .. |
| Chile | 1948 | .. | 12,619 | 5,873 | 6,786 | .. | 6.51 | 3.03 | 79.87 | 31.94 | 318.0 |
| Venezuela | 1944 | 105,941 | 50,000 | 20,000[b] | 30,000[b] | .. | .. | .. | 8.61 | 0.64 | .. |
| Colombia | 1946 | .. | 28,420 | 2,120[b] | 26,300[b] | .. | .. | .. | 9.87 | 1.03 | .. |
| Peru | 1948 | 18,617 | 15,120 | 1,576 | 13,544[b] | .. | .. | .. | .. | .. | .. |
| Uruguay | 1947 | .. | .. | .. | 14,284 | .. | .. | .. | .. | .. | .. |
| Bolivia | 1937–1938 | .. | .. | 342 | .. | .. | .. | .. | 16.01 | 1.99 | .. |
| Brazil | 1947 | 846,420 | 151,390 | 18,835 | 132,555 | 29,296 | .. | .. | .. | .. | .. |
| Ecuador | 1942 | .. | 2,720 | 1,200 | 1,520 | .. | .. | .. | .. | .. | .. |
| Paraguay | 1947 | .. | .. | 1,550 | .. | .. | .. | .. | .. | .. | .. |

(Continued on page 460)

| Country | Period | Land Area | Agricultural Area | | | Unused but Potentially Productive | Hectares per Capita of Agricultural Population | | Hectares per Capita of Agricultural Labor Force | | Agricultural Labor Force per 1,000 Agricultural Population |
|---|---|---|---|---|---|---|---|---|---|---|---|
| | | | Total | Arable Land (Including Fallow and Orchards) | Permanent Meadow and Pastures | | Total Agricultural Area | Arable Land | Total Agricultural Area | Arable Land | |
| **Middle East** | | | | | | | | | | | |
| Egypt | 1948 | .. | 2,445 | 2,445 | a | .. | .. | .. | 0.57 | 0.57 | .. |
| Palestine | 1947 | 2,640 | .. | 697 | .. | 2,716 | .. | 1.21 | .. | .. | .. |
| Turkey | 1948 | 75,744 | 56,136 | 19,941 | 36,195 | .. | .. | .. | 8.691 | 3.087 | .. |
| Iran | 1943 | .. | 44,730 | 20,330^b | 24,400^b | 40,660^b | .. | .. | .. | .. | .. |
| Iraq | 1943 | .. | 7,654 | 3,654^b | 4,000 | .. | .. | .. | .. | .. | .. |
| Syria | 1948 | .. | 6,339 | 2,290 | 4,049 | 3,388 | .. | .. | .. | .. | .. |
| **Far East** | | | | | | | | | | | |
| Japan | 1948 | 36,616 | 6,841 | 5,907 | 934 | 1,786 | 0.20 | 0.17 | 0.39 | 0.34 | 503.0 |
| Ceylon | 1948 | 6,484 | 1,312 | 1,312 | a | 403 | .. | .. | .. | .. | .. |
| India | 1947 | 225,275 | 98,696 | 98,696 | a | 56,253 | .. | .. | 1.04 | 1.04 | .. |
| Philippines | 1949 | 29,741 | 9,136 | 8,180 | 956 | 2,727 | .. | .. | 2.64 | 2.37 | .. |
| China | 1947 | 944,420 | 285,173 | 91,040 | 194,133 | .. | 0.859 | 0.274 | .. | .. | .. |
| China (22 prov.) | 1947 | .. | .. | 73,230 | .. | .. | .. | .. | .. | .. | .. |
| Indonesia | 1947 | .. | .. | 11,000 | .. | .. | .. | .. | .. | 0.797 | .. |
| Burma | 1947 | .. | .. | 8,754 | .. | 5,646 | .. | .. | .. | 2.116 | .. |
| Thailand | 1948 | .. | .. | 4,751^c | .. | .. | .. | .. | .. | 0.787 | .. |
| Korea | 1948 | 20,436 | 4,390 | 4,390 | a | 1,000 | .. | .. | .. | .. | .. |
| Indochina | 1947 | .. | 4,700 | 4,700 | a | .. | .. | .. | .. | .. | .. |
| **Africa** | | | | | | | | | | | |
| Union of South Africa | 1947 | .. | 87,100 | 6,100 | 81,000 | 4,125 | .. | .. | 25.65 | 1.80 | .. |
| Tunisia | 1948 | .. | 3,866 | 3,766 | 100 | 2,720 | .. | .. | .. | .. | .. |
| Liberia | 1948 | 9,065 | 2,072 | 1,813 | 259 | .. | .. | .. | .. | .. | .. |

Source: United Nations, Food and Agriculture Organization, Yearbook of Food and Agricultural Statistics, 1949, Washington, 1950: data on land area from Table 1, pp. 13–17; data on agricultural population and labor force from pp. 24–27.

a. None, or negligible quantity.   b. Unofficial figure.   c. Area planted to main crops only.

APPENDIX 2-2. INDICATORS OF CAPITAL INPUTS: ENERGY CONSUMED, FREIGHT CARRIED, RAILROAD MILEAGE, MOTOR VEHICLES, TELEPHONES, ANIMAL UNITS

| Country | Energy Consumed per Day (Horse-power-hours per Capita) | Annual Freight Carried (Ton-Miles per Capita) | Miles of Railroad per 1,000 Square Miles of Area | Motor Vehicles per 1,000 Population | Telephones per 1,000 Population | Per Capita Utilization of Energy by Rail and Waterways | Per Capita Utilization of Energy in Industry (Kilowatt-hours, Electrical Equivalent) | Animal Units per 1,000 Population |
|---|---|---|---|---|---|---|---|---|
| Middle East | | | | | | | | |
| Egypt | 1.7 | 69 | 9 | 2 | 3.0 | 54 | 24 | 244 |
| Palestine | 1.9 | 77 | 30 | 10 | 12.0 | .. | .. | .. |
| Turkey | .. | .. | .. | .. | .. | 53 | 74 | 994 |
| Iran | .. | .. | .. | .. | .. | 3 | 5 | 603 |
| Far East | | | | | | | | |
| Japan | 6.6 | 138 | 102 | 3 | 16.0 | 115 | 863 | 83 |
| Ceylon | 1.4 | .. | 38 | 5 | 0.3 | .. | .. | .. |
| India | 0.5 | 60 | 26 | 0.3 | 0.2 | 42 | 52 | 637 |
| Philippines | 0.6 | .. | 8 | 3 | 1.9 | 18 | 48 | 443 |
| China | 0.5 | 17 | 3 | 0.2 | 0.5 | 8 | 23 | 244 |
| Indonesia | 0.4 | 9 | 21 | 1.0 | 0.6 | 15 | 37 | 166 |
| Thailand | .. | .. | .. | .. | .. | 17 | 2 | 824 |
| Korea | .. | .. | .. | .. | .. | 33 | 254 | 111 |
| Indochina | .. | .. | .. | .. | .. | 15 | 28 | 255 |
| Northern Europe | | | | | | | | |
| Germany | 17.8 | 795 | 253 | 24 | 50 | 475 | 2,671 | 573 |
| United Kingdom | 27.1 | 424 | 222 | 53 | 59 | 574 | 3,758 | 396 |
| Switzerland | 11.0 | 289 | 230 | 18 | 102 | .. | .. | .. |
| Sweden | 18.5 | 491 | 60 | 36 | 114 | .. | .. | .. |
| Netherlands | 13.9 | 174 | 140 | 18 | 46 | .. | .. | .. |
| Denmark | 11.1 | 116 | 196 | 43 | 107 | .. | .. | .. |
| France | 13.4 | 604 | 189 | 59 | 37 | 426 | 1,855 | 659 |
| Norway | 20.0 | 180 | 20 | 34 | 74 | .. | .. | .. |

(Continued on page 462)

APPENDIX 2-2—Continued

| Country | Energy Consumed per Day (Horse-power-hours per Capita) | Annual Freight Carried (Ton-Miles per Capita) | Miles of Railroad per 1,000 Square Miles of Area | Motor Vehicles per 1,000 Population | Telephones per 1,000 Population | Per Capita Utilization of Energy by Rail and Waterways | Per Capita Utilization of Energy in Industry (Kilowatt-hours, Electrical Equivalent) | Animal Units per 1,000 Population |
|---|---|---|---|---|---|---|---|---|
| Northern Europe—Continued | | | | | | | | |
| Belgium | 22.8 | 578 | 267 | 27 | 47 | .. | .. | .. |
| Eire | 10.7 | 73 | 48 | 23 | 13 | .. | .. | .. |
| Finland | 12.1 | 508 | 26 | 2 | 2 | .. | .. | .. |
| Austria | 6.5 | 464 | 139 | .. | 41 | .. | .. | .. |
| Czechoslovakia | 11.0 | 492 | 171 | 7 | 9 | 311 | 1,888 | 557 |
| Southern and Eastern Europe | | | | | | | | |
| Italy | 3.9 | 194 | 119 | 11 | 13 | 151 | 590 | 344 |
| Spain | .. | .. | .. | .. | .. | 151 | 370 | 684 |
| Greece | 1.4 | 20 | 36 | 2 | 5 | .. | .. | .. |
| Hungary | 3.6 | 229 | 159 | 2 | 15 | .. | .. | .. |
| Bulgaria | 1.7 | 218 | 46 | 0.8 | 3 | .. | .. | .. |
| Rumania | .. | .. | .. | .. | .. | 95 | 255 | 691 |
| Yugoslavia | 2.1 | 43 | 72 | 1 | 3 | 103 | 161 | 732 |
| Poland | 5.6 | 432 | 89 | 1 | 8 | 201 | 875 | 696 |
| U.S.S.R. | 6.8 | 1,134a | 14a | 5 | 3 | 392 | 752 | 828 |
| Oceania | | | | | | | | |
| Australia | 15.4 | 660 | 9 | 125 | 86 | 907 | 1,311 | 5,824 |
| New Zealand | 12.6 | 464 | 32 | 167 | 110 | .. | .. | .. |
| North America | | | | | | | | |
| United States | 37.6 | 2,977 | 80 | 250 | 148 | 1,413 | 4,265 | 1,045 |
| Canada | 30.4 | 2,611 | 12 | 125 | 114 | 1,306 | 3,145 | 1,542 |

## Caribbean and Central America

| | | | | | | | | |
|---|---|---|---|---|---|---|---|---|
| Cuba | 2.6 | 119 | 70 | 11 | 11 | 143 | 275 | 1,843 |
| Costa Rica | 1.4 | 43 | 22 | 6 | 5 | .. | .. | .. |
| Panama (including Canal Zone) | 12.3 | 26 | 17 | 23 | 11 | .. | .. | .. |
| Mexico | 2.2 | 182 | 19 | 5 | 7 | 92 | 356 | 1,768 |
| Dominican Republic | 0.5 | 0.7 | 8 | 2 | 2 | .. | .. | .. |
| Haiti | 0.4 | .. | 14 | 0.8 | 0.8 | .. | .. | .. |
| Nicaragua | 0.7 | 10 | 4 | 0.7 | 1.5 | .. | .. | .. |
| Guatemala | 0.6 | 13 | 17 | 1.0 | 0.7 | .. | .. | .. |
| Honduras | 1.4 | 19 | 17 | 1.0 | 3.0 | .. | .. | .. |
| El Salvador | 0.6 | 9 | 30 | 2.0 | 2.0 | .. | .. | .. |
| **South America** | | | | | | | | |
| Argentina | 5.0 | 671 | 23 | 21 | 27 | 432 | 508 | 5,164 |
| Chile | 10.7 | 324 | 20 | 11 | 13 | .. | .. | .. |
| Venezuela | 5.1 | .. | 2 | 10 | 5 | .. | .. | .. |
| Colombia | 1.5 | 12 | 5 | 4 | 4 | .. | .. | .. |
| Peru | 1.1 | 45 | 4 | 3 | 3 | .. | .. | .. |
| Uruguay | 3.2 | 514 | 26 | 31 | 16 | .. | .. | .. |
| Bolivia | 0.3 | .. | 5 | 0.6 | 0.9 | .. | .. | .. |
| Brazil | 1.9 | 94 | 6 | 4.0 | 5.0 | 152 | 80 | 1,752 |
| Ecuador | 1.0 | 18 | 7 | 1.0 | 3.0 | .. | .. | .. |
| Paraguay | 0.6 | 23 | 4 | 2.0 | 3.0 | .. | .. | .. |
| **Africa** | | | | | | | | |
| Union of South Africa | 10.1 | 777 | 30 | 37 | 15 | 823 | 1,072 | 2,446 |
| Nigeria | .. | .. | .. | .. | .. | 13 | 17 | 279 |
| French West Africa | .. | .. | .. | .. | .. | 18 | 29 | 464 |

*Sources:* Columns 1–5: U.S. Department of State, *Point Four*, Publication 3719, January 1950, pp. 119–20; Columns 6–8: M. K. Bennett, "International Disparities in Consumption Levels," *American Economic Review*, September 1951, p. 646.

a. European Russia only.

## APPENDIX 5-1. MEASUREMENT OF POPULATION GROWTH

In the simplest possible terms, any change in a population over time—barring migration—is determined by the relation between deaths and births. If deaths exceed births, population declines; if births exceed deaths, population increases. This simple arithmetical relation, however, tells very little about the probable future changes in a *particular* population, because the same excess of births or deaths could occur in countries having quite different demographic and ecological characteristics. Since many underdeveloped areas differ appreciably in these respects from already developed countries, these factors must be examined before the probable relation between development and population growth can be assessed.

### Crude Birth Rates an Imperfect Measure

The crude birth rate—the number of live births per 1,000 population—gives only a rough indication of the fertility of a given population. If the proportion of women to men is small the women may be exceedingly fertile even though the crude birth rate is unusually low. To borrow an illustration from Robert R. Kuczynski:

If, for example, in the State of Colorado, in the year 1860 every second female between 15 and 50 years had borne a child (which would have implied a fertility such as never has been observed in the world) the birth rate of that year would still have been only 16 per 1,000 because the females between 15 and 50 years constituted only 3.2 per cent of the total population.[1]

One reason, then, why the crude birth rate is not sufficiently informative is that it is affected by the sex composition of the population, which cannot be assumed to be always or everywhere the same.

But the age composition of the population, especially the female population, will also affect birth rates. Hence, misleading inferences and comparisons cannot be avoided merely by expressing the number of births as a fraction of the total number of women in the population. For example, if two populations were identical in size and in sex composition but differed in the age distribution of their females, the same ratio of births to females would have different implications in the one case than in the other. Since the childbearing period is shorter than a woman's life span, the percentage of women of childbearing age in the population must be taken into account in interpreting a ratio such as the number of births per 1,000 women.

One way out of this difficulty is to consider the "age-specific fertility rates" of the females in the population—the number of births per 1,000

1. Robert R. Kuczynski, *Fertility and Reproduction*, Falcon Press, New York, 1932, p. 4.

women of specified ages—in conjunction with the proportion of the females in each age group. In 1948 in New Zealand, for example, 5.8 per cent of the females were in the age category 45–49 years and this group produced on the average 1.9 live births per 1,000. In Spain (1940) 5.2 per cent of the females were 45–49 years old but they produced 8.2 live births per 1,000— more than four times as many as New Zealand women of the same age range. Or, again, women in Iceland aged 15–19 years produced 51.7 live births per 1,000 while those in Norway produced only 15.7; moreover, 8.7 per cent of all Icelandic women were in this age group but only 6.5 per cent of Norwegian women. (See Table A.)

The measures most commonly used nowadays to circumvent these difficulties, and yet give in a single figure some indication of fertility patterns in different populations, are gross and net reproduction rates.[2]

## *Gross Reproduction Rate*

The gross reproduction rate is computed from two sets of data: first, the number of females born in a given year to females of specified ages; second, the number of females of each age. By dividing the first by the second it is possible to compute the number of females born per female at age 15, 16, 17, 18 and so on, until, at some age, the figure becomes zero because the women have passed the childbearing age. The final step is merely to add together the figures so obtained for each age to get the total number of females born per (average) female throughout her lifetime. This total is the gross reproduction rate.

As the Population Division of the United Nations has pointed out, the gross reproduction rate

. . . is a rate "per woman," not "per 1,000 women" . . . [It] indicates the average number of daughters who would be born to a group of girls beginning life together, in a population where none died before the upper limit of childbearing age (and where there was no migration) and where the given set of fertility rates was in operation.[3]

In other words, the gross reproduction rate shows how many daughters— that is, potential future mothers—will be born per woman if birth patterns stay the same as they are in the year for which the rate is computed. Of course it does not say they *will* remain the same; it only shows what will happen if they do.

2. At present it is impossible to calculate gross and net reproduction rates with accuracy for most of the underdeveloped areas. Furthermore, for some time to come these areas are likely to be bothered by population growth rather than imminent decline, the kind of situation for which gross and net reproduction rates are particularly revealing. For the most part, therefore, crude birth rates and death rates, with the derivative rate of natural increase, are used in discussing the population problems of underdeveloped countries.

3. United Nations, *Demographic Yearbook, 1949–50*, New York, 1950, p. 24.

TABLE A. AGE-SPECIFIC FERTILITY RATES AND PERCENTAGE DISTRIBUTION OF FEMALES BY AGE, SELECTED COUNTRIES

| Country | Year | Average All Ages | 15–19 Years | 20–24 Years | 25–29 Years | 30–34 Years | 35–39 Years | 40–44 Years | 45–49 Years |
|---|---|---|---|---|---|---|---|---|---|
| | | Number of Live Births per 1,000 Women in Specified Age Group | | | | | | | |
| Norway | 1948 | 69.7 | 15.7 | 99.8 | 142.7 | 126.8 | 87.4 | 37.0 | 3.9 |
| New Zealand | 1948 | 89.5 | 25.3 | 175.9 | 210.1 | 148.6 | 83.1 | 25.8 | 1.9 |
| Iceland | 1947 | 94.0 | 51.7 | 181.3 | 188.6 | 161.4 | 98.4 | 41.2 | 5.1 |
| Spain | 1940 | 71.2 | 8.6 | 89.7 | 185.3 | 166.2 | 109.5 | 45.0 | 8.2 |

| Country | Year | Under 15 Years | 15–19 Years | 20–24 Years | 25–29 Years | 30–34 Years | 35–39 Years | 40–44 Years | 45–49 Years | Over 49 Years |
|---|---|---|---|---|---|---|---|---|---|---|
| | | Percentage Distribution of Females by Age | | | | | | | | |
| Norway | 1948 | 22.3 | 6.5 | 7.5 | 8.5 | 8.1 | 7.6 | 7.1 | 6.7 | 25.6 |
| New Zealand | 1948 | 26.6 | 6.9 | 7.4 | 7.7 | 7.5 | 7.3 | 6.6 | 5.8 | 28.1 |
| Iceland | 1947 | 28.1 | 8.7 | 8.2 | 7.5 | 6.7 | 6.1 | 5.7 | 8.0 | 21.0 |
| Spain | 1940 | 28.6 | 9.6 | 8.7 | 8.2 | 7.4 | 6.8 | 6.0 | 5.2 | 19.5 |

Source: United Nations, Demographic Yearbook, 1949–50, New York, 1950, Table 18, pp. 308–12, and Table 4, pp. 104–67.

## Net Reproduction Rate

The net reproduction rate, which is derived from the gross reproduction rate, takes into account the fact that some women will die before they pass beyond the age of reproduction and therefore will not produce their full complement of daughters. The net reproduction rate is simply the gross reproduction rate modified by the prevailing age-specific mortality rates of the females in the population. Of 1,000 females aged 15, for example, a certain number will die before age 16 and of those remaining some will die before age 17—and so on for each year up to the end of their years of fertility. The net reproduction rate merely "corrects" the gross rate by allowing for these deaths. As the Population Division of the United Nations expresses it:

Net reproduction rates are obtained by multiplying the specific fertility rates of each group by the proportion of survivors to that age in a life table and adding up the products. The net reproduction rate may be interpreted, in analogy with the gross rate, as the average number of daughters that would be produced by women throughout their lifetime if they were exposed at each age to the fertility and mortality rates on which the calculation is based.[4]


## Relation between Gross and Net Rates

Gross and net reproduction rates can be highly informative, both in comparisons between countries and in their relation to one another for any particular population. A net reproduction rate of 1 would mean that—with existing fertility and mortality rates among females—the population was exactly replacing itself: every female would produce, net, only one female. A rate of 1.50 would mean a 50 per cent increase in population each 28 to 30 years, this being the time it takes for a generation of women to pass through the childbearing years. If the gap between the gross and net reproduction rates is small, then the inference is that even economic development or improved health conditions will not increase population growth much, because the gross rate already indicates the limit in this direction under the *prevailing age-specific fertility conditions.* For the gross rate shows what births would occur, granted the proviso in italics, if no females died before they ended their productive period.

The proviso is important, since the prevailing age-specific fertility conditions may be due to special factors which can be expected to disappear. Perhaps the most important variable is the marriage pattern, that is, the proportions of women in the various age groups who are married. In Western Europe after World War I, for example, an unusually high proportion of women in the productive age groups remained unmarried as a

4. *Ibid.*

TABLE B. GROSS AND NET REPRODUCTION RATES, SELECTED COUNTRIES, 1938 AND 1948

| Country | Gross Reproduction Rate | | Net Reproduction Rate | |
|---|---|---|---|---|
| | *1938* | *1948* | *1938* | *1948* |
| Canada | 1.314 | 1.667 | 1.163 | .. |
| United States | 1.113 | 1.542 | 1.011 | 1.462 |
| Chile | 1.983 | .. | 1.147 | .. |
| Belgium | .. | 1.188 | .. | 0.996 |
| Finland | 1.220 | 1.666 | 1.011 | 1.403 |
| Norway | 0.914 | 1.233 | 0.832 | 1.126 |
| Sweden | 0.879 | .. | 0.802 | .. |
| England and Wales | 0.897 | 1.158 | 0.810 | 1.070 |
| Portugal | .. | 1.667 | .. | 1.216 |
| Australia | 1.069 | 1.451 | 0.984 | 1.326 |
| France | 1.040 | .. | 0.910 | .. |
| U.S.S.R. | 2.190 | .. | 1.540 | .. |
| | *1931* | *1941* | *1931* | *1941* |
| India | 2.99 | 2.76 | 1.25 | 1.30 |
| Egypt | 3.1 | .. | 1.4 | .. |

*Sources:* United Nations, *Demographic Yearbook, 1949–50,* New York, 1950, Table 24, pp. 366–70; figures for the U.S.S.R., India and Egypt from *Population Index,* April 1952, pp. 165–72.

result of the war casualties. The gross reproduction rate was therefore lowered. The same situation in aggravated form has prevailed in Western Germany since the end of World War II. In comparing gross reproduction rates for different countries and periods, therefore, it is important to make sure that no special factors of this kind have influenced the results.[5]

Notwithstanding these possible qualifications, the differences among countries in their gross and net reproduction rates remain striking. For example, in the United States in 1938 the gross rate was 1.113 as against a net of 1.011, but in the U.S.S.R. in that year the gross rate was 2.190 and the net rate 1.540, and in Chile the rates were even further apart—1.983 gross as compared with 1.147 net. (See Table B.) In both Chile and the U.S.S.R., therefore, any drop in the mortality of women in the productive ages would substantially increase the rate of population growth.

*Paucity of Data for Underdeveloped Countries*

Most underdeveloped countries do not have the statistical data necessary to compute gross and net reproduction rates for their populations. All the evidence, however, points to high gross reproduction rates and a large spread between the gross and net rates. Egypt in 1931 had a calculated

5. Development itself, of course, may modify the social and cultural factors that determine the gross reproduction rate.

gross rate of 3.1 and a net of 1.4. One calculation for India shows a gross rate of 2.99 for 1931 as against a net rate of only 1.25, which is lower than the net rate for Australia in 1948. By 1941 the gross rate in India had fallen to 2.76 but the net had risen ominously to 1.30.

If data were available for other underdeveloped countries, they would almost certainly show a relation between gross and net rates similar to those for India and Egypt. Consequently, any drop in mortality in the under-developed areas—such as can reasonably be expected with improved pro-ductivity, higher living standards and better health conditions—will pro-duce sharp increases in their rates of population growth, *unless* their gross reproduction rates should fall proportionately. But gross reproduction rates, given the sex and age composition of the populations, seem to depend upon a variety of economic, social and cultural factors which are neither easily specified—much less subject to quantitative measurement—nor quickly altered.

# INDEX OF AUTHORS

# Index of Authors

# SUBJECT INDEX

# Subject Index

ABBINK, John, 288

Administrators, 24

Afghanistan: Export-Import Bank loans to, 371(t)

Africa, 3; agriculture: land and labor, 33, 34(f), 35(f), 460(t); population growth, 93(t); partition of, 170*n;* land tenure, 244; U.S. grants and credits and loans by International Bank, 367(t); Export-Import Bank loans, 371(t), 372; indicators of capital inputs, 463(t)

Agricultural cooperatives, *see* Cooperatives

Agricultural Industry Service (UNRRA), 278

Agriculture: efficiency, 23, 24; land suitable for, 34(f); natural fertility of land, 35(f); land-labor ratios, 36, 256–59, 458–60(t); capital resources in, 38, 39–40; peasant vs. plantation farming, 40*n*, 45, 96, 249–52, 436; productivity, 44–46, 237–40, 238(f); disguised unemployment in, 44, 45; technological improvements, 126–31, 157–60, 240–43, 252, 253, 267*ff*, 270, 271–72, 280*ff*, 419*ff;* developments: in England, 126–31, 149; in France, 154, 172–73; in Germany, 154–56, 172–73; in Japan, 177, 178, 179–80, 183, 188; in Russia, 190–92, 195(t), 204–08, 207(t), 247, 416; reforms in taxation and land tenure, 243–47, 253–54, 330, 419*ff;* in world economy, 255–56, 259–66, 411*ff;* processing of farm products, 271–72; private U.S. direct foreign investment in, 348(t)

Albania: agricultural area and labor force, 458(t)

Alsace-Lorraine, 162

American Red Cross: U.S. grants and credits to, 364(t)

Angell Report, 400

Anglo-Saxon law, 82*n*

Animal units: as capital-input indicator, 461–63(t)

Argentina: crude death and infant mortality rates, 11(t); Export-Import Bank loans to, 370(t); agricultural area and labor force, 459(t); indicators of capital inputs, 463(t)

Art, 4

Artisans, 179*n*

Asia, 3; agricultural land in, 33, 34(f), 35(f); population trends in, 93(t), 109; income taxes, 325(t); taxes on foreign trade, 327(t); consumption taxes, 330(t); attitudes toward foreign capital, 344; U.S. postwar aid to, 367; government grants and credits and loans by International Bank, 367(t); Export-Import Bank loans, 371(t); *see also under names of individual countries*

Australia, 3; price stabilization, 316*n;* agricultural area and labor force, 459(t); indicators of capital inputs, 462(t); gross and net reproduction rates, 468(t)

Austria: pig iron production, 220(t), 222(t); population growth, 225(t); Export-Import Bank loans to, 370(t); agricultural area and labor force, 458(t); indicators of capital inputs, 462(t)

Autarchy, 267

BACON, Francis, 121

Bakewell, Robert, 129

Balance of payments, 66–67; problems of, in underdeveloped areas, 382–401; *see also* International trade

Bank of Japan, 184

Banks and banking systems: Japanese, 184–85; savings banks, 305–06; commercial banks, 306–07, 308, 312, 337–38; central banks, 308, 313, 338–40; *see also* Investment; Public finance; Savings

Barbados: crude death and infant mortality rates, 11(t)

Belgium: land-labor ratios, 37, 458(t); manufacturing, 141, 223(t); early industrialization, 165–66; output: of coal, 218(t), 219(t); of pig iron, 219, 220(t), 222(t); population growth, 225(t), 226(t); Export-Import Bank loans to, 370(t); indicators of capital inputs, 462(t); gross and net reproduction rates, 468(t)

Bell Mission (to the Philippines): recommendations, 271–72, 289, 333; evaluation of import controls, 320; fiscal and monetary stipulations, 390

479